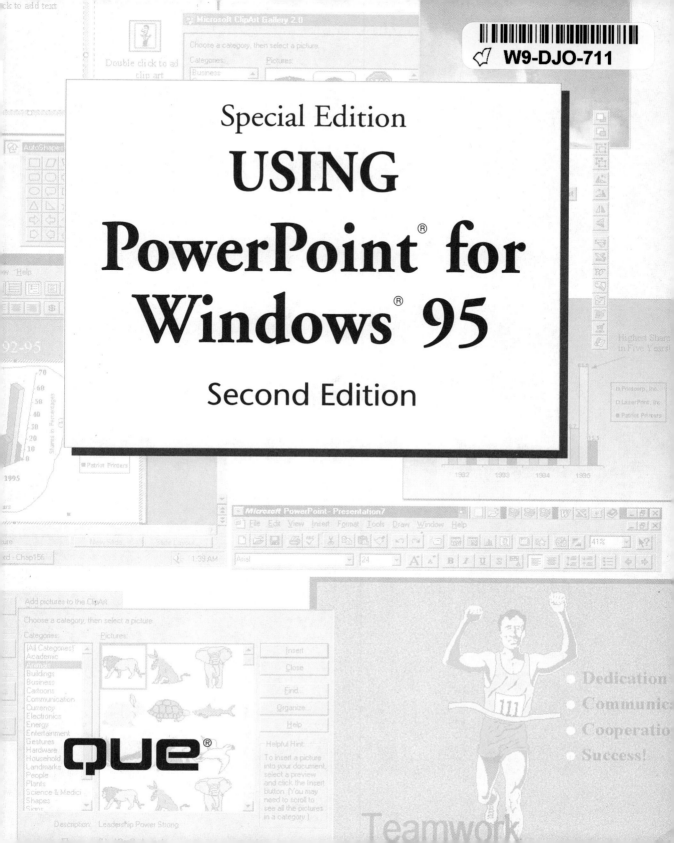

Special Edition

USING
PowerPoint® for
Windows® 95

Second Edition

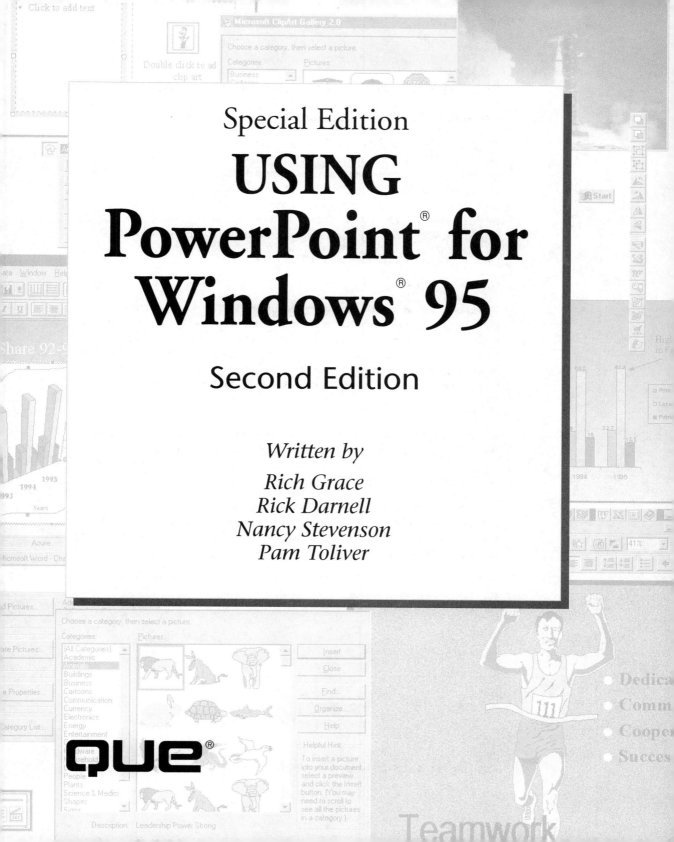

Special Edition Using PowerPoint® for Windows® 95

Library of Congress Catalog No.: 95-78881

ISBN: 0-7897-0464-1

97 96 95   6 5 4 3 2 1

Interpretation of the printing code: the rightmost double-digit number is the year of the book's printing; the rightmost single-digit number, the number of the book's printing. For example, a printing code of 95-1 shows that the first printing of the book occurred in 1995.

Screen reproductions in this book were created using Collage Plus from Inner Media, Inc., Hollis, NH.

Composed in *Stone Serif* and *MCPdigital* by Que Corporation

Credits

President
Roland Elgey

Vice President and Publisher
Marie Butler-Knight

Associate Publisher
Don Roche Jr.

Director of Marketing
Lynn E. Zingraf

Editorial Services Director
Elizabeth Keaffaber

Managing Editor
Michael Cunningham

Senior Series Editor
Chris Nelson

Acquisition Editors
Nancy Stevenson
Jenny L. Watson

Product Director
Stephanie Gould

Production Editors
Thomas F. Hayes
Julie A. McNamee

Editors
Elsa Bethanis
Amy Perry
Silvette D. Pope
Christine Prakel
Paige Widder

Assistant Product Marketing Manager
Kim Margolius

Technical Editors
Janice A. Snyder
Nanci C. Jacobs
Elizabeth Eisner Reding

Acquisitions Coordinator
Tracy M. Williams

Operations Coordinator
Patty Brooks

Editorial Assistants
Carmen Phelps
Jill Byus

Book Designer
Ruth Harvey

Cover Designer
Jay Corpus

Production Team
Angela D. Bannan
Troy Barnes
DiMonique Ford
Amy Gornik
Mike Henry
John Hulse
Darren Jackson
Damon Jordan
Michelle Lee
Bill Levy
Kevin J. MacDonald
Julie Quinn
Bobbi Satterfield
Tina Trettin
Marvin Van Tiem
Karen York

Indexer
Mary Jane Frisby

Dedication

This book is humbly dedicated to:

My martial arts instructor, Master Gordon Sproul, at American Martial Arts in Encinitas, California.

About the Author

Rich Grace has been bumping around the computer industry for years, primarily as a technical writer and software analyst. He's written dozens of articles for computer publications, and his work currently appears in *InfoWorld* and *Mac Home Journal*. He also has appeared in *InfoWorld Direct, MicroTimes, Windows User, PC Home Journal, PC Today, Electronic Engineering Times*, and *Imaging Magazine*. He is the author of Que's *Word 6 for Windows Quick Reference*, Prentice-Hall's *The Benchmark Book*, and co-author of Que's *Using PowerPoint 4 for Macintosh*. Rich owns far more computer equipment than is good for him, and tries to strike a balance with martial arts studies, art collecting, and jazz guitar. He can be reached at CompuServe 72672,2266.

Pamela R. Toliver is an independent contract trainer and owns *Soft-Spec*, a corporate training firm based in Montclair, Virginia. She has over 15 years of training and teaching experience and has taught courses in computer and business education at the high school and university levels. In addition to conducting computer training for private and governmental agencies across the country, Pam has written a variety of educational texts for educational publishers and training manuals for an international training firm on a waide range of computer applications. She received her Bachelor's degree from Souther Illinois University in Carbondale and her Master's Degree from Louisiana State University, Baton Rouge.

Nancy Stevenson is a freelance writer, teacher, and consultant. Her most recently completed book, *Using Word for Windows*, was published by Que in the spring of 1995. Ms. Stevenson teaches technical writing at Purdue University in Indianapolis. Prior to going freelance, she was a Publishing Manager at Que, and before that worked as a trainer, consultant and product manager at Symantec Corporation in California.

Rick Darnell received a B. S. in Mass Communications from Kansas State University. He has worked as part of a creative services agency in Wyoming and as a freelance journalist in Kansas, Wyoming, and Montana. Rick has worked with computers since being introduced to a Radio Shack Model I in the late 1970s. He currently lives in Missoula, MT with his wife and daughter, where he serves on a volunteer fire department and writes about the midwest, prairie fires and software.

Acknowledgments

Thanks to Microsoft Corporation, without which this project would not have been possible. Thanks also for Microsoft's excellent press relations support, represented by Waggener Edstrom in Seattle, Portland, and San Jose. In particular, Isabelle Boucq was a steady and forthcoming contact at the San Jose office. Amy Stone at the Portland office arranged for me to get a copy of Word for Windows NT, on which all my work on this book was produced without a single crash or system failure.

Ralph Bond of Intel Corporation went far out of his way to provide me with crucial information on handling video and sound objects in PowerPoint presentations. He's a good friend, and I appreciate his efforts on my behalf.

Thanks to my agent Matt Wagner of Waterside Productions, who has gone to bat for me many times, given much needed advice, and literally helped me build my career. To quote Will Durant, success has many fathers; failure is an orphan.

I especially wish to thank Macmillan Publishing and Que for giving me the opportunity to revise my previous work. It's been a fulfilling and valuable experience, though sometimes painful when I discovered just how many goofs I made before. Thanks to Don Roche and Jenny Watson for giving me that chance. Above all, I want to thank Stephanie Gould for her patience, advice, and support and Tom Hayes for keeping the project on target and making sure the text was correct.

I also want to thank the writers who chipped in with important chapters during the tight production schedule. Nancy Stevenson, Pam Toliver and Rick Darnell each provided valuable input to this project.

We'd Like to Hear from You!

As part of our continuing effort to produce books of the highest possible quality, Que would like to hear your comments. To stay competitive, we *really* want you, as a computer book reader and user, to let us know what you like or dislike most about this book or other Que products.

You can mail comments, ideas, or suggestions for improving future editions to the address below, or send us a fax at (317) 581-4663. For the online inclined, Macmillan Computer Publishing has a forum on CompuServe (type **GO QUEBOOKS** at any prompt) through which our staff and authors are available for questions and comments. The address of our Internet site is **http://www.mcp.com** (World Wide Web).

In addition to exploring our forum, please feel free to contact me personally to discuss your opinions of this book: I'm **sgould@que.mcp.com** on the Internet.

Thanks in advance—your comments will help us to continue publishing the best books available on computer topics in today's market.

Stephanie Gould
Product Development Specialist
Que Corporation
201 W. 103rd Street
Indianapolis, Indiana 46290
USA

Contents at a Glance

Techniques from the Pros 703

Techniques from the Pros

Contents

II Working with Text   163

6 Entering and Editing Text   165

III Adding Illustrations   261

10 Drawing Objects   263

11 Selecting, Editing, and Enhancing Graphic Objects   287

12 Adding Clip Art and Scanned Art   307

IV Creating Charts

13 Working with Datasheets

14 Creating Basic Charts

15 Customizing Charts 385

16 Creating Organizational Charts 419

V Output and Color   449

17 Printing Slides and Other Kinds of Output   451

18 Working with Color   479

24 Customizing PowerPoint 95   687

VII Techniques from the Pros   703

25 Making PowerPoint Presentations Fast, Fast, Fast   705

26 Preparation, Practice, and PowerPoint   711

Introduction

Microsoft PowerPoint for Windows 95 is among the leaders in a competitive and growing category of computer software: graphics presentations. This book presents the information necessary to successful use PowerPoint 95 and to integrate the latest version of PowerPoint with other Windows 95 applications.

PowerPoint is appropriately named because the program combines the most powerful features of not one program category, but several. These include:

- *Drawing.* PowerPoint offers a wide selection of drawing and art creation features that rival dedicated drawing programs. While it can never re-place, for example, CorelDRAW!, many presentation artists may find that PowerPoint is all they need. An extensive clip art library offers instant art content to the presentation creator, and the ability to import vast art collections for use therein.

- *Charting.* PowerPoint offers a highly flexible and feature-rich charting and graphing capability. You type the numeric data you want to present (sales for a company department for the four quarters of the year, for example) into a simple spreadsheet, and then choose from among the many dozens of chart styles. Custom chart styles can be saved and used in any presentation file.

- *Outlining and Word Processing.* PowerPoint offers an easy and intuitive Outlining feature in which you can add any amount of text, choose your favorite fonts and typeface sizes, and quickly create bulleted lists. Spell checking is provided, as is Search and Replace. For the first time, PowerPoint also offers the same grammar checking features found in Microsoft Word. You can construct an entire presentation and study its logic in Outline view, and export those outlines to Word for Windows 95. Outlines also can be imported into PowerPoint from Word.

■ *An Artist's Palette.* PowerPoint utilizes the graphics power of the Windows 95 platform to offer you enhanced color scheme features for your slide shows, and hundreds of predefined graphic backgrounds for various presentation motifs. If a predefined scheme doesn't please you, it's remarkably easy to create your own. The template system has been simplified, and a new black-and-white view is provided for top-quality monochrome laser printouts.

■ *An Output Program.* PowerPoint gets the most from your output devices. PowerPoint handles color printing and slide output with aplomb. You can easily create overhead transparencies. If you want professional color output, use the GraphicsLink program to send your files to Genigraphics Corporation, a service bureau that makes the slide output for you. Since PowerPoint is now the industry standard, many service bureaus now accept PowerPoint files for output.

■ *Corporate Communications.* PowerPoint's mission, ultimately, is to empower and expand your delivery of corporate communications. Multimedia support has been drastically enhanced in PowerPoint for Windows 95. Special Wizards assist you in efficient delivery of a presentation over networks to other users' screens, combined with telephone conferencing. All the tools listed above are placed in the service of providing you with the most efficient, integrated program available for making your corporate communications ring with conviction and authority.

Unlike a drawing or charting package, in which one screen at a time is created, programs like PowerPoint enable you to create extensive multiple-slide presentations at once. You can create as many slides as the memory on your system can contain. PowerPoint has perhaps the greatest flexibility of any program in its field for this purpose.

If you have multiple slides in your presentation file, you can make use of PowerPoint's handy Slide Sorter to rearrange slides by simply dragging and dropping. You can delete and add slides in the Sorter, and change the entire color scheme of the presentation at once. You also can apply different color schemes to individual slides. You can quickly and easily add any type of data to your presentation that your computer can support—including sounds, movie clips, and photo-realistic pictures.

How does PowerPoint for Windows 95 work? *Special Edition Using PowerPoint for Windows 95* answers that question.

This version of PowerPoint represents a substantial leap in capabilities from its previous version. It reflects many advances pursued in its new operating system, Windows 95. Multimedia and animations run more efficiently. System resource bottlenecks have been removed. Every capability and feature in PowerPoint is integrated into a seamless, interdependent whole. PowerPoint also associates even more closely with fellow Microsoft applications programs in the Office suite. OLE 2.0 is now quicker and easier to use and also reflects the advances in Windows 95.

You may need to create a presentation from scratch, define a color scheme, create a common background for your slide show, create the titles and basic outline for the slides in your show, write the body text for your slides, or create 3-D pie and column charts from company sales data. You may need to import Lotus 1-2-3 or Excel spreadsheets on which to base those charts, add film clips and sounds from the sales force, define a specific font (perhaps 40-Point Arial) for all the titles in your presentation, or define another font for your body text and bulleted points. In addition, you may need to add framing effects to all your objects for a custom effect, arrange the objects on your slides for a clean, organized appearance, add a company logo to all the slides in the presentation, import bitmap pictures, create tables, spell check your presentation, and save and print your file in color transparencies.

And it all has to be done yesterday!

If you had to specify each step in the presentation process by name, you would never get it done. Fortunately, with PowerPoint you don't have to. Just point and click with the mouse. With a couple of mouse clicks, even the most complex-sounding features can be mastered rapidly. Many features have been streamlined for quicker access and execution. The same drop-down color palettes and menu options are used in dozens of operations.

When you point to the desired feature or object and select it, you're using a Graphical User Interface (GUI, or goo-ey), a front end for a program or even for an entire computer system, which uses the mouse and a color display to simplify the use of your computer. Windows, of course, is a popular example of a GUI. Windows 95 is a long-overdue advance that puts more power into users' hands. The advantage of using Windows and other GUIs (such as the Macintosh, for example) is the offering of another acronym that defines another advanced capability—WYSIWYG, or "What You See Is What You Get." When a slide show or document appears on your computer screen, WYSIWYG ensures that it bears close resemblance to what you see on paper or, in PowerPoint's case, the on-screen slide show, color transparencies, or color slides.

You don't have to be a graphics designer to use PowerPoint. On the contrary, PowerPoint is designed for those users who need to apply their expertise—corporate communications—to a visual presentation; and to do it quickly and effectively. To this end, PowerPoint offers over 60 different sample templates for the quick creation of appealing and effective slide shows. More than twenty complete presentation structures (called AutoContents) enable the user to quickly build presentations designed for many crucial missions, without time-consuming design sessions. PowerPoint's templates offer many of the basic elements of an outstanding slide show, such as attractive color schemes, title fonts, placement of graphic objects, and the logical flow and basic content of the presentation.

PowerPoint for Windows 95 offers an expanded set of Wizards for content creation, online Help, networked presentation conferencing, and even packing up your presentation for easy transport to another site. Even though you might use the AutoContent Wizard to define the basic structure of your show, you can change the words, the outline, and the content of your presentation at will and craft a slide show with a top-notch professional appearance. PowerPoint's Wizards and many other features free you from having to sweat the basic details of using the program—often with some otherwise very complicated processes—letting you focus on what's most important: what to say, and what images you want to convey.

PowerPoint combines vast power in a friendly and approachable package. You can become a power user almost as soon as you begin, and using the program will soon become second nature. At first, however, you can profit by reading about the program. PowerPoint offers such a depth of features that you're likely to miss many of them unless you take a little time to seek them out. Helping you discover PowerPoint's possibilities for your corporate communications is the mission of this book.

What Is in This Book

Like the PowerPoint software itself, *Special Edition Using PowerPoint for Windows 95* endeavors to make the power of the program easily accessible. The book opens with basic features and functionality and gradually moves to more advanced and complex topics. It's recommended that you start by learning the basics; and when you feel at home with the fundamentals, you can progress to more advanced topics. Be reassured, though: Even the most complex features of PowerPoint are surprisingly straightforward and accessible and most are accomplished with a couple of mouse clicks.

This book is divided into six parts that split the PowerPoint program into several discrete areas of study: PowerPoint Basics, Text, Drawing, Charts, Output and Color, and Advanced Techniques.

Part I: PowerPoint 95 Basics

Chapter 1, "An Overview of PowerPoint for Windows 95," offers a quick road map of many of PowerPoint's most significant upgrades and enhancements, including PowerPoint's new toolbars, Wizards, drag and drop, and other features.

Chapter 2, "Getting Acquainted with PowerPoint 95," describes how to work with the mouse and keyboard, to work with the menus and pop-up lists, get help, and understand the new features of PowerPoint's user interface that help speed you on the way to successful presentations.

Chapter 3, "Creating Your First Presentation," ties many of PowerPoint's most important features together in a basic exercise for creating your first presentation in PowerPoint.

Chapter 4, "Setting Up Your New Presentation," describes the interlocking tools of PowerPoint that cooperate in helping you create the best possible presentation: PowerPoint's Masters and Views.

Chapter 5, "Creating and Using Templates," describes how to work with the fundamental building block of any presentation: PowerPoint's templates. You also learn how to import templates from other presentation programs.

Part II: Working with Text

Chapter 6, "Entering and Editing Text," describes basic text entry techniques, text object manipulation (including PowerPoint's enhanced drag-and-drop capabilities), and using fonts and text styles. Text editing is extensively discussed.

Chapter 7, "Creating Speaker's Notes & Audience Handouts," shows you how to produce your personal notes for the slide show, including formatting, changing, and printing Notes Pages. It also takes you through the process of creating audience handouts of slide printouts and background information for your presentation.

Chapter 8, "Creating Presentation Outlines," discusses the creation of presentation outlines; how they determine the content of your presentation; and how to edit, rearrange, and import them from other applications.

Chapter 9, "Creating and Working with Tables," shows you how to create, edit, and format tables of text data with Word for Windows 95, and embed those tables into your PowerPoint presentation.

Part III: Adding Illustrations

Chapter 10, "Drawing Objects," shows you how to use PowerPoint's numerous drawing tools and special drawing techniques.

Chapter 11, "Selecting, Editing, and Enhancing Graphic Objects," describes the process of using, moving, aligning, and changing object placeholders on PowerPoint slides. The processes of enhancing object placeholders (with framing and shadowing) and graphic objects (with a wide variety of effects) are explained.

Chapter 12, "Adding Clip Art and Scanned Art," shows you how to work with PowerPoint's extensive ClipArt library feature, how to place clip art into your slide show, and how to work with photo-realistic images in PowerPoint.

Part IV: Creating Charts

Chapter 13, "Working with Datasheets," shows you how to create and edit the building blocks of every chart you'll ever create—the numeric datasheet.

Chapter 14, "Creating Basic Charts," discusses how to choose chart types, describes the various elements of a chart, and explains the basics of how to change various elements on a chart.

Chapter 15, "Customizing Charts," digs deeper into the process of changing your chart's appearance, offering more detailed discussions of changing chart elements, drawing objects, and adding custom colors to charts, among other subjects.

Chapter 16, "Creating Organizational Charts," introduces you to the process of creating organizational charts to depict a corporation's or department's structure, using PowerPoint's bundled OrgChart application program.

Part V: Output and Color

Chapter 17, "Printing Slides and Other Kinds of Output," describes printing the various elements of a presentation, including handouts, notes, and slides, and using the Genigraphics service bureau for final color slide output.

Chapter 18, "Working with Color," discusses basic color theory and how color really works in PowerPoint, and some additional topics on applying color to PowerPoint objects.

Part VI: Advanced PowerPoint Techniques

Chapter 19, "Using Links to other Applications," discusses how PowerPoint 95's famous OLE (object linking and embedding) works, and how it can help you work more effectively with other data types and application programs.

Chapter 20, "Using Advanced Charting Features," further explores sophisticated chart types and chart customizing techniques, the process of saving custom chart types, and how to import Excel spreadsheets for charting use in PowerPoint.

Chapter 21, "Using Multimedia Elements in PowerPoint 95," discusses PowerPoint's dramatically expanded multimedia support, how to combine build animations and transitions with sound effects, how to employ a CD music soundtrack, and effective management of multimedia events.

Chapter 22, "Advanced Presentation Management," discusses animated build effects and slide transitions, and their appropriate use in presentations.

Chapter 23, "Using Advanced Color, Text, and Special Effects," describes PowerPoint's color systems, the use of fonts, and the use of the equation editor. It also touches on operations such as scaling objects for different screen resolutions, importing custom color palettes, and recoloring pictures.

Chapter 24, "Customizing PowerPoint 95," describes how to create custom toolbars and change PowerPoint's user interface to your liking.

Part VII: Techniques from the Pros

Chapters 25 through 27, are devoted to interviews and discussions with experienced PowerPoint users, including a major communications magazine publisher, a corporate communications specialist with Hughes Aircraft, and a communications specialist from Intel Corporation who creates PowerPoint presentations and speeches for the company's top executives.

Who Should Use This Book

Why read a book about PowerPoint if the software is so "intuitive"? Especially with a new PC-based operating system, Windows 95, that supposedly sets new standards for ease of use? Although virtually every feature in PowerPoint can be used and activated with a few mouse clicks—even advanced features such as changing color schemes or rotating charts—references like this book are valuable. PowerPoint doesn't require you to know sophisticated commands or memorize an arcane set of keystroke combinations. Nor is it necessary to know graphic arts. (Though it certainly doesn't hurt!) But knowing software isn't the whole story.

This book is aimed at anyone who wants to create more effective communications. Read this book to become acquainted with the myriad possibilities contained in the PowerPoint software package. Because of its new operating system, PowerPoint's capabilities are greater than ever. You can easily copy a presentation template or any of its default elements and make them your own. To use a presentation template, however, you must know that it's available for your use. Creating effective and attractive charts is easy in PowerPoint. But how do you know what types of charts to use? A book like this one, is more a catalog of possibilities than a simple how-to instruction manual. This is the approach attempted throughout this book, eschewing the practice of simply rewording the program's documentation.

What do you do if you need to harness advanced features but don't have the time to fish around in the software? Much of the program's power will certainly be lost to you because there's so much to offer. Consider multimedia, traditionally a sensitive and difficult topic in Windows. Windows 95 and PowerPoint combine to make multimedia more manageable and useful than PC users have ever seen. The feature depth in this area is substantial, and it's easy to miss things. A reference providing lucid, understandable accounts of the effective use of multimedia is still a rare commodity. We hope, with this book, to change that.

This book is aimed at intermediate and advanced users and any Windows user who appreciates an alternative way to use graphics on his or her computer. It isn't aimed at graphics specialists or software experts, though either can profit by reading it. Graphics specialists can learn about an alternative use of computer graphics in the workaday business world, and thus understand more about the needs of the business community. A software expert can gain insight and advice about creating high-quality graphics.

Special Edition Using PowerPoint for Windows 95 also is written for corporate communications specialists and business presenters who want to create their own presentations. This book shows you how to use the program in step-by-step, task-oriented examples. Guidelines, explanations, margin tips, and highlighted notes keep you firmly on course and help you get the most out of PowerPoint in the shortest period of time. Liberal quantities of illustrations aid in depicting features and procedures in the program.

Special Features in This Book

Que has over a decade of experience writing and developing the most successful computer books available. With that experience, we've learned what special features help readers the most. Look for these special features throughout the book to enhance your learning experience.

Chapter Roadmaps

Near the beginning of each chapter is a list of topics to be covered in the chapter. This list serves as a roadmap to the chapter so you can tell at a glance what is covered. It also provides a useful outline of the key topics you'll be reading about.

Notes

Notes present interesting or useful information that isn't necessarily essential to the discussion. This secondary track of information enhances your understanding of Windows, but you can safely skip notes and not be in danger of missing crucial information. Notes look like this:

> **Note**
>
> The scroll bar at the right side of the screen is called the Slide Changer. When you click the mouse on it, a Screen Tip appears that shows the slide number and its title. An example appears in figure 2.1.

Tips

Tips present short advice on quick or often overlooked procedures. These include shortcuts that save you time. A tip is shown in the margin as an example.

Tip

For quick help on any toolbar function, press Shift+F1 and click any tool.

Cautions

Cautions serve to warn you about potential problems that a procedure may cause, unexpected results, and mistakes to avoid. Cautions look like this:

> **Caution**
>
> Watch your close buttons. If you accidentally click on one, you may close your file or the application without intending to. Fortunately, the program will ask if you want to save before you exit. Save your work frequently!

Troubleshooting

No matter how carefully you follow the steps in the book, you eventually come across something that just doesn't work the way you think it should. Troubleshooting sections anticipate these common errors or hidden pitfalls and present solutions. A troubleshooting section looks like this:

Troubleshooting

I can't find the text formatting tools on PowerPoint's toolbar.

You probably need to display more toolbars on the screen—namely the Formatting toolbar. To do so, choose View, Toolbars to open the Toolbars dialog box. Click the Formatting check box, and then choose OK or press Enter. The text formatting tools appear on the PowerPoint screen.

Index of Common Problems

This feature goes hand in hand with the Troubleshooting elements. If you are having a problem with Windows 95 and don't know where to look in the book for an answer, look to the Index of Common Problems, located near the back of the book, immediately preceding the index. Use the Index of Common Problems to find all the Troubleshooting sections in the book and other discussions of common problems and fixes.

Cross-References

▶ See "Understanding PowerPoint's Views," p. 66

Throughout the book in the margins, you see references to other sections and pages in the book, like the one next to this paragraph. These cross-references point you to related topics and discussions in other parts of the book.

In addition to these special features, there are several conventions used in this book to make it easier to read and understand. These conventions include the following.

Underlined Hot Keys, or Mnemonics

Hot keys in this book appear underlined, like they appear on-screen. For example, the F in File is a hot key, or shortcut for opening the File menu. In Windows, many menus, commands, buttons, and other options have these hot keys. To use a hot-key shortcut, press Alt and the key for the underlined character. For instance, to choose the Properties button, press Alt and then R.

Shortcut Key Combinations

In this book, shortcut key combinations are joined with plus signs (+). For example, Ctrl+V means hold down the Ctrl key, press the V key, and then release both keys (Ctrl+V is a shortcut for the Paste command).

Menu Commands

Instructions for choosing menu commands have this form:

Choose File, New.

This example means open the File menu and select New, which in this case opens a new file.

Instructions involving the new Windows 95 Start menu are an exception. When you are to choose something through this menu, the form is

Open the Start menu and choose Programs, PowerPoint.

In this case, you open PowerPoint. Notice that in the Start menu you simply drag the mouse pointer and point at the option or command you want to choose (even through a whole series of submenus); you don't need to click anything.

This book also has the following typeface enhancements to indicate special text, as indicated in the following table.

Typeface	Description
Italic	Italics are used to indicate key terms and variables in commands or addresses.
Boldface	Bold is used to indicate text you type, and Internet addresses and other locators in the online world.
`Computer type`	This typeface is used for on-screen messages and commands (such as DOS copy or UNIX commands).
MYFILE.DOC	File names and directories are set in all caps to distinguish them from regular text, as in MYFILE.DOC.

Also, throughout this book you will notice a new feature icon in the margin. This icon points out where new PowerPoint features are specifically discussed. Look for this icon throughout.

Several chapters in this book deal with the process of creating and customizing charts. The word chart is used in this book when describing such objects as bar charts, pie charts, column charts, and so on. Although PowerPoint's graphing and charting application is named Microsoft Graph, all its menu commands, options, and help menus use the word chart in their commands, so that standard is used throughout this book except when specifically referring to the Microsoft Graph program by name.❖

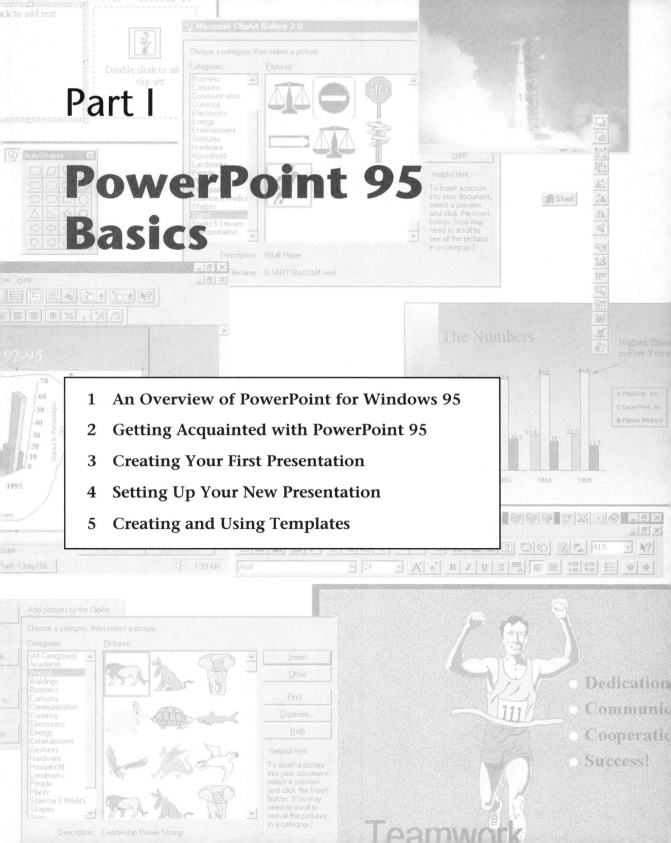

Part I

PowerPoint 95 Basics

Chapter 1

An Overview of PowerPoint for Windows 95

by Rich Grace

PowerPoint for Windows 95 is a major upgrade from the previous version, PowerPoint 4 for Windows 3.1. Although in many ways Microsoft's presentation package offers the same functions and methods as its predecessor, the new program provides even greater efficiency, stability, and power. Thus PowerPoint 4 users will feel right at home with the new version, but they also will find many new features and capabilities. Some of the most important improvements in PowerPoint for Windows 95 include:

- An enhanced interface, revised to reflect the changes presented by Windows 95 yet consistent with the previous version

- Menu bars, toolbars, and dialog boxes offering functions that are even more closely tailored to its companion programs, Word for Windows 95 and Excel for Windows 95, as part of the Microsoft Office for Windows 95 application suite

- Complete 32-bit rewrite for increased performance and stability

- Powerful new wizards that simplify and speed up formerly complex and time-consuming processes, such as getting help online (the Answer Wizard) and gracefully transporting complex presentations (the Pack and Go Wizard)

- Increased multimedia support, including a new Animation Toolbar

- Streamlined procedures in all areas of the program, such as charting and multimedia integration

- Improved *Object Linking and Embedding (OLE)* 2.0 Drag and Drop features, including greater speed and stability

- Multicolor gradient fills, built-in color schemes, and simplified template selections

- Powerful new presentation management features, such as the Meeting Minder and the ability to make presentations over networks

PowerPoint is the undisputed market leader in presentation software. According to market surveys, PowerPoint occupies more than 70 percent of the Windows presentation software market. Most people who work in a corporate environment are familiar with presentations. But what is a presentation? It's a slide show and much more. True, the key mission of PowerPoint is to produce slide shows. You do this using elements like bulleted lists, charts, tables, graphics, clip art, and multimedia objects such as sound clips and motion video.

However, using PowerPoint to create a slide show is only one part (though an important one) of a presentation. A presentation is a slide show combined with hard-copy elements that complement and complete it. They can include audience handouts, Speaker's notes, and outlines, which the presenter uses to build the structure of the presentation. PowerPoint enables you to produce these hard-copy elements as well as slides.

In this chapter, you learn about

- PowerPoint's enhanced multimedia support

- Expanded presentation delivery features

- 32-bit performance

Later chapters cover many smaller upgrades to capabilities that have long existed in the program.

32-bit Power and Performance

PowerPoint has been completely rewritten to take advantage of the enhanced multitasking, better memory protection, and faster 32-bit performance available in Windows 95. Because Windows 95 marks a serious break with the ancient legacy of MS-DOS, applications such as PowerPoint 95 offer liberation from unexplained memory conflicts, and sluggish performance of the past.

Virtual Elimination of Resource Limitations

System resource shortages are a thing of the past. It is hard to overstate how important this is. In previous versions of Microsoft Office for Windows, you encountered system failure if you ran Word, Excel, and PowerPoint at the same time. Now, you can buy as much memory as you want for your PC and actually get real benefits from it. PowerPoint 95—and all other Office 95 applications—multitask much more seamlessly than ever. Try running Word 95, Excel 95, and PowerPoint 95 at the same time. You will find far less degradation in performance on your production system (assuming you have enough memory).

Better Multitasking

Windows 3.1 uses a method of "cooperative multitasking," in which programs share the same resources and are vulnerable to system failures. Windows 95 offers a form of *preemptive multitasking*, in which each application runs in its own memory address space. PowerPoint 95 prominently uses this powerful feature. What does this do for you? It gives you far fewer system crashes and greater reliability. It also frequently enables you to access other programs and successfully run them while PowerPoint is performing a background task, such as printing slides or notes. Though the multitasking architecture of Windows 95 is still not as powerful as that of Windows NT (or OS/2), it is a significant step forward.

Better Speed

PowerPoint 95 is *faster*. Along with better multitasking and system resource use, PowerPoint is now a full 32-bit application. You will immediately notice a boost in speed in PowerPoint 95, compared to PowerPoint 4 running under Windows 3.1.

PowerPoint 95 (and Office 95) also make use of advanced multithreading operations to allow for true background printing, simultaneous screen redraws during menu pull-downs, and other program operations. Multithreading means that while you're performing one intensive task, the program can actually perform another function in the background without impacting your present work. This feature could not exist in Windows 3.1, and represents an exciting advance for PowerPoint users.

Enhanced Usability and a Consistent Interface

Though PowerPoint 95 has some changes and runs under a new operating system, any user of PowerPoint 4 should quickly feel comfortable. PowerPoint 95 retains many streamlining features, but it also improves on them. Shortcut menus, activated by clicking the right mouse button, have been expanded. Wizards, Chart AutoLayouts, and toolbars are all still present in PowerPoint 95, and they all work the same way. Cue Cards, which provide step-by-step help, have been enhanced to use both simple text-based procedures and more complicated graphics-based procedures. The program menus are largely the same. PowerPoint 95 is a completely new program, but it has continuity with the past.

Powerful Program Streamlining

PowerPoint 95's screen has changed substantially. Mostly, it reflects the changes in screen appearance provided by the Windows 95 operating system, and are not necessarily PowerPoint-specific. If you have used PowerPoint 4, many of the features described in this section will seem like old friends, thus easing your acceptance of this powerful new version.

As you progress through PowerPoint 95 (and any other Office 95 application) you find many speed improvements at all levels. Microsoft conducted large usability studies with their user base and incorporated their findings into the redesign of the program. They eliminated many dialog boxes and combined the functions into one, making frequent use of the notebook "tab" metaphor. The new program tends to be far less confusing than the already solid PowerPoint 4. The new dialog boxes as shown in figure 1.1 are a good example of these improvements.

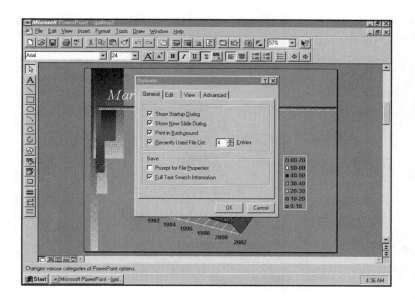

Fig. 1.1
A typical
PowerPoint-related
dialog box,
showing several
"tabs" that each
contain program
features.

Shortcut Menus

Many areas of the program are accessible with a startlingly simple feature—
clicking the right mouse button. Clicking virtually anywhere on the
PowerPoint screen brings up a specialized menu that provides easy access to
relevant program features.

Whenever you click the right mouse button on an object on the PowerPoint
screen, such as a slide background, a drawing, a chart, or a slide title, you
display a special shortcut menu similar to the one shown in figure 1.2.

What's the point of a shortcut menu? What is the biggest advantage to using
the right mouse button? Ever get tired of constantly reaching up with the
mouse to pull down a menu? Or of hunting for the right menu option? By
clicking the right mouse button over the desired object on-screen, you can
skip these tedious steps.

Customized Toolbars

PowerPoint 95 allows you to define exactly how you want your program
screen to appear. The program offers a substantial set of toolbars, any or all
of which can be displayed on the program screen at any time, as shown in
figure 1.3.

Fig. 1.2
The shortcut menu displays options for changing a slide background.

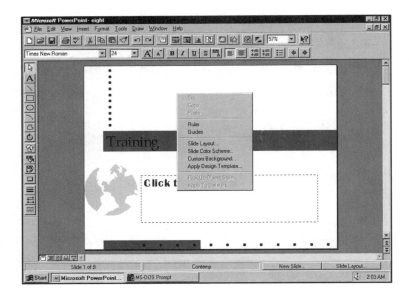

Fig. 1.3
PowerPoint's toolbar set.

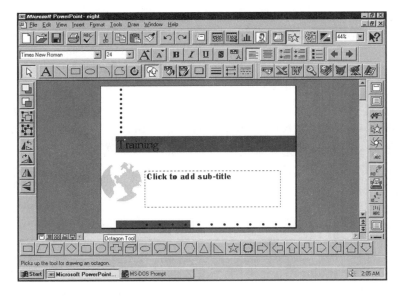

Of course, a toolbar arrangement such as the one in figure 1.3. is probably not to your liking. Most users wouldn't want half the screen occupied by superfluous icons. How does the arrangement in figure 1.4 compare?

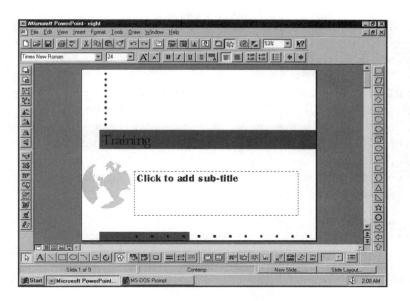

Fig. 1.4
The same
PowerPoint
toolbars, rear-
ranged.

▶ See "Using
  Toolbars,"
  p. 50

▶ See "Using
  Floating
  Toolbars,"
  p. 51

Because PowerPoint's toolbar set can be moved and rearranged at will, a given toolbar can be moved to any margin of the screen. Toolbars also can "float" over the PowerPoint screen by simply dragging them, as in figure 1.4. You have great flexibility when tailoring your PowerPoint screen.

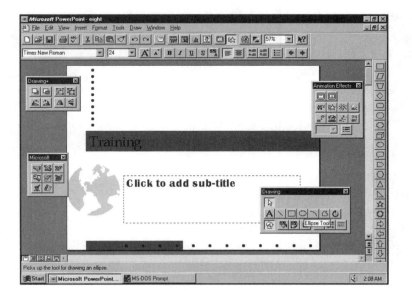

Fig. 1.5
More toolbar
customizing, using
floating toolbars.

▶ See "Customiz-
ing Toolbars,"
p. 692

You can place any PowerPoint function on a toolbar by choosing from the program's generous selection of toolbar icons. Users can change existing toolbars to suit their needs or add any desired number of new ones.

Status Bar, Screen Tips, ToolTips, and Dialog Box Hints

PowerPoint 95's ease of use doesn't stop with mere toolbars and icons. Its front end provides help every step of the way, from the most basic procedures to the most complex. It all starts with the status bar. Any action you perform, any menu option you select, or any button, icon, or tool that you pass the mouse over causes the status bar to display a helpful message, succinctly describing the exact action you're about to perform.

All of PowerPoint's dialog boxes provide a running narrative of the actions you perform and the options you select. You'll never get lost inside PowerPoint.

ToolTips is an intelligent and unobtrusive feature that displays a small text balloon when you pass the mouse over any button on a toolbar. Even advanced users will appreciate the secure feeling of knowing exactly what that cryptic icon is on the custom toolbars they have created.

You may be uncertain of the use of some dialog boxes in PowerPoint 95. Click the right mouse button on the element of the dialog box in question. A Screen Tip will appear as shown in figure 1.6. The Screen Tip is a paragraph of context-sensitive help that describes the feature.

> **Note**
>
> This is a different feature from the shortcut menu. Shortcut menus appear when you click the mouse button on an *object*, such as a drawing, chart or text paragraph, that's displayed on the PowerPoint screen. Clicking the right mouse button on a PowerPoint window displays a Screen Tip.

Feature Consistency, Standardized Menus, and Office Binders

PowerPoint 95 uses a standard menu arrangement that bears a close resemblance to those in Microsoft Word 95 and Excel 95. In fact, only one menu heading is different in each of the three programs, as shown in figure 1.7.

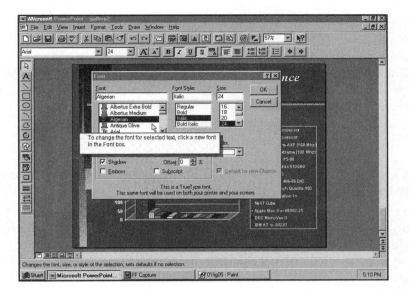

Fig. 1.6
Use Screen Tips context-sensitive help by clicking the right mouse button on a dialog box element.

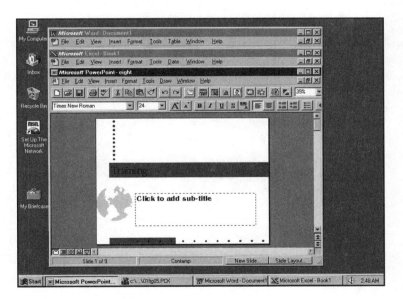

Fig. 1.7
Word, Excel, and PowerPoint menu bars.

Consistency doesn't stop with mere appearance. The AutoCorrect feature, offered in Word for Windows, is now part of PowerPoint. Veteran users also will greatly appreciate PowerPoint 95's support for multiple Undo's—another feature that was only available in Word.

Given the closer relationships between PowerPoint and other Office 95 applications, it would be a shame if there weren't a way to efficiently collect files from those applications into a convenient format. Now there is. Using Office Binders (which can be considered an "electronic paper clip," in Microsoft's words), you can tie together all the files in a project. Users can quickly store presentation files, spreadsheets, and word processing documents in one place, and print them together with continuous page numbering. This makes project management easier.

Wizards for Template and Style Selection, Outlining, Online Help, and Portability

Sometimes you may be forced to produce presentations on a tight schedule. This isn't easy, especially if you have had little experience in creating presentations. To help you get a running start in producing a complete presentation, PowerPoint offers an enhanced AutoContent Wizard. Using AutoContent ensures that you can quickly create a consistent and attractive look for your presentation, and a reasonably complete and organized style and structure before entering content and graphic elements.

The AutoContent Wizard helps you define what the basic message and appearance of your presentation is going to be (see fig. 1.8). The quick four-step process helps you decide what you're going to say and how you're going to say it, as illustrated in figure 1.9.

Fig. 1.8
Use the AutoContent Wizard to take you through the basics of your presentation.

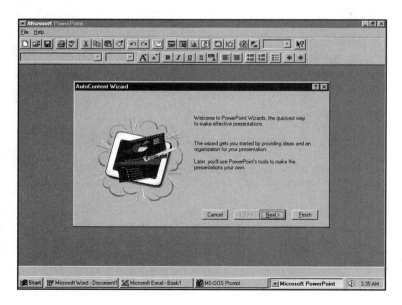

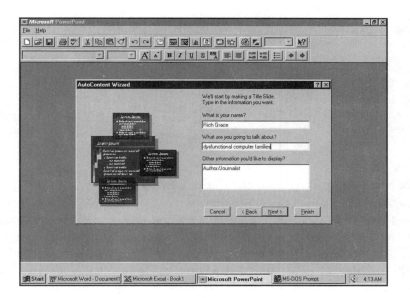

Fig. 1.9
The AutoContent
Wizard helps you
define your
message.

When you're making your presentation at another location and have to
gather sound and video files to take there, you have a difficult job ahead of
you. Another thing that often bothers users is getting lost in online Help, or
spending more time there than you want. Two new Wizards, Pack And Go
and Answer, address these important issues.

The Pack And Go Wizard (see fig. 1.10) assembles your presentation for carrying to other sites. In five simple steps, Pack And Go gathers together your
presentation file and all your linked files (such as audio clips and motion
video files), compresses them, and bundles them into a convenient single-
floppy package. (If the presentation is too big to compress onto one floppy,
Pack And Go automatically uses as many disks as it needs.) No more strug-
gling with linked files. No more making sure that everything is in the right
directory when you set up at another site. No more embarrassment when
your presentation doesn't find the multimedia clips it needs for your show.
For busy users, this new feature is a blessing—and reason enough by itself to
make the upgrade.

The Answer Wizard automates the use of online Help. Located on
PowerPoint's Help menu, the Answer Wizard accepts a word or task and tries
to match it with all the relevant subjects in the Index. The process eliminates
several steps of wading through the Help system.

Fig. 1.10
PowerPoint's Pack And Go wizard makes portable presentations convenient and easy.

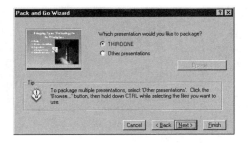

AutoLayouts for Quick Slide Layouts

Instead of having to design slides yourself, you can use PowerPoint 95's expanded set of 24 slide AutoLayouts that combine many types of slide layouts (see fig. 1.11). AutoLayouts bring together six different slide elements in various combinations: charts, tables, titles, body text, media clips, and graphic objects. Choosing a slide AutoLayout is as simple as a double-click with the mouse. Any slide layout can, of course, be modified by the user to suit his or her needs.

Fig. 1.11
PowerPoint's AutoLayout feature displays several pre-defined layouts.

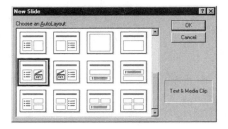

Tighter Application Integration with OLE 2.0

PowerPoint is not just a remarkably powerful application program—it's also part of a larger product called Microsoft Office for Windows 95, which combines Microsoft Word 95, Excel 95, and PowerPoint 95 into an integrated "super-app" that simplifies the process of creating powerful and complex documents. Microsoft Office 95 enables the user to create documents combining many types of data: charts, spreadsheets, databases, formatted word processing text and layouts, graphics, clip art, and even multimedia elements such as movie clips and sound files. Although many office workers may never need to create a document containing all these elements, the power is there for them to tap into at any time.

PowerPoint 95, along with the other Microsoft Office products, supports a powerful concept called *in-place editing*. It's a system in which the various Office programs can be made to work in one window, without the need to open up several applications and tediously switch back and forth between them. If you're working in PowerPoint and you want to use Word 95 to create a table and then paste it onto a slide, all you need to do is click a button on a toolbar. The PowerPoint screen remains, but the PowerPoint toolbars and menus disappear and are replaced by those for Microsoft Word, as shown in figure 1.12.

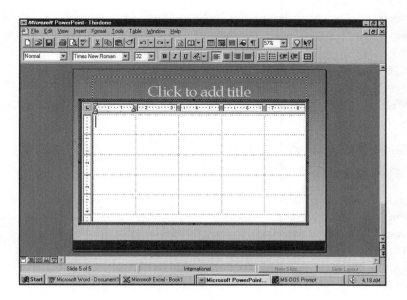

Fig. 1.12
Using OLE's application interoperability in PowerPoint, in this case, Microsoft Word's Table features.

The feature that makes this interoperability possible is Microsoft's OLE 2.0—Object Linking and Embedding, version 2.0. It allows you to copy and paste virtually any type of data between application programs that support OLE, and to bind those applications into a seamless, potent, mutually supportive mega-application program. All the programs in the Standard Edition of Microsoft Office 95 offer this powerful interapplication capability. But because of the enhancements in power offered by Windows 95, OLE 2.0 is even more potent and graceful than before.

The Microsoft Graph application takes full advantage of OLE 2.0 to integrate itself closely with PowerPoint, offering complete consistency between it and the parent PowerPoint application. As a result, PowerPoint's color palettes and color schemes are fully supported in Graph. In fact, most users won't realize that Graph is a separate application program, because it works so closely with PowerPoint 95. (Word 95 also can make use of the Graph application.) Also, veteran Excel users may notice that PowerPoint 95's charting features are largely identical to those for the powerful spreadsheet program. This similarity is yet another example of the ever tighter integration of Microsoft Office programs.

PowerPoint 95's use of objects, and its definition of an object, have been greatly expanded. Anything that's placed on a slide is now considered a PowerPoint object—even another presentation from PowerPoint or any other presentation program. Any data type that's supported as an object by Microsoft Windows can be embedded or linked into a PowerPoint slide show.

▶ See "Using OLE 2.0," p. 514

Improved drag and drop, perhaps the greatest OLE improvement in PowerPoint 95, allows you to quickly bring Word and Excel information into your presentation. Why reenter information if you already have it somewhere else? Drag and drop's improvements are in its performance and efficiency, surpassing the somewhat cumbersome and sluggish Windows 3.1 version. Though the mechanism is exactly the same for the user, the process is smoother and cleaner.

Improved Multimedia Support and Animation Features

PowerPoint 95 reflects and takes advantage of dramatic enhancements in Windows 95's multimedia support. Users will appreciate the increase in control of sound and video playback, and the overall boost in performance. It takes much less time to read in sound and video data. PowerPoint offers a much greater level of multimedia support than previous versions and has substantially caught up to the competition in this important area.

PowerPoint 95 offers a new, closely integrated Media Player application. The new Media Player has enhanced video clip properties and options, and can demonstrate them in real time. Playback timing of multimedia objects during a presentation is now much easier. Control of volume, balance, and other settings for a variety of audio sources is now part of the program.

As with many other PowerPoint objects, you can use menu shortcuts with the right mouse button to enable video and sound editing and playback. PowerPoint's newly expanded animation features can be applied to multimedia objects.

▶ See "Using Multimedia in PowerPoint 95," p. 591

Because you also can apply PowerPoint's animation features to any graphic object, you can choose from a large array of features. Builds, of course, can be applied to any text segment. Some build effects also are available in a new Animation Effects toolbar, which you can customize to provide more effects at the touch of a button. Also, the program features a set of stock sound effects that are easy to apply to Build objects.

Improved Color Support

PowerPoint 95 wouldn't be complete if it hadn't enhanced the already strong color capabilities of the previous version. In several ways, it helps both the beginning and experienced user to handle color in more creative and useful ways.

Multicolor Gradient Fills

PowerPoint 95 now enables you to use preset and custom multicolor gradient fills in graphic objects and slide backgrounds. It offers a default set of multicolor fills to the rushed presenter with a rapidly approaching deadline. Users with an artistic bent can create their own multicolor fills and save them as part of the library. For the first time, PowerPoint 95 offers a *semitransparent* shadow option, which can be applied to objects and object *shadow* for a new three-dimensional effect.

▶ See "Using Visual Editing (Editing in Place)," p. 515

Built-In Color Schemes

Novice PowerPoint 95 users can simplify the task of finding new color combinations for polished-looking presentations, by using the program's new built-in color schemes. Experienced users can create their own color schemes for future use. Figure 1.13 illustrates this new time-saving feature.

Fig. 1.13

You can use PowerPoint 95's new built-in Color Scheme to polish your presentations.

▶ See "Under-
standing Color
in PowerPoint
95," p. 480

How does this help? By using built-in color schemes, PowerPoint 95 eliminates the different directories of presentation templates that were used in
previous versions of the program. Figure 1.13 shows a set of default slide
show color schemes: from left to right, one for on-screen shows, one for color
overheads, and one for black and white. Simply clicking on one of the
scheme thumbnails changes the slide or slides to the new scheme. You also
can save as many custom schemes as you want.

Simplified Templates with Black and White View

Instead of having to use a separate set of templates for black and white displays and printing, now you can simply switch to a special Black and White
view. This feature automatically enables you to print slides on a monochrome
laser printer, thus avoiding the problem of having those spectacular color and
gradient fills, fades, and other graphic effects look muddy and unreadable on
a laser printout. Printed black and white slides now look sharp and impressive. Like many new features in PowerPoint 95, this one can be customized
by experienced users.

Expanded Drawing Features and Clip Art Library

PowerPoint 95 offers drawing features that put greater artistic power in your
hands. Using PowerPoint, you don't have to resort to a drawing program to
create simple artwork. You can quickly draw many different types of polygons, including squares and rectangles, as well as circles and ellipses. You also
can take advantage of 24 different hard-to-draw AutoShapes that allow a fast
starburst, thought balloon, or other complex shape to be drawn quickly with
a couple of mouse clicks. Other new tools include drop-down color palettes
for lines, object fills, and shadows.

PowerPoint 95 provides a special text rotation feature, and in Microsoft
Graph you can rotate axis labels 90 degrees. (PowerPoint 95 now offers the
ability to easily apply Build and animation effects to drawn objects.) In
PowerPoint 95, you can now fit text to curves. Graphics and text objects can
be extruded into three dimensions.

PowerPoint's clip art library has been expanded to more than 1,400 pieces,
created by professional graphic artists at Genigraphics Corporation. The clip
art is organized into 26 categories. An improved ClipArt Gallery (see fig. 1.13)
organizes the categories of clip art into easy-to-view thumbnails, enabling the
user to preview any artwork before deciding to include it in the presentation.

The ClipArt Gallery has been made easier to use, particularly in its methods for importing other art for use in the Gallery. Many clip art operations have been streamlined and simplified. Finally, using PowerPoint's drawing tools, you can completely change any piece of clip art to suit your needs.

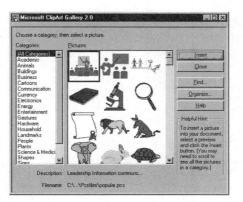

Fig. 1.14
PowerPoint's ClipArt Gallery, showing a selection of artwork.

Enhanced Presentation Rehearsal, Control, and Annotation

PowerPoint 95 simplifies the crucial processes of rehearsing, setting the timing of events, and managing slide show delivery. By simply watching a digital clock and pressing the mouse button during a slide show rehearsal, you can trigger each event that occurs during a presentation at a specific time, so that your actual presentation in front of an audience goes like clockwork. Multimedia elements work exactly as they should during a slide show.

A new tools menu available during slide shows offers a wide variety of real-time presentation tools (see fig. 1.15). Opened by clicking the button at the bottom left of the screen, it furnishes, among other features, a Slide Navigator, a Meeting Minder, and a Slide Meter for tracking slide show timings "on the fly."

The Slide Navigator allows the user to switch quickly to any slide in the active presentation. For example, if a member of the audience asks you a question about a previous slide, all you need to do is click the right mouse button, choose "Go To," and select the desired slide from the list of slides that pops up. No more guesswork!

During your presentation, a member of the audience may ask a question requiring you to expand on a certain point in your discussion. Use the Pen tool on the presentation screen to help you answer the question with hand-drawn annotations (see fig. 1.16). The Pen tool can use any of several different colors, too.

Fig. 1.15
Slide shows now offer a new array of tools.

New pop-up menu shows the list of new presentation management tools

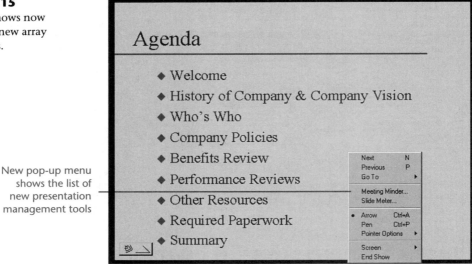

Fig. 1.16
PowerPoint's Pen tool allows you to add a top line on the graph during a presentation.

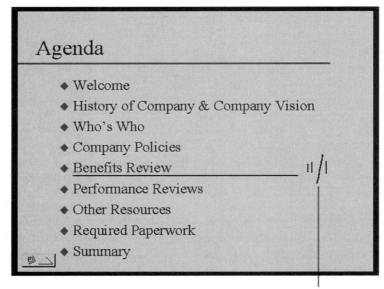

Annotated markings added using the Pen tool

You can easily hide one or more individual slides with PowerPoint 95's Hide Slide command. PowerPoint 95 uses OLE to allow an innovative method of branching between presentations. Figure 1.17 shows three different presentations that have been loaded as objects into a parent presentation.

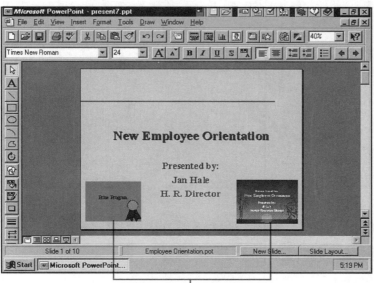

Fig. 1.17
Three presentations loaded as objects into another presentation.

Each thumbnail image, when double-clicked, branches your slide show to another presentation

Branching offers tremendous advantages, because the user can combine any number of presentations into a "super presentation" containing numerous tangents and different tracks that the audience can request during the show.

PowerPoint also lets you build Play Lists for running several presentations in sequence. Play Lists simply offer a quick way to combine several presentation files together for a longer show.

PowerPoint 95's new Meeting Minder (see fig. 1.18) provides a graceful way to manage the process of taking notes, listing action items, and gathering information during the presentation meeting. Instead of relying on cumbersome hard-copy note taking during a presentation, the user can have all the information already in electronic format for use and follow-up after the presentation. It runs simultaneously with the slide show and can output files in Microsoft Word format. The Meeting Minder represents part of Microsoft's effort to accommodate important needs of their customer base.

► See "Branching between Presentations," p. 642

► See "Rehearsing Your Presentation," p. 657

Fig. 1.18
PowerPoint 95's new Meeting Minder.

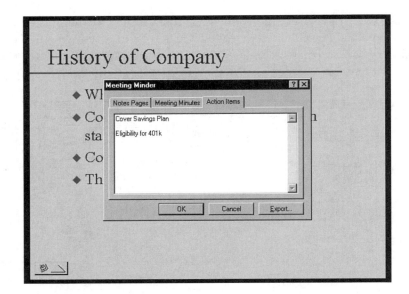

Expanded Support for Other Presentation Formats

PowerPoint 95 now imports Lotus Freelance for Windows 1.x and 2.x presentation files, along with those of various versions of Harvard Graphics. Of course, it directly supports PowerPoint 4 files. For Macintosh users, Microsoft will make available online a special filter, that enables PowerPoint 4 for Macintosh users to read and import PowerPoint 95 files.

Conferencing and Lotus Notes Support

PowerPoint's new Presentation Conferencing feature (see fig. 1.19) allows you to take advantage of Local-Area or Wide-Area Networks to deliver remote presentations. A special Stage Manager feature lets you track note, take minutes, and record action items on your computer while your entire remote audience watches only the slides. Given the expanded multimedia capabilities of PowerPoint 95, make sure you have enough network bandwidth to support your users!

Fig. 1.19
PowerPoint's new
Presentation
Conferencing
Wizard helps you
deliver remote
presentations.

PowerPoint 95 has expanded its OLE properties to include remote browsing and viewing in Lotus Notes View and on NetWare and Windows NT servers. Microsoft PowerPoint also supports Notes/FX's OLE Properties user interface.

There's actually more. PowerPoint is clearly not just a rewrite for Windows 95. It is a dramatically expanded, feature-rich program. Even with its increased depth, the program is more graceful to use, more efficient, and anticipates many more needs of the user.❖

Chapter 2

Getting Acquainted with PowerPoint 95

by Rich Grace

Windows 95 applications offer you many advantages. A key advantage is that once you know how to use one major Windows 95 program, you know how to use most of the basic features of many other Windows software packages.

In this chapter, you look at the standard Windows features of PowerPoint 95 and examine most of its important user interface features. You also learn about

- PowerPoint's toolbars and ToolTips
- PowerPoint's status bar
- Opening and closing program and document windows
- Program and document window tools

> **Note**
>
> Windows 95 offers many basic features common to all applications—clicking and dragging objects with the mouse, choosing menu options and program features by using the mouse or keyboard, changing the size of windows, and minimizing and maximizing windows, to name just a few. If you aren't already familiar with these basic Windows operations, refer to Que's *Special Edition Using Windows 95* for complete explanations.

Using the Mouse

To perform many PowerPoint actions, you can use either a mouse or a keyboard command; however, because many sophisticated PowerPoint 95 functions can be performed only with a mouse, you do need a mouse to use the program. In many cases, you may find keyboard commands more convenient to use because they offer handy shortcuts.

Normally, you use the mouse to start a PowerPoint feature, especially when the feature is a dialog box option. Click the option once to select it, and then click OK to run the feature. Alternatively, you can double-click the option to run the feature. Using the mouse this way speeds up your use of the program.

In many situations, you will need to drag the mouse. Highlighting text is just one example. You may, for example, need to move items from one place to another or to select a group of objects. To drag the mouse, you click and hold down the left mouse button and then move, or "drag," the mouse to a new position on-screen. This is especially frequent when you use OLE (Object Linking and Embedding) to bring data between Microsoft applications or PowerPoint document windows.

Selecting Multiple Objects and Scrolling

Many times in PowerPoint, dragging the mouse defines a box that changes size as you move the mouse. Drawing a box around several objects selects all those objects at once. In some situations, if you want to select several objects, you also can hold down the Shift key while you click the mouse button on each; and they will remain highlighted.

Using the mouse, you can move to any visible screen area by moving the pointer to that position and clicking. Sometimes, your PowerPoint slide or program window may not be entirely visible on-screen, particularly if you've been moving and resizing windows. To scroll through a slide or program window, use the scroll bars, which lie on the right side and bottom of each window. Each scroll bar contains two scrolling arrows and a scroll box, which enable you to see hidden portions of the window. Click and hold the mouse on the scroll bar to move it.

> **Note**
>
> The scroll bar at the right side of the screen is called the Slide Changer. When you click the mouse on it, a Screen Tip appears that shows the slide number and its title. An example appears in figure 2.1.

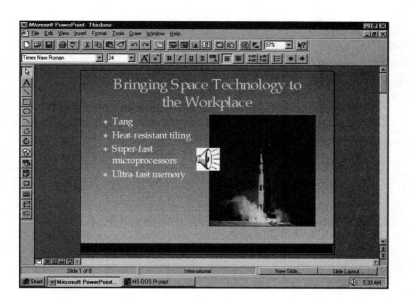

PowerPoint 95 Basics

Fig. 2.1
Clicking the Slide
Changer reveals a
Screen Tip that
displays the slide
number and its
title.

The Changing Mouse Pointer

The mouse pointer can assume several different shapes while you use it.
The arrow pointer is the most common shape. Use the arrow for pointing,
choosing from menus, selecting objects, and so on.

When the pointer changes to an I-beam (resembling an uppercase I), use it to
highlight text or click where you want to enter new text. (When you do this,
as you type, your position is indicated by a blinking vertical bar, which is
called the insertion point. This point is very likely to be separate from where
the I-beam is.)

For drawing shapes such as rectangles, ellipses, lines, and freeform polygons,
and for some other functions in the program, the mouse pointer appears as a
crosshair. When the program is completing a task and you have to wait, the
pointer turns into an hourglass. When you are resizing windows and objects
in the PowerPoint screen, the pointer appears as a two-headed arrow. The
two-headed arrow is diagonal when you are resizing horizontally and vertically at the same time. In some places, a four-headed arrow allows you to
move items with the keyboard rather than drag them with the mouse.

Using the Right Mouse Button

New programs such as PowerPoint 95 offer expanded mouse functionality.
In many places in the program, you can use the right mouse button to access
program features. Clicking once with the right mouse button on many

different kinds of items in the PowerPoint screen displays a special menu called the shortcut menu (see fig. 2.2). The features and commands on the shortcut menu depend on the type of item or object that you have selected on-screen.

Fig. 2.2
Clicking the right mouse button activates the shortcut menu in Windows 95.

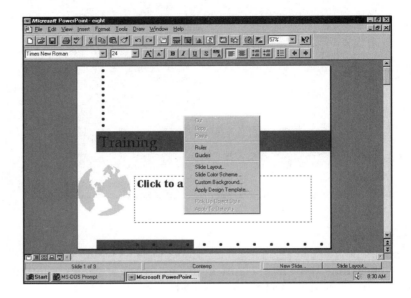

To display an object's shortcut menu, you do not have to select the object first. Right-clicking an object or screen area automatically selects it and opens the shortcut menu at the same time. The shortcut menu frees you from having to move the mouse to the top of the screen to choose menu options, thus allowing you to perform fast changes on objects.

Manipulating Windows

PowerPoint 95 conforms to all the Windows 95 standards for minimizing, maximizing, closing, moving, and resizing windows. A typical PowerPoint 95 screen appears in figure 2.3.

As with PowerPoint 4 and other Office applications, PowerPoint 95 offers a feature called Multiple Document Interface (MDI), which enables you to have multiple documents open at once within the program. If you have a presentation file open in PowerPoint, you can open a second and a third file and then minimize and maximize their windows, just as you can in Windows.

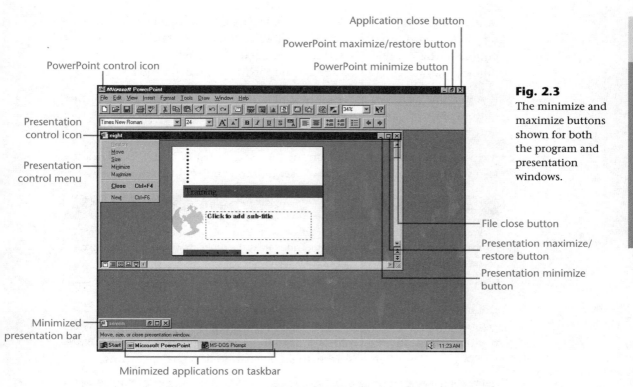

Fig. 2.3
The minimize and maximize buttons shown for both the program and presentation windows.

The PowerPoint application screen has a new Control icon, which vaguely resembles a computer monitor displaying a screen. Clicking it displays the Control menu, which allows you to close the application, minimize it, and restore it, among other functions. (The Control menu works much the same way in Windows 95 as it does in Windows 3.x.) Presentation windows also have their own Control menus, which are triggered by clicking a new Document icon in the top right, next to the caption displaying the document's name. Though both Control menus are similar, their different icons (a new Windows 95 feature) help the user see the difference between them.

The minimize button and maximize buttons, which respectively shrink and enlarge windows, are located at the top right corner of open windows. The buttons for the program window are located at the far right end of the PowerPoint title bar. A maximize/restore button (which changes its appearance depending on the state of the window) either forces the window to occupy the whole screen or enables the window to take up only a part of the screen or the application window. The same buttons are used for both application windows and document windows.

Maximizing a program window causes it to fill all the available space on-screen. Minimizing a program reduces it to an item in the task list at the bottom of the Windows 95 screen. If a program or presentation window is minimized, the task is still running, and the file is still open and active.

If you minimize a presentation window, a small document bar appears at the bottom of the program screen. This bar displays the name of the file, a restore button, a maximize button, and a close button.

A close button also is provided on the top right corner of both the application window and the document (presentation) window. Its icon is a big X.

Caution

Watch your close buttons. If you accidentally click on one, you may close your file or the application without intending to. Fortunately, the program will ask if you want to save before you exit. Save your work frequently!

Double-clicking the Control menu icon in a presentation closes that file. Double-clicking the Control menu icon in the program window enables you to close and exit the PowerPoint program. If you haven't saved the file you're working on, PowerPoint asks whether you want to do so before exiting.

Note

PowerPoint, as with other Office 95 applications, has drop-down menus. When you click a menu and display it, slide the mouse across the menu bar. The other menus are automatically displayed without clicking on them.

What Happened to Program Groups and Program Manager?

Many changes have taken place in the Windows 95 user interface. While this isn't a book about how to use Windows 95, a few important aspects call for explanation.

First, bear in mind that Windows 95 operates using a *folder* concept. A folder is roughly analogous to an old-style DOS or a Windows 3.1 directory. A directory contains files and subdirectories. Folders work exactly the same way, but look completely different. They are shown as little file folder icons.

Subdirectories are also considered to be folders under Windows 95. (Thus you can have folders within folders to any desired level.) Icons representing files can be dragged and dropped from folder to folder.

Figure 2.4 shows a fairly typical Windows 95 screen. The Start button, where you usually start programs, rests at the lower left corner of the screen, on the left end of the Windows 95 taskbar. Clicking the Start button opens the Start menu, which is your avenue to locating programs and files. Clicking Start and dragging the mouse up the menu reveals cascading menus, which display more menus or show program icons that you can select for running under Windows 95.

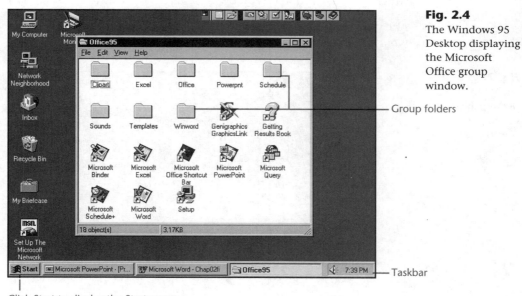

Fig. 2.4
The Windows 95 Desktop displaying the Microsoft Office group window.

Group folders

Taskbar

Click Start to display the Start menu

Your applications and documents are still gathered into "groups," just as in Windows 3.1. You can even display those groups in windows like you do in Windows 3.1. It's the method of accessing and displaying those groups that is so different. There is no Program Manager, on which your computer's desktop was arranged or "shoehorned in." Now, all elements of your desktop—Windows 95's "Recycle Bin," program groups, and the like—are arranged directly on the screen without the Program Manager straitjacket. The Windows 95 screen, as shown in figure 2.4, is now called the Windows Desktop.

Another important feature of the Windows 95 screen is called the taskbar. Shown in figure 2.4, each open program or folder is listed from left to right across the taskbar at the bottom of the screen. When you minimize a Windows 95 application like PowerPoint, it will be listed on the taskbar. Clicking any of the folders or programs displays them on the Windows 95 screen.

Starting PowerPoint

Because PowerPoint 95 is a Windows 95 application program, you can use it only within Windows 95. (PowerPoint 95 also runs under Windows NT 3.51, which offers an optional Windows 95 Graphical User Interface add-on.)

After you start Windows 95, you see a screen similar to the one in figure 2.5 (your screen should resemble, but may not be identical to this).

Fig. 2.5
The Windows 95 Desktop, before starting PowerPoint.

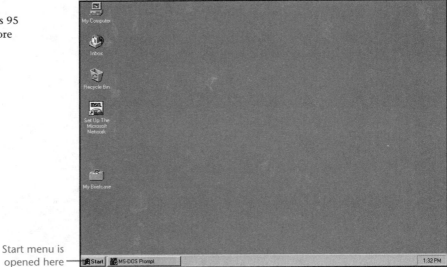

Start menu is opened here

To start PowerPoint, open the Start menu and choose Programs, Microsoft PowerPoint. During this process, the pop-up Start menu appears, showing a list of the currently installed folders. Sliding the mouse up over Programs in the Start menu will automatically display the submenu without clicking. PowerPoint appears in that submenu.

After you drag the mouse to PowerPoint, the program starts. If you are running PowerPoint for the first time (and that's the assumption here), you will see a screen titled "What's New in Microsoft PowerPoint 95," as shown in figure 2.6.

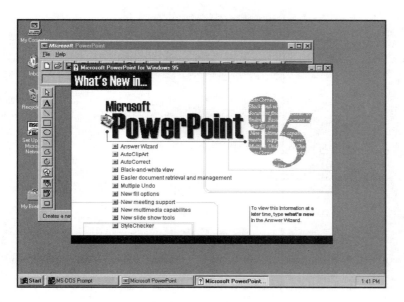

Fig. 2.6

The "What's New in Microsoft PowerPoint 95" screen. You see this when you start up PowerPoint for the first time after installation.

To close the "What's New" screen, press Alt+F4 or click the Close button. Next, PowerPoint's opening screen will show the Tip of the Day (see fig. 2.7), which offers a set of simple tips for easier use of the program.

Fig. 2.7

The Tip of the Day.

If you want the Tip of the Day to appear whenever you start the program, leave the check mark in the Show Tips at Startup check box. (The program automatically gives you this feature unless you turn it off.) If you don't want to see the Tip of the Day, click the check box to deselect the check mark.

Click OK to quit the Tip of the Day dialog box and go to the basic PowerPoint screen. (It also is available in PowerPoint's Help menu.)

Next, the PowerPoint dialog box appears. This is where you select a Wizard or other method to help you create a new presentation or where you open an existing one. It is shown in figure 2.8.

Fig. 2.8
The PowerPoint dialog box, offering key options for starting your work.

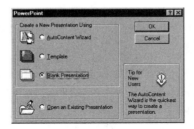

The PowerPoint dialog box options are briefly listed below:

<u>A</u>utoContent Wizard	Quickly designs the types of slides you want for your new presentation
<u>T</u>emplate	Selects a template for a presentation
<u>B</u>lank Presentation	Creates a new, blank presentation
<u>O</u>pen an Existing Presentation	Opens a presentation file. This option is dimmed when you start the program for the first time. Otherwise, choosing this option opens the File Open dialog box, allowing you to search for presentation files on the Windows Desktop.

When you quit the Tip of the Day, you see the PowerPoint dialog box as just described. After you open a presentation file or use a wizard to create a new one, you will see the main PowerPoint screen, which displays several toolbars and other basic screen elements.

Getting Familiar with the PowerPoint Screen

This section describes the PowerPoint screen and the elements that make it unique. PowerPoint is familiar because it is a Windows program, but many of its tools and screen elements require a brief explanation.

The title bar at the top of the PowerPoint program window displays the title Microsoft PowerPoint. If a file is open and maximized in the program, the title bar also displays the name of that file, as figure 2.9 illustrates. The menu bar rests just below the title bar, displaying the menu choices File, Edit, View, Insert, Format, Tools, Draw, Window, and Help.

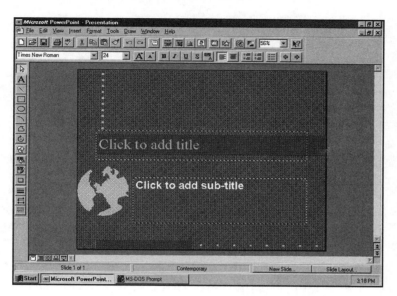

PowerPoint 95 Basics

Fig. 2.9
The PowerPoint 95 screen, with an active maximized presentation that occupies the entire PowerPoint window. Several PowerPoint toolbars are displayed.

If the active presentation file isn't maximized in PowerPoint, it has its own title bar, which appears below the menu bar (see fig. 2.10).

At the bottom of the PowerPoint screen, above the Windows 95 taskbar, is PowerPoint's status bar. In figure 2.10, the words "Slide 1 of 9" appear at its left end. The message displayed in the status bar changes whenever you do something with the program or display another slide. If you ever "get lost" while using a program feature, glance at the status bar to find out where you currently are in PowerPoint.

The center of the status bar displays the template upon which the current slide show is built. For example, in figures 2.9 and 2.10, the word Contemporary is shown. It indicates that while the Training template has been used to help define the content of the presentation, the Contemporary design template has been applied for the presentation's appearance.

At the right end of the status bar are two buttons—New Slide, and Slide Layout. Clicking New Slide inserts a new slide into your presentation, and clicking Slide Layout opens a dialog box where you can select a new slide layout.

Fig. 2.10
The active presentation is not maximized and therefore floats within the PowerPoint window.

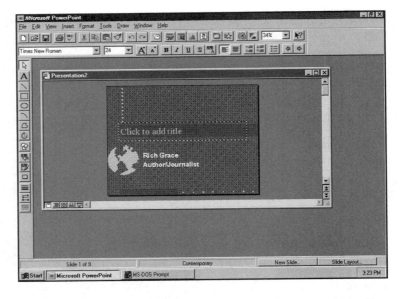

Tip
You also can press Ctrl+M to begin the process of adding a new slide.

The far right side of the PowerPoint screen is occupied by the Slide Changer. The Slide Changer works like a regular Windows scroll bar, except that as you drag up or down on the scroll bar, other slides in your presentation appear.

Understanding the Toolbars

Toolbars are one of the most important parts of PowerPoint. PowerPoint 95 offers a substantial set of toolbars that allows single-click access to many key program features. You also can create customized toolbars and add new tools to existing ones. When you start up PowerPoint for the first time, three toolbars are displayed: two at the top of the screen and one on the left side. The three toolbars represent important areas of PowerPoint's operation: Standard, Formatting, and Drawing. There are seven different toolbars in PowerPoint's basic set, as shown in figure 2.11, any or all of which you can display in the main PowerPoint screen.

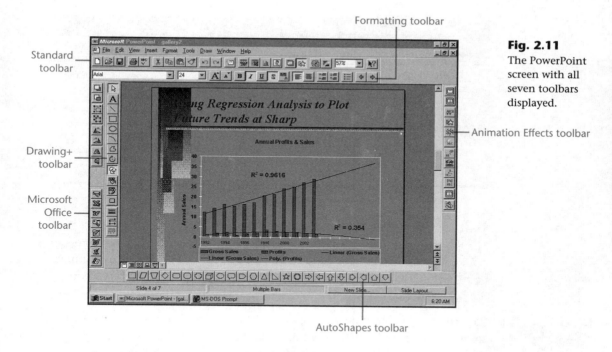

Formatting toolbar

Standard toolbar

Drawing+ toolbar

Microsoft Office toolbar

Animation Effects toolbar

Fig. 2.11
The PowerPoint screen with all seven toolbars displayed.

PowerPoint 95 Basics

AutoShapes toolbar

Table 2.1 describes the toolbars shown in figure 2.11.

Toolbar	Description
Table 2.1 PowerPoint Toolbars	
Standard	Offers many standard PowerPoint program functions such as opening, saving, and printing files; handling files; and cutting, copying, and pasting.
Formatting	Provides text formatting functions such as bold, italic, justification, and font selection.
Drawing	Offers basic drawing functions such as drawing basic shapes, arcs, and curves; applying color fills; and grouping drawn objects.
Drawing+	Provides extra and advanced drawing functions, such as applying fill colors to objects and lines, applying line styles, adding arrowheads, and grouping and ungrouping.
Animation Effects	Activates a set of Build animation effects that can be applied to selected text or graphics objects.

(continues)

Table 2.1 Continued	
Toolbar	**Description**
AutoShapes	Provides automatic drawing of 24 polygon shapes, including stars, speech balloons, sunbursts, and other hard-to-draw objects.
Microsoft Office	Provides single-click access to other Microsoft Office applications, plus other programs such as FoxPro and Publisher that are not part of the Office 95 suite. Naturally, these buttons will only work if you have copies of the applications properly installed on your system.

Using Toolbars

The toolbars pictured in the preceding section offer fast access to many crucial PowerPoint 95 features. You use the toolbars only with a mouse or similar pointing device. To use them, simply click the tool (button) that represents the command or program function you want to execute.

 PowerPoint now offers a new tool on the Standard toolbar for getting quick context-sensitive help. Clicking this tool (which shows an arrow and question-mark icon as shown in the margin of this paragraph) and then clicking a PowerPoint screen element such as another tool or the status bar will display a one-paragraph description of that feature.

As you've noticed, not all the toolbars are displayed when you first start the program. You decide which toolbars you want to display and where they will appear on-screen. Toolbars are always accessible, regardless of where they are, because they always float over your program screen.

Tip
For quick help on any toolbar function, press Shift+F1 and click any tool.

To display or remove toolbars from the PowerPoint screen, follow these steps:

1. Choose View, Toolbars.

   The Toolbars dialog box appears (see fig. 2.12).

2. The dialog box lists seven toolbars. Clicking any empty check box places a check mark inside it, meaning the program will display the desired toolbar. Clicking on a check box that has a check mark inside it removes the check mark.

3. To show color buttons on the toolbars, click the Color Buttons check box. (It's enabled as the default, so you may not have to do this.) Another check box, Show ToolTips, also appears. When enabled with a check, this allows white boxes called ToolTips to appear whenever

you pass the mouse over a button on a toolbar, displaying the name of the tool. Select Large Buttons to enlarge the on-screen size of the toolbars.

4. To display the toolbars as you have set them up, choose OK or press Enter.

Fig. 2.12
Use the View, Toolbars feature to change the number of toolbars displayed in the program. The dialog box shows a set of checkboxes that enable or disable toolbars on the PowerPoint screen.

Note

The Customize button also is offered in the Toolbars dialog box. Clicking it starts up PowerPoint's toolbar customization feature. This capability is described in Chapter 24, "Customizing PowerPoint 95."

When you need help using a particular tool, click the Help tool on the Standard toolbar and then click the tool in question. If the Help tool isn't available, press Shift+F1 and then click the tool you need help with. PowerPoint displays a Screen Tip to show you how to use the tool. To close the Screen Tip, click the screen outside of it.

Using Floating Toolbars

Floating toolbars are toolbars you can detach from their normal places at the top or side of the PowerPoint screen, so that they "float" over the presentation.

You can do this to any toolbar in the PowerPoint program (see fig. 2.13). Simply click and hold the mouse button on any gray area of the toolbar that isn't occupied by a tool button (such as the top or bottom end of a toolbar) and drag it. The toolbar changes shape as you drag it around the screen. Drag the toolbar to where you want it, and release the mouse. Toolbars can be dragged to the top, bottom, or sides of the screen.

Tools in a floating toolbar work exactly the same as they otherwise would, and you can drag them to any margin of the PowerPoint screen. You also can drag any edge of a toolbar to reshape it.

Fig. 2.13
Floating toolbars
in the PowerPoint
screen.

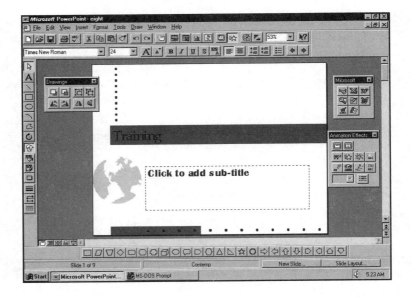

When you place toolbars in new locations on-screen or display new toolbars, PowerPoint automatically displays them in their new arrangements when you start the program again. PowerPoint thus allows you to arrange the screen exactly as you see fit.

> **Note**
>
> The PowerPoint screen can get a little crowded if you want to display all your toolbars, particularly if your computer is running in VGA mode. If your monitor and computer's video card support it, you should run Windows at higher screen resolutions, such as 800x600 or 1024x768, and thus relieve the crowding. You should then have plenty of room for your toolbars. Consult your Windows documentation or the manual for your computer's video card for more information if you're not sure how to do this.

Using ToolTips

ToolTips are a simple and unobtrusive form of "balloon help" that help you quickly understand the functions of the tools on the various PowerPoint toolbars. If the ToolTips feature is enabled (as it is by default), a small white box with text in it appears as you pass the mouse over any toolbar tool on the screen (see fig. 2.14). If you compare the ToolTip and the status bar at the bottom of the PowerPoint screen, you'll notice that their messages are the same. The status bar also provides a brief description of the tool's function.

Given the propensity of Windows programs like PowerPoint 95 to succumb to "iconitis" (the practice of assigning every possible program function an icon or a tool button), you may find it hard to keep all the tools straight. ToolTips provide an easy and convenient way to navigate all the button functions without getting lost or, even worse, doing something you didn't intend to do.

If for some reason the ToolTips feature is not enabled and you want to turn it on, follow these steps:

1. Choose <u>V</u>iew, <u>T</u>oolbars.

2. Click the Show ToolTips check box at the bottom of the dialog box to place a check mark in it.

3. Choose OK or press Enter to start up the ToolTips feature.

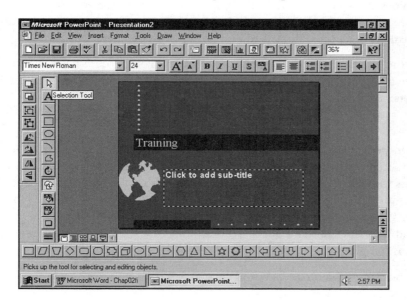

Fig. 2.14
Using ToolTips on the PowerPoint screen.

The ToolTips work whether you're in PowerPoint, in Microsoft's Graph charting application, or in any of the program's views, such as Outline view or the Slide Sorter.

▶ See "Understanding PowerPoint Views," p. 66

PowerPoint 95 Basics

Troubleshooting

I can't find the text formatting tools on PowerPoint's toolbar.

You probably need to display more toolbars on the screen—namely the Formatting toolbar. To do so, choose View, Toolbars to open the Toolbars dialog box. Click the Formatting check, and then choose OK or press Enter. The text formatting tools appear on the PowerPoint screen.

Using PowerPoint's Menus

PowerPoint's menu bar is a complement to the toolbars and offers access to literally every function of the program. Earlier, you learned the basic menu names and where they are located on the PowerPoint screen; now you'll dig into them in a little more detail. Later chapters contain comprehensive discussions of all the options and functions mentioned here.

While the toolbars offer fast access to many of PowerPoint's basic features, the menu bar, with its many options, allows you to attend to every possible detail of program management in PowerPoint.

Reviewing PowerPoint's Menus

Another advantage of using PowerPoint with other Windows applications (especially other Microsoft applications) is that its set of menus closely mirrors those of other applications. You almost always see the File and Edit menus in Windows applications. Other Microsoft programs, such as Word for Windows 95 and Excel offer other common menus—Insert, Window, and Help, for example. Of course, there are differences, but the basics of most programs are the same.

Table 2.2 gives a broad view and general description of the basics of PowerPoint's menus.

Table 2.2 The PowerPoint Main Menu Bar	
Menu	**Description**
File	Lists PowerPoint's file-handling options, such as Open, Close, New, Print, Save, Pack And Go, and Exit. It also provides a list of recently opened files that allows you to open files again quickly.
Edit	Offers access to many of PowerPoint's most important editing features, such as Cut and Paste, Paste Special, and Find and Replace.

Menu	Description
View	Offers access to the various views and screens within PowerPoint, including the default Slide view, the Slide Sorter, Outline view, and notes pages. From here you also can enable the current Slide Show, enable and disable Toolbars, control various screen viewing options such as Zoom level, and view Rulers and Guides.
Insert	Offers access to program features for inserting new entities of various types into a presentation—anything from inserting a new slide into a presentation to placing new objects of various descriptions onto a slide, such as pictures, clip art, charts, and video clips. Slides from other PowerPoint files can be inserted from here.
Format	Controls every possible feature for changing and defining the appearance of every aspect of your presentation, including fonts, presentation templates, color handling, bulleted text, text alignment, and picking up formats from objects and applying them to other objects of the same type.
Tools	Controls many of PowerPoint's most powerful add-ons, such as the Spelling Checker and AutoCorrect (for instantaneous correcting of spelling and grammatical errors). Others include transition timing for special effects in a presentation, customizing toolbars, and using or disabling Smart Quotes and Smart Cut and Paste. Many of PowerPoint 95's most important new features are located here, including the Meeting Minder, the Write-Up feature for creating Speaker's Notes, and the Style Checker for catching inadvertent errors in slide formatting. Tools also offers Animation Settings.
Draw	Controls most of PowerPoint's basic graphics handling features, such as grouping and ungrouping objects, layering drawn objects (Send to Back and Bring to Front), setting precise sizes and scales of objects, and rotating and flipping of objects.
Window	Lets you arrange PowerPoint's presentation windows on the screen: Tiling, Cascading, and Fitting the current presentation window onto the screen. The Window menu also lists currently open documents.
Help	Contains various kinds of help, including a comprehensive online Help system, the new Answer Wizard feature (which offers a fast Help Index and Search capability), the Tip of the Day, and information on the version of the software being used. Technical support information and system information are available as dialog box options under the About Microsoft PowerPoint menu option.

Choosing Menu Commands

Each PowerPoint menu, as in any other Windows application, opens when you click its menu name in the menu bar. Clicking a menu name displays a pull-down menu, so-called because the menu is normally "pulled," or dragged, downward from the menu bar at the top of the screen.

Some menu options have a submenu that pops out beside the originally selected menu. This menu is called a cascading menu or *submenu* (see fig. 2.15).

Fig. 2.15
Using submenus to locate additional features in the program.

Arrowheads indicate a cascading menu

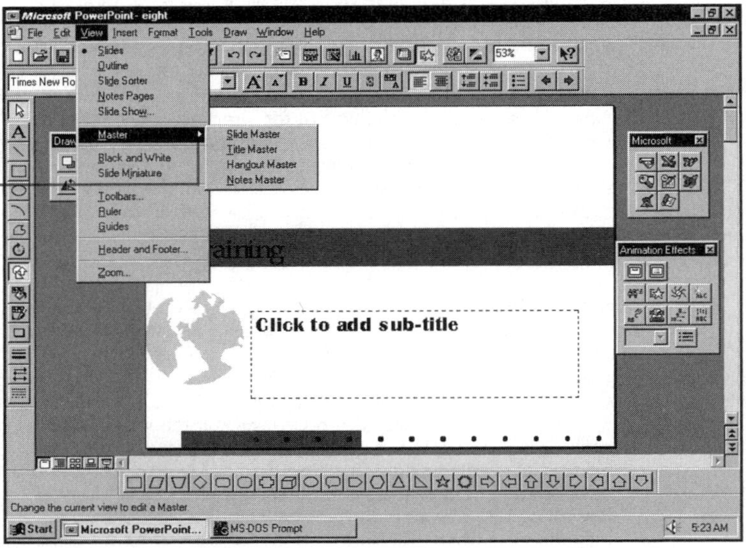

As you can see, more program options are offered on cascading menus. Cascading menus are indicated on the pull-down menu by a small arrow on the right edge of the menu.

To access a menu command by using the keyboard mnemonics, follow these three steps.

1. Pull down the menu from the menu bar with an Alt+keystroke command, such as Alt+F to pull down the File menu.

2. Press the appropriate key for the menu option you want to run.

3. If there is a dialog box associated with the menu command, use the Alt key in combination with the dialog box option.

Tip
An ellipsis (…) after a menu option indicates that a dialog box appears when you select that option.

Choosing Dialog Box Options

When you pull down any menu, you'll notice a pattern. Each menu has certain options that are followed by an ellipsis (…), such as New or Open on the File menu.

> **Note**
>
> If a menu option doesn't have the ellipsis, it simply means that when you select that menu command, it is performed immediately. For example, if you select the Date and Time command from the Insert menu, the current date is inserted as a text object.

A pair of typical dialog boxes are shown in figures 2.16 and 2.17; together they show the various dialog box elements in PowerPoint.

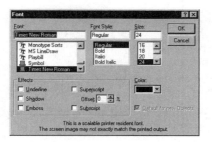

Fig. 2.16
An example of a typical PowerPoint dialog box.

Fig. 2.17
Some dialog boxes contain tabs, which include more options.

Dialog boxes contain various items. Each item type and how you use it in the program are described below:

■ *Tab.* Options are grouped into related topics on a single tab. The tabs resemble the category tabs you sometimes see in school notebooks. Tabs occur frequently in PowerPoint 95 dialog boxes.

To open a tab in a dialog box, simply click the tab at the top; the new group appears.

■ *Text Box*. A box in which you can type and edit text, dates, and numbers.

To use a text box, click the mouse inside it. A blinking bar, or insertion point, appears. You can use the Delete and Backspace keys in these boxes. To select a word in a text box, drag the mouse across the word(s) or double-click on it.

■ *Option Button*. A round button that gives you one choice from a group of options. Each option has a button. (They also are sometimes called radio buttons.)

To choose an option button, click it.

■ *Check Box*. A square box that can be turned on or off. A check in the box means that the option is enabled.

To select or deselect a check box, click the mouse inside it.

■ *List Box*. A list or drop-down list that scrolls to display available alternatives.

To select and use a list box, either click on the list item if it's visible; or click on the scroll arrow to scroll down the list to view other items, and then click on the desired item. You also can click on a list item and use the down arrow or up arrow keys to scroll along the list.

■ *Spin Box*. A box for entering a number, with up and down arrow buttons to increase or decrease the number.

■ *Command Button*. A button that completes or cancels a command. Some command buttons also provide access to additional options.

> **Note**
>
> With Windows 95 and the Office 95 applications, Microsoft has introduced a new term for part of the user interface. It's called a "sheet." Sheets (see fig. 2.18) are a special kind of dialog box that are used only when you select a "property" or "properties" of a program. PowerPoint's File, Properties command displays the properties of your currently active file:

As you can see, you click tabs in the Properties sheet to reveal new pages. File Properties provides a lot of useful information about your PowerPoint files. For example, the Statistics page shows how many minutes you've spent editing the current file, along with the number of slides, the number of media clips you've added to the file, and much more. The Contents page provides a summary of the document's contents.

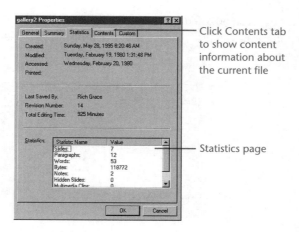

Click Contents tab to show content information about the current file

Statistics page

Fig. 2.18
In Windows 95, property boxes are called sheets, and opened tabs are referred to as pages.

PowerPoint 95 Basics

A sheet works much the same way as a dialog box, but uses slightly different terminology. The Windows 95 Control Panel's Display feature is another example of a Properties sheet.

> **Note**
>
> Many of the program aspects take much longer to describe than to use. As you work with the program, you'll find many of these elements becoming second nature during your progress.

Understanding PowerPoint Slides

Slides are the core of PowerPoint presentations. You must place and arrange on slides all objects you create for your 35mm slides, your overhead transparencies, or your on-screen shows.

Each slide in a presentation has a specific purpose—to deliver a message, or an aspect of a message, efficiently and effectively. Decide upon a particular slide design depending on the type of slide you want. When you want to add a new slide to a presentation, you have 24 AutoLayout choices to pick from. Figure 2.19 shows the AutoLayout feature.

The next chapter describes how to create new slides, along with how to complete a basic presentation. For now, take a look at figure 2.19. The dialog box displays several small thumbnails, each of which represents a slide layout. Each layout has a specific purpose and is intended to have certain kinds of content. Some of the thumbnails depict a slide containing charts, while others depict a bulleted list of points, or an argument. Other slides may offer combinations of both. Thus, the context or design of each slide frames its message.

Fig. 2.19
Viewing
AutoLayout's slide
type thumbnails.

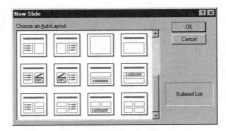

Understanding PowerPoint Templates

Templates supply the basic unifying graphical "look" of a presentation and thus are another crucial aspect of creating presentations. They also are a powerful time-saving feature in PowerPoint 95. In PowerPoint 95, there are two types of templates: presentation templates, which are a collection of slides, with a content theme, and Presentation Design templates, which apply a coordinated set of colors and graphics to a presentation. This section talks mostly about Design templates.

Why a template? If you're a busy person and suddenly have to pull together a sales pitch for an important meeting in only one hour, you definitely don't want to go through the process of creating the graphic arts layout for your slide show. If you're not a professional artist or colorist, or if you're just pressed for time, PowerPoint's substantial array of predefined design templates provide you with a sharp, attractive color background on which you can then build your case.

You can apply a design template to an existing presentation, or you can create a new presentation by using the design template of an existing one. If you have time, you also can create your own templates.

Choosing PowerPoint Template Files

PowerPoint 95 has greatly simplified its collection of templates from the Windows 3.x versions, reducing the three sets of design templates for specialized purposes to one all-encompassing set.

Each of PowerPoint's design templates is based on a certain theme. For example, one of the templates is entitled Blue Diagonal. (Notice that all the template names reflect the long-overdue Windows 95 feature of long file names.) The template displays blue diagonal lines in the slide background.

To browse through the templates, follow these steps:

1. Choose File, New.

   The New Presentation dialog box appears, as shown in figure 2.20.

2. Click the Presentation Designs tab. PowerPoint displays the folder containing all of its template files without your having to do any searching.

3. Click any of the icons that are displayed, such as Blue Diagonal or Color Boxes. You can scroll through the icon list to find others in the Presentation Designs tab.

   The dialog box Preview displays a thumbnail preview of the template. The OK button will be enabled.

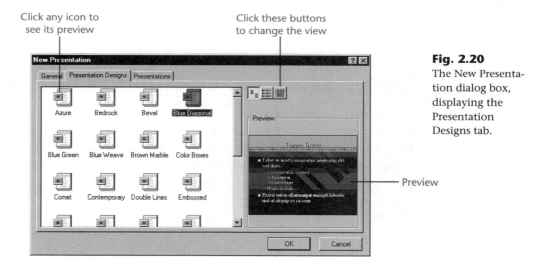

Fig. 2.20
The New Presentation dialog box, displaying the Presentation Designs tab.

4. If you want to use the template, click OK.

   The New Slide dialog box, showing the Slide AutoLayouts, appears.

5. Choose a slide type from the Choose an AutoLayout list.

6. Choose OK. A new presentation will be created, with the first slide showing the template you've chosen.

or

To create the presentation without adding a new slide, click Cancel or press Esc.

Tip
On the CD version of Windows 95, you can find additional design templates in the Pptmpl folder within the Valupack folder.

When you create a new presentation, you also can use the AutoContent Wizard to help you choose between templates.

There's another element of templates that you need to know about—the Slide Master. It's important because it helps determine the appearance of your presentation. It's described in the next section.

> **Note**
>
> PowerPoint 95 also allows the use of Headers and Footers in your slide shows. That feature is described later in this book.

Understanding PowerPoint Masters

The Slide Master defines the contents of the template. Every presentation has a slide master. In turn, presentation templates actually have several masters that control various parts of a presentation. The Outline Master, the Notes Master, and the Handout Master all have a role to play in producing effective, powerful messages.

Tip
You must have an active presentation open to view any of its masters.

Tip
To view the Slide Master you also can hold the Shift key and click the Slide View button just above PowerPoint's status bar.

Using the Slide Master

Slide Masters control the background in a slide show and define the styles of the text and titles that appear in your presentation. They also can contain any objects you want to appear in every slide of a presentation, such as a company logo.

To view the Slide Master, follow these steps:

1. Open the presentation whose master you want to view. You also can simply open a template.

2. Choose View, Master. A cascading menu appears. Choose Slide Master. Your current presentation's display is replaced by its Slide Master. An example of a Slide Master is shown in figure 2.21.

Figure 2.21 shows the way slides for the current presentation will appear when you add text statements and bulleted lists to them. Notice also that the Slide Master provides several levels of bullets. You can apply new fonts or any other available text style to the titles and text.

The statement Click to Edit Master Title Style will not actually appear in any of your slides. That statement is a placeholder that contains the styles for slide titles and their formatting information.

Using the Title Master

The Title Master defines the formatting and arrangement of the *title slide* of your presentation. It allows you to define a unique appearance for your title slide, using any template available. Figure 2.22 illustrates a typical Title Master.

Text styles are shown in the place-holders

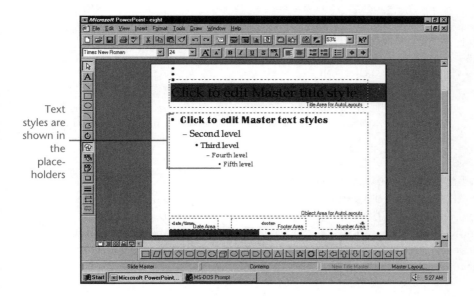

Fig. 2.21
Viewing a Slide Master, with its default text formatting and color scheme.

The Title Master bears many similarities to the Slide Master. As with the latter, you can add a company logo, date and time information, and other items that you want displayed on your Title slide. The Title Master's use is very similar to that of the Slide Master, but it's used only on the Title slide of the presentation. In PowerPoint 95, you can have a title slide that has a different appearance from all the other slides in your presentation.

Fig. 2.22
Viewing a Title Master for a typical presentation. Note the slide layout and background are different from that in figure 2.21, though it's the same presentation.

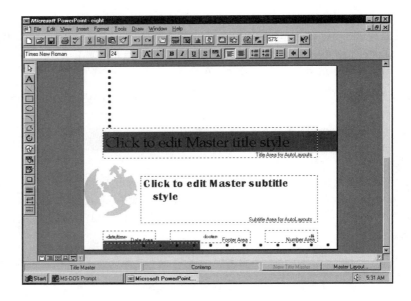

To view the Title Master, follow these steps:

1. Open the presentation you want to edit.

Tip
To view the Title Master, you also can hold the Shift key and click the Notes Pages view button above PowerPoint's status bar.

2. Choose View, Master. A cascading menu appears. Choose Title Master. Your current presentation's display is replaced by its Title Master.

Using the Notes Master

PowerPoint's Notes Master offers a handy way for you to organize an upcoming presentation. Combining a miniaturized view of each slide with the contents of its text, the Notes Master enables you to create notes pages to organize your talk without being forced to gaze at the screen whenever you need to make a point. A typical Notes Master is shown in figure 2.23.

The Notes Master defines the appearance and organization of each notes page. Several placeholders contain and uniformly format the Notes Page contents. Header and Footer placeholders allow easy placement of Header and Footer information such as company names, presenter names, and so on. You can add page numbers to the Notes Master that correspond to the slides in your presentation, and apply color schemes to the notes.

Under the slide graphic, using the Notes placeholder (refer to fig. 2.23), you can format your notes just as you do normal text—with fonts, text styles, centering, and so on. Every notes page will then use those formatting characteristics. You then print your notes pages with the slide images and each slide's notes.

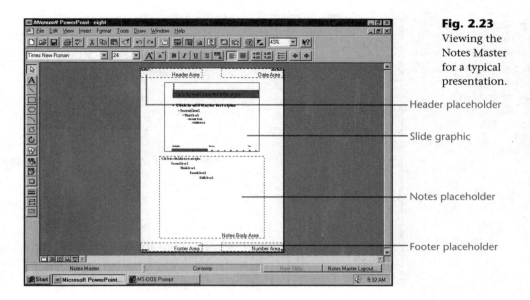

Fig. 2.23
Viewing the
Notes Master
for a typical
presentation.

Header placeholder

Slide graphic

Notes placeholder

Footer placeholder

To view the Notes Master, follow these steps:

1. Open the presentation you want to edit, or create a new presentation by using the Wizards or by opening a new template.

2. Choose <u>V</u>iew, <u>M</u>aster. A cascading menu appears. Choose <u>N</u>otes Master. Your current presentation's display is replaced by its Notes Master.

Using the Handout Master

The Handout Master is similar to the Notes Master, but is used to conveniently format the handouts you want to pass out to your audience. The Handout Master displays several slide image placeholders, which are the overlapping boxes shown in figure 2.24.

As with all the other masters, you can add background page numbers, dates and times, headers and footers, and graphic objects to your handout pages. You must arrange them outside the graphic placeholders on the master handout page for them to appear properly. Any text that you type in the Handout Master will appear on every page of your handouts. You also can change the layout of the Handout Master.

Figure 2.24 also shows guides and rulers, which can help you design and measure items in every Master and View (not just the Handout Master) in PowerPoint 95. Guides are a tool that may be familiar if you've used desktop publishing programs; they can aid in object placement and in layout for slides, handouts, and any other View and Master in PowerPoint.

Fig. 2.24
The Handout
Master. Dotted
lines are Guides;
overlapping
dashed-line boxes
are Slide image
placeholders.

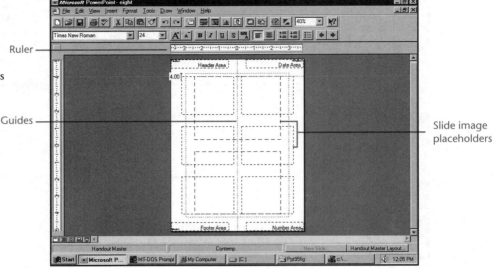

Ruler

Guides

Slide image
placeholders

Tip
To view the Hand-
out Master, you
also can hold the
Shift key and click
the Outline View
button above
PowerPoint's
status bar, near
the bottom of
the screen.

To view the Handout Master, follow these steps:

1. Open the Presentation you want to edit.

2. Choose View, Master. The cascading menu appears. Choose Handout Master. Your current presentation's display is replaced by its Handout Master.

Understanding PowerPoint Views

The various views in PowerPoint roughly correspond to the program's Masters. PowerPoint has an Outline view, a Slides view, a Notes Pages view, and a special Slide Sorter. Several of the views interact with each other and offer unique convenience features that put additional power in your hands.

Using the View Buttons

PowerPoint's views include a Slide Changer feature, which allows you to scroll through your slides by clicking and dragging the mouse. Also, several view buttons are displayed just above the PowerPoint status bar, in the bottom left corner of the screen (see fig. 2.25). Each button, when clicked, displays a different view in the program. In fact, the view buttons let you access all the various views, and also the presentation Masters, without choosing menu options.

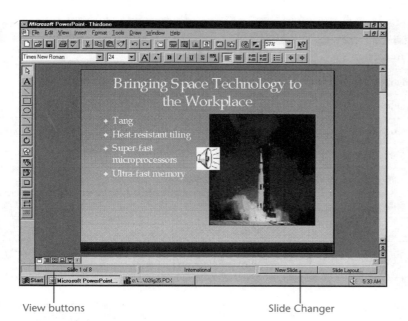

Fig. 2.25
Inspecting one of
PowerPoint 95's
View screens (in
this case, the
Slides view).

View buttons   Slide Changer

Clicking the Outline button displays the entire outline for the presentation, showing all the actual text with the proper indents for each slide.

The Slide Sorter is a drag-and-drop view that allows you to view multiple slides at varying magnifications. It also allows rearranging of slides, somewhat like a deck of cards when you're playing Solitaire.

The Notes Pages view allows you to study and page down all the notes pages corresponding to each slide in your presentation.

In PowerPoint 4 and PowerPoint 95, you can use the view buttons to toggle between Masters and the views, by using the Shift key. To access the Masters for each type, you must hold down the Shift key while you click the button. The view buttons are described in table 2.3.

Table 2.3 The View Button Functions	
Action	**Displayed Result**
Slide View	Individual slides view
Shift+Slide View	Slide Master

(continues)

Table 2.3 Continued

Action	Displayed Result
Notes	Notes Pages view
Shift+Notes	Notes Master
Outline	Outline view
Shift+Outline	Handout Master
Slide Sorter	Slide Sorter view
Shift+Slide Sorter	Handout Master
Slide Show	Run the slide show
Shift+Slide Show	Specifies slides to use in show, rehearses timing, and runs slide show

Note

Watch the status bar while you pass the mouse over each button. Then press the Shift key with the mouse over each button. The status bar tells you the function of each button. Also, if ToolTips is enabled, the ToolTips change as you move the mouse over each button, both when you are holding down Shift and when you aren't.

Viewing Slides

If you're creating presentations, you spend most of your time in the Slide view. This is where you perform many of PowerPoint's creative functions, such as building charts and tables, editing text, and drawing. You can move from slide to slide by using the Slide Changer. When you drag the scrolling tool up or down on the Slide Changer, a small Screen Tip pops up next to the Changer (refer to fig. 2.25), showing the number and title of the slide. As you scroll up or down, the Tip changes accordingly. You also can page down the slides by clicking in the vacant area of the Slide Changer.

Viewing the Slide Sorter

The Slide Sorter is a quick and dirty method for moving slides around, changing their order, and adding basic special effects. As seen in figure 2.26, the Slide Sorter displays rough thumbnails of the slides in your presentation.

To view the Slide Sorter, simply click the Slide Sorter button, just above the status bar at the bottom left corner of the screen.

Transition list   Build list

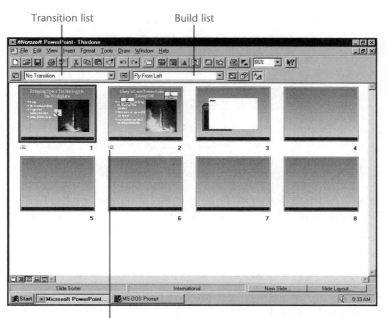

PowerPoint 95 Basics

Fig. 2.26
Viewing the Slide
Sorter displaying a
set of slides.

Icon next to slide with transition style applied

When you enter the Slide Sorter, PowerPoint displays the Slide Sorter toolbar, which offers several key functions that you can apply to any slide in your presentation. Two drop-down lists allow you to apply special animation effects—transitions and builds—to any displayed slide.

Transitions set up different ways for slides to appear and disappear during a slide show. You can apply any one of 45 transitional effects to any slide, including various fades, wipes, and explodes. You can set them to occur randomly, or you can assign a specific effect to a slide. When you apply a transition to a slide in the Sorter, a small icon appears at the bottom of its thumbnail, indicating that you have applied an effect to it.

As opposed to transitions, which govern entire slides, builds apply to individual text elements in a slide. PowerPoint 95 offers an expanded set of 37 builds, including effects that make body text objects fly onto the slide from the left, right, top, or bottom, or dissolve onto the slide. In the Slide Sorter, you apply builds from another drop-down list. (Although PowerPoint 95 allows you to apply Build effects to graphic objects like charts or graphics drawn in PowerPoint, or to slide titles, you cannot apply those effects to individual objects in the Sorter. In the Sorter, you can apply them only to entries in the slides' body text.)

To summarize, the Slide Sorter is a very effective way to manage your slides. You can drag any slide to any position in the slide order; the other slide changes places with the one you're dragging. You can delete slides from the Slide Sorter view, as well as from the Slide view.

> **Note**
>
> Although the Standard toolbar is displayed in the Slide Sorter, some of its functions work only in other views. Watch the status bar for information about tool functions.

Viewing Notes Pages

As you've seen from the discussion of the Notes Master, a notes page displays a slide in the upper half of a page; the lower half of the page shows any notes and narrative you enter for that slide.

Notes pages are especially helpful when you have a lot of content to communicate for a particular slide. Usually a lot of information will not fit on a slide. In fact, a good design rule is to limit the amount of information on a slide and verbally give amplifying statistics, narrative, or other information.

 To view the notes pages, simply click on the Notes Pages button at the bottom of the PowerPoint screen, just above the status bar. The Notes Pages view is displayed (see fig. 2.27). Or, choose View, Notes Pages.

Fig. 2.27
Viewing the Notes Pages for the active presentation.

Click inside the place-holder to add your notes text

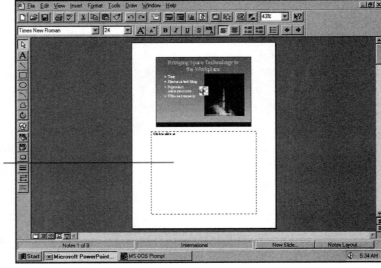

To edit notes in Notes Pages view, click the mouse inside the notes area on the page. You enter, format, and edit notes as you would any other text element in PowerPoint.

Viewing Outlines

The Outline interacts powerfully and handily with other views in the program, notably the Slide view. In Outline view, you can add slides, delete slides, and edit, format, and alter slide text. You can rearrange slides, along with body text elements, at the click of a mouse, and indent text (called promoting and demoting). Unless you manipulate multimedia elements or create graphics, you probably won't have to look at anything besides Outline view because many key program functions are available here (see fig. 2.28). To view the Outline for the active presentation, choose <u>V</u>iew, <u>O</u>utline.

Icons are shown for each slide

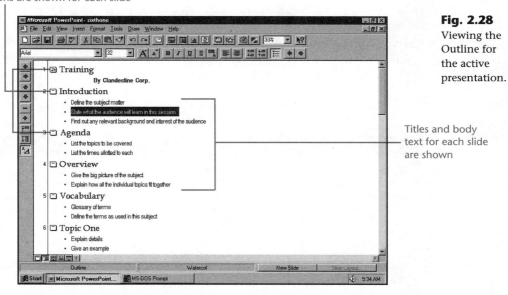

Fig. 2.28
Viewing the Outline for the active presentation.

Titles and body text for each slide are shown

Outline view is a good place to plan your presentation and to look at the logical progression of your arguments. Later chapters discuss Outline view in greater depth.

Viewing the Slide Show

The Slide Show button allows you to preview or rehearse the results of your masterpiece. Simply click on the Slide Show button above the status bar to start the show at the currently selected or displayed slide. The PowerPoint screen disappears, replaced by a full-screen display of each slide.

PowerPoint 95 Basics

Once you start the slide show, click the mouse (or press the spacebar or Enter) to display each successive slide. PowerPoint also displays any build effects with each mouse click or keystroke.

To end the slide show at any time, press the Esc key.

Slide Show view provides numerous other useful functions and features, which later chapters discuss in depth. These include rehearsals, transitions, timing slides, rearranging slides, and using the Slide Navigator and the Meeting Minder.

Getting Help

PowerPoint 95 sports an improved, streamlined online Help system, which you can access in three different ways: by using the mouse to pull down the Help menu, by pressing Alt+H, or by pressing the F1 key. The Help system provides concise descriptions and procedures for virtually every PowerPoint topic. It also proffers suggestions on the most effective use of the program's features. Also, every dialog box contains a Help button that provides quick access to an explanation of the features and options you're about to use.

Table 2.4 lists the options on the Help menu.

Table 2.4 Help Menu Options	
Option	**Description**
Microsoft PowerPoint Help Topics	Displays the main Help sheet, bearing four pages: Contents, Index, Find, and Answer Wizard.
Answer Wizard	Automatically displays the Answer Wizard tab in PowerPoint.
The Microsoft Network	If this feature is enabled, choosing this option gives you access to Microsoft's online service, which provides another, deeper level of help through its discussion forums and service technicians.
Tip of the Day	Gives you tips on effective program operation.
About Microsoft PowerPoint	Displays information about the version of the program that's running and system information. A button in the dialog box provides technical support information.

To access PowerPoint's Help system, simply choose <u>H</u>elp, Microsoft PowerPoint <u>H</u>elp Topics.

Figure 2.29 shows PowerPoint 95's new Help display. The main Help dialog box offers four tabs: Contents, Index, Find, and Answer Wizard.

The Contents tab (shown in fig. 2.28) shows a set of general topics that explain the main procedures in the program. Each topic is displayed in the form of a "closed book" icon. Double-clicking on any of the closed books reveals layers of subtopics that become increasingly more specific. When a topic appeals to you, double-click it or choose Display.

Closed Book topic icons

Subtopics

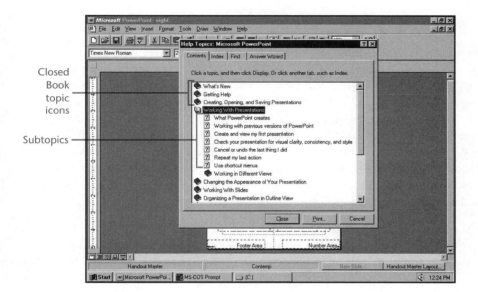

Fig. 2.29
The Help dialog, showing the Contents tab.

The Index tab provides a long, alphabetized, list of specific terms and functions. Double-clicking on a word or phrase in the Index list displays a window describing the function.

To make effective use of the Help Index, follow these steps:

1. In the entry box labeled <u>T</u>ype the First Few Letters of the Word You're Looking For, perform that action. Alternatively, you can scroll down the list labeled <u>C</u>lick the Index Entry You Want... until you locate your topic, and click on that entry. The Help information for that entry appears.

2. Choose <u>D</u>isplay.

Fig. 2.30

The Help dialog, showing the Index tab.

The Find function on the Find tab is wide ranging. When, for some reason, you can't locate a particular term or phrase in the other Help tabs, it's quite possible that you'll find it here. Find's Select list automatically adjusts to display the closest matches for the name or command you specify. (You can specify Finds to occur either after you have entered the entire term or after every keystroke.) You can, of course, scroll down the list to find the desired term. The Select list covers almost every conceivable topic in the PowerPoint program. You must carry out two steps in the Find process: specifying a command or word pertaining to the subject you need information on, and then displaying the information.

As mentioned earlier in this chapter, you can tell PowerPoint to display the Tip of the Day automatically whenever you start the program. You also can access it from the Help menu whenever you're curious about what it has to offer.

The About Microsoft PowerPoint option displays a dialog box showing the version number of your software and the user information entered when you first installed the program.

Click OK or press Enter to close the dialog box. Or, if you would like to find a great deal more about your system, click the System Info button to display the System Information dialog box.

The Microsoft System Information dialog box offers a tremendous amount of information about the inner workings of your computer. You can look up information about subjects such as system configuration or Printing setup. You can obtain a list of the Dynamic Link Libraries used under Windows 95 and its applications or a list of graphics filters and text converters. This is just a sampling of the vast amount of information you can learn from this dialog box.

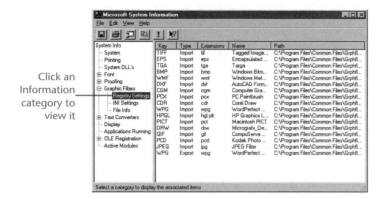

Click an
Information
category to
view it

Fig. 2.31
Using the
Microsoft System
Information dialog
box to investigate
the workings of
your computer.

Finally, the Answer Wizard ties the functions of the other three Help tabs together and adds another dimension—the ability to guide you through the selected task.

Note

Microsoft has heavily revised PowerPoint's Help system and consolidated its numerous windows, even though the number of Help topics and features has grown dramatically. At the same time, there are many fewer steps you have to go through to find a given topic.

To exit Help, click the Close button on the Help screen or press Alt+F4. The Help system is a separate program in a window that multitasks along with PowerPoint. The Help system can run even if PowerPoint is turned off.

In this chapter, you've had a chance to inspect PowerPoint's screen, and learn what some of those icons mean. You've also learned about some of PowerPoint's most basic and important features, such as templates and its on-line Help system. Now, it's time to actually do something with the program!❖

Chapter 3

Creating Your First Presentation

by Nancy Stevenson

In the last chapter, you were introduced to many of the tools you use to create presentations. In this chapter, you will learn how to make a simple presentation with the help of PowerPoint's AutoContent Wizard

For many people, the procedures used to create this type of simple presentation might be all they need for their day-to-day work. AutoContent Wizard can virtually design your presentation for you. Then, all you have to do is add specific text and graphs, and you're all set. The basic tools to do all this are covered in this chapter. By experimenting with these tools, and trying more advanced techniques covered in later chapters, you can make your presentations as complex and creative as you like. But first, the basics.

In this chapter, you learn about

- Using a Wizard to create a fast presentation design
- Creating and working with slides
- Adding and editing text
- Understanding Objects
- Creating a chart
- Saving and printing a presentation

Using AutoContent Wizard

When you first start PowerPoint, you are greeted by the Tip of the Day dialog box. After profiting from its advice, click the OK button to get it out of the way.

> **Note**
>
> Tip of the Day appears by default when you first enter PowerPoint. It can be turned off by deselecting Show Tips at Startup when it appears; so if it doesn't appear on your screen, somebody (maybe you?) has turned it off.

The next thing that appears is the PowerPoint dialog box (see fig. 3.1).

Fig. 3.1
Choose the way you want to begin a new presentation from this dialog box.

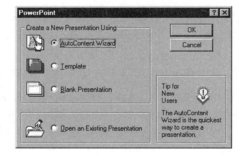

There are four choices available to you in this dialog box:

- AutoContent Wizard walks you through the process of setting up a presentation.

- Template provides a predesigned format for your slides.

- Blank Presentation is just what it says: blank slides to which you add the design and content.

- Open an Existing Presentation if you wish to work with a previously saved PowerPoint file.

The AutoContent Wizard is the easiest way to set up a new presentation. This handy Wizard gets your input on the type of information to be included and the purpose of your presentation. Then, it gives you an appropriate framework for your presentation to give you a head start as you begin to work.

Using Templates

As a result of using AutoContent Wizard, a template for your presentation will be automatically assigned, based on the choices you make while in the wizard. It may be useful to review the components of templates offered in PowerPoint and how they affect your work in the program.

The PowerPoint package offers 23 predesigned templates. Each template has certain common elements that are used in every presentation. These elements are part of *master pages*. The various kinds of output in PowerPoint (slides, audience handouts, and so on) have a blueprint for that output called a master page. A template assigns certain design elements to each master page:

- ■ *Slide Master.* The Slide Master sets up the design of every slide in the presentation. Text and objects that you place on the Slide Master appear on all the slides in your presentation. For more information, see the section "Understanding the Slide Master" in chapter 4.

- ■ *Outline Master.* The Outline Master organizes each outline page of the presentation. See Chapter 8 for more information on outlines.

- ■ *Notes Master.* Speaker's Notes Pages for a slide provide a reduced image of the slide at the top of the page and your edited notes about the slide and its contents at the bottom of the page. Slide images are resizable in the Notes Master; thus notes can be as detailed as necessary. The Notes Master contains the elements that appear on every notes page. Chapter 7 discusses Notes Pages in more detail.

- ■ *Handout Master.* Handouts can be produced for distribution to the audience. The Handout Master defines the format and appearance of handout pages and the elements that appear on each handout page, including a company name, date, or logo. When handouts are printed and given to the audience, they can be laid out with two slides per page, three slides per page, or six slides per page. Chapter 7 talks about handouts in more depth.

Starting a New Presentation with the AutoContent Wizard

To start creating the presentation, click the AutoContent Wizard option button in the PowerPoint dialog box pictured in figure 3.1. The first dialog box of the AutoContent Wizard appears. It shares a few common elements with all the other dialog boxes in the Wizard's sequence. Its elements are displayed in figure 3.2.

Fig.3.2
The AutoContent Wizard starts by welcoming you, and introducing you to the four buttons used to navigate around it.

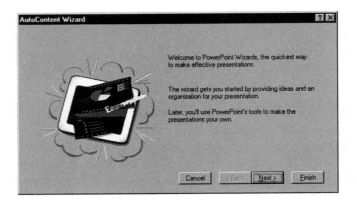

The four buttons displayed on the bottom of the dialog box are used to move through the Wizard:

Cancel	Clicking Cancel ends the Wizard outright without implementing its previous choices.
Back	The Back button (which is ghosted in the first dialog box) enables you to backtrack if you change your mind and want another option.
Next	After you make your choice from the options offered by the Wizard at each step, click the Next button to go to the next box.
Finish	The Finish button cuts the Wizard short, but implements the presentation's design based on the information it already has.

> **Note**
>
> At the top right hand corner, there is a question mark button. This is your entry to context-sensitive help while working in dialog boxes. If you'd like more information about a particular choice, just click on the question mark. Your pointer will change to a question mark/arrow symbol. Next, click on the item you need help with and information will appear. To get rid of the Help box, simply click anywhere outside its border.

The first AutoContent Wizard dialog box is simply an introduction. The following step-by-step example shows you, with illustrations, how to create a structured outline with a specific type of content for your first presentation:

1. With the first AutoContent Wizard dialog box displayed, click the Next button. The second AutoContent Wizard dialog box appears, as shown in figure 3.3.

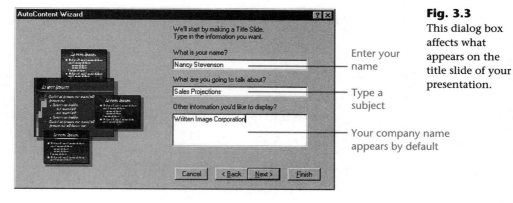

Fig. 3.3
This dialog box affects what appears on the title slide of your presentation.

Enter your name

Type a subject

Your company name appears by default

PowerPoint 95 Basics

2. Click the mouse inside each text box to enter your own data. The company name you entered when you first installed PowerPoint appears by default in the Other Information you'd like to display text box? If you want to change this, simply select it and type new information.

3. When you're done, click the Next button to go to the next step. The third AutoContent Wizard dialog box appears (see fig. 3.4).

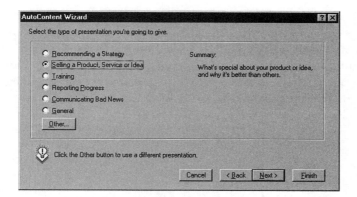

Fig. 3.4
Choose your general approach to your presentation here.

4. The next step of the AutoContent Wizard requires a little bit of thought: it gives you a choice among six different logical approaches to your presentation. Six option buttons are displayed, each of which displays a general content proposal:

- Recommending a Strategy
- Selling a Product, Service, or Idea
- Training
- Reporting Progress

■ Communicating Bad News

■ General

The Other button takes you to the Select Presentation Template dialog box where there are more options.

◄ See "Understanding PowerPoint Templates," p. 60

A description (labeled in the dialog box as Summary) of the selected approach appears to the right of the option buttons. When you select one of these, PowerPoint will assign a template which provides a look that complements that type of presentation. A template typically consists of a background color and pattern, some graphic element or elements, and typeface formatting for your text placeholders.

5. Click on your choice of presentation and click Next.

The steps for this task continue in the next section.

Defining Your Presentation: Length, Output and Handouts

The next part of AutoContent Wizard's journey takes you into the realm of refining your presentation's look and content.

The next dialog box, shown in figure 3.5, allows you to choose a style for the look of your presentation, including Professional or Contemporary. At the bottom of this box, you also can indicate the approximate length of the presentation: less than thirty minutes or longer, which will affect the number of slides provided by AutoContent Wizard. If you're not sure about either of these, it's okay to just leave the default choices.

Fig. 3.5
Here's where you begin to mold the style and length of your presentation.

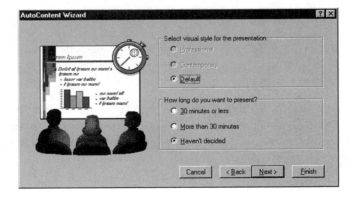

6. Make your selections, then click on Next.

The dialog box in figure 3.6 appears. This box gives you a choice of output, and whether or not you will print audience handouts derived from the content of your presentation.

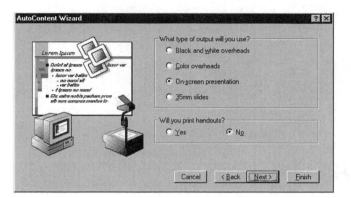

Fig. 3.6
It's important that you think about your presentation output early in the process.

PowerPoint 95 Basics

Different output devices may use different page sizes, so it's important that you designate the output before you begin to design your presentation. If you don't and you change it later on, it may impact the layout of the slides you've so carefully designed. What kind of output do you want? Four options are offered:

▶ See "Creating Handouts," p. 215

- Black and White Overheads
- Color Overheads
- On-Screen Presentation
- 35mm Slides

> **Note**
>
> It's often a good idea to provide your audience with hard copy, especially if you have a large number of people in your audience. Handouts in PowerPoint are generally split into multiple sections, each of which contains a small representation of each slide. Audience handouts also can be structured to have space for taking notes.

7. Make your selections and click Next.

When you make your selection in this screen, and click on Next, you've actually finished the AutoContent Wizard (see fig. 3.7). The basic content and outline of your new presentation have been created. Now it's up to you to refine the titles and text of each slide to convey your specific message.

Fig. 3.7
This flag tells you you've reached the finish line in the race to complete AutoContent Wizard.

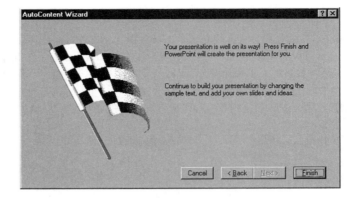

8. Click the Finish button to conclude the Wizard.

Troubleshooting

I clicked cancel by mistake before I finished AutoContent Wizard. I don't see a button or menu choice for getting into AutoContent Wizard again. How do I get my Wizard back?

AutoContent Wizard is always a choice on the opening screen when you first open PowerPoint. But if you want to use it to start a new presentation after the program is already open, select File, New. In the New Presentation dialog box, click on the Presentations tab, then double-click on the AutoContent Wizard icon to start the Wizard's sequence from the beginning.

Looking at What Wizard Has Done

The PowerPoint screen reappears, displaying the title slide with the content you entered in Wizard's opening screen. (see fig. 3.8). A background color, typeface and design options, such as a divider line between the slide title and bullet points and use of bullets, have all been determined by your choices while in AutoContent Wizard.

Note

If you used the Pick-a-Look Wizard in the previous version of PowerPoint, you'll notice it's gone. Most of its functions are now covered by the AutoContent Wizard, which now deals with the content and appearance of your presentation.

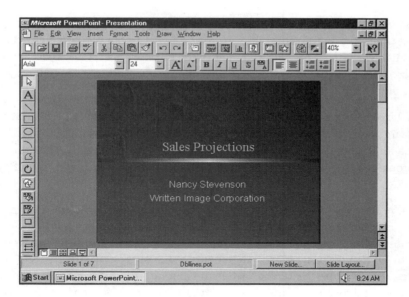

Fig. 3.8
AutoContent Wizard has applied color, typeface, and an overall 'look' to your presentation.

But PowerPoint has done more than create a look for your presentation. It's created a logical sequence of information for the type of presentation you've chosen. To see the organization of these slides, switch to the Outline view by clicking on the Outline View button just above the status bar at the bottom left of the screen. The Outline view shown in figure 3.9 gives you a text-only view of your presentation's content.

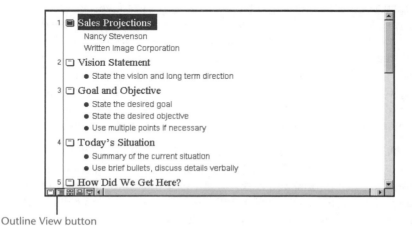

Fig. 3.9
The overall organization of your presentation is easy to see in Outline view.

Outline View button

The outline is one of the most important aspects of PowerPoint because it represents the organization of the entire presentation in text form. Every slide can be edited and its text contents changed in this view. Points and arguments made in each slide can be promoted or demoted in the outline, and slides can be rearranged in the outline as well. Even if you prefer working in Slide view, it's a good idea to refer to the outline on a regular basis because it provides a larger view of the presentation, making it easier to see flaws in the argument and to see its logical flow.

Each slide is numbered and is also marked with a small icon. The slide title is in large type, and body text outlines for each slide are shown in bullets and smaller indented text under each slide title. All the text under each title through each lower level of indented text represents the contents of each slide.

You're not married to the outline structure created by AutoContent Wizard. You can add or delete whole slides or edit the content of any that the Wizard created. Any statement in the outline can be made into a slide title in its own right. In many cases, bulleted statements in the outline may merit a slide of their own because the level of detail and amount of information under consideration may be substantial. And you can make changes to the outline right in the Outline view, or on individual slides.

Now that you've put the basic framework in place by using the Wizard, you need to deal with the process of adding the actual content—charts and text.

Working with Slides

Whether you use a Wizard or template to set up your presentation, or you start with a blank presentation, many new elements need to be added. You might want to add a new slide to the presentation. (Your presentation outline is automatically expanded as you add new slides to a presentation.) The text for each slide may need to be edited to suit your specific subject matter and formatted to suit your sense of design. You might want to add a logo, drawn artwork, or a custom graphic element to your slides. You also may need to add charts to your slide show to add impact to statistical comparisons.

PowerPoint allows you to edit your text in either Outline or Slide view, depending on what's more comfortable for you. Some people prefer simply typing text in an outline and checking the look of each slide later. However, if you make changes while in Slide view, objects can be edited and added at will while providing immediate visual feedback on the results. If something doesn't look right, you know it immediately.

Back in figure 3.8, the first slide in your new presentation was displayed in Slide view. The lines of text in this slide are, quite simply, objects. The slide title and bullet points (the body text) are all editable units that can be changed, reformatted, and moved around.

AutoContent Wizard created what it thought was an appropriate number of slides for the presentation based on your responses to its questions. Each of these slides has a logical title and several statement placeholders for your type of presentation, for example Vision Statement and Goal and Objective in a Sales presentation. Nonetheless, say you discover that you need another slide to make one more point about last year's sales. The new slide, to be titled Yearly Sales Figures, can be inserted between the current first and second slides in your presentation, Sales Projections and Vision Statement. Adding this new slide couldn't be easier.

Adding a New Slide

When you choose to insert a new slide, it will appear following the slide currently on screen (although it can be moved around in the presentation at a later time).

All that's involved in inserting a new slide is selecting an AutoLayout for it. AutoLayouts are predefined slide layouts that are based on the arrangement of typical objects and data types that are laid onto slides during the course of creating a presentation.

▶ See "Rearranging and Deleting Slides in Outline View," p. 232

With the first slide in the presentation on-screen, click on the Insert New Slide button on the toolbar. The New Slide dialog box in figure 3.10 appears. This provides a scrollable list of AutoLayout thumbnails that, when you look them over, pretty much cover every possible combination of charts, bulleted lists, clip art, and slide titles that you could think of. As you can see, some AutoLayouts offer simpler slide types than others. Some combine a title with only a chart or bulleted list of argument points, while others offer two columns below the title, combining a chart with a bulleted list.

Note

You also can add a new slide using the New Slide button on the status bar, or by selecting Insert, New Slide from the menu, or pressing Ctrl+M.

The AutoLayout thumbnails are displayed in rows of four. A description window on the right side of the New Slide dialog box tells you the type of layout that's currently selected.

Fig. 3.10
Columns, charts—
even a blank slide
are all choices in
the New Slide
dialog box.

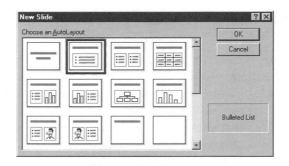

Tip
To apply a layout
to an existing slide,
display it and click
the Slide Layout
button. Make a
selection from the
New Slide Layout
dialog box.

Chart or clip art elements in an AutoLayout are simply object placeholders. They don't contain any data that directly relates to your subject matter; they are items that you edit to construct and illustrate your own logical procession of ideas.

Once you've selected a slide layout, choose OK or press Enter. A new slide is inserted into your presentation. Its appearance should resemble figure 3.11.

Fig. 3.11
Placeholders are
surrounded by
dashed lines on
a new slide.

The new slide is inserted after the slide that was displayed when you started the process of creating a new slide.

Moving from One Slide to Another

As your presentation grows in size, it's helpful to know how to move from slide to slide. There are several straightforward methods for navigating among slides in PowerPoint.

First of all, you can use the PageUp and PageDown keys. Pressing PageUp displays the previous slide. Pressing PageDown displays the next slide in the presentation sequence.

You also can use the Slide Changer, which is pointed out in figure 3.11. Clicking the doubled up arrow or doubled down arrow icons moves you up or down through the slide sequence in the same way as using the PageUp or PageDown keys.

Dragging the scroll box in the slide changer also moves you up or down the slide sequence. PowerPoint displays a ToolTip indicating the slide number as you drag the scroll box. Also, notice that when a slide is displayed, its slide number (for example, 3 of 9) is displayed on the far left of the status bar.

Working with Text

Working with text in an actual slide is a simple process. Nonetheless, many powerful features are available to you. With both title text and body text, you can change fonts, select new font styles and effects (any text font that is available under Windows can be used in your slides), change the font size, and much more.

Adding Text

If you're familiar with editing or entering text in other applications, such as a word processor, you'll find this an easy process. Just remember that each block of text is an object, which can be moved around and edited once you've selected that object.

Using the navigation techniques described above, move to the slide you wish to edit. To add a title and bulleted text to the slide:

1. Click on the slide title above the chart object, which reads `Click to add title`.

    The text `Click to add title` disappears and is replaced by a highlight bar with the blinking insertion point at the left.

2. Type your title.

3. Click the mouse pointer anywhere outside the title text. The slide should appear with a new title as shown in figure 3.12.

Fig. 3.12
When selected for editing, the title object shows with a gray border around it.

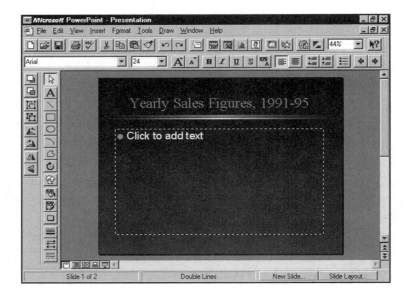

4. Click the mouse inside the bullet item reading `Click to Add Text`. Notice that the bullet item text disappears and is replaced by a blinking insertion point. Also notice that the line is highlighted, ready for editing.

5. Type the text for your first bullet point.

6. Press Enter. This adds a second bullet point, followed by the blinking insertion point.

7. Type your next bullet point.

8. Repeat step 7 until you've added all the points for the slide.

9. Click anywhere outside the text block you just edited to view how the text will look on your slide (see fig. 3.13).

Selecting and Editing Techniques

As you have seen from the examples above, it's easy to add text in Slide view. There are many convenient ways to speed the editing of text in a presentation. PowerPoint supports a wide variety of simple keystroke combinations for selecting and editing text. The same is true for using the mouse—a significant number of mouse actions are supported for editing and selecting. There are also handy shortcut menus available.

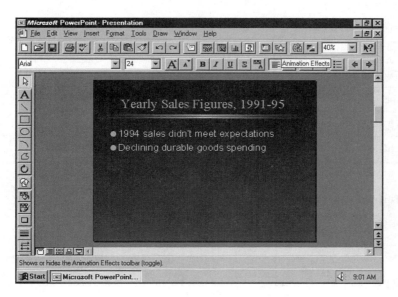

Fig. 3.13
Bullet points form the basis of many PowerPoint presentations.

Titles and body text, when clicked on, show the blinking insertion point, which is used to delete and enter text in the item. When the blinking insertion point appears in a text object, you can use the keystrokes listed below to carry out many different editing and selection procedures without using the mouse. Below is a summary of basic keystrokes and mouse actions that can be performed on titles and body text in Slide view:

Table 3.1   Keystrokes and Mouse Actions for Use in Slide View

Editing Keystrokes

Key or Key Combination	Result
Del or Delete	Deletes the character after the blinking insertion point
Backspace	Deletes the character before the blinking insertion point
Ctrl+Del	Deletes the word after the blinking insertion point
Ctrl+Backspace	Deletes the word before the blinking insertion point

(continues)

Table 3.1 Continued

Selecting with Keystrokes

Shift+left arrow	Selects the character before the insertion point
Shift+right arrow	Selects the character after the insertion point
Shift+up arrow	Selects the line preceding the insertion point
Shift+down arrow	Selects the line following the insertion point
Ctrl+Shift+left arrow	Selects the word before the insertion point
Ctrl+Shift+right arrow	Selects the word after the insertion point

Selecting with the Mouse

Single-click	Places the insertion point in sentence or line of text
Double-click	Places the insertion point and selects word
Triple-click	Places the insertion point and selects entire bullet item
Click and drag	Selects any text with left mouse button held down
Drag & Drop Move	Select and drag with the mouse
Drag & Drop Copy	Press and hold Ctrl and select and drag with the mouse

You also can drag the mouse to select any or all parts of a sentence in body text or a title.

Formatting Text

Formatting text means changing things like the size of the type and effects such as bold and underline. Giving text the right look can have a great impact on the appearance and effect of your words on your audience. In this section, you format text items in Slide view.

▶ See "Editing and Enhancing Text in Outline View," p. 231

To format text, you select it with the mouse or keyboard as described in the preceding section and then apply the formatting. Menu commands can be used for this. However, the quickest way to format text on a slide is by using the mouse and the PowerPoint Formatting toolbar. The Formatting toolbar simplifies many tedious text formatting tasks and, in many ways, simplifies the process.

PowerPoint's Formatting toolbar contains many tools for formatting text:

 Drop-down list for selecting a font

 Drop-down list for selecting a font size, or a new font size in points can be entered with the keyboard

 Tool for increasing font size to the next predefined point size (from 32 to 36 points, and so on)

 Tool for decreasing font size to the next predefined point size (from 36 to 32 points, and so on)

 Tool for applying Boldface style to selected text

 Tool for applying Italic to selected text

 Tool for applying underlining to selected text

 Tool for applying shadowing to selected text

 Drop-down palette for applying new colors to selected text

 Aligns selected text to left margin of placeholder

 Aligns selected text to center of placeholder

 Increases paragraph spacing to selected text

 Decreases paragraph spacing to selected text

Adds or deletes bullets from selected sentence

Tip
Another efficient way to alter and edit text is to use PowerPoint's Outline view. In Outline view, all the text contained in the presentation is displayed, ready for editing, and there's no need to flip back and forth through slides to make changes or to select each individual text object in order to edit it. All text also can be formatted in Outline view. Press Ctrl+A to select all the text in Outline view.

PowerPoint 95 Basics

Promotes selected text sentence (decreases its indent level)

    Demotes selected text sentence (increases its indent level)

To apply formatting:

1. Select the text.

2. Click one of the formatting buttons on the toolbar.

3. Click anywhere outside of the bullet object.

Your formatting is complete. For some Formatting toolbar buttons, such as Bulleting or Boldfacing, the formatting that is added to selected text also can be removed by selecting the text and then clicking the proper button again or by using the Undo/Redo feature.

With a text object selected, you also can click on the right mouse button and get a shortcut menu like the one in figure 3.14. This brings the most common editing functions right to your workspace for easy access. PowerPoint's Format menu also offers the same range of choices and options as the Formatting toolbar. Chapter 6 in this book discusses formatting techniques in greater detail.

Fig. 3.14
Shortcut menus are accessed with the right mouse button for fast formatting.

For those of you who are more comfortable with keystrokes, there are several that can be used in formatting text. Here's a short list of keystrokes you can use:

Tip
All the key combinations can toggle their formatting on and off.

Ctrl+B	Boldfaces selected text
Ctrl+I	Italicizes selected text
Ctrl+U	Underlines selected text
Ctrl+=	Subscripts selected text
Ctrl+Shift+=	Superscripts selected text

Caution

Try to avoid using the visual 'busyness' of too many type effects on a single slide. Also, make sure bold type doesn't blur the individual letters of your words together when printed on a slide or overhead.

Adding Bullets to Text

Bullets can be added to paragraphs in a slide. Bullets can be of several different styles, and that style can be different for each indented level of bullets.

In PowerPoint, a paragraph, or bullet point, is any length of text that is ended by a carriage return. A paragraph can be one word, a few words, a short sentence, or a sequence of sentences of any length—just like in a word processing document. The act of pressing Enter at the end is what creates the paragraph. To make a multiple line bullet point, you can press Shift+Enter and no new bullet will appear at the beginning of the new line. It is still part of the original paragraph. By definition, bullets are added only to the beginning of paragraphs.

If you don't want your paragraphs to be preceded by a bullet, simply select the paragraph(s) you want and click the Bullet On/Off button on the Formatting toolbar. To reinstate bullets before each paragraph, select them again, and click the Bullet On/Off button again. The Bullet button is a toggle function, turning bullets on and off like a light switch in your house.

A fun feature of bullets is their flexibility of character style; bullets can use any element from any available typeface, including fonts that use symbols instead of letters and numbers. The bullets that appear by default are determined by the template you use. If you don't use a template, the default style in a blank presentation is circles, but a variety of characters can be used. Generally, a bullet is culled from "Dingbats," or a font that contains a bunch of oddball characters.

Here's how to choose a new bullet style for a bulleted list in a slide:

1. Select the bulleted list whose style you want to change.

2. Click your right mouse button, and select Bullet from the shortcut menu. (You also can do this from the Format menu.)

   ◀ See "Understanding PowerPoint Templates," p. 60

   The Bullet dialog box appears displaying the following options:

   ■ Use a Bullet: When selected, uses bullets on selected paragraphs and removes them when not selected.

  ■ Bullets From: List of fonts available from which bullets can be chosen.

  ■ Special Color: Drop-down palette of colors that can be applied to bullets.

  ■ Size: Up and Down Size adjuster box to determine the size of the bullet in relation to the point size of the paragraph's font.

3. Click any bullet character from the displayed font on the grid in the dialog box. A small Zoom pops up, showing a close-up of the bullet character you chose.

4. After choosing the bullet and its formatting, choose OK or press Enter. Your new bullet characters are applied and displayed on your slide.

Working with Objects

Before we begin adding other elements to slides, you should understand some things about objects. The idea of an object is probably one of the most important things you deal with in PowerPoint—and in other Windows applications as well. What is an object, exactly?

Object is really a pretty straightforward concept. An *object* is simply any type of data item, such as a picture you draw, a text container such as the title object or bullet point object, a chart you create in Excel or PowerPoint, a sound that you record with your Sound Blaster sound card and save as a file, or a piece of prerecorded music, that can be cut and pasted between applications and documents or moved around on a slide or between slides.

If you draw a simple graphic in PowerPoint, that's an object. If you create a chart, that's an object too. Pieces of clip art are considered objects. The main thing to know about objects is that they must be selected to make changes to them, and that they can be moved around your slide. Even a text box, with many words or lines of text, can be moved as a single entity because it's an object.

Working with Placeholders

You've been using and manipulating placeholders for objects all along. Placeholders are used when you create a new presentation using the AutoContent Wizard described earlier in this chapter, or add a new slide to an existing presentation. Placeholders of various types, like the ones shown in figure 3.15, are used to set aside spaces on a slide for a specific purpose.

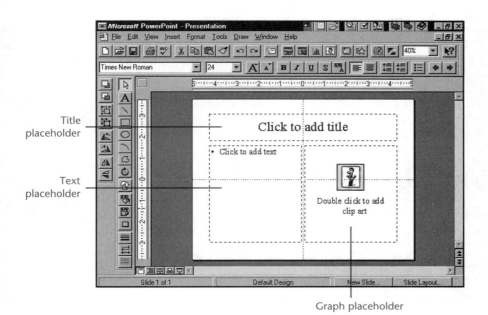

Title placeholder

Text placeholder

Fig. 3.15
There are Title, Text, Graph, Table, Organizational Chart, and ClipArt Placeholders.

PowerPoint 95 Basics

Graph placeholder

Whenever you create a new slide, using the AutoLayouts, placeholders are set up to aid in the layout and proper placement of objects in the slide. After that's done, it's up to you to define each placeholder's content.

Inserting a Placeholder or Object

You also can insert different types of placeholders into any slide in your presentation. There are four Insert toolbar buttons that allow you to place different types of objects on a slide:

 Creates and inserts a table from the Microsoft Word for Windows applications program into the PowerPoint slide.

 Creates and inserts a spreadsheet from the Microsoft Excel applications program into the PowerPoint slide.

 Inserts Graph Object (created with Microsoft Graph) into the PowerPoint slide.

 Selects and inserts a PowerPoint clip-art image from the ClipArt Library.

▶ See "Using
the ClipArt
Gallery," p. 308

Any of these objects, once inserted, acts not only as a placeholder, but as a linked object, because double-clicking any of them enables you to change, alter, or substitute for the particular item using the program feature or application program that created it.

◀ See "Tighter
Application
Integration
with OLE 2,"
p. 26

Right now, we'll only take a quick glance at the possibilities. Various chapters later in this book deal with every aspect of inserting and changing the different types of objects available to you.

Creating a Chart

Creating charts is one of the more important operations you perform in PowerPoint. Given the at-a-glance nature of most presentations, charts and graphs often provide a powerful communications tool that gives your audience a lot of information in an easy to comprehend format. An entire section of this book is devoted to the process of creating charts out of statistical data, but let's look at some of the basics now.

Charts are a commonly used tool to illustrate statistics of many kinds. Charts are used to support points in a presentation, to present sales figures, to show market shares between companies in a specific business realm, and to indicate long-term trends in the fortunes of a business. Charts can be used to show progress or comparisons among two or more sets of data. They can be used in combination to illustrate sales figures or company earnings in conjunction with other figures such as a company's long-term growth or stock price. Creating a simple chart is not difficult, and will enhance your presentation with visual interest and impact.

Understanding Microsoft Graph

PowerPoint employs a separate charting program called Microsoft Graph 5.0 for creating charts. In Microsoft Graph, you encounter two specific elements when you make a chart: the chart itself, which is the graphical representation of your data, and the datasheet, which contains the actual statistics used to generate the chart. It is the datasheet that you actually work with.

Spreadsheet users are very familiar with the concept of a datasheet, which is essentially rows and columns of numbers under specific headers that are used to describe the categories of the data. Figure 3.16 shows a picture of a typical datasheet.

> **Note**
>
> PowerPoint's nomenclature for Graph and Chart is confusing. The charting application in PowerPoint is called Microsoft Graph, but every command in the program uses the word chart. Also, when you create a new slide from AutoLayouts, one AutoLayout type is called Graph, and the placeholder it uses says "Double click to add graph". In no other area of PowerPoint (including Help) is the word Graph used; the word chart is used to describe features. Because of this, we use the word chart almost exclusively in this book, except when reference is made to the program Microsoft Graph, also referred to as just "Graph."

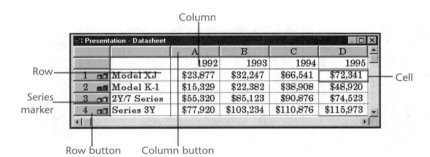

Fig. 3.16
The rows and columns of data in a datasheet determine the size of the graphic elements on a chart.

All of Graph's datasheets work essentially the same way: you type in rows and columns of numbers that are structured to fit into one or more series for display in a chart. Each column and row is numbered with a 3-D button on the edge of the datasheet that can be clicked to select the entire row or column.

Notice the small colored markers on the row buttons 1, 2, and 3. They're series markers, showing how the data displayed in the sheet and in the chart will be visually organized.

Each rectangular space in a datasheet is called a cell. In the default datasheet, there are three rows of four cells each. You click the mouse inside any cell on a datasheet to enter a new value or to edit an existing one.

Starting Up Graph

Graph is a separate program from PowerPoint, but when you use the program it doesn't appear that way. When you start the Graph application, a new toolbar appears at the top of the PowerPoint window and the menu bar also changes. To open the Microsoft Graph application:

1. Use the Insert New Slide button to insert a new slide with title and graph placeholders, as shown in figure 3.17.

2. Click on the title placeholder, and type **Sales History** as the title.

3. Double-click anywhere within the graph placeholder (which says `Double click here to add graph.`)

Graph starts up. The Microsoft Graph application toolbar and menu bar appear with a default chart and datasheet (see fig. 3.17).

Miscrosoft Graph
toolbar and menus

Fig. 3.17
A default datasheet appears the first time you open a new chart, with three rows and four columns of data.

Datasheet

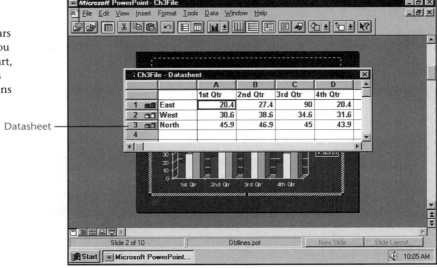

To create a new chart, it's only necessary to enter a new set of data values and labels (in other words, to edit the datasheet) and to select a new chart type if necessary.

Replacing Data in the Data Sheet

Here's a short list of keystrokes you can use to edit datasheets:

Left arrow	Move to the next cell to the left
Right arrow	Move to the next cell to the right
Down arrow	Move to the next row down

Up arrow	Move to the next row up
Shift+left arrow	Selects each successive cell to the left
Shift+right arrow	Selects each successive cell to the right
Shift+down arrow	Selects each successive cell down through the column
Shift+up arrow	Selects each successive cell up through the column
Delete or Del	Erases the cell's contents
Backspace	Erases the previous digit in the cell when directly editing a cell's contents. If the entire contents of the cell are selected, pressing Backspace deletes the contents.

To enter and delete data in a Graph datasheet, follow these simple steps:

1. Click on the first cell (Row 1, Column A) in the default datasheet shown in figure 3.17.

2. Type in a numeric value to replace the value 20.4.

3. Using the keystrokes listed above, enter in the rest of your data.

4. For the 1st Qtr, 2nd Qtr, 3rd Qtr, and 4th Qtr labels and the East, West, and North labels at the top of the datasheet, substitute labels for your data.

Selecting and Changing the Graph Type

Now, you choose a new chart type. You use Graph's toolbar and menu options to perform this operation.

> **Note**
>
> There are two key types of charts, 2-D and 3-D. Two-dimensional charts are easier to format and work with because they're not as complex, but 3-D charts can be more visually attractive. The default chart type is a 3-D column chart.

1. Click the Chart Type down arrow button on the Graph toolbar.

   A drop-down list appears displaying 14 icons showing the different basic chart types (see fig. 3.18).

Fig. 3.18
Many chart types
are available to
customize your
presentation
of data.

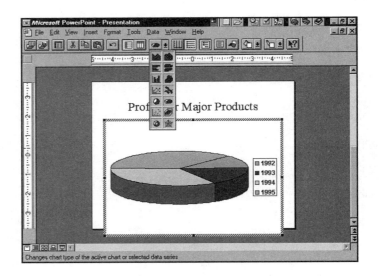

The chart types, listed as they appear in the drop-down list, are:

2-D Area	3-D Area
2-D Bar	3-D Bar
2-D Column	3-D Column
2-D Line	3-D Line
2-D Pie	3-D Pie
Scatter	3-D Surface
Doughnut	Radar

> **Note**
>
> Chapters 14, 15, and 16 discuss the numerous chart types and how to customize them in greater detail.

2. Click on the chart type of your choice.

3. Click anywhere outside the highlighted chart to view the chart on your slide.

The Graph toolbar and menu bar disappear and are replaced by the more familiar PowerPoint screen elements. The chart has now been embedded into the slide and looks something like figure 3.19.

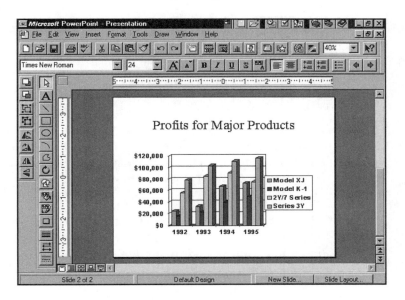

Fig. 3.19
The data you've entered is instantly turned into a visual element.

To start up Graph and edit the chart again, simply double-click anywhere inside the chart object on the slide. The Graph screen elements appear and the chart and datasheet display, ready for editing.

As you can see, you haven't even scratched the surface of PowerPoint's charting features. Charts can have many custom effects applied to them, which are covered in depth in Chapter 14, "Creating Basic Charts" and Chapter 15, "Customizing Charts."

Saving Your Presentation

Saving your presentation is, needless to say, a very simple but very important operation. Any time you create something new in your PowerPoint presentation, you should save your work. Here's how to do it:

1. With your presentation displayed in any view choose File, then Save.

If you're saving a new file for the first time, the File Save dialog box appears, as shown in figure 3.20.

Tip
A good rule of thumb for saving your work is to save every five minutes. Frequent saving minimizes the risk of losing important work.

Fig. 3.20
The File Save dialog box offers options for saving your presentations.

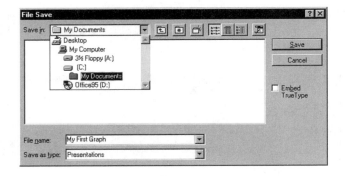

2. Click the mouse inside the File Name text box and type the file name you want: My First Graph, for example. Backspace or delete any other characters in the text box. PowerPoint adds the extension PPT automatically.

3. The Save As Type list should show, as its default, Presentations. You could save a file as a PowerPoint 4 file, a text file, or a template that you can use as the basis for other presentations. But most commonly, you'll simply save as a PowerPoint presentation; so leave this selection alone.

4. You may want to save your file in a different directory and even a different drive. You can use the drop-down box called Save In, or the buttons across the top of the File Save dialog box to move to the directory and drive you want.

5. Choose Save or press Enter.

Printing a Presentation

A substantial number of printing options are offered for your presentations. You can print your presentation as slides, an outline, handouts, or speaker notes. If you're planning to use several of these elements during your presentation, you need to print your presentation in each separate format.

Tip
For a quick save, click the Save button on the toolbar, or press Ctrl+S.

To print your presentation, follow these steps:

1. Choose File, Print to display the Print dialog box (see fig. 3.21).

2. Select the options you want, and click OK or press Enter.

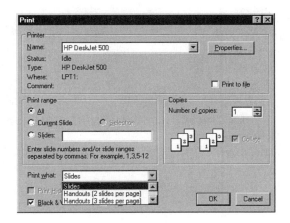

Fig. 3.21
Tell PowerPoint where to print to, how many and what kind to print all in one place.

Options available in the Print dialog box are:

Printer. Designates the printer to send the output to. Click on the Print to File check box if you want to send your output to a file rather than hard copy.

Print Range. Specifies which or how many Slides to print: All, the Current Slide, or separate slides and separate ranges of slides specified in the Slides text box.

Copies. Specifies the number of copies of the page or document to print (type in a number or use the up- or down-arrow icons to increase or decrease the value).

Print What. From the drop-down list here you can specify the type of output: Slides, Notes Pages, Handouts (2 Slides Per Page), Handouts (3 Slides Per Page), Handouts (6 Slides Per Page), or Outline View.

Check boxes at the bottom of the window enable you to select to print hidden slides, to print in black and white rather than grayscale, scale the slide output to the size of the paper, or print a border around your printed slides.

Exiting PowerPoint

When you finish working on your presentation, it's a good time to save your work again before you exit the PowerPoint program:

1. Choose File, Save; or press Ctrl+S.

2. After the presentation file is saved, choose File, Exit; or press Alt+F and then **X**.

► See "Printing Slides, Notes, Outlines and Handouts," p. 460

Tip

For a fast exit, double-click on the Control Menu button in the upper-left corner of the screen, or press Alt+F4.

This chapter has given you a brief look and overview at almost every major part of PowerPoint for Windows 95. You saw the first phases of designing and creating a presentation, then added new slides. You took the briefest of glances at how objects of various kinds work in PowerPoint and found out exactly what objects are. You typed in text and created charts. You also saved and printed your presentation file. In the next chapter, "Setting Up Your New Presentation," you'll get more specifics about beginning a presentation and planning its content.❖

Chapter 4

Setting Up Your New Presentation

by Rich Grace

As you saw in the last chapter, there are several major parts of a presentation: the notes pages, the outline, the handouts, and finally the slides. Slides, the flashy and colorful part of the whole business, are only part of the entire production. If you focus all your attention on working with slides—and ignore the other phases of working with PowerPoint 95—you'll cheat yourself out of some of the program's most helpful and powerful productivity features.

In this chapter, you get

- A more detailed look at the process of starting a new presentation

- A closer look at PowerPoint's various views

- A closer look at PowerPoint's Masters and how they interact with each other

Understanding the Presentation Process

PowerPoint 95 is the leading presentation and slide show package currently on the market. But PowerPoint isn't just about slides. It's about organizing ideas and arguments into the most effective presentation. In many situations, you're not just displaying pretty pictures to dazzle your clients—you're trying to persuade them that your proposed course of action is the best, or that they should buy your product. You're trying to sell your ideas. Delivering a presentation requires discipline and organization.

While it is possible to produce a presentation by working exclusively in Slide view, doing so defeats the purpose of 90 percent of PowerPoint 95's features. In fact, if you want to save yourself a lot of work, the wisest move for creating the basics of a brand-new presentation is to use the Slide Master, one of several Masters available in the program. After you create the basic appearance for your new presentation with the Slide Master, use the other masters to rapidly expand and change many elements of your presentation. You learn the basics of these important techniques in this chapter.

Starting a New Presentation

It is not necessary to use any templates at all to create a new presentation. If you like to do everything for yourself, this is the chapter where you begin to do so.

You can start a new presentation in several ways: by using a Wizard, by simply selecting a template, or by creating your own blank presentation. Because Chapter 3 deals with Wizards in considerable detail, this chapter focuses on starting from scratch. Although it might sound difficult, it's remarkably easy to build a new presentation from nothing in just a few steps. Doing so, you begin to see the myriad possibilities for exercising your own creativity.

To begin a new presentation, follow these steps:

1. Open the Start menu, and choose <u>P</u>rograms, Microsoft PowerPoint (see fig. 4.1). The application starts, and the PowerPoint dialog box appears (see fig. 4.2).

Fig. 4.1
Starting up Power-
Point by opening
the Start menu.

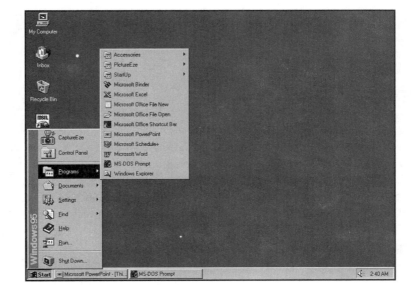

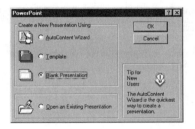

Fig. 4.2
After loading PowerPoint, you will see the Power-Point dialog box, offering several options for loading and creating presentations.

You have probably seen the PowerPoint dialog box before, especially if you read Chapter 3. This is where you select the <u>A</u>utoContent Wizard for a complete presentation layout. You also can choose from three other option buttons: <u>T</u>emplate, <u>B</u>lank Presentation, and <u>O</u>pen an Existing Presentation.

2. To create a presentation from scratch, select the <u>B</u>lank Presentation option and click OK (or press Enter).

   Next, you are prompted to choose the AutoLayout for the first slide, as shown in figure 4.3.

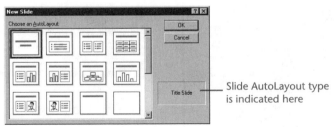

Slide AutoLayout type is indicated here

Fig. 4.3
Selecting a slide AutoLayout for the first slide in the presentation.

You have seen the New Slide dialog box before, too. This time, you're not using the New Slide dialog box to add a slide to an existing presentation—you're using it to help create a new presentation from scratch.

3. Click the Title Slide thumbnail (the upper-left AutoLayout). The text in the lower-right corner of the dialog box shows the AutoLayout slide type.

4. Choose OK or press Enter. The results appear as shown in figure 4.4.

   The new title slide appears with no formatting. Now you can explore ways to change and enhance the appearance of a slide show, using the Slide Master.

Fig. 4.4
Continuing the process of creating a new presentation, you're viewing a newly created slide.

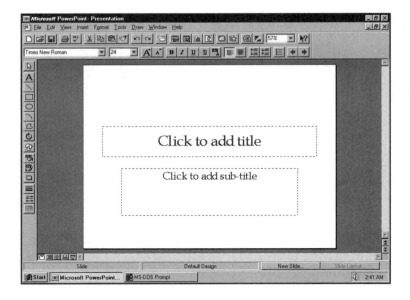

5. Choose View, Master, Slide Master. The Slide Master appears displaying the blank slide (see fig. 4.5).

Fig. 4.5
The unformatted slide appears in the Slide Master.

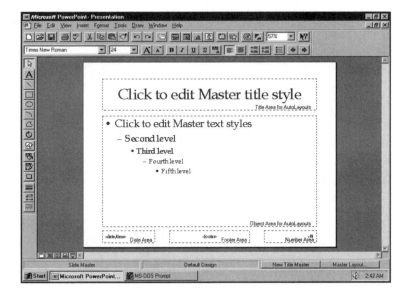

Tip
As you work more with PowerPoint, you'll become very familiar with the features you experiment with in the next several steps.

6. Just for fun, do a couple of simple formatting tricks. Choose Format, Custom Background.

The Custom Background dialog box appears, as shown in figure 4.6. This is where you decide on the color backgrounds, shading, patterns, and general appearance for the entire presentation. Though the first appearance of the dialog box is very stark and minimal, you can access a variety of PowerPoint 95 features here.

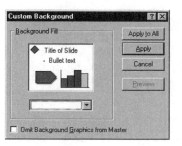

Fig. 4.6
The Custom Background dialog box is the front line for modifying a blank presentation without a template.

7. Click the drop-down list under the Background Fill thumbnail. A list of background customization options appears (see fig. 4.7).

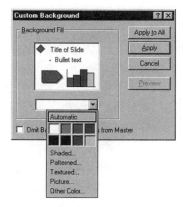

Fig. 4.7
From the Background Fill drop-down list, you can choose Shaded, Patterned, or another customizing feature.

8. Choose Shaded. The Shaded Fill dialog box opens.

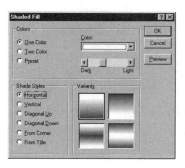

Fig. 4.8
Here you can adjust the color and style of the shade.

As you can see, there are quite a few options to experiment with in the Shaded Fill dialog box.

Fig. 4.9
The Color drop-
down list, from
which you choose
the Other Color...
option.

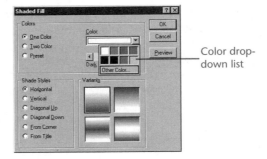

Color drop-
down list

9. From the Color drop-down list, choose the Other Color option as shown in figure 4.9.

   The Colors dialog box appears. It has two tabs: Standard and Custom. As shown in figure 4.10, the Standard tab is displayed. It shows a selection of 127 colors. Choose any color by clicking it.

Fig. 4.10
The Color dialog
box shows the
standard 127-color
palette.

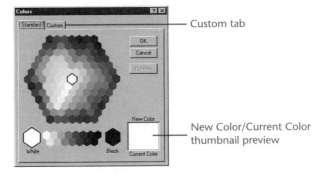

Custom tab

New Color/Current Color
thumbnail preview

Tip
To select a color in
the Standard tab
and return to the
Shaded Fill dialog
box, just double-
click the color.

10. In the 127-color palette, choose a light blue color. The chosen color appears in the New Color/Current Color thumbnail preview.

11. Choose OK or press Enter. The Shaded Fill dialog box reappears, and the Variants section shows the effects of the new color.

12. In the Variants section, choose the top right shading box (actually called a thumbnail), which shows a light-to-dark shading from top to bottom.

13. Click the Light arrow of the Light-Dark slider bar once to adjust the color mix to a lighter shade.

14. Choose OK or press Enter. You return to the Custom Background dialog box.

15. Finally, choose Apply or press Enter. The results resemble figure 4.11.

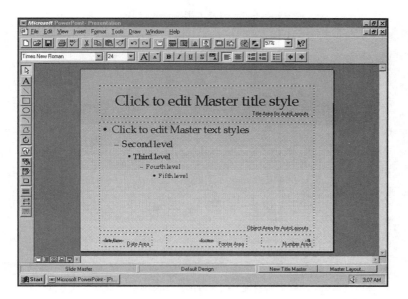

Fig. 4.11
The Slide Master shows the effects of shading and color adjustment on a previously blank template.

In this example, you added shading effects to a blank template and played with color. The text and title remained in a uniform black color. Because you have not adjusted the color for the entire presentation, you might not be able to read the text against the background. In the Slide Master, it's easy to make all your slides readable.

If you want to change the color of just one text item, such as the title, follow these steps:

1. Begin by selecting the text. Click inside the title text. The insertion point appears.

   Triple-click the mouse to select the entire text of the title. (You also can drag the mouse over the text for the same purpose.)

Note

Click the Text Color tool on PowerPoint's Formatting toolbar for a menu of colors and color options that you can apply to selected text.

2. Choose F<u>o</u>rmat, <u>F</u>ont. The Font dialog box appears.

3. Click the <u>C</u>olor drop-down list. The eight-color default palette appears, along with the Other Color option and a new box displaying the previously selected "other color" that you applied to the slide background (see fig. 4.12).

Fig. 4.12
The Font dialog box, showing its Color drop-down list for changing text colors.

Color drop-down list

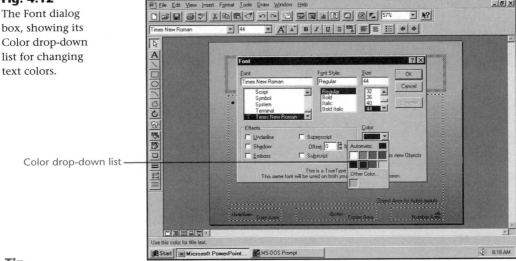

Tip
You can change the color of text and titles just as you can with many PowerPoint slide and master objects.

4. Choose Other Color from the Color drop-down list. The Colors dialog box appears, displaying the Standard tab and its 127-color palette.

5. Click the "brightest" yellow from the palette. (It's highlighted in figure 4.13.)

Fig. 4.13
Choose a color for the Title font.

Choose this color

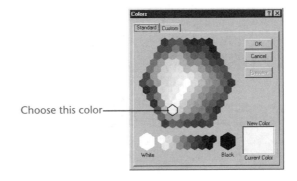

6. Choose OK or press Enter. The Font dialog box reappears.

7. For a final touch, choose Bold from the F<u>o</u>nt Style list.

8. Choose OK or press Enter. The dialog box disappears and your changes are carried out.

   Now the title text is much more visible against the shaded background (see fig. 4.14).

9. To view the results of your work on the actual slide or slides of your new presentation, choose <u>V</u>iew, <u>S</u>lides.

PowerPoint 95 Basics

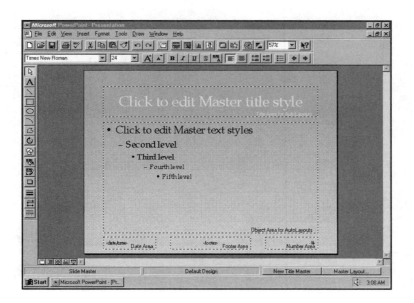

Fig. 4.14
You can view the changes for the new presentation in the Slide Master.

You literally have created a new presentation from scratch. All the other slides you add to the presentation are the same format you defined in this exercise.

There is one key point to carry away from this section: the importance of the Slide Master. When creating a new presentation with your own specifications, this is where it should all happen. You've also had a glance at some very important color and text customization features. More Slide Master tips and information can be found later in this chapter.

Save your work by choosing <u>F</u>ile, <u>S</u>ave. Specify a file name for your new presentation, and click OK. The following section is a continuation of your present work.

Understanding the View Options

Views and Masters bear considerable similarities to one another. Most primary functional areas of PowerPoint 95—slides, outlines, handouts, and notes pages—have both a Master and a view. (There is an Outline view, but no Outline Master, which was deemed redundant by Microsoft given the nature of an outline.) For PowerPoint 95, there is also a new Title Master. You can use PowerPoint's various views by choosing menu commands, or by choosing the View buttons above the PowerPoint status bar near the bottom of the screen (see fig. 4.15).

Fig. 4.15
PowerPoint's View buttons appear just above the status bar.

Slide Show button

Notes Pages View

Slide Sorter View button

Outline View button

Slide View button

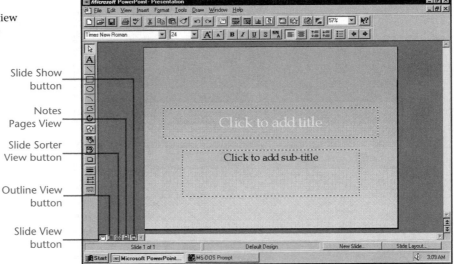

Using the View Buttons on the PowerPoint Status Bar

PowerPoint's View buttons are not located on a toolbar—they are located at the bottom of the screen, just above the status bar (refer to fig. 4.15). Each View button is briefly described in Table 4.1.

Table 4.1 PowerPoint 95's View Buttons		
Button	**Name**	**Action**
	Slide View	Changes the view to directly edit a slide
	Outline View	Changes the view to show the title and body text from all slides
	Slide Sorter View	Changes the view to show miniatures of all slides
	Notes Pages View	Changes the view to edit speaker's notes
	Slide Show View	Runs or rehearses a slide show

Clicking any of the five View buttons displays their respective sections of the program.

Viewing Slides

In Slide view, you can edit, change, and add elements on the currently displayed slide. Figure 4.15 shows an example of a presentation in Slide view. Use the Slide Changer to page through each slide in your presentation; you also can use the Page Up and Page Down keys. You can do virtually every operation that you can perform on slide objects in Slide view, such as creating charts, drawing graphics, placing clip art, entering and formatting text, and so on. All these issues are discussed in later chapters.

Viewing the Outline

PowerPoint 95 offers greater flexibility than the competition because of the various tools it offers—in particular, its Notes Pages, the handout feature, and especially its powerful and straightforward outlining capabilities. Outlining, in particular, is the key feature for organizing your ideas and critiquing your argument for logical flow and impact. A single slide view can never provide such a viewpoint.

The outline is one of the hidden sources of power in PowerPoint 95. A sample Outline view is shown in figure 4.16.

Fig. 4.16

Studying
PowerPoint's
Outline view,
which shows the
text contents of
each slide in your
presentation.

Outline
toolbar

Slide
icons

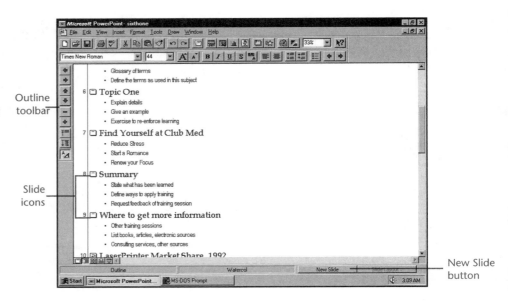

New Slide
button

Outline view offers intelligent tools for rearranging and editing an entire
presentation at a glance. Each slide in the presentation is numbered; click the
slide's number to select it. When you select a slide, you can drag, delete,
copy, and cut and paste it—you also can format the text of a slide.

To enter Outline view:

1. Choose <u>V</u>iew, <u>O</u>utline.

PowerPoint's Outline view appears (see fig. 4.16).

The slide icon is a key element of Outline view (refer to fig. 4.16). You can
drag and drop the slide icons at any location in the outline, providing an
easy way to rearrange your slides. Clicking any slide icon also selects the entire text contents—title and body text—available in the slide for formatting
and editing functions.

The Outlining toolbar (a special toolbar that's used only in Outline view)
covers most of the key functions for working with an outline. Table 4.2 describes each button.

Button	Name	Action
	Promote (Indent less)	Moves selected text to a higher level
	Demote (Indent more)	Moves selected text to a lower level
	Move Up	Moves selected slide up the slide sequence
	Move Down	Moves selected slide down the slide sequence
	Collapse Selection	Hides body text from the Outline view of the selected slide or slides (does not delete it)
	Expand Selection	Restores any body text in selected slides to the Outline view
	Show Titles	Shows only slide titles in the outline
	Show All	Shows slide titles and body text for each slide in the outline
	Show Formatting	Toggles to show text formatting for titles and body text. If formatting is off, text is shown in standard sans serif characters without boldfacing or different sizes

Table 4.2   PowerPoint 95's Outlining Toolbar Buttons

You can insert new slides in Outline view by choosing the New Slide button. However, you have no control over slide layout in Outline view; any new slide you add in Outline view is a blank slate. It defaults to a standard title and body text slide, and uses the current template.

Place the text insertion point at the end of a title line and press Enter to create a new slide. Place the insertion point at the end of a bulleted point and press Enter to create a new bulleted point in the body text for that slide. Select any text for editing to enable the use of the standard, text formatting

Tip
You can export outlines to Microsoft Word for Windows, and you can import outlines from Word into PowerPoint.

PowerPoint 95 Basics

tools on the PowerPoint Formatting toolbar. Formatting that you add to any text in Outline view is shown in the presentation. Some text formatting, such as adding colors to text, is not available in Outline view.

 By using the Outlining toolbar, you can promote and demote individual argument points in a slide. This action also appears in the presentation. Other tools allow you to view only as much of the outline as you desire. If you want an abbreviated view of the Outline, choose the Collapse Selection button on the Outline toolbar. Select all the desired Outline text (the easiest way is by choosing Edit, Select All) and click the button; you'll see a simplified outline like the one in figure 4.17.

 In a collapsed outline, each slide entry that has collapsed text is shown with a ghosted gray underline. You can still see the text in slides; this just provides a truncated outline. To return to the full outline, choose Edit, Select All, and click the Expand Selection button.

 As an alternative, if you simply want to expand the entire outline to view, click the Show All button on the Outlining toolbar.

Fig. 4.17
Ghosted underlining indicates that collapsed text is present.

Tooltips also work in Outline view

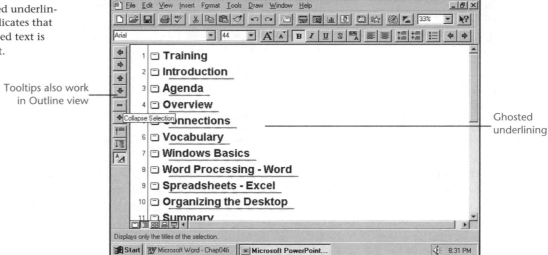

Ghosted underlining

Viewing the Slide Sorter

The Slide Sorter is a very powerful PowerPoint 95 convenience feature. As mentioned in Chapter 3, the Slide Sorter enables fast rearranging of slides to any order—just drag and drop the slide to its new place. Using the Slide Sorter, it's also easy to apply special effects to the contents of a slide, including *transition effects* that determine how a slide appears and disappears on-screen, and *build effects* to animate elements on a slide.

Simply knowing where you can apply build and transition effects to your presentation allows a wide scope for experimenting. Build effects in particular are a drastic point of improvement in the PowerPoint 95 program. In previous versions, you could only apply build effects to body text. Now you can animate titles, text, and graphics with a couple of mouse clicks.

> **Note**
>
> Not only can you apply build effects to almost any PowerPoint slide object—you can combine them with sound effects as well. (This is also true for transitions.) However, you *cannot* apply most key PowerPoint animation features in Slide Sorter view. The program's new Animation Settings feature is the key to unlocking dozens of new tricks that PowerPoint presenters have never had before. The Slide Sorter offers quick ways to add effects to any number of slides, without having to dig too deep into the program. For more information on these topics, see Chapter 22, "Advanced Presentation Management."

Applying Special Effects in the Slide Sorter

To apply transition or build effects in the Slide Sorter, follow these steps:

1. With your presentation displayed, choose View, Slide Sorter.

2. In the Slide Sorter, click the slide to which you want to apply special effects.

3. With the slide selected, choose either the Transition drop-down list or the Build drop-down list, and choose the effect you want. (For a fast choice, choose Random Effects from either list.)

4. As the effect is applied, the slide shows a brief demonstration of the applied effect.

Table 4.3 PowerPoint 95's Slide Sorter Toolbar Buttons		
Button	**Name**	**Action**
(icon)	Slide Transition	Displays the Slide Transition dialog box, where you can specify transition speeds and playback settings
No Transition ▼	Slide Transition	Drop-down list for selecting Effects individual transition effects

Tip

Choose the Slide Sorter button to quickly view the Slide Sorter from the currently displayed view.

Button	Name	Action
No Build Effect ▼	Text Build Effects	Drop-down list for choosing individual build effects to be attached to selected slides
	Hide Slide	Forces the currently selected slide to be hidden during playback
	Rehearse Timings	Starts the slide show, using timing rehearsal features. Hit ESC at any time during the rehearsal to return to the slide sorter
A A	Show Formatting	Toggle button to show appearance of each slide in the thumb-nail images, or to show a basic image of the slide titles

When you apply effects to a slide, notice that small icons appear under each effected slide thumbnail (refer to fig. 4.18). The icons correspond to the Transition tool and Build tool icons shown on the toolbar, indicating whether one or both classes of effects are applied to the slide.

Tip

Double-click a slide in the Slide Sorter to display it in Slide view, ready for editing and changes.

Unlike Outline view, you can add new slides to a presentation and have full access to AutoLayouts, for deciding what type of slide you want to insert, by clicking the New Slide button.

The Slide Sorter also offers a powerful Zoom feature that enables you to make the slide thumbnails as large or as small as desired (see fig. 4.19).

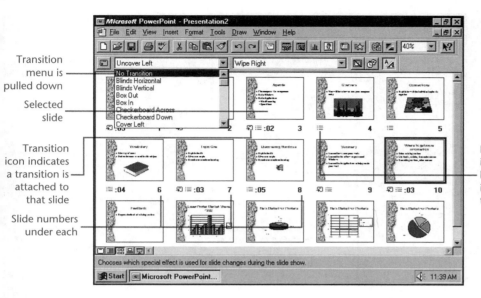

Fig. 4.18
Use the Slide Sorter to apply special effects to a slide. Each slide in the presentation is shown in a thumbnail image.

Transition menu is pulled down

Selected slide

Transition icon indicates a transition is attached to that slide

Slide numbers under each

Build icon indicates a build effect is attached to that slide

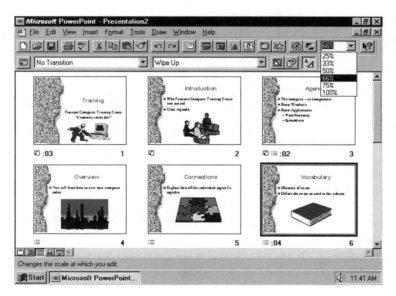

Fig. 4.19
Zooming in the Slide Sorters.

Viewing Notes Pages (Speaker's Notes)

Notes Pages offer a valuable tool to the speaker: writing and printing out extensive speaker's notes for each slide in the presentation, allowing for greater ease and confidence while conducting a show for your viewers.

As noted in Chapter 3, Notes Pages generally have one slide printed on each page, occupying the top half with space for text provided in the bottom half. Figure 4.20 shows a typical Notes Page layout.

Fig. 4.20
Viewing a Notes
Page and its
contents.

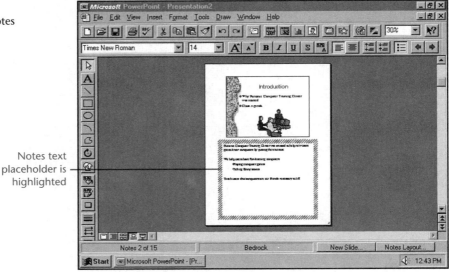

Notes text
placeholder is
highlighted

You can place special information on Notes Pages, such as headers and
footers with company names, dates, logos, and other information. You do
this with the Notes Master, which is discussed in a later section of this chapter titled "Understanding the Notes Master."

Tip
Double-clicking
the slide shown on
any Notes Page in
Notes view brings
up that slide in
Slide view.

> ### Note
>
> The Notes Master is different than Notes view. You enter speaker's notes in the Notes
> view. The Notes Master simply defines the general layout of the Notes Pages when
> you print them, including any common elements such as page numbers, logos, and
> so on.

In Notes view, each Notes Page shows a slide. Below the slide, the user can
enter and edit notes for each page. (You also can use the Notes Master to
format notes with different fonts and text effects.) To enter Notes Pages text,
follow these steps:

1. Click inside the Notes text area (also called a placeholder) for the desired page. The insertion point appears inside the placeholder.

2. If you look closely at your edits, use the Zoom feature until the view is
   comfortable for typing text. (66 percent view, from the Zoom drop-
   down list, is a good place to start.)

3. Begin typing your notes. The Notes Master determines the basic format
   of your text—but that's just the beginning. You can use the Promote
   and Demote buttons on Notes text, and add new bullets to your text.

To execute further formatting on your text, such as hanging indents, continue with these steps.

4. Choose <u>V</u>iew, <u>R</u>uler.

PowerPoint's ruler appears. You can drag the ruler's gadgets to create hanging indents and standard indents. This is especially handy for bulleted text.

5. Select the text you want to format.

6. Drag the ruler gadgets until the text is formatted the way you want. Add tabs, if necessary, between bullets and their associated text.

Viewing the Slide Show

To view the slide show, simply click the Slide Show button above the Status bar.

PowerPoint's Slide Show view provides many new program functions. Among them are the Meeting Minder and a special Slide Navigator that helps keep you from getting lost during a long presentation. While many convenience features have been added, some are still the same. Many users, particularly when using laptops to deliver a slide show in front of an audience, prefer to use keystrokes instead of mouse clicks to advance a slide show.

You can use several keystrokes for various purposes during a slide show:

Keystrokes	Action
Enter or Spacebar	Advances to next slide
Enter or Spacebar	Executes next build effect (appearance of next bulleted point in slide, if builds are applied)
Page Up	Back to previous slide
Page Down	Advances to next slide

Remember that you can perform presentation rehearsals to set the precise timing of all events that occur in each slide throughout the entire show. You use the keystrokes previously listed when you are manually advancing the slide show, and the build effects (if any) are applied to each slide.

Simply clicking the Slide Show button, however, somewhat limits your access to control features in the slide show. Choosing <u>V</u>iew, Slide Sho<u>w</u> (regardless of the view you are currently in) affords you a few more options, as figure 4.21 shows.

Fig. 4.21
Use the Slide Show
dialog box when
you are preparing
to run a Slide
Show.

The following are options available for running your slide show:

- Slides

  All. Select this option to show all slides.

  From and To. This option enables you to specify the range of slides to be shown.

- Advance

  Manual Advance. Select this option when you want to manually control when each slide and slide object or effect displays, including animation and multimedia.

  Use Slide Timings. Select this option to apply the slide timings built into the presentation.

  Rehearse New Timings. This option allows you to create new timings for the slide show, by using keystrokes to prompt the program.

- *Loop Continuously Until Esc*. Selecting this check box runs the slide show continuously until you press Esc. This feature only works if you have added event timing to your slide show.

- *Pen Color*. Choosing this option displays a color palette for assigning a new color to the Pen annotation tool, which is used by clicking and dragging the mouse on the screen during the slide show.

To run the slide show after setting your options, choose Show or press Enter.

Understanding the Master Views

You create and apply the common elements of all the parts of your presentation in the Master Views. A presentation template has several Masters that are part of the whole package, as you discover when you use the AutoContent and Wizards. The Master Views enable you to access all the components of your template and to change them for any preference, such as a company name appearing on your handouts (via the Handout Master), a company logo appearing on your slides (via the Slide Master), and the layout of all your Notes Pages (via the Notes Master). A new Title Master enables you to apply a special layout and appearance to the title slide of your presentation.

Understanding the Slide Master

The Slide Master provides the basis for the visual appearance of your presentation. As you know, a special file called a *template* defines the look of your Slide Master and slide show. The template's color scheme, graphic objects, and other common elements of each slide are based in the Slide Master; you can edit and change them there.

Using the Slide Master

To display the Slide Master for your presentation, perform the following steps:

1. Choose <u>V</u>iew, <u>M</u>aster.

    A cascading menu pops up, offering four menu choices: Slide Master, Title Master, Handout Master, and Notes Master (see fig. 4.22).

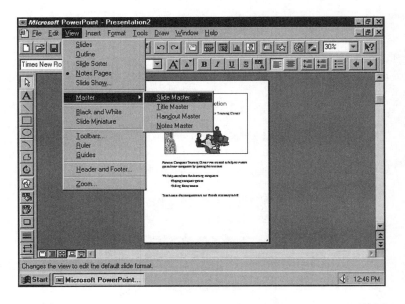

Fig. 4.22
Choose from the cascading menus to locate the Slide Master option you want.

Note

To quickly enter the Slide Master, hold down the Shift key and click the Slide View button just above the status bar. The Shift key can be used with all five buttons to reveal various Masters.

2. From the cascading menu, choose <u>S</u>lide Master.

The Slide Master appears, similar to that shown in figure 4.23.

Fig. 4.23
Viewing a typical
Slide Master with
its title and body
text placeholders.

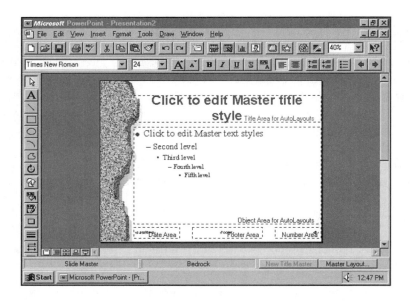

 In Slide Master view, the middle box of the status bar displays the name of the currently used template in the slide show. Notice that the template used is the Multiple Bars template, in the C:\OFFICE95\TEMPLATES\PRESENTATION DESIGNS folder. To apply this template:

1. Choose F<u>o</u>rmat, Apply Design Te<u>m</u>plate. (You also can click the Apply Design Template button on the Standard toolbar.) The Apply Design Template dialog box appears as shown in figure 4.24.

Fig. 4.24
Here you can load
a design template
in Slide Master
view.

Folder path to
the template

Preview shows
the template

2. Typically, the right template directory will automatically be found by this dialog box.

3. Scroll down the list and choose the Multiple Bars template. Click any name in the listing to see a preview image of the template.

4. Choose <u>A</u>pply or press Enter.

Now, it's time to play with some of the objects that compose the Slide Master. The Slide Master is the basis for the entire visual look of your presentation—you'll see why in the following steps.

5. Click the multi-colored graphic on the slide background (on either the left or right edge of the slide). Make sure you don't click any of the text objects. The result should appear similar to figure 4.25.

The graphic object is highlighted, showing small, square handles around it. It occupies almost the entire space of the slide.

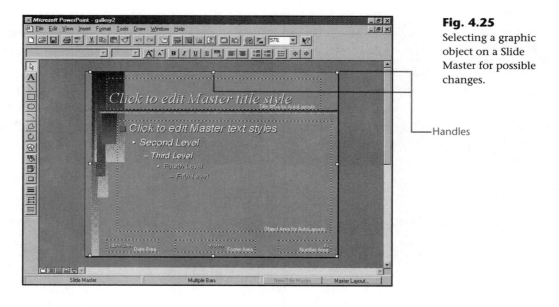

Fig. 4.25
Selecting a graphic object on a Slide Master for possible changes.

Handles

6. Choose <u>D</u>raw, <u>U</u>ngroup.

You will now see several sets of graphics, each with its own set of handles (see fig. 4.26).

7. Click outside of the graphic objects to deselect them. The handles will disappear.

Fig. 4.26
The handles are now shown around the edge of the ungrouped graphics (which are also groups of graphics in turn).

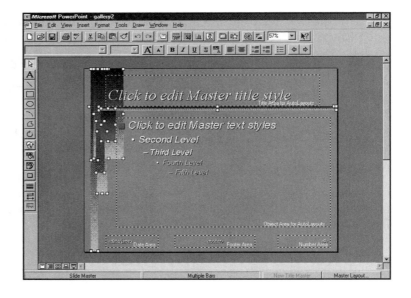

Tip
PowerPoint 95 has Multiple Undo capability. For the following step, you also can press Ctrl+Z twice to undo the last two actions.

You do this because to make changes to a single object, you must deselect all the currently selected objects first. Otherwise, you may change attributes for several graphic objects when you don't intend to.

8. Click and drag the red-colored graphic object on the left side of the Multiple Bars template across the Slide Master a couple inches with the mouse (by clicking and holding the mouse on any part of the graphic except the pressure points). (Do not perform any other actions yet.) The master looks something like figure 4.27.

Fig. 4.27
Drag a graphic on the Slide Master to demonstrate the Master's editing capabilities.

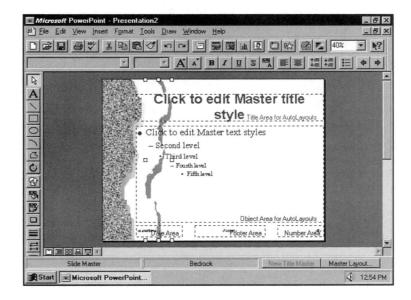

9. Choose <u>E</u>dit, <u>U</u>ndo. Then, to regroup the original graphics, choose <u>U</u>ndo again.

You really do not want to mess up your template just yet; you used the Undo commands to efface the previous action. Nonetheless, this is a very important exercise. It shows that you can move graphic objects on a slide master. Because you can move them, you can do many other things to them as well. You can change their color, and reshape and delete them. If you chose to leave the changes as they were and displayed a slide based on this template, you would see those out-of-place graphics in the slides—not just in the Master. The Slide Master is where you can design your very own graphically styled templates.

Understanding the Title Master

The Title Master differs slightly from the Slide Master. You use the Title Master only to format your *title* slides, which in PowerPoint 95 are separate from the rest of your presentation. In short, the Title Master defines the appearance of the title slide of your presentation (if you have created one), plus any other title slides that you insert into your slide show as indicators of new sections in your show. The methods and techniques used to change a title slide's appearance are the same as they are for the Slide Master. The applications for the Title Master are significant, because you may want to add a company logo, fancy graphic, date, or other embellishment to a title slide but not to any other slides in the show.

1. To insert a title slide into your presentation, choose <u>I</u>nsert, New <u>S</u>lide. The New Slide dialog box will appear, displaying the various slide AutoLayouts.

2. Choose the top left AutoLayout. The dialog box description will read "Title Slide."

3. Choose OK or press Enter.

Viewing the Title Master

To view the Title Master for the current presentation, choose <u>V</u>iew, <u>M</u>aster, <u>T</u>itle Master. You don't have to have a title slide in your presentation to do this. However, any changes you make to the title master will affect any other title slides you add to your presentation.

Tip

You can change the graphic appearance of your title slide by using the Title Master.

The Title Master is actually able to accept a custom background that is separate from the rest of the slides in your presentation. As an example, follow these steps to learn how to use Textures for a custom Title Slide background:

1. Choose Format, Custom Background.

2. From the drop-down list in the Custom Background dialog box, choose Textured. The Textured Fill dialog box appears (see Figure 4.28).

3. Select a texture from the Textures section. (Scroll through the list to see more.)

4. Choose OK or press Enter.

5. Choose Apply or press Enter. Figure 4.29 shows a typical result.

Tip
Remember to use the Preview button to see how a texture will look before you use it.

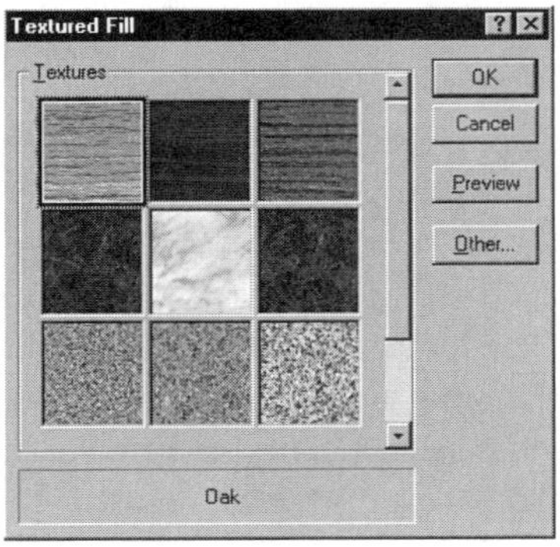

Fig. 4.28
Using the textured fill feature to apply textures to the background of a title master.

Fig. 4.29
Applying a textured fill.

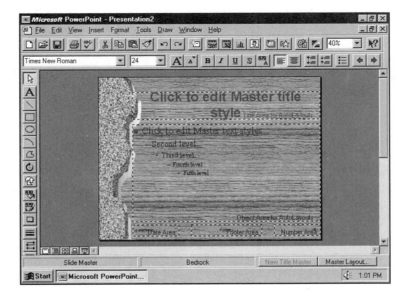

All of the customizing features you use on slides or the Slide Master also apply to the Title Master. That's why you did a texture fill for the Title; it demonstrates the program's consistency in this crucial area.

> **Note**
>
> Remember that if you make changes to the background of your Slide Master, you will have to go back and do the same thing for the Title Master. This is only the case if you want your Title Master to have the same appearance as the rest of your slides. The Title Master is unaffected by any graphic changes or rearrangements you make on the Slide Master.

Tip
If you want the Slide Master and the Title Master to have the same appearance, and you have made changes to the Slide Master, you must also change the Title Master to match.

Understanding the Handout Master

Using the Handout Master is quite simple. The dotted boxes are placeholders that hold images of slides in the presentation. Although the appearance of the slide image placeholders on the Handout Master seems complex, the only time they ever come into play is when you print the Handout Master. You do that, as you might remember, by choosing File, Print. It's just as simple to add dates, page numbers, and other elements to the Handout Master as it is to other masters.

Viewing the Handout Master

To view the Handout Master for the current presentation, choose View, Master, Handout Master. Figure 4.30 shows a typical Handout Master.

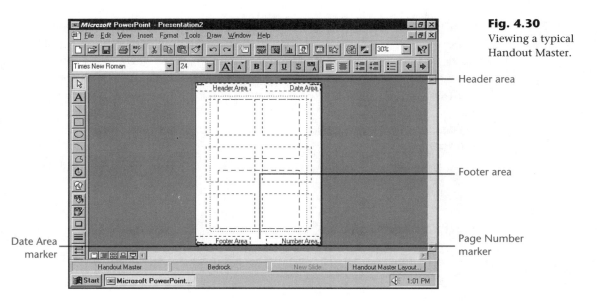

Fig. 4.30
Viewing a typical Handout Master.

Header area

Footer area

Date Area marker

Page Number marker

Using the Handout Master

To insert some background objects into the Handout Master, follow these steps:

1. Select the sample text inside the Date Area marker, on the Handout Master.

2. Choose Insert, Date and Time. The Date and Time dialog box appears (see fig. 4.31).

Fig. 4.31
There are many styles of dates and times to choose from.

3. Choose a date and time from the list, and then choose OK or press Enter.

   A date or time (or both) appears in the middle of the Date Area marker, showing the current date and/or time.

4. (Optional) Drag the date marker to an appropriate location on the margins of the page. You can use the placeholder margins as a guide if necessary.

The Handout Master is an extremely simple document. The most meaningful operations you'll have to do with it are to insert dates, times, and page numbers, and possibly change the layout to show two, three, or six slide graphics per page. That's the significance of the dotted-line placeholders on the page. The dotted lines show where slide images will be printed on each handout page. You can't select the placeholders or move them, but two, three, or six slide images per page can be printed. Each image represents a single slide in the presentation sequence.

Understanding the Notes Master

The Notes Master, because it automatically contains some graphic elements (namely, images of a slide on each Notes Page), offers some room for creativity. You can resize the slide image on each Notes Page with the mouse, as you can the placeholder for notes text. As you can see in figure 4.32, the Notes Master bears a very close resemblance to the Notes view discussed earlier in this chapter. To view the Notes Master, choose View, Master, Notes Master.

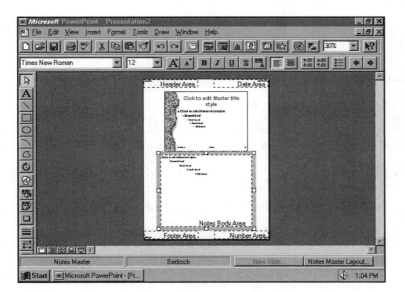

Fig. 4.32
Use the placeholder for Notes Master text formatting.

Note

There are two Notes Masters: one for Title Slides, and one for the rest of the presentation. You won't discover this unless you apply a different background appearance or other change to the Title Master. Then, if you're viewing a Title slide, its Notes Master will be different. If you want to view the Notes Master for a title slide, simply display the title slide in your presentation and choose View, Masters, and then Notes Master.

Using the Notes Master

Using the Notes Master is quite similar to working in Notes Pages view. In fact, because you don't enter notes in the Master, it is actually simpler.

To resize the slide image to a smaller size and reformat the Notes Master text, follow these steps:

1. Click the slide image in the Notes Master to select it.

2. With the mouse, grab a corner handle and drag it to shrink the slide image. The slide resizes symmetrically and retains its visual proportion.

3. Drag the slide to a centered place on the page, if necessary.

To reformat the sample text in the Notes Master text placeholder:

1. Click inside the text placeholder.

2. To reformat all the placeholder text, click and drag the mouse to select the placeholder's contents. The text is highlighted.

3. Use the tools on the Formatting toolbar, such as Fonts, Font Size, Bold-face, and so on, to format the text in the desired way. You also can Zoom and use the Ruler to aid in effective formatting for indents.

    The result should look similar to figure 4.33.

Fig. 4.33
The placeholder shows the new text formatting.

Slide image shrunk

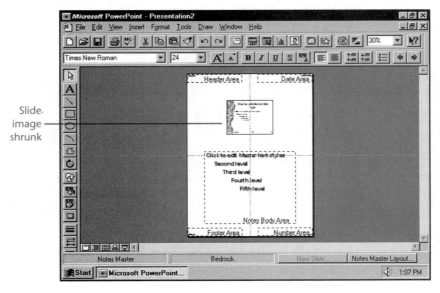

As with the other masters you work with, you can quickly and easily place dates, times, page numbers, and other items on the Notes Master. Use the same method you used with the other masters you looked at. For example, to place a date on a Notes Master, follow these steps:

1. Select the sample text inside the Date Area marker at the bottom of the page.

2. Choose Insert, Date and Time.

3. Choose a date and/or time from the list, and choose OK or press Enter.

   A date marker appears inside the Date Area marker of the Notes Master page.

Troubleshooting

I can't display any of the Masters.

Make sure you have a presentation open and active.

My outline text doesn't show its formatting in Outline view.

Click the Show Formatting tool button on the Outline toolbar. As the default, the Outline toolbar appears on the right side of the PowerPoint screen when you're in Outline view. The Show Formatting tool is the bottom button on that toolbar.

My Notes Pages don't have any text placeholders or slides on them.

There's an easy way to fix this. Display your Notes Master (not an individual Notes Page, but the Notes Master for your presentation), and choose Format, Notes, Master Layout. (Notice how the Format menu changed to reflect the Master type.) Select the two check boxes that appear in the Notes Master Layout dialog box: Slide Image and Body. Other placeholders to specify here include Date, Page Number, Header, and Footer. Choose OK or press Enter. Your Notes Master now displays the desired elements for your Notes Pages.

This technique is common to all the Masters. If any of your Masters don't have a standard element, use the Format, Master Layout command. You'll be able to fix many problems there.

Chapter 5

Creating and Using Templates

by Pamela R. Toliver

Templates contain the basic design elements that form the background for your presentation slides. As a result, comprehending how these design elements mesh with other presentation components will make it easier to understand what goes on behind the scenes as you create your presentation. Fortunately, PowerPoint comes equipped with a number of professionally designed templates, which makes working with templates easier and more effective.

In this chapter you learn to

- Recognize elements on which templates are built

- Apply PowerPoint templates to existing presentations

- Create new presentations using PowerPoint's sample presentations

- Design and create a new template

Reviewing Template Elements

Templates consist of discrete Master components, which form the character of your presentation. The role of Masters is fundamental to the overall creation of a presentation because Masters contain the basic components—page numbers, logos, company name, and dates—that you want to appear on every slide, Notes Page, or handout of your presentation.

In addition to these standard components, Masters may contain design elements that dress up your presentation. By changing the basic color scheme, background color, placeholder font and bullet characters, and adding drawings and blends, you can use the Slide Master to create your own special design template. As you can see, the Slide Master is at the core of any slide show.

Using Templates

Whether you choose to apply a template as you create a new presentation or to change the look of an existing presentation is a matter of personal preference. While some people prefer to focus on the presentation content and apply a template after it is complete, others enjoy seeing the effects of the template as they create each slide.

Applying a Template to a New Presentation

One of the options for creating a new presentation is to select the Template option from the PowerPoint dialog box. This option was not presented when you clicked the New button on the Standard toolbar to create a new presentation (that action automatically created a new blank presentation), but it can be activated by choosing File, New to create a new presentation.

To apply a template to a new presentation as you start PowerPoint, follow these steps:

1. Start PowerPoint and respond to the Tip of the Day, if necessary.

   The PowerPoint dialog box appears, as shown in figure 5.1.

Fig. 5.1
The PowerPoint dialog box enables you to choose a presentation template for a new presentation.

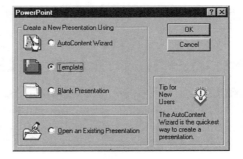

I

2. In the Create a New Presentation Using section of the dialog box, choose <u>T</u>emplate and click the OK button.

The New Presentation dialog box opens, as shown in figure 5.2.

Presentation types

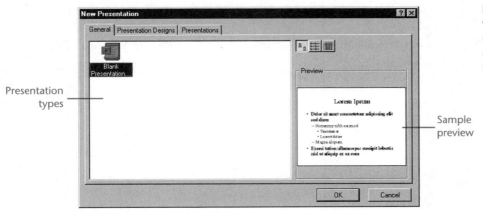

Sample preview

Fig. 5.2
The New Presentation dialog box arranges the templates by type.

3. Click the Presentation Designs tab to display the design templates.

The design templates tab of the New Presentation dialog box is displayed, as seen in figure 5.3. You may have a different selection of presentation designs, depending on what was selected when PowerPoint was installed.

Extensions   View buttons   Preview area

Alphabetical listing

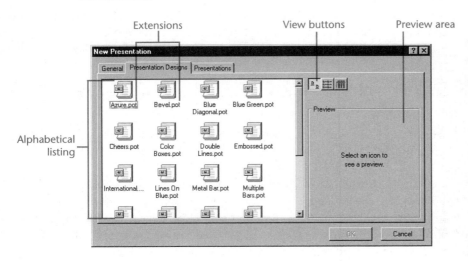

Fig. 5.3
The presentation design templates are arranged in alphabetical order and displayed in the default Large Icon view. Notice that presentation design templates appear to have standard file names but the file extension is .pot instead of .ppt.

> **Note**
>
> The next time you create a new presentation using File, New without exiting PowerPoint, the New Presentation dialog box will automatically display the Presentation Designs sheet.

Tip
To view extensions, deselect Hide MS-DOS File Extensions in Explorer's View options.

4. Select a template name and view the design in the Preview area of the dialog box.

5. Continue to select and preview template designs until you find one you like.

6. Click OK to activate the template.

7. Select the AutoLayout format you want to use for the first slide and click OK.

8. Complete the presentation using the template.

To apply a template to a new presentation after starting PowerPoint, follow these steps:

1. Choose File, New.

   The New Presentation dialog box displays the tab containing the template used to create the previous presentation. If the presentation you created before this was a blank presentation, the General tab which contains the Blank Presentation design appears; if you created a new presentation using a presentation design template, the Presentation Designs tab appears.

2. Select the design template you want to use for the new presentation and click OK.

3. Select the AutoLayout format for the first slide of the new presentation and click OK.

Another point to consider as you explore the templates that come with PowerPoint is the method you plan to use to deliver your presentation. If you are going to use the computer or a computer projection device, it is fun to use the "full living color" format of the templates. You can also print your slides onto paper to use as handouts or onto transparencies for viewing with an overhead projector. If you have a color printer, you can print the slides in color, but keep in mind that printing in color requires more time than printing in black and white. It can also be helpful to remove the background color to make the transparency easier to read. PowerPoint makes it quick and easy to change the format from black and white back to color if you aren't satisfied with the result. To change the format of a template from color to black and white or from black and white to color, follow these steps:

1. Apply the template you want to use by following the steps outlined above.

2. Choose <u>V</u>iew, <u>B</u>lack and White or click the B&W View button on the Standard toolbar.

   The color template is formatted using black and white and shades of gray as shown in figure 5.4.

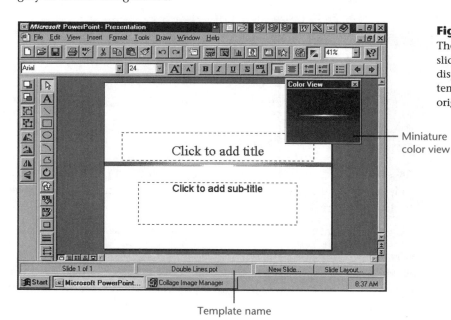

Fig. 5.4
The Color View slide miniature displays the template in its original colors.

Miniature color view

Template name

Modifying an Existing Presentation by Applying a Template

If you have a presentation open and you're not satisfied with its appearance, you apply a different template to the file by following these steps:

1. Display the presentation that you want to change.

2. Choose F<u>o</u>rmat, Apply Design Te<u>m</u>plate.

Tip
You can also open the Apply Design Template dialog box by double-clicking the design or template identified in the status bar.

The Apply Design Template dialog box appears, as shown in figure 5.5.

Fig. 5.5

The Apply Design
Template dialog
box lists the same
presentation
designs viewed
earlier, but places
them in a list on
the left and
displays the
preview on the
right in the default
Preview view.

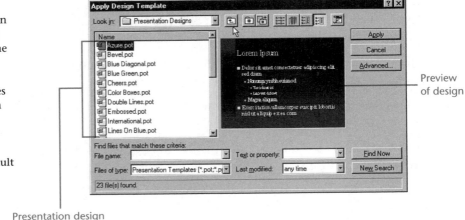

Presentation design
templates

Preview
of design

3. Click a template Name listed and use the thumbnail preview to the right to help you pick out the one you want.

4. Choose Apply or press Enter.

The dialog box disappears and the currently displayed presentation begins to undergo its facelift. If you have any charts in the presentation, a message is displayed on-screen:

```
Charts are being updated with the new color scheme
```

After a moment or two, the process is complete and your presentation gets its new look. Text, default object colors, slide backgrounds, bullet characters, and charts all have a new color scheme; and many times the alignment of objects on the slides is changed. As a result, you may want to review each slide to make sure the design template is suitable for the information you have on the slides.

Importing Templates from Other Presentation Packages

PowerPoint supports the direct importing of presentation files from Lotus Freelance 4 for DOS and Harvard Graphics 2.3 and 3.0 for DOS. PowerPoint automatically converts color schemes, objects, and charts to its own format. The procedures you use are very straightforward.

To import a presentation from another program, follow these steps:

1. Choose File, Open or click the Open button on the Standard toolbar.

   The File Open dialog box appears, as shown in figure 5.6.

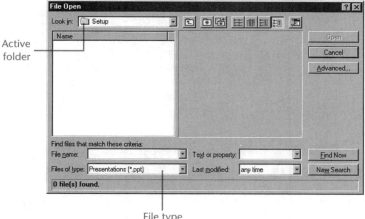

Active folder

File type

Fig. 5.6
You will need to change the folder you want PowerPoint to look in for the new file type.

2. Click the down arrow in the Files of Type drop-down list and choose the file type you want to import.

3. Change the path in the Look In text box to the drive and folder containing the Harvard Graphics or Lotus Freelance presentation.

4. Choose the presentation file you want to import from the Name list.

5. Choose OK or press Enter.

If the file is compatible with PowerPoint, the imported presentation file will be converted to a PowerPoint presentation. Many of its original colors, data, and charts will appear unchanged. If the file is not compatible, an error message will appear advising you that the file cannot be imported into PowerPoint.

▶ See "Creating a Presentation from an Imported Outline" p. 228

▶ See "Using Outline Tools," p. 229

> **Note**
>
> You can also import outlines in several text formats by using the File Open dialog box. Along with the various presentation formats supported in the preceding example, the list also includes Outline, with six different file formats directly supported for text importing of outlines for a presentation:
>
> *.DOC—Microsoft Word for Windows
>
> *.WPD—WordPerfect for windows
>
> *.XLS—Microsoft Excel Worksheet
>
> *.XLW—Microsoft Excel Workbook
>
> *.RTF—Rich Text Format (export format supported by many word processors)
>
> *.TXT—Standard ASCII text file format
>
> Selecting All Outlines in the Files of Type text box enables you to locate the desired outline file. Importing the outline automatically converts it to a PowerPoint outline with slide titles and body text placed appropriately.

Using PowerPoint's Sample Presentations

PowerPoint comes with quite a variety of different presentations containing numerous slides already formatted with an effective template design and instructive text to guide you through preparing a presentation. As a result, depending on what you hope to accomplish with your presentation, you may choose a sample presentation and change the wording and narrative to fit your particular needs. Each sample is formatted with a design template especially effective—according to the experts—for the specific nature of the presentation.

These presentations are identified on the third sheet of the New Presentation dialog box. The tab on this sheet identifies the samples simply as Presentations. The following list gives you an idea of the types of presentations you can create using samples provided by PowerPoint.

Business Plan.pot

Communicating Bad News (long).pot

Communicating Bad News.pot

Company Meeting.pot

Creativity Session.pot

Employee Orientation.pot

Financial Report.pot

General (long).pot

General.pot

Marketing Plan.pot

Recommending a Strategy (long).pot

Recommending a Strategy.pot

Reporting Progress.pot

Selling a Product or Idea (long).pot

Selling a Product or Idea.pot

Top Ten List.pot

Training (long).pot

Training.pot

Notice that each sample presentation listed above is identified as a template by the .pot extension. Notice, too, that some of the sample presentations appear identical in name except that one is designated as long and the other is not. The long presentations generally contain from two to six slides of sample text more than their "standard" or "short" counterpart for slides that may or may not need to be included in your presentation. You may want to explore both formats of these sample presentations to identify the differences between them before deciding which better meets your needs.

While each sample presentation is formatted as a template, you may wish to change the template design, thus, leaving the sample instructive text. You can easily use the procedures outlined earlier in this chapter to apply a different template. Sample text remains unaffected by the design change.

As I am sure you are aware, a presentation you may need to prepare might not be available in the sample presentations. When you need to develop a presentation that doesn't really fit into the pattern of any of those listed, use the first item listed on the Presentations sheet of the New Presentation dialog box to access the AutoContent Wizard. This Wizard helps you create an outline of a presentation based on a question and answer setup. Once you have answered all the questions, the Wizard formats a presentation and creates instructive text to help you develop your presentation.

Viewing PowerPoint's Sample Presentations

The sample presentation titles identify the nature of the sample presentation and help direct you to the topic you wish to develop in your new presentation. As you learned when selecting a template, you can preview the sample presentation before actually opening it. Simply click the presentation title, and the thumbnail of the title slide appears in the Preview window in the Open dialog box, as shown in figure 5.7.

Fig. 5.7
The Sample presentation format displays in the Preview window when you select one of the presentations.

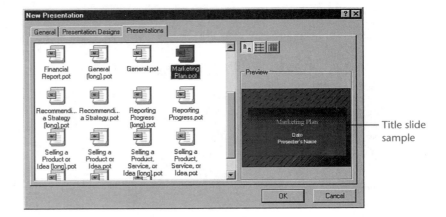

Title slide sample

To create a PowerPoint presentation using a sample presentation, follow these steps:

1. Choose File, New.

2. Click the Presentations tab to display the default Large Icon view of the sample presentations as shown in figure 5.7.

3. Choose a sample presentation, such as Marketing Plan.pot.

4. View the Preview title page.

5. Choose OK or press Enter.

   The title slide of the sample presentation is displayed, as shown in figure 5.8.

Feel free to explore the other sample presentations available. Many of them display some of the substantial graphic capabilities that you can take advantage of in PowerPoint.

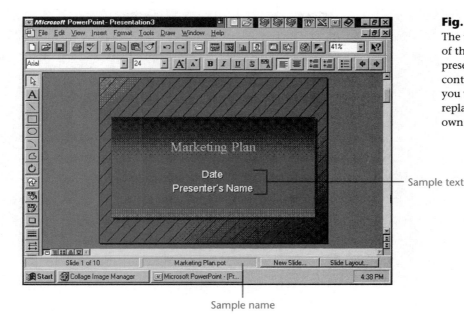

Fig. 5.8
The title slide of the sample presentation contains text that you will need to replace with your own information.

PowerPoint 95 Basics

Sample text

Sample name

Reviewing Sample Presentation Slides

Each sample presentation conforms to a specific type: a series of body text slides that when strung together, as in the samples, constitute a line of argument or a series of points made to deliver a specific message, such as a marketing plan report outlined by the framework of Marketing Plan.pot.

To review the text on the slides contained in the sample presentation, follow these steps:

1. To advance to a body text slide, click the Next Slide button (the double down-arrow button on the bottom of the Slide Changer) or press Page Down on the keyboard. If you selected Marketing Plan.pot in the preceding steps, the next slide appears as in figure 5.9.

   As you can see, the sample doesn't provide the actual content, but it does provide the logical framework for the argument you want to present.

2. Click the Next Slide button again to display the next slide in the sequence, as shown in figure 5.10.

Fig. 5.9
Slide 2 in the Marketing Plan sample presentation outlines an agenda for the meeting or report.

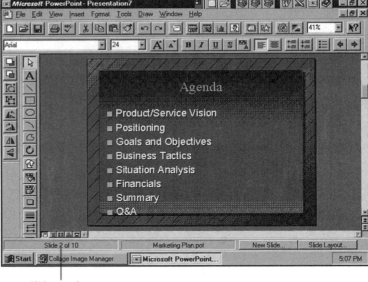

Slide number

Fig. 5.10
Most of the text on Slide 3 would be replaced with information about your own product or service.

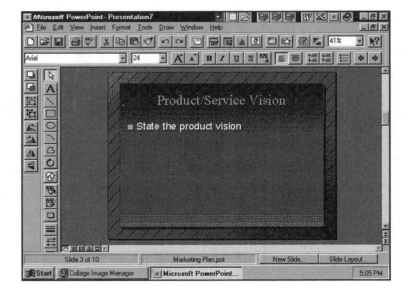

Any sample presentation can be studied in the same way. To close the sample presentation file, simply choose Close from the File menu or click the Close icon for the presentation. A dialog box will appear, prompting you to save. If you save the presentation, be sure to assign it a new file name so that the sample presentation will remain unchanged.

Using Elements from Existing Presentations and Templates to Create New Templates

As we talked about earlier in this chapter, the template designs that come with the PowerPoint program were created by professional design specialists. As a result, the planned color schemes, text formats, graphic objects, etc., complement each other and are, in general, eye-pleasing and create an effective impression. I'm the first to admit that while I have favorite colors and appreciate some of the designs more than others, I am no graphic artist. Therefore, I often find it easier to edit an existing template, thereby, creating a totally new template which better fits my needs—and I don't have to worry about colors clashing and graphic object problems.

Because so many templates are offered with the program, it makes sense to use some of their graphic elements to embellish your presentations. It's actually a simple process—essentially, a matter of copying and pasting graphic objects from one presentation to another or deleting graphic objects from an existing presentation. The key is understanding how to use the template properly. First, create a new presentation, formatting it using a template that offers graphic objects you want to use on your new presentation template or one that contains all the basic elements you want to use for the new template.

To copy a graphic object from one template to another, follow these steps:

1. Choose File, New.

2. Click the Presentation Designs tab to display the list of design templates. The list of templates appears.

3. From the list of designs, choose a template file such as Twinkle.pot.

4. Choose OK or press Enter.

5. Select an AutoLayout format for the first slide and choose OK.

   The new presentation is created, and the template is displayed. Now, to access the graphics elements of the template, you need to display the Slide Master.

6. From the View menu, select Master. A submenu appears. Choose Slide Master. The Slide Master for the chosen template appears, as shown in figure 5.11.

Fig. 5.11
The Slide Master for the Twinkle.pot template allows access to all the graphic features contained on the template.

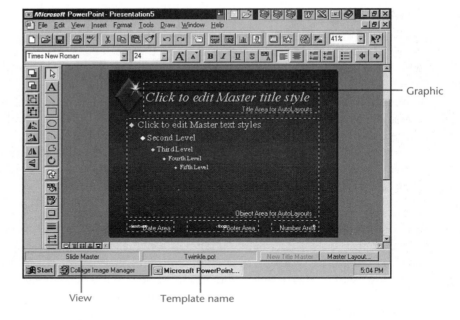

Graphic

View

Template name

7. Click the diamond in the upper-left corner of the slide. The graphic object (the diamond and the star) is selected.

Tip
You can also click the Copy button on the Standard toolbar to copy the graphic to the clipboard.

Tip
You can also paste the graphic by clicking the Paste button on the Standard toolbar.

8. Choose <u>E</u>dit, <u>C</u>opy; or press Ctrl+C.

The diamond graphic object has now been copied to the Windows clipboard.

9. Display the presentation to which you want the new graphic object added, or create a new presentation, formatting it with the template design you want to edit.

10. Choose <u>V</u>iew, Master, Slide Master.

The Slide Master for the presentation to which you want the graphic object pasted appears. If you want to paste the graphic on one slide only instead of on all of them, display the desired slide in the presentation rather than the Slide Master.

11. Choose <u>E</u>dit, <u>P</u>aste; or press Ctrl+V.

The graphic copied from the original template's Slide Master appears in the new presentation, as shown in figure 5.12.

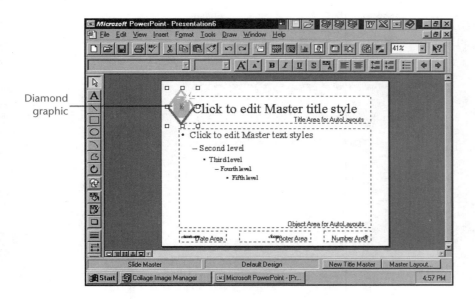

Diamond graphic

Fig. 5.12
The diamond from the Twinkle.pot template appears on the Slide Master of the new presentation, but without the color.

PowerPoint 95 Basics

Notice that the pasted graphic automatically conforms to the color palette of the presentation its pasted into. Also notice that the pasted graphic needs some rearranging for better placement on the Slide Master. The body text object and slide title object are obscured by the pasted graphic.

12. While the pasted graphic is still selected, choose Send Backward from the Draw menu, or click the Send Backward tool on PowerPoint's Drawing+ toolbar.

The graphic is sent back one layer in the Slide Master, placing it behind the body text placeholder, but it still appears in front of the title placeholder.

13. With the pasted graphic still selected, choose Send Backward from the Draw menu again.

The graphic is layered behind both text objects in the Slide Master, as shown in figure 5.13.

This example should be enough to point out some of the possibilities for borrowing graphic objects and other elements from different presentations and using them to enhance a new presentation. Items can be mixed, matched, and rearranged as needed to create just the effect you want. Additionally, you can delete graphics and other objects from existing templates when they detract from the overall effect you are trying to create.

Tip
You can also choose Send to Back from the Draw menu to move the object directly to the bottom of the objects on the slide when you know that's where you want the object. Sending backward one layer at a time allows you to explore the effects of positioning it on different layers.

For example, to create a presentation with a plain purple background and no graphics, just delete the graphic from the Slide Master before saving it as a new template following the instructions below:

Fig. 5.13
Twinkle.pot diamond graphic should be layered behind the title placeholder.

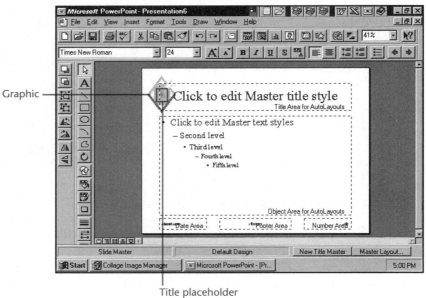

To save a presentation as a template:

1. Create the presentation, applying the desired template and editing it as desired.

2. Choose File, Save As.

3. Click the drop-down arrow beside Save as Type and select Presentation Templates (*.pot).

4. Select the Presentation Designs folder. The list of presentation templates should appear.

5. Type a file name for the new template and choose Save.

Note

If the template names are not displayed, the template will be stored on the General tab of the New Presentation dialog box with the Blank Presentation format.

The next section expands on the concept of building your own presentation template and shows you how to build a custom design from a blank presentation format.

Creating Your Own Templates

In the preceding text, you learned some of the basics of working with template elements and applying them to other presentation files. This section focuses on applying those skills to create your own custom template. Before you start, consider some of the features you want to include on the template. For example, do you want to include the company logo and colors for your template? What graphics, drawings, or other objects do you want to include on the template to make it uniquely yours—one that says *you* created it?

In the following steps, you will start with a blank presentation and create the visual effects you want by adding background color, changing the font and alignment, and changing the bullet characters. You will also be instructed to add graphics and drawings you want to use to enhance the template. These general steps enable you to apply your creative talents to complete your design.

Adding a Background Color to a Custom Template

To apply a background to your custom template, follow these steps:

1. Create a new blank presentation and select the title slide AutoLayout format.

2. Choose View, Master. When the submenu appears, choose Slide Master.

3. Choose Format, Custom Background. The Custom Background dialog box appears as shown in figure 5.14.

4. Click the drop-down arrow in the text box below the Background Fill section of the dialog box and choose the desired color or style for your background. If the color you want for your background isn't there, choose Other Color to open the color palette.

Fig. 5.14
The Custom Background dialog box enables you to choose the base color for your template.

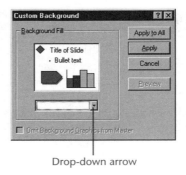

Drop-down arrow

> **Note**
>
> The procedures for selecting a shaded, textured, or patterned background are the same as those used in previous chapters.

5. Choose <u>A</u>pply. Since you are working with the Slide Master, the background color affects all slides in the presentation.

Changing Text Alignment, Font Style and Size, and Bullet Character for Custom Template Placeholders

Now that you have the background set for your custom template, you may want to customize the font for the title and body placeholders. Follow these steps:

1. Click the title text placeholder if you want to change the font, font size, or alignment of the *title* text and select the desired settings.

2. Click the body text placeholder if you want to change the font, font size, or alignment of *bulleted* text and select the desired settings.

3. To change the bullet character for a bullet level, position the insertion point in the bullet level you want to change and from the F<u>o</u>rmat menu, choose <u>B</u>ullet. The Bullet dialog box opens as shown in figure 5.15.

4. From the <u>B</u>ullets From: drop-down list, choose the character set containing the bullet you want to use and select the character, size, and color for the bullet. Choose OK.

Tip
You can also access the Bullet dialog box by positioning the insertion point in the desired bullet level, clicking the right mouse button, and selecting Bullet.

Bullet color

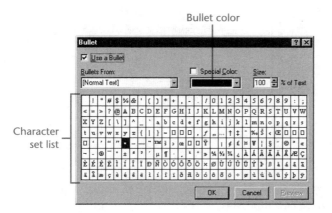

Character set list

PowerPoint 95 Basics

Fig. 5.15
The Bullet dialog box displays a palette containing characters you can use as bullets. The different bullet character sets available will be controlled by the type of printer you have.

Adding a Company Logo and Company Name to a Template

Through most of this chapter, you have used the Slide Master to create and change existing templates in the program. The Slide Master is also the key tool for another important task: adding a company name and logo to every slide in your presentation. Of course, since PowerPoint doesn't offer a selection of company logos as part of its clip-art collection, you may have to draw your own logo or import it from another source. You can use PowerPoint or another drawing program to create your company logo, if necessary. Once you have it stored in an acceptable graphic file, you can insert it onto the Slide Master so it will appear on each slide in your presentation. It can be an effective item to include as part of your custom template!

To place a company logo in your presentation, follow these steps:

Tip
When it's difficult to identify a character, click the character to enlarge it.

1. Choose View, Master, Slide Master. The Slide Master is where the company logo is placed.

2. Choose Insert, Picture

3. Identify the folder containing the logo in the Look In drop-down list and double-click the logo file.

4. Size and place the graphic object in an acceptable position on your Slide Master (in a corner of the Slide Master, for instance), as shown in figure 5.16.

Fig. 5.16

Place the graphic logo where you want it to appear on your Slide Master.

Company logo

Once it is placed on the Slide Master, the logo appears in the top-left corner of every slide. You may also want to include your company name on each slide of the presentation. The Slide Master displays the footer area of the presentation, which makes including your company name easy to accomplish. All you have to do is click on the Footer Area placeholder and type the company name. If you want to include the company name at a different location, just relocate the placeholder. To add a company name to the Slide Master, follow these steps:

1. Click the Footer Area text placeholder in the bottom center of the Slide Master.

2. Type your company name.

3. Change the font size by selecting the text and then clicking the Font Size drop-down list in the Formatting toolbar and choosing a different font size.

4. If you want to change the color of the company name, click the Text Color tool on the Formatting toolbar and choose another color (make sure it's a color that stands out well against the Slide Master background).

5. Size and position the text placeholder where you want it to appear on your slides.

Now that you have your template complete, you can save it as a template in the Presentation Designs folder using a new file name. Once it is stored among the other templates in the Presentation Designs folder, you can choose it each time you create a new presentation using the File New command.

Using Placeholders

Placeholders provide a quick way to access the different object types you may want to place on your slides. PowerPoint provides placeholders for objects such as titles, body text, graphs, tables, clip art, and movie clips on the available AutoLayout slide formats. You have already discovered that whenever you create a new slide, you choose the AutoLayout format that contains placeholders for the specific type(s) of object(s) you plan to place on the slide. PowerPoint then identifies the object and goes directly to the program or folder required to create or place the object when you double-click the placeholder.

For example, when you create a new slide using the Graph AutoLayout slide format, a chart object placeholder is added to the new slide. Double-clicking the Graph icon in the placeholder starts the Microsoft Graph application, which PowerPoint uses to create charts.

Nonetheless, that chart object is only a placeholder; it doesn't have to hold a chart. It can be modified to hold any number of different object types available on your system. Simply select the placeholder and choose a different type of object to replace the existing object. For example, you can insert a piece of clip art into the chart placeholder by following these steps:

1. Click inside the placeholder to select it.

2. From the Insert menu, choose Clip Art. After a moment, the ClipArt Gallery appears.

3. Choose a category of art from the Categories list.

4. Click an art thumbnail.

5. Choose Insert or press Enter.

The new artwork replaces the graph icon in the placeholder and assumes the shape of the placeholder.

Placeholders are simply objects on a slide that provide easy access for adding some of the most popular object types. They can be resized, cut and pasted, copied, reproduced, and deleted. They are flexible and can be changed to meet the needs of the user.

Saving Your Own Default Presentation

When you add special elements such as a company logo to a template or find a special template design that you decide to use for all your presentations, you may want to save it so that it automatically comes up each time you create a new Blank Presentation. This provides easier access to the design because you don't have to search among the other templates to find the one you want. It also ensures consistency in the image that your presentations convey. Identifying the presentation format each person in a department will use when creating new presentations is also easier. For example, several people in a corporate P.R. department might be required to use a presentation template that uses the company's specific color scheme.

It also makes it easy to identify the presentation format each person in a department should use when creating new presentations.

It is always a good idea to save the original Blank Presentation template using a different template file name before substituting another in its place. That way, you will be able to restore the original Blank Presentation template if you need to without a great deal of effort.

To store the original Blank Presentation template design using a different file name, follow these steps:

1. Create a new Blank Presentation.

2. Save the presentation as a template in either the Templates folder or Presentation Designs folder using the procedures for saving a template described earlier.

It's almost shamefully easy to make a different template the default. Here's how:

1. Display the Presentation Design that you want to make the default.

2. Choose File, Save As. The File Save dialog box appears.

3. Change the Save as Type to Presentation Template (*.pot).

4. Double-click the Templates folder.

5. Select Blank Presentation.pot in the file name list so that it will be replaced by the new dsesign.

6. Choose Save and respond Yes to replace the existing Blank Presentation.pot file.

That is all there is to it. To check your default, simply create a new blank presentation.

Troubleshooting

I made a mistake and overwrote my original blank template without saving it using a different file name.

You can restore the original Blank Presentation template by creating a new presentation; displaying the Slide Master; and removing all special objects, fonts, and alignments applied to the new design; and changing the bullet character back to the original. If you have another presentation formatted using the original Blank Presentation format, you can also open that presentation and remove the text before saving it as the Blank Presentation template. As a last option, try to locate the template on the original installation disks or reinstall PowerPoint to restore the default settings.

In the last several chapters, you've worked with many critical areas in the PowerPoint program. You learned how to create a basic presentation and glanced at many features that bear deeper study in later chapters. You will explore such topics as artwork and drawings, create organizational charts, graphs, and tables, work with text and other objects, and customize Masters in PowerPoint. In addition, you may want to explore the chapter on multimedia to learn how to add sound and video clips to further enhance your presentations. Have fun and continue to enjoy the many new features designed to add impact to your presentations!❖

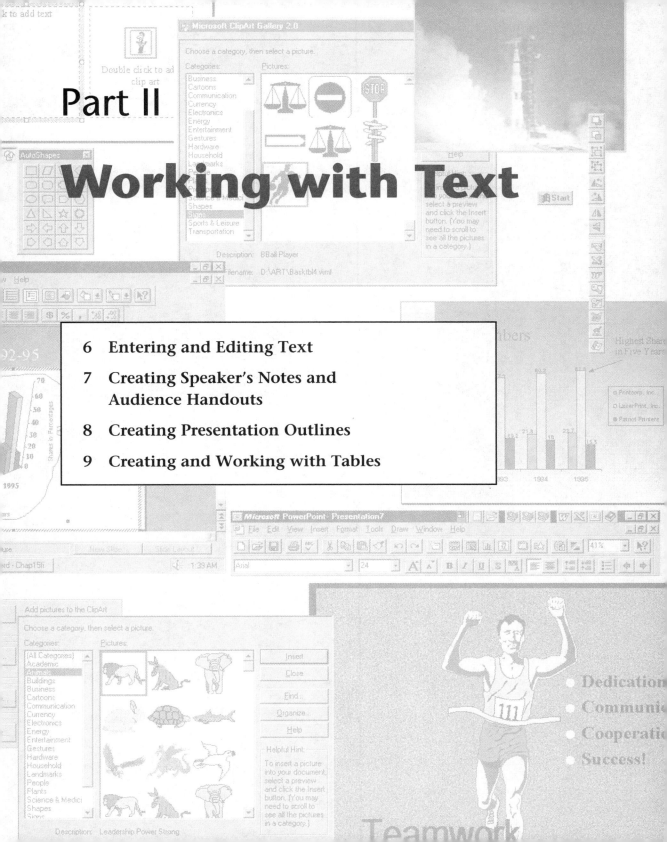

Part II

Working with Text

Chapter 6

Entering and Editing Text

by Nancy Stevenson

In most presentations, bulleted lists and other text charts predominate. A consistent look to text in each slide of your presentation is one way to help your audience focus on the content. Fortunately, PowerPoint makes it easy to create text charts and to automatically apply a consistent format to all text charts in a presentation. Features such as Smart Cut and Paste and Automatic Word Selection simplify common tasks such as copying and moving text.

In this chapter, you learn

- How to create and edit text on a slide
- Ways to modify text formatting
- How to move and copy text
- How to run a spell check
- Shortcuts for working with text

Understanding Text Placeholders

In PowerPoint, you enter all text in text placeholders, such as those shown in figure 6.1.

PowerPoint has two types of text:

- Preset text placeholders, such as those that appear in AutoLayouts. As shown in figure 6.1, these placeholders initially contain the prompt Click to Add Title (for title placeholders) or Click to Add Text (for body text placeholders). Once you add text, the prompt disappears.

Fig. 6.1

A text placeholder is actually a text object that allows you to move blocks of text easily around the page.

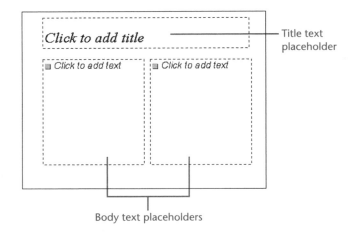

Title text placeholder

Body text placeholders

■ Text boxes that you create using the Text button (see fig. 6.2). You might use this function, for example, to create labels or other text outside the preset placeholders. Text created using the Text button does not appear in Outline view.

Fig. 6.2

Text added outside the preset placeholders using the Text button is useful for labelling a graphic element.

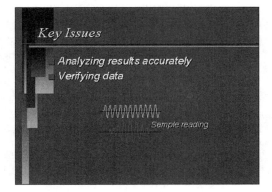

Creating Text

Creating text is as simple as clicking in a text placeholder and typing the text. If you are entering title or body text, PowerPoint has already created the text placeholders for you. If you are creating a label or other special text, you must first click the Text button, then place your cursor where you want the new text to begin before you can type the text. This section describes both of these procedures.

Creating Title and Body Text

When you create a slide, one of your first steps is selecting the AutoLayout for the type of slide you are creating. As described in Chapter 3, "Creating Your First Presentation," AutoLayouts set up the general layout for each type of slide. The various AutoLayout choices are shown in figure 6.3. The AutoLayout for a bulleted list, for example, includes a placeholder for the chart title and a placeholder for the bulleted list (see fig. 6.1). When you initially click in the bulleted list placeholder, a bullet appears; thereafter, a new bullet automatically appears whenever you press Enter to start a new list item.

◀ See "Working with Slides," p. 86

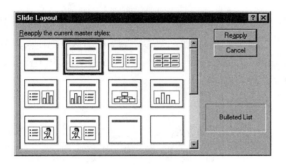

Fig. 6.3
The Slide Layout dialog box gives you choices of several master styles.

In all AutoLayouts, PowerPoint automatically creates a text placeholder for the title, and if the chart is a text chart, a second text placeholder for the subtitle or body text. Figure 6.3 shows some of AutoLayouts that are available. Scroll down to see more. One of these AutoLayouts will probably provide the only text placeholders you need.

To enter text in an AutoLayout placeholder, follow these steps:

1. Click inside the placeholder. The blinking text insertion point appears.

2. Type the text.

Later in this chapter, you learn how to edit and format the text.

Note

The shape of the mouse pointer differs depending on the type of operation you are performing. Within a text placeholder, the mouse pointer looks like an I-beam. This indicates you are in an area where you can enter and edit text.

II

Working with Text

Creating Labels and Other Special Text

Tip
You also can add labels to notes, pages, handouts, and outlines. Such labels appear only on those pages— not on the slide.

To label an object in a slide or to add special text, such as the date, use the Text button. This lets you add text anywhere on a slide.

The procedure for using the Text button depends on whether you want text exceeding a certain width to automatically wrap to a new line. For short text such as labels, this isn't a concern. You add such text by following these steps:

1. Display the slide in Slide view.

2. Click the Text button.

3. Move the mouse pointer where you want the new text to begin.

4. Click the mouse button to fix the text insertion point at that location. The gray outline of a text placeholder appears with the text insertion point inside (see fig. 6.4).

Fig. 6.4
Add text where you like on slides using the Text button.

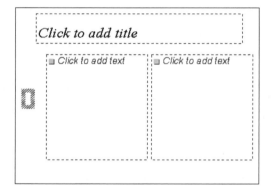

5. Type the text. The text placeholder expands to accommodate the text.

6. To start another line, press Enter. The text box automatically expands to include the next line. Type the text for that line.

The procedure just given is suitable for short labels, where automatic word wrapping isn't necessary. You can also use the Text button, however, to create a text placeholder of a specific size, where text automatically wraps to the next line when it exceeds the placeholder width. To do so, follow these steps:

1. Display the slide in Slide view.

2. Click the Text button.

> **Note**
>
> If an AutoLayout title or body text placeholder is not used (that is, if the place-holder still displays the prompt Click Here to Add...), you cannot use the Text button inside that box. If you don't need that placeholder, you can just delete it; then you can use the Text button. If you want to keep the placeholder and place a label inside it, create the label anywhere outside the existing place-holder and then move the label inside the text placeholder. To move the label, click on the label to display the gray outline of the placeholder, place the mouse pointer on the gray outline, press and hold the mouse button, drag the outline to the correct location, and release the mouse button.

3. Move the mouse pointer where you want the new text to begin.

4. Press and hold the mouse button. This sets the left edge of the new text box.

5. Still pressing the mouse button, drag the mouse pointer to where you want to fix the right edge of the new text box (notice that as you drag the mouse pointer, the outline of a text box appears and expands as you move the pointer) and release the mouse button.

   When you release the mouse button, PowerPoint creates a text box that is the selected width and one line long. The text insertion point appears inside the box.

6. Type the text. Any text that exceeds the width of the box automatically wraps to a new line, and the text box automatically expands to include the new line.

▶ See "Manipulating Text Place-holders," p. 197

You can resize any text box or placeholder. With the above method that creates a text box of a specific size, the text within automatically rewraps to fit the new size. If you used the first procedure above to create a text box of no specific size—which doesn't enable word wrapping—you can later enable word wrapping simply by resizing that text placeholder.

Tip
To enable word wrapping in any text placeholder or box, choose Format, Text Anchor, Word-wrap Text in Object, then choose OK.

Moving the Insertion Point within Text and between Text Placeholders

In a text box, the text you type is entered at the location of the insertion point, which is a vertical bar that blinks on and off. You can move the insertion point by placing the mouse pointer where you want the insertion point

II

Working with Text

to appear and clicking the mouse button. You also can use the following keys and key combinations to move the insertion point in both text boxes and text placeholders:

Press...	To Move the Insertion Point...
←	Left one character
→	Right one character
↑	Up one line
↓	Down one line
Ctrl+→	Right one word
Ctrl+↑	Up one paragraph
Ctrl+↓	Down one paragraph
Home	To the beginning of the line
End	To the end of the line

To move to another text placeholder, just click in that placeholder. You also can move to the next placeholder by pressing Ctrl+Enter. (If you press Ctrl+Enter in the last text placeholder on a slide, PowerPoint creates a new slide and moves to the first text placeholder on the new slide.)

> **Caution**
>
> Don't use tab to try to move from one box to another. Although this may move you from one field to another in other programs, here it denotes the bullet point in the outline hierarchy, rather than taking you to the next text placeholder.

Selecting Text

For many operations involving text, you must begin by selecting the text. To make existing text italic, for example, you select that text and then choose Italic (see "Changing Text Attributes" later in this chapter). Selected text is highlighted on-screen in reverse video.

Like most Windows programs, PowerPoint allows you to use the keyboard or the mouse to select text. This section describes the most common selection techniques.

Mouse Techniques

You can use the mouse to select a single word, a paragraph, or a text block of any length.

To select a word or paragraph, use these techniques:

To Select	Do This
A word	Double-click anywhere in the word
A paragraph	Triple-click anywhere in the paragraph

To select a block of text, you can use either of two methods. The first method uses the mouse:

1. Place the mouse pointer where you want the selection to begin.

2. Press and hold the mouse button.

3. Drag the mouse pointer to where you want the selection to end.

4. Release the mouse button.

The second method for selecting a block uses the mouse and the Shift key:

1. Place the mouse pointer where you want the selection to begin.

2. Click the mouse button.

3. Place the mouse pointer where you want the selection to end.

4. Press the Shift key while clicking the mouse button again.

Tip

To select all text in a placeholder, place the insertion point anywhere in the placeholder and press Ctrl+A.

> **Note**
>
> If Automatic Word Selection is on (Tools, Options, Edit), PowerPoint selects an entire word if one letter of the word is selected.

▶ See "Using Automatic Word Selection," p. 172

Keyboard Technique

To use the keyboard to select text, follow these steps:

1. Place the insertion point where you want the selection to begin.

2. Press and hold the Shift key.

II

Working with Text

3. Press the arrow keys to move the highlight to the end of the text you want to select.

4. Release the Shift key.

> **Note**
>
> The Automatic Word Selection feature, which automatically selects a word when any letter in that word is selected, does not work with the keyboard technique. See the next section for information on this feature.

Using Automatic Word Selection

PowerPoint's Automatic Word Selection feature automatically selects a word when any letter of that word is selected with the mouse. It also selects the space following a word or a period. Automatic Word Selection often speeds editing, because it eliminates the need to carefully position the mouse pointer at the precise beginning and end of text you want to select; instead, you place the mouse anywhere in the first and last words you want to select.

By default, Automatic Word Selection is turned on. To turn it off, follow these steps:

1. From the main menu, choose <u>T</u>ools, Options to display the Options dialog box.

2. Click the Edit tab as shown in figure 6.5.

Fig. 6.5
Change some of your editing options in this dialog box.

3. Select the Automatic Word Selection check box to deselect the option.

4. Choose OK.

> **Troubleshooting**
>
> *I just want to select part of a word and everytime I try to do this I get the whole word. Is there a way around this?*
>
> The easiest way is to use the keyboard. Place the insertion point where you want the selection to begin and then press and hold the Shift key while pressing the arrow keys to extend your selection; when you're finished selecting text, release the Shift key.

Editing Text

No slide presentation is perfect on the first try. In fact, chances are you will edit the text several times before you're satisfied. This section teaches not only basic text-editing techniques, but also PowerPoint shortcuts that can simplify the editing process. If you use a Windows word processing program, many of the editing techniques described in this section will be familiar.

Inserting Text

To insert text in an existing text placeholder, place the insertion point where you want to insert the text and type the text. Remember that you can use the arrow keys or the mouse to move the insertion point. To use the arrow keys, just press them (see "Moving the Insertion Point within Text and between Text Placeholders" earlier in this chapter). To use the mouse, place the mouse pointer where you want the insertion point and click the mouse button.

Deleting Text

Use the Delete or Backspace key to delete text. To delete characters one by one, follow these steps:

1. Place the insertion point where you want to begin deleting text.

2. To delete the character to the right of the insertion point, press the Delete key. To delete the character to the left of the insertion point, press the Backspace key.

To delete a block of text, select the block and then press Delete or Backspace. You can also replace a selected block with new text. To do so, just select the block and then type the new text; PowerPoint automatically deletes the original text and inserts the new text at that location.

▶ See "Editing and Enhancing Text in Outline View," p. 231

II

Working with Text

Troubleshooting

Is there a fast way to delete all text in a placeholder?

With the insertion point in the placeholder, press Ctrl+A. This selects all text in the placeholder. Then press the Delete or Backspace key.

Moving or Copying Text

▶ See "Moving and Aligning Objects," p. 295

You can move or copy text within a text placeholder and between text placeholders—even between placeholders on different slides. The procedure is the same for each case.

To move text, follow these steps:

1. Select the text you want to move.

2. Use one of the following methods to cut the text from its current location:

    ■ Press Ctrl+X.

    ■ Press the right mouse button, and choose Cut from the shortcut menu shown in figure 6.6.

Fig. 6.6
Shortcut menus make editing text quicker.

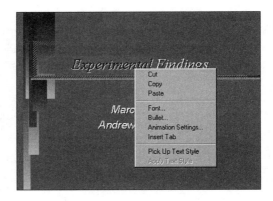

    ■ From the main menu, choose Edit, Cut.

    ■ Click the Cut button.

3. Place the insertion point where you want to insert the text.

4. Use one of the following methods to paste the text in its new location:

- Press Ctrl+V.

- Press the right mouse button, and choose Paste.

- From the main menu, choose Edit, Paste.

- Click the Paste button.

To copy text, follow these steps:

1. Select the text you want to copy.

2. Use one of the following methods to copy the text from its current location:

- Press Ctrl+C.

- Press the right mouse button, and choose Copy.

- From the main menu, choose Edit, Copy.

- Click the Copy button.

3. Place the insertion point where you want to insert the copy of the text.

4. Use one of the following methods to paste the copy in its new location:

- Press Ctrl+V.

- Press the right mouse button, and choose Paste.

- From the main menu, choose Edit, Paste.

- Click the Paste button.

With PowerPoint's drag-and-drop feature, you can also move or copy selected text to a new location within the text placeholder simply by dragging the text to the new location. You can use the drag-and-drop feature in Slide, Notes, and Outline views. The procedure is the same in each case:

1. Select the text you want to move or copy.

2. Place the mouse pointer over the selected text.

3. To move the selected text, press and hold the mouse button. To copy the text, press and hold both the Ctrl key and the mouse button.

II

Working with Text

In both cases, a box representing the text appears below the mouse pointer as you move the mouse pointer. If you are copying the text, a plus sign (+) also appears next to the mouse pointer.

4. Move the mouse pointer until a vertical gray line appears where you want to insert the text.

5. Release the mouse button to insert the text at that location.

▶ See "Copying and Pasting Objects," p. 290

When you move or copy text, PowerPoint's Smart Cut and Paste feature automatically adjusts the spaces before and after words. The Smart Cut and Paste feature appears as an option in the Options dialog box shown in figure 6.5. To display this dialog box, select Tools, Options, and the Edit tab. By default, PowerPoint selects the Use Smart Cut and Paste option. To disable this feature, clear the Use Smart Cut and Paste check box and choose OK.

Moving List Items Up and Down

To simplify editing further, PowerPoint enables you to quickly move list items up or down in the list by following these steps:

1. Click anywhere in the bulleted list.

2. Move the mouse pointer left of the list item until the pointer looks like a four-sided arrow.

3. Press and hold the mouse button. The list item is highlighted.

▶ See "Editing and Enhancing Text in Outline View," p. 231

4. Drag the mouse pointer where you want to insert the item. As you drag the pointer, it changes to a double-sided arrow. A horizontal line indicates the pointer's location in the list.

5. Release the mouse button.

Changing the Case of Text

If many persons are involved in a presentation, inconsistencies in the text are common. Inconsistent use of letter case is one of the most frequent problems. It also used to be one of the most time-consuming to fix because you had to retype the text in the correct case. Not any more. PowerPoint includes an automated Change Case feature that enables you to change selected text to any of the following cases:

■ Lowercase: these are lowercase letters.

- Uppercase: THESE ARE UPPERCASE LETTERS.

- Title case: Title Case Uses Initial Capital Letters, As Shown Here.

- Sentence case: Sentence case capitalizes only the initial letter of the first word, as in a sentence.

You also can toggle the cases in selected text so that lowercase letters change to uppercase and uppercase letters change to lowercase.

To change the case of text, follow these steps:

1. Select the text you want to change.

2. Choose Format, Change Case to display the Change Case dialog box in figure 6.7.

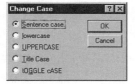

3. Select the case you want.

4. Choose OK.

Tip
You also can toggle among cases using Shift+F3.

Fig. 6.7
Quickly change the case of your letters with the Change Case dialog box.

Adding or Removing Periods at the End of List Items

Another common inconsistency is the use of periods at the end of list items. Whichever you prefer, inevitably, some list items do not conform to your convention. As you may have guessed, PowerPoint also simplifies the task of fixing this problem. You can quickly add or remove periods from the end of list items by following these steps:

1. Select the items you want to change.

2. Choose Format, Periods to display the Periods dialog box.

3. Select Add Periods or Remove Periods.

4. Choose OK.

Working with Text

Finding and Replacing Text

PowerPoint's Find feature and Find and Replace feature enable you to search for text and replace it with different text. To quickly display a slide, use the Find feature to search for text that appears only on that slide.

To search for text, follow these steps:

1. Open the slide presentation you want to search.

2. Press Ctrl+F. Alternatively, choose Edit, Find. The Find dialog box appears, as shown in figure 6.8.

Fig. 6.8

Want to check your data on quality control? Find it easily using the Find dialog box.

3. In the Find What text box, type the text you want to find.

4. To find only text that matches the case you entered, select the Match Case check box. If you enter CAMP in the Find What text box and select Match Case, for example, PowerPoint finds only CAMP. If you don't select Match Case, PowerPoint finds CAMP, Camp, camp, and all other instances of the word camp.

5. To find only whole words that match the text you entered, select the Find Whole Words Only check box. PowerPoint finds only instances where the text is preceded and followed by a space or punctuation; so if you're looking for the word bud, you won't find "budget" as well.

6. Choose Find Next. PowerPoint goes to the first instance of text that matches the Find criteria. To replace the word, choose Replace.

7. To find the next instance, repeat step 6.

8. When you finish searching, choose Close.

To search for text and replace it with different text, follow these steps:

1. Open the slide presentation you want to search.

2. Press Ctrl+H. Alternatively, choose Edit, Replace. The Replace dialog box appears.

3. In the Find What text box, type the text you want to find.

4. To find only text that matches the case you entered, select the Match Case check box.

5. In the Replace With text box, type the text you want to replace the original text.

6. To replace all instances of the original text with the new text, choose Replace All. PowerPoint does not prompt you to confirm that you want the text replaced.

   To choose the instances where the new text replaces the original text, select Find Next. PowerPoint goes to the first instance of text that matches the Find criteria. If you want to replace that text, select Replace. To find the next instance, repeat the steps in this paragraph.

7. When you finish, choose Close.

Replacing Fonts

Suppose you develop a presentation for several of your company's offices, and then find that some of the offices cannot print the fonts you use. With PowerPoint, you can quickly replace these fonts with other fonts the office can print.

To change fonts, follow these steps:

1. Open the presentation you want to change.

2. Choose Tools, Replace Fonts to display the Replace Fonts dialog box.

3. Click the Replace drop-down list button to list the fonts used in the presentation, and then select the font you want to replace.

4. Click the With drop-down list button to list available fonts; then select the replacement font.

5. Choose Replace. PowerPoint replaces all instances of the font throughout the presentation.

> **Note**
>
> You also can change a text placeholder's text in the Master Slide view and it will be changed on any slides where you haven't made specific changes to that text. However, to be sure every instance of a font is changed, use Replace Fonts.

Tip
You also can call up the Replace dialog from the Find dialog box. Just click Replace, and the box enlarges to include both Find and Replace.

II

Working with Text

Troubleshooting

To conserve space, I want to use " and ' as symbols for inch and foot (or second and minute); but whenever I press the " and ' keys, I get real quotation marks. How can I get inch and foot (second and minute) symbols?

Disable the Smart Quotes feature, which automatically enters true double and single quotation marks when you press the " and ' keys.

To disable the feature, choose Tools, Options. In the Options dialog box, clear the Replace Straight Quotes with Smart Quotes check box and choose OK. This won't change true quotation marks already in the presentation—only quotation marks you subsequently enter. If you later need true quotation marks, just reselect the Replace Straight Quotes with Smart Quotes check box.

Formatting Text

The Slide Master sets the default format for the title and body text in a slide. This includes the text font, size, and color; the bullet shape, size, and color; and the tabs, line spacing, and justification. If you want a format to affect all slides in your presentation, set the format in the Slide Master. PowerPoint automatically reformats all slides—except those where you've overridden Slide Master with individual settings—according to the new Slide Master format.

◀ See "Under-
standing the
Slide Master,"
p. 127

To change the characteristics of individual words or paragraphs in a slide, however, you must make the changes on the slide itself. A common example is when you emphasize key words by making them boldface or by changing their color. Formats you enter on individual slides are preserved even if you change the format for the corresponding text in the Master Slide.

Changing Text Attributes

PowerPoint provides you great flexibility in choosing the appearance of your text, allowing you to change the following text characteristics:

- *Font.* In PowerPoint, a font is a type family, such as Times Roman or Impact (see fig. 6.9). You can select one of the TrueType fonts, a Microsoft font technology installed with Windows (indicated by a double T symbol next to it in the font drop-down list) or any other font installed on your system.

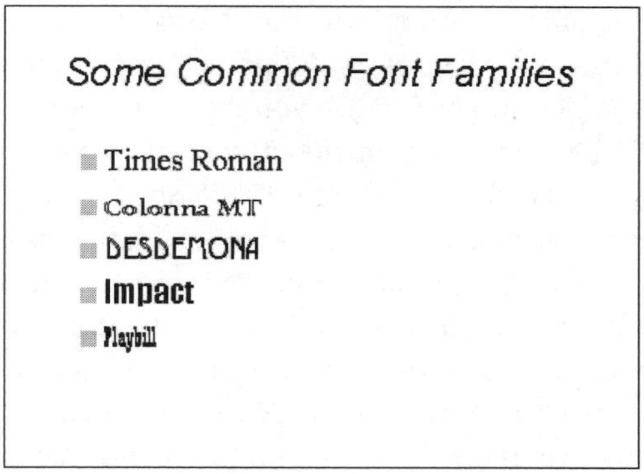

Fig. 6.9
Different fonts
convey different
feelings to your
audience.

■ *Font style.* You can make text plain, bold, italic, or both bold and italic. As shown in figure 6.10, plain text is the upright, medium-weight text you normally see. Bold text is darker than plain text. Italic text slants to the right.

■ *Font size.* Font size is expressed in points, with one point equaling 1/72 inch. The size of the font you are reading now, for example, is nine points.

■ *Color.* Color is one of the most powerful graphic elements in a slide. You can select from predefined colors or from custom colors you create.

■ *Special effects.* You can also underline, superscript, subscript, shadow, or emboss text. Shadowed text appears to have a drop shadow behind it. Embossed text appears raised.

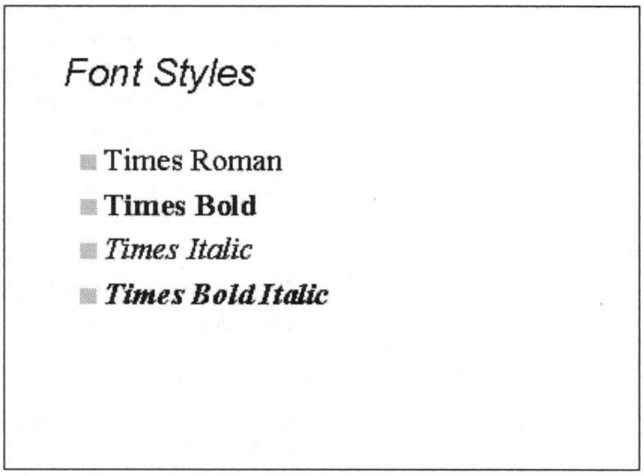

Fig. 6.10
Style can be used
to emphasize
words or phrases.

II

Working with Text

With so many possibilities, you might be confused about their appropriate use. The cardinal rule of presentation design is "Keep it simple." If you remember this as you design your slides, you create a more effective presentation, where the audience focuses on the presentation content—not a busy design. Avoid more than two typefaces on each slide. Sans serif typefaces, or any style of typeface without little flags' coming off the ends of letters, like the Impact typeface in figure 6.9, are preferred for titles, and either sans serif or serif for the body text. If you use bold, make sure it isn't so thick that letters blur together on your slide or overhead. For help in designing your presentation, use the AutoContent Wizard (see Chapter 3) or one of PowerPoint's many professionally designed templates (see Chapter 5). The typefaces used by PowerPoint's templates usually work just fine.

PowerPoint lets you use menus, the Formatting toolbar, or keystroke shortcuts to change text characteristics. The toolbar and keystroke shortcuts are the fastest methods, but they cannot be used to select some special effects, such as embossing and superscript. To select these special effects, you must use menus.

Table 6.1 describes each of the buttons on the Formatting toolbar. To use a button to format text, select the text and then click the button.

Tip

If the Formatting toolbar doesn't appear on your screen, select View, Toolbars, then choose Formatting, and click OK. The Formatting toolbar will appear.

Table 6.1 Buttons that Change Text Appearance

Button	Name	Use
	Font Face list box	Click the down arrow to display a list of fonts, and then select a font. The four most recently used fonts appear at the top of the list.
	Font Size list box	Click the down arrow to display a list of font sizes, and then select a size. Alternatively, type the size in the box.
A⁺	Increase Font Size button	Click this button to incrementally increase the font size.
A⁻	Decrease Font Size button	Click this button to incrementally decrease the font size.
B	Bold button	Click this button to toggle between adding and removing bold style.

Button	Name	Use
I	Italic button	Click on this button to toggle between adding and removing italic style.
U	Underline button	Click on this button to toggle between adding and removing underlining.
S	Text Shadow button	Click on this button to toggle between adding and removing the drop shadow effect.
A	Text Color button	Click on this button to display a color menu; then select a color.

Table 6.2 lists the keystroke shortcuts. To use these to format text, select the text and then press the keys designated in table 6.2.

Table 6.2 Keystroke Shortcuts for Changing Text Appearance	
To Select This Style	**Press**
Bold	Ctrl+B
Italic	Ctrl+I
<u>Underline</u>	Ctrl+U

You can use the menu to change any text characteristics by following these steps:

1. Select the text that you want to change.

2. Choose Format, Font to display the Font dialog box shown in figure 6.11. (You also can get here through the shortcut menu.)

3. Make your changes. If you select Superscript or Subscript, enter in the Offset box the percentage you want the super- or subscript text offset; for subscript text, enter a negative number. To choose a different color, select the Color button to display a palette, and then select a color.

4. Select OK.

II

Working with Text

Fig. 6.11
Make several
changes to your
fonts all at once
in the Font
dialog box.

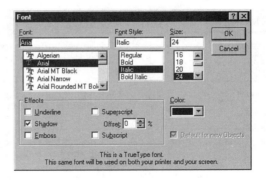

Copying Text Styles

After you format text—for example, as red 30-point italic Times New Roman—you can copy the text style to any other text. Copying text styles not
only saves you steps, it also saves you from having to remember detailed
styles.

To use the Standard toolbar to copy a style, follow these steps:

1. Select any word that has the format you want to copy.

2. From the Standard toolbar, click the Format Painter button, which is
   designated by a paintbrush icon. To apply the format to more than one
   selection, double-click the button.

3. If you want to change one word only, just click anywhere in that word.
   Otherwise, click and drag to select the text you want to change.

4. If you are applying the format to more than one selection (that is, if
   you double-clicked the button in step 2), repeat step 3. When you are
   finished, click the Format Painter button.

To use menus to copy a style, follow these steps:

1. Select any word that has the format you want to copy.

2. Choose Format, Pick Up Text Style.

3. Select the text you want to format according to the new style.

4. Choose Format, Apply Style.

Changing Bullet Characteristics

You can also change the shape, color, and size of the bullets you use in bulleted lists. Bullet size is given as a percentage of the text size. A bullet size of 80 percent, for example, means the font size used for the bullet is 80 percent of the text font size.

To change bullet characteristics, follow these steps:

1. Select all items whose bullets you want to change.

2. Choose Format, Bullet. The Bullet dialog box appears, as shown in figure 6.12.

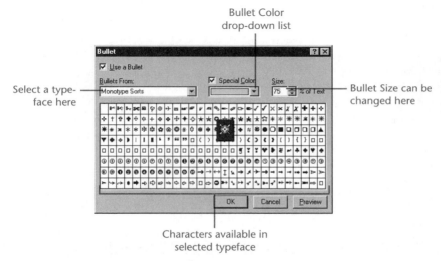

Bullet Color
drop-down list

Select a type-
face here

Bullet Size can be
changed here

Characters available in
selected typeface

Fig. 6.12
A variety of formatting options are available for the simple little bullet.

II

Working with Text

3. The bullet pallette shows all the typeface elements from the typeface shown in the Bullets From drop-down list box. To change the bullet character, select the desired character in the Character palette (refer to fig. 6.12), and it pops out as an enlarged image so you can see it more clearly. You can take a look at several of these; they won't actually be applied until you click OK to return to your presentation. To choose a character from a different font, select the Bullets From down arrow button to list the fonts and select a font; when the characters in that font appear in the Character palette, select the character you want.

4. To change the bullet color, select the color beneath the Special Color check box to display a color palette and then select the new color.

5. To change the bullet size, type a new size percentage in the Size spin box, or click the Size increment buttons to increase or decrease the percentage shown.

6. Apply your changes by choosing OK.

Setting Tabs and Indents

Tabs and indents enable you to control how text aligns. If your presentation includes columns of text, you can use tabs to set up the column format—the location of the columns and the alignment of text within the columns. To set up a bulleted or numbered list, where you want text to align at a point a certain number of spaces to the right of the left margin, use a paragraph indent. The AutoLayouts for bulleted lists, for example, use indents to set the placement of bullets and the text aligned to the right of the bullets.

Understanding the Ruler

You set tabs and indents with the PowerPoint ruler, which you can display in Slide or Notes Pages view. To display the ruler for a paragraph, place the insertion point in the paragraph and choose <u>V</u>iew, <u>R</u>uler. Rulers appear just below the main menu bar and any toolbars that are displayed and along the left side of your screen, as in figure 6.13.

Tip

If you have several columns of information to show, consider using a Word for Windows table. There is a tool on the toolbar used to quickly insert a table.

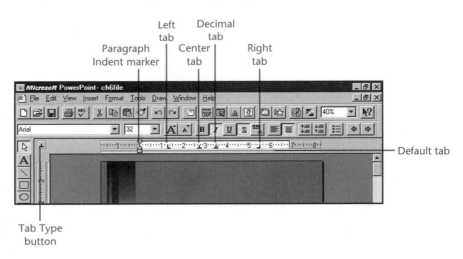

Fig. 6.13
You can set several items relating to text alignment using the ruler in Slide or Notes Pages view.

The ruler has the following features:

- *Tab Type button.* Click the Tab Type button to cycle through the four tab types, which are displayed on the ruler in figure 6.13:

- *Left.* Aligns the left end of text at the tab.

- *Right.* Aligns the right end of text at the tab.

- *Center.* Centers text on the tab.

- *Decimal.* Centers text on a period.

- *Tab markers.* The default tabs, which are left tabs spaced at one-inch intervals, are marked by ticks at the bottom of the ruler. Tabs that you set are shown on the ruler by the icon for that tab type (left, right, center, or decimal, as shown earlier).

- *Paragraph indent markers.* The top marker shows the indent for the first line of text in the selected paragraph. The bottom marker shows the indent for the rest of the paragraph. When both markers are aligned, all lines of text in a paragraph are equally indented. For most text place-holders, the default setting for both markers is zero inches; that is, there is no indent so all text in paragraphs aligns at the left margin of the placeholder. In the AutoLayouts for bulleted lists, default indents are set for the bulleted list items.

Changing the Default Tabs

You can change the default tabs for a placeholder to any evenly spaced inter-val, enabling you to quickly set up evenly spaced columns across a chart. Remember, the default tabs are always left tabs. If you want a different type of tab—for example, a decimal tab to align numbers around a decimal point—you must set a specific tab of that type, as described in the next section.

To change the default tab interval, follow these steps:

1. Place the insertion point anywhere in the placeholder you want to change.

2. If the ruler isn't displayed, from the main menu choose <u>V</u>iew, <u>R</u>uler.

3. Place the mouse pointer directly on the first tick mark and drag the tick mark to where you want the first tab. When you release the mouse button, the other tick marks adjust to be evenly spaced at the interval determined by the first tick mark.

> **Note**
>
> If in step 3 the mouse pointer isn't directly on the tick mark, you insert a tab rather than reset the default interval. If you accidentally insert a tab, you can delete it by dragging it off the ruler.

Setting Specific Tabs

You can override the default tabs by setting your own. The tab type can be left, right, center, or decimal. When you set a tab, all default tabs preceding that tab disappear. If you set a tab at three inches, for example, pressing Tab once moves the insertion point directly to the 3-inch tab. If you should remove that 3-inch tab at a later time, the default tabs would reappear.

To set individual tabs, follow these steps:

1. Place the insertion point in the paragraph you want to change, or select two or more paragraphs.

2. If the ruler isn't displayed, choose <u>V</u>iew, <u>R</u>uler.

3. Depending on the changes you want to make, follow one or more of these procedures:

   To add a tab, click the Tab Type button until it displays the icon for the type of tab you want, and then click on the ruler at the location where you want the tab. To insert more than one tab of that type, click every location where you want a tab.

   To move a tab, click it and drag it to the new location.

   To delete a tab, click it and drag it off the ruler.

4. To hide the ruler, choose <u>V</u>iew, <u>R</u>uler (the ruler toggles on and off). Hiding the ruler doesn't affect the tab settings.

Setting Indents

PowerPoint lets you choose one indent for the first line of a paragraph and another indent for subsequent lines in the paragraph. You can set up the indents so the first line begins either to the right or the left of the subsequent lines. In the first example below, the first line begins to the right; this is a standard paragraph indent. In the second and third examples, the first line begins to the left; this is called a hanging indent.

Example 1:

    The first line in this paragraph is indented. Subsequent lines in the paragraph automatically begin at the normal left margin.

Example 2:

This is a hanging indent. Notice that the first line begins to the left of
    subsequent lines.

Example 3:

- This also is a hanging indent. The bullet, which is the beginning of the first line, begins to the left of subsequent lines. In bulleted lists, the first line of text automatically moves right, so that it aligns with other text in the paragraph.

To change paragraph indents, follow these steps:

1. Place the insertion point in the paragraph you want to change, or select two or more paragraphs.

2. If the ruler isn't displayed, choose View, Ruler.

3. Depending on the changes you want to make, follow one or more of these procedures:

   To change the indent for the first line of text in the selected paragraphs: Drag the top indent marker to where you want the text to align on the left.

   To change the indent for the remaining text in the selected paragraphs: Drag the bottom indent marker to where you want the text to align on the left.

To use the same indent for all lines of text in the selected paragraphs: Align the top and bottom indent markers, and then drag the lower (square) half of the bottom marker to move both indent markers to where you want the text to align on the left.

> **Note**
>
> PowerPoint allows up to five indent levels in a text placeholder. Each level is defined by one set of indent markers. To display the indent markers for the levels already used in a placeholder, place the insertion point in any paragraph in the placeholder, and display the ruler. To add a level that isn't yet used, place the insertion point in an empty line, and press Alt+Shift+right arrow or click the Demote button to demote the line to that level. The right-most indent markers on the ruler define the settings for that indent level.

Moving to Tab and Indent Stops

When working with text, press Tab to move to the next tab stop. In placeholders containing a bulleted list, however, if you want to move the whole bullet point to the right, you must press Alt+Shift+right arrow; in those placeholders, pressing Tab indents the text away from the bullet itself. In any placeholder, press Backspace to move back one tab stop.

 To move the insertion point to the next indent, press Alt+Shift+right arrow or click the Demote button. In AutoLayouts for bulleted lists, this inserts a bullet, as well as indenting the text. To move the insertion point back an indent, press Alt+Shift+left arrow or click the Promote button.

Tab settings are simply preset positions you can use to jump your cursor across the page and place text. They do not affect indents, which are settings saved with text itself as part of its formatting. When you indent list items by pressing Alt+Shift+right arrow or by selecting the Demote button, the insertion point moves only to indent stops, ignoring tab stops. Similarly, if you set up indents to automatically indent the first line of a paragraph, the first line begins at the indent, regardless of whether you set a tab before that indent.

Indent settings, however, do affect tabs. When you press Tab, the insertion point moves to the next tab or indent stop (with the indent stop taking precedence).

Setting Margins

Margins within a text placeholder are similar to margins on a page: all text lies between the margins, which are measured from the edge of the placeholder. In PowerPoint, you can change the left and right margins jointly, but not separately. Similarly, you can change the top and bottom margins jointly, but not separately.

To change the margins in a text placeholder, follow these steps:

1. Click the text placeholder you want to change.

2. From the main menu, choose F<u>o</u>rmat. The Format menu appears.

3. From the Format menu, choose <u>T</u>ext Anchor. The Text Anchor dialog box appears, as in figure 6.14.

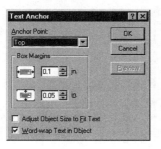

Fig. 6.14
Text Anchor is where you adjust margins for each placeholder.

4. To change the left and right margins, type a new measurement (in inches) in the top text box in the Box Margins area. Alternatively, you can click the increment buttons to the right of the text box to increase or decrease the measurement in 0.05-inch increments.

5. To change the top and bottom margins, type a new measurement (in inches) in the bottom text box in the Box Margins area. Alternatively, you can click the increment buttons to the right of the text box to increase or decrease the measurement in 0.05-inch increments.

6. Choose OK.

When you return to your slide, notice that the gray and white space on the ruler has shifted to reflect your new margins. The gray part of the ruler represents the width of the margin. Your text will fall within the space represented by the white part of the ruler.

Aligning Text

You can align text on the right, on the left, on both the right and the left (fully justified), or in the center. Generally, lists are best aligned left. Full justification, however, may be used to give a more formal appearance. Titles and subtitles may be left-aligned, right-aligned, or centered.

To change the alignment of text, follow these steps:

1. Select the paragraphs you want to change.

2. Choose _F_ormat, _A_lignment. The Alignment cascading menu appears.

3. Choose Left, Center, Right, or Justify.

A paragraph cannot have more than one type of alignment.

> **Note**
>
> There are buttons on the toolbar for left and center alignment, the most common choices. Just select the paragraph, and click one of the buttons and the text is realigned.

Setting Line and Paragraph Spacing

Line spacing is the distance from the baseline of one line of text to the baseline of the next line of text. Paragraph spacing is additional space you can add before and after paragraphs. To change line or paragraph spacing, follow these steps:

1. Select the paragraphs you want to change.

2. Choose F_o_rmat, Line _S_pacing. The Line Spacing dialog box appears (see figure 6.15).

3. To change line spacing, type a new measurement in the Line Spacing text box. Alternatively, click the increment buttons to increase or decrease line spacing by 0.05-line increments.

Fig. 6.15
Adjust spacing within or between paragraphs in this dialog box.

4. The default unit of measure is lines. If you prefer to use points as the unit of measurement, click the drop-down button displaying Lines and then select Points.

5. To change paragraph spacing, type a new measurement in either or both of the Before Paragraph and After Paragraph text boxes. Alternatively, click the increment buttons to increase or decrease spacing by 0.05-line increments.

> **Note**
>
> You also can use the Increase Paragraph Spacing and Decrease Paragraph Spacing buttons on the Formatting toolbar to adjust paragraph spacing.

6. Choose OK. The dialog box closes and the text is reformatted.

Using True Quotation Marks

With PowerPoint's Smart Quotes feature, pressing the " or ' key inserts true quotation marks (" ", ' ') rather than straight quotation marks (" ", ' '). PowerPoint is even smart enough to recognize when the quotation mark should be an opening or closing quotation mark. There may be occasions, however, when you want straight quotation marks—for example, as symbols for inch or foot. For these cases, disable the Smart Quotes feature as follows:

1. Choose Tools, Options. The Options dialog box appears.

2. If it's not already in front, click the Edit tab.

3. Clear the check box named Replace Straight Quotes with Smart Quotes.

4. Choose OK.

Disabling this feature won't affect any true quotation marks already typed.

Bulleting a List

If a text placeholder contains a simple list (that is, a list without bullets), you can change the list to a bulleted list as follows:

1. Select all items in the list.

2. Click the bullet button on the toolbar. If you want to remove the bullets, just click this button again.

3. If you want to, you can add or remove bullets, or change the bullet character (the default for first-level list items is a round bullet), Special Color, or Size by selecting Format, Bullet.

◄ See "Changing Bullet Characteristics," p. 185

4. If necessary, change the indent settings to adjust the space between the bullets and the text. Setting indents is discussed in the section "Setting Tabs and Indents" earlier in this chapter.

After you have a bulleted list, you can use the Promote and Demote buttons to add sub-items beneath the main items. To list secondary items beneath a main item, follow these steps:

1. Place the insertion point at the end of the item to which you are adding the new list.

2. Press Enter to insert a new line. A bullet automatically appears.

3. Click the Demote button or press Tab or Alt+Shift+right arrow; PowerPoint automatically indents the bullet beneath the preceding line. If the text is in a placeholder you created, the bullet character does not change. (You can change it later, as described in the section "Changing Bullet Characteristics" earlier in this chapter.) Also, the indent may not be correct; in placeholders you create, for example, there typically is no space between the bullet and the text. To fix this, you must create a hanging indent, as explained earlier in this chapter in "Setting Indents."

Tip

If you select a bulleted list and click your right mouse button, the shortcut menu that appears includes Bullet, so you can access the Bullet dialog box more quickly.

4. Type the text for the item and press Enter when you are finished. The insertion point moves to a new line that is automatically indented to the same location as the preceding item.

5. Continue adding items until the list is finished.

You can have up to five levels of lists in a placeholder, but you should limit yourself to two levels on the same slide. An audience can't digest much more than this in the short time a slide is shown. If you find yourself creating several levels of sub-points on a single slide, consider making each item into a separate slide, with the sub-points as the major bullet points. If you must add more levels, the procedure is the same as that just described for adding a secondary list.

To promote an item up one level, click anywhere in the item and then click the Promote button, or press Shift+Tab or Alt+Shift+left arrow.

> **Troubleshooting**
>
> *What's the best way to emphasize text in a slide?*
>
> In color slides, make the text a warm color, such as red or yellow (but don't mix red with green, since some people are red-green color-blind). In black-and-white slides, make the text bold or italic; bold provides a greater degree of emphasis than does italic. Some designers also use underlining for emphasis. Don't use other special effects, such as shadow or embossing, unless they fit well with the slide design.

Using the Spelling Checker

Always check the spelling in a presentation before the audience sees it. Few things are more embarrassing than an 18-inch-high typo. To check the spelling, use PowerPoint's spelling checker, which checks both spelling and letter case.

> **Note**
>
> By default, PowerPoint suggests corrections when it detects a potential error. If the spelling checker is slow, you can speed it up by disabling this feature. To do so, from the main menu choose Tools, Options, click on the Edit tab, deselect Always Suggest, and choose OK.

To use the spelling checker, follow these steps:

1. Open the presentation you want to check.

2. Click on the Spelling button, or press F7. Alternatively, choose Tools, Spelling.

PowerPoint begins checking the spelling. If it detects a potential error, the Spelling dialog box appears. As shown in figure 6.16, the potential error appears at the top of the dialog box.

Fig. 6.16

When you click the Spelling button, the Spelling dialog box appears.

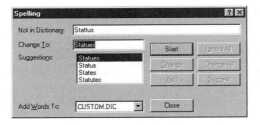

A suggested spelling or case appears in the Change To text box (unless you have disabled the Always Suggest feature). Beneath this suggestion, there may be a list of additional suggestions. You can then take one of the following actions:

- To continue without correcting the word, choose Ignore.

- To ignore this and all further instances of this word, choose Ignore All.

- To correct only this instance of the word, choose one of the suggested alternatives, or type the correction in the Change To text box, and choose Change.

- To correct this and all further instances of the word, choose one of the suggested alternatives, or type the correction in the Change To text box, and then choose Change All. PowerPoint doesn't prompt you to confirm the subsequent changes.

- To add the word in the Change To text box to the dictionary listed in the Add Words To text box, choose Add. If the word differs from the word highlighted in the slide, PowerPoint also replaces the highlighted word with the correct word. To select a different dictionary, select the Add Words To text box to list available dictionaries and then choose a dictionary.

- If you've disabled the Always Suggest feature, choose Suggest to have PowerPoint suggest a correct spelling.

After you make your selection, the spelling checker continues checking the presentation. When it has finished checking the entire presentation, it displays a message to that effect. Choose OK to close the message box.

After using the spelling checker, carefully proof the presentation for errors that a spelling checker can't detect. No spelling checker can tell you, for example, that "Sales Sour in 1994" should be "Sales Soar in 1994."

Manipulating Text Placeholders

A text placeholder is an object in PowerPoint. As such, you can treat it like any other object. You can resize, move, or copy it. And you can enhance it with a border or a different background to visually separate text areas on the slide. This section describes the basics of manipulating text placeholders as objects. You can find additional information in Chapter 11, "Selecting, Editing, and Enhancing Objects."

Resizing a Text Placeholder

After you enter text, you may find that it appears unbalanced or has awkward line breaks—for example, a bulleted list item may wrap so that only one word is on the last line. You can sometimes improve the appearance by resizing the text placeholder or box, forcing the words to wrap at a different location, or not at all. In the examples shown in figures 6.17 and 6.18, see how widening the placeholder allows all items to fit on one line.

The long word accomplishments is forced to the next line ⎯

This sentence dangles a couple of short words on the second line ⎯

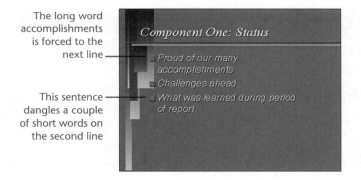

Fig. 6.17
Bullet points break at odd places due to a narrow placeholder.

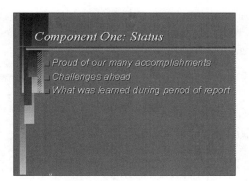

Fig. 6.18
By resizing the placeholder, the flow of bullet points is less jagged.

II

Working with Text

You also can resize a placeholder or box to extend beyond its contents. You might leave additional space, for example, to indicate to a colleague the approximate space allotted for entering her text. Text boxes you create and text placeholders automatically adjust their length to fit the text, but can be resized any way you like. However, there is a feature that can be set in PowerPoint that restrains the size of a placeholder or box to automatic sizing. If this setting has been changed from the default, you must disable this feature before you can change the length of such a placeholder. To do so, follow these steps:

1. Click anywhere inside the text placeholder.

2. Choose Format, Text Anchor. The Text Anchor dialog box appears.

3. Deselect the check box named Adjust Object Size to Fit Text if it is enabled.

4. Choose OK.

> **Note**
>
> The preset text placeholders in AutoLayouts already have this option disabled.

To resize a text placeholder, follow these steps:

1. To display the gray outline of the text placeholder, click anywhere in the text within that placeholder.

2. Click the gray placeholder to select it. Sizing handles appear, as shown in figure 6.19.

3. Place the mouse pointer over the sizing handle on the side or corner you want to move in or out. The pointer changes to a double-sided arrow (see fig. 6.19).

4. Drag the sizing handle in or out to shrink or expand the text placeholder.

Moving or Copying a Text Placeholder

Moving and copying a text placeholder is similar to moving and copying text. You just select the placeholder and use the mouse to move or copy the original to the new location. When you move or copy a text placeholder, all text inside also is moved or copied.

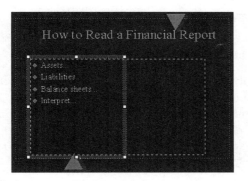

Fig. 6.19
To leave space for
your accountant to
fill in the rest of
the information,
expand the
placeholder.

Follow these steps to move or copy a text placeholder:

1. Display the gray outline of the text placeholder by clicking anywhere in the text within that placeholder.

2. Click the gray placeholder to select it.

3. Place the mouse pointer on the gray outline, being careful to avoid the sizing handles. The mouse pointer must look like a single-headed arrow.

4. To move the placeholder, press and hold the mouse button, drag the placeholder to the new location, and then release the mouse button. Alternatively, you can press the arrow keys to move the placeholder.

   To copy the placeholder, press and hold the Ctrl key, then click in the gray outline. Notice that a plus sign appears next to the mouse pointer. With the Ctrl key still depressed, press and hold the mouse button, drag the copy to the new location, and then release the mouse button and the Ctrl key.

Troubleshooting

The text in a placeholder extends beyond the placeholder. How do I fix it?

You have several options: you can reduce the font size, resize the placeholder, or edit the text so it fits. If you can edit the text without compromising clarity, this is the best method (in slide presentations, text should be as concise as possible). If you reduce the font size, make sure the audience at the back of the room can read the smaller text. To resize the placeholder so it automatically fits the text, click in the placeholder. From the main menu, choose Format, Text Anchor. In the dialog box that appears, select the check box named Adjust Object Size to Fit Text, and choose OK.

II

Working with Text

Deleting a Text Placeholder

You can delete any text placeholder by selecting it and pressing the Delete key. Text in the placeholder is also deleted.

If you accidentally delete a placeholder, you often can restore it—and its text—by using the Undo command, which reverses the last edit made, and can be used to undo several actions in sequence. To use Undo, click the Undo button on the toolbar.

Creating a Border for Text

Tip
You also can undo an action by pressing Ctrl+Z (Undo), or choosing Edit, Undo from the main menu.

To emphasize or visually separate a text area from the rest of a slide, you can create a border around the text. The border appears just inside the boundaries of the text placeholder. Figure 6.20 illustrates several line styles you can use for borders. You can also add arrows to your lines, or choose from a variety of dashed line styles in the drop-down boxes which aren't displayed in this figure. Finally, you can select the border color.

Fig. 6.20
The Colors and Lines dialog box offers a variety of line styles to choose from, such as those in the Style drop-down list.

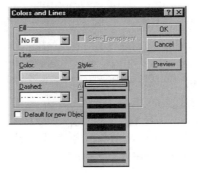

▶ See "Object Framing and Shadowing Object Placeholders,"
p. 299

To create a border, follow these steps:

1. Click anywhere in the text around which you want to create the border. The gray placeholder outline appears.

2. Click the gray placeholder outline to select it.

3. Choose Format, Colors and Lines. The Colors and Lines dialog box appears, as shown in figure 6.20.

4. In the Styles drop-down palette, select one of the line styles shown.

5. To make the line dashed as well, select one of the styles in the Dashed drop-down palette.

6. To change the border color (the default is black), select the Color drop-down palette, and then select a color.

7. Choose OK. The dialog box closes and the border appears just inside the text placeholder.

The default shape for a border is a rectangle, but you can change the shape to be any AutoShape by following these steps:

1. Create the border as described earlier in this section.

2. If the text placeholder isn't selected, select it.

3. Choose <u>D</u>raw, <u>C</u>hange AutoShape. PowerPoint displays the AutoShapes, shown in figure 6.21.

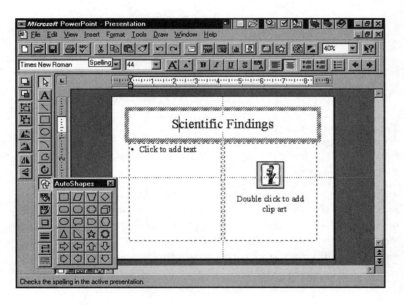

Fig. 6.21
Various border shapes are available for placeholders.

II

Working with Text

4. Select the AutoShape you want. The border changes to the new shape. (The outline of the text placeholder remains rectangular; this doesn't affect the border.) Text automatically rewraps to fit the new shape. If the text can't fit within the shape, it extends below it.

▶ See "Drawing Autoshapes," p. 278

Changing the Background Color of the Text Placeholder

To further emphasize a text area, you can change the background color of the text placeholder. If you have limited experience with combining colors, see Chapter 18, "Working with Color," for tips on when and how to use color effectively. If you then decide that a different background color is appropriate for the text, follow these steps to add the new color:

1. Click anywhere in the text for which you want to change the background color. The gray outline of the text placeholder appears.

2. Click on the gray placeholder outline to select it.

3. Choose Format, Colors and Lines. The Colors and Lines dialog box appears (refer to fig. 6.20).

4. Select the Fill drop-down palette to display the color selections, and select a color.

5. Choose OK. The dialog box closes, and the background color appears inside the text placeholder.

▶ See "Aligning Objects," p. 282

Troubleshooting

I resized a text placeholder and now the title and body text placeholders no longer align. How do I realign them?

Align text placeholders the same way you align graphic objects. Select one placeholder by clicking its gray border. Then place the mouse pointer over text in the other placeholder and press and hold the Shift key while clicking the mouse button. This selects the second placeholder and keeps selected the first placeholder. Release the keys. From the main menu, choose Draw, Align. In the cascading menu that appears, choose the alignment (for example, Lefts).

In this chapter you learned the basics of working with text and many time-saving features for editing text. The next chapter explores creating speaker's notes and audience handouts.❖

Chapter 7

Creating Speaker's Notes & Audience Handouts

by Nancy Stevenson

An effective slide presentation flows logically from one slide to the next, with each slide illustrating a few key points. This flow helps the audience follow the topic under discussion and helps the speaker make a coherent presentation. One of PowerPoint's features, Speaker's Notes, provides a useful tool to keep the presenter on track. These notes make sticking with the flow of your slide or overhead presentation simple. And they're easy to create!

For many presentation situations, it's also advisable to provide your audience members with printed material that they can follow as you give your slide presentation, or that they can take with them to review after you're done to remind them of key points. PowerPoint's audience handouts are the answer.

In this chapter, you learn how to

- Create and print Speaker's Notes

- Use the Notes Master to globally change the layout of Speaker's Notes

- Make changes to individual Notes Pages

- Add a date, time, or page number to Notes Pages

- Take advantage of handouts to increase the audience's memory retention during and after your presentation

- Create and print handouts

- Use the Handout Master page to globally change the layout of handouts

How to Use Speaker's Notes

When you present information with visual clues, such as a series of slides, overheads, or computer screens created in PowerPoint, it's important that what you're saying matches those visuals. Here are some ways you might consider using Speaker's Notes to help you do just that:

- Use notes to list each specific point you want to make under each major bullet topic.

- Put details in notes, such as the history of a situation or statistics, to substantiate your statements.

- Put the concepts behind a graph or chart's data in notes to help you explain the visual to your audience.

- Put a sentence at the end of your Notes Page to indicate what's coming next. This helps you make a transition to the next slide.

▶ See "Using the Meeting Minder," p. 662

- During an informal presentation, use the Meeting Minder feature of PowerPoint to take minutes or to add action items to your notes for follow-up after the meeting.

Creating a Notes Page

Speaker's Notes, which are made up of Notes Pages in PowerPoint, are pages that display a slide and any notes you have for that slide. You may add notes, for example, to remind you of background information for the key points illustrated by a slide. Such notes help you focus during your presentation and reduce the chance that you might accidentally skip an important topic. They also keep you from having to crane your neck around to see the slide on the wall behind you: You can focus on your content and audience for a more successful presentation.

You can create Speaker's Notes for any slide in a presentation. As shown in figure 7.1, a Notes Page displays the slide at the top of the page. Beneath the slide is a notes box where you can type notes relevant to that slide.

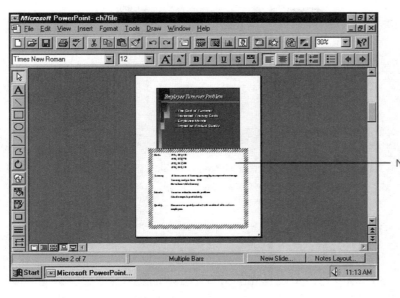

Fig. 7.1
Detailed notes help a speaker follow the sequence of ideas in a PowerPoint presentation.

Notes box

To create a Notes Page for a slide, follow these steps:

1. Display the slide for which you want to create a Notes Page.

2. From the main menu bar, choose View, Notes Pages; or click the Notes Pages View button in the set of view icons located just above the status bar. PowerPoint displays the Notes Page for the slide, as shown in figure 7.2.

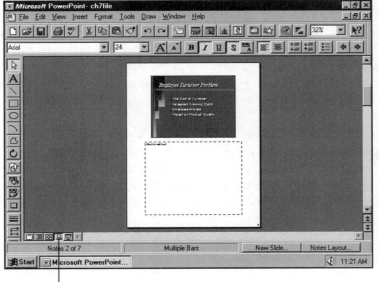

Fig. 7.2
A blank Notes Page, ready for your input.

Notes Page View button

II

Working with Text

3. Click the notes box (see fig. 7.2). The insertion point appears in the notes box.

4. Type your notes.

5. Choose File, Save to save your Notes Page. The page is saved with your presentation.

> **Note**
>
> If a presentation is new, the Save As dialog box appears. In the File Name text box, type a file name and then choose Save.

Modifying Notes Pages

PowerPoint provides a default font, color scheme, and layout for the Notes Pages. You can change these for an individual Notes Page, or globally change all Notes Pages in your presentation. You can also modify individual pages or all pages to include graphic elements.

◄ See "Formatting Text," p. 180

◄ See "Using the Notes Master," p. 64

When do you make formatting global—that is, common to all Notes Pages in the presentation—and when can you get creative with changes on each individual page? Let's say you want to use a larger typeface on all the Notes Pages so you can read it more easily during your presentation. You should do that globally. Perhaps you prefer the notes box at the top of your Notes Page on all pages. Again, make these changes globally with the Notes Master.

However, you might want to add a specific label to a graphic element on just one Notes Page. Or you might want to put the board of directors' names in boldface when they appear in your notes on slide 7, so you'll remember to acknowledge each of them when you come to that point in your presentation. These are opportunities to modify Notes Pages individually.

Making Changes to Individual Pages

Formatting elements of your Notes Pages is simple. Text is formatted just as you format text elsewhere in PowerPoint. You can also move or resize the notes box, crop the slide image itself to give you more room for notes, or change the notes background. To modify an individual Notes Page, follow these steps:

1. Display the slide whose Notes Page you want to modify.

2. From the main menu bar, choose View, Notes Pages; or click the Notes Page View button.

3. You can now make changes to the text and other slide elements just as you do in Slide view.

Modifying Text

You might want to change the text font, format, or color to emphasize certain terms or points in your presentation. Remember, you'll be reading your notes on a printed page, and possibly in a darkened room. Adjusting the font, font size, or boldness can make your notes easier to read in this situation. Modify text on a Notes Page just as you would text on a slide. Select the text, then use the tools on the formatting toolbar to change the font, size, or add effects such as bold, italic, or underline.

Tip
Your Notes Page comes up by default at less than its actual size. Use Zoom Control on the toolbar to enlarge the page.

Adding or Modifying Objects

Consider adding labels to help you remember the elements you'd like to draw your audience's attention to. Or, to give yourself a quick visual reminder, add a graphic object to your notes. Add these as you would add them on a slide using the drawing tools or the Insert menu. Note that these graphics won't show on the slide itself—just on your notes (see fig. 7.3).

◀ See "Creating labels and Other Special Text," p. 168

Sometimes it's useful to move the slide or notes box to a different position, either because it's easier to read as you make your presentation, or because you'd like to add extra elements to your Notes Page and need to rearrange things to do so (see fig. 7.3).

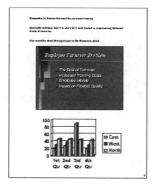

Fig. 7.3
A graph on your Notes Page gives you data to quote from at this point in your presentation.

Working with Text

1. To select the slide, click it; to select the notes box, click in the text area to display the gray border of the notes box, and then click the gray border. A selection box with square sizing handles encloses the slide or notes box, as shown in figure 7.4.

▶ See "Moving and Aligning Objects," p. 295

2. Place the pointer inside the selection box, and drag the slide or notes box to the new location. Be careful not to place the pointer directly on a sizing handle.

Fig. 7.4
Sizing handles surround the selected object. Now just drag to move it where you want it.

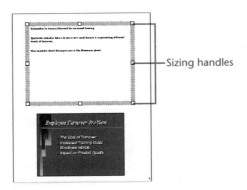
Sizing handles

◀ See "Resizing a Text Place-holder," p. 197

You can also resize the slide or notes box just as you would any object on a slide by dragging on the sizing handles shown in figure 7.4.

Sometimes it helps to crop a slide to make it fit with your notes or get rid of extraneous design elements. To crop an object, click the slide. The selection box encloses the slide. Choose Tools, Crop Picture. The crop pointer appears. Place the pointer over any sizing handle and drag it to crop the picture in the direction you're dragging.

▶ See "Resizing Objects," p. 297

◀ See "Creating a Border for Text," p. 200

Adding a border or shadow around the notes box or slide image can help you see the different elements more clearly on the printed page. Add this kind of formatting as you would add them on a slide.

Changing the Background

The background color of a notes box can be adjusted to make it more readable or attractive on the printed page. To change the background color of the notes box use the Fill Color tool on the Drawing toolbar.

To change the background design on the Notes Page choose Format, Notes Background. The Notes Background dialog box appears (see fig. 7.5).

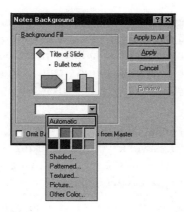

Fig. 7.5
Use the choices in
the drop-down
box to modify the
background color.

You can use this dialog box to change or shade the background color of the
notes pages:

- To change the background color, click on the down arrow to see the
  drop-down list. Choose a color from the palette, or click on Other
  Color to choose from a wider variety of standard and custom colors,
  then choose OK.

- To use a shaded background, click on Shaded in the drop-down list to
  display the dialog box in figure 7.6. Choose the direction of shading
  (for example, Vertical or Diagonal Down) from the Shade Styles group.
  If that style has one or more variations, they appear in the Variants
  group; in this case, choose the variation that you want. To adjust the
  lightness or darkness of the shading, drag the scroll bar marked Dark
  and Light at either end. To darken (add more black to) the shading,
  drag the scroll bar left. To lighten (add more white to) the shading, drag
  the scroll box right.

Fig. 7.6
Add shading to
the background
of your Notes
Pages here.

Tip

If you'd like to blend two colors in your shading, click on Two Color and a second color drop-down list will appear under the first one.

When you're done adjusting shading, click OK to return to the Notes Background dialog box. You can also use this dialog box to select a pattern or texture or to hide graphic objects, including any text added with the Text button. To do so, select Omit Background Graphics from Master using the check box at the bottom of the dialog box shown in figure 7.5 (behind the drop-down list).

After you've made your changes in the Notes Background dialog box, you can preview what these changes will look like by clicking on Preview. When you do, the on-screen view will show the suggested changes. You can move the dialog box to one side to get a better look.

When you're happy with what you've got, you can apply the changes to the single Notes Page or to all Notes Pages in the presentation. To apply the changes to only the displayed Notes Page, choose Apply. To apply the changes to all Notes Pages, choose Apply To All. To cancel the changes, select Cancel.

Tip

You can also apply changes to all pages by choosing Format, Notes Background to open this dialog box from the Notes Master view and applying changes to the Master.

To change the color scheme of the notes: From the Format menu, choose Notes Color Scheme. The Notes Color Scheme dialog box appears (see fig. 7.7). If it's not already chosen, click on the Custom tab. The Scheme Colors palette in this dialog box shows the current colors for the title text, the background, and other items in a Notes Page. In this palette, the Accent colors refer to additional fill colors, such as those used for additional bars in bar charts. To change a color, double-click on the color or select the color and then choose Change Color. In the dialog box that appears, choose a color from the color palette (or choose More Colors, complete the More Colors dialog box, and then choose OK). You return to the Notes Color Scheme dialog box, where the new color scheme is previewed in a thumbnail sketch at the lower left of the dialog box.

Fig. 7.7

If it's easier for you to see a dark background and white letters on your notes pages, change the text color here.

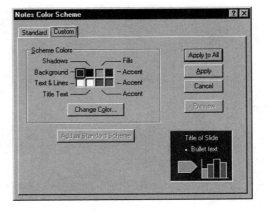

If you aren't comfortable creating your own color scheme, you can let PowerPoint suggest one. In the Notes Color Scheme dialog box, click on the Standard tab. The tab is shown in figure 7.8. PowerPoint displays seven suggested color schemes. To choose one of these schemes, just click on it.

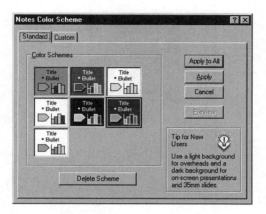

Fig. 7.8
Choose one of PowerPoint's standard color schemes from this tab of the Color Scheme dialog box.

After you've made your changes in one of the tabs in the Notes Color Scheme dialog box, you can apply the changes to the single notes page or to all notes pages in the presentation. To apply the changes to the displayed notes page only, choose Apply. To apply the changes to all notes pages, choose Apply to All. To cancel the changes, choose Cancel.

Changing Everything at Once with Notes Master

To change the font, color scheme, or layout for all Notes Pages in a presentation, use the Notes Master. This enables you to make the changes just once—to the Notes Master page. The changes to the Notes Master page automatically apply to all Notes Pages in that presentation, giving the pages a consistent appearance. You can also use the Notes Master to add graphics or text (such as the date or page number) that you want to apply to all Notes Pages in your presentation.

If you make changes to individual slides either before or after changing settings in Notes Master, the individual settings will take precedence over the master changes. If you want to reapply the Notes Master settings, select Format, Notes Layout and click next to Reapply Master.

To use the Notes Master, follow these steps:

1. Open the presentation for which you want to modify the Notes Master.

2. From the main menu bar, choose View. The View menu appears.

II

Working with Text

3. From the Underline{V}iew menu, select Underline{M}aster, and then choose Underline{N}otes Master. The Notes Master page appears, as shown in figure 7.9.

Fig. 7.9
You can rearrange placeholders and apply formatting globally from a Notes Master page.

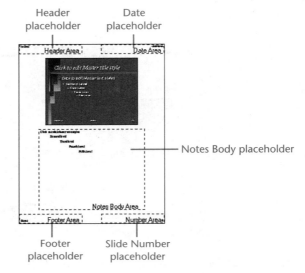

Header placeholder

Date placeholder

Notes Body placeholder

Footer placeholder

Slide Number placeholder

4. Follow one or more of the procedures given earlier for modifying individual Notes Pages. Those changes will appear on all Notes Pages in the presentation. If you want to move or resize the notes box, you can select the notes box on the Notes Master page simply by clicking the dashed border of the box. You can edit the text size or font, move the notes above the slide image—whatever changes you want to appear on every slide.

5. Choose Underline{F}ile, Underline{S}ave to save the new format. The new master page is saved with your presentation, and all Notes Pages in the presentation are modified according to the new settings in the master page (except, of course, those individual slides on which you've made specific changes).

▶ See "Deleting Objects," p. 298

Troubleshooting

I accidentally deleted the slide image or notes box from my Notes Page. Can I restore it?

You can restore the slide image or notes box to a Notes Page at any time by selecting Format, Notes Underline{L}ayout. In the Notes Layout dialog box that appears, click on the element that you deleted (Slide Image or Body), and then choose OK. If the notes box you deleted contained text, the text won't be restored. Slide images, however, are restored.

If the deletion was your last action, you can also use Undo, which reverses your last action.

Inserting the Date, Time, and Page Number

Notice that there are placeholders for date, page number, header, and footer on the Notes Master page. To have the date, time, or page number automatically appear on all Notes Pages, select View, Header and Footer. Then follow these steps, using the dialog box in figure 7.10:

Fig. 7.10
Make global changes to header and footer contents from this dialog box.

1. To insert the date, click on Date and Time and choose Update Automatically and select a date format from the drop-down list, or select Fixed and type in the text box.

2. To include a page number within the Notes Page, just click on Page Number.

3. To add text to a header or footer, simply click on that item, and type the text in the box below it.

4. When you're done, click on Apply to All.

You can change around the position of these elements on your Notes Pages by moving their placeholders on the Notes Master page. The positioning of these elements cannot be overridden from the individual pages.

Printing Notes Pages

To print your Notes Pages, follow these steps:

1. From the main menu, choose File, Print. The Print dialog box in figure 7.11 appears.

◀ See "Print a Presentation," p. 104

II

Working with Text

Fig. 7.11
Here's where you
tell PowerPoint
that you want to
print Notes Pages.

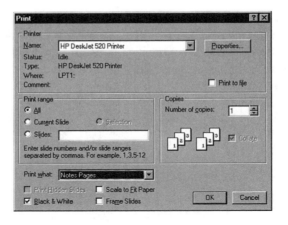

2. From the Print **W**hat drop-down list, select Notes Pages.

3. Make any other selections you want, such as number of copies or destination printer, and choose OK.

> **Note**
>
> You can also send miniature images of the slides in your presentation to Word for Windows and use its word processing features to add notes, if that's more comfortable for you. Choose Tools, Write Up and select a layout for your Word page. You can also create a link from your Word document to your PowerPoint presentation by selecting PasteLink; so if you make changes in PowerPoint, they will take effect in Word, as well.

Making the Best Use of Handouts

You can make your presentation even more effective by providing your audience with handouts. Handouts relieve your audience of the need to take extensive notes so they can focus on your presentation instead. Handouts also provide a common reference for participants in question and answer sessions. In PowerPoint, audience handouts are basically reproductions of your presentation slides in a smaller format, sometimes with added text or graphics.

People have differing opinions about the use of handouts in a presentation. Some presenters feel that the audience is reading the material in hand rather than paying attention to what's being said. Some are even disturbed by the rustling pages as the audience follows along.

Employee Turnover

Executive Committee Meeting, 8/15

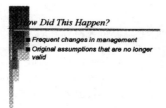

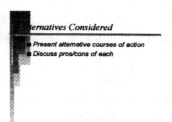

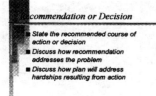

Fig. 7.13
A handout with
text added at
the top.

> **Note**
>
> One way around this is to add text to the Handout Master, then print, say, only three slides by indicating that range in the Print dialog box. Go back, change the text on the Handout Master, and print the next set of three slides. This way, you can add slide-specific notes to your handouts. Or export the slide images to Word for Windows by selecting <u>T</u>ools, <u>W</u>rite-Up. Then add as much text as you like to each slide image.

To add text or graphics to the Handout Master, follow these steps:

1. Open the presentation for which you want to modify the Handout Master.

2. From the main menu, choose <u>V</u>iew. The View menu appears.

3. From the View menu, select <u>M</u>aster, and then choose <u>H</u>andout Master. The Handout Master page appears, as shown in figure 7.14. Placeholders on the page show the layout for two, three, and six slides per page. (For three slides per page, the layout is shown by the three slides on the left side.)

Fig. 7.14
The Handout Master has placeholders for 2, 3, or 6 slides.

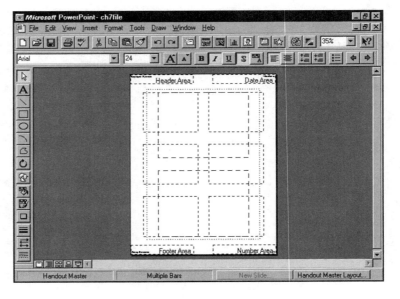

▶ See "Adding Clip Art and Scanned Art," p. 307

4. Add graphics, draw, or import artwork as you would on any slide.

5. To add text, click the Text button, position the insertion point where you want the text to appear, click the mouse button to create a text object, and type the text, as in figure 7.15. You can format the text as you would text in any slide. You can also move these text boxes around the Handout Master page.

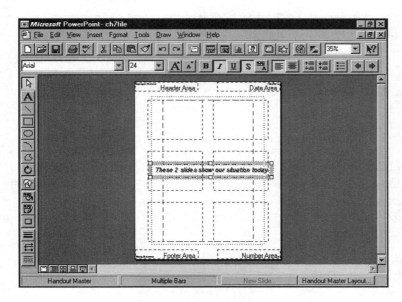

Fig. 7.15
A text item added to the Handout Master page.

II

Working with Text

Troubleshooting

I placed some text on the Handout Master, but all the words didn't print out. Did I do something wrong?

Be sure to place any graphics and text outside the placeholders for the layout you intend to use; otherwise, the slide images print over the graphics and text. To be sure of your object placement, select all the text items, and click on the Bring Forward button on the Draw toolbar. This places all the text boxes on top.

Modifying Placeholders on Handouts

You can move the four placeholders for date, footer, header, and number around the page on the Handout Master. When you do, they will be moved to the new position on every handout. You can also resize, or choose to omit, any of these placeholders from your printed handouts.

To move a placeholder, follow these steps:

1. Display the Handout Master (choose <u>V</u>iew, <u>M</u>aster, <u>H</u>andout Master).

2. Click on the dashed lines that surround the placeholder you want to move. A gray border appears.

3. Click anywhere in the gray border of the placeholder, being careful not to click on any of the sizing handles.

4. Drag the placeholder to a new position, and release the mouse button.

To resize a placeholder, simply click on its border; then click on a sizing handle, and drag in the direction you want to expand or shrink the placeholder.

 Finally, to omit a particular placeholder from your printed handouts, click on the placeholder to select it, then press delete or click on the Cut button on the toolbar. To get the placeholder back, click the Handout Master Layout button in the status bar or select F<u>o</u>rmat, Handout Master <u>L</u>ayout to see the dialog box in figure 7.16. Just click to select the item you want to appear on the master.

Fig. 7.16
If you want to replace a missing placeholder, select the item here.

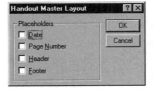

Printing Handouts

▶ See "Printing Slides, Notes, Outlines and Handouts," p. 460

To select the number of slides per handout and print the handouts, follow these steps:

1. From the main menu, choose <u>F</u>ile. The File menu appears.

2. From the <u>F</u>ile menu, choose <u>P</u>rint. The Print dialog box appears (see fig. 7.17).

3. From the Print What drop-down list, select one of the following:

   Handouts (2 slides per page)

   Handouts (3 slides per page)

   Handouts (6 slides per page)

4. Make any other selections you want and choose OK.

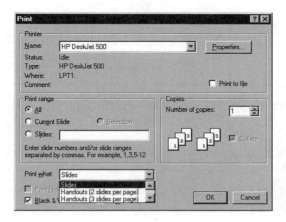

Fig. 7.17
You determine the
layout of your
handouts in the
Print dialog box.

It's sometimes easier to read handouts if you frame the slide content (see fig. 7.18). Simply click on Frame Slides in the print dialog box to do so.

Working with Text

Fig. 7.18
Frames sometimes make your slides easier to read.

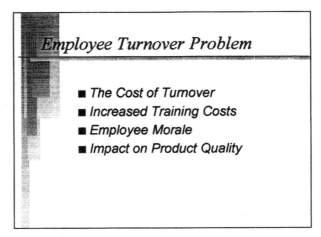

These 2 slides show our situation today

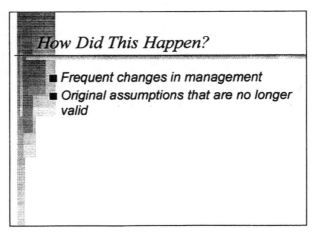

Much of what you can do to manipulate the elements on a notes page is identical to the way you do it on individual slides. For other information relating to manipulating the elements included in notes, take a look at Chapter 6, "Working with Text," which covers most aspects of creating and editing text, including selecting, editing, and formatting text, searching and replacing text, and using the spelling checker. Also, information on creating and manipulating drawing objects can be found in Chapter 10, "Drawing Objects," Chapter 11, "Selecting, Editing, and Enhancing Objects," and Chapter 12, "Adding Clip Art and Scanned Art."❖

Chapter 8

Creating Presentation Outlines

by Pamela R. Toliver

An effective slide presentation flows logically from one slide to the next, with each slide illustrating a few key points. You may, in the past, have created slides and formatted text using the Slide view. From the slides in your presentations, you may have created speaker's notes and handouts to help you prepare and give an effective presentation.

At times, you may have developed an outline of your presentation and found that creating slides in the Slide view was somewhat tedious. Since you already had an outline, it would have been quicker and more efficient to type the text from your outline on one page and have PowerPoint automatically create slides using the outline text. At other times, you may have wanted to view just the narrative title and body text of a presentation to check the flow before you finalize it. PowerPoint has such a tool—the Outline view.

With Outline view, you can type the title and body text for all slides in your presentation using a format that's similar to typing text in a word processing program. Then PowerPoint automatically creates slides directly from the text you type. So using the outline is a snap!

When you have a presentation already developed and you need to make quick edits to some of the text, displaying the Outline view condenses the title and body text of all slides so that you can move from slide to slide more quickly, checking the flow as you make the edits. When you're working with a presentation, one important point to remember is that regardless of the view you use, the presentation is a complete, cohesive unit. So changes you make to text are the same whether you add it or edit it in Slide view or Outline View. Changes you make in Slide view are immediately reflected when you switch back to Outline view and vice versa. You can add, modify, rearrange, or delete *slides* in Slide, Outline, Notes Pages, or Page Sorter view, and you can see the results in any view. You can add *text* to slides only in Slide view and Outline view.

In this chapter you learn to

- Create presentations using Outline view

- Review existing presentations using Outline view

- Print outlines

Previewing Outline View

The Outline view in PowerPoint provides a different way of viewing the information in your presentation. It helps you organize and focus your thoughts and view the flow of your presentation. The Outline view displays only the title and body text for each slide on a notebook-like page—without the distractions of graphics, color, and other objects you include or may eventually add to your slides. Graphic objects and other enhancements included on slides may be *added* only in Slide view. The complete slide image appears in miniature form in Notes Pages view and Handouts view; but a slide icon identifies each new slide in Outline view, and each slide is numbered so that it's easy to locate (see fig. 8.1). The Graphic Slide icon identifies slides containing objects other than title and body text.

 To display Outline view, open or create a presentation. Choose View, Outline, or click the Outline View button at the bottom of the presentation window (see fig. 8.2).

Note	
If you're creating a new presentation, your screen won't contain any text.	

Icon indicating graphic object   Title text

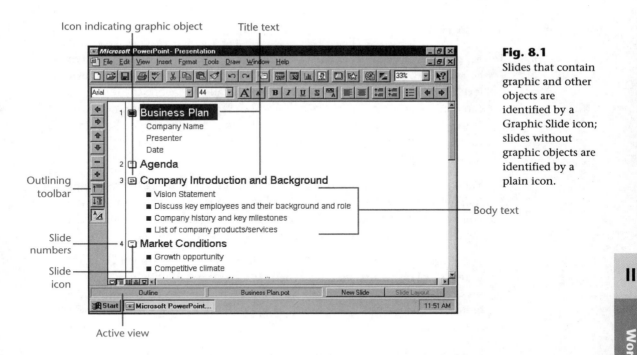

Outlining
toolbar

Slide
numbers

Slide
icon

Active view

Body text

Fig. 8.1
Slides that contain
graphic and other
objects are
identified by a
Graphic Slide icon;
slides without
graphic objects are
identified by a
plain icon.

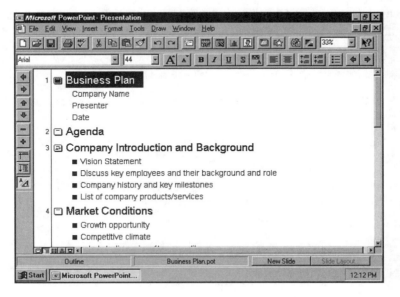

Fig. 8.2
The Outline view
button at the
bottom of the
presentation
window switches
you to Outline
view.

II

Working with Text

Working in Outline View

An outline can have up to five indent levels for bulleted items and subitems beneath each slide title. You press Tab to indent each level from the previous level. Indenting text to a new subtext level is called *demoting* the text. You can demote an item that's already typed by placing the insertion point on the item and pressing Tab or by clicking the Demote button on the Outlining toolbar. For those of you who prefer keystrokes, you can also press Alt+Shift+right arrow.

You can also move text to the previous indent level by using the techniques for *promoting* text. Press Shift+Tab once for each indent level to the left that you want to move the text. You can also promote an item one level by clicking the Promote button or by pressing Alt+Shift+left arrow.

You'll find that as you work in Outline view, PowerPoint remembers the indent level of the text you just typed. As a result, it won't be necessary to press Tab or use one of the alternate methods each time you want to add a bullet item or subitem. PowerPoint assumes that you want to continue working at the same text level until you tell it to move to a different indent level.

You can insert new slides by using any of the techniques you used to insert slides in other views. In addition, you can press Ctrl+Enter after the last bulleted item in the previous slide. The four methods for adding slides in Outline view are:

- Click the New Slide button on the status bar.

- Click the Insert New Slide button on the Standard toolbar.

- Press Ctrl+M.

- Press Ctrl+Enter

Now that you have a basic understanding of how to work in Outline view, let's create a new presentation using Outline view.

Creating Presentations Using Outline View

Once you have developed your outline on paper, you're ready to use it to create a presentation on the system. PowerPoint provides you with the tools necessary to create and manipulate the outline on the system—and it even uses the information from your outline to create slides for your presentation!

Those of you who prefer to type your outline using a word processing program will find PowerPoint equally satisfying. You can type your outline using your favorite word processing program and create a new presentation using the outline.

Creating a Presentation Outline in PowerPoint

To create a presentation outline, you use Outline view. Follow these steps:

1. Create a new blank presentation. Choose <u>V</u>iew, <u>O</u>utline.

   Outline view displays the number 1 and a slide icon in the left margin, as shown in figure 8.3.

First slide
number   Slide icon

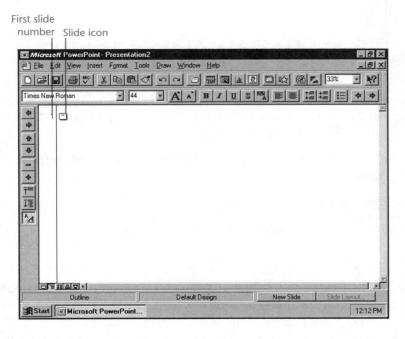

Fig. 8.3
The blank outline positions you to start typing the title for the first slide.

2. Type the title of the first slide in your presentation and press Enter.

   A slide icon and number appear for slide 2 (see fig. 8.4).

3. To enter a bullet point for Slide 1 instead of moving on to Slide 2, press Tab or use one of the alternate methods described above.

   PowerPoint automatically indents the line and inserts a bullet.

4. Type the text for the first bullet point.

II

Working with Text

Fig. 8.4
When the new slide appears, you can either type the title for the second slide or continue working on Slide 1 by pressing Tab.

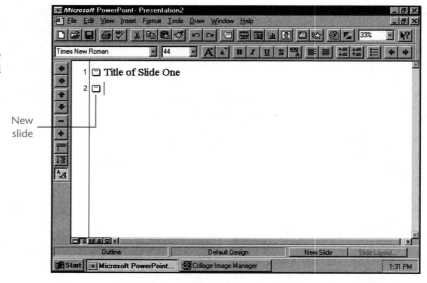

New slide

5. To add another bullet point, press Enter. PowerPoint automatically indents the next line and inserts the bullet. Repeat steps 4 and 5 until you've entered all the bullet points.

6. At the end of the last bullet point for the slide, press Ctrl+Enter to create the next slide.

7. Type the title of the next slide.

8. Repeat steps 3 through 7 to complete your outline.

Creating a Presentation from an Imported Outline

You can also create a presentation from an imported outline. It is important to note that PowerPoint generally imports outlines and text from word processing applications pretty cleanly. Sometimes, however, indent levels are thrown off when the document or outline is imported. This is especially true when styles and other formatting codes are part of the original outline document.

To import the outline, follow these steps:

1. Choose File, Open or click the Open icon on the Standard toolbar.

   The Open File dialog box appears.

2. Change the Look In folder to the one that contains the file you want to import.

3. From the Files of Type drop-down list, select All Outlines.

    PowerPoint lists those files in the document folder that you can open as outlines. If your outline doesn't have an extension as part of its name, or if it has an extension that isn't listed, you may need to choose All Files from the drop-down list.

4. Select the outline file you want to import.

5. Choose Open.

    PowerPoint automatically displays the text from the imported outline in Outline view. You can then use the techniques described later in this chapter to view the slides (see "Viewing Slides Created in Outline View" later in this chapter).

If PowerPoint can't use the extension to readily identify the program you used to create your outline, it may ask you what program you used to create the file. Select the word processing application you used. If PowerPoint can't open the file because it isn't an appropriate text file, you'll see an error message telling you that you cannot open the file in PowerPoint. The best action to take at this point is to launch the source application and save the file in ASCII or an acceptable Text file format.

Displaying an Outline for an Existing Presentation

You can also use Outline view to review the outline of an existing presentation. Just open the presentation and click the Outline View button at the bottom of the presentation window. The presentation appears as an outline, with the title and body text displayed for each slide. The outline does not show graphic objects or text you entered using the graphic Text button from the Drawing toolbar.

After you have an outline, you can use it to view, delete, modify, and rearrange slides. The next sections describe how.

Using Outline Tools

Outline view includes a special toolbar that makes manipulating, modifying, and reviewing an outline easy.

Tip
If the toolbar isn't displayed, choose View, Toolbars. When the Toolbars dialog box appears, select the Outlining check box and then choose OK. You can also point to any toolbar that's displayed and click the right mouse button. Select Outlining from the Quick List.

Table 8.1 describes each of the tools on this toolbar.

Table 8.1	Outlining Toolbar	
Tool	**Name**	**Action**
	Promote (Indent less)	Moves the paragraph containing the insertion point one level left one indent and changes the bullet character to match other bullets at that level.
	Demote (Indent more)	Moves the paragraph containing the insertion point one level right, which indents the paragraph and changes the bullet character to match other bullets at that level.
	Move Up	Moves the paragraph containing the insertion point above the preceding item one line at a time.
	Move Down	Moves the paragraph containing the insertion point below the next item one line at a time.
	Collapse Selection	Compresses all levels of text for *a slide* so that only the slide title appears. A line below the slide title indicates that the text is collapsed. To use this tool, place the insertion point anywhere in the text for that slide (can be at any level of text), and click the Collapse Selection tool.
	Expand Selection	Restores text for a *slide* that has been collapsed. To use this tool, place the insertion point in the slide title text and click the Expand Selection tool.
	Show Titles	Collapses all levels of text for *all slides* so that only slide titles appear in the entire outline. The insertion point can be anywhere in the outline to use this tool.
	Show All	Expands the outline so all levels of text for *all slides* appear. The insertion point can be anywhere in the outline to use this tool.
	Show Formatting	A toggle that lets you decide to display actual character formatting (for example, font and type size) or plain text. Plain text, which is a smaller type size, enables you to see more of the outline on-screen. The insertion point can be anywhere in the outline to use this tool.

Viewing Slides Created in Outline View

When you create a presentation using Outline view, PowerPoint automatically creates slides with the titles and text you entered in the outline. To view one of the slides in Slide view, place the insertion point on the slide title in Outline view. Then double-click on the slide icon to the left of the slide title or choose View, Slide to display the slide in Slide view.

Once you have returned to Slide view, you can then use the techniques explored in a previous chapter to move from slide to slide in your presentation. Refer to Chapter 2, "Getting Acquainted with PowerPoint 95," for more information.

In Slide view, you can edit the slide as you would any slide. Outline view automatically adjusts to reflect any changes you make in Slide view, so you don't need to worry about having different versions of the same presentation. After you edit slides in Slide view, you may want to redisplay the presentation in Outline view to obtain an overall view of the changes.

Tip
You can also click the Slide view button in the status bar to display the slide in Slide view.

Tip
You can also display the slide in Slide view by double-clicking on the Outline view slide icon for the slide you want to view.

Editing and Enhancing Text in Outline View

You can edit and enhance text in Outline view just as you can in Slide view. To make text italic, for example, select the text and then click the Italic button on the Formatting toolbar. Working with text—including formatting, copying, and moving text—is as easy in Outline view as it was in Slide view. Any changes you make to text in Outline view are reflected on the slide.

You can use the Show Formatting tool on the Outlining toolbar to display text formatting. This tool is a toggle icon that you can also use to remove text formatting from display in the Outline view. When it's on, text appears with all the enhancements, font size, font color, and so on, that you applied. When Show Formatting is off, text appears the standard default font size (generally 10 or 12 points with no enhancements) with no distinction in text size between title and body text. As a result, you can see more of the outline when Show Formatting is off, but you can view the effectiveness of text enhancements when Show Formatting is on.

In addition to editing and enhancing text, you can delete slides and rearrange slides using a variety of techniques.

◀ See "Editing Text," p.173

◀ See "Formatting Text," p.180

II

Working with Text

Troubleshooting

I changed the indent or tab settings in my text chart, but Outline view doesn't reflect those changes. Can I change the tab or indent settings in Outline view?

No. Outline view has default tab and indent settings that cannot be changed. When you return to Slide view, however, your charts retain the tab and indent settings you selected.

Rearranging and Deleting Slides in Outline View

Tip
You can use a variety of methods to relocate a slide in a presentation. Some methods are easier than others. By exploring different techniques, you can find the one with which you're most comfortable.

Slide Sorter view is the most efficient view for rearranging and deleting slides in a presentation, but you can also use Outline view to accomplish these tasks. Before you can rearrange or delete a slide in Outline view, you must first select it.

To select a slide in Outline view so that you can move or delete it, click the slide icon for that slide. PowerPoint highlights the icon and all the outline text associated with that slide.

One method you can use to move the slide to a new location is to drag the slide. Follow these directions, being careful to note the mouse pointer shape required:

1. Select the slide you want to move by clicking on the slide icon. The mouse pointer must be a four-headed dark arrow (see fig. 8.5).

Four-headed dark arrow

Fig. 8.5
The mouse pointer must be a four-headed dark arrow to select a slide.

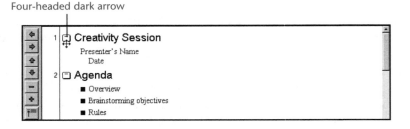

2. Position the mouse pointer on the slide icon again, making sure you see the same four-headed dark arrow. Click and drag the slide up or down to its new location.

As you drag, the mouse pointer shape becomes a two-headed dark vertical arrow, and a horizontal dark line identifies the new location of the slide (see fig. 8.6). You can easily tell where the slide will appear when you release the mouse button.

New slide location   Selected slide to move

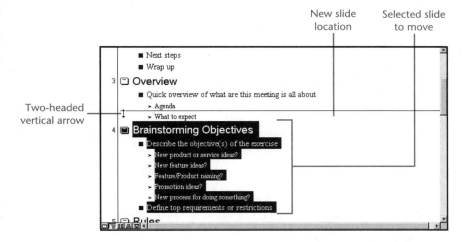

Two-headed vertical arrow

Fig. 8.6
The horizontal line identifies the new location of the slide.

Tip
You can also use these techniques to rearrange bulleted items on a slide. Just position the pointer on the bullet for the item you want to relocate and use the techniques described here.

3. When the dark line is positioned where you want the slide to appear, release the mouse button to drop the slide.

If your first movement with the mouse is right or left rather than up or down, a two-headed horizontal arrow and a vertical line appear (see fig. 8.7). This motion enables you to demote or promote selected information.

> **Caution**
>
> Your first motion when you drag, either up/down or left/right, restricts movement to the left/right or up/down direction. As a result, you can't start dragging left/right and then decide you want to drag the selected text up/down without dropping the text and starting the procedure over again. When this happens, use the Undo feature to restore the text to its original position before starting again.

PowerPoint automatically renumbers slides in the outline so that slides appear in the appropriate order in Slide view.

Deleting a slide is an easy task in PowerPoint. It's important to realize that when a slide is deleted, all graphics and other enhancements included on the slide are also deleted. So you may want to view the slide in Slide view to

II

Working with Text

make sure that it doesn't contain graphics and other objects that need to be copied to another slide before you remove the slide.

Fig. 8.7

The vertical line identifies the indent level for text being promoted or demoted.

Two-headed horizontal mouse pointer

Vertical promote/ demote position

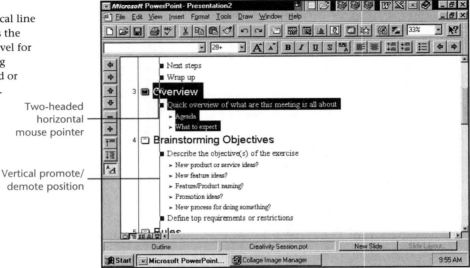

To delete a slide or bulleted information after you select it, just press Delete or choose Edit, Delete Slide.

Troubleshooting

I used the Text button to add text to my chart, but it doesn't appear in Outline view. How can I display it in Outline view?

You can't. Outline view doesn't show text created with the Text button or any graphic objects.

I accidentally dropped a slide at the wrong location and created a real mess. How can I quickly fix it?

Use the Undo feature in PowerPoint to reverse an action. In the new PowerPoint, the default settings enable you to undo the last 20 actions. You can change the number of actions PowerPoint remembers by choosing Tools, Options and selecting the Advanced tab. Increase or decrease the number of undos by clicking on the nudge buttons or by typing the desired number.

Each time I try to relocate selected text in Outline view, I get a hollow selection arrow and a small outline of a page with a short dotted vertical line. What did I do wrong?

(continues)

(continued)

You forgot to look for the four-headed dark arrow. Be sure to position the mouse pointer on the slide icon or bullet before you drag the selected information to a new location.

Each time I try to relocate a slide or bulleted item, I can't move the mouse up or down; it only wants to go left or right. How do I get it to move the slide up or down?

The first motion of the mouse after you select a slide controls the movement of the mouse. You may be trying to select text by clicking and dragging from left to right starting at the slide icon or bullet. Remember that all text for a slide is automatically selected when you click on the slide icon, so there is no need to drag to select text. After you click on the slide icon, you can click again and drag up or down—the first motion of the mouse is extremely important. You may find the Undo feature your best friend.

Printing an Outline

You can print an outline to prepare an overview of your presentation to include with audience handouts or to use as a table of contents for a report. Printing an outline is different from printing other presentation materials because it requires you to adjust the outline display *before* you print it.

An outline prints as it appears in the Outline view at the time you issue the Print command. If you turned off text formatting and collapsed the entries, for example, the outline will print presentation titles without text formatting. The outline also prints at the same zoom scale displayed in Outline view when you print. So before you print an outline, make sure that Outline view displays the settings you want for the printout.

To print an outline, follow these steps:

1. Choose <u>F</u>ile, <u>P</u>rint or press Ctrl+P.

    The Print dialog box appears.

2. From the Print <u>W</u>hat drop-down list, select Outline view.

3. Select other options you want and choose OK.

Tip
To print an outline using the Print icon on the Standard toolbar, you must first display Outline view. Otherwise the Print dialog box will not open.

II

Working with Text

Note

Working in Outline view provides you with a quick and efficient means of typing title and body text for your presentation. For those times when you need a presentation in a hurry, Outline view can help you make a favorable impression in relatively little time. Once you have the title and body text developed and entered, you can dress up the presentation with graphics, tables, charts, and background color to further impact the effects of the presentation.

Chapter 9

Creating and Working with Tables

by Pam Toliver

Using tables is a way to effectively communicate some types of information. A table can be used to list a number of specific points with short, explanatory notes beside them. Although you can show the same information using a text box and tabs for spacing, the table makes your job much easier. Using a table, you can quickly format text into perfectly aligned rows and columns so that information can more readily be grasped by your audience. You can use the power of Microsoft Word for Windows 95 to create and manipulate tables— without leaving PowerPoint!

To use the Microsoft Word table option, you must have Word for Windows 95 installed on your computer. If you do not, then this feature is not available. With both applications installed on your system, PowerPoint and Word work together to make creating tables quick and easy. You can use a variety of techniques to place a table on a slide, but regardless of which approach you use, a module of Word starts and places a table frame on your slide. Then you actually use Word's menus and functions to create the table. You know you are still working in PowerPoint because the title and status bars display PowerPoint information.

In this chapter, you learn to create and work with a Microsoft Word for Windows 95 table inside of PowerPoint. This chapter teaches you how to

- Open the Word table function and select the table size

- Enter, format, and edit information in the table

- Adjust column and row widths in a table

- Add borders and shading to a table

- View the table on the PowerPoint slide

- Create a chart using table data

Creating a New Table

You can use three basic methods to insert a table from Word on your PowerPoint slide: the menus, the toolbar, or an AutoLayout format, which contains a table placeholder. Regardless of the technique you use, you see the menus and most of the tools on-screen change from PowerPoint menus and tools to Word menus and tools.

Creating Tables Using the Menus

Many people find using the menus an easier way to control the size of the table. To use menus to create a table, follow these steps:

1. Display the slide on which you want to insert a table.

2. Choose Insert, Microsoft Word Table.

   The Insert Word Table dialog box appears, as shown in figure 9.1.

Fig. 9.1
The Insert Word Table dialog box enables you to type the number of columns and rows you need for the table.

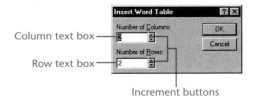

3. Enter the number of columns that you need for your table in the Number of Columns spin box. For example, enter **3** columns. You can also click the up- or down-arrow buttons to the right of the spin box to increase or decrease the number of columns.

4. Enter the number of rows that you need for your table in the Number of Rows spin box. For example, enter the number **4**. Again, you can type the number of rows needed or click the up- and down-arrow buttons to increase or decrease the number of rows.

The maximum number of rows that you can insert from this dialog box is seven. You can add additional rows later if space allows.

5. Choose OK.

PowerPoint automatically accesses Word's table function and displays a blank table within a table box. Figure 9.2 displays a table that is three columns by four rows. Notice that the columns are all the same width, and the rows are all the same height.

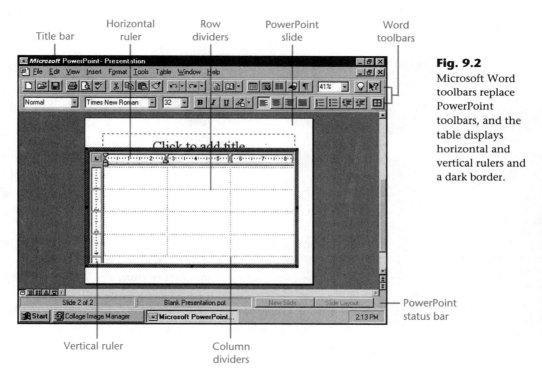

Fig. 9.2
Microsoft Word toolbars replace PowerPoint toolbars, and the table displays horizontal and vertical rulers and a dark border.

Creating Tables Using the Toolbar

The Standard PowerPoint toolbar includes an Insert Microsoft Word Table tool that you can use to create a table. To use this tool to create a table, follow these steps:

1. Click the Insert Microsoft Word Table button.

The table grid box appears, as shown in figure 9.3.

Fig. 9.3
Highlight the number of rows and columns you want in your table in the table grid box.

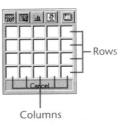

2. Click and drag the mouse pointer across the grid box to indicate the number of columns and rows that you want in your table. For example, to create a three row and four column table, select three rows down and four columns across, as illustrated in figure 9.4.

Fig. 9.4
This illustration would create a table containing three rows and four columns.

Tip
If at any time while you are working on the table you accidentally click outside the table area, the PowerPoint toolbars will reappear. Just double-click the table object to return to the Word table.

As you drag across the grid boxes from the upper left corner, you see the word `Cancel` at the bottom of the grid box replaced with `1 x 1 Table`. The first number indicates the number of rows selected for the table, and the second number indicates the number of columns. In addition to the number indicator at the bottom of the box, you see the grid boxes filled with a different color. When the number of rows and columns for your table appear on the grid box, release the mouse button. PowerPoint accesses Word's table functions and displays an empty table grid on your slide (refer to fig. 9.2).

Note

It appears from the grid box that the largest table you can construct is four rows and five columns. As you drag the mouse down or across the palette, the number of columns and rows expands to increase the size of the palette. The largest table you can create using the grid is 6 × 9. You can add additional rows and columns later as space permits.

Creating Tables Using an AutoLayout Format

Perhaps one of the quickest ways to create a table in PowerPoint is by using the Table AutoLayout format, which contains a table placeholder. Because the placeholder provides an automatic means of starting the application required to create the object, many people find it the most efficient method as well. Here's how:

1. Create a new slide, selecting the Table AutoLayout format, as illustrated in figure 9.5.

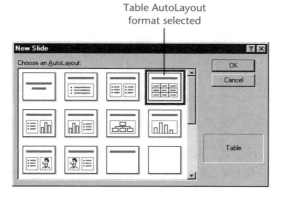

Table AutoLayout
format selected

Fig. 9.5
The Table AutoLayout format can be used to automatically access the table feature in Microsoft Word.

2. Double-click the table icon to start Word.

   The Insert Word Table dialog box opens (refer to fig. 9.1).

3. Type the number of columns and rows you want your table to contain and choose OK. The Word table appears on your side, ready for you to enter data.

Troubleshooting

When I click the Insert Microsoft Word Table button, either nothing happens or I get an error message. What's wrong?

You must be sure that you have Microsoft Word for Windows 95 correctly installed on your computer. You must have the Windows 95 version.

II

Working with Text

Entering Table Data

Tip
You can also select
all text in a col-
umn by position-
ing the cursor in
any cell in the
column and
choosing T*a*ble,
Select *C*olumn.

Table text and data can be entered by positioning the insertion point in the cell to contain the data and typing the data. Entries that expand beyond the width of the table cell automatically wrap to the next line of the same cell, and the cell expands vertically to accommodate the data. In addition, you can enter more than one line of text in each cell by pressing Enter to move to a new line. Once you have data entered in one cell, you can use a variety of methods to move from cell to cell. This section introduces you to some of these techniques.

Typing Table Data

By default, when you first create a table, the cursor is located in the first cell—the upper left corner of the table. Text default font size and type conform to the default font set in Microsoft PowerPoint rather than in Word. Entering text into a cell is simply a matter of typing. For the first cell type:

States With Highest New Home Sales

In figure 9.6, you see the results of using the default font and font size. Notice that the word wrap feature is active. You learn techniques to adjust cell height and width later in this chapter.

Fig. 9.6
Data entered in
the first cell of
the table.

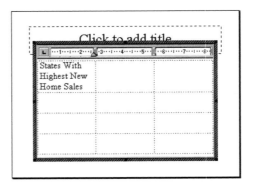

Moving from Cell to Cell

You can use many of the same techniques to move from cell to cell in a PowerPoint table that you use to access different cells in a spreadsheet program or columns in a word processing tabulation. If you are typing data in one cell, perhaps the most efficient way to move to the cell to the right is by pressing the Tab key because you don't have to move your hand away from the keyboard. If you are in the last cell in the row, pressing Tab automatically positions you in the first column of the next row.

If you are skipping around the table, adding data randomly in different cells, you may find the mouse or arrow keys an easier means of accessing the cell you need. To position the cursor in a cell, simply click the mouse on the cell to contain the data or press the arrow keys until the cursor is in the cell.

- Pressing the right-arrow key moves the cursor to the next cell to the right if you are at the end of the active cell entry.

- The down-arrow key moves the cursor to the cell immediately below the active cell if you are in the last line of the cell.

- The up-arrow key moves the cursor to the cell above the active cell if you are in the top line of the cell. When the cursor reaches the first row and you press the up-arrow key again, your computer beeps at you.

- The left-arrow key moves the cursor to the left one character at a time until it reaches the last character in the cell; then it moves to the cell to the left.

Try each of these methods of moving around your table by entering the following practice text into cells of the table. Follow these steps:

1. Press the down-arrow to move to the first cell in Row 2 and type **California.**

2. Press the down-arrow key and type **New York**.

3. Press the down-arrow key again and type **Virginia**.

4. Press the right-arrow key once and the up-arrow key three times and type **May**.

5. Press the Tab key and type **June**.

6. Continue moving from cell to cell until the data displayed in figure 9.7 is complete.

II

Working with Text

Tip

If, at any time while you are working on the table, you accidentally click outside the table area, the PowerPoint toolbars will reappear. Just double-click the table object to return to the Word table.

Fig. 9.7
Your table should
resemble this table
if you entered the
practice data.

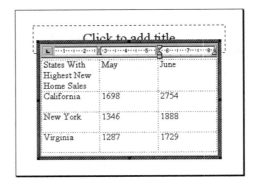

States With Highest New Home Sales	May	June
California	1698	2754
New York	1346	1888
Virginia	1287	1729

Formatting Text

As you enter information into your table, you quickly see whether the default format settings are adequate or whether you need to make adjustments to the table structure or text format. As you can see in figure 9.7, the font is too large for the text to fit on one line in all the cells. As a result, the text in the first cell was broken in the wrong place, and you ran out of rows after only three states.

This section and the next show you how you can format table text and change the table structure to improve your table. Because both PowerPoint and Word share many common features, you will find that you can use many of the text-editing techniques discovered earlier. Editing the text format helps create a more effective table.

Selecting Table Entries

◀ See "Editing Text" p. 173

◀ See "Formatting Text" p. 180

To adjust the formatting of text that has already been entered, you must first select the table entry. You can also select all text in a cell or an entire row, column, or table in PowerPoint and change the formatting all at once. This can help maintain consistency and continuity within your table.

To select the text in a single cell, use one of the following techniques:

- ■ Double-click any character in a word to select the word.

- ■ Triple-click any word in the cell to select all contents of the cell.

- ■ Position the mouse pointer to the left of the cell until it changes to a hollow right-pointing arrow and click to select all text in a cell.

To select an entire row of text, follow these steps:

1. Position the mouse pointer to the left of the first column in the row so that the pointer is a right-pointing white selection arrow, as shown in figure 9.8.

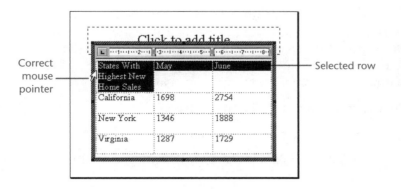

Correct mouse pointer

Selected row

Fig. 9.8
The mouse pointer must be a right-pointing arrow to use this technique.

2. Double-click to select all text in the row.

To select an entire column of text, follow these steps:

1. Position the mouse pointer at the top of the column you want to select, making sure that the pointer changes to a down-pointing dark arrow, as pictured in figure 9.9.

2. Click the left mouse button to select all text in the column.

Tip
You can also select all text in a column by positioning the cursor in any cell in the column and choosing Table, Select Column.

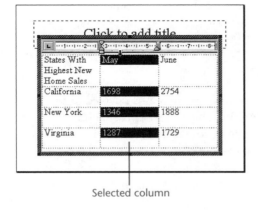

Selected column

Fig. 9.9
The mouse pointer must be a dark down-pointing arrow to select the column.

Tip
You can also position the cursor in any cell of the row and choose Table, Select Row.

II

Working with Text

Working with Fonts

Font styles available in Word are the same fonts you used to format text in PowerPoint and vary from machine to machine, depending on the printer and fonts installed on your system. Font styles can be used to distinguish different parts of the table or to emphasize specific pieces of information.

Because some fonts are easier to read than others, you may need to experiment a little to see which fonts contribute the most to your presentation. Remember that a consistency of font styles from slide to slide in your presentation helps maintain continuity. Using too many different fonts creates a distraction and can make your presentation ineffective.

To change a font style, follow these steps:

1. Select the text you want to reformat.

2. Click the down-arrow beside the Font drop-down list box in the Formatting toolbar.

   A list of available fonts appears.

3. Scroll through the list until you find the font that you want to use and click the font name.

   The selected font name appears in the Font text box on the toolbar, and your selected text is reformatted using the selected font.

Caution

Be careful not to press a keyboard character or the space bar while the text is selected or the selected text will be replaced with the character you press. If this happens, click the Undo button on the toolbar, press Ctrl+Z, or choose Edit, Undo Typing to restore the text.

The text you just reformatted remains selected until you click the mouse somewhere within the table frame. This enables you to change the font again if you are not satisfied with the new font. While it is still selected, you might want to add enhancements such as bold, italics, or underlining, or change the text color. To add enhancements available from the Formatting toolbar, just click the Bold, Italic, or Underline button. To change the font color, follow these steps:

1. Select the text you want to color.

2. Choose Format, Font.

   The Font dialog box opens. The Word Font dialog box is the same as the PowerPoint dialog box used in Chapter 6, "Working with Text."

3. Click the drop-down arrow beside the Color text box.

   A color palette drops down, showing you the font colors available.

4. Select the desired color and choose OK.

   Because of the highlighting, selected text does not display the color you choose until you deselect the text.

In addition to changing the typeface, or font style, you can also change the sizes of scalable fonts. Fonts that are not scalable may come in preset sizes. For example, the font named LinePrinter, comes in only one font size, 8.5. Others, such as Courier, come in two sizes, 10 and 12. Scalable fonts are generally available in sizes ranging from 8 to 72 *points*. Points measure the height of typed characters. There are 72 points in each inch, so if the font you select is 36 points, characters will be one-half inch high. Most TrueType fonts, which are designated by the double T symbol in front of the font name on the list, are scalable fonts.

Tip
Because this table will be on a presentation slide, the text must be visible from the back of the room in which you will deliver your presentation. Use a font at least 20 points.

To change the font size of your text, follow these steps:

1. Select the text you want to resize.

   If you are working with the example started earlier in this chapter, select the text on row one of the table.

2. Click the down-arrow button beside the Font Size drop-down list box on the Formatting toolbar or choose Format, Font.

   The current font size for the selected text is highlighted. If no font size is highlighted, the selected text has been formatted using different sized fonts for different words.

3. Select the desired font size for the selected text.

   If you are working with the example started earlier in this chapter, select a font size smaller than 32 points. This decreases the size of your letters. Select 28 points for your text.

Working with Text

II

Note

You would not normally change the text in a single cell because this can distract the audience from the point that you are making. For example, you would not increase the size of the word May in the second cell to 72 points, and leave the word June as 28 points, unless you wanted to specifically draw attention to the column labeled May. Because the text in the first cell is not directly associated with the other four columns, you may want to adjust the text size for the first cell independently.

The table is coming together into a more acceptable format, but you still must make some adjustments and explore other functions before it's complete.

Changing Cell Data Alignment

You can easily change the alignment of text in a cell, column, row, or selected cells to improve the readability of a table. The same four alignments are available for formatting cell data that you used to format text in placeholders in Chapter 6—and in Word, they are available directly from the Formatting toolbar. Of course, you can also change the alignment by accessing the Paragraph dialog box from the Format menu as you did for some alignments in PowerPoint, but the Formatting toolbar buttons are much more efficient.

	Align Left	Aligns text with the left margin of selected cells
	Center	Centers text within selected cells
	Align Right	Aligns text at the right edge of selected cells
	Justify	Spreads text from left to right across the cell. When text is justified, words may be stretched with extra space between letters so that the text fills the cell. Font size is not changed—only spacing between letters and words.

To change the alignment of text in your table, follow these steps:

1. Select the cells containing text you want to align.

2. Click the alignment button on the Formatting toolbar that represents the desired alignment for text in the selected cells.

Adding Borders and Shading to a Table

By adding borders and shading to your table, you can draw attention to selected information within the table. The gridlines that appear in the table
are not printed or visible once you place the table on the PowerPoint slide.
Therefore, you must add shading to cells or place borders around cells before
returning to PowerPoint. The table feature in Word makes shading cells and
adding borders quite easy.

To add shading to cells in your table, follow these steps:

1. Click the Borders button on the Formatting toolbar.

   The Borders toolbar appears beneath the Formatting toolbar, as illustrated in figure 9.10.

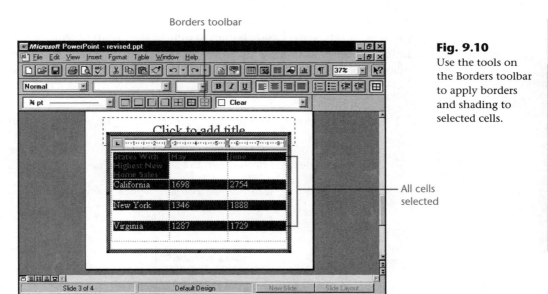

Fig. 9.10
Use the tools on
the Borders toolbar
to apply borders
and shading to
selected cells.

2. Select the cells to which you want to apply shading; for example,
   select the top row of cells.

3. Click the down-arrow beside the Shading drop-down list box on the
   Borders toolbar.

   A drop-down list of different shading styles appears, as shown in
   figure 9.11.

Fig. 9.11
The shading style palette displays various degrees of shading you can apply to selected cells.

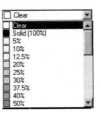

4. Select the desired shading you want to apply to the selected cells.

The cells are automatically formatted using the selected shading.

Sometimes you may want to outline only selected cells in a table with a border while most of the time you will want to outline all cells individually to make distinguishing each cell easier for your audience. When you have more than one cell selected and you want to border each selected cell separately, you need to apply an outside border to outline the group of selected cells and an inside border to separate the selected cells. You can select a different line style for each border you apply, if desired.

Follow these steps:

1. Display the Borders toolbar and select the cells you want to outline with a border.

2. Select the Line Style drop-down list.

A palette of different line styles available appears, as shown in figure 9.12.

Fig. 9.12
Choose the line style you want for the border you just applied.

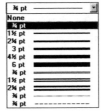

3. Select the line style you want to border your cells.

4. Click the Outside Border button to apply an outside border.

A border is placed around the group of selected cells using the line style you selected.

5. Select a different line style for the inside border, if desired.

6. Click the Inside Border button to separate individual cells if more than one cell is selected.

A border using the line style you selected is placed between selected cells. Deselect the table by clicking inside the table frame.

Editing Table Structure

You can make changes to the structure of a table by adding rows and columns or changing the size of columns and rows. In this section, you learn to use the Word for Windows 95 toolbars and other techniques to edit a table structure.

Changing Column Width

PowerPoint uses many of the same techniques to adjust the width of columns in a table that you use to adjust the width of columns in spreadsheet applications. You can adjust the column width for individual columns separately or select multiple columns to adjust the column widths more uniformly. In addition, you can adjust all columns in the table by instructing Word to provide the column width based on the information contained in each column.

For example, you may want to make a column that contains a primary point wide and the text large and bold. The next column with the explanatory information for each point can be narrower and the text smaller.

To adjust the width of a single column in your table, follow these steps:

1. Position the mouse pointer on the column gridline to the right of the column you want to change making sure that the mouse pointer becomes a two-headed arrow, as shown in figure 9.13.

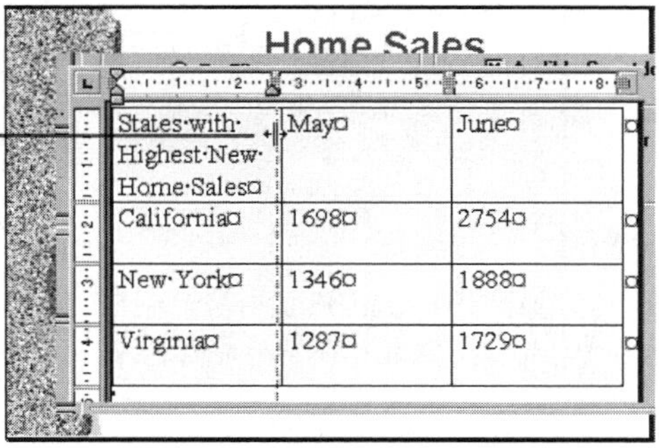

Mouse pointer ———

Fig. 9.13
The mouse pointer changes to a two-headed arrow so that you can adjust the column width.

States·with·Highest·New·Home·Sales☐	May☐	June☐	☐
California☐	1698☐	2754☐	☐
New·York☐	1346☐	1888☐	☐
Virginia☐	1287☐	1729☐	☐

Home Sales

II

Working with Text

2. Click the left mouse button and drag the column gridline to its new width.

   This method adjusts the column width for the column to the left of the gridline. All other columns are compressed into the space available in the table object.

To adjust the width of several adjacent columns, follow these steps:

1. Move the mouse pointer to the top of the first column you want to adjust.

2. When the mouse pointer changes to a down-arrow, click and drag across the columns to be adjusted. Selected columns are highlighted.

3. Double-click any of the vertical gridlines for the selected columns. PowerPoint automatically adjusts all the columns so that they fit the longest data entry in each column.

Tip

The Cell Height and Width option is also available on the shortcut menu when you click the right mouse button after selecting the table.

To automatically adjust all the columns of your table to best fit the information in your table without selecting the columns, follow these steps:

1. Choose Table, Select Table.

   All cells in the table are highlighted.

2. Choose Table, Cell Height and Width.

   The Cell Height and Width dialog box appears, as shown in figure 9.14.

Fig. 9.14

You can use the Cell Height and Width dialog box to make adjustments to all cells in a table or to individual cells.

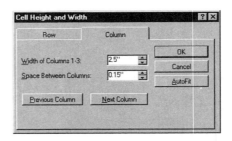

3. Click the Column tab to display the information about column width.

   The selected columns are identified. If they vary in width, no number appears in the Width of Columns #-# text box.

4. Type the desired width for the selected columns in the <u>W</u>idth of Columns spin box or choose <u>A</u>utoFit to let Word make the adjustments for you. The width must be between 0.16 and 7.3.

5. Change the <u>S</u>pace Between Columns to specify the amount of white space you want to place between your columns. The maximum space allowed is 1.24 inches.

> **Note**
>
> If you have at least one column selected when you display the Cell Height and Width dialog box, you can use the <u>P</u>revious Column or <u>N</u>ext Column buttons to adjust the width of the previous or next column in your table without closing the dialog box.

Adjusting Row Height

In addition to being able to change width of columns in your table, you can change the distance between rows in a table by adjusting row height. The procedure for adjusting the height of a row is similar to changing the width of a column. You found that all cells in a column adjusted to the same width when you changed the column width. Adjusting the row height changes all cells in the row to the same height, and you can adjust each row individually or select multiple rows and format them for consistency.

To adjust the height of a row, follow these steps:

1. Position the mouse pointer on the vertical ruler on the left of the table.

   The bottom of each row is identified by a double line marker in the vertical ruler (refer to fig. 9.2). When you position the mouse pointer on the marker, it changes to a vertical two-headed arrow.

2. Select the row marker at the bottom of the row you want to adjust.

3. Drag the row marker up to make the row narrower or down to widen the row.

   The row gridline moves with the marker.

4. When the row is sized appropriately, release the mouse button.

Working with Text

II

You can also use the Cell Height and Width dialog box to change the height for a single row or multiple rows. To use this dialog box, follow these steps:

1. Select the row or rows you want to adjust.

2. Choose Table, Cell Height and Width or choose Cell Height and Width from the shortcut menu.

   The Cell Height and Width dialog box appears.

3. Click the Row tab.

4. Select one of the following options from the Height of Rows drop-down list:

   ■ *Auto:* Automatically adjusts the row height to fit the largest size text in the row.

   ■ *At Least:* Automatically formats the row height to a minimum value but widens the row to accommodate larger text.

   ■ *Exactly:* Sets a specific row height point size.

5. Type the row height you want in the At spin box or click the up or down arrows until the desired height is shown.

6. In the Indent From Left text box, enter the distance from the left edge of the cell you want your text indented.

7. Select the desired Alignment for text in each cell in the row.

8. Select the Allow Row to Break Across Pages check box to indicate that the text in a row can be broken across a page when necessary.

9. Choose OK to apply the changes.

> **Note**
>
> You can also adjust the Previous Row or Next Row from the Cell Height and Width dialog box. Use the same procedures described previously to format column width for the previous or next column.

Inserting and Deleting Rows and Columns

If you decide that the table you have created is too small to display the information you need, you can add additional rows and columns. In addition, many people forget to include a row and/or column for row and column labels when they set up their tables. To modify the size of your table, you can use Word for Windows 95 tools to insert or delete rows and columns. Word even contains a button on the Standard toolbar once it is displayed, which provides a shortcut for adding rows or columns.

To add a row at the top or in the middle of a table, follow these steps:

1. Create a table on the desired slide and position the insertion point on the row where you want the new row to appear.

2. Click the Insert Rows button on the Standard toolbar or choose Table, Insert Rows.

    A new row appears at the insertion point location, as shown in figure 9.15.

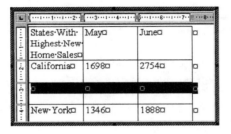

To insert a row at the bottom of a table, follow these directions:

1. Position the cursor in the last row and in the column to the far right of the table (the last cell in the table).

2. Press Tab.

    A new row appears at the bottom of the table.

To insert a column at the beginning or in the middle of the table, complete the following:

1. Position the insertion point at the top of the column where you want the new column to appear, making sure that the mouse pointer is a filled down-pointing arrow.

2. Click the left mouse button to select the column, as shown in figure 9.16.

Tip

To access the Word toolbars from an existing table on a PowerPoint slide, just double-click the table object to return to edit the table.

Fig. 9.15
The new row appears at the insertion point location.

II

Working with Text

Tip

If you add a row in the wrong location, click the Undo button to remove the row and try again to place it appropriately.

Mouse pointer

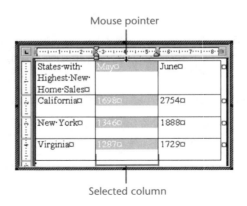

Selected column

The selected column appears, as shown in figure 9.16. PowerPoint knows that you have a column selected and decides you probably want to perform a column action. As a result, the button on the Standard toolbar that you used to insert rows can now be used to insert columns.

3. Click the Insert Columns button on the Standard toolbar or choose Table, Insert Columns.

A new column assumes the position of the selected column, and the selected column moves to the right.

Tip
You can also select
a column, position
the mouse pointer
on the selected
column and click
the right mouse
button to display
the shortcut
menu. Choose the
Insert Columns
option to add a
new column.

To add a column on the right side of a table, follow these instructions:

1. Position the mouse pointer above the area to the right of the last column and outside the table.

The mouse pointer changes to the same down-pointing dark arrow illustrated in figure 9.16.

2. Use one of the procedures described earlier to insert a column.

When you increase the number of rows or columns in a table, PowerPoint does not automatically increase the size of the table object on the slide. As a result, before you can see the new column, you may need to drag a resize handle to increase the size of the table frame. Figure 9.17 shows a table with numerous rows and columns. Notice how the table extends over the edge of the slide at this time. You can easily use your mouse to drag the table frame back onto the slide.

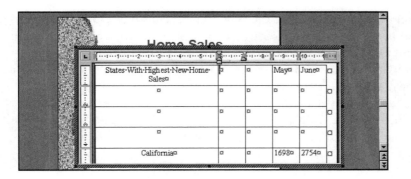

Troubleshooting

When I tried to resize a column by dragging the column selector on the ruler, only one cell in one row changed size. All the rest of the cells in the column stayed the same size; what happened?

When using the column selector on the ruler, if you select a row, then only the selected row is affected when the column border is moved. You can sidestep this problem by dragging the column gridline instead of the column selector, or by deselecting the row first.

Returning the Table to PowerPoint

After your table is complete, it is time to return to PowerPoint and view the table as it appears on the slide. The table you created is placed on the PowerPoint slide as an embedded object because you used Microsoft Word for Windows to create the table. However, because you only opened a module of Word through PowerPoint, the object "belongs" to PowerPoint and is not stored as a separate object outside the presentation. Therefore, you will not be able to open the table the next time you start or use Microsoft Word for Windows.

Does that mean you can't use the table in Word or Excel or any other Windows application? Of course not! You can select the table object on the PowerPoint slide and copy it to the Windows Clipboard. After starting another Windows application and opening a document, you can paste the table from the Clipboard into the document. You learn more about the different techniques you can use to share information in Chapter 19.

II

Working with Text

For now, you want to place the table you just constructed onto your slide. To do this, simply click the mouse pointer outside the table frame. The Microsoft Word for Windows menus and toolbars are replaced with the PowerPoint menus and toolbars, and the table appears in its default size on the slide, as shown in figure 9.18. Notice that the table object remains selected so that you can use the size handles to resize the object using the same techniques you used to resize graphic objects. Use figure 9.18 as a guide to adding the final column width and text alignment adjustments to your table.

Fig. 9.18
The table remains selected when you return it to PowerPoint so that you can easily size and position it.

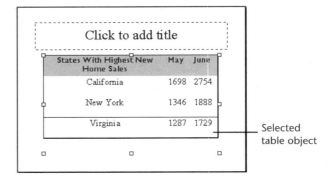

At times you will need to edit the data or table structure of an existing table on a PowerPoint slide. To start the Word module so that you can revise your table, simply display the slide containing the table and double-click the table.

Creating a Chart from a Table

When your table contains labels and numeric values, you can use the information to create a chart. It's really quite easy. Follow these directions:

1. Display the slide in PowerPoint that contains the table you want to graph.

2. Double-click the table object to start the table feature in Microsoft Word.

3. Select the cells you want to include in the graph, making sure to include the column and row headings for the values you select.

4. Choose Insert, Object.

    The Object dialog box opens, as shown in figure 9.19.

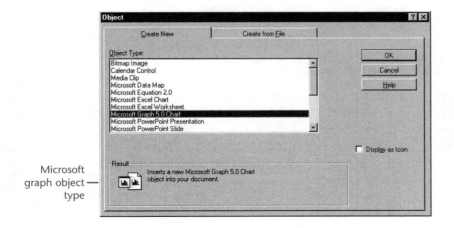

Fig. 9.19
The Object dialog box lists the different types of objects you can insert into a PowerPoint presentation.

Microsoft graph object type

5. From the Create New tab, select Microsoft Graph 5.0 and choose OK.

   The Microsoft Graph application opens and displays the ChartWizard.

6. Select a chart type from the ChartWizard and choose Finish.

   The chart appears in Microsoft Graph.

7. Choose File, Exit & Return to *filename*.

   Microsoft Graph closes. Your chart appears below the table on your Word Table window on the PowerPoint slide, as shown in figure 9.20.

8. Click the slide outside of the Word Table window to apply the table and graph to the PowerPoint slide.

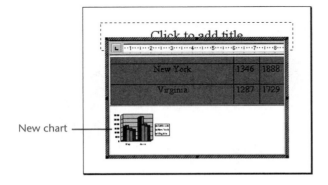

New chart

Fig. 9.20
The chart appears below the table on your PowerPoint slide.

You can leave the graph exactly as it appears, size it, move it to a new location, or copy it to another slide in your presentation. You learn more about graphing in Chapters 14, "Creating Basic Charts"; 15, "Customizing Charts"; and 16, "Creating Organizational Charts."

Tables can be an effective way to summarize information in a presentation so that you can review it efficiently. It also provides a basis for creating a graph, when necessary. Remember that Microsoft Word for Windows 95 must be installed on your system before you can adequately use the table feature in PowerPoint. In addition, Microsoft Graph must be available for use when you want to graph table data. This integration of a number of different applications can be an effective tool which, when used properly, can richly enhance your presentations.❖

Part III

Adding Illustrations

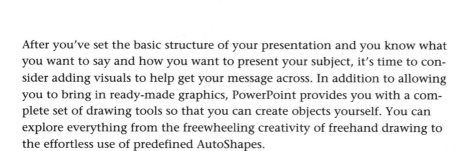

Chapter 10

Drawing Objects

by Nancy Stevenson

After you've set the basic structure of your presentation and you know what you want to say and how you want to present your subject, it's time to consider adding visuals to help get your message across. In addition to allowing you to bring in ready-made graphics, PowerPoint provides you with a complete set of drawing tools so that you can create objects yourself. You can explore everything from the freewheeling creativity of freehand drawing to the effortless use of predefined AutoShapes.

With PowerPoint, you can use shapes and color to emphasize a specific point or piece of information. Figures can be scaled, rotated, or have shadows applied to them to fit your needs. This chapter shows you how to use the PowerPoint drawing tools to help you create a visually striking presentation that can inform and persuade your audience.

In this chapter, you learn to

- Draw lines, arcs and polygons, and use AutoShapes

- Use vertical, horizontal, and 45-degree angle lines

- Draw lines, arcs, and polygons from a center point

- Use guides and grids to align objects

Using PowerPoint's Drawing Tools

For many presenters, the stylized backgrounds that come with PowerPoint provide enough of a visual framework for their presentations. Other people may want to add a company logo or graph. Still others find a need to draw an image of their own to get a point across—a bold arrow pointing to a key point, for example—or to provide a simple diagram of a product, process, or organizational structure (see fig. 10.1). With PowerPoint's professional drawing tools, you can draw and revise shapes, lines, text, and pictures to create the professional presentation you're aiming for. Each of the objects you draw for your slide is infinitely adjustable.

Fig. 10.1
A simple line drawing of the product drives home the point in the text.

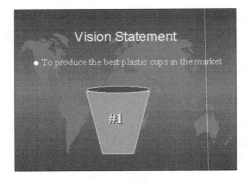

▶ See "Manipulating Objects," p. 288

▶ See "Customizing Toolbars," p. 692

The PowerPoint window contains a complete set of drawing tools on the Drawing toolbar. By default, this toolbar is located along the left side of your window. The Drawing toolbar has 15 tool buttons. You can add buttons to the toolbar, move the toolbar, or cause it to be a free-floating object, depending upon your needs. There's also a Drawing+ toolbar, which is used mainly for manipulating objects once you've drawn them.

The Drawing tools are described in table 10.1.

Table 10.1	Drawing Tools	
Icon	**Tool Name**	**Use To**
⬚	Selection Tool	Select any object. This tool is selected by default.
A	Text Tool	Enter text in a text box.
⬚	Line Tool	Draw a single straight line.
⬚	Rectangle Tool	Draw boxes or rectangles.

Icon	Tool Name	Use To
	Ellipse Tool	Draw ellipses and circles.
	Arc Tool	Draw curved lines from two selected end-points.
	Freeform Tool	Draw a many-sided figure. It enables you to continue to draw lines until you connect the beginning point with the endpoint.
	Free Rotate Tool	Rotate an object by one of the four corner points. Any object can be rotated in a full 360-degree circle.
	AutoShapes	Display the AutoShapes toolbar from which you can select a predefined shape. These shapes can be manipulated the same way other shapes or lines are.
	Fill On/Off	Automatically apply or remove the default fill pattern to the selected object.
	Line Color On/Off	Apply or remove color to a line to make it visible.
	Shadow On/Off	Automatically apply or remove the default shadow type to the selected object.
	Line Style	Choose line styles and thicknesses to apply to the selected line.
	Arrowheads	Add arrowheads to the selected line.
	Dashed Lines	Choose dashed line styles to apply to the selected line.

95

95

III

Adding Illustrations

Drawing Basic Shapes

Many of the most complicated drawings start with the simplest shapes: the line, the arc, and the polygon. If you use these objects for the basis of your drawings, you can create the emphasis that you want to make your point. You don't need to be an artist to create these simple shapes with PowerPoint.

But if you're ready to create more complex drawings, you can also easily combine pieces of a drawing to complete a single drawing. For example, the cup in figure 10.1 combines an AutoShape for the base of the cup and an ellipse for the mouth of the cup.

Drawing Lines

Let's start with something simple. The line is the most basic building block of drawing. To draw a line, follow these steps:

1. Open the slide that you want to draw on.

2. Click the Line Tool button on the Drawing toolbar.

3. Move the pointer to the slide and to the beginning point of your line. Notice how the mouse pointer changes to a crosshair when you cross onto the slide boundary.

4. Click and hold down the mouse button at this point and then drag the pointer to the endpoint of your line.

5. Release the mouse button to indicate the line's endpoint. The line appears with a sizing handle on each end (see fig. 10.2).

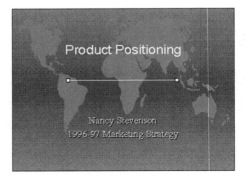

Fig. 10.2
When selected, a line drawn on your slide appears with sizing handles.

Manipulating and Moving a Line

Any PowerPoint object can be manipulated or moved to anywhere on your slide. You can quickly resize, move, or tilt a line. To adjust your line, follow these steps:

- To move the object, place the mouse pointer at the center of your line and click and hold down the mouse button. The solid line changes to a dotted line. Now drag the line to its new location.

- To resize the line, click and drag one of the handles at the ends of the line.

  You can extend the line by simply moving the handle in the same direction as the rest of the line.

- To tilt the line, drag it up or down (see fig. 10.3). The opposite endpoint remains stationary throughout these movements.

Fig. 10.3
Drag one of the ends up to tilt your line at an angle.

Drawing an Arc

Of course, not every line is a straight line and not every item that you want to show in your slide can be illustrated by using straight lines. With PowerPoint, you also have the capability to draw arcs. An arc is a curved line between two points. You can adjust the curve of the arc to fit your specific needs.

To draw an arc or curved line, follow these steps:

1. Select the Arc tool by clicking it once.

2. Move the pointer to the place where you want to begin the arc. Click and hold the mouse button.

3. Drag the pointer to the endpoint of your arc and release the mouse button. Your arc looks something like the one shown in figure 10.4.

Notice that there are two types of handles that appear on a selected arc. You use the eight square handles that surround it to resize the object; drag on these, and the arc stretches out to the left or right. To resize the arc, move the mouse pointer down to the midpoint handle on the right and drag it to the middle of your screen. Your arc has been stretched. The beginning point has remained stationary, while the endpoint has moved further to the right along the same plane.

III

Adding Illustrations

Fig. 10.4
An arc can be both resized and reshaped using the handles that appear here.

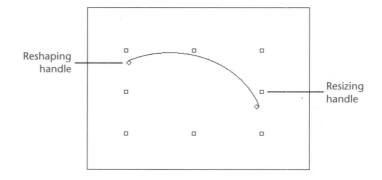

Use the two diamond-shaped handles at either end of the line to reshape it. When you drag on these handles, the arc is widened, making the pie-shaped piece bigger or smaller. If dragged far enough, a reshaping handle can create a 360-degree arc, which is actually a full ellipse. To reshape the arc, click on a reshaping handle and drag up to make a smaller arc, and down to make a larger arc.

Do not hesitate to experiment with your drawing. Try each of the handles to see just what it does. As you try each movement, you'll gain confidence in your drawing abilities. Figure 10.5 shows a series of arcs used with a clip art telephone to create a sound wave effect on a slide.

Fig. 10.5
You can combine clip art with arcs or other kinds of lines to create a special effect.

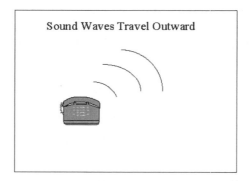

Sound Waves Travel Outward

Note

To delete an object you've drawn, simply click the object to select it, and then press Del or Backspace.

Drawing Freeform Objects

Polygons, or freeform shapes, can be used to draw many things with multiple or uneven sides, such as the star shape or the hand in figure 10.6. These shapes can be either closed or open. A polygon is closed when the beginning and endpoints meet, and it's open when the endpoints do not meet. When polygons are made up of a series of straight lines, they can have a sharp geometric accuracy, as the star does. For the less-sophisticated, but sometimes appropriate look of hand-drawn art, you can use a truly freeform polygon.

Fig. 10.6
The star and hand can both be drawn with different methods using the Freeform tool.

To draw a geometric freeform shape, follow these steps:

1. Click the Freeform tool.

2. Move the pointer to the slide and click the left mouse button once to anchor the beginning point. Do not hold down the button.

3. Move the pointer to the next corner and click the mouse button again. This anchors the next point. You can draw as many lines as you like in any direction, even crossing back over lines you already drew.

4. To finish the polygon, do either of the following:

■ Close the polygon by clicking the end drawing point on the beginning point. PowerPoint immediately changes the pointer from a crosshair to the arrow, applies the default fill pattern or color, and displays the eight resizing handles around the polygon.

■ Double-click the mouse button or press Enter.

Either of these actions completes an open polygon, and the eight resizing handles surrounding the polygon display again.

III

Adding Illustrations

Drawing in the less-structured freeform mode is similar in that you can create as many segments as you want, and you end the drawing mode in the same way.

1. Click on the Freeform tool.

2. Move your cursor to the slide, and click on the beginning point.

3. Hold down the mouse button. You see the pointer shape change to a pencil. You can then use the mouse to "draw" on your slide as if with a pencil.

Troubleshooting

I made a mistake on a freeform drawing. How do I back up and correct it?

Simply press Backspace. This deletes the last endpoint you made. You can back up as far as you need by pressing the Backspace key. Each previous endpoint is deleted up to, but not including, the beginning point.

You may want to try this method, but it takes a very steady hand to draw successfully in this manner. With practice, though, you can get better, and there are times when you may want this less-polished look.

> **Note**
>
> If you make a mistake while drawing and want to modify your shape, you can. Just double-click the drawn object, and several black reshaping handles appear on its lines. Drag on any of these to reshape the object. With the first type of freeform object, you are allowed, in effect, to move the end points of the lines that form it. With the second type of drawing, there are many more reshaping handles, allowing you to manipulate almost every point along your freeform line to reshape it.

Using Rectangles and Ellipses

In addition to lines, arcs, and freeform drawing, you also have access to tools that help you draw standard geometric shapes such as circles, ellipses (oblong circles), squares, and rectangles. By using these tools, you can draw a more exact figure without the potential jagged edges and bumps associated with the freeform objects or even with a geometric form created from four separate lines.

To draw an ellipse, follow these steps:

1. Click the Ellipse tool.

2. Move the crosshair pointer to the slide. To place an ellipse, click and hold the pointer at the position where you want to place one of the corners of the ellipse object.

3. Drag the pointer until the ellipse is the shape and size you want and then release the mouse button. You have an ellipse similar to one of those shown in figure 10.7. Remember, you can always drag the ellipse to another location or adjust its size and shape with the sizing handles if it's not quite in the place or at the size that you need.

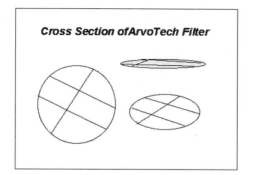

Cross Section of ArvoTech Filter

Fig. 10.7
This slide shows various ellipse shapes combined with lines to form simple product diagrams.

Troubleshooting

When I draw an object it appears in a very pale gray that's almost impossible to see. How do I make it easier to view on my screen and printouts?

If the default color for new objects has been changed from black, when you first draw an object it may appear to be only a pale line. You need to use the Line Color tool to change it to black. You can also select Format, Colors and Lines, select black line color, and make it the default for new objects. Now anything you draw will have a black outline.

To draw a rectangle or square, follow these steps:

1. Click the Rectangle tool.

2. Move the crosshair pointer to the position on the slide where you want to start your rectangle. You draw a rectangle by showing PowerPoint where you want the two opposite corners placed.

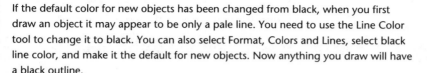

3. Click and drag the pointer to the opposite corner for this rectangle and release the mouse button.

You now have either a square or rectangle with dimensions and location on the slide defined by your beginning and ending points.

Enhancing an Object with Fills, Color, and Shadows

In addition to drawing an object, you can enhance an object by applying colors, fill patterns, and shadows. By using color, you can make your presentation more attractive and emphasize a particular point or object. Fill patterns are useful when you must show your presentation in a non-color printed form. You can apply various fill patterns or shadings instead of using color. Shadows can be used to give your slide more of a 3-D effect. With PowerPoint, you can adjust shadows to give a greater feeling of depth.

Modifying Colors and Lines

▶ See "Enhancing Placeholders and Objects," p. 299

You can change the style of line that surrounds and defines the shape of your object. You can also add various colors, patterns, and textures to fill the area inside the defining line. And you can combine these techniques to create other effects.

To access the Color and Lines dialog box, where changes to lines and fills are made, follow these steps:

1. Select an object, such as the star shape drawn earlier. Remember, an object is selected when the eight object handles surround it.

2. Click the right mouse button to display the shortcut menu, which appears at the mouse pointer's location.

3. Choose the Colors and Lines option from the shortcut menu. You now see the Colors and Lines dialog box, as displayed in figure 10.8.

Note

Each drawn object consists of two parts. The *border* is the first part, and it appears as a line. A rectangle's border consists of the four lines that create it, while a circle is comprised of a single line.

The second part of an object is its *interior*. You can change the attributes for each part of an object from the Colors and Lines dialog box.

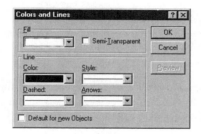

Fig. 10.8
The Colors and
Lines dialog box
controls both the
outer edge and
inner fill of an
object.

From the Colors and Lines dialog box, you can change many attributes of the objects that you draw. Almost all these options can be combined to create the specific effect that you're looking for.

In the Colors and Lines dialog box, select from the following options to change the appearance of lines:

- ■ *Color.* Select a color for the line or border of the object. You can choose No Line if you want to use a fill pattern with no border on a closed object.

- ■ *Dashed.* Select one of the five styles of dashed lines. The style you choose is applied to the border line surrounding the selected object. The default selection is a solid line.

You can also make changes to this line by using the Dashed Lines tool on the Drawing toolbar.

- ■ *Arrows.* When you want to use a line to point out another object or to show the flow from one part of a process to the next, select one of the three styles of arrowheads. You can choose to have an arrowhead on the left, right, or both ends of your line. The default option, again, is a solid line without arrowheads. This option is available only for objects with two endpoints, such as a line, arc, or open polygon.

You can also add arrows using the Arrowheads tool on the Drawing toolbar.

- ■ *Style.* Choose from six solid lines of various widths and four other styles of multiple lines. You can also make your line style selection using the Line Style tool on the Drawing toolbar.

Troubleshooting

I know that I've drawn an object and made it invisible by selecting No Fill and No Line. How do I find this object again?

Using the Selection Tool, draw a selection box that surrounds the entire slide. You now see the resize handles for each object on your slide, including the invisible object. Click one of the resize handles with the right mouse button and change the line or fill type to a color. Your object can now be seen.

You can also change what appears inside the lines that form the border of your object.

If you want to be able to see through whatever effect you apply to any objects beneath it, you can select Semi-Transparent to get a shaded effect.

To determine which color or effect will be applied, click on the arrow on the Fill drop-down list. From the Fill drop-down list, you can choose from these options:

▶ See "Using Colors and Patterns Effectively," p. 665

- *Eight color block selections.* This option provides a quick way to select any of the default color settings that are always available to you.

- *No Fill.* This option is selected if you do not want a fill pattern or color to be applied.

- *Automatic.* This option applies the default fill color

- *Background.* This option applies the default background color or pattern to the selected object.

- *Shaded.* This option displays the Shaded Fill dialog box. You can use this dialog box to select some specialized shading effects.

- *Patterned.* This option displays the Pattern Fill dialog box. You select from 36 different pattern options. You can also select different background and foreground color options.

- *Textured.* This option offers a variety of textures, such as marble, paper, fabric, or wood, so you can fill your object.

- *Other Color.* This option displays the Colors dialog box, from which you can select from a palette of 144 colors on the Standard tab. If you click the Custom Tab, you can mix your own unique colors. Your options are limited only by your video graphics adapter and your monitor. When you select other colors, they're added to the bottom of the Fill drop-down list. You can add up to eight other colors. When you add a ninth color, the first color of the eight you selected drops from the group. You can always reselect it, but you're limited to a maximum of 16 colors on the drop-down list.

The Shaded, Patterned, and Textured items in the Fill drop-down list each take you to another dialog box to make your choice. Try applying a Patterned look to see how this works.

1. Select the Patterned option from the Fill drop-down list. The Pattern Fill dialog box appears.

2. From the Pattern Fill dialog box in figure 10.9, select the fill pattern to use, and then click OK.

    You return to the Colors and Lines dialog box, where the selected pattern appears in the Fill box in the Colors and Lines dialog box.

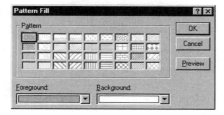

Fig. 10.9
You can choose from many patterns to fill objects in PowerPoint.

3. If you want, select an option from the Line Color drop-down list. This list is similar to the one displayed by the Fill option. You can select a color for your line from the default block of eight colors or add colors by choosing other colors and using the Colors dialog box.

> **Note**
>
> When you add other colors in the Fill drop-down list, those same colors are added as choices in the Color drop-down list and vice versa. Change one, and the other changes as well.

In the Color drop-down list, you can also select the option No Line. PowerPoint shows your object without a line surrounding it.

Tip
If both your background and foreground color selections in this dialog box are white, no patterns will show. You must adjust these colors to get darker or lighter patterns, and then make your choice.

III

Adding Illustrations

> **Caution**
>
> If you create an object that has the same fill pattern or color as your slide and then select the No Line option, your object becomes invisible. It's still there, but you can't see it. Click in the area where the object is in. When you finally click one of its lines, the selector box displays around the object.

4. To see your effects applied, click OK in the Colors and Lines dialog box. Figure 10.10 shows you how the choice of a very thick line style combined with a Textured pattern looks when applied to the star shape.

Fig. 10.10
An object with a textured fill and thick line style.

 Finally, you can make these settings the default settings for colors and lines by selecting Default for <u>N</u>ew Objects while in the Colors and Lines dialog box.

Placing Shadows

▶ See "Using Special Background Effects," p. 674

Placing a shadow behind an object adds a 3-D effect to your slide. To place a shadow, follow these steps:

1. Select an object to apply a shadow to—for example, a simple ellipse or rectangle.

2. From the Format menu, choose Shadow. The Shadow dialog box appears (see fig. 10.11).

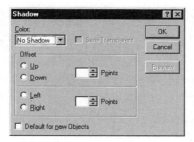

Fig. 10.11
The Shadow dialog
box helps you add
effects that give a
3-D feel to objects.

3. From the Color drop-down list, select a color that's darker than your
   object and background. This list shows the eight default color blocks
   and the four options: No Shadow, Automatic, Embossed, and Other
   Color. If you have added other colors, the color blocks appear at the
   end of the drop-down list.

   After you select a color for a shadow, notice that two of the buttons in
   the block labeled Offset are turned on and that numbers are placed in
   the two text boxes labeled Points. From here you control the perceived
   location of the light source and the distance of your object from the
   background.

4. If your light source is supposed to be coming from above and to the
   left, your shadow should be offset down and to the right. This means
   that you should click the Down and Right buttons.

5. To make your object appear farther from the background, increase the
   numbers in the two Points text boxes. Alternatively, decrease the numbers if you want your object to appear close to the background.

6. Choose Down and enter the number of points that you want the
   shadow to appear from your object.

7. Choose Right and again enter the number of points that you want the
   shadow to appear from your object.

8. Click OK to apply your shadow. Figure 10.12 shows a shadow applied to
   the object on the slide.

Tip
Be careful to use
the same shadow
settings for various
objects on a single
slide so the light
source is consis-
tent.

III

Adding Illustrations

Fig. 10.12
The drawn object now has a shadow effect at the bottom and to the right.

▶ See "Shading," p. 675

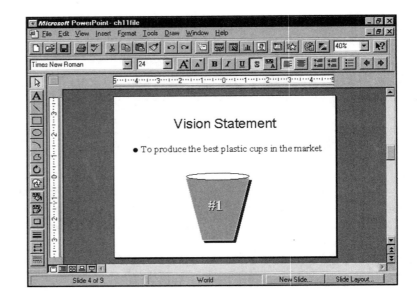

Drawing AutoShapes

PowerPoint for Windows comes equipped with a number of predefined shapes called AutoShapes. These shapes are fully adjustable in size, and many include an additional adjusting handle to reshape the object in some way. You access AutoShapes by clicking on the AutoShape tool on the Drawing toolbar. When you click on this tool, the AutoShapes toolbar shows a button for each of the shapes. By simply clicking an AutoShape button and dragging, you can place the shape on your slide.

You have already become familiar with two AutoShapes that appear on the Drawing toolbar: the ellipse and the rectangle. The other AutoShapes are used in a similar way.

The AutoShapes toolbar shown in figure 10.13 displays the 24 AutoShapes available to you. Some of the shapes include a starburst, a star, several forms of arrows, a cross, a box, and a voice balloon.

Fig. 10.13
Draw everything from stars to starbursts easily using an AutoShape.

As with all the drawing tools, you can combine AutoShapes with each other and with freeform shapes to build complex objects. To use AutoShapes, follow these steps:

1. Click the AutoShapes button on the Drawing toolbar. The AutoShapes toolbar appears. By default, the AutoShapes toolbar docks above the slide window.

2. Select the Thin Up Arrow tool and move the pointer to the slide.

3. Click the pointer to anchor the beginning point and drag to the endpoint for this object. Then release the mouse button. Your arrow should look something like the arrow on the left in figure 10.14.

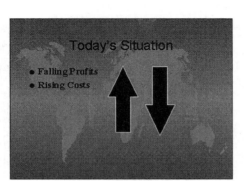

Fig. 10.14
Use AutoShapes to emphasize points in the text graphically.

Tip
You can make the AutoShapes toolbar into a floating toolbar. Just click anywhere around its edge (avoid the Close button or a shape button) and drag it where you want it.

4. When selected, an AutoShape object has eight handles around it. Several shapes, including this arrow, also have a small yellow diamond, which is an adjusting handle. Move the pointer to the adjusting handle and drag it forward toward the arrow's point. Notice that the pointer changes shape from the traditional arrow to a small arrowhead.

While not all AutoShapes have an adjusting handle, all AutoShapes do have the normal complement of eight resizing handles.

Note

To draw multiple copies of the same shape one right after the other, double-click the shape in the AutoShapes toolbar. Then draw as many objects of that shape as you like. To finish, click on another AutoShape or click to close the Autoshapes toolbar.

III

Adding Illustrations

Rotating Objects

Any object created in PowerPoint for Windows can be rotated with the Free Rotate tool. You can even rotate title bars and text boxes. The capability to freely rotate an object gives you a great deal of creative freedom—you're no longer limited to displaying objects and text in a single horizontal plane.

You can easily draw objects, add text, and then move these objects and rotate them to suit your own requirements. To see how the Free Rotate tool is used, follow these steps:

1. Draw an object in a slide, and select it.

2. Select the Free Rotate tool on the Drawing toolbar. Move the selector to one of the four corner handles of the object on the slide (see fig. 10.15).

3. Click and drag the object to its new location. Figure 10.15 shows an object after it was rotated, with the corner rotator handles still visible.

Fig. 10.15
Rotate this a cube to give the impression of an object tumbling through space.

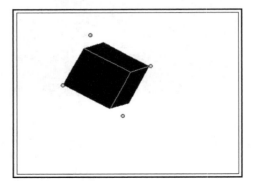

You can even draw an object, place text within it, group the two objects together, and then rotate them as a unit.

Drawing Precisely

▶ See "Layering Objects," p. 302

When creating a presentation, neatness counts almost as much as content. The last thing you want to do is distract your audience with sloppy drawings. You can use several methods to help you to use your drawing tools accurately.

Drawing Vertical, Horizontal, and 45-Degree Angle Lines

At times, you won't want to draw lines freehand. You want a line that is exactly horizontal, vertical, or at a 45-degree angle, but you don't need a rectangle or right triangle. You can easily draw such lines with PowerPoint for Windows.

To draw perfectly horizontal, vertical, and 45-degree angle lines, follow these steps:

1. Click the Line Tool button on the Drawing toolbar.

2. Move the pointer to the slide.

3. Press and hold Shift, click and hold down the mouse button, and drag to create your line. With this method, you can't place the endpoint of the line on anything other than a perfect vertical, horizontal or 45-degree angle from the beginning point. Once the line is drawn, though, you can drag either endpoint to angle it any way you like.

Drawing Uniform Shapes

When you try to draw a perfectly round circle with the ellipse tool, you have to count on your own judgment. But PowerPoint provides a method to draw shapes like circles and perfect squares precisely. These uniform (also called regular) shapes include squares, circles, and other shapes that can be drawn within a square. Regular shapes are symmetrical, and can include the AutoShapes buttons. You cannot turn a freeform-drawn shape into a regular shape.

To draw uniform shapes, follow these steps:

1. Select the Ellipse tool from the Drawing toolbar and move the pointer to the slide.

2. Press and hold the Shift key and click and hold the mouse button, and then drag an ellipse on the slide. PowerPoint for Windows forces the shape to be a regular circle on your slide.

> **Note**
>
> You can also turn a non-regular shape, such as an ellipse or a rectangle, into a regular shape quickly. Simply double-click any of the resizing handles. The object changes to a regular shape: an ellipse to a circle, a rectangle to a square. If you use this method, you always change your shape into a regular shape along the shorter of the up/down and left/right axes.

Drawing Objects from a Center Point

You can also easily draw an object outward from a center. This can be especially helpful if you know exactly where you want an object to be placed on your slide. You can use this technique with any object except for objects drawn with the freeform tool.

To draw an object from a center point, follow these steps:

Tip
You can draw an object using both the center point and uniform shape methods by pressing Ctrl + Shift, then dragging to draw the object.

1. Select the tool to draw with—for example, select the Rectangle tool.

2. Move the pointer to the position on the slide that corresponds to the center point of the object that you want to draw.

3. Press and hold Ctrl and the mouse button as you drag the rectangle on your slide. Notice how PowerPoint draws a mirror image of the rectangle on the opposite side of the center point as you drag the pointer.

4. When your object is the size that you want, release the mouse button and then the Ctrl Key to complete the object.

> **Note**
>
> If you release the Ctrl key as you draw an object, your object will immediately be redrawn, or shifted, so that your starting point of the drawing becomes the opposite corner instead of the center point. If this isn't what you want, press and continue to hold Ctrl again. Your drawing will again snap to the position that it was in, with the starting point as the center point again.

Aligning Objects

Aligning objects in relation to the edges of the slide and to each other can make the difference between an attractive, balanced design and a sloppy slide. PowerPoint for Windows has two methods that can help you align your objects. One tool is called *guides,* and the other is a set of *gridlines.* These tools are available to you from the menu bar.

Using Guides

To give your slides the most professional appearance possible, you may want to align some or all of your objects. Use guide lines to help you provide vertical and horizontal axes lines that meet in the exact center of your slide. You can move the guide lines from their origination point at the exact center of your slide. PowerPoint for Windows provides an on-screen measurement that represents how far from the center point you moved the guide line. For example, you could use guide lines if you have a slide that shows an arrow and a hexagon and you want to place the center of both objects one inch below the horizontal center of the slide.

To align two objects, follow these steps:

1. From the View menu, choose Guides. Two dotted lines appear on your slide—one vertical and the other horizontal. As figure 10.16 shows, they intersect at the exact center point of your slide.

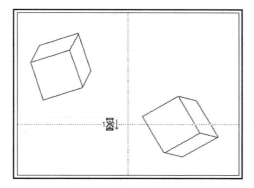

Fig. 10.16
Guide lines provide a precise measurement on-screen for exact placement of objects.

2. Click the horizontal guide line and drag the line down. When you click on the line, you see the mouse pointer replaced by the number 0.00. As you drag the line, notice that the number increases. You also see an arrow to the right of, or beneath, the number (see fig. 10.17). This arrow indicates whether you're above, below, left, or right of the center point.

3. Drag the line down until you reach the point where you want to align your objects. For the example given above, you'd drag the mouse until the number reads 1.00 and then release the mouse button.

Fig. 10.17
While moving guide lines, a measurement shows exactly how far from the exact center you're moving.

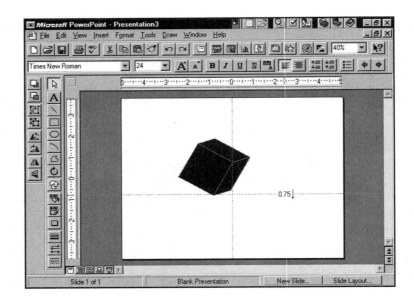

4. Now you can move the objects until they are centered on the horizontal guide line. If you move the objects slowly across the line, you see them snapping to the guide line.

> **Note**
>
> If you need to align different groups of objects at different points, simply place the guide lines for the first group and then align them. Move the guide lines for the next objects to be aligned and align them. The first objects do not move with the guide lines. Once an object has been aligned in a specific position, moving the guide lines has no further effect unless you move the object again.

5. Remove the guide lines by choosing Guides from the View menu again. This removes both the guide lines and the check mark from the menu option.

Using the Grid

PowerPoint for Windows comes equipped with another alignment method called the grid. You can turn the grid on or off at any time. The grid consists of a series of invisible lines, both horizontal and vertical, that are located across your slide screen. When the grid is turned on, your objects automatically snap to the closest gridline. If you use the gridlines and drag two objects to the same approximate location, they are likely to snap into exact alignment.

Depending on the measurement system that you selected for PowerPoint for Windows, you have either 12 gridlines per inch or five gridlines per centimeter. Draw any object, such as an ellipse or rectangle, and then follow these steps:

1. Click on the Zoom Control drop-down list, and increase the magnification to 300%. Turn on the guide lines by selecting <u>V</u>iew, <u>G</u>uides.

2. From the Draw menu, choose Snap to Grid.

> **Note**
>
> The Snap to Grid option is normally on by default when you first start PowerPoint. If a checkmark is displayed beside the menu option, Snap to Grid is on.

3. Select and drag an object upward. Notice that it does not move smoothly with the mouse pointer, but in small steps with a jerky motion.

4. Place the mouse pointer on the horizontal guide line and drag it up. You see the numbers change from 1.00 to 0.92 to 0.83, for example. These are the distances from one gridline to the next. You see that the distance is not even, because 12 gridlines per inch does not work out to an exact two decimal point number.

To see how objects move without the gridlines, follow these steps:

1. From the Draw menu, choose Snap to Grid to turn off the gridlines and remove the checkmark displayed to the left of the menu option.

2. Select the horizontal guide line and drag it up again. Notice that the change in the measurement increments is as little as 0.01 inch now.

3. Select the object again. Drag it up and down the slide. Notice that the movement is now smooth, not jerky. PowerPoint for Windows is no longer snapping the object from one gridline to the next.

The gridline option is always turned on by default in PowerPoint for Windows. If you want to place objects with greater precision than that enabled by the grid, turn it off and align your objects.

Tip
You can temporarily turn off the Snap to Grid action by pressing Alt as you drag an object.

III

Adding Illustrations

In this chapter, you have learned about the various drawing objects you can create with PowerPoint. In the next chapter, "Selecting, Editing and Enhancing Graphic Objects," you will learn more about moving, resizing, framing, and scaling objects.❖

Chapter 11

Selecting, Editing, and Enhancing Graphic Objects

by Nancy Stevenson

PowerPoint handles many different types of data in a convenient and consistent way. Every data type you can possibly include in a PowerPoint presentation—charts, drawings, imported pictures, clip art, body text, organizational charts, movies, and sound—is considered an object in PowerPoint. With rare exceptions, all these data types are handled similarly and are manipulated and changed on slides in the same way. That's what this chapter is about: The basic mechanics of handling objects on the PowerPoint screen.

In this chapter, you learn how to

- Select, delete, and move objects

- Copy and paste objects

- Rotate and flip objects

- Apply background colors, patterns, and shading to objects

- Layer and group objects

III

Adding Illustrations

Understanding Placeholders

A *placeholder* reserves space on a slide for a specific type of object. Most object types on a PowerPoint slide are contained by placeholders. Placeholders are the main tool by which various PowerPoint objects are manipulated and changed. There are placeholders for:

▶ See "Under-
standing
PowerPoint's
Charting Fea-
ture," p. 329

▶ See "Using the
ClipArt Gal-
lery," p. 308

◀ See "Creating a
New Table,"
p. 238

- Charts created in Microsoft Graph

- Organizational Charts

- Clip art from PowerPoint's ClipArt Library

- Tables created in Microsoft Word

- Slide titles and body text

- Object placeholders for embedded and linked objects, such as sounds, movie clips, imported pictures, Excel datasheets, and other types of objects available in Windows

Figure 11.1 displays an AutoLayout slide with three different placeholders in it.

Fig. 11.1
A title, text, and clip art place-holder are all part of this AutoLayout.

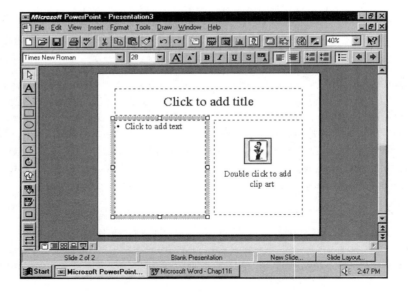

Manipulating Objects

Placeholders are not objects in and of themselves, but they're capable of containing objects of various kinds.

Before you can perform operations on placeholders or objects, you have to select them. How do you know when a placeholder or object has been selected? The Text placeholder in figure 11.1 has eight small boxes, or resize handles, which are actually used for sizing the placeholder or object. There is

also a shaded gray selection box around its edge. To move a placeholder, drag
this gray selection box. When an object is selected, the eight handles indicate
its selection, but there is no shaded selection box, as with placeholders. To
move an object, you simply click somewhere within the eight handles and
drag the object where you want it.

Many features described in this chapter require the use of the two drawing
toolbars offered as part of PowerPoint 95's standard toolbar set. To place the
Drawing and Drawing+ toolbars on the PowerPoint screen (if they are not
already on-screen), select View, Toolbars. The Toolbars dialog box appears.
Click on Drawing and Drawing+, and then click OK to return to your presentation.

The Drawing and Drawing+ toolbars appear on the PowerPoint screen. The
Drawing tools are defined in Chapter 10, "Drawing Objects." The Drawing+
tools are shown in table 11.1.

Table 11.1   Drawing+ Toolbar Tools

Tool	Tool Name	Description
	Bring Forward	Layers one object in front of another
	Send Backward	Layers one object behind another
	Group Objects	Allows you to group several objects together so you can manipulate them as a single unit
	Ungroup Objects	Changes grouped objects back into separate entities
	Rotate Left	Rotates objects 90 degrees to the left
	Rotate Right	Rotates objects 90 degrees to the right
	Flip Horizontal	Flips an object from left to right or right to left
	Flip Vertical	Flips an object upside down

You can drag either of these drawing toolbars to a convenient place on the screen, if necessary, by simply clicking on their edges and dragging them.

Selecting Multiple Objects

Selecting a single object is as simple as clicking on it with the mouse. Selecting multiple objects is done in several ways. To start, display the slide that contains the objects you want to select.

Drag the mouse diagonally across the displayed slide from one corner to the other, drawing a "box" around the objects you want to select.

All the objects on the slide that the mouse was dragged around are selected, as in figure 11.2.

Fig. 11.2
By dragging your mouse across several objects, each individual objects handles display.

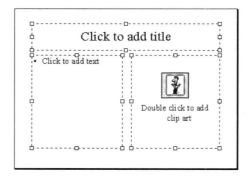

Another way to select multiple objects is to hold down the Shift key and click on one object. While you hold the Shift key, click on each successive object until you have selected all the objects you want.

If you want to select all the objects in a given slide, you also can use a third method. From the Edit menu, choose Select All.

Copying and Pasting Objects

You can copy objects from one slide to another, or even from one presentation to another. To copy and paste any object, select the object you want by clicking on it with the mouse. Choose Edit, Copy or use the Copy button on the toolbar. PowerPoint places the copy on the Windows clipboard, waiting for you to paste it elsewhere in the document, or even into another PowerPoint document or a document created in another application.

> **Caution**
>
> You can only keep one object on the clipboard at a time. If you copy or cut another object, it will overwrite the first one.

Display the slide where you want to paste the copied object. Choose Edit, Paste, or use the Paste button on the toolbar. This action simply pastes a copy of the object into the currently displayed slide.

Pasting Objects from Other Programs

You also can paste anything from the clipboard, whether or not it exists in a PowerPoint presentation, into a slide using a command called Paste Special. This command also allows you to display objects such as detailed graphics as icons. If you're working with a slide with several charts or clip art images on it, this saves you the time it takes to display such graphics on screen as you're working on your presentation.

Paste Link allows you to paste an object from another program into your PowerPoint presentation and create a link to the other program at the same time. Paste Link means that if you change the object in the program that created it, the change is automatically added in your PowerPoint file. For example, if you place an Excel spreadsheet into your slide and you link it, then when you change the numbers for current sales in the spreadsheet in Excel, they will automatically update in your presentation. That way you don't have to to open PowerPoint, open the presentation file, and paste the changed picture back into the slide.

From the Edit menu, choose Paste Special. The Paste Special dialog box appears (see fig. 11.3). Choose the object type to paste onto the slide from the As list in the Paste Special dialog box.

If the object on the clipboard is a graphic, chart, or imported picture, you can paste it either as an object or as a simple picture. If the object is a specific type that is generated in another program, that specific object type displays in the As list as well.

If you paste your object using either Paste or Paste Special, it retains all the typical properties of an object of its source program, which could be a PowerPoint object like a title text object, a chunk of body text, or just about

Tip
You also can click the right mouse button and choose Copy or Paste from the shortcut menu, or use the key-strokes Ctrl+C and Ctrl+V to copy and paste.

▶ See "Using Links to other Applications," p. 513

III

Adding Illustrations

Fig. 11.3

The Paste Special dialog box allows you to put various types of objects into your presentation.

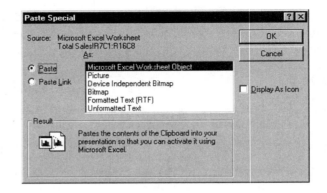

anything else. For example, if the object is a bitmap Paintbrush picture, you can paste it into the slide. Then it becomes an object that exists in PowerPoint, but also retains a connection to the program it was created in. It's not just a graphic object. It also can be edited or changed by double-clicking the picture on the slide. Then the Paintbrush application will open and you can make changes to the picture. This is called creating an embedded object.

▶ See "Creating an Embedded Object," p. 516

If you paste the object as a picture, the pasted item is placed as a simple bitmap on the slide and the picture cannot be edited by double-clicking within PowerPoint.

If you don't intend to make any changes to a picture once it's placed in your presentation, you should paste it as a picture. You can still resize it, or place other objects on top of or behind it, but you can't change its shape, color, or elements without going back to the original object and recreating it. If you might want to modify the object, perhaps by changing its color to match your presentation background, paste it as an object.

The As list displays the object type of whatever is on the clipboard. It can show any object type that your system supports, such as a chart made in Microsoft Graph, an OrgChart, a Word table, an Excel datasheet, or any other data type that's imported from another program. If the object is a PowerPoint object, such as a title or body text from a slide, you only see the words Object and Picture.

You also can display the pasted object as an icon to save the time PowerPoint may take to display several graphic objects on screen, or to reduce the on-screen clutter as you work. You can do this by choosing the Display as Icon check box. When you're done with your selections, choose OK or press Enter to complete the Paste Special operation.

Rotating and Flipping Drawn and Text Objects

In Chapter 10, the Free Rotate tool was discussed. Combined with the Rotate Right, Rotate Left and Flip Horizontal, Flip Vertical tools on the Drawing+ toolbar, you can get even more flexibility in reorienting objects. You can manipulate not only the angle of an object on your slide, but also change it to a mirror image of itself. PowerPoint allows the freeform rotation of text objects, such as titles or body text, and of objects drawn on the PowerPoint screen. Objects such as imported pictures, sound file objects, movie clips, and charts cannot be directly rotated because they're objects that were created in other programs.

Using the Rotating Tools

Rotating objects is done to make them fit better with other objects on a slide, or to create design interest. Rotating several objects in a sequence often gives a sense of motion or sequence. For all object types, the procedure for rotating is the same:

1. Click on the object you want to rotate.

2. Click the Free Rotate Tool button on PowerPoint's Drawing toolbar.

The mouse pointer changes its shape to a pair of arrows circling each other. Also, another visual clue appears: the eight boxes around the border of the selected object turn into four, one box for each corner of the selected object.

The status bar at the bottom of the PowerPoint screen reads:

```
Position the mouse pointer over any handle.
```

3. Click and hold the mouse on one of the four handles of the selected object.

The status bar at the bottom of the PowerPoint screen reads:

```
Drag to rotate the selection; press Shift key to constrain
angle.
```

4. Drag the mouse in any direction. As you do so, the status bar displays the message

```
Rotated by X degree(s); Press Shift key to constrain angle.
```

describing the number of degrees around a circle by which the object has just been rotated.

III

Adding Illustrations

5. To constrain the angle of the rotation to every 90 degrees, press and hold the Shift key while you rotate the object. You also can use the Rotate Right and Rotate Left tools on the Drawing+ toolbar. These automatically rotate the object exactly 90 degrees.

6. When you finish rotating the object, click on an empty part of the slide.

An object rotated to varying angles might look like the one in figure 11.4.

Fig. 11.4
Changing the rotation of an object can give the feeling of sequence or motion.

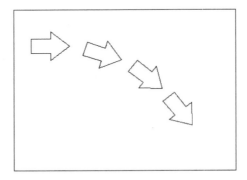

Note

It's possible to rotate more than one object at a time. Simply hold the Shift key, select the objects you want to rotate, and choose the Free Rotate tool. Click any selected object's handle and drag. All selected objects are rotated at the same angle. Alternately, grouped objects also can be rotated together. See more about grouping later in this chapter.

Flipping Objects

Flipping an object turns it over (see fig. 11.5). Flipping vertically is like flipping something upside down: the top goes where the bottom was and vice versa. Flipping horizontally moves what was the left side of the object to the right, as if you were looking at it in a mirror.

To flip an object, simply click on the object, then on the Flip Vertical or Flip Horizontal tool on the Drawing+ toolbar. That's it! To flip it back again, just click on the same tool again.

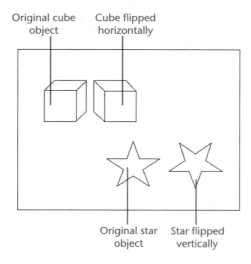

Original cube object

Cube flipped horizontally

Original star object

Star flipped vertically

Fig. 11.5
Flip Horizontal and Flip Vertical change the orientation of your objects.

Moving and Aligning Objects

Objects are moved according to the type of object they are. Text objects must be selected and dragged by the selection box surrounding them. Other kinds of objects can simply be dragged from anywhere within the object.

To move a text object:

1. Click the edge of the text object. Its selection box appears.

2. Drag the selection box of the object.

To move any other object, simply click anywhere on the object and drag it where you want to place it.

Tip
If you'd rather use menus, choose Draw, Rotate/Flip, and a side menu will offer you the choices of Rotate Left or Right, Flip Horizontal or Vertical, or Free Rotate.

III

Adding Illustrations

> **Caution**
>
> Be careful when clicking on embedded objects, such as an Excel spreadsheet or a Paint drawing. If you inadvertently double-click on them, they open up the program they were created in. If you open its application accidentally, you can move the object while you're still in that application by clicking on its selection box and dragging.

When you're moving objects around on a slide, you may find that you want to align one or more objects more precisely than you did when you dragged the object into place. Placeholders and objects can be aligned to each other on a slide in many different ways. They can be aligned to their bottom edges, tops, left sides, or right sides. If you have two objects that you just can't seem to get lined up properly or if you just want a fast way to do it, here's how:

1. Select the two or more objects that you want to align to each other.

2. From the <u>D</u>raw menu, select <u>A</u>lign.

   A cascading menu listing six different alignment options appears (see fig. 11.6).

Fig. 11.6
Six alignment options allow you to line up objects exactly.

3. Choose the alignment option you want: Lefts (align objects' left sides), Centers (align objects to their centers), Rights (align objects' right sides), Tops (align objects' top edges), Middles (align objects to their middles), or Bottoms (align objects to their bottom edges).

Note

If you have one object on the left side of your screen and one on the right side, left-aligning the objects moves the object on the right over to the left side of your screen, with the left sides of each object aligned. Conversely, right-aligning moves the object on the left of your screen over to the right, with the right sides in a line.

You align placeholders the same way that you align drawn objects.

Troubleshooting

When I click in a title placeholder and try to drag it, it won't move.

Placeholders can be moved by dragging them from their inside areas or from their border. If the placeholder won't move when you drag on its interior area, it's a place-holder that was originally put in your Slide Master, and consequently, it appears in all the slides in your presentation. This is often the case with slide title placeholders, for example. In that case, for the slide you're working in, you must click and drag on the placeholder's border to be able to move it.

Resizing Objects

After you've created an object, you might want to make it larger or smaller. Most types of objects are resized in two ways.

You can resize an object proportionally so that it retains its original proportions, but on a larger or smaller scale. Any time you have something like a diagram to scale, you definitely want proportional sizing.

You also can resize an object freely with the mouse, which can distort the original proportions in various ways. This creates effects not unlike the fun house mirror that makes objects seem oddly proportioned. Sometimes you use this disproportional sizing for a creative effect, or to help you fit a picture or other object alongside other objects on a slide. Use this only when exact proportions are not vital.

Note

Some object types, such as imported pictures and movie clips, can be resized only proportionally. Other object types, such as clip art placeholders, are resized in any way that the mouse can be dragged.

III

Adding Illustrations

Resizing is done with placeholders that hold objects such as imported pictures, clip art, charts, and multimedia data types such as movie clips. Clicking and dragging a corner handle of any of those placeholders automatically resizes the object proportionally if the object type is already inside the placeholder. The object (and the placeholder that contains it) retains its shape regardless of its size. However, clicking and dragging on any handle other than a corner handle resizes the object and placeholder only in one direction, which causes it to lose its original proportions.

> **Note**
>
> If you hold down Shift while resizing an object, the resizing process in PowerPoint is not affected as it would be in some other drawing programs. Pressing Control while resizing will cause the object to resize outward from the center in both directions at once, rather than just expanding the side you're dragging on.

Proportionally Resizing Placeholders

Empty placeholders of any kind can be resized proportionally by holding Shift while you drag a corner handle with the mouse. Doing so retains the default shape of the placeholder (usually a square or rectangle) but shrinks or enlarges it depending on the direction in which the mouse is moved.

Randomly Resizing Placeholders

An empty placeholder is resized randomly by grabbing a handle and simply dragging the mouse. The placeholder can then be reshaped and resized at will.

Resizing an empty placeholder at random does not affect the quality or proportionality of an inserted object such as a bitmap picture or clip art object; it merely affects the size of the object when it's inserted into the placeholder.

Deleting Objects

You can delete any object, but if that object is within a placeholder, deleting it doesn't delete its placeholder. Deleting an object *and* its placeholder is a two-step process. First, the contents of the placeholder (the actual object) must be deleted, and then the placeholder is deleted.

To delete an object within a placeholder, follow these steps:

1. Click the border of the object you want to delete.

2. To delete the object in the placeholder, choose Edit, Clear. Alternately, you can highlight the object, such as text, and press Backspace or Delete.

Tip
If you choose to clear an object, it's deleted and not placed on the clipboard so you can retrieve it later. On the other hand, if you select Cut, it is placed on the Windows clipboard and can be pasted elsewhere.

The object contents are deleted and the placeholder originally containing the object appears, selected for deletion.

3. To remove the placeholder, choose Clear or Cut from the Edit menu; or press Backspace or Delete.

If the object you're deleting is an object drawn with PowerPoint's drawing tools, which don't use placeholders, click anywhere on the object, and then press Delete or Backspace to remove the drawn object.

Note

Whenever you are resizing or deleting objects, you may find that you want to reverse your previous action to get back what you started with. Use the Undo button to undo an action immediately after you have taken it, or undo several actions in sequence. This also works when you clear an object, even though it is not on the clipboard. To return a picture to its original size, choose Draw, Scale, and make it 100 percent of its original size.

Enhancing Placeholders and Objects

You can use PowerPoint's drawing tools to enhance object placeholders in much the same way as you do with objects themselves. You can add line styles to placeholder borders, add color fills and shading to their backgrounds, and align them to each other for a uniform and organized appearance. Placeholders can have shadows applied to them. The colors applied to placeholder color fills have the same range and availability that is offered when you're working with drawing, chart objects, and slide backgrounds.

Framing and Shadowing Object Placeholders

Placeholders for clip art, text, titles, and other objects can have line weights and styles applied to their borders. You also can apply shadows to placeholders to add emphasis to the presence of the object on the slide.

To add a different line style to an object placeholder, follow these steps:

1. Click the border of the desired placeholder.

2. Click the Line Style button of PowerPoint's Drawing toolbar. A drop-down list of 10 line styles and weights appears.

3. Click the line style or line weight you want.

III

Adding Illustrations

Fig. 11.7
A shadow applied to a text place-holder adds a shadow to both the border and text.

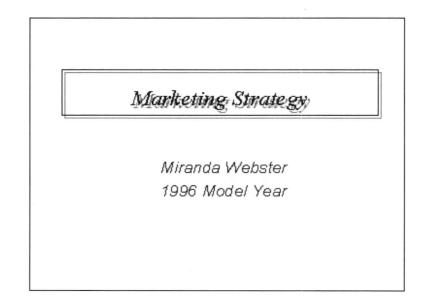

Fig. 11.8
Make choices about how your shadow will appear in the Shadow dialog box.

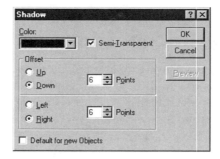

The selected placeholder has the line style applied to its border.

You can combine line styles for width and dashed lines on the same place-holder. Select the Arrowhead tool and click on the placeholder and then the Dashed Lines button on the Drawing toolbar.

You also can apply shadows to any placeholders on a slide, as shown on the title placeholder in figure 11.7. Click the border of the desired placeholder. Then click the Shadow On/Off tool on the Drawing toolbar.

If you want to be able to modify the color or offset of the shadow from the placeholder line and text, choose Format, Shadow. The Shadow dialog box appears, as in figure 11.8.

Choose from the following options to adjust and apply shadow effects:

- *Color.* Drop-down eight-color palette that offers the basic presentation color scheme, the No Shadow option, the Automatic option, an Embossed shadow style, and the Other Color option for adding colors from the expanded Other Color table.

- *Semi-Transparent.* Sets the shadow so you can see through it.

- *Up* or *Down.* Sets the shadow to project Up or Down from the object by a specified number of points.

- *Left* or *Right.* Sets the shadow to project Left or Right from the object by a specified number of points.

- *Default for New Objects.* Applies the settings to new objects you draw.

Try different combinations from this dialog box to see their effects, including the options in the drop-down list for Color. Here you can choose other colors, or an embossed look. Embossed gives the placeholder a raised look, as on an embossed invitation. Different offset amounts can particularly make text in the placeholder more or less legible. You also can choose to apply these settings as the default for new objects by clicking that option here. When you're done with your choices, click Preview to change the appearance of the object on the screen behind the dialog box, but not actually apply the changes. Click OK to apply them.

Filling, Shading, and Patterning Objects

Any placeholder or object—a chart object, an empty placeholder for a piece of clip art, a title, a body text object—can have a fill applied to it, and the fill can be any style, such as a solid color, a shading, or a pattern fill.

III

Adding Illustrations

When you draw polygons and other shapes in PowerPoint, as discussed in Chapter 10, "Drawing Objects," you use the same techniques for adding shading, shadows, patterns, and color fills as you do for placeholders. Line styles and color and shading fills can be combined to lend an attractive appearance to a placeholder, particularly if the placeholder is used for text objects such as body text and titles.

To add a color fill and shading to a placeholder in PowerPoint:

1. Click the border of the text object placeholder.

2. Click the Fill Color button in the Drawing toolbar. The drop-down color palette and option list appears.

3. Choose a color from the palette. The fill color is applied to the placeholder background.

4. To add shading to the color, click the Fill Color button in the Drawing toolbar again.

5. From the drop-down list, choose Shaded. The Shaded Fill dialog box appears.

6. Choose a Shade Style from the six Shade Styles option buttons.

Layering Objects

Sometimes for design reasons, or to fit more on a single slide, you may want to layer objects so that they overlap each other in some way. For example, you might want a text object to fit with a drawn object, as in figure 11.9. In this figure, the white letters of the word "spotlight" have been brought forward, which places the shaded ellipse behind so the letters are visible. If the ellipse were brought forward, you wouldn't see the letters at all.

Every object you place on a slide occupies its own layer. Whether you have three or 100 objects on a slide, each object can be Sent Backward or Brought Forward relative to any other object.

If you want to reverse the order of the objects, follow these steps:

1. Click the first object.

2. Click the Bring Forward button on the Drawing+ toolbar. The first object is brought forward one layer, as with the text object in figure 11.9.

3. Click the Send Backward button on the Drawing+ toolbar to move the object behind the other again.

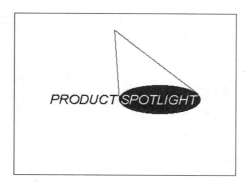

Caution

Sometimes when you have several objects in close proximity or on top of each other, it's difficult to select the one you want. You may have to move them away from each other so that a corner of each is clearly distinct, select them, send backward or forward, then move them back into place.

Layering applies to any objects on a PowerPoint slide (that includes placeholders, the objects you put in those placeholders on the slide, and drawn objects). Object placeholders can be layered over each other, and you can draw objects by using PowerPoint's drawing tools and layering the objects over each other—and over text, too.

Grouping Objects

Another common ground that placeholders and drawn objects share is the capability to be grouped together for easier moving and manipulation. After objects are grouped, they act as a single object. That object can then be resized, flipped or rotated, deleted, copied, or moved like any other object. When you're done manipulating the multiple-object group, you can simply ungroup it, and the object are once again separate.

For example, let's say your law firm's logo consists of a circle, with a picture and text within the circle. You can create or insert the various objects, group them, then move the logo around as a single unit. If you want to edit them

III

Adding Illustrations

later, say to add a new partner's name in the company name, just ungroup them, work with the text, then regroup them.

You group object placeholders exactly the same way you group drawn objects. Hold down the Shift key, and click on the objects on the slide that you want to group together. You must select two or more objects, but there is no limit to the number of objects you can group together.

 Click the Group button on the PowerPoint Drawing+ toolbar. Or, from the Draw menu, choose Group.

 The selected objects are grouped, and a set of handles appears over the area occupied by all the selected objects. Now you can use those handles to resize the group object, or click and drag to move the grouped object wherever you like. To ungroup the objects, simply select the grouped object, and click on the Ungroup Objects tool. You can also choose Draw, Ungroup.

Scaling Objects

Dragging sizing handles to resize an object involves eyeballing the final size of the object. Sometimes, you need a more precise way to resize things. PowerPoint's Scale feature is an easy and efficient way for users to accurately resize pictures, charts, movie clips, and other objects on PowerPoint slides. It allows you to do several things: resize any selected object (or more than one object at a time) by percentages to be smaller or larger than its current size; resize an object to an optimum size based on the screen resolution of your slide show; or restore a resized picture or object to its original proportions.

The Scale feature resizes pictures and other objects while retaining their original proportions. You will not see any distortion of the object during resizing.

To rescale an object, follow these steps:

1. Click the object(s) you want to rescale. (You can select more than one object for rescaling by holding down the Shift key and clicking on each object in turn.)

2. Choose Draw, Scale. The Scale dialog box appears.

3. In the Scale To spin box, type a number for the percentage you want to resize the picture to. Higher numbers enlarge it, smaller numbers shrink it.

   If you're giving a slide show presentation, and you want to make sure that the selected object or objects are the best size for the screen when you give the actual presentation, click the Best Scale for Slide Show

Tip

To regroup objects you just ungrouped, leave them still selected and just click the Group Objects tool again. Or, from the Draw menu, select Regroup.

Tip

To return the picture to the size it was when you imported it, click the Relative to Original Picture Size check box. Used with a scale of 100%, this resizes the picture to its original proportions.

check box. This is especially handy for the best resolution for multimedia movie clips, which are discussed in more detail in chapter 21.

To check your scaling changes before closing the feature, click the Preview button. (Move the Scale dialog box if it happens to cover up the object.) Although the image changes on-screen, the changes have not yet been applied.

4. When you're satisfied, choose OK to apply the changes.

Fig. 11.10
You can use the scale dialog box to resize an object to an exact percentage.

This and the previous chapter offered instructions on many of the tools and basic techniques for creating and working with different types of drawn objects. The next chapter, "Adding Clip Art and Scanned Art," shows you how to add existing artwork to your presentations for visual interest. To learn about adding and working with tables and charts, see Chapter 9, "Creating and Working with Tables," and Chapter 13, "Working with Datasheets." Finally, look at some more advanced drawing features in Chapter 23, "Using Advanced Color, Text, and Special Effects."❖

III

Adding Illustrations

Chapter 12

Adding Clip Art and Scanned Art

by Rich Grace

PowerPoint 95 comes with a variety of professionally drawn pictures known as *clip art*, which you can use in your slides. These drawings are professionally done and save you time when you need to put together a polished presentation in a hurry.

PowerPoint goes farther by allowing you to use pictures from other sources. For example, by using a scanner with special software, you can scan your company's logo in a bitmap (.bmp) file and include it in a presentation. You also can include pictures from other applications such as word processors, drawing programs, or desktop publishing packages. Many of these packages include thousands of pieces of clip art. They can all be integrated into a booming PowerPoint ClipArt Gallery. PowerPoint 95 is able to read and import more than 20 different graphics file formats.

In this chapter, you learn to

- Insert clip art from the ClipArt Gallery

- Search for and organize clip art in the ClipArt Gallery

- Insert clip art from another application

- Add scanned art to a slide

Using the ClipArt Gallery

More than 1,400 clip art pictures are included with PowerPoint. With that kind of selection, there is a good chance you'll find one or two pictures that will work well in your presentation. If you don't find what you're looking for among the clip art included with PowerPoint, you can use pictures from other applications. When you're ready to place clip art onto a slide, you do so using the ClipArt Gallery, discussed later.

PowerPoint's ClipArt Gallery allows you to manage a large collection of clip art, organized into a number of predefined categories: business, landmarks, communications, animals, and many more. You also can use the ClipArt Gallery to organize every picture in your collection and add new categories of artwork. This includes not just what's on your hard disk, but on floppy disks, network hard drives, and CD-ROMs as well. Like a library, the ClipArt Gallery maintains an index containing the location of each picture in the gallery. Using this method, you can keep track of a large collection of useful artwork without having to use up valuable hard disk space.

The first time you start the ClipArt Gallery (which may or may not also be the first time you start up the PowerPoint program), you have to initialize it. PowerPoint creates a clip art database used by the Gallery to locate the clip art in the system. To begin with, you'll probably want to install and view all the clip art categories that PowerPoint offers as part of its standard package.

When the Add New Pictures dialog box opens, the clip art is shown as being split up into *packages*, such as the Animals Package and the Background Package. There are dozens of packages, each with a selection of art. All are automatically selected. They correspond with the artwork categories installed in the Gallery.

To access the ClipArt Gallery, follow these steps:

1. Choose Insert, ClipArt or click the Insert ClipArt button on PowerPoint's Standard toolbar. On an AutoLayout slide, you can double-click a clip art placeholder.

2. To initialize and install the artwork packages, simply choose Add All.

Keep in mind that the process of building the art database can take a few minutes. Once it has been created, the ClipArt Gallery dialog box appears, as shown in figure 12.1. Let's survey its elements.

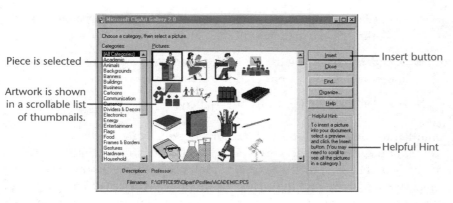

Piece is selected

Artwork is shown in a scrollable list of thumbnails.

Insert button

Helpful Hint

Fig. 12.1
Using the ClipArt Gallery.

To the left, make a selection from the Categories list to view a set of pictures by a category. The default selection is All Categories. With this chosen, every piece in PowerPoint's original ClipArt Gallery can be scrolled through. Because that long scroll can be rather tedious (although initially impressive), it's best to click a category for more convenience, as shown in figure 12.2.

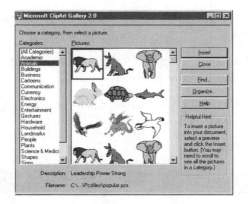

Fig. 12.2
Displaying a single art Category.

III

Adding Illustrations

The larger section to the right is labeled Pictures. It is an image gallery that displays thumbnail graphics for each piece of art. Scroll through the thumbnail list and click a desired piece of art. It's shown in figures 12.1 and 12.2.

At the right side of the ClipArt Gallery dialog box are several buttons, labeled Insert, Close, Find, Organize, and Help. Their functions are as follows:

- *Insert.* Inserts the selected art into the slide as a ClipArt object.

- *Close.* Closes the Gallery without making a selection.

Tip
Double-click a thumbnail in the Pictures list to automatically insert a piece of art in your presentation slide.

- *Find.* Clicking this starts a Find operation through your system for any artwork that's compatible with the Gallery.

- *Organize.* Enables you to search for and add new artwork to the gallery, and provides instructions on other Gallery operations.

- *Help.* Online Help for the ClipArt Gallery.

Another handy feature is the Helpful Hint section, located in the lower-right corner of the ClipArt Gallery. You find Helpful Hints throughout PowerPoint, in many of the major dialog boxes. They tell you how to perform the principle task associated with the dialog box; in this case, selecting and placing a piece of clip art onto a slide. If you need additional information, choose the Help button.

Placing Clip Art From the Gallery Onto a Slide

As you certainly know, it's simple to place clip art from the Gallery into a slide. Keep in mind that a presentation must be open first. Place clip art onto a slide by following these steps:

1. Display the ClipArt Gallery dialog box by choosing Insert, ClipArt, or by clicking the Insert ClipArt button on the toolbar.

2. In the ClipArt Gallery, choose a category from the Categories list to view. The default selection in the list is All Categories.

3. Scroll through the gallery of pictures in the Gallery and make a selection by clicking the desired picture.

4. Choose Insert or press Enter.

> **Note**
>
> You also can choose Insert, Picture, to place artwork that is not in the ClipArt Gallery onto a slide. Click the Look In drop-down list, and select a desired drive and folder. (By default, the Files of Type list will show "All Pictures.") Make your selection from the File Name list, and then choose OK or press Enter. Either method results in the picture being placed on the current slide.

Searching for Clip Art

You can search the ClipArt Gallery for a specific picture or group of pictures. When you click the Find button in the ClipArt Gallery, the Find Picture dialog box appears. The Find Picture dialog box allows you to narrow or expand your search criteria by the text used in the picture description, file name, and picture (file format) type. This function *only* works for art that is placed in the Gallery.

To search for clip art, follow these steps:

1. Display the ClipArt Gallery dialog box by choosing Insert, ClipArt, or by clicking the Insert ClipArt button on the Standard toolbar.

2. Choose Find. The Find ClipArt dialog box appears, as shown in figure 12.3.

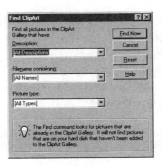

Fig. 12.3
Using the Find feature to locate specific pieces of art.

Three text boxes use drop-down lists to provide criteria for searching:

- The Description drop-down list performs a search based on the text in a picture description. For example, typing **Household** causes PowerPoint to search for all pictures in the gallery with this word in their descriptions. PowerPoint displays all clip art having this word in its description.

- The Filename Containing list grows as you add entries to it and allows you to search for art by a name or part of a name. Figure 12.4 shows a typical list with some new entries. In practice, this feature doesn't work too well with the basic clip art library in the gallery, because all the art is organized into packages and categories. Those categories are the only valid names that work with this feature on the base library.

III

Adding Illustrations

Fig. 12.4
Adaptive lists keep
track of your
search criteria.

Tip
Whenever you
click a piece of art
in the Gallery, its
description and
filename pop up at
the bottom of the
dialog box. That's
a tip-off to what
you're expected
to enter in the
Description and
Filename Contain-
ing drop-down
lists of the Find
ClipArt dialog
box.

■ The Picture Type drop-down list allows you to specify the file
format type to search for. Examples include Windows Bitmaps,
Targa, Windows Metafiles, Tagged Image File Format, JPEG Filter,
CorelDraw, and many others.

3. Make selections from the drop-down list to define your search and click
Find Now. After a moment to do the search, the ClipArt Gallery displays the pictures matching your criteria. If no pictures match, the dialog box shows the message The ClipArt Gallery could not find any
pictures matching your criteria. Click OK and try another after
changing search criteria.

Note

We've noted that the Find feature isn't all that effective with the basic clip art libraries
offered with PowerPoint. That's because PowerPoint organizes its basic library in
categories, and not in individual files. With the base ClipArt library, you can only
search by category and not by file name, or the general appearance of a clip. However, bear in mind that the Gallery accepts other sets of clip art, virtually all of which
is offered in individual *.TIF, *.EPS, *.BMP, or other file formats. When you install a
large quantity of such art, this makes a search much more comprehensive, and the
feature becomes increasingly useful with the more artwork you add to the Gallery.

Managing the ClipArt Gallery

Choosing the Organize button in the ClipArt Gallery dialog box causes the
Organize ClipArt dialog box to appear (see fig. 12.5). You use the Organize
ClipArt dialog box to manage the ClipArt Gallery, adding and updating clip
art and clip art categories. Organize also provides brief information about
other functions in the Gallery, such as deleting pictures, changing a picture's
category, and deleting or changing a category.

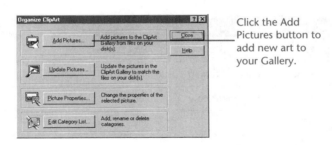

Click the Add
Pictures button to
add new art to
your Gallery.

Fig. 12.5
Using the Organize
feature.

Adding Clip Art to the Gallery From Other Applications

You can take advantage of PowerPoint's wide array of graphics filters to import vast clip art libraries into the ClipArt Gallery. You can literally add tens of thousands of new pieces to the convenient Gallery browser and place them in their own categories.

As noted earlier, many Windows applications such as word processors, drawing packages, and desktop publishing programs come with a variety of pictures saved in various file formats. For example, Word for Windows includes pictures saved in Windows Metafile (.WMF) format. CorelDRAW! offers libraries of images on CD-ROM discs in TIF, EPS, and CDR formats. Programs that enable you to create and edit images, such as CorelDRAW! and Adobe Illustrator, allow you to save images in multiple file formats.

PowerPoint's ClipArt Gallery lets you add pictures from many different file formats (as shown in table 12.1) to your clip art collection. Notice that many of these file formats are native to a specific software package such as DrawPerfect or AutoCAD.

Table 12.1   File Types You Can Add to the ClipArt Gallery

File	Extension
Windows Bitmaps	BMP
Windows Metafile	WMF
HP Graphic Language	HGL
Computer Graphics Metafile	CGM
Encapsulated PostScript	EPS
CompuServe GIF	GIF

(continues)

III

Adding Illustrations

Table 12.1 Continued	
File	**Extension**
Tagged Image File Format	TIF
Micrografx Designer/Draw	DRW
PC Paintbrush	PCX
AutoCAD Format 2-D	DXF
CorelDRAW!	CDR
DrawPerfect	WPG
HP Plotter Print File	PLT
Kodak Photo CD	PCD
Macintosh PICT	PCT
Targa	TGA
JPEG Filter	JPG

Choose the <u>A</u>dd Pictures button in the Organize dialog box to search for and add one or more clip art files to the ClipArt Gallery. When you choose <u>A</u>dd Pictures, the Add Pictures to ClipArt Gallery dialog box appears, as shown in figure 12.6. Use this dialog box to select a drive, folder, and file type to locate.

In the following example, we'll use a CD-ROM disc that contains a substantial amount of artwork, just to show it's possible to add clip art from other sources to the Gallery.

Fig. 12.6
Using the Add Pictures to ClipArt Gallery dialog box to search for new clip art.

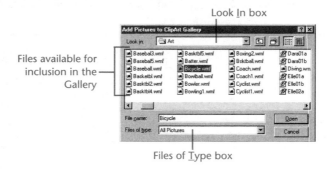

Look <u>I</u>n box

Files available for inclusion in the Gallery

Files of <u>T</u>ype box

To add clip art from another application to the PowerPoint ClipArt Gallery, follow these steps:

1. Display the ClipArt Gallery dialog box by choosing <u>I</u>nsert, <u>C</u>lipArt, or by clicking the Insert ClipArt button on the Standard toolbar.

2. Choose the <u>O</u>rganize button. The Organize ClipArt dialog box appears.

3. Choose the <u>A</u>dd Pictures button to display the Add Pictures to ClipArt Gallery dialog box (shown in fig. 12.6).

   In the Look <u>I</u>n box, choose the desired drive and folder in which the clip art for importing is to be found. In the example, a CD-ROM disc is in drive D:, in the Art folder. Figure 12.6 shows a long list of *.WMF files. This provides another clue to the user: the Add Pictures to Gallery utility automatically sees any files in its search criteria and displays them. (Note that the Files of <u>t</u>ype box at the bottom reads All Pictures. This means that the utility automatically looks for files of all the types listed in table 12.1.) It's a real convenience feature.

4. As shown in figure 12.7, select a piece of art shown in the file list. In the sample disc I'm using for this exercise, there are over 500 WMF files to choose from.

5. To select a range of consecutive items, press the Shift key while clicking the first and last file names you want. Hold the Crtl key down to select non-contiguous files in the list. Figure 12.8 shows how it could look.

Tip

Hold the shift key down as you click, to choose a range files in the list for selection.

Fig. 12.7
Selecting a single piece of art in the Add Pictures to Gallery dialog box.

III

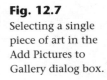

Adding Illustrations

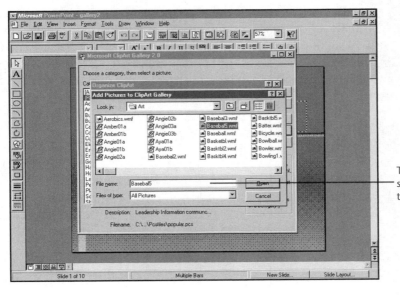

The File Name box shows the name of the selected file.

Fig. 12.8
Selecting multiple pieces of non-contiguous art (by holding the Ctrl key) in the Add Pictures to Gallery dialog box.

The File Name box lists all the names of the selected file

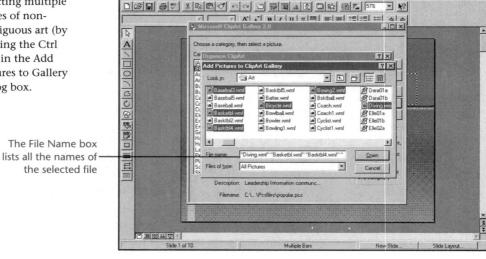

Tip
To select non-consecutive within the list, press Ctrl while clicking various file names.

6. Choose Open or press Enter.

Whether you select one piece of art or more than one, the Picture Properties sheet appears, as shown in figure 12.9.

The Picture Properties sheet represents a great improvement in Power-Point 95. Several excellent convenience features are built into the dialog box. To begin with, a thumbnail preview of the first new art piece in question is shown at the top left. You can create your own art categories by clicking the New Category button, or insert the artwork into an existing one by choosing one from the scrollable list. There's also a very interesting checkbox at the bottom, called Add All Pictures to the Selected Categories. If you have multiple files of the same type, this can be very powerful (as you soon see).

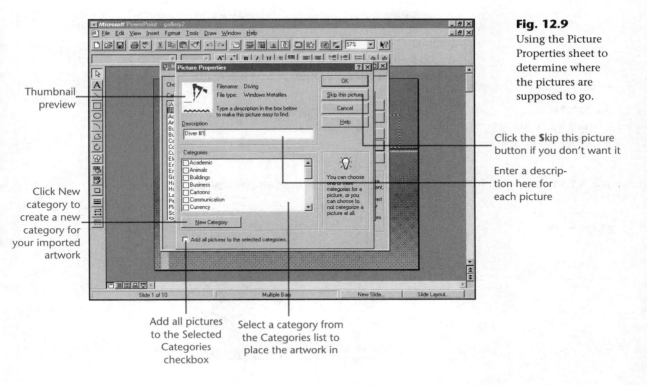

Thumbnail preview

Click New category to create a new category for your imported artwork

Click the **S**kip this picture button if you don't want it

Enter a description here for each picture

Add all pictures to the Selected Categories checkbox

Select a category from the Categories list to place the artwork in

Adding Your Own ClipArt Categories to the Gallery

You might notice in the example that the WMF files selected in figure 12.8 all have sport-related titles like DIVING.WMF, BICYCLE.WMF, and so on. Because they're all in a neat category and the ClipArt Gallery does not have a "Pro Sports" category (it does have a Sports & Leisure category, though), why not create one?

1. To create a new category for your art, click the <u>N</u>ew category button. The New Category dialog box appears.

2. Type in the desired category name in the New Category dialog box, as shown in figure 12.10. The example is ProSports, but it could be anything you want. Then choose OK or press Enter to return to the Picture Properties sheet. The new category is shown in the Categories list (see fig. 12.11).

III

Adding Illustrations

3. If you don't want to create a new category or know that the art you're bringing in will fit into an existing one, choose a category from the Categories list to insert the current picture into. Otherwise, the pictures are added to the All Categories group by default.

Fig. 12.10
Creating a new art category.

Fig. 12.11
The new art category is now placed in the Categories list.

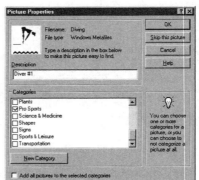

Tip
If you add clip art from a CD-ROM disc, the Gallery automatically looks for it on the CD-ROM. The art is not installed on your hard drive.

4. Enter a description for the current artwork in the Description box.

   But wait. If multiple files are selected, you'll have to enter a description for each of them. Adding descriptions for dozens or hundreds of pieces of artwork can become drudgery.

   If all the selected files are of similar subject matter, like Aliens, click the Add All Pictures to the Selected Categories checkbox. Make sure that the desired category is selected with a check in its checkbox in the Categories list.

5. Choose OK or press Enter.

The artwork has thumbnails created for the Gallery and is inserted into the desired categories. Suddenly, you have lots of new artwork to play with. It works! If the art is brought in from CD-ROM, the art is not copied over to your hard disk, but remains resident on the CD. If you try to insert clip art from a CD that isn't in your CD-ROM drive, you will get a "Cannot find file" error. The program is intelligent, and will then request that the proper disc be installed in your drive.

Deleting and Renaming ClipArt Pictures and Categories

A clue to finding out how to delete and rename ClipArt categories is actually found by clicking the right mouse button on an art thumbnail in the Gallery.

The ClipArt Gallery now makes use of the shortcut menus common in other areas of the PowerPoint program. To access these shortcut menus, point to a picture on the ClipArt Gallery and right-click. The exercises for deleting and renaming pictures work from these shortcut menus.

Deleting Pictures from a Category

To delete a picture from the Gallery, follow these steps:

1. Click the desired picture with the right mouse button.

2. From the shortcut menu, simply choose Delete Picture. A new dialog box appears, as shown in figure 12.12.

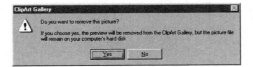

Fig. 12.12
Deleting a piece of art from the Gallery.

The dialog box asks you if you want to remove the picture. It also points out that although the preview is removed from the Gallery, the picture file remains on your hard disk.

3. To delete, choose Yes or press Enter. To avoid removing the preview, choose No.

Moving Pictures to Another Category

To move a picture to another category you use the same shortcut menu. You also can change the category of a picture. To move a picture between Gallery categories, do the following:

1. Click the desired picture with the right mouse button.

2. From the shortcut menu, choose Picture Properties.

   The Picture Properties sheet shows the description (if any) of the art-work in the <u>D</u>escription box (see fig. 12.13). (You can, of course, change

III

Adding Illustrations

this if you want to.) The Categories are also listed. The category the picture currently belongs to has a check mark in its box.

Fig. 12.13
Using the Picture Properties sheet to move a picture between categories.

Tip
When you delete a category of clip art, all its thumbnails are also removed from the Gallery.

3. Click another category name in the Categories list to place a check mark by it.

4. Click the category name the picture is currently associated with to remove its check mark from its box.

5. Choose OK or press Enter. Figure 12.14 shows a typical (though hopelessly mismatched) result.

Deleting a Category

Working with ClipArt categories is quite similar to working with ClipArt pictures. You can rename and delete categories within the Gallery. When you delete a category, PowerPoint also deletes the picture thumbnails previously assigned to that category. (Bear in mind that you can reassign pictures to other categories before you delete the original one.) Figure 12.15 shows the shortcut menu displayed when you click the right mouse button on a category name.

To delete a category, follow these steps:

1. Click the right mouse button on a category in the Categories list in the Gallery. The Category shortcut menu appears.

2. From the shortcut menu, choose Delete.

   The program displays a prompt reading: `Are you sure you want to delete the category (category name here)`? Previews that are only in this category will be removed from the ClipArt Gallery.

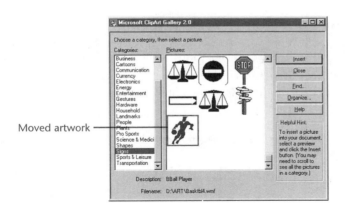

Fig. 12.14
A piece of art has been swapped between categories.

Moved artwork

Fig. 12.15
Using the Category shortcut menu.

3. To perform the deletion, choose <u>Y</u>es. If not, choose <u>N</u>o.

Renaming a Category

When you rename a ClipArt category, all pictures grouped under the old category are reassigned to the new one. Follow these steps to rename a category:

1. Click the right mouse button on a category in the Categories list in the Gallery. The Category shortcut menu appears.

2. From the shortcut menu, choose Rename Category.

3. A small Rename Category dialog box appears (see fig. 12.16).

4. Type a new name in the box, and choose OK.

The new category name appears, with all its existing artwork still placed in it.

Fig. 12.16
Renaming a category.

III

Adding Illustrations

Adding a New Category

To add a new category to the list, you don't have to use the Organize feature. Simply click any category name with the right mouse button and choose New Category from the shortcut menu. The New Category dialog box appears. Choose OK or press Enter when you're done entering the new category name, as seen in figure 12.17.

Fig. 12.17
Adding a new category to the Gallery.

The Edit Category List option on the shortcut menu simply allows you to delete, add, and change category names the Edit Category List dialog box. The buttons in this dialog box display the same dialog boxes you have seen in the last few exercises.

Updating the ClipArt Gallery

When you add artwork to the ClipArt Gallery, it records the location of each picture in your collection. Sometimes, the art is in another folder of your hard disk. Sometimes, it's on a CD-ROM. You may need to move pictures located in a certain folder to a new location on your hard drive—or even to a diskette—to conserve space, or you might simply delete some artwork you no longer need. When you do so, it is a good idea to update the ClipArt Gallery.

To update the ClipArt Gallery, follow these steps:

1. Display the ClipArt Gallery dialog box by choosing Insert, ClipArt, or by clicking the Insert ClipArt button on the Standard toolbar.

2. Choose the Organize button.

> **Note**
>
> You'll remember that you can change a picture's description when you add and rename artwork. A good practice for heavy use of the Gallery is to add description text that allows you to perform precise searches (using the Find button) based on picture descriptions.

The Organize ClipArt dialog box appears.

3. Choose the Update Pictures button to begin the process of updating the Gallery. The Update dialog box appears, as shown in fig. 12.18.

The dialog box shown in figure 12.18 reads: `Click Update to match previews in the ClipArt Gallery with files on your disk(s). To add previews to the ClipArt Gallery, click Cancel, then click Add Pictures.` This means that you aren't adding pictures by using this command, but simply updating the Preview thumbnails to show the current selection of artwork.

Check Network
Drives checkbox

Check Removable
Drives checkbox

Fig. 12.18
Updating the
ClipArt Gallery.

4. If you have installed art from removable drives (such as CD-ROMs, file server or network hard drives, or optical drives) and drives on a network file server, the Update feature is crucial in ensuring that your Previews show the artwork from those drives in the Gallery. The program must check on those drives to update the Gallery. If you need to do this, make sure that either (or both) the Check Network Drives or the Check Removable Drives checkbox is enabled.

5. To perform the update, choose Update in the Update dialog box. The proper drives will be searched. If any cannot be found, you are prompted to either Browse, Remove File, Skip it, or Cancel the operation.

Entries for clip art in the Gallery that cannot be found are deleted. The updated Pictures lists are displayed in the Gallery.

Troubleshooting

I attempted to add a new image to the ClipArt Gallery by using the Organize feature, but there are too many files to scroll through to find the name of the image I want.

Use the Files of Type drop-down list to specify the specific file format of the file you need. If the image was created by a drawing package such as CorelDRAW!, change the Files of Type to CorelDRAW! (.CDR). Also note that you can still use DOS wild cards such as *.*, ??.*, and so on. If you have hundreds of files of a certain type in your folder and still must winnow down the choices, use wild cards. If you have a file called POWERBK9.TIF and there are 500 TIF files in the folder but only ten files with the name POWERBK, search using the criteria POWERBK*.* or POWERBK?.*. You might have to experiment a bit, but your search methods will be made much more effective.

(continues)

III

Adding Illustrations

(continued)

I used PowerPoint's SETUP program to add more clip art images to my system, but when I try to access them from PowerPoint, they don't show up in the ClipArt Gallery.

To use the new images, you must let PowerPoint know where they are located on your disk drive. Choose Organize and then Update in the ClipArt Gallery dialog box to scan the drive for the images. The images are added to the ClipArt Gallery, and you can add them to your slide presentations.

My company has grown quickly, and I have numerous divisional logo images I'd like to use in PowerPoint. I used the Organize feature of the ClipArt Gallery to create a new category for the logos, but my company has gone public and changed its name. The category name I used for the images is no longer correct.

In the ClipArt Gallery dialog box, use the Rename Category feature in the shortcut menu to rename it to match your new company name.

I mistakenly deleted a category of images in the ClipArt Gallery, and I need an image from the deleted category.

The images in the category you deleted are not gone, just removed from the Gallery. You can use the Organize feature to find the old category of art. To recover the image you need, use the instructions for adding pictures to the Gallery in this chapter.

Adding Scanned Art

Scanners allow you to copy a variety of important material such as company logos, drawings, photographs, and text into your computer directly from paper. There are two basic types of scanners: *handheld* and *flatbed*. While flatbed scanners offer a wider range of options and features, high-end ones can cost as much as a personal computer. (Prices have been dropping, however.) Handheld scanners, on the other hand, tend to be priced much lower, making them popular PC accessories. Another device that is becoming popular is the digital camera, which works the same way as a regular camera in many respects, but stores images in a bank of memory. You then download the images into files on a desktop or laptop system for printing, image processing, and other operations.

Scanners in particular work in a specific way; they copy an image and save it to a file on your PC. Many flatbed scanners allow you to scan color as well as black-and-white images. Flatbed scanners that do this make three passes over a color image using blue, red, and green light. Good color handheld units also produce images that appear in shades of gray or in color.

If you can afford it, flatbeds are usually more powerful and versatile. Flatbeds can scan two-dimensional art of any kind, photographs, films, and slides. They're also far and away the best choice for OCR (Optical Character Recognition) tasks. Scanners are rated in terms of two things: color depth and resolution. A good color flatbed should support at least 24-bit color for good reproduction of photographic images on the screen and on paper. (Some good ones support 30- and 36-bit color depths.)

Scanner resolution is measured in Points Per Inch (PPI) or Dots Per Inch (DPI), just like a laser printer. Some inexpensive color flatbeds offer "pure" 300-DPI scanning with "interpolated" 600- or 1200-DPI resolution. This means that the scanner package uses software to boost the "apparent" resolution. Usually, the results aren't that good. Given that laser printers average 600-DPI printout and even up to 1200-DPI, you want to get as much quality as you can afford.

Bear in mind that the DPI of the scanner and of your printer aren't the same as on your screen. Typically, your Windows screen runs at a mere 96 DPI!

The software that usually comes with your scanner manages the scanning operation, uses interpolation if desired, and allows you to edit and print the image. Most software packages also give you more than one file format choice, into which you can save the scanned image. Typical file formats include TIF, EPS, BMP, and others. All are easily read by PowerPoint.

Placing a Scanned Image onto a Slide

There is no big secret to adding scanned images to your slides. You have to save the scanned image in a format that PowerPoint can read (see table 12.1 for a list). Then, you can simply choose Insert, Picture or even incorporate the scanned artwork into your ClipArt Gallery.

To add the scanned picture to a slide from the Gallery, add the art to the Gallery using the methods described earlier and follow the steps given earlier in this chapter's section "Placing ClipArt from the Gallery onto a Slide."

◀ See "Selecting, Editing, and Enhancing Graphic Objects," p.287

In this chapter, you have had a good look at PowerPoint's revamped ClipArt Gallery. You've learned how to place clip art as well as other types of pictures into presentations. You may want to explore other art-related chapters in this book. You may also want to start exploring those CD-ROM clip art disks gathering dust on your shelf to see what else you can use in the Gallery.❖

III

Adding Illustrations

Part IV

Creating Charts

Chapter 13

Working with Datasheets

by Rich Grace

Charting is one of the key facilities in PowerPoint 95. Charts are created using rows and columns of numeric data. In PowerPoint, those rows and columns are called a *datasheet*. The process of creating and editing datasheets is important to effective charting in the program.

This chapter begins by discussing how datasheets are created and used. Creating them is similar to table creation, discussed in previous chapters. Datasheets, however, are used solely to create charts and are not intended for direct display on a slide. (This can easily be done, however.) To create datasheets and charts or to edit existing ones, you must begin with PowerPoint 95's Graph program.

In this chapter, you learn how to

- Start PowerPoint's charting features

- Place data series in rows or columns

- Edit datasheets

- Work with rows and columns

- Format chart data

Understanding PowerPoint's Charting Feature

PowerPoint 95's charting features represent a minor level of improvement over PowerPoint 4, its predecessor. PowerPoint 95 focuses more on improvements in charting efficiency and speed—saving users steps to achieve the same result. It is in many other areas of the software that PowerPoint 95 has made tremendous strides. The charting, already made strong in the previous release, has simply been made easier to work with, containing many fine details showing competent and subtle design work.

PowerPoint 95's charting is in a program called Microsoft Graph. When you install PowerPoint 95, Graph also is installed. Graph is actually an entirely separate program, intended to be used in other Microsoft Office applications such as Word for Windows 95. For this purpose, Graph uses a technique called *object linking and embedding* (*OLE*) to place charts into PowerPoint slides.

▶ See "Using OLE 2.0," p. 514

How does it work? Whenever you double-click a chart or new chart object in a PowerPoint slide, Microsoft Graph appears, taking over the PowerPoint window. That's why you don't see the name Microsoft Graph pop up when you start it to create charts for your slides. It doesn't look like a separate application program at all—but it is. This illustrates an important OLE feature called *in-place editing*. Object linking and embedding is a method (invented by Microsoft) for allowing applications to share various types of data between them. It's been used for a few years as a major feature in many Windows programs. Windows 95 and Office 95 now represent the state of the art in OLE integration.

This chapter, and all the other chapters that talk about charting, will refer to Microsoft Graph as a separate program.

Starting the Charting Application

You begin the examples in this chapter by creating a new chart. To create a new datasheet and chart, follow these steps:

1. Open the presentation in which you want to embed a new chart object.

2. Display the slide on which you want to insert a chart.

3. Click the Insert Graph button on the PowerPoint toolbar. The Microsoft Graph application program starts.

Note

You also can create a new slide with a chart object embedded in it by clicking the New Slide button at the bottom of the PowerPoint screen and choosing a slide template with an embedded chart object. When the slide is created, a column chart icon appears in the middle of the chart object, with the caption Double-click to Add Graph underneath.

The Microsoft Graph standard toolbar appears at the top of the PowerPoint screen, and a new datasheet is displayed with a chart object just behind it (see fig. 13.1). The PowerPoint menu bar also changes to Graph's set of menus and functions.

Graph menu bar

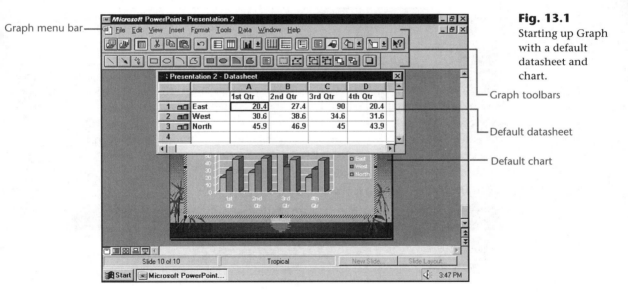

Fig. 13.1
Starting up Graph with a default datasheet and chart.

Graph toolbars

Default datasheet

Default chart

Note

Graph's Standard toolbar offers buttons to perform many functions. Other important functions for changing the look of datasheets are available in Graph's Formatting toolbar, which is displayed by default. Finally, Graph's Drawing toolbar allows you to use a large number of drawing tools to help embellish your charts. To display or remove any toolbar from Graph's screen, choose View, Toolbars and place or remove check marks in the Toolbars list. Choosing OK will remove or display the desired toolbars.

Notice that the new datasheet has a set of default values that make up the sample data displayed. The chart shown just behind it is a default 3-D column chart. The following sections lead you through the process of editing the chart and choosing different types of charts to reflect the changes in your datasheet.

Troubleshooting

My datasheet doesn't appear when I double-click the chart to start Graph!

That chart may default to "hiding" the datasheet. To fix this, choose View, Datasheet. The datasheet for that chart appears. When you finish editing, don't remove the datasheet from view before re-embedding the chart. This ensures that it will appear should you need to edit it again.

Tip
Press Alt+V+D to display the current datasheet in Graph.

Understanding Datasheets

The process of creating and editing datasheets is quite simple and closely resembles editing tables, which is described in Chapter 9, "Creating and Working with Tables." The key difference is that when you are editing datasheets, they are used to create charts for display in your presentation. Unlike tables, datasheets are not displayed on slides after you edit them—they are only used to generate charts. That is why you must double-click an existing chart before the associated datasheet will appear.

> **Note**
>
> Datasheets are used to create charts. They aren't displayed on slides as tables are. They only appear when you want to insert or edit a chart.

Each rectangle containing text entries in a datasheet is called a *cell*. Some cells, such as the ones displayed on the top row and in the farthest left column of the datasheet shown in figure 13.2, are meant to hold text that is used to label each row and column in the chart. Most other cells hold data values. In many PowerPoint charts, several categories of data are compared against each other. Each category of data, in turn, is called a *data series*. In the sample datasheet in figure 13.2, the series are labeled East, West, and North. Each series has four values, which are in turn labeled 1st Qtr, 2nd Qtr, 3rd Qtr, and 4th Qtr. The time period labels are displayed on the top row of the datasheet. Those labels are called a *measurement scale* or *timeline*.

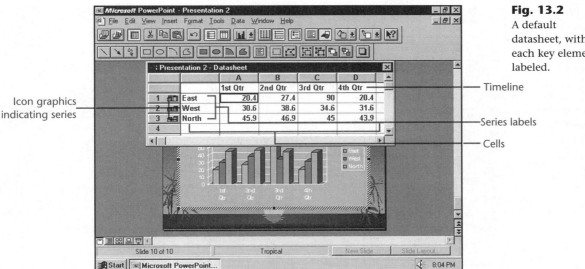

Fig. 13.2
A default datasheet, with each key element labeled.

Icon graphics indicating series

Timeline

Series labels

Cells

Each row and column is numbered, just as in a typical spreadsheet. The rows in the example are labeled 1 through 3, and the columns are labeled A through D.

Placing Data Series in Rows or Columns

An important aspect of editing charts is knowing where to place your data values for best effect. A *data series* can be defined as a single set of values that have a close relationship to each other. For most charts, data values are placed in rows in the datasheet to create each series. Each successive value represents another entry for the series on the timeline represented in the chart. Notice that the PowerPoint default is to place data series in rows, as shown in figure 13.3. Sometimes, series are placed in columns for a different charting effect.

In figure 13.3, each row label has a small graphic placed next to it, indicating the chart type in which each series appears. For this example, the series label graphics indicate that 3-D columns are used and show the colors used for each series. Putting the series in rows emphasizes the timeline values (1st Qtr, 2nd Qtr, 3rd Qtr, and 4th Qtr in the default example), each of which compares the figures for East, West, and North for each quarter. Placing the data series in rows creates the best and most workable chart in many cases. This

Tip
Look for the label graphics to quickly see whether the data series are organized in rows or columns.

Fig. 13.3
Looking at Graph's default datasheet and its elements.

Graphics indicate the chart type and color for each series

Series are in row as default

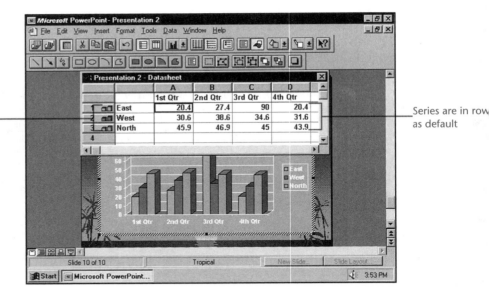

applies to almost every chart type you create. Exceptions to this rule are discussed in later chapters. But it's easy to change the series orientation, and there may be cases where you'll want to.

For example, you may want to emphasize the East, West, and North data sets by defining the yearly quarters to be the data series rather than the regions. Then, the data for each quarter is broken down by columns in the datasheet (with one value from each series for each quarter), so the data series need to be redefined in columns.

To redefine the data series from rows to columns, perform the following steps:

1. Display the slide containing the chart you want to change.

2. Double-click the chart to select it and bring up the Graph toolbar.

3. Click the View Datasheet button on the Graph Standard toolbar to display the datasheet.

4. Click the By Column button on the Graph Standard toolbar.

Notice that the series label graphics migrate to the column labels A through D on the datasheet. That indicates that the series labels have been transferred to the columns. Thus, the series are now the quarters rather than the regions.

The chart also reflects these changes. Notice how the four sets of three columns in figure 13.3 have become three sets of four columns, shown in figure 13.4. Also notice how the East, West, and North labels have been placed on the axis at the bottom of the chart, replacing the original quarter labels. The data for each region is broken down in columns in the datasheet instead of the data for each quarter.

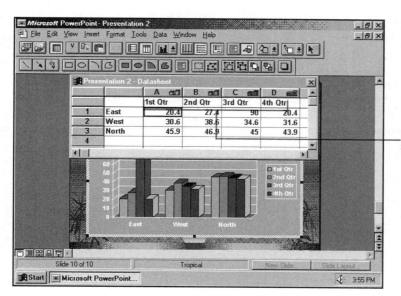

Fig. 13.4
Changing the datasheet series orientation to Columns from the Rows default.

Series have been swapped to columns

Editing Datasheets

In PowerPoint 95, editing a datasheet is a relatively painless process. PowerPoint's default datasheet offers a default set of data series that can either be deleted or simply typed over when you want to enter new values. There are a few generic rules to follow when editing datasheets:

- Use the arrow keys to move from one cell to another.

- To move through each successive cell in a row, press the Tab key.

- To completely remove a cell, row, or column's contents, press the Delete key.

- When the desired cell is selected, simply type in the new value or entry, and the old one is overwritten.

Table 13.1 shows a sample data set you can enter into the datasheet. It's a fictitious listing of the market share for laser printers split between three companies over a three-year period.

Table 13.1 Laser Printer Market Share (entirely fictional)				
	1992	**1993**	**1994**	**1995**
Printcorp, Inc.	22.1	23.5	21.8	22.7
LaserPrint, Inc.	57.1	57.3	60.2	61.8
Patriot Printers	20.8	19.2	18.0	15.5

To enter the data shown in table 13.1 into the datasheet, follow these steps:

1. Click the mouse once inside the cell labeled 1st Qtr in the default datasheet.

2. Type **1992**, and then press Tab or the right-arrow key to move to the cell labeled 2nd Qtr. Type **1993**, which overwrites the previous entry. Repeat the same step to enter **1994** in the next cell. Move to the next cell and type in **1995**. Press Tab or click the mouse anywhere outside of the 1995 cell.

   Notice that the 1995 entry automatically is right-aligned when you click outside it. In Graph datasheets, cell entries default to right alignment. The company labels, however, default to left alignment.

3. Click inside the cell labeled East and type **Printcorp, Inc**. The original entry, as with the previous ones, is overwritten. Next, press the down-arrow key to move to the cell labeled West.

4. Repeat step 3, replacing West and North with **LaserPrint, Inc.** and **Patriot Printers,** respectively.

5. Use the arrow keys, or click in the desired cells, to replace the default values with those in table 13.1. When you're finished, the datasheet should look like that shown in figure 13.5.

Notice that in the datasheet in the preceding example, the column containing the series labels PrintCorp, Inc., LaserPrint, Inc., and Patriot Printers is too narrow for the long company names; they override the boundaries of their cells and are not visible beyond the cell border. You learn how to solve this problem later in this chapter, in the section titled "Changing the Column Width."

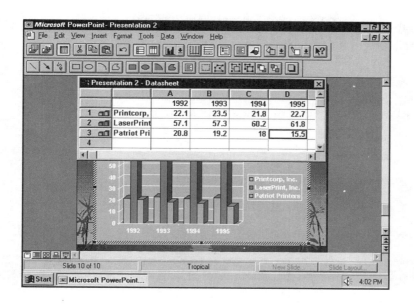

Fig. 13.5
Your newly edited
datasheet.

IV

Creating Charts

Editing Cells

Editing a cell is quite simple, but keep in mind a couple of generic rules when doing so:

- To edit the contents of a cell without overwriting its contents, double-click inside the cell and then place the I-beam at the place in the cell text where you want to edit.

- To edit and overwrite the contents of a cell, simply click the cell once to select it and begin typing.

You may not want to overwrite the contents of a cell to change its contents. Say, for example, that you want to change LaserPrint, Inc., to read LP.

1. Double-click inside the cell labeled LaserPrint, Inc. The cell contents are highlighted, and the entire text "pops out" and seems to overwrite the next cell to the right. (Don't worry about this. The other cell's contents are untouched.)

2. Notice that when you pass the mouse over the highlighted cell, it turns from a cross into an I-beam for editing. Click the mouse once again at the end of the text entry you highlighted. The text insertion point blinks at the end of LaserPrint, Inc.

3. Press the Backspace key until you are left with LaserP in the entry, and type a period to indicate an abbreviation. With the arrow key, move the insertion point to the end of the first word and Backspace over it until the cell reads LP.

Notice that when editing a cell, you can also use the Delete key to delete characters to the right of the text insertion point.

Copying Cells

Copying cell contents to another cell is a simple process, but there is a subtle trick to watch for. Following these steps helps ease the process:

1. Select the cell you want to copy by clicking once inside it with the mouse. The cell border is bolded.

2. Choose Edit, Copy; or press Ctrl+C.

3. Click once inside the datasheet cell to which you want to copy.

4. Choose Edit, Paste; or press Ctrl+V.

> **Note**
>
> In many Windows software packages, you're probably used to double-clicking a word to select it before you delete it, copy it, or move it. When you edit datasheets in PowerPoint 95, you are now able to do that: It's a new feature! When you double-click a cell, the contents are highlighted, and the Ctrl+C and Ctrl+V (Cut and Paste) commands work as they do with typical editing tasks. You could not do this in PowerPoint 4 datasheets. You can still copy cell contents to the Clipboard, by clicking just once on the desired cell and performing your Copy command.

To use the right mouse button to copy a cell's contents, follow these steps:

1. Click the right mouse button on the cell you want to copy. The Edit shortcut menu appears.

2. Choose the Copy command. The cell's contents are copied to the Clipboard. The cell's contents can now be pasted into a new cell.

As you can see, there are several simple ways to get the job done.

Dragging and Dropping Cells

It's simple to drag and drop a cell's contents to another location in the datasheet. Just select the cell, and then click and hold the mouse over its border. (When you select a cell or group of cells, the border surrounding them is highlighted in a thicker black line.) Drag the mouse to the new location on the datasheet. While you drag the cell, you see an outline of the cell as you drag. You can also hold down the Ctrl key while you drag, if you want to drag and drop a copy of the cell to a new location. A plus sign (+) appears next to the pointer when you drag while holding down the Ctrl Key.

> **Troubleshooting**
>
> *Even though I'm double-clicking a cell value to select it, I can't use any of the menu options on it. What's wrong?*
>
> You cannot double-click a datasheet cell to select it for many operations. Most menu options dealing with editing and formatting are dimmed. In PowerPoint 95, single-clicking has the same effect. To change the font and formatting for cells in a datasheet, you must select the entire row or column.
>
> *I can't get drag-and-drop to work!*
>
> The feature may be turned off. To enable dragging and dropping of cells, choose Tools, Options. Several tab options appear. If it is not already shown, click the Datasheet Options tab. If the Cell Drag and Drop option is not selected, click once inside its check box to enable it, and choose OK or press Enter. You should now be able to use drag-and-drop on your datasheets.

Working with Rows and Columns

Datasheets allow editing of individual cells and their values. In PowerPoint 95, the process of editing and working with rows and columns of data is intuitive and simple. Each cell in a datasheet can be altered, or an entire row or column, several selected rows and columns, or groups of selected cells can be copied and moved to another section of the datasheet. Columns, rows, and cells can also be selected for exclusion from a chart.

Selecting Rows and Columns

Selecting rows and columns for editing and moving is a straightforward process. Datasheets in the new PowerPoint have a series of 3-D buttons along the top and left side, each of which represents one column or one row of data. Clicking one of these buttons automatically selects the entire row or column. All these buttons are lettered or numbered; numbers represent rows, and letters represent columns.

Tip
Click the row or column button with the right mouse button to both select it and bring up the short-cut menu.

Use the following techniques to select rows and columns:

- To select an entire row, click the numbered button (1, 2, 3, and so on) to the left of the row you want to select. The row of data values is highlighted.

- To select an entire column, click the lettered button (A, B, C, and so on) at the top of the row. The column of data values is highlighted.

- To select more than one row or column at a time without selecting the entire chart, hold down the Shift key as you click each successive button.

- Once the row(s) or column(s) is highlighted, press Ctrl+C to copy the contents to the Clipboard.

You also can click the mouse over the first cell to be selected and drag the mouse over all the other cells you want to include in the group. The rule applies to a row of cells, a column of cells, or to any number of rows and columns in combination. All the cells selected are highlighted in black, and can then be copied and pasted into other places in the datasheet.

Clearing Rows and Columns

PowerPoint 95 has made some small but important improvements in the way users work with datasheets. For example, in PowerPoint 4, simply selecting the column (or row) to delete and pressing the Delete key or Ctrl+X was not enough to remove the column. You could then wind up with unexplained empty areas in your charts and not quite know how to get rid of them. PowerPoint 95 has eliminated this minor logical glitch. Now, pressing the Delete key clears the selected cell, column, or row of all its contents, removing them as an entity in the chart. Cut and Clear commands both also accomplish this.

> **Note**
>
> Pressing the space bar also erases the entry, but it leaves a space bar character in the datasheet cell. Pressing Backspace opens the Clear dialog box, which works just as well but imposes an extra step. The quickest way, and the safest and easiest for good datasheet editing practice, is to use the Delete key.

1. Click the column button labeled D at the top of the datasheet. The entire column is highlighted.

2. Press the Delete key, or Ctrl+X for Cut.

 3. To restore a deletion of any datasheet cells, press Ctrl+Z or click the Undo button on Graph's Standard toolbar.

You cannot select more than one cell with the right mouse button. A single cell, or a single column or row button, can be selected.

IV

Creating Charts

Inserting New Rows and Columns

If you discover that you need another row or column in your datasheet, it's a simple matter to add one. In fact, you can do so in several ways. Again, there are a few generic techniques that can be followed:

■ To insert a new row above any other row, click the row button (1, 2, 3, and so on) for the row above which you want to insert a new one. Then choose Insert, Cells.

Suppose that you want to add a new row to the top of the datasheet displayed in figure 13.5. You need to reset the chart for Series in Rows and add the new row, by following these steps:

1. Click the By Row button on the Graph toolbar. PowerPoint returns the series to the Rows in the datasheet.

2. Click the row button labeled 1. The entire datasheet row labeled PrintCorp, Inc., is selected.

3. Choose Insert, Cells.

   A new row is inserted above the PrintCorp, Inc., row. The datasheet row labeled PrintCorp, Inc., moves down to row 2. You are now in the process of adding another series of data to the chart.

   Notice that the chart itself does not yet change or add any space for more columns.

4. Click the mouse in the cell above PrintCorp, Inc., and type **Color Laser Ltd.** Press the right-arrow key to move to the next cell.

5. Type the values **17.1**, **15.5**, **14.9, and 15.3** in columns A, B, C, and D respectively.

As you enter the values for the fourth series, you see that the chart adjusts to place a fourth column in each yearly group (see fig. 13.6). The new columns in the series are automatically assigned a new color in the chart, and the name Color Laser Ltd. is added to the legend.

You don't have to select an entire row to insert a new one:

1. With the left mouse button, click any cell in the row (except its row number) above which a new row is to be inserted.

2. Choose Insert, Cells to display the Insert dialog box (see fig. 13.7).

3. Choose from the following options:

Fig. 13.6.
Adding a new row
to the datasheet.

Chart has added
room for the
new series.

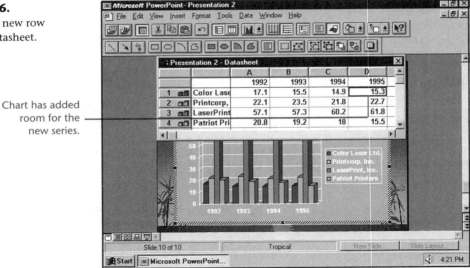

Fig. 13.7
Using the Insert
Cells command to
add a new row to
the datasheet.

■ *Shift Cells Right* enables you to shift the cell or cells you have selected to the right by one cell (or column).

■ *Shift Cells Down* enables you to shift the cell or cells you have
selected down by one row.

■ *Entire Row* inserts an entire new row into the datasheet.

■ *Entire Column* inserts an entire new column into the datasheet.

For this example, choose Entire Row.

4. Choose OK or press Enter.

> **Note**
>
> The Insert dialog box appears only if you select a cell or a group of cells. If you select
> an entire row or column (by clicking their buttons), choosing Insert, Cells automati-
> cally adds the new one.

Dragging and Dropping Rows and Columns

Graph's datasheet editor also enables you to drag and drop cells, groups of cells, rows, and columns. It's a fast rearranging feature that was not present in the previous version of Microsoft Graph.

To drag and drop one or more rows or columns, follow these steps:

1. Select the cell(s), row(s), or column(s) you want to move to a new place on the datasheet.

2. Click and hold the mouse on the border of the selected cells. Drag the cells to the new location on the datasheet. Make sure not to overwrite other datasheet elements you want to keep. If you accidentally do so, Graph warns you and prompts whether you want to replace the contents of the destination cells. Choose Cancel. If you drag rows or columns to a blank location, you can undo the drag and drop by choosing Edit, Undo Drag and Drop.

Tip

To drag and drop a copy of any datasheet contents, hold down the Ctrl key while dragging to drag a copy of the selection and leave the original in place.

Formatting Chart Data

Datasheets bear a resemblance to conventional spreadsheets because chart data can be formatted in a variety of ways. You can apply different fonts to the datasheet to change its appearance. You can change the style of numbers used in the datasheet. You can set the alignment of cell data to be left-aligned, right-aligned, centered, or justified. Column width can be adjusted for more readable values. Most of these operations, with one exception, do not affect the chart that you are creating with the datasheet; they are used to improve the datasheet's readability.

The only datasheet formatting specification that can alter the results of your chart display is formatting of numbers. This feature has a crucial bearing on the resulting display of your chart.

Changing the Numeric Format

Changing the numeric format of the chart is simply a matter of specifying that you want your data values to be of a specific format. Numbering systems are offered in a wide variety of formats and can be closely associated with the type of charts you are trying to create. Table 13.2 lists the numbering categories available for use in PowerPoint 95.

Table 13.2 Numbering Categories	
Category	**Description**
Accounting	For ledger sheets and accounting charts
Currency	Adds currency signs to dollar values
Date	Formatting for various dating standards (m/d/yy) and others)
Fraction	Used for stock quotes and Open-High-Low-Close stock charts
General	PowerPoint default; automatically adjusts numbers to most precise value
Number	Various standard number formats up to eight characters including commas and decimal points
Percentage	Expresses values as percentages and attaches percent signs
Scientific	Applies scientific notation to datasheet values
Time	Formatting for various timing standards (h:mm:ss and others)
Text	Standard Arabic text numbers

Each category has a selection of specialized numbering types. Sometimes, if a number format is too long for the size of the cell holding the data value, the number is displayed in scientific notation. At other times, if the number is far too big to be displayed at all, it is shown as a series of hatch marks (#), in which case the column must be widened to properly display the data value.

Each numbering format affects the actual value in different ways. Table 13.3 shows a partial list of samples of various number, date, and time formats.

Table 13.3 Number Formatting Examples	
Type	**Result**
General	5
0	5
0.00	5.00
#,##0	5

Type	Result
#,##0.00	5.00
$#,##0_);[Red]($#,##0)	$5
$#,##0.00_;[Red]($#,##0.00)	$5.00
0%	500%
0.00%	500.00%
0.00E+00	5.00E+00
m/d/yy	1/5/94
d-mmm-yy	5-Jan-94
mmm-yy	Jan-94
h:mm AM/PM	11:00 AM
h:mm:ss AM/PM	11:00:00 AM
h:mm	11:00
h:mm:ss	11:00:00
m/d/yy h:mm	1/5/94 14:00

When changing the numeric format in a datasheet, the values displayed on the Y or value measurement axis in the accompanying chart change to reflect the chosen number format.

To change the number format for one cell on a datasheet, follow these steps:

1. To quickly change the number format of a cell in Graph, click the right mouse button on the cell to select it and bring up the shortcut menu.

> **Note**
>
> You also can click once with the left mouse button on the cell to select it, and then choose Format, Number. Don't make the conventional mistake of double-clicking the cell to select it. The Number menu command is ghosted and unavailable.

2. Choose the Number command. The Number Format dialog box appears (see fig. 13.8).

Fig. 13.8
Using the Number
Format dialog box.

Numbering formats ——

Sample result ——

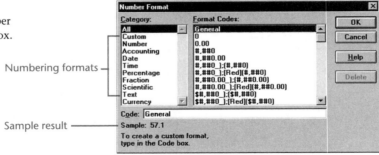

3. Select the numbering Category, and then choose the desired numbering format.

Although many number formats are rather complex to look at, you can see their end result on the Sample line just underneath the format list. The formatting code you select is shown in the Code text box.

4. Click the OK button.

To change the numbering format for all cells in a datasheet, drag the left mouse button over the desired cells to select them. The cells are highlighted in black. Click the right mouse button over any of the selected cells and choose the Number command; or choose Format, Number.

To change the numbering format for a single row or column, simply click the row or column heading button to select it, and then choose Format, Number or click the right mouse button over the selected cells to pull down the short-cut menu.

To convert the numeric values in the sample datasheet to percentages to reflect the purpose of the chart, which is to display market share in percentages, follow these steps:

1. Select any cell in the datasheet.

2. Choose Format, Number to display the Number Format dialog box.

3. From the Category list, select Percentage.

4. From the Format Codes list, select the Percent numbering format you want.

5. Choose OK or press Enter.

Tip
You also can customize any numbering code in the Code text box by deleting or adding your own formatting characters.

Tip
Use the Formatting toolbar's Increase Decimal and Decrease Decimal buttons to add or subtract significant digits from decimal values.

Percent signs appear on the selected numbers in the datasheet.

> **Note**
>
> The Formatting toolbar contains several buttons that can be used to manipulate number formatting. They include Currency, Percent, and Comma Style buttons, and buttons for adding significant digits to decimal numbers (from 20.3 to 20.30, for example) and subtracting them (from 20.30 to 20.3, and so on).

As you may have noticed by now, there are several ways to do just about any basic operation in a datasheet. Most people are used to using the left mouse button (the normally used one) to pull down menus and select options. Using the right mouse button takes a minor conceptual leap but has the potential to save time by cutting the necessary number of steps to select values and formatting menu options in half.

Changing the Fonts in a Chart

Changing the font in a datasheet is simply a cosmetic process to improve the datasheet's appearance. Changing the font in a datasheet does not affect the display in a chart; text elements in a chart must have their fonts changed separately. With this in mind, selecting datasheet elements and changing their font works much the same way as with changing number formats.

PowerPoint 95 supports both TrueType and Adobe fonts for datasheets and charts. You can only change the font displayed on an entire datasheet; you cannot change the font or text formatting (boldface, italics, underlining, and so on) for just one cell, row, or column. (You can, however, do those things in an Excel spreadsheet.)

To change the fonts displayed in a datasheet, perform the following steps:

1. Click the right mouse button over any cell containing a datasheet value. The shortcut menu pops up.

2. Choose the Font command to display the Font dialog box.

3. After the dialog box opens, you can choose from the actions listed here:

   ■ Choose a new font from the Font list by clicking a name displayed on the list, or scroll down the list by pressing the down-arrow key when the insertion point is in the Font text box. Each successive font name is highlighted and displayed in the Preview window.

- Choose a new Font Style: Bold, Italic, Regular, Bold Italic, or whatever is shown in the list (some fonts you install in your system may not have all those options available).

- Choose a new font Size, if desired. Each size change is shown in the Preview window.

- You can choose an Underline style: Single, Double, or None.

- The displayed font Color can be changed to any color available in the palette.

- Three text Effects can be selected: Strikethrough, Superscript, or Subscript.

4. When the options are set the way you want, choose OK or press Enter.

The Formatting toolbar can also be used to add Bold, Italic, Underline, and to change the font and the font size. Also, a pull-down list is provided on the Formatting toolbar that offers quick access and selection of any available font on your system.

Changing the Column Width

Looking back at figure 13.5, you remember that the entry PrintCorp, Inc., on the sample datasheet is too large for the margins of the cell in which it's entered. That's also true for the other series labels. The column width can be changed to show the entire contents of the offending cell. Individual cells cannot have their margins adjusted.

To adjust the width of a selected column, follow these steps:

1. Click the column button for the column you want to adjust.

2. Choose Format, Column Width; the following options can be selected:

Tip
Double-clicking the right border of the column's heading is the fastest way to adjust a column width beyond the default.

- You can manually adjust the width by entering a new number value in the Column Width text box.

- Click the Best Fit button for an automatic adjustment of the column to the width needed to accommodate the PrintCorp, Inc., entry.

- The Use Standard Width check box can be used to adjust the column to the default width values in the datasheet.

3. Choose OK or press Enter. If you chose the <u>B</u>est Fit button, the width of the column is adjusted, and the entire company name appears. Figure 13.8 shows the results of this operation.

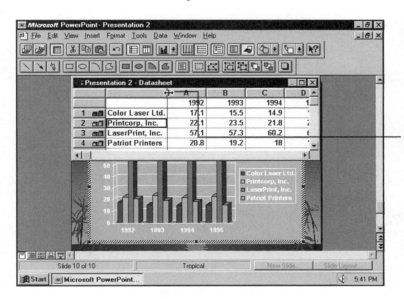

Fig. 13.9
Changing a column width for readable datasheet text.

You can adjust columns by dragging the border of the column button.

Troubleshooting

I can't drag and drop any rows or columns of data.

You're probably trying to click directly on a selected row to drag it. It won't work. Click the row or column button to select the entire row or column; then click and drag the black border of the selected row (column). Move the mouse to the desired location on the datasheet and release the button. Drag and drop works slightly different in Graph datasheets than it does in other applications. The method also works for individual cells or blocks of cells in a datasheet, except for their method of selection.

Now that you are familiar with working with datasheets and arranging data, you are ready to begin building PowerPoint charts. Chapter 14, "Creating Basic Charts," builds on what you learned about datasheets in this chapter and takes you through the process of creating bar, column, pie, and other chart types from datasheet values.❖

Chapter 14

Creating Basic Charts

by Rich Grace

As noted in chapter 13, PowerPoint 95 features greatly enhanced and more closely integrated charting capabilities. For native PowerPoint 95 use, a solid and well-designed charting engine offers excellent color scheme integration, a wide selection of chart types, flexibility in chart formatting, and many other features. It supports Microsoft Graph objects from PowerPoint 4, and any user of that program (or Excel) will immediately feel at home in it. The program also is more welcoming to newer users.

PowerPoint 95 offers sophisticated charting options that can help you convey powerful images to your audience—or, just as easily, confuse them. The key is to make the right choices, and to place no more information on the chart than is needed to illustrate your ideas. Besides presenting a road map of basic and essential charting features, this chapter also offers brief design tips to help ensure the most effective charts for your presentations.

In this chapter, you learn how to

- ■ Create several basic types of charts

- ■ Select chart types for maximum effectiveness

- ■ Add and edit various chart elements, including labels and titles

- ■ Change colors and patterns in your chart

- ■ Add a chart to your slide

> **Note**
>
> Throughout this chapter, please bear in mind that Graph is a separate program from PowerPoint. Whenever you use the program to create and modify charts, the Microsoft Graph program "takes over" the PowerPoint screen and displays its own toolbars. If this issue is a little confusing, please read the first section of Chapter 14, which offers a more complete description of Microsoft Graph's basic operations.

Using Chart AutoFormats

For its basic chart-generating engine, Graph uses a feature called *Chart AutoFormats*. It's where you begin when you want to create any of a dozen chart types, without spending a lot of time designing. As noted earlier in this book, Graph's Chart AutoFormat feature closely resembles the chart creation features of Microsoft Excel. Graph also allows you to create custom chart types and save them as AutoFormats for later use. (That feature is described later in this book.) Chart AutoFormats offer every major predefined chart type available in PowerPoint 95. Figure 14.1 shows the AutoFormat dialog box.

Fig. 14.1
Viewing the Chart AutoFormat feature.

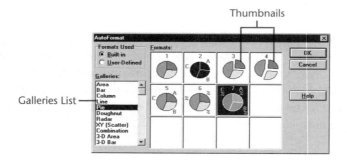

The AutoFormat dialog box is your key to having the greatest possible number of chart types to choose from. For example, in figure 14.1, Chart AutoFormat offers seven different types of 2-D pie charts, each of which are displayed in a thumbnail picture. Each thumbnail is numbered from 1 to 7. Double-clicking any of the thumbnails containing a desired chart type changes the selected chart to the new style.

To the left of the thumbnails rests the Graph Galleries list box. This is where you select every chart category offered by PowerPoint. When you select a different category, a different set of thumbnails appears, and you can select any of these for a new chart format. Table 14.1 lists the available charts:

Table 14.1   Chart AutoFormat Types

Gallery Type	# of AutoFormats Offered
2-D Area	5
2-D Bar	10
2-D Column	10
2-D Line	10
2-D Pie	7
2-D Doughnut	7
2-D Radar	6
2-D XY (Scatter)	6
Combination	6
3-D Area	8
3-D Bar	5
3-D Column	8
3-D Line	4
3-D Pie	7
3-D Surface	4

To choose a chart AutoFormat, perform the following steps:

1. Double-click the chart object on the PowerPoint slide to bring up Graph. (The process works both for existing charts and for newly created ones; for example, slides created with a Slide AutoLayout.)

2. Choose Format, AutoFormat.

   The AutoFormat dialog box appears.

3. Choose a chart type from the scrollable Galleries list.

   A new set of thumbnails appears in the Formats section.

4. Click on a thumbnail that contains the desired chart type.

5. Choose OK or press Enter.

Tip

A double-click on the desired thumbnail selects it and applies it to the chart.

Note

It's a simple matter to insert your completed chart into your slide. When you're ready, click once anywhere outside the selected chart object. The PowerPoint main screen reappears with its menus and toolbars, and the chart is now on the slide.

Tip

When you use the Chart Type button to change chart types, its appearance changes to match the currently selected chart type.

There are other ways to choose chart styles (including the Chart Type button on the Graph toolbar, which scrolls down an icon-based list of 14 basic chart types), but AutoFormat offers the fastest access to the greatest number of options for any given chart. Unless otherwise noted, this chapter uses AutoFormat for choosing chart styles.

Also, remember that you're not limited to the charting choices displayed in the AutoFormat thumbnails. You can create as many of your own custom chart types as you have room for on your hard disk. In the current chapter, you'll stick with the built-in chart types.

Understanding the Elements of a Chart

Chart elements are the pieces that compose a chart. The presenter manipulates, customizes, and formats chart elements to produce a desired visual effect. Some AutoFormat styles base their uniqueness solely on whether the chart displays certain text labels, or whether gridlines are present in the background to aid in visual measurement. (These are relatively minor differences between chart types.) The next several sections discuss those elements and how to work with them.

Knowing basic chart elements is the key to effectively designing and customizing charts. It also will help you when you explore the chart creation and modification examples later in this chapter (and later in this book). Most chart types share the elements and principles described in the paragraphs that follow.

The various chart elements fall into two categories—those that are common to 2-D charts, and those that are unique to 3-D charts. Two-dimensional charts exist only in a flat, two-dimensional visual plane, while three-dimensional charts add a third dimension that gives the illusion of visual depth.

Elements of Two-Dimensional Charts

Figure 14.2 shows a sample 2-D column chart with each chart element identified.

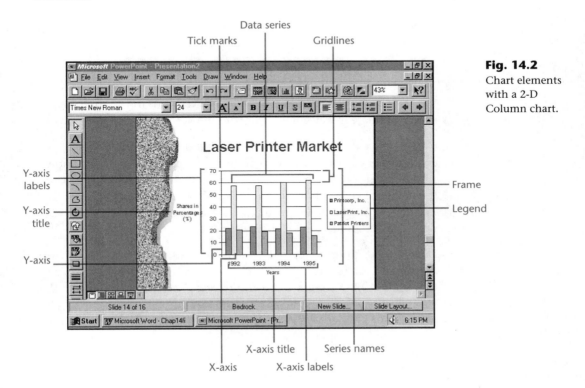

Fig. 14.2
Chart elements
with a 2-D
Column chart.

Not every chart will need all of these elements to get your point across—and some chart types just get confusing if they contain too many elements. The following short sections describe each of the chart elements.

- *X-Axis.* The horizontal axis, which normally appears along the bottom of the chart. Each series has a single column for each increment along the X-axis. Figure 14.2 shows increments along the X-axis for the labels 1992, 1993, 1994, and 1995.

- *X-Axis Title.* Identifies the X-axis and what each axis label represents. In figure 14.2, the X-axis title is Years.

- *X-Axis Labels.* Labels for the increments along the X-axis. The audience uses the labels to determine what data each bar represents. In figure 14.2, the X-axis labels are 1992, 1993, 1994, and 1995.

- *Y-Axis.* The vertical axis against which the height of each column is measured. The increments and range of the Y-axis are directly based on the values in your data. The Y-axis value range starts at zero, or below your most negative data value, and extends beyond your highest data value. In figure 14.2, the increments of the Y-axis are evenly spaced from the bottom to the top of the range, in increments of 10 from 0 to 70.

- *Y-Axis Title.* Helps clarify what the data values in the chart represent. In figure 14.2, the data values, and hence the columns in the chart, are shown as Share in Percentages (%) for each company.

- *Y-Axis Labels.* Provide a scale for measuring the heights of bars and columns. As you can see, the labels on the Y-axis in figure 14.2 simply show the values of each increment, from 0 to 70. The viewer compares the height of each column to the axis and labels to learn the approximate value. For example, the market share for Printcorp, Inc. in 1992 was just over 20 percent by visual estimate.

Tip

Limit the number of series to four or less to keep the chart from becoming crowded or cluttered. For more than four series, use two or more charts.

- *Data Series.* A group or set of data defined by a specific criterion, such as all the data values associated with a company. PowerPoint displays all the columns of one series in the same color and relative location in the chart. In figure 14.2, the series for Printcorp, Inc. appears in the first column of each group in the chart. The series for Laser Print, Inc. appears in the second position of each column group. Finally, the series for Patriot Printers appears in the third position, or the rightmost columns, of each group in the chart.

- *Legend.* Provides information about the data in a chart, including the name for each series and the color for the columns (or bars, or pie slices, or whatever chart type you select). The legend in figure 14.2 indicates which series represents each company's yearly market shares and displays the color for the columns of each series.

- *Series Names.* Provide information about what the data series represent. The series names appear in the legend of the chart. In figure 14.2, the series names are Printcorp, Inc., Laser Print, Inc., and Patriot Printers.

- *Frame.* Appears behind the chart and works with the Y-axis as a scale with which to measure the columns' values. You can add gridlines to a frame, as figure 14.2 shows. (That figure shows only horizontal gridlines as an example.)

- *Gridlines.* These appear on the frame behind the chart; they extend from each axis across the frame. Gridlines displayed from the Y-axis appear behind the chart and help you measure the height and value of columns. Gridlines displayed from the X-axis help visually separate each group of yearly columns.

- *Tick Marks.* Tick marks help mark measurement levels on a chart axis. In fig. 14.2, each tick mark has a label next to it showing the value measurement at that level in the chart (10, 20, 30, and so on). You can have Major and Minor tick marks to almost any density on an axis.

Elements of Three-Dimensional Charts

In many cases, a 3-D chart may not be absolutely necessary but may provide visual attractiveness and impact, without detracting from the message. In other cases, 3-D charts offer compelling advantages. You can adjust viewing angles with many 3-D chart types, and add spectacular special effects such as rotation and perspective. The following paragraphs describe chart elements that are unique to 3-D charts.

Figure 14.3 shows a sample 3-D column chart with each chart element identified.

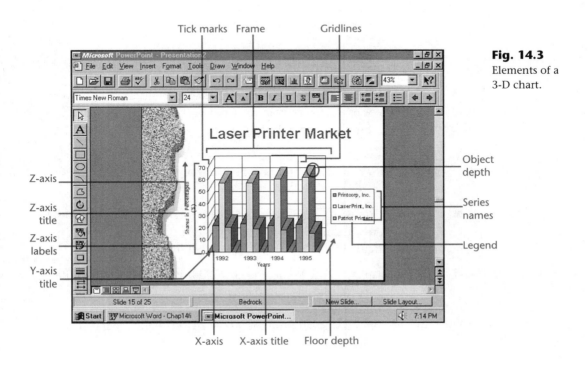

Fig. 14.3
Elements of a 3-D chart.

■ *Z-Axis*. The X- and Y-axis elements described for 2-D charts apply to all charts you can create in Microsoft PowerPoint. X- and Y-axes give shape to 2-D charts—charts that have no visual depth. Three-dimensional charts have a third axis, called the *Z-axis*. The Z-axis helps create the depth that defines the shape of a 3-D chart.

In a 3-D chart, the Z-axis is actually the vertical axis—unlike 2-D charts where the Y-axis is the vertical one. Imagine a 2-D chart flopped over on its side, with the previously vertical Y-axis now lying on the "floor." The Z-axis is then drawn perpendicular to the plane created by the X- and Y-axes. The Y-axis gives the illusion of depth to the chart, and the Z-axis takes its visual place. The Z-axis is generally labeled with a series of tick-mark labels, used to measure values.

Tip

The Z-axis lends depth to a 3-D chart and acquires the measurement tick marks that otherwise would be on the Y-axis if the chart were 2-D.

■ *Z-Axis Title*. Identifies the Z-axis and what each axis label represents. Figure 14.3 shows that the Z-axis title is Market Share %.

■ *Z-Axis Labels*. Labels for the value increments along the Z-axis, numbered from 0 to 70.

> **Note**
>
> In 3-D charts you normally use the X- and Z-axes to provide clues about the data presented in your chart. Most 3-D charts don't provide three axis titles or enable attachment of labels or increments to them. For that matter, adding a title to just one of the axes can provide all the information you need about the contents of a chart.

■ *Object Depth*. Applies only to 3-D charts. *Object depth* is the thickness of the column or other object from the front of the chart to the back. Two-dimensional charts are flat and have no depth.

■ *Floor*. Applies only to 3-D charts. The *Floor* helps define how deep the bottom of the chart is and helps define how much room there is between each series.

■ *Frame*. Displays behind the chart and works with the Z-axis as a scale with which to measure the columns in the chart. Gridlines can be added to a frame in a 3-D chart, as they are in figure 14.3.

■ *Gridlines*. Display on the frame; they extend from each axis across the frame. Gridlines displayed from the Z-axis are seen behind the chart and help you measure the height and value of the column. In 3-D charts, gridlines displayed from the X-axis help visually separate each group of yearly columns.

■ *Tick Marks.* Tick marks help visually measure values on a chart axis. As with 2-D charts, tick marks can have value labels next to them that help measure values quickly. In figure 14.3, tick marks are attached to the Z-axis and numeric labels are attached for easier value measurement. Again, Major and Minor tick marks can be applied.

Selecting the Best Chart Type for Your Data

PowerPoint 95 offers a wide selection of chart types, including 2-D and 3-D line charts, XY scatter charts, combination charts, doughnuts, 3-D surface charts, and radar charts. A complete breakdown of all chart types and their uses is beyond the scope of this chapter and this book. Brief accounts of many other types are offered in this book, and you'll meet more of them in Chapter 20.

In many cases, selecting a chart type is a matter of taste. As explained later in this chapter and in this book, you can manipulate many other charting design features to modify and customize charts for maximum effectiveness, but there's another issue to consider. What kinds of charts work best for which situations? Here are some simple guidelines that may help you select from the various chart types.

■ Audiences appreciate bar charts because of their visual simplicity, and their common frame of reference—the size or length of horizontal bars representing the data values. When the audience walks out of the conference room, they tend to remember images of bars and how they differ in size rather than specific values and percentages. The secret to effective bar charting is simplicity—providing bars in your images that the audience can easily see and compare. In other words, don't pack a chart with too many bars.

■ Use column charts when you have data values that you want your viewers to compare, such as the sales of different products over a period of time. Viewers can quickly see differences in values and spot trends in the data. Column charts are popular in every charting and spreadsheet program on the market. Both bar and column charts—2-D and 3-D alike—can be used to display more than one series of data. So what's the difference between bar and column charts? Simply, bars are measured horizontally, while columns are measured vertically.

■ Bar and column charts of both types also have special sub-types, such as stacked bars and stacked columns. An example of a stacked column chart can be seen in figure 14.4. 3-D column charts are a type that places each series in its own rank, offering direct visual comparisons of values in each series, while showing their relationships to the other series in the chart.

■ Pie charts are most effective when you're displaying one set of data values for direct comparison. For example, a pie chart is effective when you're conveying information such as a set of companies' market share in a particular business for one year. You can pull a single slice of the pie away from the rest to emphasize a value. Putting too many values in a pie chart creates a crowded and unreadable slide. 2-D and 3-D pie charts work in much the same way, but 3-D pies can offer visual stimulation.

■ Line charts offer a tremendous number of options to the user. They can display multiple data series, and you can put them in both 2-D and 3-D formats. One specialized line chart type is the Stock chart, otherwise known as an Open-High-Low-Close chart. OHLC charts show the progress of a company's stock prices over a period of time. They're also unique in that a very large number of data sets can be displayed—as anyone who has seen a Dow Jones stock price history can attest.

Chapter 13, "Working with Datasheets," used the example of a datasheet containing fictional market-share statistics for three major laser-printer companies: Printcorp, Inc., Laser Print, Inc., and Patriot Printers. This chapter uses the same datasheet, shown in table 14.2, to step through the process of creating and customizing various basic kinds of charts within PowerPoint.

Table 14.2 Market Share Datasheet				
Title	**1992**	**1993**	**1994**	**1995**
Printcorp, Inc.	22.1	23.5	21.8	22.7
Laser Print, Inc.	57.1	57.3	60.2	61.8
Patriot Printers	20.8	19.2	18.0	15.5

2-D and Stacked Column Charts

The options available for column charts reflect many of the major features available in PowerPoint charting. You have ten different 2-D column chart types and eight different 3-D column chart types from which to choose. After you've entered the information, such as that shown in table 14.2, into the datasheet, you can begin to create charts.

The data set in the example lends itself well to a stacked column chart. In this example, stacked columns offer a visual representation that the audience can take in at a glance of how the three companies divided 100 percent of an industry's market share for each year. Each stacked column has several differently colored segments that show how much of each column is occupied by their respective data value. Stacked columns are also a good way to display several series of data.

Tip

Remember: Microsoft Graph is an OLE 2.0 application program that appears directly in the PowerPoint screen.

To create a 2-D column chart, follow these steps:

1. In the PowerPoint screen, double-click the chart object in your slide that you want to modify. Graph appears, displaying your chart for editing.

2. Choose Format, AutoFormat.

   The AutoFormat dialog box appears.

3. In the Galleries list box, select Column. Clicking Column once brings a set of 10 thumbnails into the Formats section.

4. For a basic 2-D column chart type, select chart type 1 or 2. For most simple data sets, either type will do.

5. Choose OK or press Enter.

Here's how to create a stacked column chart:

1. In the PowerPoint screen, double-click the chart object in the slide. Graph appears, displaying the chart for editing.

2. Choose Format, AutoFormat.

3. In the Galleries list box, select Column. Clicking once on Column brings the set of 10 thumbnails into view.

4. For the proper 2-D stacked column chart type, select chart type 3.

5. Choose OK or press Enter.

The chart should appear similar to that in figure 14.4.

IV

Creating Charts

Fig. 14.4
Creating a simple stacked column chart.

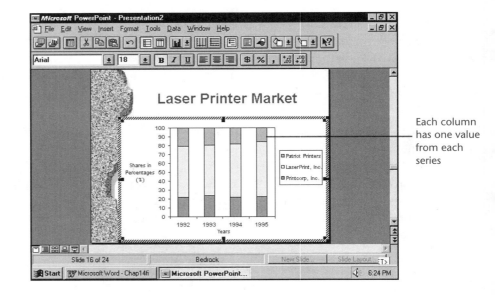

Each column has one value from each series

In the figure, a legend provides information about the series values.

Tip
To draw attention to dominant statistics or series values, place them on the bottom of a stacked column chart. (Place the series containing those numbers on the top row of the datasheet.)

Two-dimensional column chart type #9 works just as well and is essentially the same type of chart, except that linking lines are added between each company value. Linking lines visually separate series values in a stacked chart, making them easier to read. Also notice that when you create the chart, the Laser Print, Inc. values are in the middle of the stacks, which can be visually undesirable. This type of chart is more visually appealing as well as easier to read if the largest stacked column segments are at the bottom.

For that matter, in a basic column chart, it's a good idea to put column values in ascending order (smallest to largest) from top to bottom, to provide a congenial track for the viewer's eye.

Pie Charts

Pie charts are an exceptional option for comparing a set of values across series in a datasheet. For example, it's easy to split up the market shares for the three companies Printcorp, Inc., Laser Print, Inc., and Patriot Printers into three separate pie charts, one for each year. If you have several series of data, you'll need to split them up into several pies for maximum effect.

As the datasheet stands, the series are organized in rows. Each row represents four years' market share percentages for each company. To create a pie chart from this data, follow these steps:

1. In PowerPoint, double-click the existing market-share chart to open it. Click the View Datasheet button to display the datasheet.

> **Note**
>
> Before you make any serious changes in the data in this exercise, take the time to make a backup slide containing the market-share chart you already have. You'll need it later in this chapter. Choose Insert, New Slide and then copy the chart to it. Save the file to make sure you keep its contents.

2. With the column chart displayed, click the By Column button on the Graph Standard toolbar.

   The series indicators are transferred to columns A, B, C, and D of the datasheet.

3. Drag across the column B, C, and D buttons at the top of the datasheet to select all three columns.

4. With the B, C, and D data columns still selected, choose Edit, Cut. The data is cut to the Clipboard.

   ◄ See "Selecting Rows and Columns," p.339

   You make the first pie chart with the contents of column A in the datasheet. For the time being, the other two series of data remain in the Clipboard until you're ready to bring them back.

5. Choose Format, AutoFormat. The AutoFormat dialog box appears.

6. In the Galleries list box, select Pie.

   This brings a set of seven new thumbnails into the Formats section. They represent several types of pie charts, which differ largely by the types of data labels they bear and whether any pie slices are separated.

7. Choose Formats, chart 7.

8. Choose OK or press Enter.

   Several things have happened. Your column chart with its three series no longer exists. It's been replaced by a pie chart with one percentage for each company, representing each company's market share for 1992 (see fig. 14.5). Each pie slice has two labels: the company name, and the market share percentage.

Fig. 14.5
Creating a pie
chart.

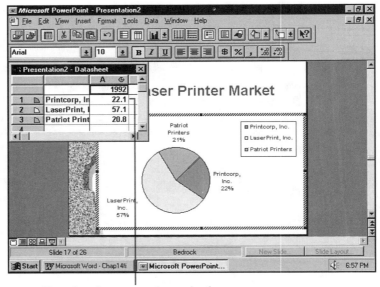

The values for one year (one value from
each series) compose the pie chart

Also notice that a small pie has replaced the series indicator on the
button for column A in the datasheet. Small pie slice graphics have
appeared in the 1, 2, and 3 row buttons as well, each correctly representing a value in the pie.

9. Click once on the slide to embed the chart.

10. To retain your data for 1993, 1994, and 1995 and create charts for
them, create new slides, and cut and paste each set of the datasheet
information to its own slide.

There are some problems with the chart as we've created it, however. First,
the legend isn't needed anymore because the slice labels contain all the
needed information. With this type of chart, a legend just clutters up the
slide. Also, in many cases, like this one, the default pie size may be too small.

To fix these problems, follow these steps:

1. Double-click the pie chart to bring the chart back on-screen.

2. Click the legend once to select it.

3. Press the Delete key. The legend disappears.

4. Click once just outside the pie. A ghosted box should appear, showing that you've selected the pie as a whole.

5. Click on one of the corners of the box. Drag the mouse so that the pie is larger, and release it. You can resize it until you're comfortable with it. Notice that the labels automatically resize with the pie.

6. To move the pie, click on it. Once again, a ghosted box appears around it, showing that it's selected. Click and hold anywhere on the border of the box, and drag it until the pie is where you want it inside the chart object. The labels will come along for the ride, moving automatically with the chart.

Tip
To select a pie for moving or resizing, click just outside its contents.

The pie should resemble the results shown in figure 14.6.

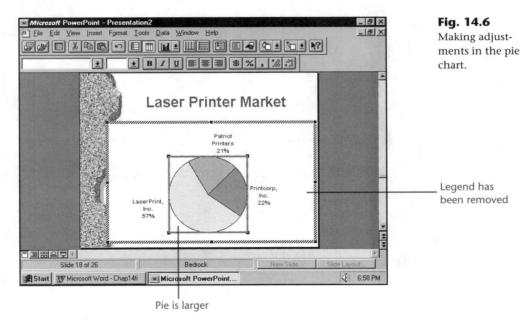

Fig. 14.6
Making adjustments in the pie chart.

Legend has been removed

Pie is larger

The exercises you just went through demonstrate only a few of the many ways to change and customize charts in PowerPoint 95, all of which you'll find discussed in later chapters. In this next exercise, we assume you're already displaying the chart in Microsoft Graph, ready for editing. Before moving on, follow these steps to change the pie chart to 3-D:

1. Choose F̲ormat, A̲utoFormat.

2. In the G̲alleries list box, select 3-D Pie.

   Seven new thumbnails appear in the F̲ormats section.

3. Select chart 7 to display the result shown in figure 14.7.

Fig. 14.7
Switching the pie chart to 3-D.

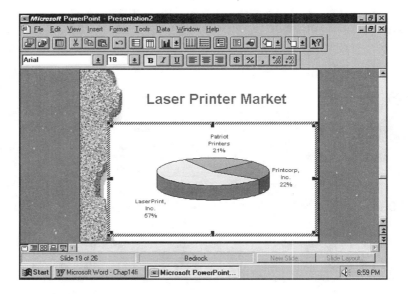

You can resize and move a 3-D pie in the same way as described earlier for a 2-D pie.

Bar Charts

Bar charts are popular among presentation planners. PowerPoint 95 provides ten types of 2-D bar charts, and five types of 3-D bar charts. As we've mentioned, differences between many of the chart types are minimal—gridlines present or absent, linking lines, and the like—so the choices usually aren't that difficult. All the default bar chart types in Microsoft Graph are horizontal. This means you don't have to worry about confusing bar charts and column charts, because column charts are always vertical.

To create a 2-D bar chart, follow these steps:

1. In PowerPoint, double-click your original market-share chart (showing all four years' worth of data) to select it for editing. Graph will appear.

2. Choose Format, AutoFormat.

3. From the Galleries list box, select Bar. Ten bar chart thumbnails appear, each representing a different type.

4. From the Formats thumbnails, choose chart 1.

5. Choose OK or press Enter.

   The chart appears similar to the one in figure 14.8, except that a legend and axis titles have been added to explain the chart.

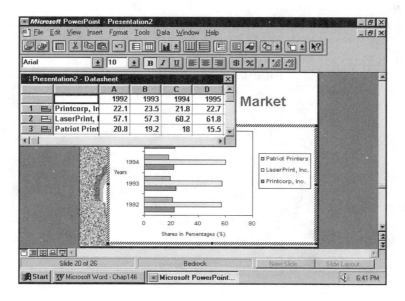

Fig. 14.8
Creating a basic bar chart.

6. Click the Datasheet button on the Graph toolbar to display the datasheet. Notice that the label graphics on the row selection buttons have changed to tiny horizontal bars: one set for each data series. This provides a clue to how bar charts work. They can be slightly confusing, and the next section explains them.

The process of choosing and using a bar chart is very much the same as it is for other charts, including 3-D bar charts. Nonetheless, bar charts differ significantly from other types of charts. Here's why.

Bar charts have an additional level of complexity, plus a few oddities that set them apart from other chart types:

■ *X-axis.* In bar charts, PowerPoint displays X-axis values and labels on the vertical axis, which is on the side of the chart. You can still use the X-axis for categories and series labels. (To understand this quickly, simply change the chart type from a 2-D bar to a 2-D column chart. The X-axis switches positions from vertical to horizontal respectively.)

■ *X-axis title.* Identifies the X-axis (vertical, in this case) and what each axis label represents.

■ *X-axis labels.* Labels for the increments along the X-axis. The viewer uses the labels to determine what data each bar represents.

■ *Y-axis.* In 3-D bar charts, the Y-axis defines the depth of the chart. That's why Y-axis labels aren't available for this chart type. Figure 14.9 is a 3-D bar chart. The horizontal axis labels shown in figure 14.9 are actually the Z-axis labels.

Fig. 14.9
Studying the elements of a 3-D bar chart.

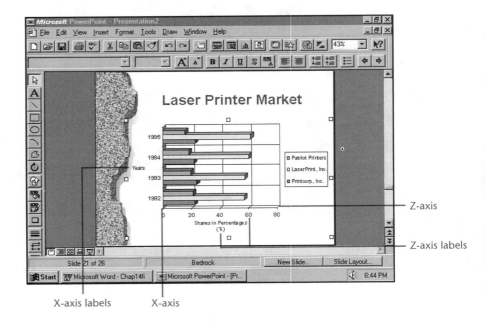

■ *3-D bar chart.* In a 3-D bar chart, the Z-axis is the horizontal axis—unlike in 2-D bar charts, where the Y-axis is horizontal.

Imagine a 2-D bar chart rotated 90 degrees, with the horizontal Y-axis rotating 90 degrees to the "back," while still lying on the "floor."

The vertical X-axis rotates in place. The Z-axis is then drawn in the position previously occupied by the Y-axis, perpendicular to the vertical plane created by the X- and Y-axes. It usually has another series of tick-mark labels, because values are measured against it.

Tip
The Z-axis is the axis of measurement in 3-D bar charts.

Troubleshooting

My columns or bars are in the wrong order.

It's quite possible that your data series have been set up for Series By Columns rather than Series By Rows. Click the By Rows button on Graph's Standard toolbar.

Line, XY, and Stock Charts

Line charts are an interesting and subtle way to help your audience draw visual conclusions from your numeric data. Line charts are deceptively simple—line charts can convey messages that aren't so apparent in other types of charts. In figure 14.10, Laser Print, Inc.'s market-share curve shows steady if unspectacular growth over the last four years. On the other hand, Patriot Printers is steadily losing market share to its competitors. A line chart drives this fact home with emphatic clarity. A major advantage of a line chart is that it can communicate multiple messages with a minimum of clutter.

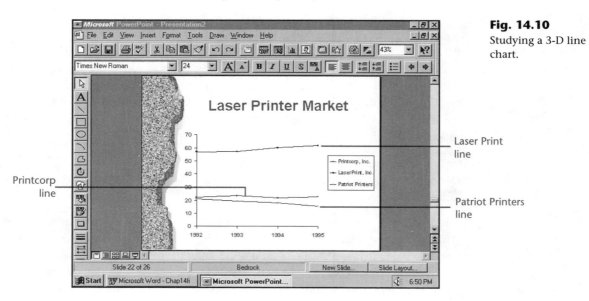

Fig. 14.10
Studying a 3-D line chart.

Printcorp line

Laser Print line

Patriot Printers line

Line and XY Charts

Line and XY charts are very useful when you have a large number of values in each series that would otherwise create a very crowded bar or column chart. XY charts plot their data against two axes—the X- and Y-axes—because each point, line, or sized object needs to be measured against each axis to determine its location. In figure 14.10, for example, each point on each line has a year value that ranges from 1992 to 1995, and a numeric value ranging between 0 and 70. A requirement common to all XY charts is that each data item have two values, which create and locate the graphic object denoting the series value.

Stock Charts

Graph doesn't put stock charts in a separate section under AutoFormats; instead, it groups them with the line charts. Nonetheless, stock charts are so different and require such a different set of data that they deserve their own space in this book, and they're discussed in Chapter 20. The same is true, of course, with combination charts, the building of which may be the most challenging chart-building task you will undertake.

Stock charts require different data sets from those that we used in our previous examples. In fact, one type, a High/Low/Close stock chart, requires exactly three series of data—Low stock price values, High values, and Closing values.

Tip

OHLC charts can also be used to show types of data such as temperature fluctuations over a period of time.

An Open/High/Low/Close chart requires four series. The Open value is the price the stock had when trading opened for the given time period, which is indicated by markers. High values are the highest price at which the stock traded during the given time period. Low values are the lowest values at which the stock traded in the time period—a day, a week, or whatever period the marker represents. Closing values show where the price of the stock settled at the end of the trading period.

The four series can be tremendously long; as mentioned earlier, the Dow Jones stock price poster you see in any stockbroker's office is a classic example of an OHLC chart.

▶ See "Using Combination Charts," p.555

Combination charts can combine stock price information with profit, sales, or market-share statistics to provide a compelling picture of the overall fortunes of a company. Generally, combination charts combine columns with lines or columns with OHLC numbers. They require two distinct data sets. They form their own category of chart and take a substantial amount of work to create.

Editing Chart Objects

Now that you've been introduced to creating charts, it's time to take a first look at some of Microsoft Graph's basic chart customization features. Even the simplest charts have quite a few elements; by the time you finish this chapter, you'll be familiar with all of them.

Taking a close look at Graph's Format menu, you'll notice changes in one of its menu options as you select different chart elements to edit. When you double-click a chart on a slide to start Microsoft Graph (remember, Graph is PowerPoint's separate charting application, even though it doesn't look that way when you use it), the top item on the Format menu is Selected Chart Area, as shown in figure 14.11.

Fig. 14.11
Graph's Format menu, shown in its opening version.

If you click the chart's legend before opening the menu, however, the first menu item is Selected Legend, as shown in figure 14.12.

Fig. 14.12
Here's how Graph's Format menu looks when you've selected a chart legend.

If you select a chart axis, the menu item changes to Selected Axis, and so on. Whenever you decide to change a chart element and select it, the Format menu changes its top option to address the selected object.

> **Note**
>
> Alternatively, you can use the right mouse button to help you edit chart elements. Click and hold the right mouse button on the desired chart element (axis, legend, and so on) and a shortcut menu appears. Its formatting options are the same as, and work exactly the same as, the options on the pull-down menu at the top of the screen. Over time, you may prefer using the right mouse button.

Selecting Objects

In Graph, you select chart objects the same way as you do objects on PowerPoint slides. You can select almost any object on a chart:

- Axes, bars, pie slices, columns, lines—anything that represents a data series or data value

- Chart and axis titles

- Data points or data series

- Gridlines

- Legends

- Chart plot areas (the area that contains the chart)

Many types of chart objects have similar formatting methods and similar ways of accessing formatting features. In every case, you must select a chart object before you can change it.

> **Note**
>
> You can use the mouse in three different ways on chart objects: single-clicking selects them; double-clicking automatically brings up formatting options; and clicking with the right mouse button brings up a shortcut menu for changing the elements.

Tip

Dragging a handle of a selected object resizes the object. Dragging its box moves the object.

As mentioned earlier, the normal method for selecting charts and chart objects is a single click with the mouse. Figure 14.13 shows an example of a selected chart, in this case a 2-D pie chart. Notice the ghosted border around it and the eight small dots (called handles). The box and handles indicate that the object has been selected. Dragging on a handle resizes the chart. Dragging on the border of the box allows you to move the chart around the screen along with its labels.

After you select a chart object, you can do several different things. You can format it in various ways. Dragging a portion of the box that isn't a handle drags the object and any fonts attached to it to another location in the chart. Click and drag the mouse on a handle to resize the object.

Handles

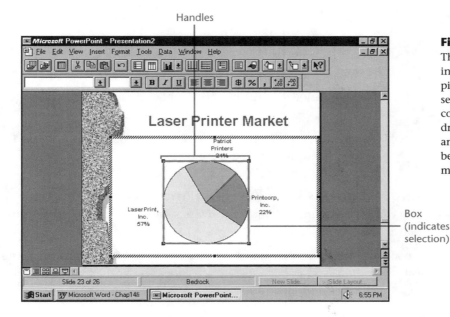

Fig. 14.13
The ghosted box
indicates that the
pie chart is
selected. The
corners can be
dragged to resize
and the sides can
be dragged to
move the chart.

Box
(indicates
selection)

Now, let's turn to the numerous elements that you can add and change
within a chart.

Adding a Title

You can add a title to any chart to explain its contents. You should always (or
almost always) use titles, because they're a big help to an audience. To add a
chart title, follow these steps:

1. Double-click the chart object to select it and bring up Microsoft Graph.
   The full chart object is automatically selected.

2. Choose Insert, Titles.

   The Titles dialog box appears, as shown in figure 14.14.

   The last two title options are normally disabled, unless you're working
   with combination chart types. Sometimes, particularly with pie chart
   types, only the Chart Title option is available. Since there are no axes of
   measurement in a pie chart, this stands to reason.

Fig. 14.14
The Titles dialog
box, used for
inserting chart and
axis titles.

3. Click the Chart Title check box to select that option.

4. Choose OK or press Enter.

   The word Title appears in a small text box, currently selected.

5. Click once inside the Title object. The I-beam pointer blinks inside the text.

6. Type a new title and then click a location outside the Title object. The new title is deselected and displayed.

Choosing Axis Line Weights and Tick Marks

You can alter axis line weights to lend visual emphasis to an axis or to enhance its visibility.

Good charts often use tick marks. They're very useful for helping to measure values on the Y-axis, and to separate categories on the X-axis for easier viewing, as can be seen in figure 14.15.

Fig. 14.15
Displaying tick marks on a column chart.

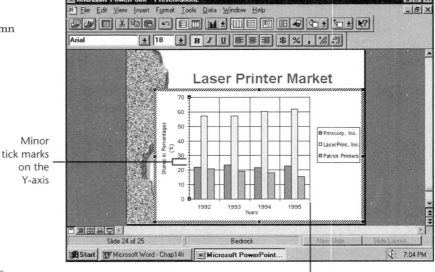

Minor tick marks on the Y-axis

Major tick marks on X-axis

Tip
Minor tick marks are an important tool for measuring precise values, and you can select them as easily as Major tick marks.

Major tick marks occur at each major increment on the axis scale; if your scale is measured by 10, 20, 30, 40, and so on, Graph places a major increment tick mark at each one. Minor tick marks, which are smaller, are used for more precise measurements.

In chart types that normally display axes, such as bar, column, scatter, XY, and combination, you can create different line weights and tick marks by performing the following steps:

1. Click the desired chart axis once to select it.

2. Choose Format, Selected Axis.

   The Format Axis dialog box appears (see fig. 14.16).

Tip
Make sure you click directly on the axis, or you may select another chart element instead.

Fig. 14.16
Using the Patterns tab on the Format Axis dialog box to change axis line weights.

3. Click the Patterns tab.

4. To change the line weight of the selected axis, click the down arrow of the Weight drop-down list. You'll see several line weights, with the lightest weight on top and the heaviest on the bottom. Click the desired weight to select it.

5. To assign and place labels for tick marks on the selected axis, select an option from the Tick Mark Labels area of the dialog box:

Tip
Change the line style for the selected axis by choosing a style from the Style drop-down list. Choose a line color by choosing a color from the Color drop-down list.

Option	Description
None	No tick mark labels displayed
Low	Displays tick-mark labels on the "low" side of the axis, which means directly next to the tick marks for the axis concerned
High	Displays tick-mark labels on the "high" side of the chart, which means "on the other side" of the chart from the axis bearing the tick marks
Next to Axis	Places labels directly next to axis (for X-axis, effect is same as for Low)

6. To assign the placement and type of the tick marks themselves, choose options from the Tick Mark Type area of the dialog box. First choose either Major to assign major tick marks or Minor to assign minor tick marks. Then choose from the following options:

Option	Description
None	Place no tick marks on the axis
Inside	Tick marks on the inside of the axis
Outside	Tick marks on the outside of the axis
Cross	Tick marks that cross the axis

7. Choose OK or press Enter.

Specifying Colors and Pattern Fills

Colors and pattern fills are among the most important chart customizing features. Although PowerPoint's built-in templates automatically assign specific colors to certain chart elements (and Graph automatically uses those colors), you're not locked in to those predefined choices. You can use any color available in the current Windows palette for a chart object. Using colors is, as with many other chart features, largely a matter of taste.

Generally, you should use colors that help chart objects stand out from the slide background and the chart background. A pattern fill is a graphic pattern that fills the area of an object to its borders. Colors work exactly the same way and fill objects such as bars, columns, and data markers with a distinctive color that sets them apart from other data sets.

Graph offers numerous color and pattern options. It supports a 56-color palette in all templates and provides a good selection of pattern fills, which you can combine with colors to create custom effects.

Here are some general rules that may make it easier to select colors and patterns:

- You can change the color (and usually, the pattern) of any object on a chart—such as a set of data markers, lines, axes, bars, pies, pie slices, fonts for chart titles, axis titles, tick-mark labels, gridlines, or chart background.

- Objects are generally split into two parts for color changes: borders and areas. A border, the outside edge of an object, can have various line weights, colors, and line styles. An area, the interior of an object, can be filled with colors and patterns.

- Clicking once on any chart object selects it for color and pattern changes.

    After you've selected a chart object, the easiest way to make color and pattern changes is to use the Selected command at the top of the Format menu. When you do so, the Patterns tab automatically appears so that you can make changes.

Once you change the color or pattern of one chart object, you can do so for just about anything else by using the same methods. Suppose, for example, that you want to change the color of the chart background by following these steps:

1. Click an area of the chart that isn't occupied by any other chart object.

2. Choose Format, Selected Chart Area.

    The Format Chart Area dialog box appears, as shown in figure 14.17, with the Patterns tab options displayed.

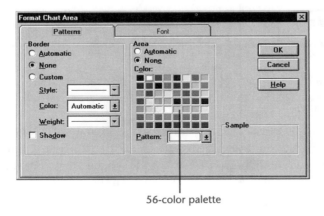

56-color palette

Fig. 14.17
The Patterns tab offers numerous colorizing options.

3. Create the type of border you want by selecting options from the Border area of the dialog box:

Option	Description
Automatic	Default border color

(continues)

(continued)

Option	Description
None	Removes border from display
Custom	Defines custom border settings
Style	Drop-down list to assign a new line style
Color	Drop-down list to assign a new line color
Weight	Drop-down list to assign a new line weight
Shadow	Add a shadow effect to the border of the object

Tip

Clicking any color or pattern selects it. You can also mix colors and patterns.

4. "Color in" your object to your taste by selecting from the Area section of the dialog box:

Option	Description
Automatic	Default, automatically displays default color
None	Ensures a transparent chart background or object background
Color	Select colors from the current color palette
Pattern	Pop-up box displays the color palette and a selection of 18 different pattern fills

▶ See "Studying PowerPoint's Color Schemes Basic Color Palette," p.481

▶ See "Changing a Presentation's Color Schemes," p.486

5. To apply your color of choice, choose OK or press Enter. Graph applies the new color to the object border or object area.

This section has barely touched on the basics of handling color in PowerPoint. You can customize palettes; you can define, mix, and apply new colors; and you can manipulate whole color schemes to change the look of an entire presentation. Later chapters touch on the many associated subjects regarding color.

▶ See "Changing a Slide's Color Scheme," p.488

▶ See "Using Colors and Patterns Effectively," p. 665

▶ See "Using Special Background Effects," p. 674

Selecting Fonts

Using Graph's Fonts features, you can select the type, style, size, color, and background for all the fonts in your chart. You can apply font changes to any chart element containing text, including legends, axis labels, chart titles, tick-mark labels, and comments. You can alter any of those elements individually without affecting other elements in the chart.

To change the fonts in a chart, follow these steps:

1. Select the line, legend, axis, or other chart item containing the text you wish to change.

2. Choose Format, Font.

   The Font tab appears in a dialog box, as shown in figure 14.18.

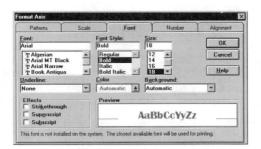

Fig. 14.18
Formatting the font for the axis labels.

3. Choose a new font from the Font list, or scroll down the list by pressing the down-arrow key when the cursor is in the Font name box. Each successive font name is highlighted and displayed in the Preview window.

4. Choose a new Font Style: Bold, Italic, Regular, Bold Italic, or whatever is shown in the list (some fonts in your system may not have all those options available).

5. Choose a new font size, if desired. The Preview window shows each size change.

6. If you wish, choose an Underline style: Single, Double, or None.

7. If you wish, change the displayed font Color to any color available in the palette. Click on the down arrow in the Color drop down list and click on the desired color.

8. Select any of the three text Effects, if you desire: ~~Strikethrough~~, Superscript, or Subscript.

9. When the options are set properly, choose OK or press Enter.

Tip
You can use the same set of font formatting options repeatedly for any Graph object by taking advantage of the Format Selected dynamic menu option.

For some chart objects, the Font tab offers another option: Background. You can set the background color of an axis title, chart title, or the chart itself to be opaque or transparent, or to use a specific color or pattern—or any combination thereof.

Adding and Editing Labels on an Axis

Adding an axis label works exactly the same way as adding a chart title. The purpose of an axis label is different, however. It tells what the axis increments measure (the Y-axis in most charts, and the Z-axis in 3-D charts) and identifies the categories of the data sets (on the X-axis). Axis labels can thus be extremely helpful in many charts.

Troubleshooting

I can't add titles to my pie chart.

The only title that you can add to a pie chart is a chart title. There are no axes on a pie chart—hence, you can't attach titles to them. Most pie charts offered in the AutoFormats automatically attach percentage labels or slice labels, or both, to a chart.

To add or edit labels on an axis, follow these steps:

1. Double-click the chart object in the slide to bring up Graph's menu and toolbar.

2. Choose Insert, Titles to display the Titles dialog box.

Tip
You can attach a title to an axis without selecting the axis first.

3. Click either the Value (Y) Axis or the Category (X) Axis check box to select it. (Or, to remove its selection, click in the check box again.)

4. Choose OK or press Enter.

   The axis title appears, remaining selected on the chart.

   Once you insert an axis title, you may need to format it with font changes, size changes, or other adjustments. You can also rotate an axis label if it interferes with the readability of tick-mark labels (an axis label longer than a few letters may very well do so, particularly a vertical axis label). Figure 14.19 shows an example of an axis title that interferes with the axis tick-mark labels.

5. With the axis title selected, choose Format, Font.

   The Format Axis Title dialog box appears, with the Font tab in front.

6. If you want, select a new font type, size, style, or color, and set your options for filling the background of the axis title with a color or pattern, and for making it transparent or opaque. In that respect, Graph treats axis titles like other objects.

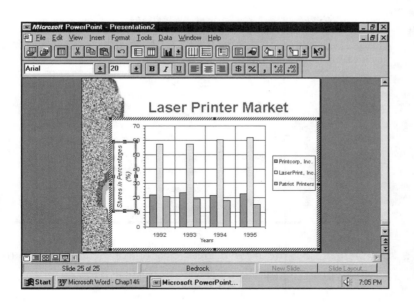

Fig. 14.19
Here the axis title
writes over the axis
tick-mark labels.

7. After you choose the font settings you want, click the Alignment tab to
display the options shown in figure 14.20.

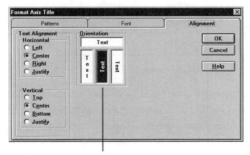

Orientation icons for title rotation

Fig. 14.20
Viewing the
Alignment tab of
the Format Axis
Title dialog box.

8. To change the alignment of text for the axis, choose an option from
either the Horizontal or Vertical option button groups in the Text
Alignment section of the dialog box:

Section	Option	Description
Horizontal	Left	Left aligns text in the object.
	Center	Centers title text in the object.

(continues)

(continues)

Section	Option	Description
	Right	Right aligns title text in the object (aligns text to the right edge).
	Justify	Justifies title text in the object.
Vertical	Top	Aligns text at the top of the object.
	Center	Aligns text midway between the top and the bottom of the object.
	Bottom	Aligns at the bottom edge of the object.
	Justify	Vertically justifies the text in the object.

9. To rotate the axis title by 90 degrees, click one of the four icons in the Orientation area of the Alignment tab in the dialog box.

Tip

Click and drag a handle to resize or change the shape of a selected axis title.

Rotation can be either normal or 90 degrees to either the left or the right. Or you can align the text vertically, with each letter below the previous one. A rotated axis title often is very attractive on a chart.

10. Choose OK or press Enter to implement your changes.

Troubleshooting

My axis titles still interfere with value labels on the axis.

Despite specifying a rotated axis title or a different font size for the title, you may still experience problems getting an axis title to lie properly on the chart. To fix this, click on the area holding the actual chart (the region between the X- and Y-axes of the chart). Then, grab one of the handles on the border of the selected area and resize it to allow more space. The title moves along with the chart border.

Next, click on the axis title and then grab the border of the title and drag it. You may have to experiment a few times to get it right.

Adding and Moving Legends

The legend, the small box in your chart that identifies the data series, is on the right side by default. But you can move the legend to any other location on the chart. You can also resize it and change its font to any font available in your system.

Many chart styles don't automatically add a legend. Some charts, such as a labeled pie chart, don't need one. Nonetheless, it's a simple matter to add a legend:

1. Double-click the chart you want to edit.

The Graph toolbar and menu appear.

2. Choose Insert, Legend.

A legend automatically appears in the chart showing the series names and their assigned colors.

You can move the legend to any location on the chart simply by dragging it, or you can let PowerPoint find the best location for it by the following means:

3. Choose Format, Selected Legend.

The Format Legend dialog box appears.

4. Click on the Placement tab to display the options shown in figure 14.21.

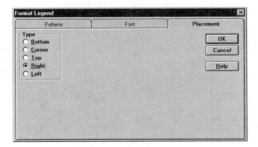

Fig. 14.21
The Format Legend dialog box with the Placement options displayed.

5. Choose from the five options: Bottom, Corner, Top, Right, and Left.

If you choose Top, for example, Graph formats the legend automatically as a single-row legend and places it above the center of the chart, automatically allowing for proper spacing. This feature allows for easier manipulation of legends without having to struggle with resizing the chart.

6. Choose OK or press Enter to execute your changes.

Tip
Use the Format Legend feature's Placement tab to easily place a legend in the proper place with good spacing around the chart.

Note

If you want to format a portion of your legend separately from the rest of it, click on it after selecting the entire legend. Then format it as you would any other text element.

There are so many different ways to do so many basic tasks in PowerPoint—and in its charting facility Microsoft Graph—that it's a matter of taste as to how you decide to use the program. In this chapter you've done most of the basic grunt work of creating charts. The next chapter will be a little more fun. The chart customization and alteration features of PowerPoint 95 are among its major improvements.❖

Chapter 15

Customizing Charts

by Rich Grace

Charting is one of the most creative ways to use PowerPoint 95. This chapter builds on the basic chart creation and manipulation features discussed in Chapter 14. When you move beyond those and start customizing charts, manipulating color, and creating and saving custom chart types (a process described in depth in chapter 20), you become more aware of the true strengths of PowerPoint 95, including especially its powerful charting engine, Microsoft Graph. This chapter explores PowerPoint's charting features more deeply.

In this chapter you learn to

- Draw various objects on a chart
- Use drawing tools to add arrow pointers and colored polygons to a chart
- Add colors, shading, and shadowing to drawn objects
- Rotate charts with the mouse and with specified rotation values
- Apply color palettes in a chart

Customizing Chart Elements

Besides the numerous chart elements discussed in the last chapter, many others are available for adding custom effects. Most of the examples in this chapter use the same data set as the two previous chapters, representing the fictional market-share split for three major companies in the laser printer business (see table 15.1).

Table 15.1 Market Share Datasheet				
Title	**1992**	**1993**	**1994**	**1995**
Printcorp, Inc.	22.1	23.5	21.8	22.7
LaserPrint, Inc.	57.1	57.3	60.2	61.8
Patriot Printers	20.8	19.2	18.0	15.5

Figure 15.1 shows the Market Share datasheet represented in a typical 2-D column chart. The sections that follow will demonstrate PowerPoint's flexibility and power by adding several new types of chart elements and objects to it.

Fig. 15.1

The Market Share column chart.

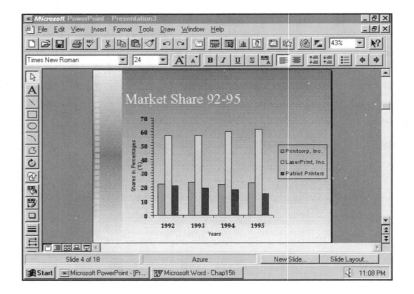

Displaying Gridlines

The column chart in figure 15.1 could benefit from a few additional touches to aid its readability. One of those touches is *gridlines*. Gridlines rest inside the vertical plane created by the X- and Y-axes in 2-D charts and provide more accurate visual measurement of data values. You can use them in conjunction with tick marks (they fill much the same function), or in place of tick marks.

Gridlines bear another similarity to tick marks. You can specify them in major and minor increments in the same way. Figure 15.2 shows the Market Share chart with its major Y-axis gridlines enabled.

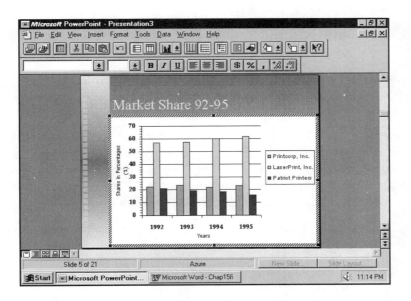

Fig. 15.2
Major Y-axis gridlines are now on the 2-D column chart.

Notice how the gridlines intersect with the major tick marks on the Y-axis. Most chart types offer gridlines as an option, including bar, column, line, area, and scatter charts in both 2- and 3-D formats. To add gridlines to the Market Share chart, and to any other chart type that can use them, follow these steps:

1. Double-click the chart to enable its editing in Graph. The Graph toolbar appears and the chart is automatically selected.

2. Choose Insert, Gridlines.

   The Gridlines dialog box appears, as shown in figure 15.3.

Fig. 15.3
The Gridlines dialog box.

The four options for 2-D chart types are for major and minor gridlines on the X- and Y-axes. As you'll see shortly, it's usually not a good idea to go nuts on the gridlines—you can easily render a chart almost unreadable by using too many.

3. For the Market Share chart, choose the Major Gridlines check box for the Value (Y) Axis.

4. Choose OK or press Enter.

Your chart should now appear similar to figure 15.2.

At this point, the new Y-axis gridlines now enhance the readability of the column chart. The values of each column are much easier to estimate. In particular, one company—LaserPrint, Inc.—is shown to have crossed the 60 percent threshold in market share in 1993, while the other two companies have either held steady or lost slight amounts of market share.

On the other hand, figure 15.4 shows what happens when you enable the major and minor X-axis gridlines along with the Y-axis minor gridlines.

Fig. 15.4
Too many major and minor gridlines on the X- and Y-axes make the chart difficult to read.

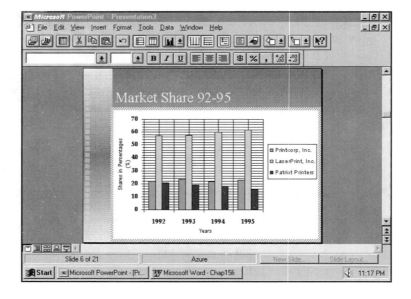

Although the chart is still functional, it poses a few risks. The viewer's eye is distracted by the additional work of having to read a closely packed succession of gridlines to see the columns' values. Also, if a large television monitor is being used for your display, those packed horizontal gridlines can be painful to view for both you and your audience.

Adjusting Gridline Scales

It *is* possible to use major and minor gridlines in combination effectively—you just need to adjust the scale of the gridlines on your chart. To adjust the Y-axis gridline scale for easier reading on minor gridlines, follow these steps:

1. Click any of the Y-axis gridlines displayed on the chart (whether major or minor doesn't matter, because the steps will apply to any gridline on the desired axis).

2. Choose Format, Selected Gridlines.

   The Format Gridlines dialog box appears. It contains two tabs: Patterns and Scale.

3. Choose the Scale tab.

4. Choose from the following scale options for the Y-axis gridlines:

Section	Option	Description
Auto	Minimum	Sets Minimum Y-axis value
	Maximum	Sets Maximum Y-axis value
	Major Unit	Sets the increment for each major gridline
	Minor Unit	Sets the increment for each minor gridline
	Category [X] Axis Crosses At	Sets Y-axis placement where X-axis crosses the chart
Logarithmic Scale		Useful for charts that have widely ranging values
Values in Reverse Order		Switches the Value [Y] axis increments from top to bottom or bottom to top; reverses position of X-axis
Category [X] Axis Crosses at Maximum Value		Places the X-axis at the highest Y-axis value on the chart if the chart is resized

5. For the market share example, you can simply adjust the minor gridlines to a better value. To do so, click inside the number entry box beside the Minor Unit option and type 5 to set the minor gridlines to

an increment of five ticks on the Y scale. This insures a wider gridline spacing, enabling easier readability.

6. Choose OK or press Enter. Figure 15.5 shows the example chart.

The sheer number of options may seem daunting, but this is a place where you can do a lot of experimenting with very little trouble. Using only the Format Gridlines dialog box, you can execute some simple but sophisticated effects.

Fig. 15.5
Adjusting the minor gridlines to 5 maintains the chart's readability, while offering more precise value measurement.

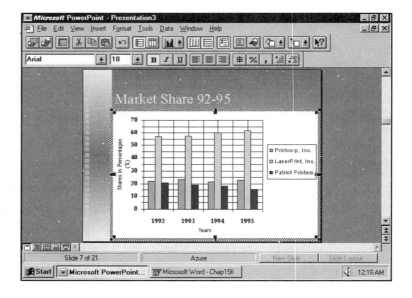

As you can see, it's easy to use major and minor gridlines to design a powerful chart. Now, by proper adjustment of the minor gridline increment, you've made it even easier for the audience to estimate column values, yet you haven't drowned the chart in distracting horizontal lines.

Note

Chapter 20, "Using Advanced Charting Features," discusses in greater detail the use of the Gridlines dialog box to customize charts.

Displaying Data Labels

Sometimes it may be helpful to your viewers to see explicit data values on your chart. In the Market Share column chart shown in figure 15.1, they can roughly estimate values. The chart, although attractive, is also somewhat minimalist in style. The two previous sections on gridlines discussed one method of ensuring accurate visual estimates. If you don't want to provide estimates, but do want to display concrete number values on your chart, you can easily attach data labels to your columns or put other data marker types on your chart.

To display actual values as data labels on your chart, follow these steps:

1. Click the data series marker (a column, bar, or other type of object representing a data value on the chart) to select it. All markers belonging to the same series are selected.

2. Choose Format, Selected Data Series.

   The Format Data Series dialog box appears.

3. Choose the Data Labels tab to display the options shown in figure 15.6.

Tip
Graph applies data value labels to one series at a time.

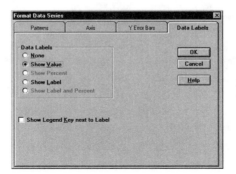

Fig. 15.6
The Format Data Series dialog box, showing the Data Labels tab.

4. Choose the Show Value button to display data values on the chart.

   Other options for displaying data labels:

Option	Description
Show Percent	Disabled except for pie charts; displays percentage represented by pie slice
Show Label	Displays Category Label
Show Label and Percent	Displays Value and Category Label

IV

Creating Charts

5. Choose OK or press Enter.

6. Repeat the same process for each data series in your chart. The end result for the chart should resemble figure 15.7.

Fig. 15.7
The chart with data labels attached to the series.

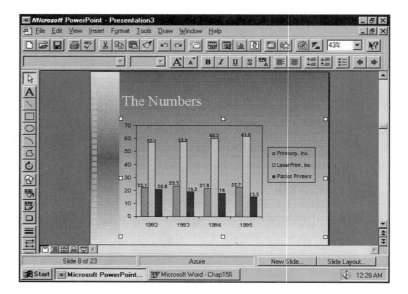

If the font for the labels is too big, you can reduce it to a more graceful size by clicking any label for each data series and choosing F̲ormat, F̲ont. (You can also double-click any data label and the Format Data Labels dialog box appears, displaying the Font tab and its contents.) Choose a new size from the Size list, and choose OK or press Enter.

Adding Arrows

You can add *arrows* with various styles of arrowheads to draw attention to an outstanding or interesting feature of the chart. After you place an arrow, you must enter any text to be used with it.

Here's how to add an arrow:

1. Double-click the chart to edit it in Graph.

2. Choose V̲iew, T̲oolbars. The Toolbars dialog box appears.

3. Select the Drawing check box in the Toolbars list, and choose OK or press Enter. This causes the Drawing toolbar to appear while you are editing charts.

4. Click the Arrow button on Graph's Drawing toolbar.

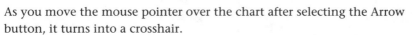

   As you move the mouse pointer over the chart after selecting the Arrow button, it turns into a crosshair.

5. Click and drag the mouse from the desired starting place of the arrow to the desired end point. When you release the mouse, an arrow appears (see fig. 15.8). The arrowhead appears at the point where you released the mouse.

6. Click anywhere outside the chart to embed it into the slide.

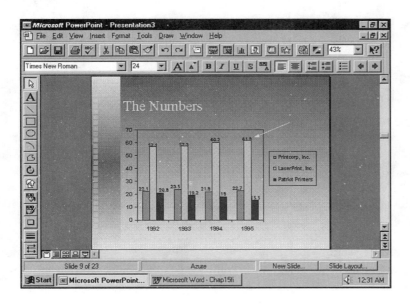

Fig. 15.8
The chart with an arrow pointing to the highest data value.

To add a caption to the arrow, follow these steps:

1. Click the Text Tool button in the PowerPoint Drawing toolbar.

2. Click the mouse in the slide where you would like to put the caption. The I-beam appears in a new text object. Type the text you want and click outside the text object to embed it. The results should resemble figure 15.9.

Fig. 15.9
Fig. 15.9
The chart with an
arrow and a
caption added in
PowerPoint.

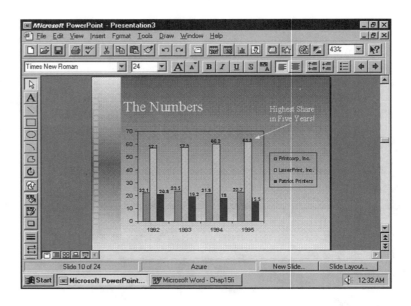

> **Note**
>
> Sometimes it's necessary to leave the Graphing facilities to add a text caption to an arrow. This is true for any text object that isn't directly related to a series value, an axis, or any chart object that has a direct provision for a text label.

What if you want to format the arrow? Change its line weight? Change the style of the arrowhead? For PowerPoint 95, Graph provides formatting features for arrows and numerous other minor chart objects. You can choose from a number of different arrowhead types. To add a different arrowhead style to an existing arrow, follow these steps:

Tip
Double-click the
mouse on the
arrow to quickly
display the Format
Object dialog box
with the Patterns
tab showing, or
click with the
right mouse but-
ton to display the
shortcut menu,
and select Format
Object.

1. Double-click the embedded chart on the slide to edit it. Graph appears with its associated toolbars.

2. Click once on the arrow in the chart.

3. Choose Fo_r_mat, _S_elected Object.

   The Format Object dialog box appears.

4. If it isn't already displayed, choose the Patterns tab.

5. If you want to change the line style, select from these options:

Option	Description
Automatic	Default line style
None	Removes line from display
Custom	Defines custom line style settings: Style, Color, and Weight

6. If you want to change the arrowhead style, select from these options:

Option	Description
Style	Drop-down list of five types for assigning an arrow head style
Width	Drop-down list of three types for assigning a head width
Length	Drop-down list of three types for assigning a head length

7. Choose OK or press Enter.

Resizing Drawn Objects within a Chart

The Properties tab in the Format Object dialog box offers an interesting feature: with the Object Positioning option, you can automatically resize the selected object with the chart, or you can make it retain its size even if you shrink or enlarge the chart. If you turn off resizing (by selecting the Don't Size with Chart option), the selected arrow or other object stays its original size even if you resize the chart. If you select the Size with Chart option, Graph resizes the arrow or other object to keep its aspect ratio with the rest of the chart.

Tip
You can automatically resize drawn objects in Graph along with the chart.

Changing Axes

Chart axes can play a key role when you're customizing a chart's appearance. Earlier in this chapter, you learned how to scale gridlines in different increments. Scaling an axis works very much the same way, which stands to reason because a gridline scale is identical to an axis scale. In 2-D charts, the X- and Y-axes scales each have different properties, just as the X and Y gridlines do.

Scaling Axes

Changing the scale for the X-axis involves changing the frequency at which labels appear on the axis. In the Numbers column chart, for example, the X-axis categories are 1992, 1993, 1994, and 1995. Frequently, you create charts that have more than four categories on the X-axis. Sometimes you may even create charts that have more X-axis categories than you can display effectively. For example, a column chart depicting the quarterly sales of a firm over the last five years in theory can have as many as 20 categories on the X-axis. It isn't always necessary to include all the X-axis category labels; if you do, you'll get a cluttered chart, which is visually distracting to the viewer.

Tip
The more X-axis categories you have, the more advisable it is to limit the number of labels on that axis.

To adjust the scale for the X-axis, follow these steps:

1. Click the X-axis once to select it.

2. Choose Format, Selected Axis.

   The Format Axis dialog box appears.

3. Choose the Scale tab to display the options shown in figure 15.10.

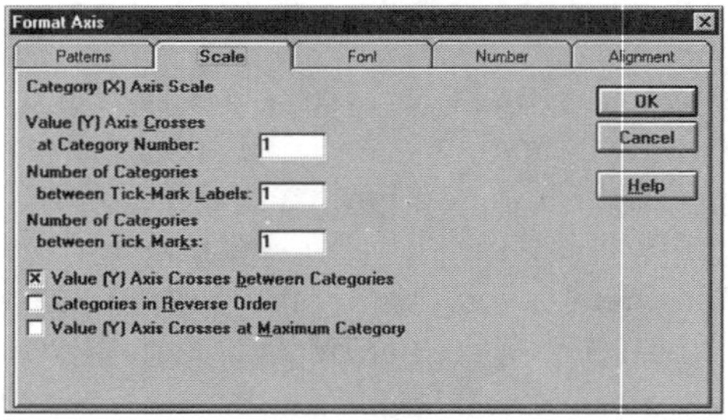

Fig. 15.10
The Format Axis dialog box, with the Scale tab displayed.

4. Select from the following Scale options for the X-axis:

Option	Description
Value [Y] Axis Crosses at Category Number	If set to 1, the Y-axis remains in its customary position on the left side of the chart. The Y-axis can be placed anywhere else, with major effects on the custom appearance of the chart.
Number of Categories between Tick-Mark Labels	If set to 1, this option means that each X-axis category bears a label on the chart. If set to 2, every other category is labeled. If set to 4, every fourth one is labeled, and so on.

Option	Description
Number of Categories between Tick Marks	When this option is set to 1, every category on the X-axis has a tick mark. Setting this entry box to a higher number (such as 2) means that every other category (first, third, fifth) has a tick mark assignment on the chart for the X-axis.
Value [Y] Axis Crosses between Categories	Check box option. Enables the placement of the Y-axis somewhere along the X- or Category axis, the location of which is determined by the value you enter in the Value [Y] Axis Crosses at Category Number text box.
Categories in Reverse Order	Check box option. Sets the categories in reverse order on the X-axis.
Value [Y] Axis Crosses at Maximum Category	Check box option. Places the Y-axis to cross at the highest value on the X-axis, placing the Y-axis on the other side of the chart.

5. When you've finished making your selections, choose OK or press Enter.

Changing the scale for the Y- or value axis is somewhat more straightforward. Here's how to do that on a 2-D chart:

1. Click the Y-axis once to select it.

2. Choose Format, Selected Axis.

The Format Axis dialog box appears.

3. Choose the Scale tab.

4. Select from the following Scale options for the Y-axis:

Section	Option	Description
Auto	Minimum:	Sets Minimum Y-axis value
	Maximum:	Sets Maximum Y-axis value
	Major Unit:	Sets the increment for each major tick mark
	Minor Unit:	Sets the increment for each minor tick mark

continues

Section	Option	Description
	Category [X] Axis Crosses At	Sets Y-axis placement where X-axis crosses the chart (default is 0, so X-axis rests at the bottom of the chart)
	Logarithmic Scale	Useful for charts that have widely ranging values
	Values in Reverse Order	Switches the Value [Y] axis increments from top to bottom or bottom to top; reverses position of X-axis
Category [X] Axis Crosses at Maximum Value		Places the X-axis at the highest Y-axis value on the chart

As mentioned earlier, you can do a lot of things to charts just by adjusting the axis placement and label values. While there isn't space in this chapter to do justice to all the possibilities, figures 15.11 and 15.12 illustrate some of the things you can do to change the appearance of even the simplest column chart.

Hiding Axes

Hiding axes, thankfully, is a more straightforward process than changing the display style of axes, which is all by itself a way of designing custom charts. In figure 15.13, the Y-axis and its labels are absent, and the chart has a pleasing minimalist effect.

To hide the Y-axis, follow these steps:

1. Click the Y-axis to select it.

2. Choose Format, Selected Axis.

   The Format Axis dialog box appears.

3. Click the Patterns tab if it isn't already displayed.

4. To remove the Y-axis from the chart display, click the None option under the Axis options list.

5. Under Tick-Mark Labels, click None. This removes the tick mark increment labels from the chart.

6. Choose OK or press Enter.

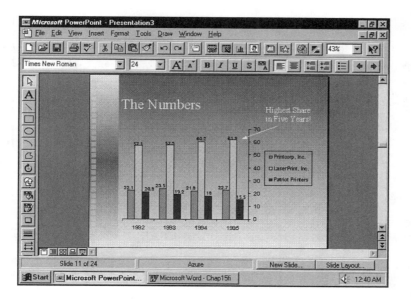

Fig. 15.11
The Number column chart, with the Y (value) axis moved across the chart to cross at the maximum value of the X (category) axis.

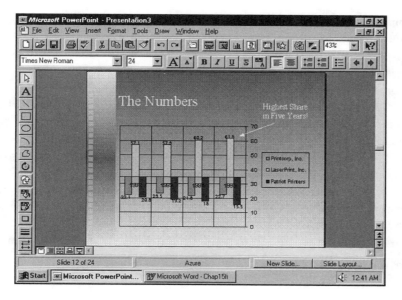

Fig. 15.12
The same chart, this time with the X-axis crossing halfway up the Y-axis. The X- and Y-axis gridlines are enabled, lending structure to the chart.

IV

Creating Charts

Fig. 15.13
The Numbers chart, with its Y-axis removed. Gridlines have also been removed.

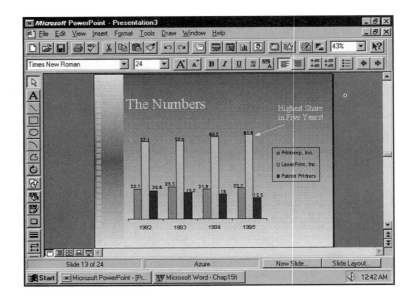

Considering that figure 15.13 already has the column values displayed above each column, it really isn't necessary to show the Y-axis.

Using a Logarithmic Scale

If some series values are too big for your chart, you may need to use a logarithmic scale. It's a particularly handy feature to have if you have a chart in which you want to display two widely ranging sets of data, such as sales figures for an age group 10 to 15 years old and for an age group 60 to 65 years old. If you set up your age groups on the X-axis, the age groups will be so far apart on the X-axis that they will distort the chart. Instead, you can use an X-axis logarithmic scale. If one set of sales figures is an order of magnitude greater than another (one company has $10 million in sales, while another has $150 million, for example), then you can apply a logarithmic scale to the Y-axis. You can even apply it to both axes if necessary. Here's how to apply a logarithmic scale to a selected axis:

1. Click the axis to be scaled.

2. Choose F̲ormat, S̲elected Axis.

3. Click the Scale tab.

4. Click the L̲ogarithmic Scale check box.

5. Choose OK or press Enter.

The selected axis automatically adjusts to encompass the values. The data markers adjust themselves to be more proportional on the chart, while still providing for visual measurement. Notice that you can click on a gridline (if there are any on the desired axis) to follow the same procedure.

Colorizing Charts

In PowerPoint 95, color schemes are completely consistent between Graph and PowerPoint. Graph seamlessly transports the color scheme from the template in PowerPoint to its own charting facilities and conforms to those facilities whenever you create new chart elements. This, of course, doesn't mean that you can't assign your own colors to chart elements of every description.

This section digs deeper into PowerPoint's enhanced color support, its improved color palettes, and its method of assigning specific colors to individual chart elements, among other features.

Understanding the Basic Color Palette

Graph's color palette has expanded to 56 colors. It also boasts 18 different patterns that the user can apply in chart objects, in borders, and in color and pattern fills, and can combine with colors from the palette. Patterns enable you to create custom effects and to visually distinguish large numbers of series values from one another.

PowerPoint assigns certain colors in every presentation template to specific chart and presentation elements, and understanding the basic use of color is part of the foundation for what happens in later chapters.

To study Graph's color palette, perform the following steps:

1. With a chart displayed in Graph, choose Tools, Options.

   The Graph Options dialog box appears. It displays a magnified version of the 56-color palette that you've seen in several of Graph's tabs and dialog boxes.

2. Choose the Color tab to display the options shown in figure 15.14.

Fig. 15.14
The Graph Options color palette. The colors for the first four data sets in the column chart correspond to the first four colors in the Chart Fills group.

Chart Fills color group

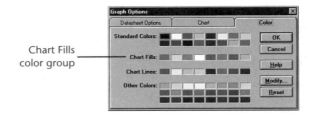

The 56 colors in the palette are split into four specific categories:

- Standard Colors: This 16-color palette set contains the 16 basic colors used in the Microsoft Windows color palette.

- Chart Fills: This eight-color palette set is used for color fills in data series markers, such as the columns in the Numbers chart.

- Chart Lines: This eight-color palette set is used for lines and borders in a chart.

- Other Colors: This 24-color palette set is a group of additional colors that are "leftovers" but are also available because they are matched to the palette and template in current use.

You can use any of the colors for any purpose, but PowerPoint's color defaults are used for a reason: colors chosen for a specific set are generally the ones best suited for the task. Color palettes, and the individual colors in each set, also change depending on the template that you use to create your presentation. Compare the first four colors in the Chart Fills group to those used in the Numbers graph. They are the same, which provides a clue to how PowerPoint organizes its color palettes. But you're not limited to the colors provided in the palettes.

From the Color tab, it's possible to modify any chosen color into a new one, and if you especially like a color palette that you've modified, you can copy it from one slide to another, thus creating consistency of custom colors in your slides. When you modify a color in any of these groups, that new color is communicated throughout the program and appears in all of the color palettes where you work with color in Graph. Any objects already using a color that you change here will show the new color. Chapter 18, "Working with Color," and Chapter 23, "Using Advanced Color, Text, and Special Effects," discuss the uses of color in greater detail, including customizing and changing colors, copying palettes, and using color effectively.

Selecting and Coloring Chart Elements

Most chart elements consist of two parts: borders and areas. Objects of these types include the following:

- Data markers such as columns, bars, and pie slices

- Drawn objects such as polygons and freeform shapes

- Floors, backgrounds, and walls of charts

For all object types, you need to choose color and pattern fills for the area and line colors for the border. You can change the style, color, and weight of borders for a selected object, as well as the pattern and color for its area. For example, suppose that you want to change the color fill of the data markers for the LaserPrint, Inc. series, which are the tallest columns in the sample chart shown in figure 15.15.

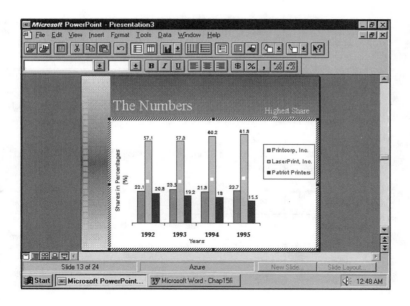

Fig. 15.15
The Market Share chart, before adding color changes to the LaserPrint data series.

To change the color fill for a data series, follow these steps:

1. Double-click the chart to bring up Graph's toolbar and menus.

2. Click once on any of the data series you want to change. In the example, click any three of the columns representing LaserPrint (the tallest columns in each data set). Clicking once selects the entire series.

3. Choose F<u>o</u>rmat, S<u>e</u>lected Data Series to display the Format Data Series dialog box, with the Patterns options tab showing (see fig. 15.16).

Fig. 15.16

The Format Data Series dialog box, showing the Patterns tab.

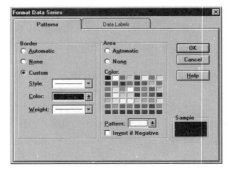

4. If you desire, change the options for displaying the chart object's border:

Option	Description
<u>A</u>utomatic	Default, automatically displays Border
<u>N</u>one	Removes border from object display
Custom	Defines custom border settings: <u>S</u>tyle, <u>C</u>olor, and <u>W</u>eight

5. To change the color of the selected area, choose from these options in the Area section of the dialog box:

Option	Description
A<u>u</u>tomatic	Default, automatically displays the area in the default color. Also select this option if you want to clear custom formatting and return to the defaults.
No<u>n</u>e	Removes area from object display (in effect, makes the objects transparent)
C<u>o</u>lor	Thumbnail display of the 56-color palette. Click any color to assign it to the selected object(s).

For the example, click the third color from the left, second row down, in the Color palette. It should be dark blue. When you choose a color, it will appear in the Sample box at the bottom right of the dialog box.

6. If you want to assign a pattern to the selected area, select a pattern from the Pattern drop-down list. The top-left pattern is a transparent one and shows only the color already chosen. Patterns can change the appearance of the color on a chart.

> **Caution**
>
> Patterns can render other parts of a chart unreadable, particularly if applied to chart backgrounds or if a chart object happens to lie behind a text object such as a data label. Watch your effects to make sure chart visibility is preserved.

7. If you want to invert the pattern assigned in step 6, select the Invert if Negative check box. If selected, this option inverts the pattern ascribed to a series value if that value happens to be a negative number (such as a company losing money during the last quarter). The color will be recognizably similar as part of the same series, but the color inversion indicates a major shift in the numbers within the series. Otherwise the option doesn't affect the colors or patterns selected.

8. Choose OK or press Enter.

The entire LaserPrint series should now be in the new color. Choose Edit, Undo Format Data Series (or press Ctrl+Z) if you want to return to the original color.

> **Note**
>
> You can change the color of a single data marker. It's a simple but somewhat tricky step using the mouse.
>
> Click once on the series data marker you want to change. This selects the entire series. Pause for a second or two, and click again on the same data marker. This selects it alone. Then choose Format, Selected Data Point to change the border or area of the data marker. The functions are the same as for a series.

Tip

3-D charts have walls, which can have different colors and patterns applied to them.

In 3-D charts, you have another option for changing the chart's appearance. 3-dimensional charts actually have walls containing the data markers. Graph allows you to change the colors of the walls surrounding a 3-D chart.

1. With the chart displayed in Graph, click once on the border of the chart wall.

2. Choose Format, Selected Walls.

A tip-off that you've selected the correct chart object is that the Format, Selected command will read whatever object you chose (Walls in this case). If it doesn't, you'll be working with the wrong element.

The Format Walls dialog box will appear, as shown in fig 15.17. Notice that there are no tabs in this dialog box. You can change the appearance of the border or the color fill of the wall.

Fig. 15.17
The Format Walls dialog box.

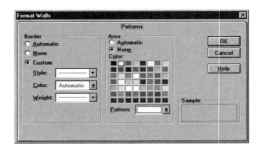

3. Choose a color from the 56-color palette. You can also apply a pattern from the drop-down list beneath the palette.

4. If you want to change the appearance of the wall's border, choose from the options: Automatic, None, or Custom settings (Style, Color, and Weight).

Does this dialog box look familiar? As you can see, the process works the same way as for many other chart objects.

5. When you've finished making your color and pattern selections, choose OK or press Enter.

Troubleshooting

What can I do if I get my colors mixed up and I want to change my objects back to the original colors?

This is an easy place to get mixed up. Sometimes, a color change may wind up clashing with the color scheme, and you may find it difficult to change the values back to their original settings. Click the chart object in question, such as a data series (but this applies to almost any chart object) and choose Format, Selected Data Series. From the Area section of the Patterns tab, click the Automatic option and then choose OK. Graph will reset the colors to their defaults.

IV

Rotating Three-Dimensional Charts

Rotating charts is one of the fastest, most flexible ways to customize a chart, and you can do it easily with the mouse or the keyboard. There is one limitation: it is possible only with 3-D charts. In this section, you will begin to explore 3-D chart types. Before moving on to PowerPoint's chart rotation feature, convert the 2-D Market Share column chart to 3-D columns by following these steps:

Tip
Rotation only works for 3-D chart types.

1. Double-click the chart on the slide to start Graph.

2. Choose Format, AutoFormat.

   The AutoFormat dialog box appears.

3. From the Galleries list box, choose 3-D Column.

   A set of eight thumbnails, each representing a 3-D column type, appears in the Formats section.

4. Choose thumbnail (or chart type) 1.

5. Choose OK or press Enter (you can also double-click the thumbnail to select it and return to Graph).

6. Click outside the chart to embed it into the slide.

The Numbers chart should appear much as it does in figure 15.18.

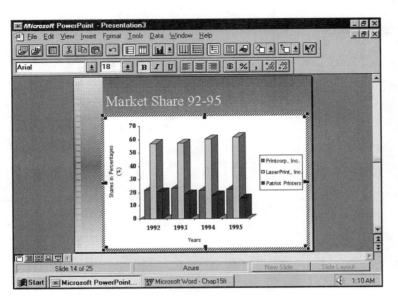

Fig. 15.18
The Numbers chart, converted to a basic 3-D column chart.

Assigning Explicit Rotation Values to Charts

The Graph program offers flexible, powerful, and surprisingly simple methods for rotating charts to add a custom look. The many items you can adjust include viewing elevation, perspective adjustment, and left and right rotation values. It's also quite easy (almost too easy) to rotate a chart solely by using the mouse. To change the view of your 3-D chart (which is a rather attractive chart to begin with), first you'll need to use the keyboard to specify rotation values:

1. Double-click the chart to start Graph.

    The Graph toolbar appears and the chart is automatically selected.

2. Choose Format, 3-D View.

    The Format 3-D View dialog box appears, as shown in figure 15.19.

Fig. 15.19

The Format 3-D View dialog box.

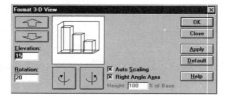

3. To start with, choose from the options displayed for formatting 3-D chart views:

Option	Description
Elevation	Adjusts the view elevation (overlooking the chart). Two arrow buttons, one pointing up and one pointing down, let you adjust the Elevation values by increments of 5. You can, of course, also type in the number.
Rotation	Rotates the chart around the vertical axis. Two Rotation buttons, one left rotate and one right rotate, adjust the Rotation values by increments of 5. You can also type in the number you want.
Auto Scaling	Enabled by default. Used when changing a 2-D chart to 3-D, it helps retain the size of the chart.
Right Angle Axes	Enabled by default. Controls axis orientation, showing axes at right angles to one another. Turning off this option enables 3-D Perspective features. For an example of Right Angled Axes versus Perspective, compare figure 15.19 with figure 15.23 later in this chapter.

IV

Creating Charts

Option	Description
Height: % of Base	Text box. Enter a value here to adjust the perspective of your 3-D chart. If the Auto Scaling and Right Angle Axes are both enabled, you can't make perspective adjustments, and this text box will be disabled. Perspective is primarily used to adjust the height of your chart view. In the present example, this option is disabled.

Tip
To quickly restore the rotation defaults in 3-D charts, click the Default option.

For this example, in the Elevation box, type a value of **30**. In the Rotation box, type a value of **40**.

4. Choose OK or press Enter.

The Numbers 3-D column chart should resemble figure 15.20.

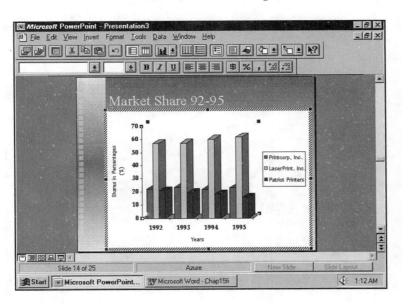

Fig. 15.20
The 3-D Column chart, with adjustments for elevation and rotation.

As you can see, even the minor adjustments just performed have significantly altered the chart's appearance.

Rotating Charts with the Mouse

You can also perform three-dimensional rotation with the mouse, with somewhat less predictable, but amusing results. It's also a great convenience, because you can simply drag the mouse, view the results, and undo the action you just performed; then, you can repeat the process again until you get it right, skipping the tedious but more precise process of going through the Format 3-D View dialog box. To rotate a 3-D chart with the mouse, follow these steps:

1. Double-click the chart to start Graph.

    The Graph toolbar appears, and the chart is automatically selected.

2. Click the mouse once within the area defined by the axes of the chart (but not on any of the data markers). The chart area is highlighted.

3. Click and hold the mouse on any of the pressure points on a corner of the selected chart. The mouse changes to a small crosshair.

4. Drag the mouse in any direction. The 3-D chart changes to a transparent wire-frame box, which rotates according to the movement of the mouse.

5. Release the mouse. The chart may, or may not, resemble figure 15.21.

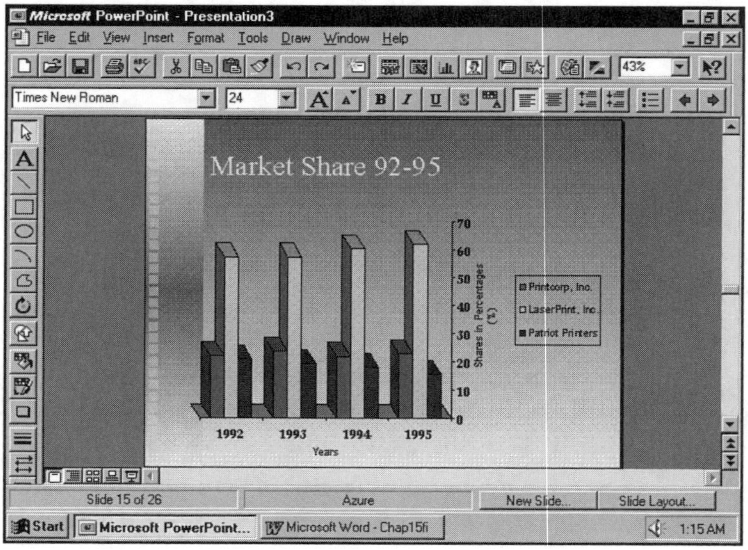

Fig. 15.21
The 3-D Column chart, showing an example of mouse-directed rotation.

Tip
Choose the Format, 3-D View command to check the actual values of the mouse-directed rotation.

After you wreak havoc on what was a perfectly respectable 3-D chart, you can check the actual rotation values by choosing Format, 3-D View. The Elevation and Rotation values will reflect the new position created with the mouse.

Choose Edit, Undo 3-D View command if the results aren't to your liking.

Adjusting for Three-Dimensional Perspective

Three-dimensional Perspective changes the viewing angle from the perspective of the viewer. Perspective is handy when you have a large number of data values to display because it creates a better sense of visual proportion. It also is a remarkably powerful way to customize any 3-D chart type that can benefit from it (3-D Pie charts are an exception). The perspective value that you specify is the ratio of the front of the chart to the back of the chart, and the value can range from zero to 100.

To change the 3-D perspective of a chart, follow these steps:

1. Double-click the chart to start Graph.

The Graph toolbar appears and the chart is automatically selected.

2. Choose Format, 3-D View.

The Format 3-D View dialog box appears.

3. To enable the Perspective feature, click the Right Angle Axes check box to deselect it. The Perspective feature pops up in the dialog box, as shown in figure 15.22.

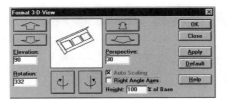

Fig. 15.22
The Format 3-D View dialog box, after deselecting Right Angle Axes. The Perspective feature appears.

4. Enter a value into the Perspective text box. For example, type **80**.

5. Choose OK or press Enter.

Tip
The Perspective feature isn't available unless the Right Angle Axes check box is unchecked.

Perspective has specific (and radical) effects on a 3-D chart. More perspective makes data markers at the back of a chart smaller than markers at the front of a chart, which creates a visual impression of distance to the data markers at the back. The 3-D column Market Share chart may resemble figure 15.23.

The section you've just read should give you some idea of the possibilities inherent in 3-D chart creation. Even though you used just one simple chart type, 3-D Columns, you created many special effects that can actually be considered new chart types and can provide striking visual effects in your presentation.

▶ See "Using Custom Chart Types as AutoFormats," p. 578

Fig. 15.23
The 3-D Column
chart, with
perspective
adjustments
added.

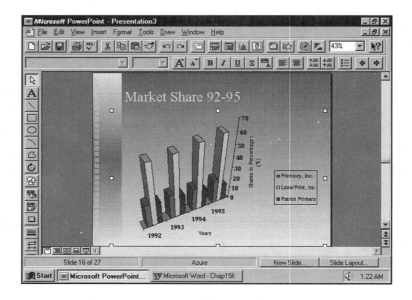

Drawing Shapes and Graphics on Charts

Presentations often use artwork to emphasize a point or add aesthetic appeal. PowerPoint 95 enables you to add the special effect of artwork quickly and efficiently, and you don't even need any special artistic talent! For instance, you can draw polygons and freeform shapes directly on a chart. The new version of Graph offers a special toolbar containing all its key drawing functions, which closely resembles the Drawing toolbar of the main PowerPoint program. If you know how to draw shapes in PowerPoint's main screen, you can draw shapes in Microsoft Graph.

> **Note**
>
> Some shape drawing features aren't available in Graph. The AutoShapes toolbar, for example, isn't available. Nor can you add clip art from PowerPoint's ClipArt Gallery directly to a chart.

Graph's Drawing toolbar lets you draw filled polygons such as ellipses, rectangles, and freehand shapes. You can also alter their color fills and borders as you would other chart objects. Before drawing shapes and other objects on the chart, display the Drawing toolbar in Graph.

1. With Graph displayed, choose <u>V</u>iew, <u>T</u>oolbars.

   The Toolbars dialog box appears.

2. Click in the Drawing check box.

3. Choose OK or press Enter. The Drawing toolbar appears, as shown in figure 15.24.

Fig. 15.24
Graph's Drawing toolbar.

Adding Ellipses, Rectangles, and Freeform Shapes to a Chart

To add an ellipse to a chart, follow these steps:

1. Double-click the chart to start Graph.

2. With the chart selected, click the Ellipse button on the Drawing toolbar.

   The mouse changes to a crosshair when it passes over the chart object.

Tip
To draw a perfect circle, hold down the Shift key while you draw the ellipse.

3. Click and drag the mouse to draw an ellipse. When you release the mouse button, an ellipse will be on the chart. The ellipse is transparent (without a color or pattern fill), as shown in figure 15.25.

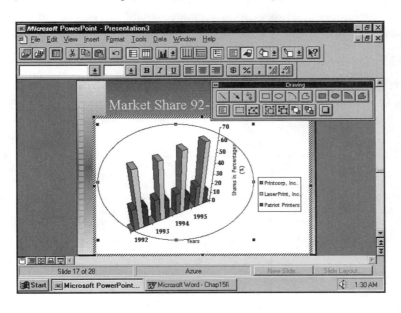

Fig. 15.25
An ellipse is drawn on the chart.

4. To draw an ellipse with a color fill, click the Filled Ellipse button on the Drawing toolbar.

To add a rectangle to a chart, follow these steps:

1. Double-click the chart to start Graph.

2. With the chart selected, click the Rectangle button on Graph's Drawing toolbar.

   The mouse changes to a crosshair when it's moved over the chart object.

3. Click and drag the mouse to draw a rectangle. Hold the Shift key down as you draw if you want to create a perfect square. When you release the mouse button, a rectangle appears on the chart. It will be transparent (without a color or pattern fill).

4. To draw a rectangle with a color fill, click the Filled Rectangle button on the Drawing toolbar.

You can see the pattern developing here. Drawing simple graphic objects is the same whether you draw a filled shape or one without a color or pattern fill.

Drawing freeform polygons is a more complex process. Freeform objects are editable: Any handle available on a selected freeform shape can be grabbed and moved to change the shape of the object. You can draw freeform objects with or without color fills with the appropriate buttons, just as you can other shapes on the Graph drawing toolbar.

To add a freeform polygon object to a chart, follow these steps:

1. With the chart selected, click the Freeform or Filled Freeform button on the Drawing toolbar.

   The mouse changes to a crosshair when it passes over the chart object.

2. To draw a freeform object, click and hold the mouse and draw until the shape is the way you want.

   Before you can finish drawing the freeform shape, you have to close it.

3. Release the mouse, and then drag it to the point where you began drawing the shape. Click the mouse again. This closes the freeform shape you just drew. Otherwise, when you release the mouse button, it continues adding new segments to the shape as you move the mouse over the chart object.

   The freeform object rests on the chart, as shown in figure 15.26.

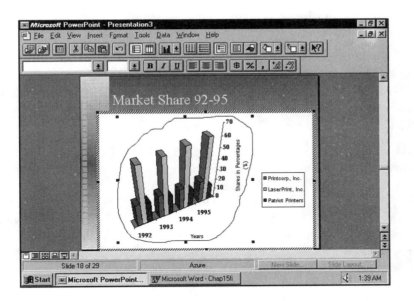

Fig. 15.26
A "quick and
dirty" freeform
shape drawn on a
chart.

When selected, the freeform shape has a standard set of eight handles that
you can use to resize or reshape it. To edit the shape in detail, however, use
the following steps:

1. Select the freeform shape that you want to edit.

2. Click the Reshape button on the Drawing toolbar.

The freeform shape acquires a large number of editable points on its
border (see fig. 15.27).

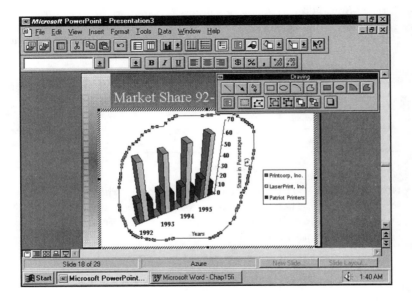

Fig. 15.27
A freeform object,
selected and
enabled for
Reshaping. Note
the large number
of handles, any of
which can be
dragged to reshape
the object.

3. Click and hold the mouse over the desired handle. Dragging the point changes the shape.

Though freeform shapes offer a lot of flexibility, they're not the easiest objects to draw accurately. It's best to have a specific shape or outline in mind before you begin to draw. Then, draw each segment of the shape. Each handle (called a *vertex* in dedicated drawing programs) lets you adjust the shape more precisely.

Also bear in mind that you can't layer drawn shapes behind the chart. Although you can layer drawn shapes over one another (with the Format, Object Placement cascading menu), you can't place them behind a chart. This means that a drawn object in Graph, unless very carefully chosen, can wind up obscuring part of the graph. For most purposes, you're probably better off drawing objects in PowerPoint, where you enjoy much more flexibility in layering and other effects.

Changing Graphics Colors

As with many Graph objects, many of the shapes you draw on a chart can change their color fills or pattern fills. When you draw a filled shape on a chart, you can change borders and areas in the same ways.

To change graphic colors, follow these steps:

1. With the chart displayed in Graph, click the freeform object to select the object you want to edit.

2. Choose Format, Selected Object.

   The Format Object dialog box appears, displaying the Patterns tab.

3. Select from the color fill or border line style options as desired. These options are described in detail earlier in the chapter.

4. When you're satisfied with the color fill or border line style, choose OK or press Enter.

Troubleshooting

Can I apply shading effects to objects drawn in Graph?

No, unfortunately, you can't. Nor can you apply shading to chart backgrounds or series markers such as bars or columns. To do so, you have to draw objects directly on the PowerPoint slide. Although Graph has numerous drawing tools, PowerPoint fortunately boasts many more.

Working with Chart Group Options

Occasionally you may find that you have too many columns on a 2-D bar chart, so that the chart winds up looking crowded. Is there a way to fix this without deleting important values from the datasheet? Absolutely. It requires using a feature called Format (Chart Type) Group. It's on the bottom of the Format menu. Format (Chart Type) Group is another dynamic menu option that changes according to the chart type you're dealing with.

If you have a bar chart and want to make some custom changes to it, after you choose Format, the menu will read Bar Group. If you have a Column chart, the command will read Format, Column Group. This customization holds true for any chart type.

The (Chart Type) Group menu command does not have a letter-based hot key; the hot key is a number. Thus, for changing bar chart characteristics, the command would read 1 `Bar Group`. For a column chart, 1 `Column Group`.

This also applies to 3-D charts of these types. If you're making changes to a combination chart (one which combines two different charts, such as a bar/line chart), you get *two* Group commands at the bottom of the menu:

1   Bar Group

2   Line Group

For this example, you confine yourself to changing the overlap on a set of bars to save room on your chart. *You can do this only for 2-D bar charts and 2-D column charts.* In so doing, you glimpse even more possibilities for chart customization.

1. With your chart displayed in Microsoft Graph, choose F**o**rmat, **B**ar Group.

   The Format Bar Group dialog box appears.

2. Click the Options tab if it isn't already displayed (see fig. 15.28).

3. In the Overlap text box, type a value of **30**. As a result, 30 percent of the width of each bar is overlapped by its neighbor.

   It's also possible to set a gap between columns, if you want to set them apart from each other, by using the Gap Width adjustment.

4. Choose OK or press Enter to execute your changes. Your 2-D columns are more closely grouped, resulting in a more spacious chart.

IV

Creating Charts

As you can see, there is much more to this feature than can be described here. Chapter 19 discusses the Format (Chart) Group and Format Chart Type commands in greater detail.

Fig. 15.28

Using the Options tab to adjust gap widths and overlapping on a bar chart.

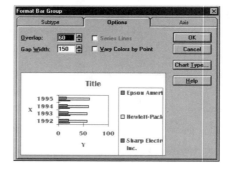

A book could be written on PowerPoint's chart customization capabilities. In fact, though this discussion has covered many subjects, it has barely scratched the surface. If you want to know more about associated charting and drawing subjects, take a look at the following chapters: Chapter 18, "Working with Color," offers a deeper discussion of basic color mechanics in PowerPoint. Chapter 20, "Using Advanced Charting Features," offers more information about powerful chart customization features.❖

Chapter 16

Creating Organizational Charts

by Rich Grace

Organizational charts are another important charting feature offered in PowerPoint for Windows 95. An organizational chart describes the structure of a company, including company officers, assistants, departments, and employees. Organizational charts resemble a computer programmer's flowchart, and denote another way they can be used.

Though the actual name of the program is Microsoft Organization Chart, for brevity's sake we will refer to it as OrgChart for the balance of this chapter. OrgChart is a separate application program that comes with PowerPoint 95. It enables you to create organizational charts as another graphical object, which can be embedded into a slide, and then cut and pasted to any other slide in your presentation.

In this chapter, you learn

- The basic components of an organizational chart

- How to create and embed an organizational chart

- How to edit and change relationships in an organizational chart

- How to change the colors in an organizational chart

Installing Microsoft Organization Chart

Microsoft Office 95's Setup program does not automatically install OrgChart, even though it's an included object type in the PowerPoint program. When you create an OrgChart slide in your presentation for the first time and double-click the object to edit it, you will receive an error message indicating that "The server application cannot be found." This of course is not acceptable to the user. You must then rerun the Office Setup program to install the OrgChart program. Here's how:

1. In the folder titled C:\Office95 (or whatever name you have assigned it: C:\Office, C:\MSOffice, and so on), double-click the Setup program icon.

2. Setup may request that you place the Office 95 CD in your CD-ROM drive. Choose OK or press Enter after making sure the right CD is in your CD-ROM drive. The Office 95 Setup dialog box will appear.

3. Choose the Add/Remove button. The Office 95 Maintenance dialog box will appear (see fig 16.1).

Fig. 16.1
Running Office 95 Setup to install Microsoft Organization Chart.

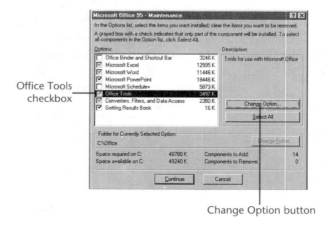

Office Tools checkbox

Change Option button

Some Setup program options will have ghosted checkboxes. Ignore them, because you don't want to delete any applications here.

4. Click in the Office Tools checkbox.

5. Choose the Change Option button. The dialog box will then display the list of "Tools" or bundled applications, including the Organization Chart program, the Equation Editor, and several others (see fig 16.2).

Place a checkmark in the Organizational Chart checkbox

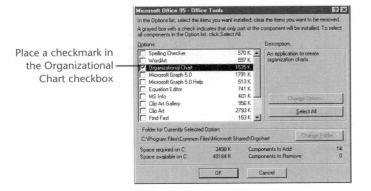

Fig. 16.2
Choosing Office Tools to install Organization Chart.

6. Click on the Organizational Chart checkbox to place a checkmark inside it.

7. Choose OK or press Enter.

8. Choose Continue.

The Setup program will run the installation of the OrgChart program, and update the system to make sure you can use it in PowerPoint. You may have to reboot your system to run properly.

Elements of an Organizational Chart

Organizational charts are quite straightforward. They're an organization tree of a company or department. The OrgChart feature of PowerPoint, however, offers many tools for creating organizational charts that might seem confusing to the user. When you bring up the OrgChart program for the first time, your screen looks like figure 16.3.

OrgChart is an application program; you can create charts of remarkable complexity. Any element of an organizational chart can be customized with different box and line styles and color fills. Boxes of various kinds can be added with the click of a mouse.

Fig. 16.3

The OrgChart program, displaying one of its chart templates.

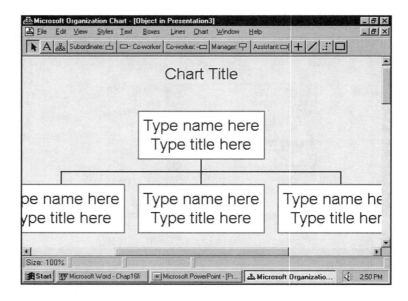

A toolbar, which is called the icon bar in this application, is located at the top of the OrgChart window, which offers the following tools:

![Selection Arrow tool]	OrgChart's Selection Arrow tool enables you to reactivate the mouse pointer after you've used another tool in the program.
![Text tool]	The OrgChart Text tool enables you to type in captions and notes anywhere on the chart window.
![Zoom tool]	The Zoom tool allows you to take a closer view at any box or section of a chart. When you zoom in, the face of the tool changes to an organization chart.
Subordinate:	The Subordinate Box tool allows you to insert a new Subordinate box in the chart and attach it to a superior's box.
:Co-worker	The Co-worker Left Box tool allows you to attach another box to a worker at the same level in the organization to the left of the original box.
Co-worker:	The Co-worker Right Box tool allows you to attach another box to a worker at the same level in the organization to the right of the original box.
Manager:	The Manager Box tool allows you to insert a Manager box entry above an employee's box.

Assistant: ☐┤	The Assistant Box tool enables you to attach an Assistant designation box to that of a manager or other employee's box in the chart.
+	The Horizontal/Vertical Line tool allows you to draw a straight line at 90 degrees, across or up and down, on the OrgChart.
/	The Diagonal Line tool allows you to draw a line at any angle on the OrgChart.
⦂	The Auxiliary Line tool allows you to draw dashed lines between boxes in a chart to show special relationships between them.
☐	The Rectangle tool allows you to draw filled boxes for special entries in a chart. Drawn boxes default to the same style as the boxes in the basic template.

The last four tools, Horizontal/Vertical Line, Diagonal Line, Auxiliary Line, and Rectangle, only appear when you activate them by choosing View, Show Draw Tools, or by pressing Ctrl+D. We will cover these tools in more detail later in the chapter.

OrgChart has two basic templates that the program starts with: a single-box chart and a four-box chart. Figure 16.3 shows the four-box type. Figure 16.4 shows a more complex organizational chart with several important elements.

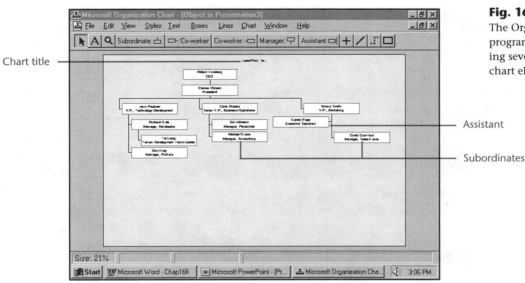

Fig. 16.4
The OrgChart program, displaying several basic chart elements.

IV

Creating Charts

Though this is a fairly simple chart, it combines enough elements to convey the flavor and functionality of the OrgChart application. The highest levels of management are shown as the top two boxes in the chart: the CEO and the President. Three coworkers, who are vice presidents, are ranked equally in a row. The VP on the far right has an assistant attached to her box, who is a separate category by herself.

All three vice presidents have subordinates ranked underneath them in various capacities. Contrary to their appearance, several of them are coworkers that work on the same level. There is even a subordinate to a subordinate. All of these elements will be used to help illustrate how OrgChart works.

> **Note**
>
> OrgChart offers four levels of magnification from the View menu: Size to Window (F9), 50% of Actual (F10), Actual Size (F11), and 200% of Actual (F12). Pressing the appropriate function key activates the corresponding Zoom level.

Building an Organizational Chart

You start by creating a new slide from an AutoLayout that contains an OrgChart object. To create the organizational chart, follow these steps:

1. From the Insert menu, choose New Slide.

   The New Slide dialog box appears, displaying the AutoLayouts available.

2. Select the AutoLayout titled Organization Chart.

   The new slide is displayed in PowerPoint, similar to figure 16.5.

3. Double-click the OrgChart object in the slide. The program displays a chart template. The default template is either one box or four boxes.

> **Note**
>
> The OrgChart program appears in its own window. This indicates a crucial difference between OrgChart and Microsoft Graph: OrgChart is an OLE 1.0 application program, which means that you must choose the Update Presentation command from the File menu when you finish editing the chart, and need to place it back in the PowerPoint slide. (We talk more about this later.)

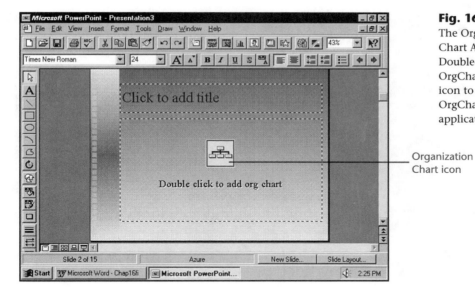

Fig. 16.5
The Organization
Chart AutoLayout.
Double-click the
OrgChart object
icon to start the
OrgChart
application.

Organization
Chart icon

Troubleshooting

*When I double-click the organizational chart on my slide, the OrgChart program doesn't
come up.*

This might be caused by one of two problems. First, you may already have OrgChart
running with the chart you've tried to open. A tip-off: if the chart you click in your
slide looks ghosted or grayed-out, it's already displayed in the OrgChart program.
You can't reopen an organizational chart if it's already being edited in OrgChart.

Otherwise, the OrgChart program may be corrupted or missing from your system.
Use the PowerPoint Setup program to reinstall OrgChart. As a last resort, if you know
that the program is installed, you can locate the OrgChart icon in a folder inside the
Office95 folder to start the program. In that case, the Windows Registry may have
lost its OrgChart entry. To fix it, a reinstall may be necessary.

Editing the Chart

You've just created an organization chart, and are about to start editing and
adding boxes to it. Then, you'll explore the different visual styles that can be

Fig. 16.6
Starting with the
basic four-box
OrgChart
template.

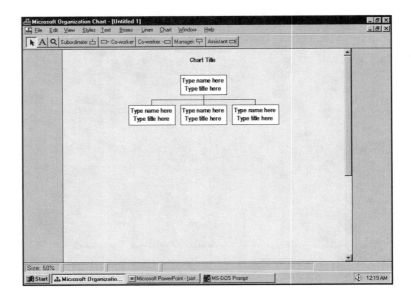

applied to sections of a chart. To start, you will reproduce the chart shown in figure 16.4 by adding some boxes and editing the text entries for each box, as well as the chart title (see fig. 16.6).

Editing the Title

To edit the title in an organizational chart, follow these steps:

1. Pass the mouse over the text object titled Chart Title. The mouse changes into an I-beam pointer.

2. Click the text object, placing the insertion point at the end of the text.

3. Backspace over the Chart Title text and type **LaserPrint, Inc.**. Of course, you don't have to use the sample text. Use your own company's management structure if you see fit. The sample text is a fictional example of a management tree at a major computer company, and bears no resemblance to what really exists.

Adding and Removing Boxes

To add boxes for employees to the organizational chart, follow these steps:

1. To add a higher manager box to the chart, click the Manager Box tool on the OrgChart toolbar. The mouse pointer changes to the shape of the Manager Box icon.

2. Click the existing Manager box in the template. It's the one that is currently highest in the chart. After clicking, a new, higher Manager box is attached above it.

   The new Manager box is filled in black, which denotes its selection and the imminent entry of text data (see fig. 16.7). The next step is to edit its contents.

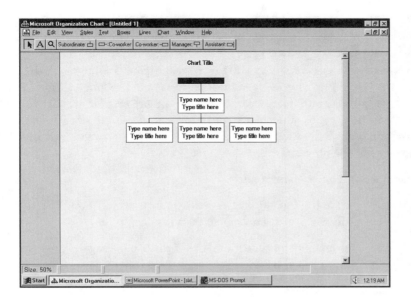

Fig. 16.7
Adding a higher management level box.

IV

Creating Charts

Note

When a box is blacked out, it has been selected either for the editing of its text contents or to have another box attached to it.

Don't be fooled by the tiny size of the box you just added. When you select it to type in the proper text, it expands to fit. That's true for any organizational chart box.

What if you want to remove a box from a chart? Here's how:

1. Click once on the box you wish to delete.

2. Choose Edit, Cut (or press Ctrl+X). The box will be removed from the chart.

Troubleshooting

How can I add two or more subordinates to a single box on a chart?

Click the Subordinate Box tool and click the box to which a subordinate is to be attached. Then, click the Subordinate Box tool again and click the same box to which you just added the *first* subordinate. A second subordinate box is added. You can add as many as you need to any box.

Editing Chart Boxes

To edit the contents of any existing box in an organizational chart, *double-click* the box. Up to four fields of information (called <Name>, <Title>, <Comment 1>, and <Comment 2>) can be entered in any organizational chart box. OrgChart boxes automatically expand to accept the length of text entered. First, you'll enter the CEO's name and title in the box that you just added to the chart in the previous exercise.

Tip

For any existing box in an OrgChart, double-click to enable editing its contents.

To edit a box, follow these steps:

1. Click inside the top "Manager" box you just created. Four fields will appear, in which text entries can be typed.

2. In the <Name> field, type the name of the top manager. For example, enter **Robert Fineberg**.

3. Press the down-arrow key. The <Title> field is highlighted. Notice that the insertion point does not move to the next box, but to the next field in the current box.

4. Type **CEO**.

5. Click outside the box you just edited.

   All OrgChart boxes work the same way. Text is entered in the fields in each box. It is automatically displayed in the chart once you enter it and click outside the chart box that you typed in. Notice that if a box is placed on a chart and is left alone for the moment, it displays two lines reading Type name here and Type title here. This obviously means the same thing, but indicates that the box is awaiting editing.

Note that for any box you place on a chart, two other text entry fields are offered: <Comment 1> and <Comment 2>. They are used for typing in remarks and information to accompany the name and title of the person in the box.

6. Click in the box just below Robert Fineberg.

7. Backspace over the Type name here field and type **Dennis Wilson**.

8. Press the down-arrow key, and type **President**. Click outside the box. The result should look like figure 16.8.

9. The next step is to add the names and titles of the three subordinate boxes below Dennis Wilson.

   For the three coworker boxes in the chart, type the names and positions of the three vice presidents in the chain of command: **Jerry Paulsen, V.P., Technology Development**; **Carla Woods**, **Senior V.P., Business Operations**; and **Sherry Smith, V.P., Marketing**, from left to right. For this example, they're all considered upper management, and will next have some levels of subordinate employees added. The figure should end up looking like figure 16.9.

Tip
Use the arrow cursor keys to move around in OrgChart boxes while you edit them.

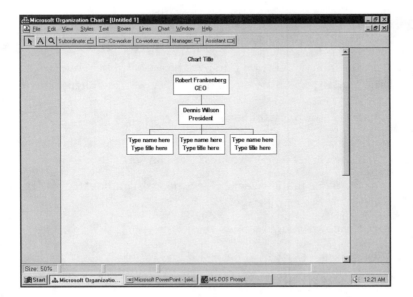

Fig. 16.8
Adding the top management levels in the sample OrgChart.

Fig. 16.9
Finishing the top management levels in the sample OrgChart.

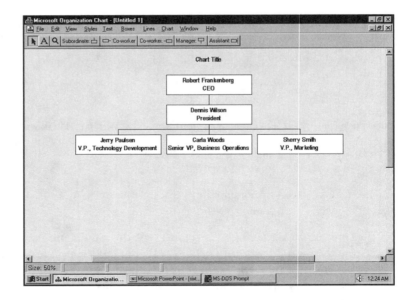

Adding and Removing Subordination Levels

Now, you'll begin adding the levels of subordinates:

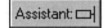

1. Click the Assistant Box tool on the OrgChart toolbar.

   Notice how the mouse pointer changes its shape again.

2. Click the mouse on the bottom-right box, labeled in figure 16.9 as Sherry Smith. An Assistant box appears below it, as in figure 16.10.

3. Click inside the Assistant box you just created.

   As you pass the mouse over the box, it changes into an I-beam pointer. When you click, the box expands to display its fields.

4. Type the name in the <Name> field of the Assistant box. For this example, type in **Candy Page**.

5. Press the down-arrow key.

   The next field (<Title>) in the box is highlighted.

6. Type **Executive Secretary**.

7. Click outside the box you just edited.

   An Assistant is one type of entity that you can add to any OrgChart. Another type is called a Subordinate. For the next several steps, you'll

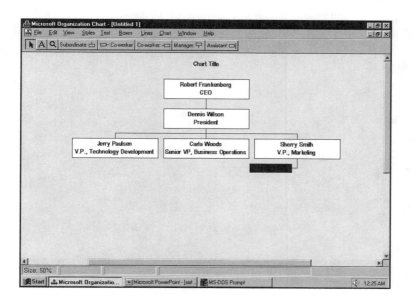

Fig. 16.10
Adding an
assistant box to a
chart level.

be adding a group of subordinate "managers" below the vice-president
level.

8. Click the Subordinate Box tool on the OrgChart toolbar.

9. Click once on the Sherry Smith box to which the new assistant attaches. A subordinate box will extend below both the Sherry Smith box
and that of her assistant Candy Page. This illustrates the fact that a
Subordinate box is different from an Assistant box.

10. Now, choose the Subordinate tool again and click the mouse on the
farthest left of the three boxes, which in figure 16.11 is labeled Jerry
Paulsen.

11. Click the Subordinate tool again and click again on the box labeled
Jerry Paulsen. A second subordinate box will appear, side by side with
the first one.

12. In the center box of the original three subordinates, which in figure
16.11 is labeled Carla Woods, add two more new subordinate boxes by
the same method as you just used for the Paulsen box.

You have just added a grand total of five subordinates to the chart. When you
select a box tool, the number of times you click it on any box equals the
number of new boxes you will (very quickly) create. Figure 16.11 shows how
your results should look.

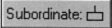

Tip
Bear in mind that
Subordinate boxes
and Assistant
boxes are different.

Fig. 16.11
Adding subordi-nate boxes to a
chart.

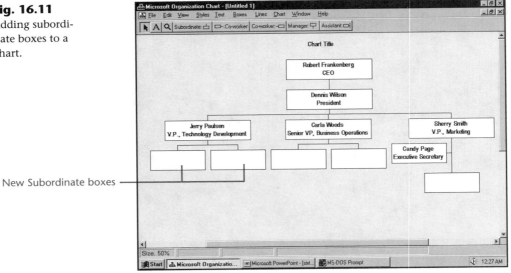

New Subordinate boxes

13. If desired, enter the subordinate names and titles in the new boxes—
from left to right—as shown in figure 16.12. The names and titles are:

Richard Gale
Manager, Notebooks

Don King
Manager, Printers

Ed Johnson
Manager, Personnel

Michael Grace
Manager, Accounting

Cindy Crawford
Manager, Sales Force

As your last step, you'll add one more box to the chart. With the Subordinate
tool still selected from OrgChart's toolbar, click the box named Richard Gale.
A new subordinate box will appear. Type in **Tsi Liang**, and the title **Taiwan
Development team leader**.

Now that all the basic elements for this exercise have been added, it's time to
analyze the chart, as shown in figure 16.13, to see how to make it more readable.

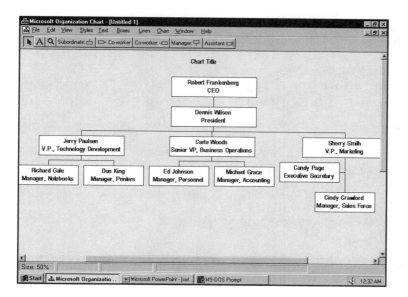

Fig. 16.12
Finishing the lower level of management in the sample OrgChart.

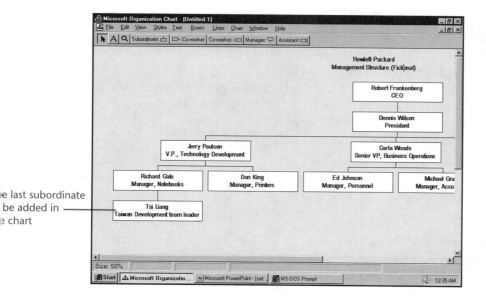

Fig. 16.13
Adding one last subordinate in the sample OrgChart.

e last subordinate
be added in
e chart

Although you've worked with many of the OrgChart application's basic tools, many more are available. The `Tsi Liang` box is actually five levels down the organizational hierarchy. Because of the way the chart is displayed—by default—that's somewhat hard to see. The next exercise lets you work with

OrgChart's styles to make the various levels in the company clearer to the viewer.

First, save your work. Instead of embedding the chart in the PowerPoint slide, save the chart as a separate file. Since OrgChart is a separate program that creates its own data files, this is easier. To save your OrgChart:

1. Choose File, Save. The Save Chart dialog box appears.

2. Click the down arrow for the Save In drop-down list. The folder structure for your computer appears.

3. Scroll down the list until you find the desired folder to save your file.

4. In the File Name text box, type the name for your file (such as **Pres3 Org Chart**).

5. In the Save as Type list box, Organization Chart (OPX) (*.OPX) is shown as the default. Use this format.

6. Click the Save button.

You will reuse this file later.

Changing the Chart's Style

OrgChart offers an innovative feature to stylize charts without affecting their essential structure and relationships. Combining the features of a pull-down menu with the qualities of a button bar, the Styles menu (as it's called) is shown in figure 16.14.

Three style categories are offered. The Group styles consist of six different chart arrangements that apply to the entire OrgChart. When the entire chart is selected, clicking any of the six Group style buttons rearranges the chart into a different style.

For example, selecting any box on a chart and choosing the Assistant style button changes the selected box to the Assistant style, which is denoted by a right-angled connecting line. (We'll explore this a bit later.) The Co-Manager style gathers several employees of the same occupation level into one group that shares the same subordinates and other resources inside the company.

You can select any number of OrgChart boxes to change the style. Many subtleties can be conveyed, some of which we'll explore in the following exercises. The simplest task is to apply a style to an entire chart.

Fig. 16.14
OrgChart's Styles
menu.

IV

Creating Charts

To adjust the style for an entire chart, follow these steps:

1. Choose Edit, Select, and then All.

   All the boxes in the chart are selected (blacked out).

2. From the Styles menu, choose one of the six Group style buttons. (If you want to change your work back, choose Undo Chart Style from the Edit menu or press Ctrl+Z.)

Tip
To quickly select all the boxes in an OrgChart, press Ctrl+A.

This is a rather brute-force method that fails to convey many of the complex relationships that frequently apply in a tree of interacting employees. The Styles are meant to be applied to *sections* in a chart for specific purposes. First, the chart needs to be made more readable.

Using Styles to Improve Readability
First, check to be sure that all officers on the same level in the firm appear on the same visual level. To do so, you'll need to select groups of employees.

1. Click the box in the middle, labeled Carla Woods. Then, hold down the Shift key.

2. Click both subordinate boxes underneath Carla Woods, named Ed Johnson and Michael Grace. When OrgChart boxes are clicked while holding down the shift key, they're highlighted in black.

   There's a special trick to doing this. If you don't want to click several boxes in succession, drag the mouse to form a dotted rectangle entirely around the Carla Woods box and her two subordinates. Those three boxes will be selected. Even though the mouse may cross the boundaries of other boxes in the chart, OrgChart is smart enough to know that those boxes aren't selected unless the mouse is dragged completely around them.

3. From the Styles menu, click the center button at the top of the Groups list. The results should resemble those in figure 16.15.

Fig. 16.15
Applying styles to lower levels of management in the sample OrgChart.

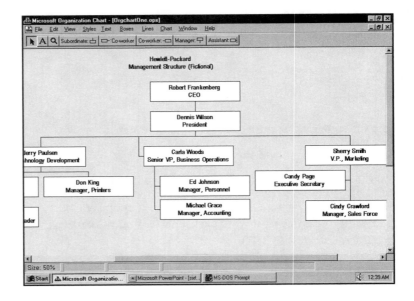

4. Next, select the box at the left, labeled Jerry Paulsen, and his three subordinates Richard Gale, Don King, and Tsi Liang.

5. From the Styles menu, click the top center button again. The results should resemble those in figure 16.16.

6. Now, select the box labeled Sherry Smith and her two subordinates, Candy Page and Cindy Crawford.

7. Click the top center button on the Styles menu again. Your chart should resemble figure 16.17.

At this point, the chart has been heavily revised by simply applying one style to several sections of the chart. But there's a subtle problem, which we talk about next.

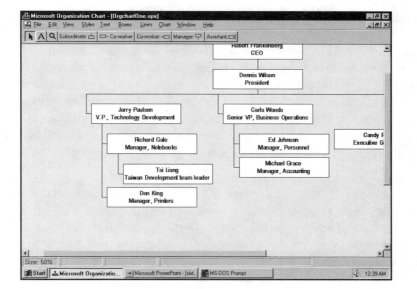

Fig. 16.16
Now, there is no doubt that Tsi Liang is five levels deep in the hierarchy. The chart is becoming much more readable.

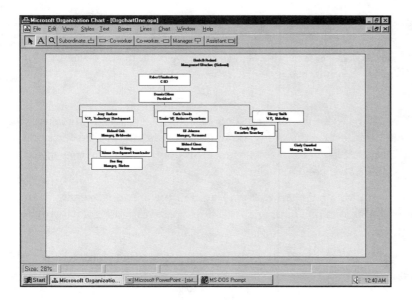

Fig. 16.17
Applying the Group Style across the entire chart.

Applying Co-Manager Styles to Change Relationships

You can see from the organizational chart in figure 16.15 that three vice-presidents are set to be officers roughly at the same level of the company. Does this mean that they're co-managers? Not necessarily. Co-managers often share the same resources (assistants, subordinates, and the like), and even the same department. The default chart style doesn't create those three vice-president boxes as actual co-managers; none of the existing vice-presidents have that status. Normally, they wouldn't, but what if they did? What if, for example, Candy Page served as the Executive Secretary for all three of them?

Can you perform the same operation based on the chart in figure 16.17, after applying the Group Style to the lower levels? Because you selected the vice-president boxes along with their subordinates in the exercise, you can't. When you applied the new Group Style to the "veeps" and their underlings, you subtly changed the vice-presidents' relationship to the higher management, removing their co-equal status. Avoid this problem by applying Group Styles only to the subordinate groups on a specific level, not to multiple levels in the chart. Here's how:

> **Note**
>
> Apply Group Styles to only one level at a time in a chart. This maintains the relationships between other levels.

In this chart, when you attempt to do an Edit, Select All Co-Managers command, the selection doesn't work. In the defaults, they are on the same level, but another step needs to be taken. At this point, you will retrieve the chart you saved in the previous exercise.

Reload your original chart that you saved in the previous exercise by using the File, Open menu command. You also can save your existing work under another filename.

Tip
The OrgChart application can have multiple files open at once.

To create a new co-manager level in the organizational chart, follow these steps:

1. While holding down the Shift key, click the three vice-president boxes labeled Jerry Paulsen, Carla Woods, and Sherry Smith.

2. From the Styles menu, choose the top-left Group button.

3. From the Styles menu, click the very bottom chart style button on the menu, next to the label reading Co-Manager.

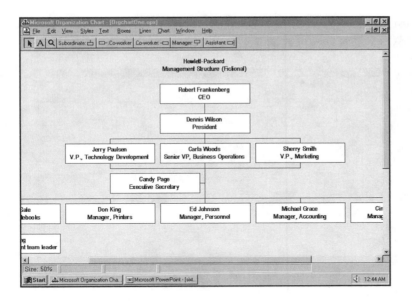

Fig. 16.18
Setting the three vice-presidents as co-managing officers at the same level, based on the chart shown in figure 16.17.

The organizational chart's connecting lines change to the arrangement shown in figure 16.18. (Compare this chart to that shown in figure 16.17.) Now a Co-Manager level has successfully been created. The subordinate levels now appear as they would if they all reported to the same group of managers.

Notice that the three vice-president boxes are connected on the top and the bottom. The boxes create a single, compact unit—as shown by the connecting lines on the bottom as well as the top— implying that the three V.P.s are officers at the same level in the corporate structure and share the same resources. Also note that, as a result, the Candy Page box connects with the three co-manager boxes. Now, because their style has changed, the three V.P.s are true co-managers and can be selected as such.

4. To make the chart more readable, select all the "manager" (Richard Gale, Don King, etc...) boxes. (*Do not select the vice-president boxes.*)

5. From the Styles menu, choose the top left Group Styles button. The results should resemble those in figure 16.19. If desired, save your work, by choosing File, Save or pressing Ctrl+S. You also can choose Save As to save your work under a different file name.

Without going through every style possibility in the program, you can now see the structuring of the OrgChart program. Styles allow you a wide range of possibilities for formatting and arranging an organization chart. But you must be a little careful about how your groups and styles are applied.

Fig. 16.19
Continuing style applications.

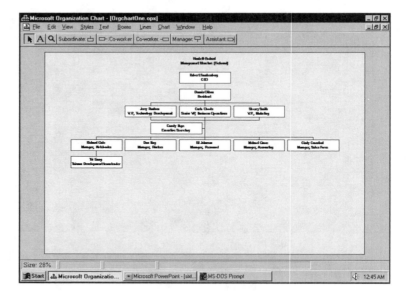

Troubleshooting

When I select a group of officers to set as co-managers, I get an error message that reads, "Co-managers must have the same manager and be adjacent within their own group. Press F1 for help." What's up?

You need to group your selected boxes together on the same level. Simply choose a Group type from the top three buttons offered in the Style menu. You will then be able to create the selected boxes as co-managers.

Working with Chart Levels

When you choose to work with parts of an OrgChart, you have access to a set of options for selecting various elements. OrgChart elements are denoted by the type of employees they represent and by specific sections of a more complex OrgChart.

Selecting Levels

When you want to make changes to all the boxes in a certain level or levels of an organizational chart, you can use selection options to choose all those boxes at once. In OrgChart, you can execute a normal Select All command by pressing Ctrl+A, but that's just one of many options for selecting the chart levels. To see the other options for selecting chart levels, choose <u>S</u>elect from the <u>E</u>dit menu.

A cascading menu appears with the following choices:

Option	Description
All	Select all chart elements without exception.
All Assistants	Select all Assistant OrgChart boxes. Assistants are a separate box type.
All Co-Managers	Select all managers of equivalent levels. Co-Managers are a specific box-and-connecting-line style.
All Managers	Select all Manager OrgChart boxes.
All Non-Managers	Select all non-manager OrgChart boxes. Non-manager types include Assistants and Subordinates, both of whom have specific boxes assigned to them.
Group	Select a group of boxes.
Branch	Select a branch of an OrgChart.
Lowest Level	Select the entire lowest level of the chart.
Connecting Lines	Select all connecting lines of an OrgChart.
Background Objects	Select any graphic objects that have been imported into the current OrgChart file.

Tip
Press Ctrl+A to select all elements in an organizational chart.

You also can select more than one box on a chart by holding the Shift key while you click each successive box.

Menu options such as All Managers, All Non-Managers, All Assistants, and Connecting Lines are very useful when you want to set those specific types of employees apart and apply a different color to them, change their font formatting, or split them into another chart.

Tip
Press Ctrl+G to select a group of boxes in an organizational chart.

Changing the Color of Boxes and Backgrounds

Any box can be changed to reflect the special status of its occupant. You can change both the color of the box and the background. For example, the CEO's box can be changed to denote his level and to draw attention to his status in the chart. To do so, follow these steps:

Tip
Press Ctrl+B to select a branch in an organizational chart.

1. Click the top box in the chart, which in the previous exercise was labeled Robert Fineberg, CEO. The box turns black.

2. From the Boxes menu, choose Color. The Color dialog box showing 32 color choices appears, as shown in figure 16.20.

3. Choose a red color or any color that stands out against the background of the presentation.

4. Choose OK and then click outside the box that you just changed (see figure 16.21).

5. To change the OrgChart background color, choose Background Color from the Chart menu.

6. Choose a color and then choose OK.

Keep in mind that the background color chosen in the OrgChart program affects the appearance of the chart in the PowerPoint slide, just like a chart created using Microsoft Graph. However, you need to choose your background color carefully to avoid clashing with your existing presentation's color scheme.

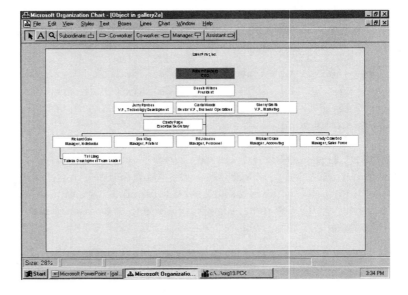

Moving OrgChart Boxes to Other Files

The OrgChart application does not support in-place editing. Because it isn't an OLE 2.0 application, you can't drag and drop boxes, branches, or charts to other files or applications. You can, however, cut and paste any number of OrgChart boxes into other OrgChart files or into other applications.

1. To select an entire branch for copying, simply click the topmost box that you want to copy.

2. Choose Edit, Select, and then Branch.

3. Choose Edit, Copy.

4. Click inside the second OrgChart file, or open the desired file.

5. In the second OrgChart file, click the new Manager box, to which the new branch or box will be attached.

6. From the Edit menu, choose Paste Boxes. The branch is attached to the box in the second file.

The process is the same if you are pasting the branch or chart to an open file in another application.

Tip

Bear in mind that Microsoft Organization Chart does not support multiple Undos. You have only one Undo action you can take at any time.

Tip

To select a branch, click the top box of the branch and press Ctrl+B.

Adding Elements to a Chart with Drawing Tools

As noted earlier in this chapter, OrgChart offers a few drawing tools to aid in adding elements to a chart. By default, these tools are hidden. To display them, choose View, Show Draw tools, or press Ctrl+D. Two line tools are offered for drawing solid lines between boxes:

- The Horizontal/Vertical Line tool is used for one purpose: to draw horizontal or vertical lines. Regardless of the positioning of the mouse, a straight line is drawn in a vertical or horizontal direction.

- OrgChart's Diagonal Line tool enables you to draw a straight line at any angle on the screen. Selecting this tool and dragging the mouse between boxes or groups draws a line at any desired angle.

- The Auxiliary Line tool allows you to draw dashed connecting lines between any two boxes on a chart, adding angles where necessary.

As an example, the CEO in the sample chart might have a special working relationship with the manager of the Notebooks division, Richard Gale, who may report directly to him for various business purposes, thus bypassing the normal chain of command. It's easy to draw a connecting line to show this relationship by following these steps:

1. Click the Auxiliary Line tool.

2. From the left edge of the President box, drag the mouse to the left and then down.

3. Drag the mouse over the box labeled Richard Gale.

A dashed connecting line is drawn between the two boxes, as shown in figure 16.22.

When you draw an *auxiliary* or connecting line between boxes on widely separated levels, the OrgChart program automatically draws the new line to avoid any intervening levels of supervisors. If a diagonal or horizontal/vertical line is drawn across several levels, the line is automatically placed behind any intervening boxes.

Fig. 16.22
Adding a connecting line to boxes on different levels.

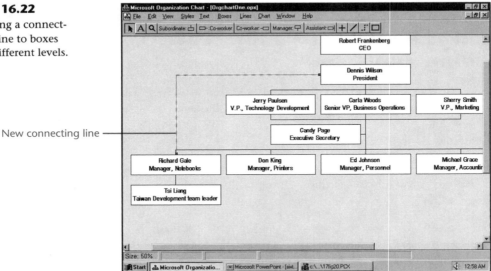

New connecting line

Placing Pictures in an OrgChart Background

You can alter the appearance of your organization chart by adding graphics from other applications. Graphics are pasted onto the background of an OrgChart. Use this method to add corporate logos or decorative wallpaper to your chart. Other applications for this include comments or arrows to indicate places in the organization where a new affiliate might be added in an acquisition or restructuring.

Since there is no Insert File or Insert Object command in the Organization Chart application, you must carry out a simple copy and paste from the originating graphics program. You can't import a graphics file either. Copy and Paste is the only convenient way.

1. From the draw or other graphics program that contains the artwork, choose Copy from its Edit menu. (Some programs may do this somewhat differently, but most are very similar to one another.)

2. Click the OrgChart program, or open the OrgChart application and display the desired file.

3. In OrgChart, with the preferred file displayed, choose Paste from the Edit menu.

As shown in figure 16.23, the graphic should be pasted onto the chart background.

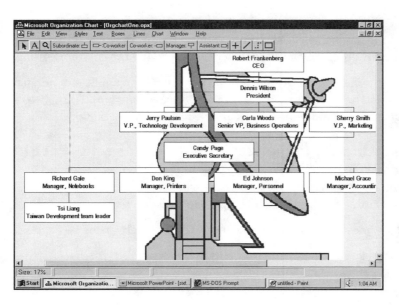

Fig. 16.23
Adding a graphic bitmap to an OrgChart.

Once the graphic is pasted in, you can drag the artwork anywhere in the active Chart window. You also can select and resize it within the OrgChart program by dragging a handle on a corner of the graphic object.

Embedding an Organizational Chart into a PowerPoint Slide

After you're finished creating your OrgChart, embed it into your slide by following these steps:

1. From the File menu, choose Update Presentation.

   Updating embeds the chart into the presentation. If the chart is as you want, you must perform this step after you create it or the chart will not be available in your presentation.

   Also notice that updating is not the same as leaving the program. You can update the chart in the presentation and remain in the OrgChart program.

   After updating the chart, if desired, return to the presentation.

2. From the File menu, choose Exit and Return to Presentation.

After you've updated the organizational chart in your slide and closed the OrgChart program, you may discover that you need to further edit the chart. To do so, double-click the organizational chart in your PowerPoint slide. The OrgChart program reappears on-screen, displaying the chart for editing.

As mentioned earlier, remember that OrgChart is an application program that can be started without using any other Office 95 program. You can save OrgChart files and import them as objects into PowerPoint 95.

Inserting an Organizational Chart as an Object into a PowerPoint Slide

If you don't have the OrgChart placeholder on your slide, you can still create an organization chart by following these steps:

1. Choose Insert, Object. The Insert Object object dialog box appears.

2. Make sure the Create New option button is selected.

3. In the Object Type area, scroll down until you find MS Organizational Chart 2.0, as shown in figure 16.24.

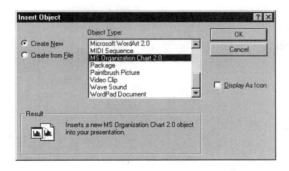

Fig. 16.24
Scroll down to find
MS Organizational
Chart 2.0.

IV

Creating Charts

4. Highlight MS Organizational Chart 2.0 and click OK. The OrgChart
   program opens and you're ready to create a new organizational chart.

The last four chapters have covered the basics of charting in the PowerPoint
95 program. A large number of major subjects are covered in the next several
chapters. Chapter 17, "Printing Slides and Other Kinds of Output," discusses
how to print your presentation in monochrome and color output, how to
produce overhead transparencies and slides, how to use the Genigraphics
slide production service, and how to print notes pages, handouts, and outlines. Chapter 18, "Working with Color," offers a more in-depth discussion of
basic color mechanics in PowerPoint. Chapter 20, "Using Advanced Charting Features," offers more information about powerful graph customization
features. ❖

Part V

Output and Color

Chapter 17

Printing Slides and Other Kinds of Output

by Rick Darnell

With PowerPoint, you can produce a variety of presentation media. The most practical method, which requires no special equipment (other than your printer), is to print your slides on paper. You can also print your outline, speaker's notes, and audience handouts on paper.

For presentation to larger audiences, consider producing overhead transparencies, 35mm slides, a computer slide show, or a network presentation. Each has its own strengths and weaknesses that you should take into consideration. Overhead transparencies are quick and easy to produce on your printer, but can be awkward to manage during a presentation. Slides take advantage of color presentations, but are more expensive and generally require several days lead time to produce. A computer slide show is a natural way to view PowerPoint presentations, since they were created on a computer, but the audience size is limited by the size of your screen. It can be shown to larger audiences with the help of specialized, albeit costly, equipment to connect the computer to a television. Network slide presentations can be shown to a large number of people who don't have to be in the same room, but all viewers must have access to the network.

In this chapter, you learn to

- Set up your printer and slides

- Print your slides and supporting materials

- Send your slides via modem to Genigraphics Corporation for quick processing

■ Create and run a slide show

■ View slide shows with the PowerPoint Viewer

■ Run slide shows with a play list

Choosing an Output Medium

Here are some guidelines for deciding what kind of output is best for you:

■ *Overheads.* This is the quick, easy, and most commonly used way. If you have a laser or inkjet printer, you can load it with transparencies specifically made for laser printers, such as 3M Scotch Laser Printer Transparencies, or 3M Inkjet Printer Transparencies. You print on these transparencies as if they were paper. The result—a set of high-quality transparencies—can be displayed using an overhead projector.

■ *35mm Slides.* If you can darken the room where the presentation will occur, you can use colorful 35mm slides with a desktop film recorder, or obtain slides by sending your PowerPoint file to a service bureau. For a large audience, 35mm slides provide the best option; you can project the slides onto a large screen. But be forewarned: You will need ample preparation time. If any of the slides seem unsatisfactory, you will have to reshoot them and have them redeveloped.

■ *Slide Show.* A slide show provides an electronic presentation using your computer. Your slides fill the screen. A variety of special effects are available, such as timings, transitions, and builds. To display your slide show for a small audience (three or four people), you can use a desktop computer. For a larger audience, you need to use other projection equipment such as a projection panel—a transparent color computer display designed to fit on top of an overhead projector.

■ *Network Presentation.* This new PowerPoint feature utilizes a computer communication network to transmit your presentation simultaneously to a virtually unlimited number of other computers. If you're giving the presentation, you can control its timing, keep notes, and record action items for future reference. If you're watching, you can use your arrow and drawing tool to point out items on the screen and make notes directly onto the slide while the show is in progress. It's the next best thing to someone standing over your shoulder and watching.

Whichever printed output you choose, the process followed to produce output stays the same. First, open the presentation you want to print, and then select the printer you want to use. Next, set up your slides by choosing the output media and orientation (portrait or landscape). Finally, choose the command that produces output.

For a network presentation, PowerPoint is equipped with the Presentation Conference Wizard, available by choosing Presentation Conference in the Tools menu. After opening the desired presentation, this utility shows you how to connect with the other computers.

Setting Up Slides

The next step in the output process is to set up your slides by using the Slide Setup option from the File menu. This option lets you identify your output medium (paper, on-screen slide show, or 35mm slides) as well as the orientation of slides, notes, handouts, and outlines (portrait or landscape).

To set up your slides, follow these steps:

1. If necessary, open the presentation you want to set up.

2. From the File menu, choose Slide Setup. You see the Slide Setup dialog box (see fig. 17.1).

3. From the Slides Sized For drop-down list, choose the output medium you plan to use: letter or A4 paper, on-screen slides, 35mm slides, overhead or custom.

   Each choice comes with preset width, height, and orientation:

Tip

PowerPoint can print your slides on any Windows-compatible printer. However, you need an inkjet or laser printer to print your own overhead transparencies.

Tip

The best time to set up your slides is when you begin creating a new presentation. PowerPoint will display your new slides using the correction dimensions of the output medium you want to use.

Fig. 17.1

Use the Slide Setup dialog box to identify the output medium you're using—paper, on-screen slides, 35mm slides, or custom.

V

Output and Color

Option	Width	Height	Slide Orientation
On-Screen Show	10in	7.5in	Landscape
Letter Paper (8.5 × 11)	10in	7.5in	Landscape
A4 Paper (210 × 297mm)	10.83cm	7.5cm	Landscape
35mm Slides	11.25	7.5	Landscape
Overhead	10in	7.5in	Landscape
Custom	10.5in	8in	Landscape

Note

To print overhead transparencies, choose Letter or A4 in the Slides Sized For drop-down list and choose Portrait orientation for your slides.

If you are planning to produce on-screen or 35mm slides, size your slides for the output medium you will use for your final presentation. Should you want to print drafts on paper, PowerPoint can temporarily scale the print output so that it fits on your printer's paper.

4. If desired, change the orientation.

In Landscape orientation, the image is wider than it is tall. In Portrait orientation, the image is taller than it is wide.

Notice that you can choose one orientation for slides, and another for notes, handouts, and outlines.

The current settings—Landscape for slides and Portrait for notes, handouts, and outlines—are good choices for almost all purposes, with one exception: overhead transparencies. For this purpose, choose Portrait orientation.

5. You can change the width and height by clicking the arrow buttons next to the Width and Height boxes, or type a number. If you make a change here, the Slides Sized For box automatically changes to the Custom option.

6. If you want to start slide numbering with a number other than 1, click the arrow buttons next to the Number Slides From box, or type the number.

Numbers do not appear on slides unless you insert them by using the Slide <u>N</u>umber command on the <u>I</u>nsert menu, the <u>V</u>iew, Header and Footer command, or the <u>V</u>iew, <u>M</u>aster, <u>S</u>lide Master command.

7. To confirm your choices, choose OK.

Choices made in the Slide Setup dialog box affect only the presentation that is open when you choose the Slide Setup command.

> **Caution**
>
> If you change the size or orientation of a presentation you have already created, PowerPoint adjusts the layout of each slide to produce the best possible balance. Review each slide individually to make sure that they still look good. You may need to adjust the position of charts and text boxes.

Setting Up Your Printer

As part of its advanced setup, Windows 95 already knows about the printers connected to your computer. But, you may need to tell Windows there is a different printer that you want to print to. This is necessary if you want to print your files at work or send your slides to a service bureau for conversion to 35mm slides. It is essential if you add a new printer.

Installing Printer Drivers with Windows 95

Many Windows users don't realize you can install a printer driver for a printer not directly attached by a cable to your system. When this printer is selected, PowerPoint uses this printer's settings, making its special capabilities available to you. You can then save or print your presentation to a file, which you can transport to a graphics service bureau or other printer. The file can be carried by hand or sent through the mail on a floppy disk, or transmitted electronically via a modem.

You should prepare your PowerPoint file using the printer that the service bureau prefers. To do so, you must install this printer driver so that Windows and PowerPoint can use it.

PowerPoint comes with the software needed to send your PowerPoint files to Genigraphics Corporation, a graphics service bureau. It can transform your PowerPoint presentation into 35mm slides, and 8-by-10-inch color transparencies or prints. You can mail your presentation to Genigraphics or, if you have a modem, upload your presentation using the GraphicsLink software, also provided. You learn more about GraphicsLink later in this chapter.

If you want to use a different printer not available on your system, make sure that Windows 95 has the right information by using the following procedure.

> **Note**
>
> Take some time to call the graphics service bureau to find out which printer driver they want you to use.

To install a new printer driver, follow these steps:

1. From the Start button, select Settings, Printers.

2. Double-click the Add Printers icon. You see the Add Printer Wizard.

3. Click the Next button. Choose Local Printer if the printer driver you are adding is cabled directly to your computer or if you are adding the driver to prepare output for the transport to another computer. Choose Network Printer if you are installing a driver for a printer connected to a network.

4. Click the Next button. Wizard provides a list of printer manufacturers and a list of printers available from that manufacturer (see fig. 17.2).

Fig. 17.2
Use the Windows 95 Printers option to install your printer. The Add Printer Wizard dialog lets you install additional printers.

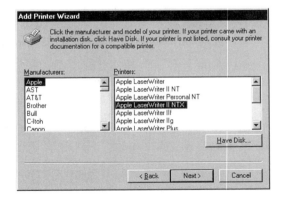

Select the appropriate make and model of your printer. If you have an up-to-date disk from the manufacturer, choose Have Disk. Otherwise, click Next.

If your printer is not listed, check your printer's documentation to see if you received a disk with the printer driver. Put the disk in the disk drive and click Have Disk.

5. Next, you will be asked to choose a port, or outlet, for your new printer. If this is a printer connected to your machine, select the appropriate port. If you are setting it up solely for transmission to a service bureau, select File: Creates a file on disk (see fig. 17.3). When you have made your choice, click Next.

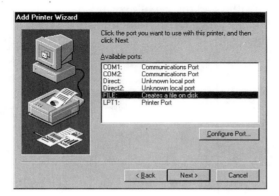

Fig. 17.3
Choose the port your printer will be connected to, or choose File if it is installed for a service bureau or other printer off-site.

6. If you would like to give your printer a different name, like New Hewlett Packard, My Printer, Ed, or something else other than the computer's generic name, type it into the box.

   You may make this new printer the default selection selecting the Yes option button. Choose Next when you are finished.

7. At this point, you can print a test page to make sure your printer is set up correctly. Choose Finish if you want the test; otherwise, click the No box before choosing Finish.

   At this point, you may be prompted for one or several of your Windows setup disks or your Windows 95 CD-ROM.

8. Repeat steps 2 through 7 to install additional printers, if needed.

9. To set a printer as the default, double-click its icon in the Printers window from Settings or the Control Panel, and select Set As Default from the Printer menu.

Tip
If you're using PowerPoint at home, install your office computer system's printer driver. If PowerPoint is installed on the office computer, you can save your presentation to a floppy disk, take it to the office, and print it there.

V

Output and Color

The default printer is the one that Windows will use unless you specifically override this choice by selecting an alternate printer, as explained in the following section.

10. Close the Printers window.

Choosing a Printer

When you choose a printer, PowerPoint prepares and saves your presentation so that it prints as well as possible on that printer. PowerPoint normally uses the printer you identified as the default when you installed your printer drivers; however, you may want to choose a different printer:

■ If you plan to send your PowerPoint presentation to a graphics service bureau, choose the printer driver they prefer.

■ If you plan to print your PowerPoint presentation at a different location, using a better printer (such as the one at work), choose that printer's driver.

To choose a printer driver from PowerPoint:

Tip

To see the current printer settings, choose the Print command from the File menu. The Printer area shows the current default printer.

1. Open the presentation you want to send to a printer other than the default printer.

2. From the File menu, choose Print or use the Ctrl+P shortcut to open the Print dialog box (see fig. 17.4).

If the Print option is dimmed, return to step 1 and open your presentation.

3. In the Printer section of the dialog box, click the drop-down list for Name. This displays a list of printers installed for your computer, choose the printer you want to use.

Tip

Don't use the toolbar's Printer icon to open the Print dialog box. It's a shortcut to send your entire file to the printer without a dialog box.

4. From this point, you can also choose the Properties button to change page orientation and size, graphics, memory management, and other details of your printer's performance.

5. Click Cancel to return to PowerPoint. (Even though you choose Cancel, PowerPoint retains the printer driver choice you made in step 3.) If you click OK, PowerPoint immediately tries to send your presentation to the new printer.

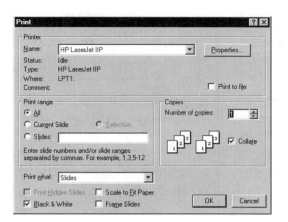

Fig. 17.4
The Print dialog box lets you change printers from the Windows default to another choice. Use this dialog box to print your slides, notes, outline, or handouts.

Note

The printer driver choice affects only the current presentation—the one that's active when you choose Print from the File menu. This choice is saved with this presentation. Your choice does not affect the printer driver setting in other PowerPoint presentations or other Windows applications.

► See "Understanding PowerPoint's Defaults: Printing Defaults," p. 688

Troubleshooting

I don't see the Genigraphics printer on my printer list.

PowerPoint now works directly with Genigraphics from the File menu, Send to Genigraphics. PowerPoint's Genigraphics Wizards appears and walks you through the process of preparing a file for transmission through GraphicsLink.

Send to Genigraphics is dimmed on the File menu.

PowerPoint does not install the Genigraphics printer driver and GraphicsLink software unless you choose the Complete/Custom option when you install PowerPoint. If you did not choose the Complete/Custom option when you installed PowerPoint, you can install the Genigraphics software by using the Add/Remove Programs icon from the Control Panel, clicking the PowerPoint program or Microsoft Office in the list, and choosing Add/Remove. You will be prompted for your setup disk or CD-ROM, and the setup program will begin. When the Setup dialog box appears, choose Add/Remove, highlight PowerPoint, and choose Change Options. Click the box next to Genigraphics Wizard and GraphicsLink, and then choose OK until installation begins.

V

Output and Color

Printing Slides, Notes, Outlines and Handouts

It won't take long for printing to become old hat. As you complete your presentations, you will probably produce several copies on your printer to review, rehearse, or proofread your work.

There is one important thing to remember before printing—check your paper tray. You don't want to print your notes and handouts on expensive overhead film. Likewise, it's not very productive to print on paper when you're ready for the final printing on a transparency.

> **Caution**
>
> If you have a laser printer, do not use heat-sensitive transparencies that are designed to be used with heat-transfer copiers. These transparencies will melt inside your printer and cause great damage. Make sure you have taken the transparency from a box labeled Laser Printer Transparencies. If you are not sure where the transparency came from, don't use it.

To send your set of slides to the printer without changing any options, simply click the printer icon on the toolbar. PowerPoint automatically sends all slides from the current presentation to the Windows default printer, or to the printer you selected from the PowerPoint Print dialog box.

Tip
If you are printing handouts, the three slides per page option is a good choice. The slides are printed large enough to be easily legible, and there is space on one side of the page for your audience to take notes.

If you need a copy of your presentation notes, outline, or handouts, follow these steps:

1. If necessary, open your presentation and set up your slides. Open the Print dialog box by choosing File, Print, or by pressing Ctrl+P.

2. In the Print What drop-down list select any part of your presentation to print—slides, notes pages, handouts, or outlines.

   At this point, you can also send your output to a file for use by another printer not connected to your machine, or a service bureau. To do this, select the Print to File check box in the printer area. To send a presentation to Genigraphics, see the next section.

> **Note**
>
> If you plan to send your PowerPoint presentation to a graphics service bureau, you may be asked to print the presentation to a file. Be sure the printer selected is one the service bureau prefers. While this is generally a PostScript printer, the specific model may vary and can make a big difference between an easy transaction and deep frustration.

3. In the Print Range area, the <u>A</u>ll option is selected for printing all slides
    in the presentation. Choose Current Slide to print the currently selected
    slide. If you selected one or more slides before choosing Print from the
    File menu, the Selection option is available.

    If you want to print a portion of your presentation only, make a choice
    in the Print Range area. To print some of the slides in your presentation
    (but not all), type the slides you want to print in the Slides text box. To
    indicate a range of slides, type the beginning number, a hyphen, and
    the end number (for example, 12-15). To indicate single slides to print,
    type their numbers separated by commas (for example, 2,4,7,11). You
    can combine these (for example, 1,4,6-7). If you type one number,
    PowerPoint starts with that slide and prints the rest of the presentation.

4. If you need multiple copies, increase or decrease the Number of Copies,
    and select the Colla<u>t</u>e check box if you want to collate the copies.

5. If there are hidden slides that you want to print, select the Print Hidden
    Slides check box.

    Frame Slides prints a line around the border of the slide.

    If you're printing to paper different than the size of your slides, select
    Scale to Fit Paper, and PowerPoint will fit the slide to the page. This is
    good for previewing 35mm slides or a presentation designed for the
    computer screen.

    To print your slide on a black and white printer, or to print a fast draft
    copy on a color printer, select the Black & White option.

6. Choose OK to confirm your choices and begin printing.

V

Output and Color

Note

If you selected Print to File during step 2, the Print to File dialog box will appear.
Select a folder and type a name for the file you are creating. Choose Save to start
printing the file.

If you are printing the file to a floppy disk to send, begin the file name by typing the
disk drive (A: or B:) that contains the disk.

Tip
Select the Black &
White checkbox
to print a draft
quickly on a color
printer.

Troubleshooting

I just printed my slides on my black-and-white printer, but they look dark and muddy and didn't photocopy very well.

Try choosing the Black & White option in the Print dialog box. This option removes color fills, which are replaced by white. The Black & White option turns all text to black and replaces all color fills with white, but it uses grayscale printing for some objects (such as decorative borders and clip art).

I just want to make a quick printout of my slides so that my assistant can double-check them. However, it's taking too long to print them. Isn't there a "Draft" printing option?

It is taking so long for your slides to print because your printer is trying to capture the colors you've used by printing gray tones. To speed up printing, choose the Black & White option in the Print dialog box, as explained above.

Preparing a Presentation for Genigraphics

If you chose Send to Genigraphics from the File menu, you see the Genigraphics Wizard (see fig. 17.5). The Wizard guides you through specifying the type of copies you want (35mm slides with plastic mounts, 35mm slides with glass mounts, color overheads, and color copies, photographic prints or posters). You can order as many of these as you like, and you can order more than one set of each.

Fig. 17.5

The opening dialog box for the Genigraphics Wizard outlines your choices for services before beginning. If you have ordered from Genigraphics before, be sure to deselect the New Customer box.

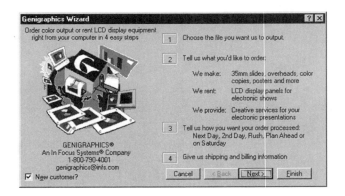

In addition, you can order an LCD panel for overhead projection if one is not available in your area. Creative services from graphic professionals are available through Genigraphics to add an extra flair to your presentations by adding sound and motion to create a multimedia presentation. More information on this service is available from Genigraphics by choosing the services you're interested in.

You can send the file via modem or diskette. If you choose the modem option, you will use the GraphicsLink software to upload your file to the Genigraphics service center. After selecting the services you need, choose the turnaround time required. Genigraphics offers everything from Rush service (in by 7 pm, delivered by 10:30 the next day) to Plan Ahead (delivery within 3 to 7 business days). The quicker the turnaround, the more expensive the price. Call Genigraphics for a current price list.

All presentations are shipped via FedEx®. Shipping charges can be added to your invoice or billed to a FedEx® account.

Using the Genigraphics Billing Information dialog box, specify where and how you want your services billed (see fig. 17.6). If you have used Genigraphics before and have an account, you have the option of direct billing. Otherwise, Genigraphics accepts American Express, Visa, and MasterCard. When you are finished filling out the information, click Next.

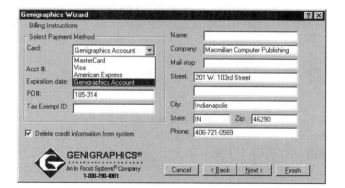

Fig. 17.6
The Billing Instruction dialog box allows you to select a different billing address from your shipping address. From the drop-down list box under Select Payment Method, you can choose a credit card, or if you're a previous customer, charge to a Genigraphics Account.

Troubleshooting

I have a Genigraphics account, but my only choices for billing are credit cards.

It's because you didn't deselect the New customer check box on the first Wizard screen. You can either keep clicking on Back until you reach the first screen, or choose Cancel to start over.

The wizard will display one final screen confirming your shipping and billing address, in addition to the products and services ordered. Choose Finish to confirm, and your presentation is prepared to Genigraphics standards.

Using GraphicsLink

If your computer system is equipped with a Hayes or Hayes-compatible modem, you can use the supplied GraphicsLink software to upload your PowerPoint presentation to the nearest Genigraphics service center. There is no charge for the telephone transmission because GraphicsLink uses 800 numbers to upload your file.

Before using GraphicsLink for the first time, you will need the following information about your modem: the port to which it is connected (probably COM1 or COM2) and the baud rate (1200, 2400, 9600, 14,400, 19,200, 38,400, and so on). GraphicsLink is preset to use a 9600 baud Hayes modem connected to COM1, but you can change these settings.

> **Note**
>
> You can use GraphicsLink with modems that are not Hayes compatible, but you will have to specify the modem initialization, dialing, and termination strings.

To upload your presentation to a Genigraphics service center by using GraphicsLink, follow these steps:

1. In Windows Explorer or My Computer, navigate to the GraphicsLink program item. You will find this in the same program group that contains PowerPoint. After the GraphicsLink dialog box appears (see fig. 17.7), select the file or files you want to send.

Fig. 17.7
The GraphicsLink dialog box. As you prepare files for transmission to Genigraphics from PowerPoint, they will appear on the list, where you can select which ones to submit.

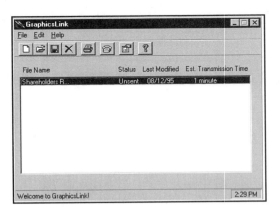

2. From the Edit menu, choose Communications Options. The Communications Setup dialog box appears, as in figure 17.8.

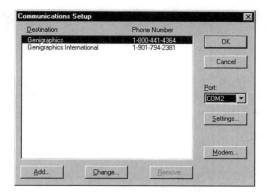

Fig. 17.8
With this GraphicsLink dialog box, choose the Genigraphics service center that you want to process your slides, transparencies, or prints. The port which is connected to your modem is also selected from this box.

3. In the Port drop-down list box, choose the port to which your modem is connected (this is probably COM1 or COM2).

4. If you are not using a 9600 baud modem (the default), you need to change the baud rate setting. Choose Settings. You see the Settings dialog box for the port you have selected (see fig. 17.9).

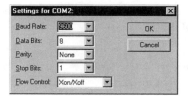

Fig. 17.9
Use this dialog box to specify your modem's baud rate and other settings.

5. In the Baud rate drop-down list box, choose your modem's baud rate. The other settings are OK as they are. Choose OK to close the Settings dialog box.

6. In the Destination list, select the Genigraphics service center to which you want to send your presentation for processing, and choose OK.

7. In the GraphicsLink window, select the presentation that you want to send. To select more than one presentation, hold down the Ctrl key and click the presentations you want to send. To send all unsent presentations, choose Edit, Select Unsent.

8. Turn on your modem, if necessary.

V

Output and Color

> **Note**
>
> If you want to change the order instructions, or if you want to take advantage of rush services, choose Edit, Order Properties or click the Order Properties button on the toolbar. The Order Properties dialog box appears with four tabs of options you selected. Change your order, if you want. To rush your order, choose the Shipping Instructions tab and select Rush in the Turnaround drop-down list. Choose OK when finished.

9. Click the Connect button on the toolbar. GraphicsLink sends your presentation to the service bureau you selected. The Send Status window appears during transmission. A Transmission Summary appears at the end of the transmission.

10. Choose OK to return to the GraphicsLink window or, if the transmission failed, click Retry Unsent.

Troubleshooting

I tried to send my presentation, but a dialog box appeared informing me that the transmission was unsuccessful.

GraphicsLink had trouble accessing your modem. Make sure your modem is plugged in, turned on, and connected to your computer. Make sure the telephone cable is plugged into the wall and the modem. If GraphicsLink still can't dial, make sure you have selected the correct port (usually COM2). If necessary, change the Port setting in the Communications Setup dialog box.

I'm sending a big presentation file to Genigraphics and it's tying up my computer.

Just switch to another application. GraphicsLink can send your presentation in the background.

I'm trying to send my file, but Call Waiting messes up my modem and transmission ceases.

With most phone systems, you can disable Call Waiting temporarily. If you have a touch-tone phone, try pressing *70. If you then hear a dial tone, you have disabled Call Waiting for the next call. Now use GraphicsLink.

Creating a Slide Show

If you want your presentation to feature the brilliant colors seen on your Windows display, you have two choices: 35mm slides or a computer slide show. In a slide show, PowerPoint's screen elements—the menus, toolbars, and scroll bars—disappear, and the first slide fills the screen. When you click the mouse, the next slide appears.

A slide show has many advantages over other presentation media:

■ You don't need substantial lead time for film development. Once you complete your presentation with PowerPoint, you can display it immediately.

■ You can give a presentation in a room that cannot be darkened (a necessity with 35mm slides).

■ You can use the mouse pointer, which is visible on-screen during the slide show, to call your audience's attention to a particular element on the slide. You can even write and draw on the screen as you give the presentation.

■ You can use professional-looking effects, such as transitions and builds. These effects add variety, interest, and emphasis to your presentation.

■ With PowerPoint's sound-equipped system and multimedia capabilities, you can include movies and sounds in your presentation.

■ You can rehearse your presentation until you have it just right. And you can keep making changes until the moment your presentation begins.

■ If you have embedded information such as a spreadsheet into a PowerPoint slide, you can open the source spreadsheet and make changes—for example, trying a "what-if" analysis—right before your audience.

■ You can give a continuous presentation, one that keeps running in an endless loop until you tell it to stop. This is a good choice for unattended exhibits.

■ You can add buttons to your slides that enable you to branch to another presentation while the slide show is in progress.

The major disadvantage of slide shows is the computer's small screen, which limits the size of your audience to three or four people. However, many organizations have projection devices that allow you to project your computer's screen with an overhead projector. With one of these, you can present a slide show to an audience of 50 or more people.

As your understanding of slide shows grows, you can add special effects, such as sounds, builds, transitions, timings, branches, and movies.

Running a Simple Slide Show

With PowerPoint, it is very easy to create a simple slide show in which slides advance when you click the mouse button.

To create a slide show using PowerPoint's default settings, follow these steps:

1. If necessary, open your presentation.

2. Switch to Slide Sorter view by clicking the Slide Sorter View button at the bottom of the window or by choosing the Slide Sorter command from the View menu.

Tip
To select the first slide quickly, press Ctrl+Home.

3. Select the first slide you want to display. To show all the slides, click the first slide.

4. Click the Slide Show button at the bottom of the screen. PowerPoint displays the first slide in your presentation.

Tip
Use the mouse pointer to call your audience's attention to features you want to emphasize.

5. To advance to the next slide, click the mouse button. You can also press the space bar, the N key, PgDn, right arrow, or down arrow to advance to the next slide.

Click and hold the right mouse button to display a shortcut menu with all slide show options, including viewing the next or previous slide, viewing hidden slides, adding meeting notes, switching between the arrow and pen, pointer options, blanking the screen, or ending the show. You can also display the slide show menu by moving the mouse pointer to the lower-left corner of the screen to display a button. Click the button to pop up the menu. To write or draw on the slide show screen with the mouse, right click to display the shortcut menu. Click and hold down the mouse button to write or draw. Choosing Pointer Options also allows you to change the color of your pencil. When you are finished, click the pencil icon again to restore the mouse pointer. The writing or drawing you make this way is temporary; it does not affect the slide's appearance after the slide show is over.

Tip
Instead of leaving a slide on-screen for a long time while you discuss a point, press B to black the screen. Press B again to return to your presentation.

6. To view all the slides in order, continue clicking the mouse button or using any of the keyboard equivalents (space bar, N, PgDn, right arrow,

or down arrow). To view the previous press one of these keys: Back-space, P, left arrow, up arrow, or PgUp.

For a list of all the key and mouse commands you can use while view-ing a slide show in PowerPoint, see table 17.1.

7. Continue clicking until you have seen all the slides. To stop the slide show, press Esc.

When the slide show is finished, you see PowerPoint again.

Note

To avoid having your audience see the PowerPoint screen after you display the last slide, end your presentation with a black slide. To do so, add a blank AutoLayout slide after your last slide. From the Format menu, choose the Custom Background command. In the Custom Background dialog box, deselect the Omit Background Graphics from Master check box. In the drop-down list, choose black in the color palette, and then choose Apply.

Tip

During a slide show, press Ctrl + P or choose Pen on the Slide Show menu to write or draw on-screen. To erase the drawing, press the E key.

V

Output and Color

Table 17.1 Mouse and Keyboard Commands for Slide Shows

To...	Do This...
View a list of the keys in this table	Press F1
View the next slide	Use any of these options: ■ Click the mouse button ■ Press N ■ Press the right-arrow key ■ Press the down-arrow key ■ Press the PgDn key ■ Press the space bar ■ Press H, even if it is hidden
View the previous slide	Use any of these options: ■ Click the right mouse button, and select previous ■ Press P ■ Press the left-arrow key ■ Press the up-arrow key ■ Press the PgUp key ■ Press the Backspace key
Go to a particular slide	Type the slide number and press Enter

(continues)

Table 17.1 Continued	
To...	**Do This...**
Return to the first slide	Hold down both mouse buttons for two seconds
Black/unblack the screen	Press B or period (.)
White/unwhite the screen	Press W or comma (,)
Hide Pointer Now	Press Ctrl + H
Hide Pointer Always	Press Ctrl + L
Change Pointer to Pen	Press Ctrl + P
Change pen to pointer	Press Ctrl + A
Show/Hide the pointer	Press A or equal (=)
Erase pen drawing	Press E
Stop/Restart an automatic show	Press S or plus (+)
Stop the slide show	■ Press Esc ■ Press Ctrl+Break ■ Press the hyphen key (-)
Rehearse Using New Timing	Press T
Rehearse Using Original Timing	Press O
Rehearse Advancing on mouse click	Press M

Running a Slide Show in a Continuous Loop

At trade shows and conventions, you may have seen computers at booths that are running a continuous slide show. You can easily do the same thing with your computer and PowerPoint.

To create a continuous slide show, follow these steps:

1. If necessary, open your presentation.

2. Switch to Slide Sorter view by clicking the Slide Sorter View button at the bottom of the window or by choosing the Slide Sorter command from the View menu.

3. From the Edit menu, choose Select All; or use the Ctrl+A shortcut to select all the slides in your presentation.

This step is necessary because the timings you choose in step 5 affect only the slides you have selected in the Slide Sorter.

4. From the Tools menu, choose Slide Transition. You see the Slide Transition dialog box (see fig. 17.10).

5. In the Advance area, select Automatically After and type the number of seconds you want each slide displayed. You can also set the same transition for all slides in your presentation by selecting an option from the Effect area.

Tip
Try displaying each slide for 15 seconds initially.

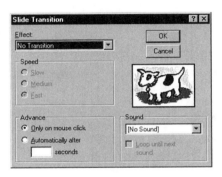

Fig. 17.10
Use the Slide Transition dialog box to specify how long you want slides to appear during a continuous presentation.

6. Choose OK.

7. From the View menu, choose Slide Show. You see the Slide Show dialog box (see fig. 17.11).

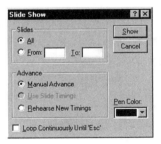

Fig. 17.11
You can use the Slide Show dialog box to create a continuously running presentation.

Tip
To prevent viewers from disturbing the show, place the mouse and keyboard behind the computer while the show is running.

8. If you want to display only some of the slides, type the number of the beginning slide in the From box and the ending slide in the To box.

If you type a number only in the From box, PowerPoint displays the presentation starting from the slide number you specify.

9. In the Advance area, choose <u>U</u>se Slide Timings. PowerPoint will use the automatic timing option you specified in the Slide Transitions dialog box (step 5).

10. Select Loop Continuously Until 'Esc'.

11. Choose Show to start your slide show.

Rearranging Slides

As you preview your slide show, you may find that one or more of the slides is out of sequence. You can easily change the order of your slides by using the Slide Sorter.

To change the order of slides, follow these steps:

◀ See "Understanding PowerPoint Views," p. 66

1. If necessary, switch to Slide Sorter view by clicking the Slide Sorter View button or choosing Slide Sorter from the View menu.

2. Click the slide you want to move and hold down the mouse button.

   The pointer changes shape to indicate that you have enabled PowerPoint's drag-and-drop editing feature.

3. Move the pointer to the place you want the slide to appear.

   You see a gray line showing where PowerPoint will place the slide when you release the mouse button.

Tip
To undo any change you have just made to the slide order, immediately choose Undo Move from the Edit menu or press Ctrl+Z.

4. When you have positioned the dotted line in the correct place, release the mouse button.

Making Sure Your Slide Show Looks Good

Now that you have created colorful, attractive slides, added charts, graphs, text, and clip art, and put everything in the right order, you have one more item to think about—the equipment you're using for your presentation.

Connecting Your Computer to Other Displays

There are several other options for displaying your presentation to larger audiences beyond hard copies, transparencies and slides. Some may be affordable to your organization, while some will probably only be available through a conference center or college.

Four tools are available that hook directly into your computer:

■ *Projection Panel.* This is similar to a printed transparency, only it plugs into the video connection on your computer. The panel sits on an overhead projector and displays your images in color or black and white, depending on the panel. Many come with a Y cable to connect to a monitor and the panel simultaneously. For portability, panels can be paired with a laptop computer for easy use and small size on the road. Overhead projectors are also available that have the projection panel built in. Many colleges, universities, and conference centers will have some form of projection panel available for use.

Cost: $1,300 to $5,000

■ *Data Projector.* Similar to a projector, this little black box uses the images from your computer for its slides. The quality of these machines has improved dramatically in the last two years, although they are still not as crisp as a video projector (see below). These are also available with color or black and white capabilities. A Y cable is also very useful with this piece of equipment.

Cost: $5,000 to $10,000

■ *Video Projector.* This high-quality projector works on the same principle as a big screen television, using three tubes (red, green, and blue) to project an image on a fixed screen. This type of projector is typically found in a fixed installation in corporate or academic settings since the cost and weight rule out affordable portability. Newer projectors have direct ports for a VGA connector from your computer, while others need a special adapter to separate the signal into its three color components—computer-to-TV adapters will not always work with a video projector. It is very important to call ahead to determine if the equipment will work with your computer.

Cost: $7,000 to $60,000

■ *Television.* Probably the lowest cost and most available option, televisions are available at virtually any facility you will use. PC to TV converters are available for less than $500 to get your image from the computer to the screen. The standard models convert your VGA output to a signal usable by an NTSC monitor or big-screen TV, and allow simultaneous display on your VGA monitor. One feature to look for is a "flicker filter." Because of the differences in resolution and type of signal, lower-cost units will appear to flicker on a TV screen, which is annoying and distracting for the audience. Be especially wary of units

Tip

Always call ahead to the facility where you'll give your presentation to confirm equipment availability and compatibility. Ten minutes before show time is a bad time to discover you're missing an adapter or should have brought your whole computer.

V

Output and Color

designed for playing computer games on a TV screen—these typically have the poorest quality.

Cost: $50 to $450

Planning Ahead

If you're taking your presentation on the road for any size audience, it's important to plan ahead and make sure you have everything you need for a successful presentation.

- Allow yourself plenty of setup time to make sure all equipment will work together as planned. A couple of hours is usually adequate, although a "dry run" the day before never hurts.

- Call ahead to the host facility for availability of an overhead projector, slide or video projector, and projection screen. If you're using traditional slides, it's a good idea to see what kind of projector will be used. While carousel systems are the most common, you may need time to place your slides in a different carrier.

- If you're bringing your own projector, computer, or television, take along your own extension cord (at least 20 feet long). It may be a long way to the nearest outlet.

- Laptop and portable computers are especially good for taking a presentation on the road. But don't depend on the batteries to get you through. If your machine uses battery packs, take along an extra, or better yet, just plug the computer in to a wall outlet.

- If you choose not to use a mouse or other computer-based pointing device that takes advantage of PowerPoint's annotation features, a laser pointer is a very useful item. The size of a ballpoint pen, the pointers produce a small dot of red light which is very visible on projection screens up to 150 feet away. Cost is approximately $80.

Taking PowerPoint On the Road

Suppose you want to give a presentation while traveling. A computer is available, but PowerPoint is not installed. Does this mean you can't present your slide show? No. PowerPoint Viewer, an application included with your copy of PowerPoint, allows you to display your presentation on any computer with Windows. Simply bring a disk containing your presentation and PowerPoint Viewer.

PowerPoint Viewer also comes in handy when you want to send your presentation to a computer user who does not have PowerPoint. Just include PowerPoint Viewer on the disk with your presentation. You may duplicate PowerPoint Viewer for others without violating the law or your software license.

Using the Pack and Go Wizard

You need at least one 1.44M (high-density) floppy disk to create a portable version of your presentation. If your presentation includes many graphics, charts, or equations, it can take several, so be sure and have plenty of disks on hand.

To create disks that contain PowerPoint Viewer and your presentation, follow these steps:

1. Select Pack and Go from the File Menu. Choose Next when the opening Pack and Go Wizard dialog box appears.

2. Select the presentation you want to package (see fig 17.12). If a presentation is open, it will be selected. To prepare more than one presentation, choose Other Presentations. You can then navigate to your other presentations and use the mouse with the Ctrl key to select more than one. Choose Next when you have picked your slide show.

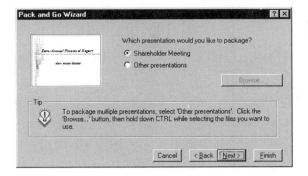

Fig. 17.12
The Pack and Go Wizard assembles a ready-to-run package incuding one or several presentations, along with a viewer if the recipeint doesn't have PowerPoint.

3. Choose your presentation's destination—a floppy drive or a folder on your hard drive. Click Next to continue.

If you selected the Other Destination option, click the Browse button to open the Specify Directory dialog box. Locate the folder where you want to store the presentation, placing its name in the Folder Name box, and then choose Select to return to the Wizard.

4. If you are not sure whether the computer on which you will run your presentation has the TrueType fonts you have used, activate the Embed TrueType Fonts option and save your presentation to the floppy disk. PowerPoint will include the fonts you have used, and they will be available when your slide show is viewed.

   Select Include Linked Files to allow the recipient to work with any linked files, such as spreadsheets, that you have included in your presentation. Otherwise, they will only be able to see the representation on the slide. If disk space is a factor, deselect this option.

   Choose Next when you've made your choices.

5. If the receiving computer has Windows, but doesn't have PowerPoint, select the Include PowerPoint Viewer checkbox to copy the viewer. Choose Next when you're done.

6. The Wizard lets you know it is ready to complete the process. Choosing Finish will compress the necessary files and save them to your chosen destination.

Installing PowerPoint Viewer on Another Computer

Now that all of your presentation files are on disks and sent to their destination, the receiver will want to know how to view your work.

PowerPoint Viewer runs too slowly from a floppy disk. For good performance, you or the person to whom you are sending your presentation must install the program and your presentation on the computer that will show the presentation.

From Windows 95 or NT:

1. Insert the first disk in the drive, and select Add/Remove Programs from the Control Panel.

2. Choose Install. Windows will check the floppy drives for the setup files. Choose Finish when the PNG setup file is located.

   Windows will run the install program, prompting you for a location to put the files. When it's finished, you have the option of running the slide show right away by choosing Yes or waiting until a later time by choosing No.

Using PowerPoint Viewer to View a Slide Show

After you have installed PowerPoint Viewer, you can display a slide show on a computer that does not have PowerPoint installed. All the features available within a PowerPoint slide show, including the special effects you may have included—such as builds and transitions—are available.

1. To view the show again, use Windows Explorer to navigate to the folder where the PowerPoint Viewer was installed. Double-click Pptview.exe to start the Microsoft PowerPoint Viewer dialog box.

2. A list appears of PowerPoint presentations that were copied to the folder. Select one, and if necessary, also select Loop Continuously Until Esc and Automatic Timings or Use.

3. Choose Show, and the Viewer will load the presentation and begin the slide show.

4. Find the pointer and pencil in the viewer by pressing the right mouse button to reveal an icon at the bottom right of the screen. To advance a slide without automatic timing, click the mouse button or use any of the keyboard shortcuts.

After the slide show ends, the Viewer Dialog box returns. Choose Quit to exit, or select another presentation.

Running Slide Shows with a Play List

Using a play list—a text file containing a list of PowerPoint presentations—you can run two or more presentations consecutively as a continuous slide show. You may do this with PowerPoint Viewer.

Creating the Play List

To make a play list, create a file with any word processor or editor, such as Windows Notepad or Word. Type the file name of the first presentation you want to display, and press Enter. Then type the second presentation's file name, and press Enter. Continue until you have typed the names of all the presentations you want to include in your slide show, as in this example: SHOW1.PPT, SHOW2.PPT, and SHOW3.PPT. Save the file in the same folder as the presentations using the extension .LST.

V

Output and Color

Running a Play List from PowerPoint Viewer

To run a play list from PowerPoint Viewer, follow these steps:

1. In Windows Explorer, navigate to the viewer.

2. Double-click Pptview.exe to show the Microsoft PowerPoint viewer dialog box.

3. Type the name of the .LST file and choose Show to open the play list and start the slide show.

Building a presentation is a challenging and rewarding experience, but like a good book, pretty worthless if no one ever sees it. With this chapter, you have gained the knowledge to transmit ideas and goals to their final recipients—the folks in the crowd who need to hear your message.❖

Chapter 18

Working with Color

by Rich Grace

Color is a very important component of slide shows, and the proper use of color can make the difference between a dull, boring presentation, and one that excites, informs, and prompts a decision.

PowerPoint 95 offers many new color features. Among the most important color features are simpler ways of working with color. Now you can change palettes and colors in almost every view and in every Master in the program. Dialog boxes are simpler and more consistent. For the first time, PowerPoint offers multicolored gradient fills so you can add a powerful custom look to your slides. A few simple steps suffice to convert an entire presentation to a black and white format.

In this chapter, you study PowerPoint's color features more intensively, and you learn how to

- Create new colors and place them on the palette

- Understand the relationship between template color schemes and color palettes

- Understand the 15-color and 127-color PowerPoint default palettes and how to change their colors

- Acquire techniques, tips, and tricks for effective color management

- Use PowerPoint 95's Built-In Color Schemes

- Create multicolor gradient fills

- Learn the simple techniques for changing slides from color to black and white

Understanding Color in PowerPoint 95

When you choose a template to create a PowerPoint 95 presentation, you also make a decision about the presentation's appearance. You have a specific set of colors to work with, but that doesn't mean that you can't change them. PowerPoint allows you the flexibility to use any color you want anywhere you want.

 The front-line tool for working with color in PowerPoint is the Fill Color tool, which is located on the Drawing+ toolbar. The tool is actually a combination of a menu list and a color palette (see fig. 18.1). A basic set of eight colors is offered there.

Fig. 18.1

The Fill Color palette displaying several menu options, the basic eight-color palette, and some extra colors to assign to objects.

Basic eight-color palette

Notice the appearance of a similar color palette in the Font dialog box (see fig. 18.2). Here you can use the palette to assign different colors to slide text.

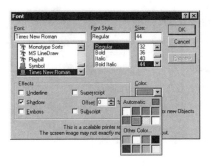

Fig. 18.2
The Font dialog box displaying the same color palette as the Fill Color tool.

The same color set is used in several different places throughout the program. PowerPoint 95 has lots of consistency of color use. Most, if not all, of the PowerPoint features that use color use the same palette, show the same drop-down list, and apply colors the same way. The shortcut menu also uses the same palette feature in many places. In PowerPoint 95, you'll rapidly become familiar with ways to apply color in the program.

> **Note**
>
> PowerPoint 95 comes with one set of masters for all uses—color slide shows, color transparencies, or black and white. All the masters default to color. (Previous versions of PowerPoint came with separate black and white versions of the master set.)

Studying PowerPoint's Color Schemes and Basic Color Palette

The eight-color palette you see in the preceding two figures is no accident. There is a reason for the placement of those eight colors. They are the eight basic colors for the entire template. When you select a design template for your presentation, those eight colors show up everywhere in your program. Each color is assigned a place and has specific uses to ensure its appropriate and proper use in the slide show. (Believe it or not, eight colors is usually more than enough for any slide show.)

PowerPoint's new Color Schemes form the foundation for working with color in PowerPoint. This is where we'll begin our exploration of color. From the Format menu, choose Slide Color Scheme. The Color Scheme dialog box appears. This is where it all begins. Figure 18.3 shows its contents.

Fig. 18.3
The Color Scheme dialog box, displaying its various elements.

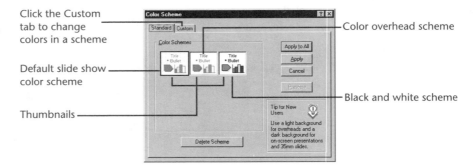

The Color Scheme dialog box shows a set of standard Color Schemes that you can select to change the appearance of one slide, or of the entire slide show. Either process is equally simple. Every template offers a set of at least three thumbnails showing color schemes, as shown in the dialog box. Some templates offer six or seven color schemes, and you can add your own schemes as well.

Your presentation template defaults to the scheme on the top left. One of the color sets is a black and white (or grayscale) version for use in producing black and white overheads.

Tip
Each pictorial object in a Color Scheme thumbnail shows how one color in the scheme is assigned.

The thumbnail color schemes merit further examination. Instead of having to choose each additional color, you're offered a choice of three or more different schemes. Each scheme is displayed as a small slide thumbnail, and the various colored elements on the thumbnails display where each of the eight colors in the scheme are assigned.

What are those eight colors?

■ Within each thumbnail, the four little columns represent the Fills color and the three accent colors automatically assigned to each scheme.

■ The title at the top of each thumbnail represents the title text color.

■ A line of sample text below the title shows the default Text & Lines color for the scheme.

■ The polygon on the left side of each thumbnail shows the default Fill color for drawn objects.

■ The background color of each thumbnail represents the background color used on the slide.

■ Finally, the shadow color is shown at the lower edge of the polygon, as a shadow, naturally. All eight colors are accounted for.

You also can change the color schemes for any of the three standard color palettes, and save them as additional color schemes in the dialog box. To have a closer look at the color palette for the currently used master, click the Custom tab shown later in figure 18.4.

You have to click the Custom tab in the Color Scheme dialog box to view the actual color palette for the current template. PowerPoint's templates determine the color appearance of your slide show. You're not limited to the colors prescribed in each template, though. Any of the colors can be changed to suit your taste. The Custom tab enables you to do this.

Notice the eight-color palette in the dialog box. These define the use of each color in the program (see table 18.1).

Table 18.1 The Slide Color Scheme Color Assignments

Assignment	Description
Top row, left to right:	
Background	Used to create the background fill colors for your slides
Shadows	The shadowing color used for text, graphic objects, other items on your slides
Fills	Default color fill from drawn objects
Accent	Accent color (used primarily for chart series items in the default)
Bottom row, left to right:	
Text & Lines	Color assigned to body text on the slides, and to lines bordering drawn objects
Title Text	Color assigned to titles on your slides
Accent	Accent color (used primarily for chart series items in the default)
Accent	Accent color (used primarily for chart series items in the default)

The functions of the buttons in the Color Scheme dialog box are described in table 18.2.

V

Output and Color

Table 18.2 The Color Scheme Dialog Box Button Functions

Button	Function
Standard tab	
Apply to All button	Applies color changes to all slides and exits dialog box
Apply button	Applies color changes to current slide and exits dialog box
Cancel button	Cancels out any changes and returns to presentation
Preview	Lets you preview any color changes to your slide before you commit to them
Delete Scheme	Deletes the selected color scheme shown in the Standard tab
Custom Tab	
Apply to All button	Applies color changes to all slides and exits dialog box
Apply button	Applies color changes to current slide and exits dialog box
Cancel button	Cancels any changes and returns to presentation
Preview	Lets you preview any color changes to your slide before you commit to them
Change Color	Click on any of the eight colors and then click this button to access PowerPoint's Histograms, from which you can select and create custom colors for your palettes
Add as Standard Scheme	Places the changed color scheme into a new thumbnail on the Color Scheme dialog box Standard tab. Does not replace the defaults. This step is recommended any time you change colors in a color scheme.

Effective color management begins with knowing the specific role of the eight colors found in the Slide Color Scheme dialog box. Those eight color boxes are considered the basic color scheme for your entire presentation, and they're used the same way for any presentation you ever create (though with different colors for any given slide show and its color scheme).

Note

Chapters 3 and 4 include information about how a slide background color and a Slide Master's background color can be changed.

When you select a template, the background color sets the tone for the rest of the elements of your presentation. While you can change the background color at any time, bear in mind that other colors also may need to be changed to compensate. The colors that usually need to be adjusted in such a case are the Text & Lines color and the Title Text color.

Also, when you select a new color scheme for your presentation, the background and text colors are the key colors selected, and the other six colors are automatically assigned. You learn how to do this a little later, in the section of this chapter titled "Changing a Presentation's Color Schemes."

While the Slide Master controls the color scheme for the overall presentation, you use the color changing techniques you learn in this section to change the color scheme for an individual slide. So one or two slides can have a completely different background color and will probably need different text colors to match. (We talk about good color matching later on in this chapter.) The Title Master also can have a different scheme.

You can activate the Color Scheme and make changes and color choices in virtually every view or Master in the program: when viewing any slide in your presentation, the Slide Sorter, Slide view, Notes Pages view, or the Outline view; viewing the Title Master, the Handout Master, or the Notes Master; or when viewing the Slide Master. The dialog box is the same, simply named after the Master or view that you're currently in. This is another prominent example of how PowerPoint's methods of operation have been both simplified and made more consistent. Many of PowerPoint 95's color-handling features differ in this way from previous versions.

Tip

If you change a background color, you should change the text or title colors to match.

Some PowerPoint views, such as Notes Pages or Handouts (or their Masters) don't default to the color schemes of the slide show, but use the Windows default colors. You can select the template color scheme in these views. In this chapter, we'll concentrate on changing the colors when you're in Slide view or in the Slide Sorter.

V

Output and Color

Note

A seldom-used but very intelligent way to manage multiple slide color schemes is to use the Slide Sorter view. Using the Sorter enables you to get the large view of where a different colored slide fits into the presentation. In the Sorter, you can access the same color changing features available in Slide view or the Slide Master. In most examples in this chapter, Slide view or the Slide Master is used, but when you change the color scheme for just one slide in a presentation, Slide Sorter view is used.

Changing a Presentation's Color Schemes

Changing a color scheme should be defined as a process separate from simply changing a color. Changing a color scheme, as noted previously, requires changing two key elements: the background color and the text color.

To change the color scheme for an entire presentation, follow these steps:

1. From the View menu, choose Slides to change to Slide view. (You can change the color scheme from any of PowerPoint's views except Slide Show.)

   Because you're changing the color scheme for the entire presentation, it doesn't matter which slide you're currently displaying.

2. From the Format menu, choose Slide Color Scheme. The Color Scheme dialog box appears.

   As we've noted, you can change a single slide or an entire presentation's color scheme here. When the dialog box appears, the three (or more) color scheme thumbnails are displayed. The scheme in use by the current slide, or by the presentation, is highlighted.

3. Click the Custom tab. The dialog box changes its appearance and shows the color palette for the currently selected scheme (see fig. 18.4).

Fig. 18.4
The Color Scheme dialog box showing the Custom tab, which displays the basic eight-color palette for the currently selected color scheme.

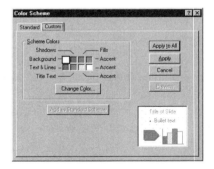

The contents of the Custom tab are described in table 18.2. The steps to change any color in the palette are the same as those described below. For our example, we'll change the background color.

4. Select the Background color in the Scheme Colors section of the dialog box, and then choose a Change Color.

   The Background Color dialog box appears. It automatically shows two tabs, also conveniently named Standard and Custom (see fig. 18.5).

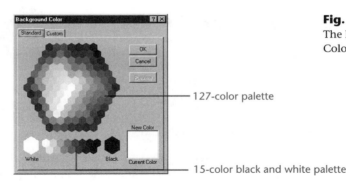

127-color palette

15-color black and white palette

Fig. 18.5
The Background
Color dialog box.

> **Note**
>
> The Background Color dialog box actually changes its name, depending on which of the eight colors in the color scheme you select in the Color Scheme dialog box. If you choose to change the Fills color, for example, the Background Color dialog box is then called the Fills Color dialog box. Otherwise, its functions are basically identical.

In figure 18.5, an expanded 127-color palette is shown (in previous versions of PowerPoint, this was a 90-color palette). The current background color is already selected in the 127-color palette, which is shown in a hexagonal shape. Just below the hexagon, another smaller palette appears, which is a 15-color black and white palette. Any of those 15 colors also can be selected.

5. To change the background color, simply click another color in the 127-color palette.

   Some colors provide a good match for the background color, and provide readable body text on your slides. PowerPoint makes an effort to select a group of colors that works with the background color, but colors by their very nature are mutable, and one person will see a particular color differently from another person. Some colors may not work quite as well as others.

6. To see the effects of a new background color without changing it permanently, choose Preview.

7. Choose OK or press Enter.

   The Color Scheme dialog box reappears. Notice that the color scheme has changed to reflect your new choices.

Tip
You use the Color dialog box the same way for all scheme colors.

Tip
You can drag the dialog box to the side of the screen for a better view.

V

Output and Color

8. Choose the Apply <u>t</u>o All button to apply the new color scheme to the entire presentation. If you choose the <u>A</u>pply button only, the new scheme is applied only to the currently displayed or currently selected slide.

   A message pops up, reading:

   ```
   Charts are being updated with the new color scheme
   ```

   The Color Scheme dialog box disappears.

9. If the color scheme doesn't quite fit your taste when you're back to your view, choose the <u>U</u>ndo Slide Color Scheme command from the <u>E</u>dit menu.

   Because you changed your background color, you'll now have to take a good look at the default color for your text and titles. To be readable, the text color must contrast against the background color.

Changing a Slide's Color Scheme

To change a single slide's color scheme, you follow almost the same steps that you did in the preceding example, which describes how you change the color scheme for an entire presentation. In this example, you use the Slide Sorter to pick a slide for a new color scheme. You start by displaying the Slide Sorter for the current presentation:

1. Choose <u>V</u>iew, Sli<u>d</u>e Sorter.

   The Slide Sorter screen appears (see fig. 18.6).

Fig. 18.6
The Slide Sorter view, showing the slides in the presentation.

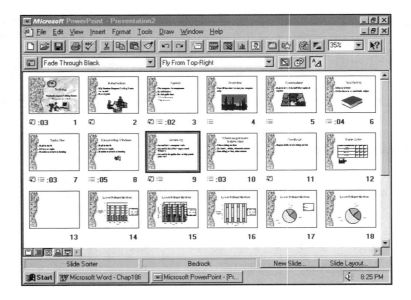

2. Click the slide with the color scheme you want to change.

3. Choose Format, Slide Color Scheme.

   The Color Scheme dialog box appears, displaying the thumbnails currently available for the template.

4. Click the Custom tab.

   The dialog box changes its appearance and shows the color palette for the currently used scheme.

5. For this example, choose the Fills color and then click the Change Color button.

   The Fill Color dialog box appears.

6. If it is not displayed, click the Custom tab.

   The Fill Color Custom tab displays PowerPoint's color histogram (see fig. 18.7).

Tip
Double-click on a Scheme Color to automatically bring up the Color dialog box (which changes its name to read Fill Color, Background Color, Title Color, Text & Line Color, or Accent Color, depending on the palette color you've selected) with its adjustable palette.

Crosshair (drag this with the mouse)

Drag this arrowhead to adjust the darkness of the selected color

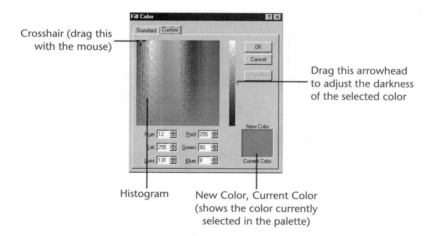

Fig. 18.7
The Fill Color Custom tab, displaying PowerPoint's histogram.

Histogram   New Color, Current Color (shows the color currently selected in the palette)

You are now at PowerPoint's most sophisticated level of color manipulation and selection. PowerPoint's histogram offers an extremely flexible and sensitive method for adjusting colors to a precise value.

The histogram represents the entire color range supported by the VGA card or Windows accelerator in your computer. You drag the crosshair on the histogram with the mouse to change the color. When you do so, release the mouse; the RGB and HSL values change their values dynamically.

V

Output and Color

The color adjuster bar to the right of the histogram also changes to reflect the colors over which the crosshair passes. You drag the small arrowhead on the adjuster bar to change the luminance on the selected color.

Notice that when you drag the arrowhead on the adjuster bar up and down, hue and saturation values stay the same and the luminance value changes. The red, green, and blue values also change because when you change the luminance, you are also changing the quantity of "light" displayed in the color, from brighter to darker or vice versa.

The two color swatches at the bottom left of the dialog box are labeled New Color and Current Color. The Current Color swatch shows the color that the object (text, title, background, etc.) is presently filled with. The New Color swatch is the mixed color produced when values are changed or the crosshair on the histogram is moved. It represents a color that's actually supported by your computer's display hardware. When you drag the crosshairs on the histogram, you can watch the New Color swatch change its color.

PowerPoint uses two different color mixing systems for custom color creation: RGB (red-green-blue) and HSL (hue-saturation-luminance). What is hue-saturation-luminance?

Hue
: The hue is simply the color shown in the color swatch. The hue determines the basic color, such as green, blue, or orange.

Saturation
: Provides the basic vividness or purity of a color. More gray in a color, less saturation; less gray, more saturation.

Luminance
: The degree of lightness or darkness in a color, which is created by mixing black and white in differing degrees to the color.

These three quantities are mixed together to create the colors you see in all the palettes, and all colors you see in PowerPoint.

HSL and RGB are very similar to each other; RGB is simply the mixture of the pure red, green, and blue brightness values to produce a mixed color. The red, green, and blue values are measured and adjusted from 0 to 255 in PowerPoint. (HSL values are also measured from 0 to 255.) A single color in PowerPoint is defined by the mix of red, green, and blue.

Think of a TV set, which uses exactly the same system to produce its photo-realistic images. A TV set has three "guns:" red, green, and blue. Each "shoots out" light of its respective color. If a color gun fails in your TV set, you immediately notice the change in the color quality of your screen. The RGB color system works exactly the same way.

Individual red-green-blue and hue-saturation-luminance values can be adjusted using the up- and down-arrow icons next to each text box. You also can type in specific values—in fact, whenever you create a color that pleases you, or is meant to be used in other presentations, make a note in a safe place of the red, green, and blue values so that you won't lose them and can quickly apply them to new jobs.

> **Note**
>
> When you create custom color schemes, you're often doing so to match the colors of a company logo, or promotional materials used by a company for its products. In cases like these, keep permanent records of color mixes you use in a presentation, particularly if you frequently use a service like Genigraphics to produce slides and presentation output.

To resume our exercise, for adding a custom fill color to a color palette:

7. Adjust the values to the level desired, or type in the Red-Green-Blue or Hue-Saturation-Luminance values desired.

8. Choose OK or press Enter.

   The Color Scheme dialog box shows the custom color in the eight-color palette.

9. Choose Preview to view the effect of the new color without closing the dialog box. (Because you can Change Color only from the Custom tab, that's what reappears after you do the color mixing.)

   The new color is applied to the selected object.

10. To keep the original color scheme but use the one you've just modified, choose the Add as Standard Scheme button. (This is a highly recommended step.) If you then click the Standard tab, you'll see that a new thumbnail has been added to the dialog box, showing the new colors you've created.

    Tip
    Choose the Add as Standard Scheme button to preserve your work and also the original palette.

11. Choose the Apply button to apply the new color scheme to the slide selected in the Sorter.

A message appears, reading:

```
Charts are being updated with the new color scheme
```

The Color Scheme dialog box disappears.

Now the slide has a different appearance, which can be an intelligent way to make it stand out and get the audience's attention. But use this trick sparingly. If you change the color scheme of every slide to get attention, you'll try the audience's patience in a short time. With a little imagination and discreet applications of color, you can ensure that your audience is never bored—and then you're halfway there.

If the final results of your color twiddling don't quite work, there are many ways to change it back. You can choose Undo Slide Color Scheme from the Edit menu. Because PowerPoint now has multiple undos (and the number of undos can be adjusted), it's even easier to change the colors back. But there are other ways.

If you kept your default color scheme by adding your custom one as another standard scheme (as described above), you can simply display the offending slide and reapply the default scheme. If you've made a record of the original color mixes, you can replace them from there.

The steps described here apply to every PowerPoint object that can have its colors changed. Depending on the slide object that you select, you also can use the shortcut menu (displayed by clicking the right mouse button) to start PowerPoint's Color Scheme features.

Basic Color Theory: What Works and What Doesn't?

Modern PCs offer many temptations. Millions of colors are available to you. Almost every major software package offers a minimum of hundreds of colors in their basic palette. The quantity of colors may tempt you into overdoing it. PowerPoint's basic palette offers the first antidote to this possibility: only eight colors are available in the basic palette. "Eight colors?" you may ask. "So what? I had that on my PC ten years ago!"

The crucial trick is not to please yourself. You must please your audience. The psychology of color is both subtle and powerful. Considering your audience and thinking ahead is what gets that crucial Purchase Order signed and on your desk. Consider the psychology and the world view of the people who will see your presentation, and you may well get the edge you need to succeed.

Keep it Simple

The first key point, keep it simple, is nearly universal in any field of human endeavor, and it definitely applies to presentation design and the use of color. Drowning a slide in vibrant colors can have precisely the opposite effect of what you intend. As you've just seen, PowerPoint automatically provides some levels of effective color management without intruding on the user. In most situations, it may be best to follow the guidelines and color schemes offered by the program.

Watch your Color Schemes Carefully

The second key point: control your color schemes wisely. As you just saw, it's possible to apply different color schemes to each slide. In most situations, this may not be a good idea. Consider that the vast majority of your slides (perhaps 70 percent) are simple text slides with bulleted lists. How do you think your audience would feel if you changed the background and text colors for every successive slide? Impatience may be a kind word for it.

A corollary to this point: You can shift gears by changing the color scheme on a slide, particularly if you change the subject and you want to provide an effective transition. It also can work if you want to forcefully bring attention to a chart illustrating a crucial point during your presentation. Just don't go overboard.

Tailor Color Schemes to Your Audience

The third key point: color schemes can be tailored to your audience. For example, if you are addressing an audience from a foreign country, try to make them feel more at home by using their national colors as a base for your presentation's color palette. How do you find this out? Check a world atlas in either book form or on CD-ROM.

Different corporate environments can require different approaches, too. In general, you may expect marketing and public relations executives to respond more favorably to a flashy and strikingly colored presentation (within limits) than a board of directors or upper management group would. Also, company cultures vary widely, regardless of the department you're addressing. Take a few minutes to do some detective work to find out a general "cultural" sketch of the people you are presenting to.

Watch Your Fonts and Color Schemes in Text Slides

Point four is the most specific tip: text slides work best with highly contrasting color schemes. The vast majority of slides in most presentations are text slides with a few bulleted points. A good rule of thumb is to use yellow or light blue text against a dark background. Also, go easy on the fonts, and use conservative typefaces, such as Times Roman, Helvetica, Garamond, and Palatino. Modern PCs offer every typeface conceived throughout the history of printing and moveable type, and it's easy to go with ornate and striking typefaces for your slides. Use them very sparingly.

Troubleshooting

My color schemes look crude and unattractive.

This probably isn't the fault of Windows, but of the video card and monitor that you use on your system. You may be running Windows in its default VGA display mode, which is 640 × 480 resolution at 16 colors. That does lend a crude appearance to even the most sophisticated presentation. Fortunately, many Windows systems can do much more. Run Windows 95 at a minimum of 256 colors for on-screen presentations. It's possible to display as many as 16 million colors in Windows and in PowerPoint. This lends a beautiful accuracy to color shadings and other effects in the program. Many modern video cards that are optimized for Windows will actually run *faster* at higher color depths. However, many presenters use laptops that tend to drag at higher color depths, so you may need to compromise at 256 colors for your work.

Also, consider using higher screen resolutions than 640 × 480. On-screen slide shows can look extremely sleek and readable and show much greater detail at 1024 × 768 or 1280 × 1024 screen resolution. A huge number of current video cards (also called Windows Accelerators, because they're designed mainly to boost Windows performance) routinely support those dramatically higher resolutions. Even an 800 × 600 screen shows a great improvement. Most modern Windows machines easily run 800 × 600 at 256 colors, and this is the minimum standard I recommend for pleasing visuals in PowerPoint.

The main flaw in this strategy is that many presenters have to use laptop computers and large TV monitors to display their shows. Television sets are very limited in the screen resolution that they can display. Typically, they can display a 640 × 480 VGA screen with an unlimited palette of colors. With a television monitor, your color range can be much more ambitious than your resolution.

Video cards usually come with a set of Windows software drivers for higher resolutions and color depths. Make sure that you have access to these drivers. They make it possible to run Windows the way it should be run. Check your Windows and video card documentation for more information on video settings and how to run them.

Applying Colors to Individual Objects

Unlike more general color schemes, applying colors to individual objects on a slide can be considered an open field of play. For colors, shading, and pattern fills of drawn objects, you can use every color you could possibly display under Windows. (This isn't the case, however, for imported graphics. You must use the original drawing or graphics program for that.)

Most of the exercises in the rest of this chapter are quite straightforward and share many common steps.

The key tools for altering colors in drawn objects are the Fill Color and Line Color tools in the Drawing toolbar. Note that all the exercises in the rest of this chapter discuss the use of color; grouping, arranging, drawing, and other operations are discussed elsewhere in this book.

> **Note**
>
> See Chapter 10, "Drawing Objects," and Chapter 11, "Selecting, Editing, and Enhancing Graphic Objects," for more methods and techniques for working with drawn objects in PowerPoint.

Figure 18.8 shows a typical slide, designed for the purpose of adding graphic objects for embellishment. Starting with this exercise, you go beyond the basic palettes offered in the drawing tools to select colors from a wider palette.

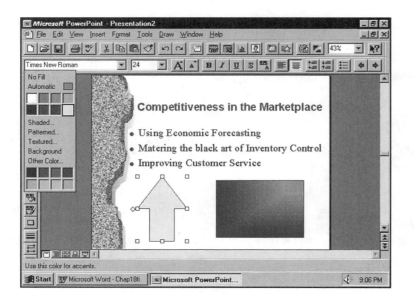

Fig. 18.8
Typical slide waiting for embellishment.

To change the color of an object, follow these steps:

1. Click the Rectangle tool on the Drawing toolbar.

2. Draw a simple rectangle on the slide.

3. Click the rectangle to select it.

4. Click the Fill Color tool on the Drawing toolbar.

   The drop-down palette menu appears.

   The automatic color is the default color from the template's color scheme for the currently selected object. The Fill Color tool offers a significant number of options.

> **Note**
>
> Notice that when you perform the previous step, a Fill Color is highlighted in the drop-down palette. It corresponds to the default color applied to the selected object.

5. You can choose any of the eight colors that are shown, or, for a custom color, click the Other Color option in the drop-down list.

   The Colors dialog box appears, as shown in figure 18.9.

Fig. 18.9
The Colors dialog box (does this look familiar?).

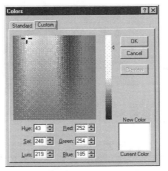

The Colors dialog box (showing the Histogram in the Custom tab) is the same one that you examined earlier in this chapter. The only difference is that its name has changed. Both the Standard and Custom tabs are available, and their functions are exactly the same.

6. Change the color using the histogram, or click the Standard tab.

7. If you click the Standard tab, choose a color from the hexagon of 127 colors shown there.

8. Choose OK or press Enter.

Here's another example of how PowerPoint's functions have been streamlined. The common points between every color-related function in PowerPoint provide a real boon to the user. You rapidly get accustomed to a large variety of features if the mechanisms they use are the same across the board. Most of the other exercises in this chapter work identically, except for menu choices in the Fill Color tool.

Applying Shadows, Patterns, and Textures to Objects

In most situations, basic colors are adequate for any task. In others, you can use special graphics effects, such as shading, gradient fills, pattern fills, or PowerPoint 95's new texture fills, for an artistic touch to a graphic object, a slide background, or an entire presentation. PowerPoint now provides more versatile gradient fills using more than one primary color. The program also bundles a set of default texture fills that can be applied to backgrounds or to drawn objects. Most of the provided textures resemble marble and wood surfaces.

Using Shaded Color and Multi-Color Gradients for Objects and Backgrounds

To apply shading to a selected graphic object, follow these steps:

1. Select the rectangle or other object for color changes.

2. Click the Fill Color tool on the Drawing+ toolbar.

   The drop-down palette menu appears.

3. Choose the Shaded option from the drop-down menu.

   The Shaded Fill dialog box appears (see fig. 18.10).

Fig. 18.10
The Shaded Fill
dialog box.

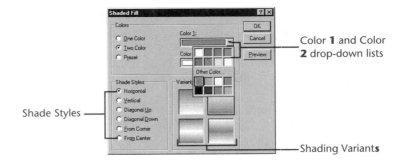

Color **1** and Color
2 drop-down lists

Shade Styles

Shading Variant**s**

The Shaded Fill dialog box displays a couple of options that may be familiar to you from earlier chapters: the Shade Styles option button list and the shading variants, which display four thumbnails showing different orientations for the same fill type. The Color 1 and Color 2 drop-down menus are similar to the Fill Color tool, except that they only give you access to the basic eight-color palette and to the Other Color palette, from which you can choose any color for the fill.

4. For an example, click the top-right shading variant. Variants provide directions the shading will move toward.

5. Click on any of the Shade Styles option buttons (Horizontal, Vertical, Diagonal Up, Diagonal Down, From Corner, and From Center), to view alternative groups of shading variants.

6. To create shading effects, choose from the buttons in the upper-left corner.

   ■ If you want to create a single-color shading effect, click the One Color option button. The set of variants changes to reflect shading using one color. You can darken or lighten the color by dragging the scroll box on the Dark-Light slider.

   ■ If you want to create a two-color shading effect, click the Two Color option button. The variants change to reflect shading using two colors.

   ■ Choose the Preset option button if you want to choose from among Microsoft's substantial default set of two-color gradient fills.

> **Note**
>
> The Preset option provides access to a pleasing selection of pre-built gradient fills. Most of them reflect natural or metallic themes, such as Early Sunset, Late Sunset, and Nightfall, or Brass, Chrome, and Silver. A Rainbow fill uses all the colors of the rainbow to create the gradient fill. Choose the Preset option button and choose from the drop-down list of sixteen presets. Remember that all sixteen preset fill types use Shade Styles as well (Horizontal, Vertical, and so on).

7. Select colors you want from the Color 1 or Color 2 lists. The Other Color options are the same as for other color features described in this chapter.

8. Click Preview if you want to see the effects on your object before you make the changes. Otherwise, choose OK or press Enter.

The result resembles figure 18.11. As you can see, it's not hard to add effects to a drawn object.

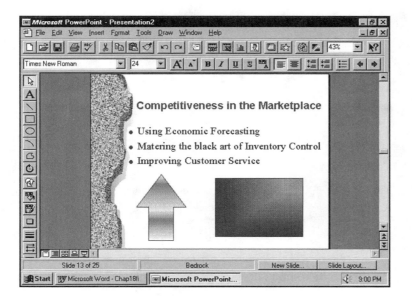

Fig. 18.11
Results from applying a shaded fill.

To apply shading or custom color gradient fills to a slide background, follow these steps:

1. From the Format menu, choose Custom Background.

2. The Custom Background dialog box appears (see fig. 18.12).

Fig. 18.12

The Custom
Background dialog
box.

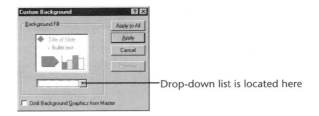

Drop-down list is located here

Tip

You also can open
Custom Back-
ground by clicking
the right mouse
button on an open
region of the slide
background (an
area that has no
other objects over
it).

This is an important dialog box, because every effect you can possibly
apply to a slide background, title master, or a slide master is located
here. These effects include applying bitmap pictures, patterns, shading,
gradient fills, and special textures to a background.

3. Click on the drop-down list at the bottom of the dialog box (see fig.
18.13).

Fig. 18.13

The Custom
Background dialog
box, showing its
drop-down list.

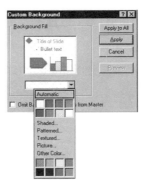

4. From the drop-down list, choose Shaded.

The Shaded Fill dialog box appears (refer to fig. 18.10). It's another
example of PowerPoint's enhanced consistency of features.

5. Choose from the various shading options, variants, and other options.

6. Choose OK or press Enter. The Custom Background dialog box reappears, with its thumbnail displaying a slide sample with the new effect.

7. Choose Apply for the current slide or Apply to All for the entire slide
show. The dialog box disappears and the shading effect takes place.

Note

To add an embossed effect to a graphic, draw an ellipse or another shape on top of the rectangle (using the rectangle as a guide for your drawing cursor to ensure that the ellipse is in proportion to the rectangle), change the color to the same as the rectangle, and add a shading variant that runs in the opposite direction.

Using Pattern Fills for Objects and Slide Backgrounds

PowerPoint offers a selection of 36 pattern fills that you can apply to any selected object. You apply pattern fills from the Fill Color tool's drop-down menu; they can be combined with any desired color.

To add a pattern fill to a drawn object, follow these steps:

1. Select the object for pattern filling.

2. Click the Fill Color tool on the Drawing toolbar.

   The drop-down palette menu appears.

3. Choose the Patterned option from the drop-down menu.

   The Pattern Fill dialog box appears, as shown in figure 18.14.

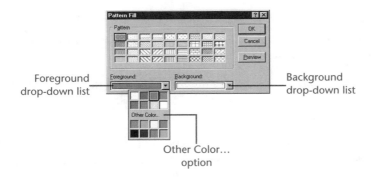

Foreground drop-down list

Background drop-down list

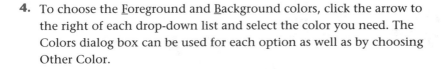

Other Color... option

Fig. 18.14
The Pattern Fill dialog box.

4. To choose the Foreground and Background colors, click the arrow to the right of each drop-down list and select the color you need. The Colors dialog box can be used for each option as well as by choosing Other Color.

V

Output and Color

Tip

Pattern fills use both a Foreground and a Background color—choose them carefully.

The foreground color is the color that the actual pattern assumes. Choose the background color so that the pattern stands out effectively. (In some cases, a well-chosen pattern and background color may actually resemble another color. That's an area where you can do a lot of experimenting. As an example, a white background color mixes well with a blue foreground color.)

5. Choose a pattern from the palette.

6. Click the Preview button to view the effect of the pattern on the object before you apply it.

7. Choose OK or press Enter.

If you select a pattern fill for a shaded object, the original shading is canceled, and cannot be recovered or combined with the pattern fill.

The process of applying pattern fills to a slide background is much the same:

1. Choose Format, Custom Background.

2. The Custom Background dialog box appears.

3. Click on the drop-down list at the bottom of the dialog box and choose Patterned.

   The Pattern Fill dialog box appears (refer to fig. 18.14 earlier).

4. Choose from the 36 pattern options, and choose your foreground and background colors.

5. Choose OK or press Enter. The Custom Background dialog box reappears, with its thumbnail displaying its slide sample with the new pattern effect.

6. Choose Apply for the current slide or Apply to All for the entire slide show. The dialog box disappears and the patterning effect will take place. To undo, choose Edit, Undo Pattern or press Ctrl+Z.

Changing Line Colors

To change line colors for the selected object, follow these steps:

1. Click the Line Color tool in the Drawing toolbar.

   The Line Color drop-down palette appears, showing the same color palette as that for the Fill Color tool.

2. Choose any of the colors displayed or choose the Other Color option. The Colors dialog box appears. To make it simpler, click the Standard tab.

3. Choose from among the 127 colors in the hexagon palette.

4. Choose OK or press Enter.

5. Finally, choose Apply.

For lines, there's another way to go. For lines or objects, you also can choose the Colors and Lines option from the Format menu or the shortcut menu. Figure 18.15 shows the Colors and Lines dialog box.

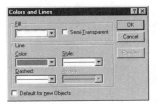

Fig. 18.15
The Colors and Lines dialog box.

The Other Color option is also liberally used throughout this dialog box. It's applied to fills and colors. In most circumstances, using the Colors dialog box will be overkill for changing line colors.

Notice also the availability of line Styles (line weights and different ornamented line styles) and Arrows (this option list is available only if you selected a line and not a closed object).

Adding Shadows and Changing Shadow Colors

Adding a basic shadow and changing the color of a shadow is a simple process, and you change the color of a shadow almost the same way you change the color for a regular drawn object. Just make sure that the shadow color you choose is appropriate for the effect you're trying to achieve.

Tip
Shadows should generally be as dark or darker than the object they're behind.

To quickly create a shadow effect, follow these steps:

1. Select the slide object that you want to attach shadowing to. Experiment! Many different objects can have shadows.

2. Click the Shadow On/Off tool in the Drawing toolbar.

A basic shadow using PowerPoint's defaults is applied to the selected object. The shadow color, by the way, is part of the default eight-color palette from your presentation's template.

To add a custom shadow effect to any selected graphic or text object, follow these steps:

1. Select the desired object.

2. Choose Format, Shadow.

   The Shadow dialog box appears (see fig. 18.16), displaying the Color drop-down list and the following options buttons for Offset:

   Up: Raise the shadow offset above the object margin by the specified number of points.

   Down: Lower the shadow offset below the object margin by the specified number of points.

   Left: Set shadow offset to the left of the object margin by the specified number of points.

   Right: Set shadow offset to the right of the object margin by the specified number of points.

Fig. 18.16
The Shadow dialog box, which you use for changing shadowing colors and offset directions.

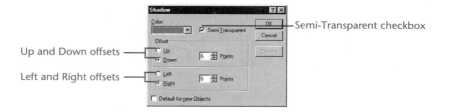

As you can see, once you learn the process of changing colors for one graphic element, such as a drawn object fill, line style, or shadowing, it's pretty much the same for all. The same color palettes are used and the procedures are the same. Nonetheless, PowerPoint offers more options for creating custom shadows, which you explore next.

Tip
You also can add shading, shadowing, and other effects to text object backgrounds, just as you can to graphic objects.

3. Adjust the shadow to the desired level (it may take some experimenting to get it right).

4. If you want to apply a different color (different from the template default shadow color) to the shadow, click the drop-down arrow icon under the Color option. The drop-down menu appears.

   The Color drop-down list functions the same as for the other examples in this chapter (see fig. 18.17).

5. Choose the desired color from either the drop-down palette or from the Colors dialog box.

6. Click the Semi-Transparent check box if it doesn't already have a check in it. A semi-transparent shadow more closely resembles what a shadow actually looks like in real life. While this won't work very well for an object that's already semi-transparent, it's a good effect to have for shadowing, if desired. When you create a shadow, the Semi-Transparent option is enabled by default.

7. Choose OK or press Enter. The shadow will be applied to the selected object.

Changing the Text Color

You can work with text objects and color on a slide in two ways: change the color of the text itself, or add a color fill, shading, or a pattern fill to the text object's background. In the first case, you're formatting the font itself; in the second, it's a matter of a simple color fill like the earlier exercises.

To change the color of title or body text on a slide, follow these steps:

1. Click and drag the mouse over the text in the text object to highlight it.

2. Choose Format, Font.

The Font dialog box appears (see fig. 18.17).

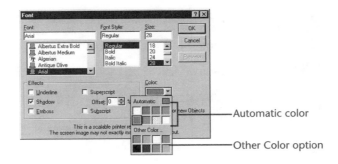

Fig. 18.17
Changing text colors with the Font dialog box.

3. Click the drop-down arrow under the Color option. The drop-down list appears.

4. Choose a color from the available palette colors, or choose the Other Color option and follow the steps described in the previous exercises.

5. Choose OK or press Enter.

To change the background color or fill of the text object, follow these steps:

1. Click once on the text object.

2. Click the Fill Color tool on the Drawing toolbar.

3. Select a color from the drop-down palette or choose the Other Color menu option. The Colors dialog box, displaying the color palette, appears.

4. To keep it simple, click the Standard tab. Choose a color from the 127-color hexagon palette. Or mix a new color by using the Custom tab with its histogram.

5. Choose OK or press Enter.

6. Finally, choose OK or press Enter again to execute the changes.

Using Textures in Slide Backgrounds

PowerPoint 95 offers a new set of texture fills that you can apply to slide backgrounds and graphic objects, in much the same way as you apply patterns and gradients. The set of textures provided with the program are marble, rock, and wood surfaces of different colors. It is also possible to import textures from other graphic files from any graphic file supported by PowerPoint filters.

1. From the Format menu, choose Custom Background.

2. The Custom Background dialog box appears.

3. Click on the drop-down list at the bottom of the dialog box.

4. From the drop-down list, choose Textured.

   The Texture Fill dialog box appears (see fig. 18.18).

Fig. 18.18
Using the Texture
Fill dialog box to
choose a texture
fill for a slide
background.

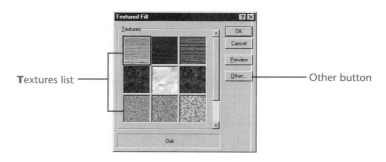

Textures list ─────

Other button ─────

5. Choose from the 12 textures shown.

6. Choose OK or press Enter. The Custom Background dialog box will reappear, with its thumbnail displaying the slide sample with the new pattern effect.

7. Choose Apply for the current slide or Apply to All for the entire slide show. The dialog box disappears and the patterning effect will take place. To undo, choose Edit, Undo Custom Background or press Ctrl+Z.

PowerPoint's Texture Fill feature allows for importing of new textures. When you do so, they will appear in the texture palette. Importing a new texture is very simple.

1. With the Texture Fill dialog box opened, choose the Other button.

2. The Add Texture dialog box appears, which in all functions is the same as the Insert Picture dialog box.

3. Locate the files you want by using the Files of Type, File Name, and Look in drop-down list boxes.

4. Highlight the desired file and make sure it's shown in the File name text box.

5. Choose OK or press Enter.

6. Choose Preview to see how the texture will affect your slide's appearance.

7. Choose Apply to apply the texture to the current slide, or Apply to All to use the pattern throughout the presentation.

The graphics file is placed onto the texture list. Bear in mind that any graphics file will be treated as a texture; thus custom effects are possible. Any bitmap picture can be placed on a slide background. Figure 18.19 shows an example, using a background bitmap from the Windows directory.

Also bear in mind that you can use the same textures to fill drawn objects, using the same steps with selected graphic objects.

Fig. 18.19

Placing a texture fill onto a slide background.

Troubleshooting

I can't find all the color tools I need.

Most of the tools used for color fills, shading, shadowing, applying line weights and line colors, and so on are in the Drawing toolbar, which may not be displayed when you use PowerPoint. Toolbars take up a lot of space on-screen. Use the Toolbars command under the View menu to make sure that all the toolbars you need display on-screen. The Drawing and Drawing+ toolbars are enabled here. Also bear in mind that you can use the shortcut menu (click the right mouse button on an object or a slide background) to access many, if not all, color features. You may actually grow to prefer the speed and flexibility of the shortcut menu instead of constantly reaching for menu options at the top of the screen. The shortcut menus also have the advantage of making cluttersome toolbars less necessary.

I've messed up my color scheme by applying the wrong color to all my slides.

You probably used the Apply to All command button when you changed a color in the palette for the current slide. When you use the Slide Color Scheme command in the Format menu, you need to understand the difference between the Apply and Apply to All buttons in the Color Scheme dialog box. If you click Apply to All, you can place the new background color, object color fill, or other palette color in many places where you don't want it to be.

When this happens, the system probably takes a minute to make all the changes. The screen message `Charts are being updated with the new color scheme` will probably also appear. After that's done, choose _E_dit, _U_ndo. The screen message reappears, and your changes are undone. Since PowerPoint 95 now has multiple undos, you should have no problem getting this done. Just don't wait too long or do too many things before you change your mind!

Color is a sophisticated tool, and a realm of knowledge in itself. While you've been digging into some principles of color theory and techniques for using color in this chapter, you still have only glanced at the basics. Still, you've seen enough in this chapter to know that color is one of the many areas of the program where PowerPoint has seen great improvements and streamlining. Feature consistency is dramatically increased, and the sheer number of ways to find those features and use them has also increased. The shortcut menu provides access to almost all the features we've discussed here. Other program features that make heavy use of color are still to come.❖

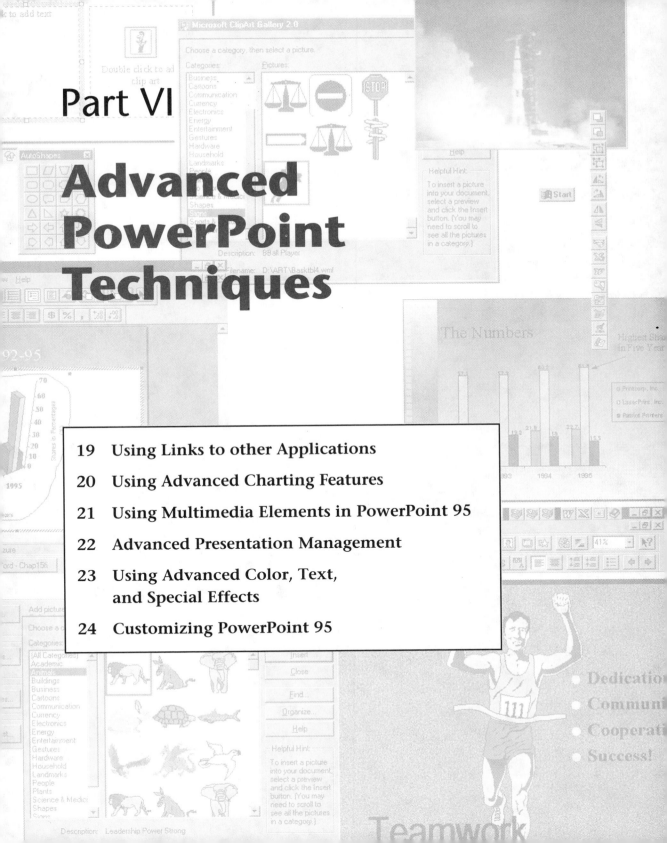

Part VI

Advanced PowerPoint Techniques

Chapter 19

Using Links to other Applications

by Rich Grace

PowerPoint 95 offers enhanced capabilities for linking and exchanging differ-ent kinds of data from other programs to your presentation. If you change the data in another program, PowerPoint updates the linked data in the pre-sentation file. The process is called Object Linking and Embedding (OLE, or Oh-Lay). PowerPoint 95 and Office 95 represent Microsoft's most ambitious effort to make Windows PCs more productive for their users. Nevertheless, they also can present some confusion to people—what exactly is an object? What does it mean for computer users?

Anything you work with in PowerPoint is an *object*—whether it's a piece of artwork, a chart created in Microsoft Graph, or a chunk of body text in a slide. Objects in a PowerPoint presentation are arranged by using placehold-ers. *Placeholders* reserve space in the slide for the particular object type they're supposed to contain.

But objects aren't just items created in your favorite presentation program. Objects also can be created from other programs, such as Microsoft Graph, Excel, and Word. Here, the true power of objects in PowerPoint 95 asserts itself.

In this chapter, you learn

- The two versions of object linking and embedding
- To link objects from other programs into your presentation
- To embed objects from other programs into your presentation
- To use drag and drop between files and applications in PowerPoint

Understanding Object Linking and Embedding (OLE)

Object linking and embedding enables users to combine various types of data into one document, and have instant access to the applications that originally created that data—without having to start and restart programs, or repeatedly copy and paste data into the Windows Clipboard.

There are two types of OLE to deal with: OLE 1.0, which many Windows applications have supported for a few years now, and the newer OLE 2.0, also called "editing in place," that Windows 95 applications support. OLE 2.0 has been updated for Windows 95 to operate with more efficiency and quickness.

Tip
Many currently released Windows applications only support OLE 1.0, so in-place editing is not available with those applications.

In Windows 95, OLE can be an extremely powerful tool. Though it takes a little time to master, you will find the productivity gains and additional flexibility to be well worth the effort. The key is that while using Office 95, it's possible for several applications to use only one program window. This goes against many users' normal ways of doing things, where they have two or three application windows open and switch back and forth between them. OLE's key function—in-place editing—changes that. Windows 95 (and Windows NT) offers great advantages for this, because of their stronger multitasking nature and improvements in interapplication operability. The rest of this chapter discusses OLE in greater detail.

Using OLE 2.0

OLE 2.0 embedding and linking work essentially the same in Windows 95 and Windows 3.x. When you edit an embedded object that originates from an OLE 2.0-compliant program in PowerPoint, you don't see the other application program window pop up. Instead, you edit the object in its original application without leaving the PowerPoint window. *Editing in place* means that you can have five or six application programs all using the same window, without having all of them open at the same time, or even having all of the other ones running.

Caution

Linking and embedding are two very different processes. Beware!

Using Visual Editing (Editing in Place)

When using OLE, PowerPoint's menus and toolbars are temporarily replaced by those of the application program that originally created the object. You have already used this visual editing technique many times, especially for creating charts in PowerPoint, because Microsoft Graph is actually a separate application and an OLE 2.0-compliant program. Every time you use Graph to create charts and paste them back onto a slide or to modify an existing chart, Graph quickly replaces PowerPoint's menus and toolbars with its own set.

Graph is an OLE *server* program. This means that Graph can "send" or produce objects for other programs. When you use Graph with PowerPoint, PowerPoint assumes the role of an OLE *client* program. So, PowerPoint can directly accept objects from other programs, like charts, Excel worksheets, Word tables, and so on. In fact, Word, Excel, and PowerPoint function as OLE clients *and* servers. See "Working with Other OLE Applications," later in this chapter for more information.

> ### Note
>
> Some applications are designed to work as OLE client and server programs, such as the Office 95 programs, but some packages don't need to do both functions. Desktop publishing programs like Corel Ventura, Adobe PageMaker, and Quark Xpress are only OLE client programs. Microsoft Graph is only an OLE server program.

The major software companies continue to develop and release Windows 95-compliant programs. Because of the variety of applications software users are accustomed to running, some exercises in the rest of this chapter will be non-specific, teaching you how to link and embed objects from other programs in a generic fashion. In most cases, however, Microsoft Office 95 applications will be used as examples.

Working with Other OLE Applications

On PowerPoint's most basic level, it's easy to create and use objects from other programs. PowerPoint's Standard toolbar offers three quick tools for doing so.

PowerPoint's Insert Microsoft Word Table tool enables you to create a table using the Microsoft Word for Windows application program for embedding into a PowerPoint slide. Using this tool requires that Microsoft Word for Windows 95 be installed on your system. This tool doesn't work for Version 6 or earlier versions of WinWord.

PowerPoint's Insert Microsoft Excel Worksheet tool enables you to create a typical Excel worksheet for embedding into a PowerPoint slide. Using this tool requires an installed copy of Excel 95 on your system; earlier versions of Excel can't be activated with this tool.

PowerPoint's Insert Microsoft Graph tool allows you to insert a new chart object into a slide, edit it using PowerPoint's screen, and embed it by clicking outside of the chart on the slide.

You also can use the Object command on the Insert menu to work with OLE applications. Using this feature, many applications that don't show up on the toolbar can easily be used as another part of your working routine.

Creating an Embedded Object

Assuming that the latest version of Word is installed on your system, here's how to embed objects from that program. A tool is provided for fast access to the program from PowerPoint.

◄ See "Creating a New Table," p. 238

To insert a Word 95 table, make sure you're in PowerPoint's Slide view, and follow these steps:

1. Click the Insert Microsoft Word Table tool on the PowerPoint Standard toolbar.

   A drop-down Table tool appears, as shown in figure 19.1.

Fig. 19.1

Use the drop-down Table tool to automatically create Word tables of up to 4 rows by 5 columns in size.

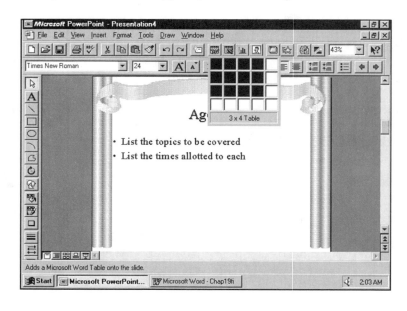

2. Drag the mouse down and across from the top-left cell in the drop-down tool. This defines the number of table entries to be created in the table.

As you drag, the cells are highlighted and the message cell at the bottom of the Table tool shows the selected table size: 3 × 3, 4 × 3, or whatever the selection is.

3. Release the mouse.

PowerPoint starts the Word for Windows application program, and then the PowerPoint toolbars and menu bar are replaced by the Word toolbars and menu bar, as shown in figure 19.2. As you can see, the Word and PowerPoint toolbars are rather similar.

Word
menu bar

PowerPoint
title bar

Word
toolbars

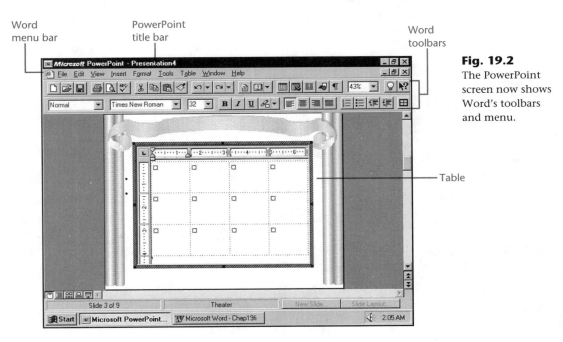

Fig. 19.2
The PowerPoint screen now shows Word's toolbars and menu.

Table

The PowerPoint slide is still displayed on-screen, but the Word screen elements and a new Word table also appear on-screen.

> **Note**
>
> For more information on Word's table editing and formatting, please see Que's *Special Edition Using Word for Windows 95* or *Word for Windows 95 Visual Quick Reference*.

VI

Advanced Techniques

4. After editing and formatting the table, click the PowerPoint slide anywhere outside the table object you just edited. It's inserted into your slide as a text object, with the color and font defaults assigned to it from within PowerPoint, as shown in figure 19.3.

PowerPoint menu bar

PowerPoint title bar

Fig. 19.3
The PowerPoint screen showing the embedded Word for Windows table.

PowerPoint toolbars

Table

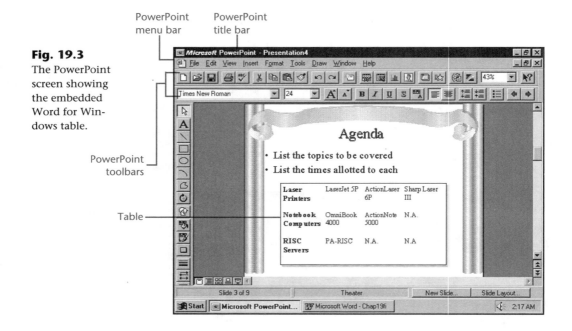

You also can create a new slide, and select a Slide AutoLayout that contains a Word Table placeholder like the one shown in fig. 19.4. Double-clicking the placeholder displays the Insert Word Table dialog box, in which you enter the number of columns and rows. Clicking OK then opens Word in the same way as described above.

The method for using Excel 95 to insert worksheet objects into a PowerPoint slide is identical to that for Word, except for the actual editing mechanics and data type of the program.

To insert an Excel worksheet, make sure you're in PowerPoint's Slide view, and follow these steps:

1. Click the Insert Microsoft Excel Worksheet tool on the PowerPoint Standard toolbar. A drop-down worksheet tool appears.

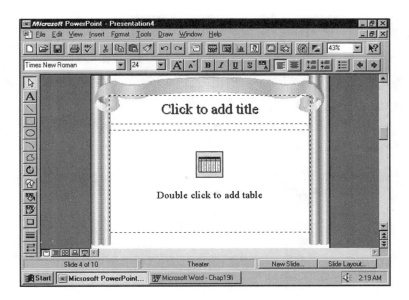

Fig. 19.4
A PowerPoint slide
AutoLayout with a
Word Table
placeholder.
Double-click the
placeholder to edit
the table object.

2. Drag the mouse down and across from the top left cell in the drop-
   down tool. This defines the number of rows and columns of cells to be
   created in the datasheet. As you drag, the message cell at the bottom of
   the table tool shows the selected datasheet size: 3×3, 4×3, or whatever
   the selection is.

3. Release the mouse button. PowerPoint starts the Excel application program, PowerPoint's toolbars and menu bar are replaced by Excel's
   toolbars and menu bar.

4. After editing and formatting the table, click the PowerPoint slide anywhere outside the worksheet object you have just edited. The worksheet
   is inserted into your slide.

As we've noted, there is another way to create a new embedded object: by
using the Insert, Object command. To do so, follow these steps:

1. Choose Insert, Object. The Insert Object dialog box appears, as shown
   in figure 19.5.

2. If not already selected, click the Create New option button.

VI

Advanced Techniques

Fig. 19.5
Use PowerPoint's
Insert Object
dialog box to select
a new object type
for insertion into
the current slide.

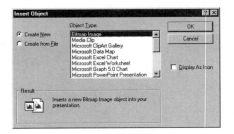

> **Note**
>
> You also can use any OLE-compliant program to create an object from an existing file, by choosing the Create from File button instead of Create New.

Tip
If you're embedding a new sound file or other object, click the Display As Icon check box. When you run the presentation, the object executes.

The Object Type list box in the dialog box shows the different types of objects (Windows Metafiles, Excel charts and worksheets, etc.) available to you under Windows. The list of OLE object types is derived from an OLE Registry list in a Windows startup file, and provides a handy reference to the specific types of files you can embed into a presentation.

3. From the Object Type list box, choose the file type you want to embed.

4. Choose OK or press Enter.

If the application program is OLE 2.0-compliant, PowerPoint's menu bar and toolbars are replaced and you can create the new object.

If the application you selected is OLE 1.0-compliant, see the upcoming section, "Working with OLE 1.0 Applications," for more information on how to proceed.

5. Click anywhere outside the boundaries of the object to embed it onto the PowerPoint slide.

The object has been successfully embedded.

Embedding an Existing Object File

It's easy to bring an existing file, like an Excel worksheet, into a presentation as an embedded object. Instead of creating a new object from scratch, as in the previous example, any drawing, chart, or other object from a program that supports OLE can be embedded. This is logical, considering that an embedded object is the actual file created by the other program. That is why presentation files with embedded objects are so easily transported.

Tip

Existing PowerPoint presentation files can be embedded as objects.

To embed an existing file, follow these steps:

1. Display the PowerPoint slide in which the object is to be placed.

2. Choose Insert, Object. The Insert Object dialog box appears, as shown in figure 19.6.

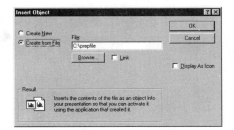

Fig. 19.6
The PowerPoint Insert Object dialog box contains options for inserting existing object files.

3. Click the Create from File option button and the File text box is displayed.

4. To locate the file to embed, click Browse and the Browse dialog box appears, as shown in figure 19.7.

Fig. 19.7
Use the Browse dialog box to locate an existing file for embedding.

VI

Advanced Techniques

Tip
An embedded sound file, video clip, or animation sequence automatically runs in a presentation. Pictures and other objects automatically appear in your slide show.

5. By using the file, directory, and drive listings, locate the desired file.

6. Choose OK or press Enter. The Insert Object dialog box appears. The desired file name should now appear in the File text box.

7. Choose OK or press Enter.

The object file is embedded into the slide. You can double-click on the object to open its originating program.

Creating a Linked Object

Creating a link from a PowerPoint presentation to an object file of another type is as easy as copying and pasting between the programs. As noted at the beginning of this chapter, the relationship of a linked object to the OLE client program is different from that of an embedded one. The process of inserting linked objects is also very different.

> **Note**
>
> Linking's biggest advantage is the ability to have multiple copies of an object in different files. For example, you could have the same CorelDRAW! picture in a Microsoft Word document, a PowerPoint slide show, and a Quark Xpress desktop publishing file. You can then edit that picture in its original application, save it as you normally would, and that picture will be automatically updated in all those files where you've placed it (the Word, PowerPoint, and Quark files). You don't have to reimport or relink the object in the other applications—the work is done for you. This is helpful for people whose work involves constantly creating complex documents.

PowerPoint's Paste Special feature is the key to effective linking of objects within your presentation.

To create a linked object, follow these steps:

1. In the application program that is used to create the source file, open the file containing the desired object for linking.

2. Select the data in the file (the CorelDRAW! picture, Microsoft Word text, Excel chart, or whatever) that you want to link.

3. Choose Edit, Copy.

4. Switch to the PowerPoint window and display the slide in which you want to insert the linked item.

5. Choose Edit, Paste Special.

   PowerPoint's Paste Special dialog box appears, as shown in figure 19.8.

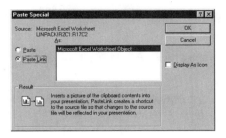

Fig. 19.8
PowerPoint's Paste
Special dialog box,
displaying the file
type to link after
clicking the Paste
Link option
button.

6. To establish a link, click the Paste <u>L</u>ink option button.

   In the <u>A</u>s: list, the file type that you already copied to the Windows
   Clipboard from the other application appears, as shown in figure 19.8.

> **Note**
>
> As described in the Result box in the Paste Special dialog box, linking places a
> "picture" of your linked data in the presentation, not the actual file.

7. Choose OK or press Enter and the linked object appears on your slide.

> **Note**
>
> Unlike OLE 2.0's embedding, double-clicking a linked object brings up the originat-
> ing program in a separate window. In-place editing is not activated.

When you double-click a *linked* object inside PowerPoint, you won't see
PowerPoint's menu and toolbars replaced by the other application's menu
and toolbars. The other program comes up in its own window! This is the
case for both OLE 2.0 and OLE 1.0 objects when they're *linked* in a
PowerPoint 95 file. In-place editing is not supported for linked objects.

When you edit the linked object and then save it (*saving the file is the crucial
step*), the linked object updates next time the presentation file is opened in
PowerPoint. When you open the PowerPoint presentation, a message appears
informing you that the presentation contains links. The link updates when
you choose Yes.

If both programs are open, the link is constantly updated, even before the file
containing the linked object is resaved. That's how linking works.

You may notice some degradation in your computer's performance while
linked files are open. Close the PowerPoint presentation if you are doing
extensive editing of the linked object. Then, when you have finished editing

the linked object, you can open the presentation and confirm that you want to update the link.

To create a link to an existing OLE 2.0 object file from within PowerPoint, follow these steps:

1. Display the PowerPoint slide in which the object is to be placed.

2. Choose Insert, Object and the Insert Object dialog box appears.

3. Click the Create from File option button and the File text box is displayed.

4. To locate the file to embed, click the Browse button and the Browse dialog box appears.

5. Use the Browse dialog box to locate the desired file.

6. Choose OK or press Enter.

7. Click the Link check box. There should be a check mark inside it.

8. Choose OK or press Enter.

The linked object appears on the slide.

> **Note**
>
> If you link an object from an OLE 1.0-compliant program like Excel 4.0 or CorelDRAW! 4.0 to a presentation in PowerPoint 95 (an OLE 2.0-compliant program), you can double-click the linked object and its original program comes up in a separate window. But if you link an object between two OLE 1.0-compliant programs, when you double-click the client program's linked object to edit it in the server program, you can't do it. The server program does not appear!
>
> This illustrates one of the subtle differences between OLE 1.0 and 2.0, and gives another reason why OLE 2.0 was created, and why OLE 1.0 is outdated.
>
> In the end, linking works similarly in both versions of OLE, except that version 2.0 now enables you to edit linked objects in a separate window.

Using OLE 1.0

As you now know, object linking and object embedding are two different processes that have subtle but important differences. If you're using the older version of OLE, double-clicking an Excel chart or spreadsheet that is placed into a PowerPoint slide brings up the Excel program in a separate window, and displays the chart or spreadsheet, ready for editing. This is called editing an embedded object, even in OLE 1.0.

You can create an embedded object from scratch, or embed an existing file into your presentation. Any embedded object, whether an Excel chart, a CorelDRAW! picture, or a sound wave form—when double-clicked in PowerPoint—brings up the application program that originally created it.

One advantage of embedding objects into your PowerPoint files is that when you relocate your presentation file, all the embedded objects are taken along for the ride—without having to bring all the original object files with you. All the objects are lodged and present in your PowerPoint file. (This does create a much bigger PowerPoint file, however.)

Linking is a different matter. Excel 4.0, CorelDRAW! 4.0, and many other programs don't appear when attempting to edit a linked object from within PowerPoint. When linking an object in OLE 1.0, you have a copy of any pictures or other items in multiple documents—say, a specific CorelDRAW! picture in five or six different PowerPoint presentations—and if you modify that picture from within CorelDRAW!, all your PowerPoint presentations that contain that picture are automatically updated.

Embedding, on the other hand, requires that when you modify an object in its original program, that object must be reembedded in each file that contains it, or the changes in the object won't appear in the files.

Double-clicking a linked object from an OLE 1.0 program *in PowerPoint 95* successfully brings up the other program in a separate window. Also, to transport a PowerPoint presentation file containing linked objects, the presentation file and all the separate files containing the linked objects (CorelDRAW! files, Excel files, and the like) must be transferred as a group with the presentation. Using the Pack And Go Wizard ensures that you can do this easily and efficiently.

◀ See "Taking PowerPoint on the Road," p. 474

VI

Advanced Techniques

Troubleshooting

When I transport a bunch of linked files with a presentation, I can't get the presentation to use them when I'm at my destination and trying to give the show.

Ouch! You have run up against a bug in Microsoft's OLE 2.0 system. It turns out that unless you place the linked files in exactly the same folder structure at your destination computer that they were in when you created the presentation (in other words, make the same folders in the other guy's computer that are in your own and copy the linked files to them), your slide show won't find them. This winds up being a real

(continues)

(continued)

pain. There is a powerful solution, though. PowerPoint 95 offers a new method to avoid this problem: the Pack And Go Wizard. This useful feature helps you bundle all the necessary files for your presentation into one convenient package. Using Pack And Go, you will never have to worry about this problem again.

Note

Applications that support OLE usually divide into two camps: "clients" and "servers." OLE client programs can accept objects such as Excel charts, CorelDRAW! pictures, or other application data types. They allow double-clicking the object for use of the original program, but OLE client programs cannot *send* objects out to other OLE-compliant programs. Desktop publishing programs are typical examples of this. On the other hand, because they can send objects to other applications, programs such as Excel or CorelDRAW! are called OLE servers. Some Windows programs, like PowerPoint 95, support both client and server functions.

Working with OLE 1.0 Applications

Because many Windows applications on your hard disk are likely to support OLE 1.0 (such as CorelDRAW! 4.0, Excel 4.0, and Word for Windows 2.0), it's important to know that these programs can still play an important role in the creation of a well-rounded presentation. Such programs are about two generations behind the state of the art, but are still in use by many people.

Those programs generally run just fine under Windows 95. Many of these programs, though they don't support OLE 2.0 features like Office 95, are still extremely powerful and sophisticated, and may offer capabilities that Microsoft application programs can't match (CorelDRAW! 4 is an example). Also, those who own and use Word for Windows 2 or Excel 4 can still use these programs as vital tools in tandem with PowerPoint 95 by employing OLE 1.0 techniques to link and embed objects. It's a little more difficult to do this, however, than to use programs that are more up-to-date.

Caution

Although most of these programs run under Windows 95, some may not. They may break under the pressure of running with a new operating system like Windows 95. Be aware of this possibility.

To embed a new OLE 1.0 object in a PowerPoint 95 slide, follow these steps:

1. Open the desired PowerPoint presentation.

2. Minimize the PowerPoint window.

3. In the OLE 1.0-compliant application program that offers the object type desired (such as Excel 4.0 or CorelDRAW!), open and select the drawing, worksheet, chart, or other object you want to embed.

4. Choose Edit, Copy to copy the object to the Windows clipboard.

5. Minimize or close the program.

6. Maximize the PowerPoint program window.

7. Choose Edit, Paste Special.

    PowerPoint's Paste Special dialog box appears, as shown in figure 19.9.

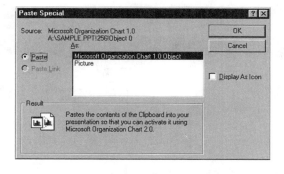

Fig. 19.9
PowerPoint's Paste Special dialog box, displaying options for inserting an existing object file.

8. To embed an OLE 1.0 object, click the Paste option button on the Paste Special dialog box.

    The file type that you already copied to the Windows Clipboard from the other application appears in the As: list, as shown in figure 19.9 (in this case, it's a PowerPoint Organization Chart 1.0 object).

9. From the As: list, choose the file type you want to embed.

> **Note**
>
> Notice that the Paste Link option is NOT used. This act of omission tells PowerPoint that the object is to be embedded rather than linked.

10. Choose OK or press Enter and the embedded object is placed into the presentation.

VI

Advanced Techniques

Double-clicking the object brings up the original application in its separate window, displaying the picture for editing. After you do so, the picture is dimmed on the PowerPoint slide. This is a tip-off that its originating application is running with the object file.

To modify an existing embedded OLE 1.0 object in PowerPoint 95, follow these steps:

1. Double-click the embedded object in the PowerPoint slide.

   The program that originally created the object appears. It's a separate window and doesn't replace the PowerPoint toolbars and menu.

2. Modify the object within the application program. When you're finished making your changes, save your work.

3. Choose File, Update.

   The program closes and the PowerPoint slide shows the changes you made to the embedded object.

Note

For OLE 1.0-compliant programs, when you edit and save the original object file, you must choose File, Update in the original program or the changes aren't placed in the presentation.

Working with Placeholders

Essentially, a placeholder is a resizeable container for objects of any description. Although you can create new slides that have specified placeholders for charts, body text, organizational charts, and titles—among other things—any placeholder can be used for any purpose. By a simple trick with the mouse, a chart placeholder can be used to contain a graphics image, as in the example that follows.

To change placeholder types, follow these steps:

1. Insert a new slide into your presentation by clicking the New Slide button (on the status bar) and choosing an AutoLayout. Select, for example, a Graph slide, as shown in figure 19.10.

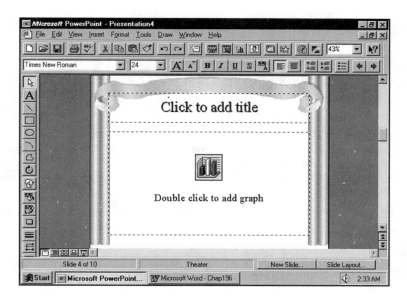

Fig. 19.10
Adding a Graph
AutoLayout slide
to a presentation.

2. Click once on the outer edge of the chart placeholder to select it. Its
    highlighted border gets thicker.

3. Choose Insert, Picture and the Insert Picture dialog box appears, as
    shown in figure 19.11.

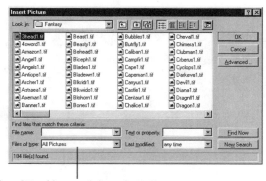

Files of Typé box and drop-down list

Fig. 19.11
Using the Insert
Picture feature to
bring in graphics
files to an existing
placeholder.

VI

Advanced Techniques

PowerPoint supports a substantial number of graphics formats, including CGM, GIF, AutoCad (DXF), CorelDRAW! 3.0 (CDR), PCX, TIF, EPS, HPGL, Photo-CD, Targa (TGA), and Windows bitmap (BMP).

> **Note**
>
> PowerPoint's CorelDRAW! graphics filter does not support any file versions newer than CorelDRAW! 3.0. Using CorelDRAW! 5 or CorelDRAW! 6 (which has been completely rewritten for Windows 95), you're better off creating an embedded OLE object rather than trying to insert a file.

4. Choose the type of file to import from the Files of Type list box, and choose the desired file from the proper drive and directory.

5. Choose OK or press Enter.

The Graph placeholder now contains a graphic, as shown in figure 19.12.

Fig. 19.12
Artwork has been placed inside the placeholder and thus in the slide.

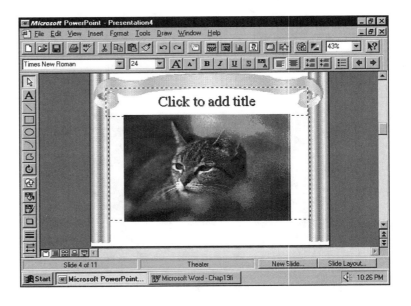

Tip
The Insert Picture feature also offers an easy way to link imported pictures by using the Link to File check box.

When changing the placeholder type and inserting the graphic inside the placeholder, make sure you click the margin of the placeholder before you insert the picture or other object. If you don't, the new object is simply pasted on top of the existing placeholder. By using the placeholder, the inserted picture is automatically resized to its dimensions.

By selecting the placeholder and choosing an option from the Insert menu, a placeholder can be used to contain any object. Bear in mind that importing a graphic by using the Insert, Picture command doesn't mean you can double-click the object and edit it with its original program. When you do this, you will normally be greeted by a dialog box that reads, `Sorry, this picture contains only a bitmap`. To import a graphic object and use OLE-type editing on it, you must use the Insert, Object command.

Troubleshooting

When I delete an object, the placeholder stays in place.

To entirely remove an object and its placeholder, you have to perform a two-step deletion process. First, click the object to select it, and then delete it. Then, click the border of the placeholder and then delete it. There's a reason why it's done this way. You can't just create a new placeholder and put it on a slide (you must create an entire slide for that), so it's a good idea to leave it in place even if you don't want to use it. An empty placeholder does not show up on a slide show.

Using PowerPoint's Drag-and-Drop Enhancements

Among PowerPoint's most important OLE features is its support of enhanced drag-and-drop. Earlier chapters covered the basics—how to drag-and-drop cells, rows or columns of data in Microsoft Graph datasheets, and text in PowerPoint slides and in Outline view. You also can drag-and-drop copy by simply holding down the Ctrl key when you perform the operation. There's much more to it, however.

With PowerPoint 95, it's simple to drag-and-drop elements between open presentation files. You can even drag-and-drop data between applications. Drag-and-drop copying is also supported between files and between applications. That particular feature is one of the key benefits available to Office 95 owners—those who own Microsoft Word for Windows, Excel, and PowerPoint 95 all in the same package.

VI

Advanced Techniques

Microsoft Office owners who are reading this section should bear a couple things in mind:

- Drag-and-drop works the same way in all levels of Windows: in a document, between documents, and between programs that support it, the keystrokes and mouse actions are the same.

- Dragging-and-dropping between applications can slow system performance. Windows 95 offers significant improvements in this area, and users will immediately notice the difference. Having plenty of memory is a must for smooth operation (16 MB is a good rule of thumb, and is more than adequate to run all three Office 95 applications at once).

What Programs Work with Drag-and-Drop?

The version numbers for the programs mentioned here (Word for Windows 95, Excel 95, and PowerPoint 95) are important. Earlier versions of all three of these programs (PowerPoint 4, Excel 5, and Word for Windows 6) all run OLE tasks very similarly to the versions we're looking at here. In those programs (and some from other vendors), you can drag-and-drop between files in the same program, or drag-and-drop between separate programs. Office 95 stabilizes and quickens OLE—veteran Office users will be quite happy with the improvements. Only the very latest versions of the three main programs included in Microsoft Office 95 (or sold separately) are discussed here.

You can buy all three main Office 95 programs separately and obtain all the features of drag-and-drop among them. Buying the Office suite simply saves you a little trouble (and possibly some money as well).

> **Note**
>
> Both Windows 95 and Windows NT 3.51 support OLE 2.0-compliant applications., as does Windows 3.x. They also both fully support Office 95, but Windows 3.x does *not*.

With these caveats, the next two sections show you how to use drag-and-drop between PowerPoint documents, and how to drag-and-drop a PowerPoint element from PowerPoint 95 to another application (in that example, Word for Windows 95 will be used).

Dragging-and-Dropping between PowerPoint Presentations

To start, make sure you have two PowerPoint 95 presentation files open and displayed, and then follow these steps:

1. Open each desired file.

2. Choose <u>W</u>indow, <u>A</u>rrange All.

It's important that both files be displayed for drag-and-drop (between files) to work.

> **Note**
>
> The next step is very important. PowerPoint 95 directly supports the dragging-and-dropping of slides (with all the contents that the dragged slide contains) between files. Dragging-and-dropping between PowerPoint files works only if both presentations are shown in Slide Sorter view.

3. Click in each file, and choose <u>V</u>iew, Sli<u>d</u>e Sorter for each.

The results should resemble figure 19.13.

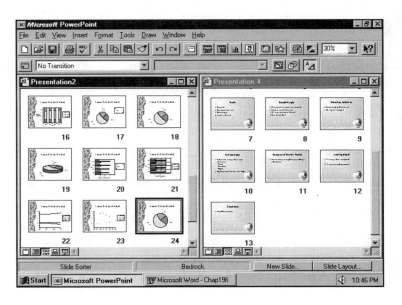

Fig. 19.13
Preparing PowerPoint for a drag-and-drop operation.

4. Click the desired slide in the file that you want to drag and drag the mouse. As you drag, you see the mouse pointer change shape to a tiny box with a down arrow attached to it, and a bracketing arrow travels along. Move the mouse over the other presentation to the location in its Slide Sorter where you want the slide to be dropped (see fig. 19.14).

VI

Advanced Techniques

Fig. 19.14
Dragging-and-
dropping a slide
between
PowerPoint files.

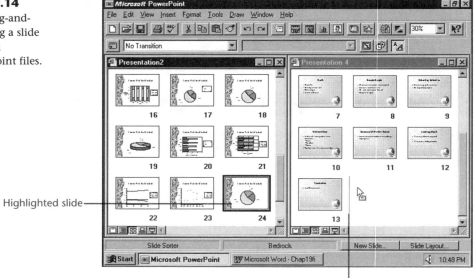

Highlighted slide

Bracket shows where the slide will be dropped in the other file

5. Release the mouse button. The slide has been dragged-and-dropped to the new file, as shown in figure 19.14.

The slide that has been dragged will automatically adopt the template of its new presentation. This is a new PowerPoint 95 feature that can really help the user (see fig. 19.15).

Fig. 19.15
The slide has been
successfully
moved between
PowerPoint files.

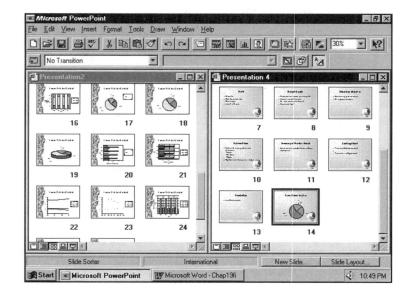

Does this procedure look familiar? It's almost identical to rearranging slides in the Slide Sorter. The major difference: the slide is moved to the other file. To retain the changes, *both* files must be saved by choosing File, Save for each file. If you only save the file you dragged to, you in effect simply copy the slide over.

> **Note**
>
> You also can drag-and-drop copy slides between presentations. Simply press and hold the Ctrl key as you drag the slide thumbnail from one file's Slide Sorter to the other file.

Dragging-and-Dropping between Applications

Windows applications that support OLE 2.0 are the only type of program that can support drag-and-drop and drag and drop copy between programs. Upon the release of Windows 95, the only packages that support those features are PowerPoint 95, Excel for Windows 95, and Word for Windows 95. Certainly, many others will quickly follow. In the next example, a PowerPoint file has an Excel worksheet copied to it.

1. Display the PowerPoint file that you want to drag-and-drop to.

2. Next, open Microsoft Excel 95 for Windows and display a worksheet from which you want to drag data.

   You may want to organize the two programs side by side or in another arrangement for easier viewing and dragging, as in figure 19.16.

3. Display the PowerPoint presentation that you want to drag to, as shown in figure 19.16. For the example, Slide view is sufficient.

4. In the Excel worksheet, select the data that you want to copy.

5. While holding down the Ctrl key, click the border of the selected data in the Excel worksheet and drag over to the PowerPoint window. Drag the mouse over the border of the selected data in the Excel worksheet. Release the mouse button to place it.

   Figure 19.17 illustrates the result.

Tip

Whenever possible, instead of executing drag and drop of Excel worksheets and charts, simply import them into Microsoft Graph.

VI

Advanced Techniques

Fig. 19.16
Excel and
PowerPoint
arranged for easier
dragging.

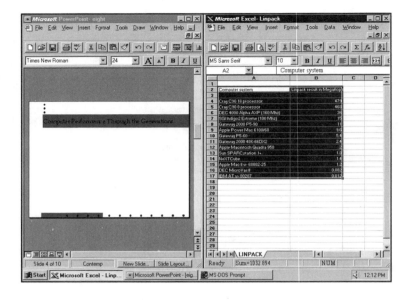

Fig. 19.17
An Excel spread-
sheet placed in a
PowerPoint slide.

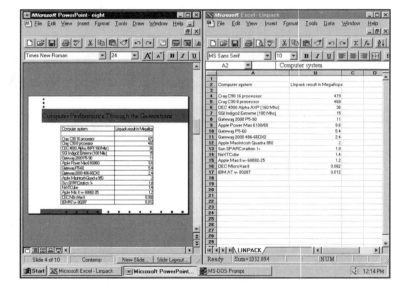

The worksheet that's now in the PowerPoint slide is an Excel object. Double-clicking the copied worksheet in the PowerPoint slide starts PowerPoint's OLE 2.0 capabilities. PowerPoint's menu and toolbars are replaced with Excel's toolbars and menu, and the worksheet can be edited, formatted, and resized as if you were actually using Excel. So, after the drag-and-drop copy is done, you're back to the process of in-place editing, which was described earlier in this chapter.

You can copy and paste Excel worksheet rows and columns from the embedded Excel object into a Graph worksheet in your presentation.

There's more. When you select the worksheet and drag-and-drop it from Excel to PowerPoint, any chart that's based on that Excel data also comes. You can drag one of the pressure points on the new object in the PowerPoint slide to display more of its contents, as shown in figure 19.17. What about other Office applications? For starters, you can copy an entire PowerPoint slide to a Word document. Here's how:

1. Display the Word 95 file that you want to drag-and-drop to.

2. Open your PowerPoint presentation in Slide Sorter view. (Dragging-and-dropping, or drag-and-drop copy, works in either Slide Sorter or Notes Pages view.) Then, select a slide that you want to drag to the Word document.

3. Hold down the Ctrl key.

4. Click and hold the mouse over the selected slide in PowerPoint. You will notice that the mouse pointer shows a small box with a plus sign above it. You may want to organize the two programs side by side or in another arrangement for easier viewing and dragging.

5. Still holding the Ctrl key down, drag the mouse over to the Word application window. Then, release the mouse. After a moment, the slide image will appear in your Word file.

Now, when you double-click the slide illustration in the Word document, PowerPoint's menu bar and toolbars take over the Word screen, and you are actually running PowerPoint (even though the Microsoft Word title remains in the window). Click outside the slide graphic and Word reasserts itself.

These are just basic examples. Dragging-and-dropping between programs is phenomenally improved in Windows 95. Microsoft Graph allows you to directly import Excel 5 and Excel for Windows 95 worksheets and charts, which is an easier and more efficient use of resources. On the other hand, dragging-and-dropping Excel data to a Microsoft Word document can be a very useful action.

VI

Advanced Techniques

Troubleshooting

I can't embed Excel worksheets or Word tables in my slides.

It's very likely that you don't have the latest versions of either program, or at least have not installed them if you have purchased Microsoft Office in addition to the PowerPoint 95 application. If you are running Word for Windows 6 or Excel 5, be aware that although those programs do support OLE 2.0, you can't use PowerPoint 95's Insert Word Table or Insert Excel worksheet tools with those older version programs for those purposes.

There are limits to how data can be dragged-and-dropped, and which views in PowerPoint you can perform the operation in. As you've seen, you can only copy slides from one presentation to another when both files are in the Slide Sorter view. You can't, for example, drag-and-drop a single chart from one slide to another, even if both slides are displayed in the program.

The enhanced drag-and-drop features in PowerPoint 95 (and in Microsoft Office) are sophisticated and demanding features. You should have plenty of memory and computer horsepower before you attempt such operations.

There's also lots of scope for experimenting with Object Linking and Embedding; the examples explored in this chapter are just the tip of the iceberg. Imagine what will be possible when more applications from other software publishers support drag-and-drop copy between them.

Troubleshooting

I can't get OLE to work at all on my Windows 95 system.

Using the Windows Explorer or some other method, check the Windows System folder on your hard disk (normally, C:\WINDOWS\SYSTEM) for the following files:

OLE2.DLL

OLE2CONV.DLL

OLE2DISP.DLL

OLE2NLS.DLL

OLE32.DLL

OLEAUT32.DLL

OLECLI.DLL (OLE 1.0 client support software)

OLECLI32.DLL

OLESVR.DLL (OLE 1.0 server support software)

OLESVR32.DLL

OLECNV32.DLL

OLEDLG.DLL

OLETHK32.DLL

If none of these files are on your system (especially in the C:\WINDOWS\SYSTEM folder, which is where they must be located), or if any are missing, you have two choices: reinstall Windows and PowerPoint, or copy the proper compressed files (which are called OLESVR.DL_, and so on, instead of OLESVR.DLL) directly from the Windows 95 CD-ROM to the WINDOWS\SYSTEM folder. Then use the MS-DOS EXPAND command to decompress the files. (Since EXPAND is not part of Windows 95, you will probably have to boot your system from a DOS floppy to get this job done, or exit Windows 95 in DOS mode. That is a shutdown option from the Win95 Start button.) All the files in the Windows 95 installation CD-ROM are compressed to save space, hence the underline in each file name. Use either the DOS Prompt or the Windows Explorer to do the file copying. This may take less time than a complete reinstall. In most cases you're better off doing the reinstallation, though.

Also bear in mind that Microsoft offers a special package called the Windows 95 Resource Kit. Versions are also available for Windows 3.x, Windows for Workgroups, and Windows NT. The Windows 95 Resource kit is extremely helpful and valuable for anybody who wants to dig further under the hood of Windows 95, and understand more about how OLE works.

If you reinstall Windows, copy all your existing *.INI and *.GRP files from the Windows directory to another directory or a floppy. Those files are important and will help restore your system a lot faster. This is just as true for Windows 95 as it is for Windows 3.x.

VI

Advanced Techniques

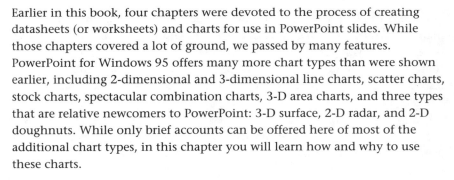

Chapter 20

Using Advanced Charting Features

by Rich Grace

Earlier in this book, four chapters were devoted to the process of creating datasheets (or worksheets) and charts for use in PowerPoint slides. While those chapters covered a lot of ground, we passed by many features. PowerPoint for Windows 95 offers many more chart types than were shown earlier, including 2-dimensional and 3-dimensional line charts, scatter charts, stock charts, spectacular combination charts, 3-D area charts, and three types that are relative newcomers to PowerPoint: 3-D surface, 2-D radar, and 2-D doughnuts. While only brief accounts can be offered here of most of the additional chart types, in this chapter you will learn how and why to use these charts.

In this chapter you learn to

- Understand alternative chart types

- Understand and use trendlines

- Save custom charts and create new default charts

- Export and import charts to and from various applications

PowerPoint offers too many chart types to allow comprehensive coverage in this book. The following sections, however, give examples of many alternative chart types you might consider using. We make an attempt to explain how some of these specialized charts can be used, and times when it's better to make another choice. Some exercises in this chapter require quite a few separate tasks; once you've gone through them you'll gain insight into how powerfully charts can illustrate your ideas.

Using 2-D Line (XY) Charts

In standard charting nomenclature, line charts, area charts, scatter charts, and stock charts are all examples of XY chart types. *XY charts* are so named because their values are calculated against both two-dimensional axes: x and y.

> **Note**
>
> In PowerPoint, Microsoft has split line charts and XY (scatter) charts into separate categories. But there is no *functional* difference between them, because they are calculated the same way. This can confuse the user, because there are numerous redundant chart types offered between them. It's easier, in this book, to split them into specific categories such as stock, line, and scatter chart types so that you can see the uses and subtle differences between them.

Line charts can help your audience draw visual conclusions from your numeric data. Line charts are deceptively simple—messages can be found in line charts that may not be apparent in other types. In figure 20.1, you can see that a line representing Patriot Printers, Inc. shows their market share for the last four years. What you may also notice is that Patriot's market share has gradually declined. In short, Patriot Printers, Inc. is in a recession. At the same time, Printcorp, Inc. has maintained a steady level of market share, as has LaserPrint, Inc. In a line chart, those facts are driven home with emphatic clarity. (Please bear in mind that this is an entirely fictitious chart and scenario!) This is one major advantage of a line chart—multiple messages can be conveyed with a minimum of screen clutter.

Line charts and scatter charts are handy and useful tools when you need to display some long data series in a chart. *Lines* and *points* are displayed in both types. (As noted earlier, there is no functional difference between a scatter and a line chart.) Points represent the actual data values in each series, and the graphic shapes used to define those points are called *markers*.

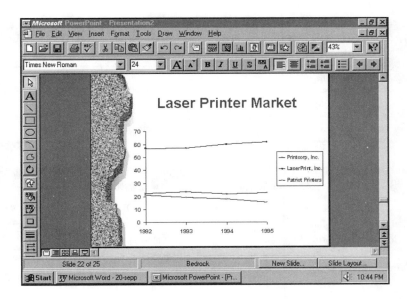

Fig. 20.1
Market share data
shown in a 2-D
line chart.

Creating a Line Chart

In PowerPoint 95, line charts are often called XY charts because their data is
charted against two axes—the x- and y-axes—and because each point, line, or
sized object needs to be measured against each axis to determine its location.
In figure 20.1, for example, each point on each line has a year value that
ranges from 1992 to 1995 and a numeric value ranging between 0 and 70.
The common element across all XY charts is the requirement for two values
for each data item. These two values are used to create and locate the markers
representing each series value.

Here's how to create a chart like the one shown previously in figure 20.1:

1. In PowerPoint, click the Insert Graph button on the standard toolbar.
   Microsoft Graph appears.

2. Select the default data in Graph's datasheet and then choose Edit, Clear
   All to delete it. Type the sample data set shown in table 20.1.

VI

Advanced Techniques

Table 20.1 Market Share Datasheet				
Company Name	**1992**	**1993**	**1994**	**1995**
Printcorp, Inc.	22.1	23.5	21.8	22.7
LaserPrint, Inc.	57.1	57.3	60.2	61.8
Patriot Printers, Inc.	20.8	19.2	18.0	15.5

> **Note**
>
> Graph's Clear command is a cascading menu offering three options: All, Contents, and Formats. Selecting Contents removes the data, but retains the fonts or other formatting you've applied in the selected cells for fresh data entry. Clearing Formats removes the fonts or other visual changes you've applied to datasheet numbers and labels.

3. Choose Format, AutoFormat. The AutoFormat dialog box appears.

4. From the Galleries list box, choose Line.

5. Select chart #1.

6. Click OK.

7. Click one of the lines in the chart.

8. Choose Format, Selected Data Series.

   The Format Data Series dialog box appears, displaying the Patterns tab.

9. In the Line section of the Patterns page, choose a heavier line weight from the Weight drop-down list.

10. Click the Smoothed Line check box.

11. Choose OK or press Enter.

12. Follow the same procedure for the other lines in the chart (steps 7 through 11).

You may consider changing the colors of the lines in the chart to ensure that they show up better. You do this by using the Patterns tab and its Line and Marker sections. For data markers, which denote series data values, you must specify both the Background and Foreground colors for a complete color change. Figure 20.2 shows where the various features are located. Many other functions can be used, such as smaller fonts for the legend and axes.

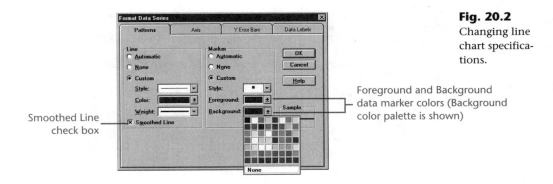

Fig. 20.2
Changing line chart specifica-tions.

Smoothed Line check box

Foreground and Background data marker colors (Background color palette is shown)

Using 2-D Scatter Charts

You may have realized at the end of the last exercise that line charts don't necessarily work well with series that contain only a few numbers each. Lines can be too crude and one-dimensional. In many cases, you won't need lines in a chart at all, but simply points or data markers. Bare points on a chart are what create the scatter effect of the *scatter chart*, in which the points show their relationships to each other by the common colors or shapes of the markers.

In scatter charts, the height of the points along the line represents the data values in the chart. Scatter charts are plotted against two axes—the x- and y-axes—because each point, line, or sized object needs to be measured against each axis to determine its location. (Hence, they're a type of XY chart.)

Why use a scatter chart? When you have more than four series, connecting lines may confuse the viewer or obscure some of the data markers on the chart. In that case, scatter charts without lines may be just the thing to dis-play a large number of series. Data markers (which are very small entities on the chart) enable the user to display almost as many series as possible. A scat-ter chart is very useful if you have only a few series, but also have a large number of values in each series, as shown in table 20.2 and in figure 20.3.

Table 20.2 Revised Market Share Datasheet								
Company Name	**1992**	**1993**	**1994**	**1995**	**1996**	**1997**	**1998**	**1999**
LaserPrint, Inc.	57.1	57.3	60.2	61.8	52.2	48.4	43.2	46.2
Printcorp, Inc.	22.1	23.5	21.8	22.7	28.7	28.4	34.7	27.7
Patriot Printers, Inc.	20.8	21.2	18.0	15.5	21.1	23.2	22.1	26.1

VI

Advanced Techniques

Fig. 20.3

The expanded Market Share datasheet, showing a significantly more detailed chart.

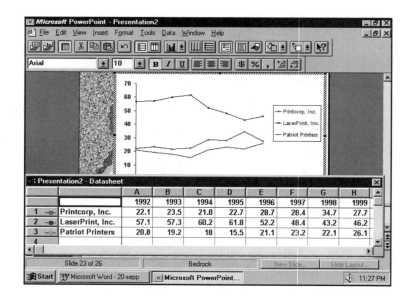

Looking at the chart above, you can see the effect that using longer series has on a line chart. Now, trends and dramatic shifts can be spotted, and the chart provides far more information.

Handled properly, a scatter chart can be used to bring together many disparate sets of data, such as demographic surveys of customers in the marketplace. Logarithmic scales can be used to tie together values from widely ranging statistical areas, such as surveys of different age groups.

For the next chart example, the Market Share datasheet is expanded through a few more years to provide a wider scatter chart:

1. In PowerPoint, click the Insert Graph button on the standard toolbar. Microsoft Graph appears.

2. Select the default data in Graph's datasheet and choose Edit, Clear All to delete it.

3. Type the sample data shown in table 20.2.

4. Choose Format, AutoFormat. The AutoFormat dialog box appears.

5. From the Galleries list box, choose XY (Scatter).

6. Select chart #1.

7. Click the OK button.

The resulting scatter chart is shown in figure 20.4.

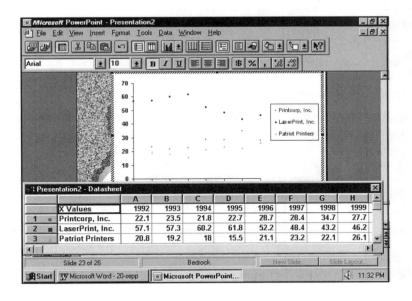

Fig. 20.4
A scatter chart
using the ex-
panded Market
Share data.

Scatter chart types are quite similar to several line charts in the Gallery. Scatter chart #2, in particular, is functionally identical to some line chart types. Most other scatter chart types add gridlines or, in the case of scatter chart #4, a logarithmic scale is automatically added to the chart. If you had a series whose values ranged between 10 and 15, and another series that showed values of another order of magnitude (say, 100 to 150), a logarithmic scale is a good option.

Scatter chart type #6 is a smoothed line chart without data markers. The same feature can be enabled on any line chart (or scatter chart displaying lines) by enabling the Smoothed Line check box option when you format lines under the Format Data Series dialog box.

To make line and scatter charts more readable, you will probably have to tweak their color and line weight settings for better visibility. Try to use dark colors against a light background. It's possible to use light colors against a dark background, but the results aren't as good, especially with printed output.

VI

Advanced Techniques

Troubleshooting

My scatter chart data markers are almost invisible on-screen.

You have to do some work with the chart's color scheme (and very likely its slide as well) to make your scatter chart markers more visible. On many occasions, a scatter chart will need a different color scheme from the rest of the presentation because of the difficulty of making the markers visible.

A good rule of thumb is to use bold, bright primary colors for scatter chart markers, and to use a dark background color on the slide. First, click on the scatter markers, each series in turn, and choose Format, Selected Data Series. Change the marker colors to reflect your needs (making sure, of course, that each marker series is a different color). If you must use gridlines (which can be a good idea with a scatter chart) use black for their color to ensure that your markers show up. Then select a dark color for your slide background.

Using Stock Charts

In Microsoft Graph, *stock charts* are not offered as a separate section under the Graph Gallery; they are, instead, grouped with the line chart type in the PowerPoint program. Nonetheless, stock charts are so unique, and require such a different set of data, that they deserve their own space in this chapter. The same is true, of course, with combination charts, the building of which may be the most challenging chart-building task you undertake. They're described in the next section.

Stock charts require different data sets from those used in previous examples—one type, a *High/Low/Close stock chart*, requires three series of data, one that represents a series of low stock price values, one that shows high values, and one that shows closing values. An *Open/High/Low/Close chart* requires four respective series. The *open value* is the price at which the stock opened trading for the given time period. A sample stock chart is shown in figure 20.5.

What are the elements of stock charts? Some unfamiliar element names will pop up here, and they bear some explanation.

High-low lines are used to show the extent of stock price fluctuations. *High lines* extend above the Up-down colored bar for each series. *Low lines* extend below it.

Up-down bars indicate the open and close values of the data series. Keep in mind that the Up-down bar can represent a value that closes lower as well as higher, and that a high or low value can be the same as a close value. In such a case, no high or low line extends from the Up-down bar. Up-down bars only apply to one type of stock chart, the Open/High/Low/Close (*OHLC*) chart. In the High-Low-Close (*HLC*) chart type, a short horizontal line pointing to the right is used to indicate the closing value. Hi-lo lines are still used in HLC charts.

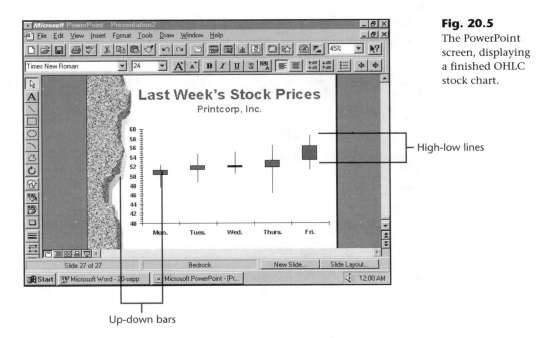

Fig. 20.5
The PowerPoint screen, displaying a finished OHLC stock chart.

High-low lines

Up-down bars

The open price is located on either the top or the bottom edge of the colored Up-down bars for each trading day (or week, or year, and so on), and the open price value is measured against the y-axis. If a price went up for the time period, the open value is on the lower edge of the Up-down bar. If it went down, it's the top edge of the bar.

The low price is located on the bottom end of the hi-lo line combination, and it's the lowest price at which the stock traded for the given time period, whether that's a day, week, or month. It's measured against the y-axis. The high price is located on the top end of the hi-lo line combination. It's the highest price level at which the stock traded during the given period, and it's measured against the y-axis. The high value isn't necessarily the value that the stock closed at; if it is, no high line extends beyond the Up-down bar.

Tip
Up-down bars are named according to their closing value. If the value is lower, it's a Down bar. If the value is higher, it's an Up bar.

VI

Advanced Techniques

The closing price is located on either the top edge or the bottom edge of the Up-down bars for each trading period, and it's measured against the y-axis. The closing price is the price at which the stock rests at the end of each given trading period. A closing price data marker can be placed to clearly mark its position for each trading day. If a price went up for the time period, the closing value is on the upper edge of the Up-down bar. If it went down, it's on the lower edge of the bar.

Creating a Stock Chart

Table 20.3 is a simple table displaying four series of data for Printcorp, Inc., that are used for the stock chart example.

Table 20.3 Printcorp's Stock Prices for a One-Week Period				
Day	**Open**	**High**	**Low**	**Close**
Mon.	50.25	52.375	47.5	51.25
Tues.	51.25	54.5	48.75	52.25
Wed.	52.25	55	50.5	51.75
Thurs.	51.75	56.5	46.25	53.25
Fri.	53.25	58.5	51.25	56.25

The values as shown in the table display what should be the typical OHLC chart data format. For this type of chart, series should be in columns. HLC (High-Low-Close) datasheets are also structured the same way.

Here's how to create a basic stock chart:

1. In PowerPoint, click the Insert Graph button on the standard toolbar. Microsoft Graph appears.

2. Select the default data in Graph's datasheet and delete it using the Clear All command from the Edit menu. Type the sample data set shown in table 20.3.

3. Click the By Column tool on the Graph Standard toolbar.

4. Choose Format, AutoFormat. The AutoFormat dialog box appears.

5. From the Galleries list box, choose Line.

6. Select chart #9. This is the OHLC chart option.

7. Click the OK button.

The OHLC stock chart appears, as shown in figure 20.6.

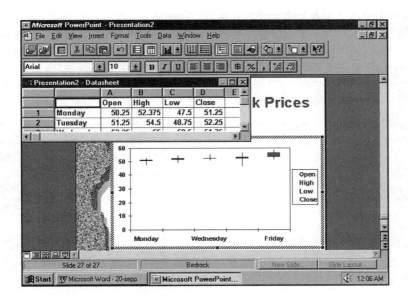

Fig. 20.6
The PowerPoint screen, displaying its default stock chart.

Modifying Stock Charts for Better Visualization

As you can see, there are quite a few problems with the chart in figure 20.6 versus the finished version shown in figure 20.5. The color scheme is off, and the stock values are unreadable. In a chart of this type, the legend is almost superfluous. The OHLC markers are out of proportion with the chart, which needs to be re-scaled. Except for its basic type, it barely resembles the chart in figure 20.5. It's time to do some clean-up.

1. Click the Legend tool on the Graph toolbar to delete the legend. (This frees up some room in the plot area of the chart.)

2. Click on the y-axis.

3. Choose Format, Selected Axis.

   The Format Axis dialog box appears. Five tabs are displayed: Patterns, Scale, Font, Number, and Alignment.

VI

Advanced Techniques

4. Click the Font tab, and choose a smaller (but not too small) font size for the y-axis labels.

5. Choose OK or press Enter.

Adjusting the Axis Values for a Stock Chart

While the chart is already significantly improved, it needs a few more adjustments before it resembles the final chart in figure 20.5. If you take a close look at the y-axis in figure 20.5, you see that the y-axis does not start at zero. The y-axis value range is set to display a range between 40 and 60 to give a better sense of proportion to the chart.

This illustrates an important point: why have vast amounts of open space in a chart when you don't need it? Also, the color of the Open-Close boxes is set to a more visible color than the default version you just created. Finally, the y-axis labels need to be displayed for each increment.

1. Click on the y-axis to select it.

Tip
Double-clicking the axis selects the axis and opens the dialog box.

2. Choose Format, Selected Axis.

3. Click the Scale tab.

4. In the Minimum text box, enter the value **40**.

5. In the Major Unit text box, type **2**.

6. Choose OK or press Enter.

   The y-axis scale is reset to the new values. The minor and major tick marks are also labeled.

7. To change the x-axis labels to a better point size, click the x-axis.

8. Choose Format, Selected Axis.

9. Click the Font tab.

10. From the Size list, choose 14 to set a smaller point size.

11. From the Font Style list, choose Bold.

12. Choose OK or press Enter.

    At this point, the stock chart is becoming quite serviceable.

Formatting a Stock Chart's Up-down Bars

The next step is to change the color of the Up-down bars to make them more visible against the slide background.

1. Click on any of the Up bars. Recall that Up bars indicate where the stock price closed. The closing value marker rests on the top edge of an Up bar.

   Notice that the bar for Wednesday's data is not selected. If you click Wednesday's Down bar, it's the only one selected because Up bars and Down bars are treated as separate groups. If you click any other bar, all the rest of them in this example are selected because they are all Up bars (representing a higher value than the previous one).

2. Choose Format, Selected Up Bars.

3. Choose a color from the Color palette in the Area section of the dialog box. Try to select colors that show up best against the slide's background color.

4. Choose OK or press Enter.

5. Click the Down bar in Wednesday's chart entry.

6. Choose Format, Selected Down Bars.

7. Click a blue color (or whatever color you prefer) from the Patterns Area palette. The same rule applies, of course: choose a color that has high visibility against your slide's background.

8. Choose OK or press Enter.

Formatting a Stock Chart's Data Markers

The final step is to make the closing value data markers more visible. Viewers otherwise may not be able to see them in your slide.

1. In the chart, click on any place where a closing value on an Up-down bar meets a high line. The result should appear as shown in figure 20.7.

2. Choose Format, Selected Data Series.

   The Format Data Series dialog box appears.

VI

Advanced Techniques

Fig. 20.7
The stock chart, with reformatted Up-down bar colors and a readable y-axis scale. The closing data points are highlighted.

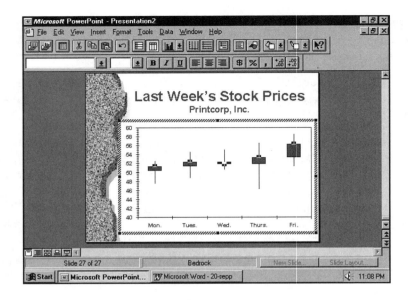

3. Click the Patterns tab if it isn't already displayed.

4. Click the Custom option button in the Marker section of the dialog box.

5. From the Marker Style drop-down list, choose a square marker.

6. From the Marker Foreground and Background drop-down palettes, choose any color you prefer.

7. Choose OK or press Enter. You may just barely be able to see the markers.

8. Click outside the chart to embed it into the slide.

As you can see, you can add some interesting touches to a stock chart. Stock charts can display a huge number of series values, as anyone who's seen a Dow Jones stock price history chart can attest. It's a classic type that is a good addition to any presenter's arsenal. HLC charts work much the same way, but discussions and examples of every chart type offered by PowerPoint are beyond the scope of this book. Nonetheless, with a little experimentation, any stock chart of either type can be customized and altered to suit your needs. They can also be added to a combination chart. (A concept that is full of possibilities for conveying knowledge to your readers.)

Troubleshooting

How can I get all my axis tick mark labels to display properly? Some of them are erased when I display the chart.

Often, Graph does not display all your axis tick mark labels because the font that's assigned to the axis is too large. When that happens, sometimes labels overrun each other, and the Graph program tends to drop some of them. To fix this, reduce the font size by clicking on the offending axis and choosing the F<u>o</u>rmat, <u>F</u>ont command.

Sometimes you run into the same problem in a 3-D chart. The cure for this is two-fold: change the font size and adjust the 3-D Rotation values as described in this chapter.

I can't get my stock charts to display properly.

The key to correct stock charting is having the correct number of series, and display-ing your series By Columns on the datasheet. An OHLC (Open-High-Low-Close) stock chart must have four series, one each for the Open, High, Low, and Close data sets, and an HLC (High-Low-Close) chart must have three series. When your data series are properly entered, also make sure to click the By Column button on Graph's Standard toolbar.

Using Combination Charts

Combination charts are an especially powerful and complex chart type that is primarily used to define and illustrate relationships between different sets of data. Combination charts can have elements of stock charts, bar charts, line charts, and column charts within them.

Combination charts combine elements from many different types of 2-D charts and enable you to plot data in two or three different ways on the same chart. Charts of this type are often used to draw relationships between, for example, gross revenues and profits, where yearly gross revenues might be shown in columns and yearly profits in a line. Powerful and informative messages can be conveyed with this chart type.

Combination charts (or *overlay charts*) are so named because one type of chart is overlaid on another chart. As a result, a combination chart displays, at a minimum, two y-axes and one x-axis. It's also quite possible to display two x-axes and two y-axes on the same chart, though that can become somewhat visually confusing. Combination charts, as you can imagine, also require a

Tip

Combination charts can display two x- and two y-axes on the same chart.

VI

Advanced Techniques

slightly different set of data than that used in previous examples; a sample set of data is provided to build the example in this section. Combination charts, incidentally, are only available in 2-D types. Figure 20.8 shows an example of a combination chart.

For combination charts, PowerPoint 95 displays x-axis values on the horizontal axis, shown on the bottom of the chart. In line charts, the x-axis is used to denote categories and series labels. Figure 20.8 shows increments along the x-axis labeled 1992, 1993, 1994, and 1995.

Tip

For combination or overlay charts, the y-axis is also called the *Y1 axis* in many charting applications.

The Y1 axis is the vertical axis on the left of the chart against which the numeric values of one series are measured. The increments and range of the Y1 axis are based on the values in your data. The Y2 axis works the same way, but is located on the right side of the chart in figure 20.8 and measures the other data set in the chart. In figure 20.8, the Y1 axis is used to measure the 2-D columns in the chart, and the axis is scaled from 0 to 25, in increments of five. The Y2 axis is used to measure the values of the 2-D line in the chart.

The *Y2 axis* is the third axis in your combination chart and is the basis by which your second set of data is measured. It's the second vertical axis shown

Fig. 20.8
A combination chart showing 2-D columns and lines.

Y1 axis, used to measure columns

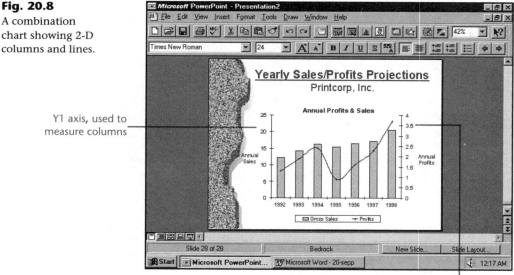

Y2 axis, used to measure the line

on the right side of the chart. Notice that the scale of values in the Y2 axis is very different from the scale of values in the Y1 axis. In figure 20.8, the Y2 axis is scaled from 0 to 4, in increments of 0.5. It's used to measure the line that is overlaid on the 2-D columns and it represents yearly profits.

The Y2 axis labels are used to coordinate with the legend and to describe the values on the chart that the Y2 axis measures. In figure 20.8, the label, Annual Profits, is attached to the Y2 axis. The legend shows that Profits are described with the yellow line and markers and thus are measured against the Y2 axis.

Note

In combination charts, it's a good idea to be explicit and generous with your axis labels—and to add a legend. A tremendous amount of information is conveyed in a chart of this type, and it's easy to forget a label that provides the viewer with the critical visual link to interpret the data.

Creating a Combination Chart

You take a slightly different approach to the creation of this type of chart, because the steps required are more complex and the details must be endured to get the chart right. Because of the myriad possibilities of this type of chart and space considerations, only one exercise can be used in this section. One exercise is enough, however, to illustrate the power of this chart option, its complexity, and the number of customization options available.

Table 20.4 gives you the sample data set that figure 20.8 is based on.

Table 20.4 Printcorp, Inc.'s Annual Sales and Profits, 1992-1998							
	1992	**1993**	**1994**	**1995**	**1996**	**1997**	**1998**
Gross Sales	12.2	14.3	16.2	15.4	16.4	17.1	20.6
Profits	1.3	1.9	2.4	0.9	1.6	2.3	3.7

Using this data, you create a combination chart from scratch in Microsoft Graph. The data set is deceptively simple. Many steps must be followed to properly create and customize the chart as seen in figure 20.8.

VI

Advanced Techniques

1. In PowerPoint, click the Insert Graph button on the standard toolbar. Microsoft Graph appears.

2. Select the default data in Graph's datasheet and delete it (the Del key is sufficient). Type the sample data set shown in table 20.4.

3. Choose Format, AutoFormat. The AutoFormat dialog box appears.

4. From the Galleries list box, choose Combination.

5. From the Formats thumbnails, choose chart type #2. It appears as a chart bearing a set of bars, a line, and two y-axes, as shown in figure 20.9.

Fig. 20.9
The AutoFormat dialog box, showing combination chart options.

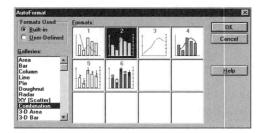

6. Choose OK or press Enter.

A rough combination chart appears, as shown in figure 20.10.

Fig. 20.10
A basic combination chart, showing 2-D columns and lines.

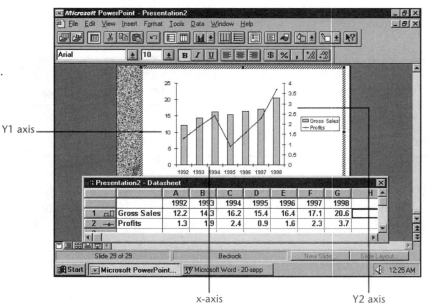

Note

You don't have to use the AutoFormats to change the appearance of combination charts. You can use the Format, Chart Type and Format, Group commands to alter the overlays in your chart. A section near the end of this chapter, "Customizing Combination Charts," describes these techniques in more detail.

Improving the Look of the Chart

The default combination chart type you selected has actually turned out very well. Axes are in place, value labels are correct, and the values can easily be read. Now, you'll change some colors, and go through several other procedures for cosmetic improvements.

1. Double-click any of the Gross Sales columns.

   The Format Data Series dialog box appears.

2. In the Patterns Area section of the dialog box, click a desired color in the palette, choosing a color that stands out clearly against your slide background. (Against a white or yellow slide background, a more subdued violet or magenta hue might be suitable. Against a dark background, a yellow hue works well.)

   If any of your column values are negative in a chart of this type, you can choose the Invert if Negative checkbox in the Patterns tab so that negative value columns will stand out clearly from other values. If all your values are over 0 this option will have no effect.

3. Choose OK or press Enter.

4. Double-click the Profits line in the combination chart.

   The Format Data Series dialog box appears.

   Note

   Despite the wildly different appearance of the series on the chart, formatting either of them uses mostly the same procedure. The only real difference is the type of marker that is used: lines or columns, in the current example.

5. In the Patterns Line section of the dialog box, choose the Custom option button.

VI

Advanced Techniques

6. From the Patterns Line Color drop-down list of the dialog box, choose a color that will stand out against both the background and the color you chose for the column group.

7. In the Patterns Marker section of the dialog box, choose the Custom option button.

8. In the Patterns Marker Foreground and Background drop-down lists of the dialog box, choose the same color as selected in step 6.

9. Choose OK or press Enter.

Changing the Line Weight

As a visibility enhancement, you can make the line thicker in the chart to make it easier to see.

1. Double-click the line.

   The Format Data Series dialog box appears, displaying the Patterns tab.

2. In the Patterns Line section, choose a heavier line weight from the Weight drop-down list.

3. Click the Smoothed Line check box to round out the jagged points on the line.

4. Choose OK or press Enter.

Adjusting the Proportion of the Fonts

To make the axis fonts more proportional to the chart (they're a little large in the default), start by double-clicking the Y1 axis (the y-axis on the left of the chart). The Format Axis dialog box appears. Then follow these steps:

1. Click the Font tab.

2. From the Size list, choose 14 to set a smaller point size.

3. From the Font Style list, choose Bold. Also, from the Color list, choose a suitable color.

4. Choose OK or press Enter.

5. Follow steps 1-4 for all three axes on the chart.

To make the legend more proportional in size to the rest of the chart, double-click the legend. The Format Legend dialog box appears. Then follow these steps:

1. Click on the Placement tab.

2. In the Placement Type area, choose the <u>B</u>ottom option button. The legend will automatically be centered at the bottom of the chart.

3. Click the Font tab.

4. From the <u>S</u>ize list, choose 14 to set a smaller point size.

5. From the F<u>o</u>nt Style list, choose Bold. From the <u>C</u>olor list, choose a suitable color.

   Once you place the legend at the bottom of the chart, some more room may open up inside the chart placeholder. You can drag the side of the chart's plot area to resize it, select the legend again, and use the Placement Type feature again as described above to re-center the legend. The chart will resemble figure 20.11.

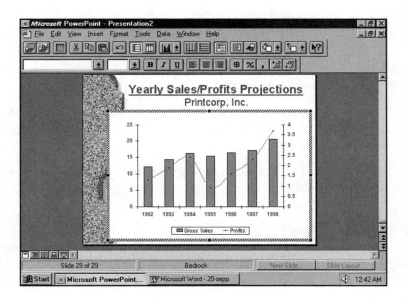

Fig. 20.11
A column-line combination chart with a legend centered at the bottom.

6. Choose OK or press Enter.

Adding Axis Labels to a Combo Chart

Now, you add the y-axis labels:

1. Click the Y (Y1) axis to select it.

2. Choose <u>I</u>nsert, <u>T</u>itles.

   The Titles dialog box appears.

3. Choose the <u>V</u>alue (Y) Axis and Second Value (<u>Y</u>) Axis check boxes.

4. Choose OK or press Enter.

   A Y appears next to the left-hand y- (or Y1) axis. A Y2 appears alongside the Y2 axis to the right of the chart.

   Note

   As noted, the second y-axis in a combination or overlay chart is also called the Y2 axis. When Graph puts the Y2 in the title entry, it's leaving you a clue about what axis you are adding a title to.

   ---

5. Click the mouse on the y-axis label to select it, and again inside the label to activate the I-beam pointer.

6. Delete the Y and type **Annual Sales**. To save room, place a carriage return between Annual and Sales. (In some situations, Sales may automatically move to a second line.)

7. Click the mouse on the Y2 axis label to select it, and again inside the label to activate the insertion point.

8. Delete the Y2 and type **Annual Profits**. To save room, place a carriage return between Annual and Profits. (In some situations, Profits may automatically move to a second line.)

   You may need to resize the chart to compensate for any overwriting of titles and axis labels.

Adding the Chart Title

As you can see, it takes quite a few steps to create an effective combination chart. Hang in there, you're almost done. To add a chart title, follow these steps:

1. Choose <u>I</u>nsert, <u>T</u>itles.

2. Click the Chart <u>T</u>itle check box. (Make sure you keep the y-axis checkboxes enabled.)

3. Click the OK button.

   The word Title appears over the chart.

4. Click the mouse in the Chart <u>T</u>itle text object that appears over the chart, delete `Title`, and type **Annual Profits & Sales**.

5. Change the font size and color if desired.

6. Now click outside the chart object to embed the finished chart in your slide. The chart should look similar to figure 20.12.

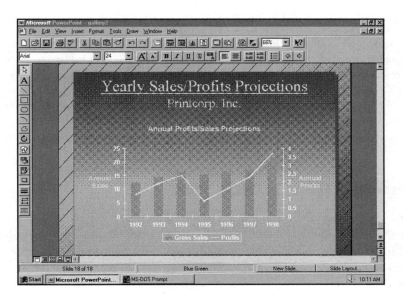

Fig. 20.12
A finished column-line combination chart.

As you can see, it takes some work to properly build a readable, useful combination chart. It's necessary to strike a balance between conveying all the information required to deliver your message and avoiding cluttering up your slide. That's why gridlines aren't used in this chart—they might only confuse the viewer.

> **Note**
>
> When you create your combination chart, take a look at the left margin of the spreadsheet holding your series data. You'll see a white dot next to the Profits series row. That white dot is the *overlay chart indicator.* It indicates that the Profits data series forms the overlay chart, which, in this case, is a line chart with markers.

Troubleshooting

I can't create combination charts when I try to use a 3-D column chart combined with a 2-D line.

It's not possible to use 3-D chart types to create a combination chart type. The other chart type will automatically be erased. Your series data in the datasheet won't be removed, but Graph won't display it in combination.

Also, if you play around with the Format, Chart Type command as described in this chapter, you will find it's possible to combine a 2-D pie chart with, say, a line chart, but the results will be almost meaningless, and you'll have a very hard time trying to define the relationship between such a combination of types. Nonetheless, the scope for experimentation is so great that even with a trial-and-error process, you may find combinations no one has thought of, and with customizing features, even be able to pull them off.

Using 2-D Radar Charts

Radar charts are often also called *spider charts*, because their general shape is like that of a spider's web. Radar charts are best used when you need to show multiple variables, such as ratings in different areas, performance levels of entities such as employees or corporate divisions, or progress in a project or other endeavor.

Radar charts require at least three categories and one series of data. They can also be somewhat perplexing to understand at first glance. Figure 20.13 shows a radar chart generated with the basic default labels and series names provided by PowerPoint.

The row labels in the datasheet are shown in the legend, and the column labels are used to label each spoke. The rows represent the three series of data, and each series is shown as a geometric shape whose appearance is determined by the position of each series value on the spokes.

Radar charts are best viewed when the series are arranged to provide maximum visibility to as many series values as possible. This means that the series must be "stacked" like pancakes with the smallest shape on top, the next largest below that, and the largest on the bottom. If they aren't, entire series can be hidden from view and thus from analysis by the audience.

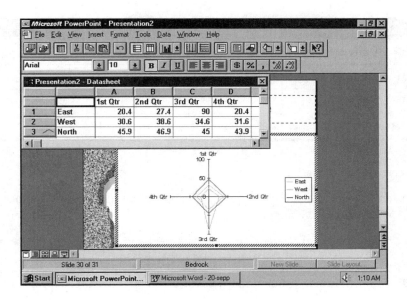

Fig. 20.13
A simple radar
chart, using
heavier line
weights.

> **Note**
>
> In figure 20.13, the series are arranged in such a way that all the series values can be measured along the spokes. Look closely at the datasheet in the figure. The East data set, which is on the top of the chart stack, is on the third row of the datasheet. Notice also that its values are consistently less than those of the next datasheet row up, the West row. Radar charts may require rearranging of chart values to get the best effect.

A standard datasheet can usually be made to work well with a radar-type chart; the key is to arrange your series for best visibility. Otherwise, axes and axis labels, series markers, gridlines, and other elements of radar charts can be selected and customized much as any other chart.

The Market Share datasheet in table 20.5 is reasonably well-suited to a simple radar chart.

Table 20.5 Market Share Datasheet				
Company Name	**1992**	**1993**	**1994**	**1995**
Printcorp, Inc.	22.1	23.5	21.8	22.7
LaserPrint, Inc.	57.1	57.3	60.2	61.8
Patriot Printers, Inc.	20.8	19.2	18.0	15.5

To create a radar chart, follow these steps:

1. In PowerPoint, click the Insert Graph button on the standard toolbar. Microsoft Graph appears.

2. Select the default data in Graph's datasheet and delete it (the Del key is sufficient). Type in the sample data set shown in table 20.5.

3. Choose Format, AutoFormat. The AutoFormat dialog box appears.

4. From the Galleries list box, choose Radar.

5. Select chart #2. This option is a radar chart without gridlines.

6. Click the OK button.

Fig. 20.14
The completed
Radar chart
without gridlines.

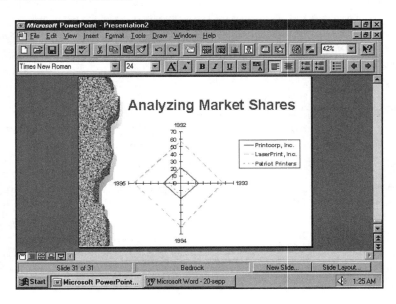

The end result, given the relative sparseness of the chart, can be rather striking and visually attractive (refer to fig. 20.14). The y-axis bears the value measurements, ranging between 0 and 70. The category labels at each of the four corners can have their fonts changed and recolored as usual, and the legend can be reformatted. The plot area of the chart can be filled in with a color that shows the values up properly. Radar lines representing the series can use heavier weights to improve their visibility against the chart background or slide background.

Tip
Radar charts can benefit greatly from somewhat heavier line weights.

Radar charts are well-suited for displaying a substantially greater number of series and data values than are given in this example. Up to six or eight data series can be accommodated in a radar chart without difficulty. They're worth considering for an offbeat and striking accent to your data—if you can ensure that your series values will be visible.

Using 2-D Doughnut Charts

Doughnut charts offer many of the same attributes of pie charts, which were described in Chapters 14 and 15. The main difference between pie charts and doughnuts is the obvious visual one: the center of a doughnut chart is hollowed out. There is one more difference: unlike a pie chart, it's possible to display more than one series in a doughnut chart. Each series has its own doughnut, one inside of another.

Otherwise, a doughnut chart provides much the same function that a pie chart does—to display the division of a finite quantity, such as a year's market share, from one series of data. The use of a doughnut chart is mainly a stylistic decision. A data series is provided in table 20.6 for use in building a doughnut chart.

Table 20.6   Market Share Datasheet, for a Single Years' Worth of Data

Company Name	1992
Printcorp, Inc.	22.1
LaserPrint, Inc.	57.1
Patriot Printers, Inc.	20.8

VI

Advanced Techniques

1. In PowerPoint, click the Insert Graph button on the standard toolbar. Microsoft Graph appears.

2. Select the default data in Graph's datasheet and delete it. Type the sample data set shown in table 20.6.

3. Choose Format, AutoFormat. The AutoFormat dialog box appears (see figure 20.15).

Fig. 20.15
The AutoFormat dialog box shows all the doughnut chart options.

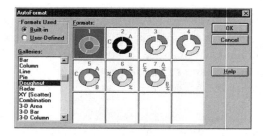

4. From the Galleries list box, choose Doughnut.

5. From the Formats thumbnails, choose chart type #1. It appears as a simple doughnut chart.

6. Choose OK or press Enter.

7. If the doughnut appears to be all one color, click on the chart (to select it) and then click the By Column tool on the Graph toolbar. The three series values should split the doughnut up properly. If not, extra column formatting is still present in the datasheet, even though there may not be any data values in those columns. Click any column buttons showing series indicators and choose Edit, Cut. The doughnut should then appear properly.

The next few steps are optional, but when using doughnut charts, it's a good idea to show values or percentages to provide visual cues for measurement or doughnut slices. This is especially true if you have slices that are close together in size.

8. Choose Insert, Data Labels.

The Data Labels dialog box appears.

9. Choose the Show Percent option button.

10. Choose OK or press Enter. Figure 20.16 shows what the results might look like.

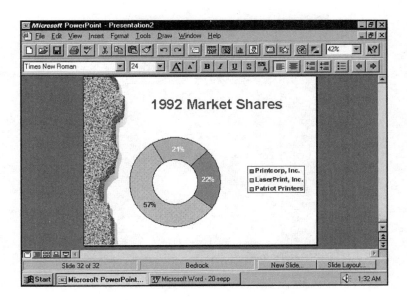

Fig. 20.16
A doughnut chart
showing values
and a legend.
Though sparse, the
chart adequately
conveys its
message.

The use of doughnut charts is straightforward—a 3-D doughnut type isn't
even available. They're a good substitute for pie charts if you want to break
the monotony of a long series of chart slides.

Using 3-D Surface Charts

A *3-D surface chart* is a specialized chart type that is generally not suited for
many conventional business tasks used by other charts in this chapter. 3-D
surface charts closely resemble topographic maps—in fact, given enough
series of data, you could actually construct a topographic map with geological
data in PowerPoint.

Surface charts are used to show surface variations established over two or
more evenly spaced values. Those evenly spaced values are the X and Y values
in your chart, and there must be a minimum of two series of data and two
categories of values to form a surface chart. The z-axis values in the chart
determine the "topography" of the chart's surface. Figure 20.17 shows a fairly
typical 3-D surface chart.

3-D surface chart types can greatly benefit from the use of major gridlines
on each axis. The 1992-1995 categories in this example are arranged on the
x-axis and the series labels are displayed on the y-axis. The major gridlines for
all axes are displayed on the chart, which makes it easier to read.

Tip

Doughnut slices,
just like pie slices,
can be pulled or
"exploded" away
from the chart.

VI

Advanced Techniques

Fig. 20.17

A 3-D surface chart.

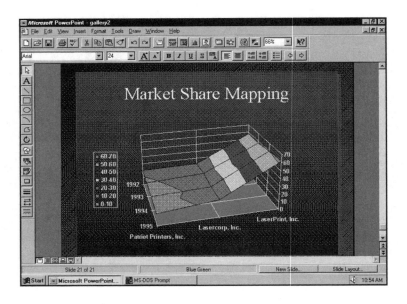

Each series label has a tick mark and a major gridline assigned to it to help show the values of each series as they move across the chart. Based on the surface altitudes, the chart assigns colors to each value range. On first glance this can be confusing—what values do the colors signify? They actually don't signify any series values, just surface transitions from one series to another. The surface traverses up several ranges of altitude, for example, between the LaserPrint series on the y-axis and the Printcorp, Inc. series.

Table 20.7	**Market Share Datasheet for a 3-D Surface Chart**			
Company Names	**1992**	**1993**	**1994**	**1995**
Patriot Printers, Inc.	20.8	19.2	18.0	15.5
Printcorp, Inc.	22.1	23.5	21.8	22.7
LaserPrint, Inc.	57.1	57.3	60.2	61.8

The surface is much flatter between the Patriot Printers, Inc. series and Printcorp, reflecting the much closer range in values between them. While the 3-D surface chart reflects the dominance of LaserPrint in this market, there are a number of other chart types that better convey this message, such as pie charts. There is great scope for creativity and experimenting with this chart type, however. The chart in figure 20.17 shows a few adjustments, such as 3-D rotation, that have been made to render the chart's values more readable.

Creating a Surface Chart

The following steps help you create the chart in figure 20.17:

1. In PowerPoint, click the Insert Graph button from the standard toolbar. Microsoft Graph appears.

2. Select the default data in Graph's datasheet and delete it. Type the sample data set shown in table 20.7.

3. Choose Format, AutoFormat. The AutoFormat dialog box appears.

4. From the Galleries list box, choose 3-D Surface.

5. From the Format thumbnails, choose chart type #1.

6. Choose OK or press Enter.

Adjusting the 3-D View

3-D surface charts can benefit from viewing adjustments. While this feature is very flexible (and in the next few exercises you'll see why), for the current chart you'll stick to some basic viewing specifications.

1. Choose Format, 3-D View.

   The Format 3-D View dialog box appears, as shown in figure 20.18.

2. In the Elevation text box, enter the value **25**.

3. In the Rotation text box, enter the value **75**.

4. In the Perspective text box, enter the value **30**.

5. Choose OK or press Enter.

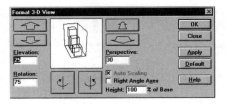

Fig. 20.18
An introductory glance at PowerPoint 95's Format 3-D View dialog box.

Adding Gridlines to a 3-D Surface Chart

Gridlines can be very useful in a 3-D Surface chart, because they create an extremely easy way to measure values in a 3-D chart that would otherwise be somewhat difficult to interpret. Gridlines are added to the walls of a 3-D surface chart by the following steps:

1. Choose Insert, Gridlines.

    The Gridlines dialog box appears.

2. Click the Major Gridlines check boxes in the Category (X) Axis, Series (Y) Axis, and Value (Z) Axis dialog box sections.

3. Choose OK or press Enter.

Moving the Legend

A final improvement for this chart is to relocate the legend to a more convenient place:

1. Click the legend.

2. Choose Format, Selected Legend.

3. Click the Placement tab.

4. Click the Left option button under the Type option list to place the legend on the left side of the chart.

5. Choose OK or press Enter.

If desired, assign a smaller font to the z-axis scale (which is the vertical axis against which the chart values are measured), and change its scale (using the Scale tab in the Format Axis dialog box) to a Major increment of 10. When you do this, the entire chart will show a wider range of color values.

Surface charts can be heavily customized, and you just had a small taste of that in the preceding example. While they're a very specialized chart type, surface charts are also attractive, and if they're chosen properly for the subject matter, they can be a striking addition to a slide show.

3-D Area and 3-D Line Charts

3-D area and 3-D line charts are two more options that you should consider for your slide shows. Both types are readily adaptable to the same kinds of data and can deliver the same message; the use of one over another is generally a matter of taste. Area charts simply fill the areas below the lines with colors or patterns, but the values defined are the same. 3-D lines and areas are easily customized in much the same way that other 3-D charts are—for different chart depths, rotated views and different perspectives, gap widths between 3-D lines, different gridlines, and more.

Lines are generally easier to see in three dimensions than in 3-D area charts, because you don't run the risk of hiding substantial areas behind other ones. Viewers see lines somewhat more distinctly, as separate series at different depths within the chart. Nonetheless, 3-D areas offer other advantages, such as a greater physical presence in the chart, particularly when one area is much greater than the others. Figure 20.19 displays such a chart.

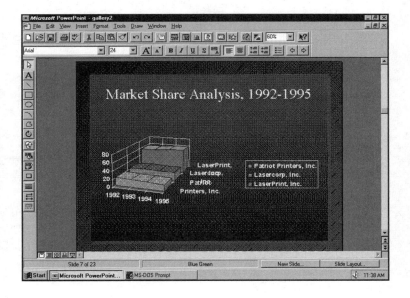

Fig. 20.19
A 3-D area chart, displaying the laser printer market share data.

To get to this point, quite a few things may need to be adjusted beyond the basic chart. The rows of data in the chart datasheet may need to be rearranged to ensure that the largest area is in the "back" of the chart. The 3-D viewing angle may need to be adjusted for better area visibility. Axis label fonts may need to be readjusted.

Creating a 3-D Area Chart

Given the numerous similarities between 3-D area and 3-D line charts, one exercise will work for both chart types. Use the data in table 20.8 to complete the next set of steps.

Table 20.8 Market Share Datasheet				
Company Name	**1992**	**1993**	**1994**	**1995**
Patriot Printers, Inc.	20.8	19.2	18.0	15.5
Printcorp, Inc.	22.1	23.5	21.8	22.7
LaserPrint, Inc.	57.1	57.3	60.2	61.8

1. In PowerPoint, click the Insert Graph button on the standard toolbar. Microsoft Graph appears.

2. Select the default data in Graph's datasheet and choose Edit, Clear All to delete it. Type the sample data set shown in table 20.8.

3. Choose Format, AutoFormat.

   The AutoFormat dialog box appears.

4. From the Galleries list, choose 3-D Area. Eight thumbnails appear in the Formats area.

5. Choose Chart #6.

> **Note**
>
> 3-D area chart types #5, #6, and #7 are all quite similar, except for the gridlines that are displayed as their default. Also, several stacked area charts are offered that vary according to their use of gridlines, labels, and other chart elements.

6. Choose OK or press Enter.

   The basic 3-D area chart appears, as shown in figure 20.20.

Deleting the Legend and Adjusting the Chart Size

For a chart of this type, you don't need both labels and a legend. One is sufficient. Which to get rid of? It's generally easier for an audience to relate to labels directly attached to a chart than to have to squint to see the colors in a legend. So, get rid of the legend.

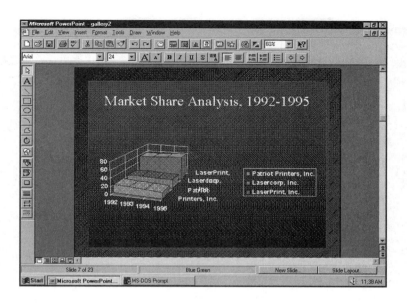

Fig. 20.20
A basic 3-D area
chart, displaying
the market share
data. Notice that
the labels and
legend are
redundant, and the
viewing angle
could bear
adjustment.

1. Select the legend and press the Delete key.

The legend disappears from the chart.

2. Click anywhere inside the chart plot area. A highlighted box appears around it.

3. Drag the right side of the chart to resize it. The chart will increase in size. It should appear roughly as shown in figure 20.21.

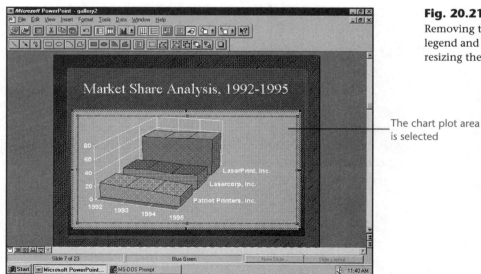

Fig. 20.21
Removing the
legend and
resizing the chart.

The chart plot area
is selected

VI

Advanced Techniques

Formatting the Axes and 3-D View

To continue the 3-D Area chart exercise, you can format the axis labels and make some viewing angle adjustments. Both procedures will help make the chart more attractive.

Tip
Remember you can double-click on many chart elements to begin formatting them, or click directly on them with the right mouse button to use the shortcut menu.

1. Click the y-axis—the axis bearing the company name labels.

2. Choose Format, Selected Axis.

3. Click the Font tab if it isn't already displayed.

4. Choose a smaller font size, such as 14 point. (This will make the labels more readable and less obtrusive.)

5. Choose OK or press Enter.

6. Repeat steps 1-4 for the x-axis.

For many charts, you need to play with the 3-D values to get it right (also, don't forget that you can rotate a 3-D chart with the mouse):

1. Choose Format, 3-D View.

   The Format 3-D View dialog box appears.

2. In the Elevation text box, enter the value **15**.

3. In the Rotation text box, enter the value **15**.

4. If the Perspective feature is not displayed, click the Right Angle Axes check box. The X should be removed, displaying the Perspective feature in the dialog box. If the Perspective feature is already displayed, proceed to the next step.

5. In the Perspective text box, enter the value **30**.

6. Choose OK or press Enter.

With the end result of this chart, as shown previously in figure 20.21, you can now measure the yearly values with better accuracy. This is an area where you can readily experiment with viewing angles and rotation to create pleasing charts, but remember, the audience must always be able to measure the values in the chart.

Creating a New Default Chart

Using a preferred chart as a default chart format has a number of advantages. First, it prevents the necessity of reentering the same set of data for a series of charts using the same datasheet, or even the tedium of clearing and pasting data between slides.

Second, every formatting specification you desire can be included in the default format, including axes, axis labels, types of gridlines, line weights, fonts attached to labels, colors, and anything else having to do with chart formatting.

To create a new default chart, follow these steps:

1. Make sure all the formatting changes are made that you want included in the new default.

2. Choose Tools, Options. The Graph Options dialog box appears, as shown in figure 20.22.

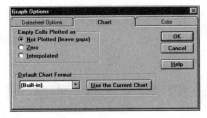

Fig. 20.22
The Graph Options dialog box, showing the Chart tab options.

3. Click the Chart tab.

   Here, an entire list of new charts can be added for new default chart types. Under the Default Chart Format section, the Graph default is called Built-In.

4. Under the Default Chart Format section of the dialog box, choose the Use the Current Chart button. An entry titled Custom Default is placed in the drop-down list.

5. Choose OK or press Enter.

You can only add one custom default chart at a time. You can, however, add as many chart types as you want to the AutoFormat list. (See the next section for more information.)

VI

Advanced Techniques

> **Note**
>
> The new default chart type is placed as an entry in the Windows text file GRAPH.INI. Whenever Graph is started up, it loads the new chart type from this file as the default format.

Using Custom Chart Types as AutoFormats

After all the work of creating a custom chart, wouldn't it be nice to be able to store that custom format so you didn't have to go through the whole mess again? It's simpler than you think. Here's how:

Tip

Before starting the steps, make sure all the formatting changes are made that you want included in the new chart type.

Fig. 20.23

Setting up a user-defined AutoFormat.

1. With the chart displayed in Graph, choose Format, AutoFormat. (For this example, we'll use the combination chart created earlier in this chapter.)

2. In the Formats Used section at the top left of the dialog box, click the User-Defined option button.

   As figure 20.23 shows, the dialog box changes.

3. Choose the Customize button.

   The User-Defined AutoFormats dialog box appears.

4. Choose the Add button. The Add Custom AutoFormat dialog box appears, as shown in figure 20.24. This is where you add your actual entry to the program.

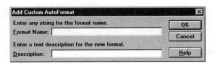

5. Type in a brief name for your new chart format. For this example, type **Combo #1**. Then, if desired, type in a description of up to 32 characters for this format.

6. Choose OK or press Enter. The User-Defined AutoFormat dialog box now shows a thumbnail of your new chart (see fig. 20.25).

7. Choose Close.

Now, your chart is part of PowerPoint's AutoFormat library.

Choose User-
Defined to
view any
custom charts

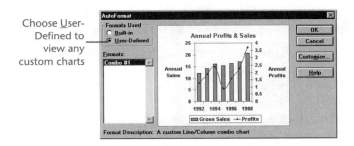

Exporting a PowerPoint Chart to Other Applications

What can you do to place those lovely PowerPoint charts in other programs? Though PowerPoint can't directly export chart objects to other applications, it's possible to save a slide as a bitmap picture for display in other programs.

1. In PowerPoint, display the slide that you want to export as a bitmap picture.

2. Choose File, Save As (see fig. 20.26).

3. In the File Name text box, type the desired name for the file, with thirty-two characters or less.

4. In the Save In drop-down list, locate the folder where the file can be saved.

VI

Advanced Techniques

Fig. 20.26
Using the File Save
dialog box to
export a slide as a
picture file.

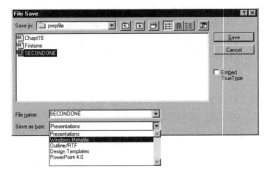

5. In the Save as Type drop-down list, choose Windows Metafile. The default file extension is WMF.

6. If you want the fonts to be included in the picture, click the Embed TrueType check box. This ensures that typefaces will show up properly in the image.

7. Choose Save or press Enter.

The slide is saved as a picture, or "screen shot," to be viewed or placed in a different application. The file can be opened up in Windows 95's Paint program and many other programs that use graphics, or imported as a bitmap into Microsoft Word and other programs. A better alternative is to use Drag-and-Drop Copy to place a slide image directly into Word or another program that supports OLE.

Importing Data and Charts

PowerPoint for Windows 95 offers direct ways to import data and charts from Microsoft Excel. Versions 4.0, 5.0, and Excel for Windows 95 are supported, and although PowerPoint has a closer relationship to Excel for Windows 95 in terms of object linking and embedding capabilities, you can still include Excel 4.0 charts and datasheets. Chapter 19, "Using Links to Other Applications," describes how to work with object linking and embedding for use between PowerPoint and other applications such as Excel. This short section describes the direct importing of data and charts from Excel files.

Importing Data

Importing Excel or Lotus 1-2-3 datasheets can be extremely handy for PowerPoint users. You may want to create your own charts in PowerPoint but have most of your data committed in datasheets from another program. Importing them can save tons of work. Doing so requires only that you be in PowerPoint's Graphing application. A good way to start is by displaying a PowerPoint default chart and datasheet in a new Graph slide. With the default chart and datasheet displayed in Microsoft Graph (not in PowerPoint), follow these steps:

1. Choose Edit, Import Data.

   The Import Data dialog box appears, as shown in figure 20.27.

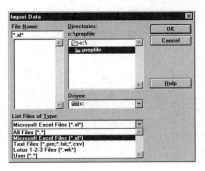

Fig. 20.27
Using the Import Data dialog box in Graph to import an Excel datasheet.

2. In the List Files of Type drop-down list, choose the desired file type. Excel files are shown as (*.xl*) and Lotus 1-2-3 files are shown as (*.wk*).

3. Choose the Directories (folder) and Drives under which the file can be located.

4. In the File Name list, click the desired file name to select it and display it in that text box.

5. Choose OK or press Enter.

   A message box appears asking whether you want to overwrite the existing data.

6. Choose OK or press Enter.

The imported data is displayed in the Graph datasheet.

Importing Excel Charts

Importing Excel charts can also be useful for PowerPoint users. You may want to create your own charts in Excel because you're used to that program, and your data may be committed to datasheets in that program. Importing them is simple and doing so requires only that you be in PowerPoint's Graphing application. A good way to start is by displaying a PowerPoint default chart and datasheet in a new Graph slide. With the default chart and datasheet displayed in Graph (not in PowerPoint), follow these steps:

1. Choose Edit, Import Chart.

   The Import Chart dialog box appears, as shown in figure 20.28.

Fig. 20.28
Importing an Excel
chart, using
Graph's Import
Chart feature.

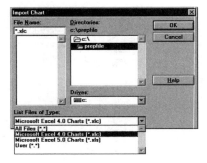

2. In the Files of Type drop-down list, choose the desired file type. Excel 4.0 files are shown as (*.xlc) and Excel 5.0 chart files are shown as (*.xls). Excel for Windows 95 files are directly supported through OLE, so importing them isn't necessary.

> **Note**
>
> If you are importing a chart from an Excel 5.0 workbook, the chart must be placed on a chart sheet as the first sheet of the workbook. Graph will not recognize an Excel chart that is part of a worksheet, even if it is placed on the first sheet. To create an Excel 5.0 chart on a chart sheet, select the worksheet data, and then choose Insert, Chart, As New Sheet. Follow the ChartWizard to create the chart. If necessary, drag the chart sheet tab to the left-most position in the workbook. Save the Excel workbook, and then the chart is available for import into Graph.

3. Choose the Directories and Drives under which the file can be located.

4. In the File Name list, click the desired file name to select it and display it in the text box.

5. Choose OK or press Enter.

A message box appears asking whether you want to overwrite the existing chart.

6. Choose OK or press Enter to import the Excel chart, automatically overwriting the existing data. If you don't wish to overwrite, choose Cancel.

The Excel chart is displayed in Graph, available for changing and editing in Graph's normal modes.

Importing Charts from PowerPoint 4

If you've built up a library of presentations and charts created in PowerPoint 4, you're in luck. It's easy to import charts from the previous version of the program into PowerPoint for Windows 95.

Essentially, all you have to do is load the old-format presentation into the PowerPoint program. Once you've done so, double-clicking on a chart in a slide automatically converts the old Microsoft Graph charts to the new version. The major difference between the versions of Graph, of course, is that the older version uses OLE 1.0, while the current version uses OLE 2.0, or in-place editing. Graph data is converted automatically, invisible to the user. Here's how the procedure is done:

1. In PowerPoint, choose File, Open.

   The Open dialog box appears.

2. From the File Name, Files of Type, and Look In lists, search for and choose the PowerPoint 4 file you want to load. Then, choose OK or press Enter.

   After a moment, the program displays a message box reading:

   ```
   This presentation uses File Format 102. It will be converted
   and opened as Read-Only.
   ```

3. Choose OK or press Enter.

4. When the file is opened, use the File, Save As command to save the opened file as a new PowerPoint for Windows 95 format file (you won't be able to overwrite the old one—the program won't let you).

5. When that's done, double-click on a chart in the presentation. The conversion is finished.

Tip
PowerPoint 3 and PowerPoint 4 files also have the file extension .PPT.

Tip
You may need to rerun Setup to install the proper files translators for converting older PowerPoint files. They should be automatically installed when you install PowerPoint, but it's possible to miss this.

VI

Advanced Techniques

Using the Slides From File or Slides From Outline command from the Insert menu under PowerPoint is an alternative method that may save you a few steps. Here's an example:

1. With your presentation displayed in PowerPoint, choose Insert, Slides from File.

   The Insert File dialog box appears.

2. From the File Name, Files of Type, and Look In lists, choose the PowerPoint 4 file you want to load and then choose OK or press Enter.

The slides from the PowerPoint 4 file (or PowerPoint for Windows 95 file, for that matter) are automatically converted and inserted into your presentation. You won't even see a screen message regarding file formats, but you may see a `Charts are being updated to the new color scheme` message for a moment as the computer does its work. Using Slides from Outline allows you to create a presentation by using an outline created in Word or PowerPoint. Importing an outline works the same way as for importing slides from a PowerPoint 4 file.

Customizing Combination Charts

PowerPoint offers other features to customize and change combination charts (and, for that matter, any chart type), by using two commands that haven't been discussed very much until now: the Format, Chart Type command and the Format, Group command. Neither command is particularly difficult, and both offer another dimension to the conventional use of AutoFormats, which you've relied on for most of the charting examples in this book.

Tip
Use the Format, Chart Type and Format, Group commands to experiment with combination chart types.

Both commands allow you to change the type of data markers that are applied to any data series in your chart. For example, if you have a combination chart that uses a line and an area, the area can be quickly converted to a set of 2-D columns. A chart of any type can be converted to any other type.

The Format, Chart Type command and the Format, Group command are closely interrelated, and they can both be accessed from one another (see fig. 20.29 and fig. 20.30).

You can see that the two dialog boxes mutually reinforce each other. The Format Group menu option is a dynamic one that changes based on the chart type you select (see fig. 20.31 for an example).

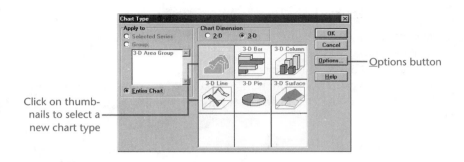

Click on thumb-
nails to select a
new chart type

Options button

Fig. 20.29
The Chart Type
dialog box
showing the
Options button,
which offers
reciprocal access to
the Format, Group
command in the
next illustration.

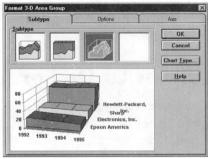

Fig. 20.30
The Format 3-D
Area Group dialog
box showing its
Chart Type button,
offers access to the
Format, Chart
Type command.

Fig. 20.31
The Format menu
will display two
chart types if
you're using a
combination chart.

You see two Group commands on the Format menu only if you're using a
combination chart. Otherwise, only one Group command is shown on the
menu.

If you click on the 1 Column Group or 2 Line Group menu commands, you
bring up the Format Column Group or Format Line Group dialog box, each
of which bears three tabs: Subtype, Options, and Axis. All of them are used to
add custom effects to your charts, and all three tabs dynamically change to
offer different features depending on the chart type that's currently selected.

In all cases, clicking on the Chart Type button in the Format Group dialog
box brings up the Chart Type dialog box in turn (refer to fig. 20.29).

VI

Advanced Techniques

Here you can change the chart type that's applied to the current chart or selected data series (or a group) in a combination chart. A *group* is any number of data series used to create a chart, and a *single series* is one set of data markers of the same color in the chart. You can have up to two groups in a chart, which results in a combination chart. Clicking on one of the groups in the Group list and then clicking on a thumbnail changes the chart type for the selected group.

It isn't as hard as it sounds. Be aware that you can change any chart to a 2-D or 3-D type by choosing the 2-D or 3-D option button in the Chart Dimension section of the Chart Type dialog box (refer to fig. 20.29), but you can't apply 3-D chart types to groups in a combination chart. The other group will be erased from view in the chart.

Using Trendlines to Do Forecasting

Trendlines are a useful tool for forecasting and illustrating trends in your charts. You can apply trendlines to most 2-D chart types; they're very useful for 2-D column charts, but they can be applied to bar, scatter, line, and area charts as well. In fact, they can be applied to any chart type in the XY category. They can also be used with a combination chart, and in such a chart a trendline can be applied to each group. They cannot, however, be applied to an OHLC or HLC stock chart. You see a 2-D column chart used generically in the trendline examples shown in this section.

Trendlines are a tool for forecasting possible future trends in your data. While they're simple to use, the concept behind trendlines is not. The theory behind trendlines is an idea called *regression analysis*. Without getting too technical, regression analysis is the basis for using your datasheet statistics to create the trendline. You can choose between six different mathematical models to create your trendline:

Linear	Exponential
Polynomial	Power
Logarithmic	Moving Average

Depending on the nature of your datasheet numbers, you may need to try two or three math models to get the most accurate trendline. How can you tell if a trendline is accurate? Check the R-Squared value. All the calculation methods listed above yield a final value between 0 and 1. The closer a trendline's R-Squared value is to 1, the more accurate it is for the purposes of your chart. If it's closer to 0, the less accurate its trend calculations will be.

Please note that many details are beyond the scope of this book; Graph's On-Line Help on this subject (which is best found by using the Search for Help On feature) is highly recommended for users who need more detail than can be provided here.

You can apply a trendline in the following steps:

1. Display your 2-D column chart in Microsoft Graph.

2. Click on the data series (a set of columns of a specific color) to which you want to add a trendline.

3. Choose Insert, Trendline.

   The Trendline dialog box appears, as shown in figure 20.32.

Options tab
Click on thumb-nails to select a trendline type

Fig. 20.32
Using the Trendline dialog box from Graph's Insert menu to set up one or more trendlines.

4. Six thumbnails are displayed showing the various trendline types that can be applied: Linear, Logarithmic, Polynomial, Power, Exponential, or Moving Average. Click on any of them (it may take some experimenting to get the best trendline type for your chart).

   You can add a name for your trendline and set other options for the trendline, such as displaying the R-Squared value.

5. Click the Options tab.

> **Note**
>
> You need at least four series values to display the R-Squared value of your trendline to determine its accuracy.

VI

Advanced Techniques

6. To display the R-Squared value for your trendline, click the Display R-Squared Value on Chart check box (see fig. 20.33).

7. To display the formula used to create the trendline, click the Display Equation on Chart check box (see fig. 20.33).

Fig. 20.33

The Trendline dialog box, showing its Options tab, offers more precise tools for trendline forecasting and setup.

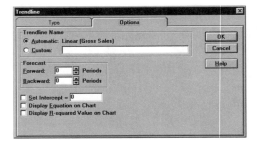

> **Note**
>
> Trendlines also offer a forecasting feature that allows you to forecast ahead to a user-specified number of time periods, based on the time periods reflected in your chart. Doing so extends your trendline beyond the scope provided by your basic datasheet. You can forecast backward or forward on your chart trendline. This feature is also called *goal seeking*. An example is shown in figure 20.34.

8. To add forecasting to your chart: under the Forecast section, type a value in the Forward Periods or Backward Periods text box or use the mouse to increment them to a desired value. Both Forward and Backward forecasting can be used at one time.

9. The Trendline name is automatically added, or you can add your own by typing it into the Custom text box.

10. Choose OK or press Enter.

You can insert more than one trendline into a chart. If you have more than one set of columns in a chart, you can attach a trendline or more than one to each of them. You can, as seen in figure 20.34, use trendlines for comparison between two analysis types—in this case, linear vs. polynomial for the taller columns.

In figure 20.34, the shorter columns have a trendline attached which bears the most accurate R-Squared rating. Forecasting for both data sets (Profits and Sales) has been added, so you see the trendlines extending beyond the limits of the data. The Profits trendline accurately shows a projected drop off in profits even though the annual sales are expected to steadily increase. You can also click on any existing trendline to format it and change its formula or analysis method.

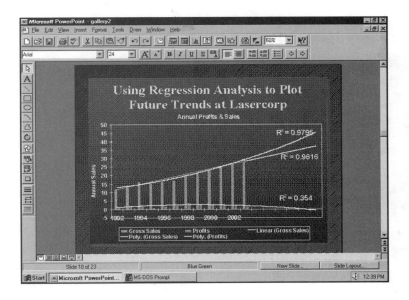

Fig. 20.34
Displaying two trendlines with differing R-Squared values for one series. Which trendline is more accurate? On the other series, the most accurate trendline has been selected.

By using trendlines, you can add a sophisticated element of forecasting and statistical trend illustration to your charts. It's recommended that you have some understanding of mathematics (or know someone who does!) so that you can make the best choice for accurate forecasts. Nonetheless, displaying the R-Squared value is a good expedient for a quick assessment of the accuracy of each of the six types of trendlines, though it does require some experimenting.

Despite the extensive looks at PowerPoint 95's powerful charting capabilities, some things were left out due to simple space considerations. An entire book could be devoted to PowerPoint's charting features alone. Hopefully, ample information has been provided to you for further explorations of charting. ❖

VI

Advanced Techniques

Chapter 21

Using Multimedia Elements in PowerPoint 95

by Rich Grace

The last few years have produced an explosion of multimedia effects and applications in the PC market. The most important additions to the roster of computer-based media are full-motion video and portable CD-quality sound. You easily can incorporate these data types, plus more, into your PowerPoint presentation. PowerPoint for Windows 95 has taken a big leap forward in enabling mainstream presenters to fully use multimedia in their shows. Windows 95 has completely revamped and rewritten its multimedia libraries and programs, and PowerPoint takes advantage of every aspect of this major upgrade in the operating system.

You learn about the following PowerPoint for Windows 95 features in this chapter:

- Adding video clips to slides

- Adding sound clips to slides

- Exploring and using Windows 95's new Media Player

- Setting video and audio playback timings and events

- Using PowerPoint's Animation Settings feature to trigger multimedia events

- Adding a CD soundtrack to your presentation

Adding Video to Your Presentations

Video is an extremely demanding but rewarding type of data for your computer. Although desktop video has been around for several years, PC users have been slow to take advantage of it. Multimedia PC hardware and software on all levels, including applications and the operating system, have had to evolve—sometimes painfully. Chronic hardware incompatibilities and performance bottlenecks have plagued PC multimedia users for years. That is starting to change. Video is now a constant in computer games, and business users are beginning to accept it as a useful tool for presentation delivery.

Video comes from several sources. One way is to place a video-capture board in your computer, such as Creative Labs' Video Blaster or Intel's Smart Video. Then you hook up a portable video camera or a VCR and you instantly have new video clips to use. Another method is to buy video clips on CD-ROM, which is a safe bet to avoid copyright infringements.

Several software standards have emerged for using video on your Windows PC; two of the most important are Apple's *QuickTime for Windows* and Microsoft's *Video for Windows*. Video for Windows supports a specific video file standard, called AVI. (See the following Note for more on this topic.) Generally, video appears in a window on-screen, as figure 21.1 shows.

Fig. 21.1
A typical video application in PowerPoint.

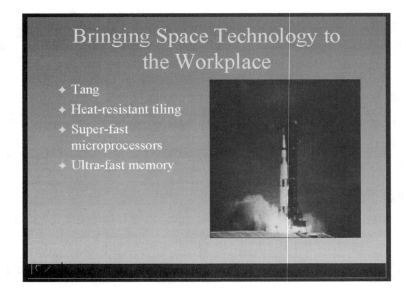

Recording video clips on your PC can be an expensive business; this process chews up hard disk space at an astonishing rate. Also, unless you run your Windows screen at VGA resolution (640 x 480), you can have some difficulty viewing your video clips. For most video recording products, the largest video capture screen is 320 x 240 pixels, and video clips are normally played back at that resolution (hence the window in fig. 21.1). If you typically run PowerPoint at 1024 x 768 or 1280 x 1024 screen resolution (which is often desirable), the video clip is roughly the size of a postage stamp. However, you can avoid this problem when running a presentation, by using the Media Player.

The PowerPoint for Windows 95 package includes an integrated video and audio editing tool, called the *Media Player*. You use the Media Player frequently in this chapter. The Media Player helps ease the process of playing video and sound clips during a presentation, as well as copying, cutting, and pasting frames or frame sequences of a video or parts of a sound file. In fact, for efficient placement of video and sound clips on your PowerPoint presentation, using the Media Player program is necessary. This chapter discusses how to use the Media Player to manipulate video and sound clips in your slides.

Note

When you load video clips as objects into PowerPoint, they normally have the file extension *.AVI (the Video for Windows file standard). Windows 95 has a set of software extensions, called *Video Compression CODECs* (for Coders-Decoders), that enable Video for Windows to run different video compression formats. The default set that comes with Windows includes RLE, Cinepak, Intel's Indeo 3.1 and 3.2, and Video 1. If you receive video clips that use any of these compression formats, Windows 95 automatically loads and plays them.

Apple's QuickTime for Windows is a good cross-platform playback program that dominates on the Macintosh. To use QuickTime, you must obtain it from Apple or a software distributor such as CompuServe.

To have a closer look at Windows 95's multimedia support, look through the Multimedia Properties sheet in the Windows Control Panel.

To begin with, we'll start with the basic process of placing video clips in your PowerPoint slides. There are two possible ways: to use the Insert, Movie command and the Insert, Object command. The big advantage to using Insert, Movie is a quicker and easier search for the correct file type.

VI

Advanced Techniques

Inserting Video Clips as Movies

Inserting video clips into any slide of your presentation is straightforward. To insert video clips and other objects, you must be in PowerPoint's Slides view. Follow these steps:

1. If you are not already in Slides view, choose <u>V</u>iew, <u>S</u>lides.

2. Select the slide that you want to insert the video clip into.

3. Choose <u>I</u>nsert, <u>M</u>ovie. The Insert Movie dialog box appears (see fig. 21.2).

   As you can see, this dialog box is the same one you use for many file loading operations. Only the title is different.

Fig. 21.2

Placing a video clip in a slide show by using the Insert Movie dialog box.

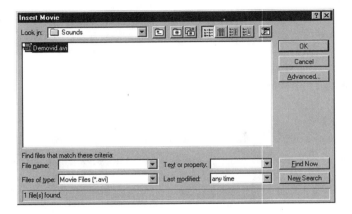

4. From the Look In drop-down list, choose the drive and folder in which your video files are located. The Files of <u>T</u>ype text box at the bottom automatically shows `Movie Files`.

   You also can initiate a File <u>N</u>ame and <u>F</u>ind Now operation if necessary. If you know it, type the name of the desired file in the File <u>N</u>ame text box, and click the <u>F</u>ind Now button.

5. Double-click the file icon.

   PowerPoint embeds the video clip into your slide.

Inserting Video Clips as Objects

Loading a video clip as an object is a slightly different process which ends up with the same result: placing a video clip in your slide. To load a video clip as an object, follow these steps:

1. Choose Insert, Object. The Insert Object dialog box appears as shown in figure 21.3.

   You can load an existing file or create a new media clip object. This example uses an existing file.

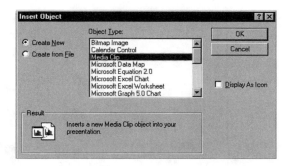

Fig. 21.3
Using the Insert Object dialog box to load a media clip.

2. In the Object Type list box, choose Media Clip.

3. Click the Create from File option button. The dialog box changes appearance to that shown in figure 21.4.

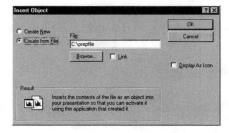

Fig. 21.4
Continuing the process of loading a video.

4. Because the dialog box probably will not automatically display the file you want (or even the right folder), choose the Browse button. The Browse dialog box appears, as shown in figure 21.5.

5. Select the drive, folder, and file you want, and choose OK.

   The Insert Object dialog box reappears, displaying the name of your selected video clip.

6. Choose OK or press Enter. The video clip is inserted into your slide. When you play the slide back, the clip appears in its own separate window, as shown in fig. 21.6.

VI

Advanced Techniques

Fig. 21.5
Browsing for a
video file during
the process of
loading it as an
Object.

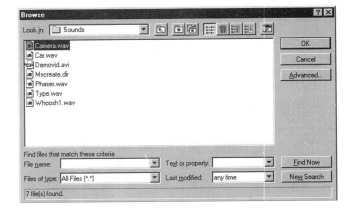

Fig. 21.6
Playing an
embedded video
clip in your
PowerPoint
presentation.

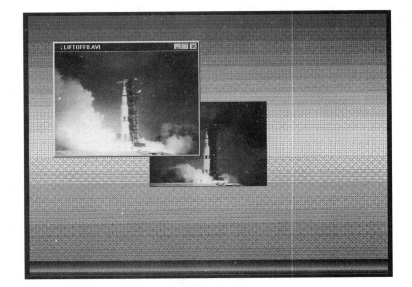

Note

You can link video clips in your presentation. The Insert Object dialog box shows a check box named Link (see fig. 21.4). Choosing Link ensures that if you edit the video in another application, the changes are maintained in the copy of the video in the presentation. Nonetheless, for most video applications in PowerPoint, you probably shouldn't link. Your video will still play during the presentation, but it will always play in a separate window, thus severely limiting your playback options. Also, linking requires that you bring the video clip as a separate file with the presentation. Therefore, for our exercises in this chapter, leave the Link check box disabled.

Note

You can display the video clip as an icon by choosing the Display as Icon check box in the Insert Object dialog box (see fig. 21.4). When you do this, you set the playback features exactly as you would if the video object were displayed as a picture on the slide, similar to what is shown in figure 21.1. However, this method gives you less control over the location of the video clip when it plays back during the slide show.

Creating a New Video Object

Choosing the Create New option in the Insert Object dialog box (shown in fig. 21.3) automatically opens the Media Player program. The PowerPoint slide on which the video is to be embedded still appears in the background. What's the difference between this and the previous example? Here, you use the Media Player to select the video clip for insertion. You do not actually record a new video—you are simply using the Media Player to bring the file in.

From the Media Player program, you must load the video file you want to insert into your slide. (Despite the deceptive "Create New" feature name, the Media Player does not record video from your computer. You use utilities provided with a video capture card for that purpose.) You may use one of two ways to place a video clip into the Media Player:

- Use the File, Open command
- Use the Insert Clip, 1 Video for Windows command

The advantage of using the Insert Clip, 1 Video for Windows command is that it automatically searches for only files that fit its description. Let's use that method:

1. From the Media Player, choose Insert Clip, 1 Video for Windows (see fig. 21.7).

   The Media Player's Open dialog box appears (see fig. 21.8). The Files of Type drop-down list displays the media file types the program can load.

VI

Advanced Techniques

Fig. 21.7
The Insert Clip menu where you can choose 1 Video for Windows.

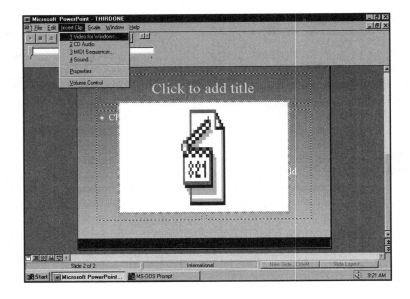

Fig. 21.8
The Media Player's Open dialog box, which is used to search for and load the desired video clip.

2. Locate the drive and directory that contain your video file, and choose the .AVI file you want to insert.

3. Choose Open or press Enter (or double-click the file name you want).

   The Media Player is still displayed, as shown in figure 21.9.

4. To embed the video object, simply click outside the clip to another area of the PowerPoint slide.

   The video clip is placed on the slide and can be resized and moved around the slide like any other object on-screen.

To preview the video, double-click it. A movie window pops up on-screen, as shown in fig. 21.10, and the clip runs.

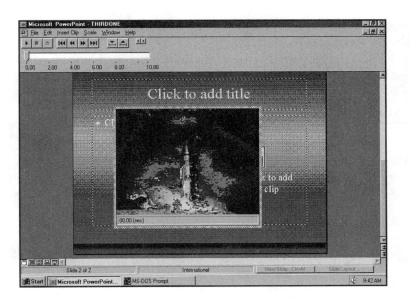

Fig. 21.9
The Media Player, after loading a video clip, displays the first frame of the video.

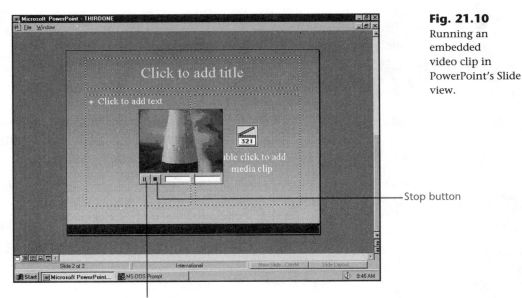

Fig. 21.10
Running an embedded video clip in PowerPoint's Slide view.

Stop button

Play/Pause button
(showing Pause)

VI

Advanced Techniques

Notice the Play and Pause buttons on the movie screen. At any time during the video playback, you can click the Pause button to stop the video. Clicking the Play button resumes the paused clip. When the clip is finished, its window disappears and you return to the PowerPoint screen.

Troubleshooting
My video or sound clip doesn't play during my presentation.
You very likely haven't brought the sound files (.WAV) or video files (.AVI) with you when you transported the presentation file. Make sure you bring all your multimedia objects with you when you deliver your presentation. The best way to do this is to always use the Pack and Go Wizard to make sure you have everything with you.

Inserting Video Clips with the Slide AutoLayout Feature

As you have seen in the preceding sections, you have several ways to load a video clip into a slide—but the video always plays in a separate window. What if you want to ensure that the video plays in a specific place on your slide, and not in a separate window? What if you want the video to play full-screen? Both of these options are easy with PowerPoint's (and Windows 95's) upgraded multimedia capabilities.

For a truly graceful integration of video into your slide, start by using the Slide AutoLayout feature that you saw in earlier chapters. With AutoLayouts, you easily can ensure that video clips are embedded properly and stay where they belong during the slide show and video playback events.

To create a new slide containing a Video Clip Object:

Tip
Press Ctrl+M to insert a new slide using AutoLayouts.

1. Choose Insert, New Slide.

   The New Slide dialog box appears showing its AutoLayouts (see fig. 21.11). Two AutoLayouts have special objects for video clip embedding—Text & Video Clip, and Video Clip & Text. The objects are the same except for a minor rearranging, and they both have a special *placeholder* for video clips. You may have to scroll the AutoLayout list to show the desired type.

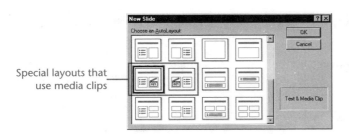

Fig. 21.11
Choosing a video clip-based Slide AutoLayout to help build a solid multimedia presentation.

Special layouts that use media clips

2. Choose either of the AutoLayouts that have video clips as part of their arrangement. (The dialog box shows the type of slide when you click it.) Double-click a slide thumbnail, or click a layout and choose OK, to insert a new slide that resembles fig. 21.12.

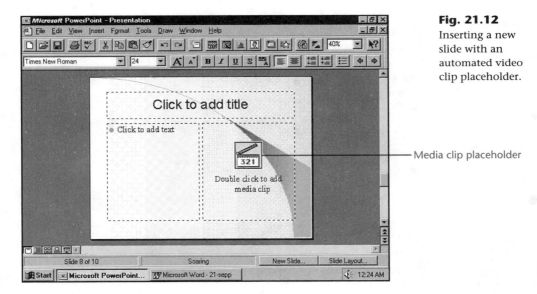

Fig. 21.12
Inserting a new slide with an automated video clip placeholder.

Media clip placeholder

> **Note**
>
> Remember from earlier chapters that placeholders are resizable, and you can copy and paste them to other slides. Placeholders also can trigger specific applications depending on the type of object the placeholder is designed for.

3. Double-click the media clip placeholder in the new slide to insert the video clip.

The Media Player program appears, taking over the PowerPoint screen (see fig. 21.13). Notice that the large icon representing the media clip is sized to fit in the placeholder.

Fig. 21.13
Getting ready to embed a video clip into the place-holder.

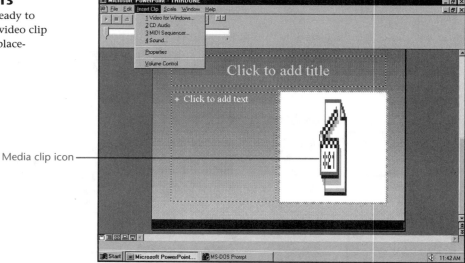

Media clip icon —

4. From the Media Player, choose <u>I</u>nsert Clip, <u>1</u> Video for Windows.

The Media Player's Open dialog box appears.

5. Locate the drive and directory that contains your video file and choose the .AVI file you want to insert.

6. Choose <u>O</u>pen or press Enter (or double-click the file name you want). The video clip is inserted directly into the placeholder (see fig. 21.14).

IMPORTANT: For now, keep the screen as it is, with the Media Player as the active application.

Fig. 21.14
Embedding a video clip into the placeholder, with the Media Player still active.

Although you set timings and sequences for multimedia events in PowerPoint, you must also use Media Player (actually a separate application) to control many aspects of multimedia objects in your presentation. The basic placement of the multimedia objects in your PowerPoint slide is not enough to guarantee the effect you want. You may need to use Media Player to help provide a cleaner and more sophisticated result.

At this point, the video clip is sized to fit inside the placeholder as a self-contained unit. Now you need to set some important playback parameters to make sure the video plays properly during the slide show. You set these parameters in three places: in the Media Player's Edit, Options and Insert Clip, Properties menu commands; and with PowerPoint's Animation Settings command. The following section explains these steps.

Tip
The Media Player is actually a separate program from PowerPoint, and controls many of your video playback settings.

Managing and Configuring Video Effects

The Media Player enables you to set a number of options for more efficient execution of video clips in a slide show. You can apply these procedures to objects that have already been embedded in a slide or when you place a new multimedia object. This section continues the exercise from the preceding section, where you embedded a new video clip. You should still be in the Media Player.

Tip
The Media Player controls many key video playback characteristics. The key menu commands are Edit, Options and Insert Clip, Properties.

VI

Advanced Techniques

To start with, an important set of video playback options is available under the Edit, Options menu command. Features offered there include automatic rewind and auto repeat of video clips, and several OLE options for playing videos with or without a border, a caption, a playback toolbar, and others. Other playback options are available under the Insert Clip, Properties command.

> **Note**
>
> To follow the exercise in this section, you need a media clip open in Media Player for a PowerPoint slide. See the preceding section for details.

To begin exploring the options in the Media Player, follow these steps:

1. Choose Edit, Options. The Options dialog box appears (see fig. 21.15).

Fig. 21.15
The Media Player's Edit, Options feature, showing the Options check boxes, as set for the current example.

A substantial number of playback options are offered:

■ Auto Rewind: Sets the video clip to rewind to the beginning after playback. (Rewind does not happen automatically, so you must select the check box.)

■ Auto Repeat: Sets the video clip to repeat in an endless loop until the user interrupts it with a mouse click during the presentation.

■ OLE Object: A selection of options for defining how the video clip appears when it is played back in the OLE client application (in this case, PowerPoint for Windows 95).

• Control Bar on Playback: Displays a control bar on the video clip, which offers the standard Play/Pause and Stop buttons pictured in figure 21.10. The user may click the control bar buttons during playback.

- Caption: Displays a caption showing the file name of the video clip during playback in the presentation. For most situations, this option may not be desirable, because it distracts from the actual content of the slide.

■ Border Around Object: Displays a window border around the video clip when it's played.

■ Play in Client Document: This option is highly recommended if you want a seamless appearance of the video clip in your PowerPoint slide show (or any OLE client application that uses video clips). Selecting this check box allows the direct playing of the clip in the slide show, without the appearance of the Media Player application during playback. This feature works best with video clips that are inside a PowerPoint media clip placeholder.

■ Dither Picture to VGA Colors: Resets the color palette of the video clip to the basic VGA 16-color palette under Windows. This is only necessary if you are running in 16-color VGA mode on your system. You do not need to click this option if you're running Windows in a 256-color or higher display mode. Also, the average video clip looks horrible in the 16-color VGA palette, so avoid this option unless you have no alternative.

2. For the current example, select the check boxes as they're shown in figure 21.15. Select only the Auto Repeat and Play in Client Document check boxes and then choose OK.

3. Choose Insert Clip, Properties to open the Video Properties dialog box (see fig. 21.16).

Fig. 21.16
The Video Properties dialog box, showing Media Player's other key set of video playback options.

4. In the Show Video In section, choose whether to run the video clip full screen or in a window during the slide show.

5. If you choose <u>W</u>indow, select a visual setting from the <u>W</u>indow drop-down list:

   ◼ <u>W</u>indow: The clip plays inside its own window on top of the slide. If you have selected to use a border around the video in the <u>E</u>dit, <u>O</u>ptions dialog box, a border will show around the video.

     • Original Size: Plays the video back on the PowerPoint slide at its original resolution. This is the default setting unless you have changed the default in the Display Properties of Windows control panel.

     • Double Original Size: The video clip is magnified by a factor of 2. This size is especially handy if you're running Windows at a higher resolution, because it eliminates the "postage stamp" visual effect that a small video window acquires at higher resolutions.

     • 1/16, 1/4, and 1/2 of Screen Size: Resizes the clip to precisely the dimensions given by each option.

     • Maximize: If you select this choice for a full-screen video clip display, the effect can be somewhat less pleasing, because the video becomes more grainy and loses some detail. Also, unless you have a *very* fast machine, playback will probably be less efficient and frames will drop. However, video card and video playback technologies are rapidly evolving, and full-screen high-resolution playback is likely just around the corner.

   ◼ <u>F</u>ull Screen: The clip automatically opens into a full-screen view and plays through its sequence. When the clip is done, it disappears and the slide show resumes.

6. When you're finished making your Video Properties selections, choose OK or press Enter. You return to the Media Player.

7. Click any open area of the slide to close the Player and return to PowerPoint. The video clip is embedded in the slide, with all the settings you just defined.

> **Note**
>
> You can adjust the volume settings for multimedia items, including any audio components of a video clip. See the later section "Controlling the Volume" for details on these options.

Controlling Video Playback with Animation Settings

Animation Settings is an upgraded feature in PowerPoint for Windows 95 that enables you to control the timing and triggering of multimedia elements in your presentation. The methods of setting playback values and events have completely changed from the last version of the program.

▶ See "Building Animation Effects," p. 647

You can easily apply timing to multimedia events in your presentation. Timing is an essential feature if you're not interested in clicking the mouse to control all aspects of your slide show when you deliver it. Animation Settings provides the final, crucial level of control to ensure smooth multimedia in your shows.

If you have followed the last two sections, you've embedded a video clip into your slide and defined many of its critical playback settings. Now you can add the finishing touches from within PowerPoint:

1. Click the video object you want to adjust.

2. Choose <u>T</u>ools, A<u>n</u>imation Settings.

   The Animation Settings dialog box appears (see fig. 21.17).

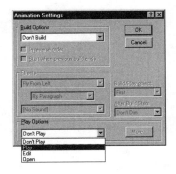

Fig. 21.17

You use the Animation Settings dialog box to define several important playback settings for your video clips.

VI

Advanced Techniques

> **Note**
>
> Although you can use Animation Settings to apply Builds to video clips as you do to text or graphic objects, we'll skip that matter for now and deal strictly with critical video playback settings.

▶ See "Applying Animation Builds to Graphic Objects," p. 655

3. From the <u>P</u>lay Options drop-down list at the bottom of the Animation Settings dialog box, select Play.

> **Caution**
>
> The video will not run successfully during a slide show unless you select Play. This step is very important.

4. After you select Play, the <u>M</u>ore button becomes active. Click it. The More Play Options dialog box appears, as shown in fig. 21.18.

Fig. 21.18
After choosing More in the Animation Settings dialog box, the More Play Options dialog box appears.

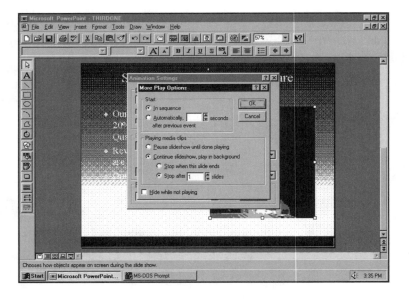

The next section describes how to use the options in this dialog box.

Specifying the Play Options

In the More Play Options dialog box, you plumb the deepest level of PowerPoint's multimedia event-triggering features. The dialog box is divided into two key sections and a check box:

■ Start: This section provides two option buttons that are mutually exclusive; if one is selected, the other is deselected. You can choose whether to run the video clip In Sequence or Automatically after an assigned number of seconds.

- In Sequence: This option forces the video clip to play in the sequence defined for the slide show. (You define that sequence using the Build/Play Object list described later in this section.) You determine the sequence *timing*, which is different, by rehearsing your slide show timings.

- Automatically, *n* Seconds after Previous Event: This option forces the video clip to play a specific number of seconds after the last event in the slide show.

  For example, if you have a build effect assigned to a text block in the slide, and you run that Build first, the video follows by the amount of time you specify. If the video is to play as the first event after the slide appears, you specify the number of seconds to pause before the video plays.

■ Playing Media Clips: This section provides a number of critical options for video event execution.

- Pause Slideshow Until Done Playing: The slide show stops while the video plays.

- Continue Slideshow, Play in Background: Mutually cancels out Pause Slideshow button; if selected, this option continues the slide show while the video clip runs in the background.

- Stop When This Slide Ends: Ends the video playback in background when the slide is passed for the next one.

- Stop after *n* Slides: User can set the number of slides in the presentation where the video plays in the background.

■ Hide While Not Playing: Hides the video clip until it executes. When finished, the clip disappears again.

You will need to experiment with these options to achieve the effect you like. For our example, follow these steps:

1. Choose the In Sequence option.

2. Choose the Continue Slideshow, Play in Background option. For now, ignore the Hide While Not Playing check box; you can use it later if you see fit. (These settings have a direct bearing on the rest of our example.)

3. Choose OK or press Enter.

   You return to the Animation Settings dialog box. Notice that the Build/Play Object list box is now active (see fig. 21.19).

Fig. 21.19

The Animation Settings dialog box, now showing the Build/Play Object drop-down list from which you select the build order for your video.

4. Click the Build/Play Object list and choose First for the video object.

   This selection ensures that the video clip starts running as soon as the slide appears. This tool is also important for setting the sequence of all your multimedia and Build events in the current slide.

5. Choose OK or press Enter to go back to PowerPoint. Choose View, Slide Show, and run or rehearse your slide show.

Fig. 21.19 is important because it illustrates how you must set your sequence of slide events for the best effect. In the preceding steps, you chose to select the In Sequence and Continue Slideshow, Play in Background options. By doing so, you can execute the video, running continuously in the background, and then execute a Build effect on any text or graphics you have (or any event you're considering doing). Figure 21.20 shows a video running while PowerPoint executes a typical word-by-word Build effect on a block of text.

After this grueling series of exercises, notice the following:

■ The video clip stays in rock-steady position, without playing in a separate window, and appears to be an organic part of the slide.

■ The video runs continuously in the background.

■ Performance, even on a middling 486-DX2 with enough memory (preferably 16M), is apt to be sufficient for such a demanding task.

Fig. 21.20
Running a video
and a Build
simultaneously
(yes, it's possible).

You have just scratched the surface of the possibilities when going through the last few exercise sequences. The few dialog boxes you have encountered seem to have countless permutations. And we haven't even discussed sound!

> **Note**
>
> If you have two or more multimedia objects in a slide, you can assign different timings to each so they trigger in sequence. You can set a sound bite to trigger two or three seconds after the start of a silent video clip, so the events run more or less simultaneously. Or, as noted earlier, a video and a Build can run more or less simultaneously.

Adding a Build to the Video Object

You can apply Builds to video objects. (Builds are simple animation effects, such as flying across the screen, that can be applied to PowerPoint screen objects.) For example, you can have your video clip fly across the screen to its assigned position and then play. Follow these steps:

1. Select the video object to which you want to apply a Build.

2. Choose Tools, Animation Settings.

   The Animation Settings dialog box appears (refer to figure 21.17).

3. The Build Options drop-down list offers two possible options for video clips: Build or Don't Build. The default is Don't Build. Choose Build from that list, and the Effects section is active.

VI

Advanced Techniques

4. If you want, select the Start When Previous Build Ends check box. Builds work the same way as for any other appropriate object.

5. Choose a preferred Build style from the drop-down list in the Effects section. Choices among several dozen include Fly from Top, Fly from Right, and many others.

▶ See "Adding Sounds to Build Effects," p. 652

6. If you want, choose a sound effect from the other drop-down list in the Effects section of the Animation Settings dialog. Default choices include Applause, Breaking Glass, and others, including the option to load your own. Note also that you can Dim video clips after they go through their motions.

7. Choose OK or press Enter to go back to PowerPoint. Choose View, Slide Show, and run or rehearse your slide show.

Important Notes about Using Multimedia Objects

You can find many products, disk-based and particularly on CD-ROM, that provide libraries of stock video footage and sound files you may use freely. When you are importing video clips and sounds, and especially if you're recording your own sound files and video, remember: don't use copyrighted material. You may be held liable for expensive royalties, or even face criminal prosecution, if you are caught using someone else's artistic or intellectual property to spice up your slide show.

Multimedia objects are a fun way to dress up a slide, but don't go overboard with them. Always be aware of your audience. Especially in Fortune 500 companies, be knowledgeable of the company's culture. Is it very conservative? Aerospace? Government contractor? Or a maverick, high-riding computer firm? The steps you've just explored are vital for ensuring that any multimedia effects you employ don't seem gratuitous, distracting, or annoying. Also consider the *size* of your audience and the place you will be delivering your talk. Is the delivery in an auditorium? Will everybody be able to *see* the video? If not, you may need to consider being more conservative with your video effects.

Presentation pacing is another serious issue. Many presenters severely limit their use of multimedia elements in their slide shows because the clips can be unpredictable. (See chapter 25 for a good example.) With careful attention to your playback and animation settings for both sound and video, using the steps in this entire video section and building on them, you will be able to master and deliver those elements effectively whenever the situation calls for it.

Adding Sound to Your Presentations

Sound can add a distinct mood to your presentation, but sound is somewhat touchier than video. Many dozens of sound cards are available, most of which enable the recording of voice, sound, and music at almost CD-quality levels. However, some products are more effective on paper than they are in the real world. Computer user groups resound with the complaints of hapless users trying to install a simple sound card. Sound is also resource-intensive. Sound recording (which is called *sampling*) can require as much as 10M of hard disk space for one minute of sound. Generally, for presentation purposes, such a sound file is impractical. It's more feasible to add lesser quality sound files, or sounds of a much shorter duration of time, to a presentation.

Understanding Sound Quality

Most higher-quality sound cards support six different recording formats, as described in table 21.1.

Table 21.1 Audio Quality Formats		
Card Size	**Frequency**	**Sound Quality**
8-bit	11 KHz	Poorest quality, smallest files
	22 KHz	Most sound files are in this format
	44 KHz	Good quality, best available for an 8-bit card
16-bit	11 KHz	Again: good quality
	22 KHz	Best compromise between CD-quality and sound files
	44 KHz	CD-quality sound, largest files
	48 KHz	Best sound quality available today Only dogs can tell the difference

Each format has mono and stereo versions, which affect file sizes as well. Typically, a stereo sound file is twice the size of a mono file if all other things are equal. Therefore, you have a grand total of twelve different audio file types available.

The 8-bit and 16-bit specifications refer to the kind of sound card and the number of bits allocated to each segment of sound recording; you can have an 8-bit or 16-bit ISA bus card, for example. The Sound Blaster Pro is an 8-bit sound card, and 16-bit ISA cards include the Pro Audio Spectrum, Sound Blaster 16, and Turtle Beach Multisound cards (just to name a few). Using 16-bit means substantially higher quality sound and substantially larger recorded files.

VI

Advanced Techniques

For most applications, you don't need to use CD-quality sound. 16-bit 22 KHz sound—or even 8-bit 22 KHz—is more than adequate for most presentation needs.

Tip

If you include high-quality sound files in your presentation, make sure the system on which you deliver the presentation has sound capabilities of its own.

The Media Player sound file standard has the *.WAV (for Waveform) file extension. As a default, these are the files you should seek for inclusion in your multimedia presentations. They are the current standard in the PC world, and under Windows.

Inserting Sound Files

You can add sound files to your presentation in two ways: by inserting the file as an object, or directly from the menu. The following example shows the menu method:

1. Choose Insert, Sound.

   The Insert Sound dialog box appears (see fig. 21.21).

Fig. 21.21
Loading a sound clip by using the Insert, Sound menu option.

Tip

Double-click an embedded sound object icon to hear the sound.

2. If necessary, choose the drive and folder where your sound files are located.

3. Select the sound file you want, then choose Insert.

   The sound file is loaded onto the PowerPoint slide, as shown in figure 21.22.

4. To test the sound, select the sound file icon. Then choose Edit, Wave Sound Object, Play.

   You can resize and move the sound object icon around the slide like any other object on-screen.

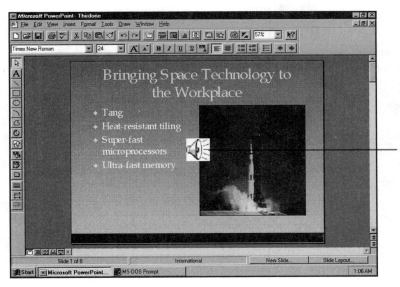

Fig. 21.22
Embedding a
sound file into a
PowerPoint slide.

Icon represents
embedded
sound file

> **Note**
>
> You also can load MIDI synthesizer sound files, which typically use the file extension
> .MID. Working with these files is very similar in all respects to working with sound
> and CD Audio files. Typically, MIDI synthesizer files are of specific MIDI instrument
> passages recorded in a sound file, or a custom composition.

Managing Sound Effects with the Media Player

The Media Player can act as an OLE server for sound files. You can use the
program to set up sound files for proper playback in PowerPoint slide shows
in much the same way you do for video. The options available are somewhat
less extensive than those for video, but they are still a deep source of features
for good management of sound-based multimedia effects.

> **Note**
>
> If you want to use the Media Player to manage your sound files and their playback,
> you *must* insert sounds as a Media Clip and choose the Create New option button. If
> you simply choose Insert, Sound, you cannot use the Media Player to change the
> sound object's playback settings.

VI

Advanced Techniques

For this new example, assume that you're inserting a brand-new sound file into the presentation. You can use the Media Player only for sound files when you're inserting a new Media Clip object from scratch or using a slide AutoLayout. The Media Player isn't available if you embed a sound file using the procedure from the earlier section, "Inserting Sound Files." For this reason, the process of using the Media Player for sound management is somewhat roundabout. When you work with sound under many circumstances, you will not actually use the Media Player, as you'll see later.

You will begin by using the Insert, Object command to start up the Media Player and load a sound file.

1. Display the PowerPoint slide in which you want to place a sound file, or click the Media Clip placeholder on an appropriate slide.

2. Choose Insert, Object.

3. In the Object Type list box, choose Media Clip.

4. Click the Create New option.

5. Choose OK or press Enter. The Media Player program takes over the PowerPoint screen, as shown in figure 21.23.

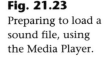

Fig. 21.23

Preparing to load a sound file, using the Media Player.

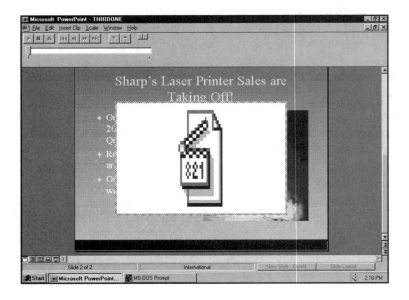

6. Notice, when you open the Insert Clip menu, that it has three good options for sound objects: CD Audio, MIDI Sequencer, and Sound. For the current exercise, choose Sound.

Troubleshooting

The Media Player does not let me load sound files! Also, the Sound Recorder doesn't work. Sounds do not play back in PowerPoint.

It's possible that you don't have a sound card installed in your system. What's the point? If you don't have a sound card, you will not be able to use the Media Player to load and work with sound files. Moreover, you will not be able to use the Sound Recorder applet to record sounds, or even play them at all on your system. If the Media Player does not show a Sound or MIDI option on its Insert Clip menu, the chances are very high that your sound card is either not working properly or not even installed in your system.

During installation of Windows 95, the operating system inspects your system to see if a sound card is in your machine. If so, usually it will automatically load the proper drivers and set itself up to use the sound card properly. If this hasn't happened, check to see if you have a compatible sound card or that you even have one at all. If not, or if you've forgotten to install it, put a sound card in the machine (when it's turned off, of course), and use the Add New Hardware program in the Windows 95 Control Panel to set it up.

The Media Player's Open dialog box appears.

7. Using the Open dialog box, locate the drive and folder that contains your sound file, and choose the sound file you want to insert.

8. Choose Open or press Enter (or double-click the file name you want). The sound clip is inserted directly into the placeholder (see fig. 21.24). For now, keep the screen as it is, with the Media Player as the active application. The next section describes the use of the Media Player to define some audio playback options.

VI

Advanced Techniques

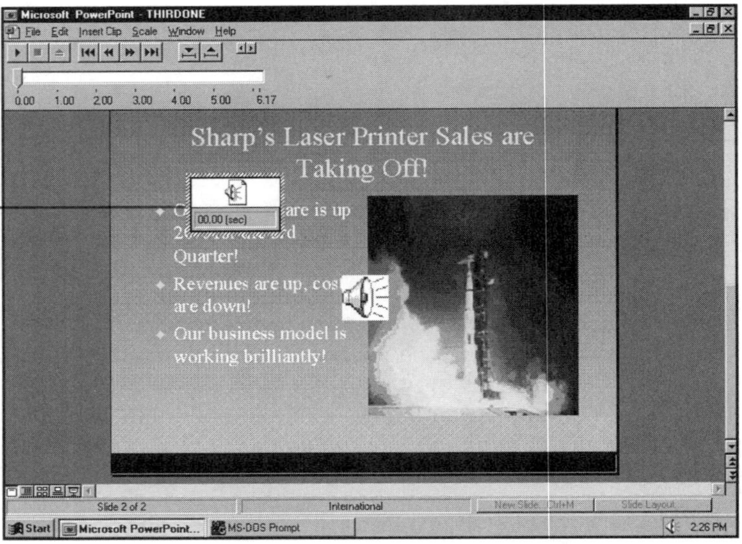

Fig. 21.24
Using the Media
Player to embed a
sound into the
placeholder.

Sound embedded
in placeholder

Using the Media Player to Set Audio Playback Options

As with videos, you need to set some playback parameters to make sure the sound file plays correctly and at the right time. Again, you set these parameters in three places: the Media Player's Edit, Options and Insert Clip, Properties menu commands; and PowerPoint's Animation Settings command. If you have worked with videos as discussed earlier in this chapter, this procedure should look familiar. It's an example of how PowerPoint has made strides in promoting consistency throughout the program. Follow these steps to set sound playback settings using the Media Player:

1. In the Media Player, choose Edit, Options.

   The Options dialog box appears (see fig. 21.25).

Fig. 21.25
Using the Media
Player's playback
Options check
boxes, set as for
our example.

The dialog box contains these audio playback options:

- Auto Rewind: Sets the sound to rewind to the beginning after playback (rewind is not automatic, so you must select the check box to rewind).

- Auto Repeat: Sets the sound to repeat in an endless loop until the user interrupts it with a mouse click during the presentation. (Be careful—continuous repeat can be very annoying.)

- OLE Object: A dialog box section containing options for defining how you can interact with the clip when it is played back in the OLE client application (in this case, PowerPoint for Windows 95).

  - Control Bar on Playback: Displays a control bar on the sound file icon, which offers Play/Pause and Stop buttons you can click during sound playback.

  - Caption: Displays a caption showing the name of the sound file during playback in the presentation. For most situations, a caption may not be desirable, because it distracts from the actual content of the slide.

- Border Around Object: Displays a window border around the sound clip and its control bar when it's played. Deselecting this option does not affect the playing of the clip, but a border is not added during playback.

- Play in Client Document: This option is highly recommended if you want a seamless appearance of the audio clip in your PowerPoint slide show (or any OLE client application that uses sound files). Selecting this check box allows the direct playing of the clip in the slide show, without the appearance of the Media Player application during playback. This feature works best with sound files that are inside a PowerPoint media clip placeholder.

2. For the current example, select the check boxes as they're shown in figure 21.25. Select the Auto Rewind, Control Bar on Playback, Border Around Object, and Play in Client Document check boxes, and leave the Caption. Disable the Auto Repeat check box. Choose OK.

3. Choose Insert Clip, Properties. Figure 21.26 shows you what you will see.

Fig. 21.26
You can set the amount of memory a single sound clip will use with the Insert Clip, Properties command.

Slider bar for audio
buffer memory

4. The MCI Waveform Driver Setup dialog box is a simple device that allows you to adjust memory use settings for audio clips.

   The slider bar enables you to set the amount of memory for "buffering the sound data." If you're using a lengthy sound, adding more buffer memory ensures efficient playback during a slide show. Otherwise, PowerPoint may have to access the hard disk during playback.

5. Choose OK or press Enter to remove the dialog box and return to the Media Player.

Controlling the Volume

The Media Player offers volume settings for multimedia items, including any audio components of a slide show. Follow these steps to adjust volume:

1. Choose Insert Clip, Volume Control. Figure 21.27 shows the Volume Control dialog box.

Fig. 21.27
Using the Volume Control dialog box to set volume levels for your sound clip.

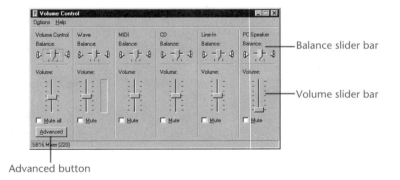

Balance slider bar

Volume slider bar

Advanced button

The slider bars in the Volume Control section on the far left of the dialog box apply to audio as well as video, or any other multimedia data type.

2. If you want, adjust the volume and/or balance settings.

3. If desired, choose the <u>A</u>dvanced button below the slider bars to adjust the treble and bass functions.

   The <u>M</u>ute All button enables you to shut off all sounds that would otherwise play in the current PowerPoint slide. Since you're working with a sound clip in this example, this probably won't be necessary.

4. From Volume Control's O<u>p</u>tions menu, choose E<u>x</u>it.

5. Click any open area of the slide to close the Media Player and return to PowerPoint. The sound file is embedded in the slide, with all the settings you just defined.

The next step is to employ Animation Settings to put the sound into its proper place in the slide event sequence.

Controlling Sound Playback with Animation Settings

As you did earlier with video, you now use the Animation Settings command to set sound playback settings and their place in the current slide's event sequence:

1. On the slide, select the sound clip.

2. Choose <u>T</u>ools, A<u>n</u>imation Settings.

   The Animation Settings dialog box appears (see fig. 21.28).

Fig. 21.28
Using the Animation Settings feature to manage sound playback in your presentation.

VI

Advanced Techniques

3. From the <u>P</u>lay Options drop-down list at the bottom, select Play (as shown in fig. 21.28).

   The sound will not play during the slide show unless you follow this step.

> **Note**
>
> Applying Builds to sound clips is perfectly legal and possible. But Builds have no effect on how the sound plays, and because sound is an audible rather than a visual experience, Builds on sound files are redundant, unnecessary, and a waste of machine resources. Don't bother with the Build Options when working with sounds.

4. Select a placement in the Build/Play Object list. This drop-down list shows numeric places (First, Second, Third, Fourth...) of all the events you have placed in the current slide. Every time you add a new event the list gets longer. By clicking an embedded object, choosing Tools Animation Settings, and selecting from this list, you can interchangeably assign event sequence positions to each object *in the current slide*. You may need to experiment with positions to get the effect you want.

5. After you select Play to enable sound playback during a slide show, the More button becomes active. Click it. For sounds, the More Play Options dialog box appears (see fig. 21.29).

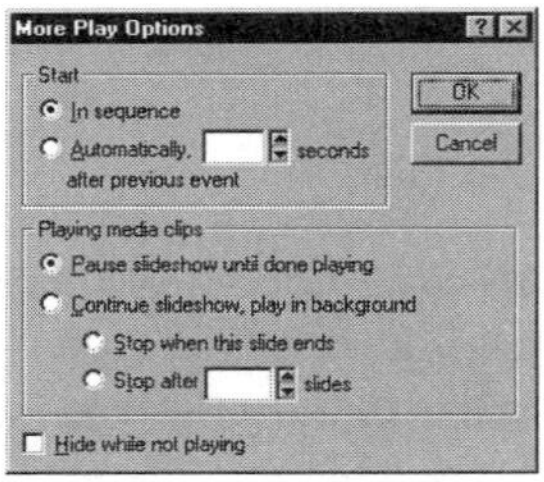

Fig. 21.29

Using the Animation Settings' More Play Options dialog box to determine more sound playback options. This set of options is important for desirable sound playback.

As you learned in the previous video sections of this chapter, the More Play Options dialog box contains two key sections and a check box:

■ Start: This section provides two option buttons that are mutually exclusive; if one is selected, the other is automatically deselected. You can choose whether to run the sound file In Sequence, or Automatically after an assigned number of seconds.

- In Sequence: Selecting this option forces the sound file to play in the sequence defined for the slide show. (You define that sequence using the Build/Play Object list described in step 4.) You determine the sequence timing, on the other hand, by rehearsing your slide show timings.

- Automatically, n Seconds after Previous Event: This option forces the sound file to play a specific number of seconds after the last event in the slide show. For example, if you have a Build effect assigned to a text block in the slide, and you run that Build first, the sound follows by the amount of time you specify. If the sound is to play as the first event after the slide appears, you specify the number of seconds of an apparent pause before it plays.

■ Playing Media Clips: This section provides a number of critical options for video event execution:

- Pause Slideshow Until Done Playing: The slide show stops while the sound file plays. Normally, this option isn't necessary or even a good idea. Sounds are meant to augment and add atmosphere to a slide show—not stop it in its tracks.

- Continue Slideshow, Play in Background: Mutually cancels out Pause Slideshow option; if selected, this option continues the slide show while the sound clip runs in the background.

- Stop When This Slide Ends: Ends the sound playback in background when the slide is passed for the next one.

- Stop After n Slides: User can set the number of slides in the presentation where the sound file plays in the background.

■ Hide While Not Playing: Hides the sound file until it executes. When finished, the file disappears again.

6. You may need to experiment with these options to get the effect you want. For our example, select In Sequence and Continue Slideshow, Play in Background. For now, ignore the Hide While Not Playing check box; you can use it later if you want.

7. Choose OK or press Enter to return to the Animation Settings dialog box.

8. Click outside the sound object to return to PowerPoint and embed the object into the slide with its new settings.

9. Run the slide show and check the sequence and timings.

Tip

Typically, you should set sounds to play in the background while other slide events occur. This will limit their impact on system resources, improve efficiency, and preserve the flow of your presentation.

VI

Advanced Techniques

Managing Your Sound Clips by Using the Sound Recorder

You can work with sound files in another easy way. Assume that you use the Insert, Sound command rather than the Insert, Object, Create New command sequence, as you did at the beginning of this discussion on sound files.

What happens? You use a familiar dialog box to load a sound file into the program, and the sound file is inserted as an object into the slide. The sound file shows up as an icon, similar to fig. 21.22. Double-click the icon, and the sound plays. From there, you can perform a wide number of operations on the sound.

Tip
You can record a custom sound by using the Sound Recorder editing utility for the currently selected sound object on a slide.

You can edit the sound file or change it by selecting the icon and choosing Edit, Wave Sound Object, Edit.

You then see the Sound Recorder editing utility, as shown in fig. 21.30. (This sequence does not occur if you have embedded a sound clip in a Media Clip placeholder with the Media player, as you did earlier. The sequence is then Edit, Media Clip Object, Edit, and the Media Player appears. If it's a MIDI Sequence, the command sequence is Edit, MIDI Sequence, then Edit.)

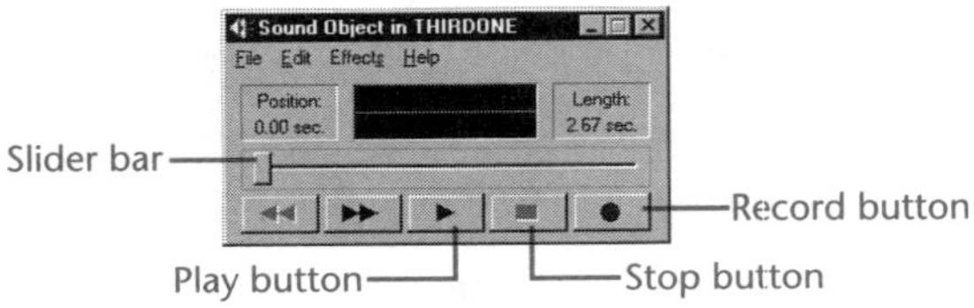

Fig. 21.30
The Sound Recorder editing utility, which allows you to perform rudimentary cuts, pastes and deletes on sound files.

If you want to substitute an existing sound file for the current one, choose Edit, Insert File from the Sound Object utility menu. A familiar Insert File dialog box appears, and you can choose a new file from the appropriate drive and directory. Choose Open or press Enter to replace the old sound with the new one.

Troubleshooting

Why can't I use Media Player to edit my sound object?

Editing techniques may be confusing, because you have two different ways to place a sound file in a PowerPoint slide. If you use the Insert, Object command and then Create New, you can use the Media Player on that sound object at any time. However, if you place a sound file quickly using Insert, Sound, the only facility you can use on the embedded sound file is the Sound Object editing utility.

Recording New Sounds

You can record a new sound in the Sound Recorder editing utility if you have a microphone hooked up to your sound card and your drivers are set up properly in Windows 95. Just click the Record button (shown in fig. 21.30) to record the sound directly into the currently selected sound object in the slide. The existing sound is completely erased from the slide (but not the original file).

Combining Sounds

You can use the Sound Recorder to combine two or more sound effects into the same sound object, making for some unexpected and possibly humorous effects. Follow these steps:

1. In Sound Recorder, play the existing sound, or scroll its slider bar, to the point in the sound clip where you want to put the new sound (without erasing the existing one).

2. Choose Edit, Mix with File. A familiar Mix with File dialog box appears, and you can choose another file from the appropriate drive and directory.

3. Choose Open or press Enter and the new sound is mixed in with the old one at the place specified in step 1.

4. Play the sound and check it out. The mix is usually seamless, with no discernible pause.

Changing the Format of a Sound File

When you combine sounds, you can create a much larger sound file than the original. You can improve this by using another of PowerPoint's (and Windows 95's) new features: change a sound file's format. You can convert sound files to various formats, including higher and lower frequencies, mono to stereo and vice versa, and 4-bit, 8-bit, and 16-bit.

To perform a sound file conversion:

1. In the Sound Recorder, choose File, Properties in the Sound Recorder utility.

   The Properties for Sound dialog box appears (see fig. 21.31). This dialog box shows you the basic information about your sound file:

   ■ How much memory the file occupies (the current example in fig. 21.31 is over 1M)

Tip

Keep track of the resources any multimedia event uses, so the whole show isn't bogged down by that special effect. If a sound uses too many resources, you can convert it to a less demanding format.

VI

Advanced Techniques

■ Copyright information (always a relevant issue)

■ Time length in seconds

■ Audio format

Audio format is closely related to the information presented earlier in table 21.1. In the example, the format is PCM 22,050 Hz (22 KHz) 16-bit stereo. This quality is very good and more than sufficient for the average presentation, but the file is a bit large.

Fig. 21.31

Using the Properties for Sound dialog box in the Sound Recorder to inspect the file format (frequency, size, quality).

The Choose From list enables the recording and playback conversion formats supported by your sound card

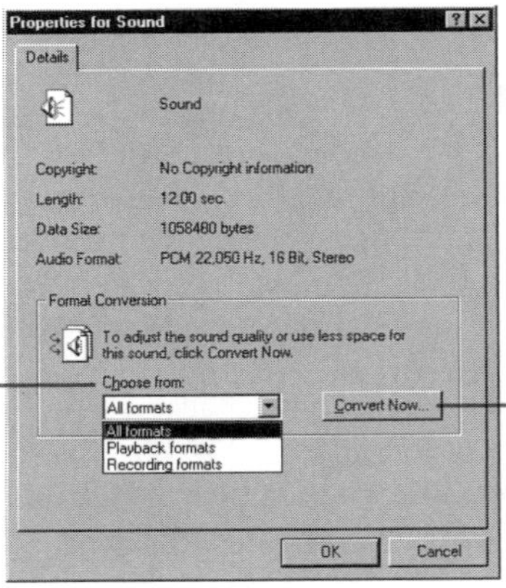

Click the Convert Now button to open the format conversion feature

2. Note the Choose from drop-down list shown in fig. 21.31. It determines what kind of sound formats you convert between. In turn, those formats are decided by the power of your sound card. The list choices are:

■ All formats: Displays all available formats, both recording and playback, supported by your sound card.

■ Recording formats: enables conversion of the sound file between the various recording formats supported by your sound card.

■ Playback formats: enables conversion of the sound file between the various playback formats supported by your sound card. Frequently, these may not be the same as Recording formats, depending on your sound card.

3. For the current exercise, choose All Formats from the Choose from drop-down list.

4. Choose the Convert Now button on the Properties for Sound dialog box to convert an existing sound file to any other audio quality format.

For example, if you want to convert a 22 KHz 16-bit stereo sound clip to 11 KHz 8-bit mono, choose this button. (The process doesn't always work quite as well in reverse, but it can significantly improve a poor sound bite.) When you choose the Convert Now button, the Sound Selection dialog box appears, as shown in fig. 21.32.

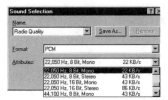

Fig. 21.32
You use the Sound Selection dialog box to convert between audio quality formats.

The various Sound Selection settings are briefly described in this list:

■ Name: This drop-down list provides convenient and generic quality selections in the Attributes drop-down list (described below): Telephone Quality, Radio Quality, and CD Quality. For example, Telephone Quality automatically displays an 11 KHz, 8-bit Mono setting. Radio Quality provides an automatic 22 KHz, 8-bit Mono setting. CD Quality provides an automatic 44 KHz, 16-bit Stereo setting. Select any of these three if you know the basic settings you want but don't have time to experiment.

■ Format: This drop-down list provides a set of audio format schemes that also affect the quality of the sound effect. The formats are CCITT A-Law, CCITT u-Law, DSP Group TrueSpeech, GSM 6.10, IMA ADPCM, Microsoft ADPCM, and PCM. All formats define industry standards for various types and qualities of sound, and describing each specific type is far beyond the scope of this book. (Consult your Windows 95 user manual for more details on this issue.) Each choice provides a set of Attributes in turn; for example, if you select PCM, you have the widest selection of sound quality settings, from 8 to 44 KHz and so on. If you select Microsoft ADPCM, all sounds will be converted to 4-bit regardless of the frequency (11, 22, or 44 KHz).

■ Attributes: This section provides the raw quality ratings by which you can gauge your conversion. Table 21.1 provides a partial list.

VI

Advanced Techniques

To convert your sound file, select from the drop-down lists for the three settings. (This area can take a great deal of experimenting—that's why the Name list can be handy.) Choose OK or press Enter to perform the conversion and return to the Sound Object utility. Play the sound to hear the effects of the conversion.

As you can see, there's more to sound clips than just using the Media Player or animation settings to set the sounds up. You can perform a lot of editing and conversion chores, such as converting demanding high-quality sound clips to lower-quality formats to save space and resources. These steps play an important part in building your multimedia presentation into a usable result.

> **Note**
>
> You can make use of quite a few mixing commands in the Effects menu of the Sound Recorder utility. You can increase and decrease speed, add echo, and reverse the sound sequence. Using the Edit, Audio Properties command, you can choose the customize button to set the default audio quality of your recordings with the same collection of specifications that you use to convert sound files (PCM, ADPCM, 16-bit 22 KHz, and so on). Defining a standard quality setting for your recordings and playbacks of all your sound objects enforces consistency and gives you a clear notion of what to expect from your sounds.

Adding a CD Audio Soundtrack

If you have a CD-ROM in your notebook computer or in the desktop machine that you're using for presentation delivery, you can use that CD drive to play a musical soundtrack from any music CD you want. The process is easy and bears considerable resemblance to the procedures you've seen in every section of this chapter, including using Animation Settings and the Media Player.

> **Note**
>
> A good place to begin a CD Audio soundtrack is on the first slide of your presentation, and at logical starting points for different phases of your presentation. Tailor the timing of your soundtrack to your audience and to the subject matter of your show. You can embed multiple CD Audio objects, each with a different song. Just make sure you have the right CD discs in the CD-ROM drive when you make use of this feature.

This final example illustrates the versatility of PowerPoint for Windows 95's multimedia support, buttressed by the major advances in Windows 95. Let's step through the entire process:

1. Place the music CD in a properly installed and working CD-ROM drive in your computer.

2. Choose Insert, Object.

3. In the Object Type list box, choose Media Clip.

4. Choose the Create New option.

5. Choose OK or press Enter. The Media Player program takes over the PowerPoint screen.

6. From the Insert Clip menu, you have three options for sound objects: CD Audio, MIDI Sequencer, and Sound.

   For the current exercise, choose CD Audio.

   An Open dialog box does not appear in this case. Instead, the Media Player's toolbar is activated, and the slider bar acquires the track-to-track sequence of the music CD, as shown in figure 21.33.

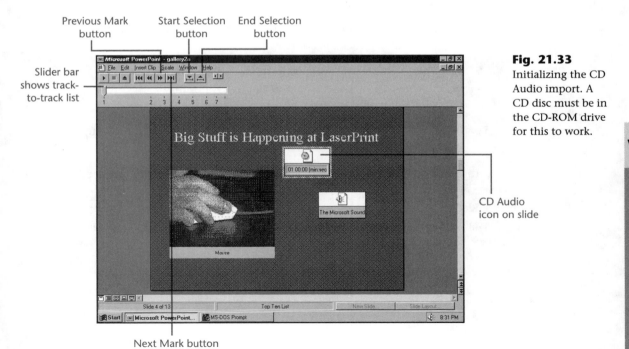

Previous Mark button

Start Selection button

End Selection button

Slider bar shows track-to-track list

Next Mark button

Fig. 21.33
Initializing the CD Audio import. A CD disc must be in the CD-ROM drive for this to work.

CD Audio icon on slide

VI

Advanced Techniques

You select the CD track or tracks you want to play through the attached speakers using the tools on the Media Player toolbar:

- The Next Mark button lets you fast-forward to the beginning of each successive track on the CD.

- The Previous Mark button does the same for successive previous tracks.

- You must use the Begin Selection and End Selection buttons for a successful selection of the music you want; you can't simply click and select CD tracks with the mouse.

> **Note**
>
> Bear in mind that you may need to attach the speakers directly to the headphone jack of the CD-ROM drive. This isn't always the case, particularly with a well-integrated sound card/CD-ROM package. Experiment to find the proper setup.

7. Click the Next Mark button to place the slider bar at the beginning of the first track you want.

8. Click the Start Selection button. A small arrowhead marks the beginning of your CD track selection.

9. Click the Next Mark button again to move the slider bar forward to the beginning of the next track. Do so again if you want to select more than one sequential track.

10. Click the End Selection button. A blue bar appears on the slider bar, indicating that one or more tracks are selected.

At this point, you've basically done the job. There is no process of embedding or copying the CD Audio tracks to the presentation. Instead, an object embedded in the current slide contains the playback settings and a call to the installed CD disc. However, you can make some more adjustments for playback in the Media Player.

1. Choose Insert Clip, Volume Control. Figure 21.34 shows the Volume Control dialog box.

Slider bar for headphone volume control

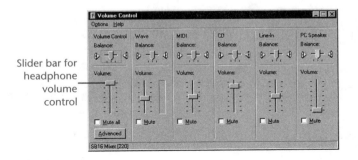

Fig. 21.34
Using the Media Player's Volume Control dialog box to set volume levels for the CD soundtrack.

2. Use the slider bar in the Volume Control section to adjust your CD Audio volume for speakers connected to a headphone jack.

3. If you want, adjust the volume and/or balance settings in other sections, particularly the CD section. You may need to experiment with the settings to find the right adjustments.

4. Choose Options, Exit.

5. In the Media Player, choose Edit, Options.

   The Options dialog box appears (see fig. 21.35). The set of CD Audio playback options is the same as the sound file options discussed earlier in "Using the Media Player to Set Audio Playback Options."

Fig. 21.35
Select CD Audio options using the Options dialog box, just as you do for sound files.

VI

Advanced Techniques

6. For the current example, select the check boxes as they're shown in figure 21.35. Select Auto Rewind, Control Bar on Playback, Border Around Object, and Play in Client Document, and leave the Caption.

7. Choose OK or press Enter. Then click the slide to embed the CD Audio object with your playback settings.

8. Now, as with the earlier sections on video and sound files, you can use the Animation Settings command to define the CD Audio object's place in the current slide's event sequence. On the slide, select the CD Audio icon.

9. Choose Tools, Animation Settings.

   The Animation Settings dialog box appears.

10. From the Play Options drop-down list at the bottom, select Play (again see fig. 21.17).

    The CD Audio will not play during the slide show unless you follow this step.

11. Select a placement in the Build/Play Object list. This option works the same way for CD Audio as for other multimedia objects discussed earlier in the chapter.

12. After you select Play to enable CD soundtrack playback during a slide show, the More button becomes active. Click it. For sounds, the More Play Options dialog box appears. (For details on these options, see the earlier section "Controlling Sound Playback with Animation Settings.")

Tip

Typically, you set CD Audio to play as a running soundtrack in the background while other slide events occur.

13. For our example, select In Sequence and Continue Slideshow, Play in Background. For now, ignore the Hide While Not Playing check box; you can always use it later.

14. Choose OK or press Enter to return to the Animation Settings dialog box.

15. Choose OK or press Enter. You're done! Run the slide show and check out the effect of the soundtrack.

Troubleshooting

Why isn't my CD soundtrack playing?

A number of reasons can cause a soundtrack not to play. First, remember that the CD Audio soundtrack you set up for your slide show is not actually embedded in the presentation file. Instead, a pointer to the CD-ROM drive is embedded in the slide that tells the program what tracks to play, what drive the CD is located in, and other things. You may not have the right music CD in the drive. Or you may have accidentally deleted the embedded CD Audio object in the slide.

If you need to bring the presentation and the music CD to another place and another machine, the other machine's drive assignments may be different from yours. If so, the CD Audio object may not be able to find the right drive and you'll need to set it up again. Finally, your playback or animation settings may be wrong somewhere. Make sure that the Play Options drop-down list in the Animation Settings dialog box is set to Play, and that the music is set to play through as many slides as you want.

Finally, there's another potential problem, which I myself have run into. When you insert a CD disc in the CD-ROM drive, Windows 95 may automatically run a CD music utility and start playing the darn music off the CD! If this happens, you will not be able to access a CD Audio option from the Media Player's Insert Clip menu. If this happens to you, simply close the Windows 95 CD music utility and you should be able to access the disc through the Media Player. (I scratched my head about this one. It's too obvious for smart people to figure out.)

Multimedia is still an inexact science on the PC. Windows 95, however, represents a big step forward. Though it's still a good idea to stick to the most standard hardware and software you can use for multimedia in your presentations, Windows 95 raises the bar and provides PC users some much-needed relief and performance improvements. Primarily because of this, PowerPoint's support for multimedia is also drastically improved. Nonetheless, some experimenting with the myriad features described in this section will help you master the techniques to make your presentations come alive.

This isn't the last you'll see of sound effects in PowerPoint. Chapter 22, "Advanced Presentation Management," offers several more uses of sound in your presentations. Build and animation effects can have sounds attached to them. Transitions can too. Those features are straightforward to use, and they're explored in the next chapter. ❖

VI

Advanced Techniques

Advanced Presentation Management

by Rich Grace

No presentation, particularly if it includes special multimedia elements such as video and audio clips, is complete without a set timing structure that enables the user to integrate those various elements without unwanted foul-ups during the actual show. Even if you have never conducted a public talk in your life, PowerPoint's transition, animation, and timing features can help you appear like David Copperfield. For effective presentation management, you need to understand and use PowerPoint's rehearsal features. Delivering an effective show is a discipline in itself, and PowerPoint for Windows 95 provides a wider selection of tools than ever before to help you build that skill.

PowerPoint for Windows 95 offers a greatly expanded selection of special effects that can be added to slide shows. Animation build effects can now be added to any drawn object in PowerPoint. Imported graphics, video clip thumbnails, and slide titles can take advantage of build effects. Animations, build effects, and transitions between slides can have sound effects added to them with the click of a mouse. In another area, rehearsal of timings for slide shows has been made easier and more precise than ever. A special Interactive Settings feature expands PowerPoint's functionality into new and unexpected realms.

In this chapter, you learn how to

- Create transitions between slides
- Add build effects to slides
- Use build effects for animations

- Rehearse and set timings for events in your presentation

- Use PowerPoint's new Interactive Settings to trigger branches and events

- Use PowerPoint's new presentation management features, including the Meeting Minder and the Slide Navigator

Controlling Slide Transition

When you run a slide show, it's quite simple to flip from one slide to the next on-screen—it's the typical 35mm slide show metaphor. It's just as easy, however, to provide graceful transitions between slides that add a more sophisticated effect. Transition styles can be assigned for any or all slides in your presentation with a few mouse clicks.

A *transition style* is the style in which a slide appears and disappears in an on-screen presentation. The concept is analogous to a slow fade or a "peeling" of the screen during a movie or a fancy video effect applied to a screen message during a football game. It's a quick segue to the next slide in your presentation. PowerPoint 95 offers 46 different transition styles that can be applied to any slide in your presentation. Styles include:

- Vertical and horizontal blinds, in which segments of the slide are revealed to the viewer

- Box In and Box Out, in which the information on the next slide appears to "implode" or "explode" onto the screen

- Checkerboard Across and Checkerboard Down, in which the contents of the next slide appear in a checkerboard pattern

- Cover Left, Up, Down, Left-Up, Right-Up, Left-Down, and Right-Down, in which the slide is assigned a direction from which it appears to be plopped down on top of the previous one

There are, of course, many more.

When you rehearse a presentation, you're actually in the process of setting the timing for all the events in your presentation—when each slide appears, when text points in a list appear on-screen, and so on. Effective use of timing in a presentation, particularly in a long and complex one, is a vital tool in preventing your audience from losing interest in your ideas. It's another valuable tool for effective management of the extensive multimedia elements and techniques that we discussed in the preceding chapter.

Knowing the timing of your slide show also points out the importance of the other parts of your presentation—the outlines, speaker's notes, and handouts that are discussed in Chapters 7 and 8. With a few extra minutes of preparation, all these tools can be used to deliver your message intelligently and cogently.

Setting a Transition Style

You can assign a transition to a slide in any PowerPoint view: Slides view, Notes Pages, Outline, and in the Slide Sorter (see fig. 22.1). Although all views offer the same method for assigning effects, the Slide Sorter has advantages because its thumbnail display of all the slides enables you to keep track of all the slides to which you have assigned effects, and to interact with the entire presentation in a way that other views don't permit. Slides can be dragged and dropped in the Sorter to a different order, for example. The Sorter also has its own special toolbar, called (naturally) the *Slide Sorter toolbar*. You will use the Slide Sorter view to assign transition effects for the examples in this chapter.

Another advantage of using the Slide Sorter to apply transitions and other effects is its display of small Transition icons underneath each slide thumbnail indicating when a transition effect has been applied to a selected slide. The icons do not appear if a slide has not had an effect applied to it.

To assign transitions to slides in Slide Sorter view, follow these steps:

1. Open the desired presentation in PowerPoint.

2. Choose <u>V</u>iew, Sli<u>d</u>e Sorter, or click the Slide Sorter View button.

   The Slide Sorter appears, as in figure 22.1.

3. Click once on the slide that you want to assign a transition.

   For a fast transition assignment, you can choose an effect from the Transition drop-down list. A transition icon appears below the chosen slide.

4. Click the Slide Transition button on the Slide Sorter toolbar to display the Slide Transition dialog box, as shown in figure 22.2.

Tip
Slide transitions can be assigned in any PowerPoint View mode.

Tip
Hold the Shift key and click on several slides to assign a transition to all of them at one time.

VI

Advanced Techniques

Fig. 22.1
Displaying the Slide Sorter for adding transitions and other features.

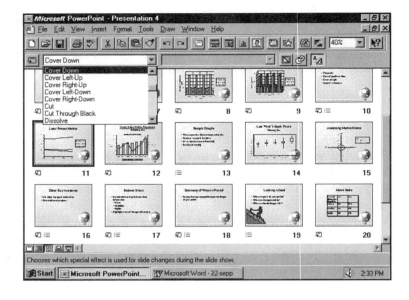

Fig. 22.2
The Slide Transition dialog box.

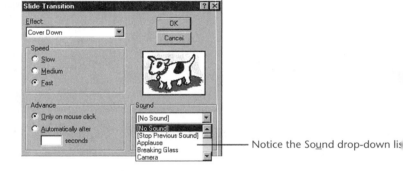

Notice the Sound drop-down lis

5. Choose the transition options you want.

6. Choose OK or press Enter. The effect will be applied to the slide.

Remember: As on the Slide Sorter toolbar, a transition effect can be applied from the drop-down list in the Slide Transition dialog box shown in figure 22.2. The toolbar list makes it fast and easy, but fewer options are offered. The dialog box must be used for a wider selection of transition options.

Tip
Hold the Shift key and click on several slides to assign a transition to all of them at one time.

Setting Transition Timing

An advantage of using the Slide Transition dialog box in the Slide Sorter or in Slide view is that you can assign speeds and specific timings to transitions.

This can be done with slides that already have assigned transitions, or with newly assigned ones.

To set the transition timing for a slide, follow these steps:

1. To assign a different speed to your transition, click on either the <u>S</u>low, <u>M</u>edium, or <u>F</u>ast option button in the Speed section of the Slide Transition dialog box. These three option buttons simply affect how quickly the transition effect is executed when the slide appears during the slide show.

2. Slides can be advanced with a mouse click, or you can set the slide to advance automatically after a specified time. Select an option for advancing your slides:

   - If you want the slide transition to advance on your prompting, click the <u>O</u>nly on Mouse Click option button.

   - To set a custom slide timing, click on the <u>A</u>utomatically After ? Seconds option button and enter the desired number, that represents the length in seconds before the next slide appears, in the text box. The timing, in seconds, depends heavily on your intentions of how you will deliver the slide show. Also bear in mind that using this setting may conflict with settings created from rehearsing your slide show.

Adding Sounds to Transitions

PowerPoint 95 offers the capability to attach sound effects to transitions in your slide show. The process is very straightforward, and its start is shown in figure 22.2.

1. Click the So<u>u</u>nd drop-down list in the Slide Transition dialog box. You can choose a default sound that's already on the list, or you can go find another one by choosing Other Sound.

   The Add Sound dialog box appears:

2. The program will automatically look for *.AVI files or any sound file that is compatible with the multimedia sound setup under Windows. You can search for them in the same way you do for files. Choose a file from the desired drive and folder, and choose OK or press Enter.

   The sound is attached to the transition for the slide(s), and will automatically play during the slide show.

VI

Advanced Techniques

Fig. 22.3
The Add Sound
dialog box.

Caution

The check box option titled Loop until Next Sound will play the selected sound
continuously until you initiate the next action in the slide show. This could prove
extremely annoying to you and your audience. Choose your sound effects carefully.

Hiding Slides in a Presentation

PowerPoint 95 offers the capability to hide one or more slides in a presentation. *Hidden slides* are especially useful if you have created a large presentation that contains elements for several different audiences—some of whom
may not need to see parts of the same slide show.

Creating Hidden Slides

Slides can be hidden when you are in Slide view, or in the Slide Sorter. The
Slide Sorter is recommended for this operation, because it's easy to keep track
of the slides on which you perform this operation.

Tip
To hide multiple
slides with a
single Hide Slide
command, hold
the Shift key as
you click each
slide in the Slide
Sorter and then
execute the Hide
command.

To create hidden slides in a presentation, follow these steps:

1. Display the presentation in Slide Sorter view.

2. Click the slide to be hidden during the presentation.

3. Choose Tools, Hide Slide.

    Or, click the Hide Slide button on the Slide Sorter toolbar.

The slide number at the bottom has a box icon stamped over it, signifying that it is hidden when the slide show is run. The hidden slide is skipped automatically.

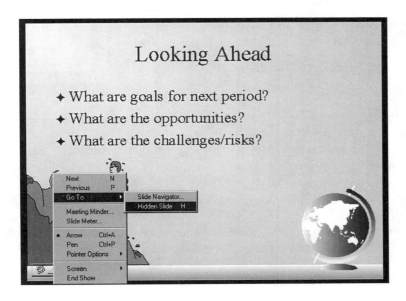

Fig. 22.4
A hidden slide can be assigned in the Slide Sorter with a simple menu selection.

If you change your mind about a hidden slide, simply execute the Hide Slide command again.

Displaying Hidden Slides

During a presentation, it may become necessary to display a hidden slide for an unanticipated reason. The procedure is a simple one and can be done during the slide show.

1. Run the slide show.

2. When a slide appears during the slide show, click the right mouse button for the shortcut menu, or choose the Slide Show pop-up icon. Choose Go To. If the slide after the current one is a hidden slide, the Hidden Slide menu option will be enabled. You will need to know where your hidden slides are located.

3. Choose the Hidden Slide menu option. The hidden slide will appear.

If your current slide is not the one immediately preceding the hidden slide, you will not be able to display the hidden slide from the pop-up menu. The Slide Navigator is actually the better option:

VI

Advanced Techniques

1. Choose the Slide Show pop-up icon, and choose <u>G</u>o To.

2. Select Slide Navigator.

3. Scroll through the Slides list to find the hidden slide. You will be able to locate any hidden slides because they will have parentheses around their slide number.

4. Double-click the hidden slide in the list.

Branching between Presentations

PowerPoint 95 offers two styles of branching: within a presentation and between different presentations. They are both clever features that offer greater flexibility for presentation delivery. Audiences may want to examine several angles of the same issue, such as studying a marketing plan in one slide show, scrutinizing the budget for that plan in a branch off one of the first slides, or seeing another branch if they want to see an assessment of competing companies' strategies. One slide can have several branches attached to it, of either type. The presenter now has the tools to anticipate any audience questions and address them in an almost stream-of-consciousness manner!

Branching to Another Presentation

Branching to another PowerPoint presentation is done using OLE, through embedding a file as an object, just like a sound file or video clip. To branch to another presentation, follow these steps:

1. Display your presentation in Slide view.

2. Display the slide from which you want to branch.

3. Choose <u>I</u>nsert, <u>O</u>bject.

   The Insert Object dialog box appears. The Insert Object dialog box lists the various types of files you can load as objects into your presentation.

4. In the Object <u>T</u>ype list box, choose Microsoft PowerPoint Presentation. (Yes, it's considered an object type.)

5. Click the Create from <u>F</u>ile option button. This step is important, because you are using an existing PowerPoint file to branch to.

   The Object <u>T</u>ype list disappears, replaced by a Fil<u>e</u> text box and a <u>B</u>rowse button that allows you to search for the exact location of your presentation file.

6. Click the Browse button to search for the specific file for embedding.

7. When the file is displayed in the File text box, choose OK.

A presentation object is displayed in your slide, as shown in figure 22.5.

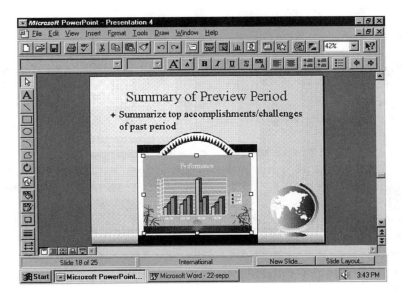

Fig. 22.5
Embedding another presentation into a slide.

If you embed another PowerPoint presentation, all its assigned timings and special effects are included—just as if it were a stand-alone presentation. Individual slides also can be embedded.

> **Note**
>
> In the same way, you can embed files from Lotus Freelance, Excel, Lotus 1-2-3 for Windows, Lotus Improv, and other presentation programs.

Loading Slides from Another Presentation

A simpler method of linking presentations is to load slides from another presentation into the current one. It's analogous to the Merge Files command in a word processor: You can merge the slides from one presentation with those of another.

To load the contents of a second slide show into the current one, follow these steps:

VI

Advanced Techniques

1. Display the slide after which the new slides are to be inserted.

2. Choose Insert, Slides from File.

   The Insert File dialog box appears.

3. Locate the desired presentation file.

4. Choose OK or press Enter.

The entire contents of the second presentation are merged with the current one. The presentation slides that have just been merged adopt the template of the current presentation, and any builds or transition effects, or Object timings and triggerings will translate intact.

Using PowerPoint's Interactive Settings

PowerPoint 95 offers a powerful new branching feature called *Interactive Settings*. This feature redefines the basic mechanism of branching. Now, by simply clicking on an object, you can branch to any other slide in your presentation, edit an object during a presentation, or even start up another application program. In most situations, users will probably prefer to use Interactive Settings as a simple yet sophisticated branching tool within a long presentation. For our main example, we'll use an AutoShape graphic object, as shown in figure 22.6.

Fig. 22.6
Choose an object for attachment of an Interactive Setting.

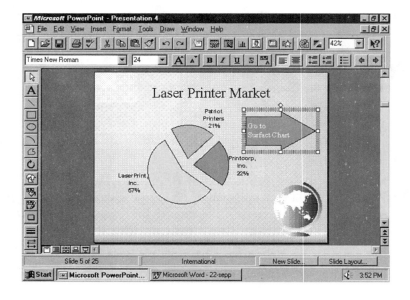

Essentially, you can use any object as a "trigger" to branch anywhere else in your current slide show. Here's how to set an object to do so:

1. Display the current presentation in Slide view, and display the slide containing the desired graphic object.

2. Click the object to which a setting will be added.

3. Choose Tools, Interactive Settings.

   The Interactive Settings dialog box appears (see fig. 22.7).

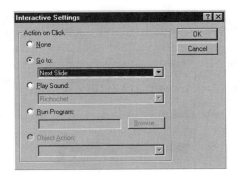

Fig. 22.7
The Interactive Settings dialog box.

For a new object, the Interactive Settings default is None. The option buttons for this dialog box are described below:

None	Disables the use of any interactive settings with the selected object.
Go To:	Drop-down list allows the selection of a destination slide: Next Slide, Previous Slide, First Slide, Last Slide, Last Slide Viewed, Slide (the option described in the steps below), and End Show.
Run Application:	Drop-down list enables you to run any Windows application program by clicking on the object, but you must furnish the entire path to the program, and make sure it's correct. Unfortunately, you can't browse from this dialog box to find the desired program. Use Windows Explorer, a DOS prompt, or another file manager to do this before you open this dialog box.
OLE Action:	Two possibilities exist in this drop-down list: Open and Edit. For objects such as charts and other OLE-

VI

Advanced Techniques

application data types, both options are quite similar. Clicking on the selected object during a slide will open the application that the item originated from: a Word table, Excel spreadsheet, Graph chart, or whatever. The program will appear over the slide show screen, ready for editing. In some cases, if you choose Open and click on the object, the item will merely play—a video clip, for instance. The Edit option is for direct, real-time editing of the object in question.

4. To set up a branch to another slide, click the Go To option button. Its drop-down list will be activated. Most of its options, such as Next Slide, Previous Slide, First Slide, and Last Slide, are self-explanatory.

5. For our example, choose Slide from the Go To drop-down list.

   As shown in figure 22.8, the Go To Slide dialog box appears.

Fig. 22.8
Choosing a slide
to branch to.

Slides list ——

—— Thumbnail displaying the
currently chosen slide

6. Choose the desired slide from the Slides list. The thumbnail on the right will show you whether or not you've chosen the right one. Make sure you don't branch to the same slide!

7. Choose OK or press Enter. The dialog box closes and returns you to the Interactive Settings dialog box. The Go To box will display the number and title of the chosen slide.

8. To place the settings, choose OK or press Enter.

The possibilities for application interactivity are immense. For specialized occasions, you can enable a teleconferencing application from within PowerPoint, or open a drawing package, to conduct a real-time illustration of a point that requires capabilities beyond the Annotate tool's abilities. While this type of function isn't something you'll see everyday, the mere fact that it is there does open new worlds to the presenter. It also reflects the real advances that Windows 95 offers the user, because such multitasking would be either impossible or a real kludge under Windows 3.x.

Note

One interesting aspect of this feature is that you can use it on objects that have builds or animations attached. So you can have multiple effects attached to one object. You also can copy an object that has an Interaction Setting to another slide, and the settings will be preserved.

Building Animation Effects

This feature represents a major change in the PowerPoint program. Previous editions of the program limited your build effects to text objects within the program. Also, you could only select entire paragraphs for builds, such as each point in an argument gliding onto the screen as you proceeded through your discussion. Now, you can apply builds to individual characters and words in a line of text! That's not all. For the first time, PowerPoint allows you to apply build features to graphic objects, giving you substantial graphic animation capabilities.

So what is a *build*? Build effects make objects on a PowerPoint slide move around the screen. Individual build effects are applied to individual items in a bulleted list, or are assigned to an entire bulleted list or text object at once. Many previous restrictions on build effects have been removed:

- You can now apply build effects to slide titles!

- Builds of any kind can now be applied to graphic objects. You can use one build on any graphic object, and can use as many builds as you have graphic objects for on your screen.

- Another multimedia aspect: Sounds can be attached to any animation build, from presets in PowerPoint's Animation Effects toolbar, to any custom sound you import from an application or CD-ROM.

Many basic animation effects (some combined with sound) can be applied using PowerPoint's new Animation Effects toolbar, which is shown in figure 22.9 below.

VI

Advanced Techniques

Fig. 22.9
The Animation Effects toolbar (shown floating on the screen).

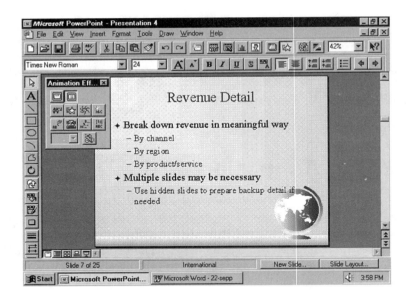

Table 22.1 shows the various Animation tools on the toolbar.

Table 22.1 The Animation Effects Toolbar

	Button	Description
	Animate Title	Allows you to apply the currently selected Title Build style to the selected title object.
	Build Slide Text	Enables you to apply the currently selected build effect to the selected text object(s). Body text will appear paragraph by paragraph.
	Drive-In Effect	Causes the selected object to fly into position from the right side of the screen. Works with text and graphic objects. A "car" sound effect is attached to this animation.
	Flying Effect	Causes the selected object to fly into position from the left side of the screen. Works with text and graphic objects. A "whoosh" sound effect is attached to this animation.
	Camera Effect	Causes the selected object to "explode" or "box" outward and assume its shape. Works with text and graphic objects. A "clicking camera" sound effect is attached to this animation.

	Button	Description
	Flash Once	Causes the selected object to flicker once on screen and disappear. Works with text and graphic objects.
	Laser Text Effect	Allows the selected object to "fly into" the screen from the top right. Uses a "laser beam" sound effect. Works with text or graphic objects.
	Typewriter Text Effect	Causes selected text to build, letter by letter, from left to right. Works only with text objects. Uses a "typing" sound effect.
	Reverse Text Build	Causes selected text to unfold from left to right ("wipe right, reverse order"). Works only with text objects.
	Drop-In Text Effect	Causes selected text to fly in from the top of the screen, word by word. Works only with text objects.
	Animation Order	A drop-down list that controls the order of animation effects you apply to the current slide. Selecting an object on a slide and then choosing a number from this list applies build effects in numerical order. For example, if you have four objects, each of which executes in a certain order (a title first, a text object second, an AutoShape graphic third, and a chart fourth), you can change their order by using this feature. When you originally assign a build to an object, it automatically acquires the order of the highest number available on the list. Similar to the Build This Object drop-down list in the Animation Settings dialog box.
	Animation Settings	Clicking this button displays the Animation Settings dialog box, which offers a wide variety of animation options and choices. This dialog box offers the most control over how your build effects will appear.

Some tools will only work with text objects, and will provide no response when you attempt to use them on graphics. For a complete selection of build effects, use the Animation Settings feature from the Tools menu or click the Animation Settings button on the Animation Effects toolbar.

VI

Advanced Techniques

Many animation features apply to builds for texts and for graphics, which provides a useful simplicity for the user. The next few examples go through the various applications of animation and build effects on slide objects.

Applying Builds to Text

Builds can be applied to text in the Slide view or the Slide Sorter, but not in Outline view. For this example, Slide view is used.

When builds are applied to *text slides*—slides that contain a bulleted list as their main component—they're called *Build slides*. Sometimes they are also termed *Progressive Transition slides*. Regardless of the semantics, you create them from the Animation Settings dialog box. To open the dialog box:

1. Display the current presentation in Slide view.

2. Click the text object (slide title, or body text) to which a build will be added.

3. Choose Tools, Animation Settings.

   The Animation Settings dialog box appears (see fig. 22.10).

Fig. 22.10
Using the
Animation Settings
dialog box to
apply build effects.

If you're a PowerPoint 4 user, you will see a number of unfamiliar elements in this dialog box. First of all, build effects are now organized in text levels. You can apply builds to a text object "All at Once," which means that the entire text object will fly around or explode onto the screen depending on which effect you've selected. In such cases, all bulleted points will appear all at once. The better choice, for point-by-point arguments, is to select one of the five text levels in the list, as seen in figure 22.11.

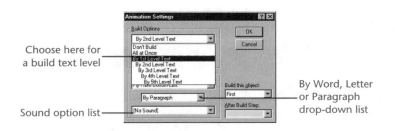

Choose here for
a build text level

Sound option list

By Word, Letter
or Paragraph
drop-down list

Fig. 22.11
Using the
Animation
Settings dialog box
continued.

Each of the five levels can have a different default build effect assigned to it. By doing so, the user can save a lot of work from laboriously reassigning builds one text item at a time throughout the slide show. (This only applies to text, and not to graphics.)

For a typical bulleted text, select By 2nd Level Text from the Build Options list. This will enable a build effect to be applied. The text levels in this feature apply to the varying levels of text you might have on your slides: a main bulleted point (2nd Level) followed by two bulleted subpoints (3rd level), for example. (Your outline for your presentation shows the flow of the text and bulleted points in your slide show, providing a quick view of the hierarchy and structure of your text.)

By using this feature, you can have subpoints in a bulleted point come in after their main or introducing point appears, providing a logical sequence.

Note

When you apply a build effect to a bulleted list, you only need to select one of the bulleted points in a text object. All the rest will adopt the same build effect. List items cannot have separate bullet effects assigned to them unless they are all separate text objects. This is also true for using sound effects and dimming.

Adding Special Effects to a Build

From the Effects section's top drop-down list in the Animation Settings dialog box, choose from one of the 35 build effects (refer to fig. 22.10).

Notice the other list box just below the build effects? Clicking on it displays a list as shown in figure 22.12. You can now use build effects in a letter, word, or paragraph sequence. Choose any you wish.

Tip
You can apply any sound effect you want to any build effect in the program.

VI

Advanced Techniques

> ### Caution
>
> Bear in mind that applying build effects a letter or word at a time can slow down your show dramatically and drive your audience to distraction. Choose these effects carefully.

Fig. 22.12
Applying builds to a letter, word, or paragraph at a time.

Adding Sounds to Build Effects

How about a sound effect? Here's another powerful new PowerPoint feature: attaching custom sounds to your animations and builds. They're available from the bottom drop-down list in the Effects section of the Animation Settings dialog box, as seen in figure 22.13.

Fig. 22.13
Choosing to use a sound with a build effect.

Choose this option to bring in a custom sound

Tip
Keep the quantity of embedded sound objects and CD Audio sound-tracks in mind. Too much sound can distract from your message.

That bottom list in the Effects section offers the ability to use a default sound (called CHORD.WAV in the figure). It also offers lots of possibilities for abuse. Be careful with this feature, especially if you're in a hurry. Sound effects are triggered on every build action, whether it's a letter, word, or a paragraph. You could easily (and mistakenly) drive your audience and yourself nuts with that Chord sound effect, if you had a letter-by-letter build!

To load a new sound effect, choose Other Sound from the drop-down list as shown in figure 22.13. The Add Sound dialog box appears, as shown in figure 22.14. Choose a sound file from the desired drive and folder, and choose Open. The sound will be loaded in and applied to the build effect for that text object only.

Tip
Don't go into overkill with the sound effects.

Fig. 22.14
Loading a sound effect.

Dimming Objects in the Slide

To dim previously bulleted items in the body text (have them fade out when you are ready to move on to the next point in your argument), click the After Build Step drop-down list in the Animation Settings dialog box (refer to fig. 22.12). Its default is Don't Dim. From this list, you can choose any color in PowerPoint's spectrum to use as a dimming color; including using the familiar Other Color option, to work with its basic 127-color palette or the histogram in its Custom tab. Colors are applied to Dim effects in the same way as many other PowerPoint elements that use color.

Tips for Using Builds

Applying builds can actually be a fairly complicated process, if you use all the options that are available to you. Here are some things to keep in mind when using builds and animation effects:

- If the build is applied to body text in a bulleted list, each bulleted item will reveal itself in sequence using the same chosen build effect. If you're applying the build using the Slide Sorter, a small icon appears denoting the slide as a build slide. The icon is the same as the Build button on the Slide Sorter toolbar.

- In a bulleted list, you can't apply one build effect to one bulleted item, and then another build effect to a second or third bulleted item. You are limited to one build effect for any text object, whether it's a single word, a slide title, or a bulleted list. If a bulleted list is contained in one selected text object, that entire list will be animated in the same way. If you build a bulleted list in which each bullet point is its own text object (a somewhat more laborious process), then a different build effect can be applied to each one.

Tip

When you load sound effects from outside Power-Point, they are added to the drop-down list in the dialog box.

VI

Advanced Techniques

■ If you copy the contents of a slide that has build effects applied to it, and paste those elements into a new or blank presentation, the build effects will come along for the ride. This is very convenient, because you can simply paste the "built" text or graphics objects into a series of other slides. By doing this, you can save a lot of time and enforce some consistency in your animation and sound schemes. As far as I've been able to determine, this is the closest you can come to saving a complex build slide for re-use in other presentations.

■ A couple of checkbox options in the Animation Settings dialog box can be very helpful. The In Reverse Order checkbox simply displays the bullet points from bottom to top instead of top to bottom. The Start When Previous Build Ends checkbox runs the build in a continuous sequence without pausing between bullet points.

Building Effects for a Group of Slides with the Slide Sorter

As mentioned earlier, the Slide Sorter offers a special toolbar with drop-down lists for transition and build effects (see fig. 22.15). Using the Sorter, it's possible to select any number of slides and apply a build effect to them all at once.

Fig. 22.15
Using the Slide Sorter view to apply builds and transitions.

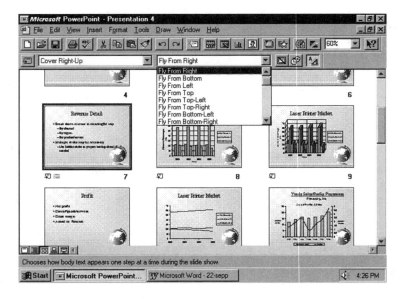

Using the Slide Sorter makes the process simple. Click on a slide (or several slides), or choose Select All from the Edit menu, and the Build drop-down list will be activated. This is more of a brute force approach, because you can't use the Animation Settings dialog box, with its many options for sound and other effects, in the Slide Sorter view. (The Sorter does avoid applying build effects to any selected slides' titles —a small bit of good programming design.) This is a much faster and simpler method.

The advantage is that if you have a long sequence of text slides in which you want to use the same build, you can click them all, apply the build, and you're done. This technique also helps the consistency of your slide show.

Applying Animation Builds to Graphic Objects

As noted at the beginning of this chapter, build effects have been extended for use on graphic objects. This includes all manner of graphic objects.

- You can apply build effects to any graphic object you draw in the PowerPoint program.

- You can apply build effects to graphic objects that you import from other programs or from the Clip Art Gallery, and to movie clips!

- You can even apply animation effects to charts created in Microsoft Graph!

The features for using builds on all five of these data types (video clips, clip art, charts, PowerPoint-drawn objects, and imported graphics) is the same, and they will be treated generically in this procedure. In fact, the process is very similar to using builds on text objects in the previous section.

1. Display the slide containing the graphic or other object that you want to apply a build to.

2. Select the graphic object to which a build will be added.

3. Choose Tools, Animation Settings.

   The Animation Settings dialog box appears.

4. Choose Build from the Build Options drop-down list.

   The Effects section is enabled.

5. Choose a preferred build style from the drop-down list in the Effects section, as seen in figure 22.16. If desired, the Start When Previous Build Ends checkbox is also available.

6. If desired, choose a sound effect from the other drop-down list in the Effects section.

Tip
The Animation Settings dialog box is not available in the Slide Sorter.

VI

Advanced Techniques

Tip
You can dim graphic objects in the same way as text.

Fig. 22.16

Applying build effects to graphic objects.

Build drop-down list

Notice the new dialog box section titled Play Options

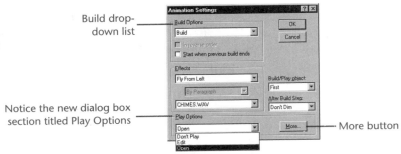

More button

Setting Play Options for Builds on Graphic Objects

◄ See "Dimming Objects in the Slide," p. 653

Figure 22.16 shows a new feature, which appears only when you're applying builds to graphics or other non-text items: the Play Options section. Though we discuss this feature more extensively in Chapter 21, "Using Multimedia Elements in PowerPoint 95," it also has a lot of bearing in this area.

The Play Options drop-down list has two choices for graphic objects:

■ Don't Play (the default), which actually has no practical effect on graphic objects. The build effect is applied.

■ Replace, which triggers the Clip Art Gallery for replacing the picture if you double-click the artwork after its build effect appears.

This is a feature provided by Microsoft for the user's convenience, but it's hard to see many scenarios where you will want to replace a piece of clip art during your actual presentation. It is convenient when you're rehearsing and decide that you want to change the artwork without following a bunch of extra steps. This is not limited to PowerPoint's clip art. If the art in question, for example, was a CorelDRAW image, you could double-click on the art to start the CorelDRAW program (because CorelDRAW supports OLE) if you decided you wanted to make some changes. This process can save you a few steps. Some PowerPoint templates, such as the Brainstorming template, lend themselves well to this kind of mechanism.

If you select a video clip and choose this feature, three choices are provided under Play Options:

■ Don't Play (the default), which prevents any video clips from being executed.

■ Open, which enables the selected video clip to play as it is moving across the screen during the build effect. As you can imagine, this last function can require a lot of processing power.

■ Edit, which opens up the Media Player during the slide show when the video appears.

None of these settings have any relevance for graphic objects; they only affect video clips, which are discussed in Chapter 21.

For more animation options, choose <u>M</u>ore. The More Play Options dialog box appears (see fig. 22.17).

Fig. 22.17
Setting playback timing for graphic objects.

Unless you're working with a video clip, the only More Play Options available are a pair of option buttons and a checkbox, which are described below.

■ <u>I</u>n Sequence places the selected item in the default sequence of objects with assigned builds. If you want the build effect to advance in the normal build sequence, use this option.

■ To set a custom slide timing, click on the <u>A</u>utomatically ? Seconds After Previous Event option button and enter the desired length in seconds (before the next slide appears) in the text box.

■ If you want the object to disappear after playback of its animation, click the <u>H</u>ide While Not Playing checkbox.

For both text and graphics, Animation Effects offers a lot of scope for experiments. You're better off not trying to use these effects when you're in a hurry to produce a presentation, because you can wind up with unintended effects or effects that don't work. When you change animation settings, check them by playing the slide to make sure they work properly. That leads us naturally into the next section of this chapter, which deals with the process of rehearsing and timing your presentation.

Rehearsing Your Presentation

When you apply build and transition effects, and include numerous multimedia elements, it's important to keep control of the timing of all the various

VI

Advanced Techniques

elements to—simply put—keep yourself from messing up in front of your audience. Rehearsing is a critical tool for putting yourself in control, and it should not be neglected.

Here's a quick course on how to rehearse your presentation:

1. Display the first slide in your presentation.

2. Choose <u>V</u>iew, Slide Sho<u>w</u>.

   The Slide Show dialog box appears (see fig. 22.18).

Fig. 22.18
Getting ready
to rehearse.

Click the Rehearse New
Timings button

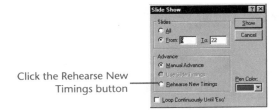

3. Choose from the rehearsal options:

Option	Description
<u>A</u>ll	Rehearse entire presentation
<u>F</u>rom	Specify range of slides to rehearse
<u>M</u>anual Advance	Use mouse click or keystroke to advance to each successive slide
<u>U</u>se Slide Timings	Use default slide timings in template
<u>R</u>ehearse New Timings	Use keystrokes and/or mouse click to set timings and trigger the events of the presentation
Loop <u>C</u>ontinuously Until Esc	If this checkbox is enabled, presentation runs in endless loop until you press Esc

   To rehearse slide and element timings (builds, etc.), choose the <u>R</u>ehearse New Timings option button.

4. Choose <u>S</u>how or press Enter.

The slide show starts, and a timer is displayed at the bottom of the screen, showing elapsed seconds as shown in figure 22.19. Click the mouse, or press the spacebar or press Enter to trigger each successive event in the slide show. You can press Esc at any time to stop and go back to the PowerPoint screen.

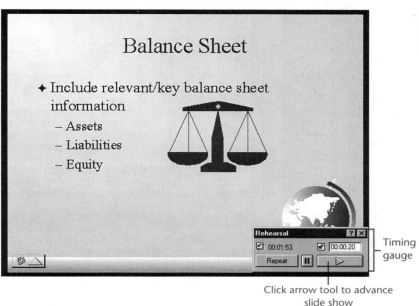

Fig. 22.19
Rehearsing a slide show.

Timing gauge

Click arrow tool to advance slide show

Remember that when you rehearse a presentation, you're rehearsing all the events that compose it—builds, multimedia event triggerings, and the length of time that each slide is displayed.

When you start up your slide show for rehearsal, a gauge will be displayed at the bottom right of the screen, which shows the time elapsed, a Repeat Slide tool, and a right arrow tool which, when clicked, conveniently advances the slide show without having to search for a PageDown key on your keyboard.

When you're finished, the program will notify you of the total time and ask if you want to save it. (When you save your file, all the timings are automatically saved within it.) If you decide to save your timings, the times for each slide will be visible in the Slide Sorter view. If not, rehearse again. When the timings are satisfactory, simply save your file and you will be ready to go.

Tip
Don't linger too long on any one slide unless the discussion calls for it.

Tools for Presentation Delivery

PowerPoint 95 offers an expanded set of tools for slide show delivery. Among the most prominent improvements is a pop-up menu that appears during the slide show, offering access to all of the program's show management features. Figures 22.20 and 22.21 illustrate the appearance of the special menu.

VI

Advanced Techniques

Fig. 22.20
The Slide Show
Pop-Up Menu
icon.

Fig. 22.21
Displaying the
Slide Show Pop-
Up Menu.

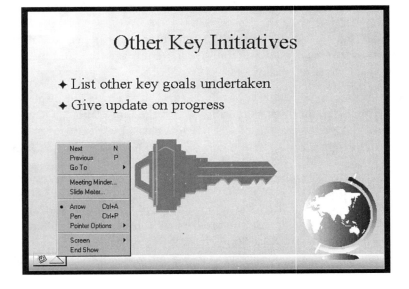

Tip
Clicking the right
mouse button
during a slide show
will also display
the Slide Show
pop-up menu with-
out having to get
to the icon at the
bottom left.

Click the icon at the bottom left corner of the Slide Show screen, and the menu pops up as shown in figure 22.21. This menu is available when you run the slide show from the PowerPoint Player as well as from within the actual application. From here, you can enable two key show management features: the Meeting Minder and the Slide Manager. Logically, these features are offered as part of PowerPoint's slide show system, instead of menu items in the main PowerPoint screen. The next few sections describe how to use PowerPoint's delivery tools.

Annotating Slides with the Pen Tool

PowerPoint also has expanded its slide show Annotation features. You can now choose a pen color for your Annotate tool, and directly choose whether or not to hide or to use the tool in the course of your show.

While you're conducting a slide show, you might find it handy to emphasize points, like a teacher at a chalkboard. PowerPoint 95 offers an easy way to do this.

1. Before running a slide show before an audience, display your presentation in Slide Show view, and click the right mouse button to show the Slide Show pop-up menu.

2. From the pop-up menu, choose Pen.

3. The Pen's color will be the default assigned to it in the color palette. The default should be sufficient for good visibility. It's easy to change the pen color, however. From the Slide Show pop-up menu, choose Pointer Options. A cascading menu will appear.

4. Choose Pen Color. Another cascading menu appears.

Tip

Press Ctrl+P during the slide show to enable the Pen tool.

Click the mouse button while in the slide show. Drag the mouse across the screen. You can draw circles around items, underline them, and draw arrows to point to slide elements.

Bear in mind that the Pen tool is not artistic. Any scribbling you do on the screen is bound to look like crude graffiti! To move on to the next slide, or the next event in the current slide, press the space bar or press Enter.

> ### Note
>
> A previous section of this chapter, titled "Using PowerPoint's Interactive Settings," provides an expanded way to annotate your presentation, by opening application programs during a real-time slide show. In rare circumstances, and particularly if you have mastery of the applications in question, you can use illustration or other programs to annotate and change objects in a slide show while you're holding it.

VI

Advanced Techniques

Using the Meeting Minder

The idea behind the Meeting Minder is to give the presenter a way to take meeting minutes and notes electronically. Those notes and minutes can then be imported into Microsoft Word and other word processors and edited, or included in another presentation outline.

To use the Meeting Minder during a presentation:

1. During the slide show, click the Slide Show pop-up menu icon or click the right mouse button.

2. From the pop-up menu, choose Meeting Minder.

   The Meeting Minder dialog box appears. It bears three function tabs, titled Meeting Minutes, Action Items, and Notes Pages. Meeting Minutes and Action Items both provide an editable screen area for typing in their respective information.

   > **Note**
   >
   > Meeting Minutes and Action Items tabs are both editable areas for minutes and notes of a meeting. You can cut, copy, and paste using editing commands (Ctrl+X, Ctrl+C, Ctrl+V, respectively) and select words and paragraphs with the mouse just as you would any text in the program.

3. The Meeting Minutes tab is normally the default display.

4. Click the Action Items tab to display an editable area for notes and information for a later date.

5. Click the Notes Pages tab to display any notes for the currently displayed slide, that were previously entered during preparation of the presentation.

6. After using the tabs as needed, choose OK or press Enter to remove the Minder. Note that you cannot proceed through the slide show while this dialog box is displayed.

Using the Slide Navigator

The Slide Navigator is a simple tool for monitoring your location within a long, complex slide show. (Notes Pages are a hard-copy tool for doing basically the same thing.) If you haven't employed PowerPoint's branching tools (described earlier in this chapter), this is a decent last-resort way of navigating around your presentation.

1. Begin your slide show.

2. Click the icon at the bottom left to display the Slide Show pop-up menu.

3. Choose Go To and a cascading menu will appear. In turn, choose Slide Navigator.

   The Slide Navigator dialog box appears, as shown in fig. 22.22.

Slides list —————

Fig. 22.22
The Slide Navigator dialog box.

4. Scroll up or down the Slides list and double-click the desired slide, or select it and choose <u>G</u>o To.

The new slide appears. Nothing to it. If you see slide numbers with parentheses around them, that indicates a hidden slide. You can simply choose the hidden slide in this way if you want to display it. Otherwise, during the normal slide show run, hidden slides will stay hidden.

Many tools for effective presentation management are presented in this chapter. Some subjects, such as builds and animation effects, have been extensively discussed, but out of necessity many detailed touches have been left out.

Chapter 23, "Using Advanced Color, Text, and Special Effects," shows how to add special effects to slide text, how to rotate text, how to do tricks with color, and how to create new color schemes. Many functions covered in this chapter can be added to a customized toolbar. See Chapter 24, "Customizing PowerPoint 95," for more information. ❖

Tip
In the Navigator, a slide number with parentheses around it indicates a hidden slide.

VI

Advanced Techniques

Using Advanced Color, Text, and Special Effects

by Rick Darnell

In addition to the basic color and text functions you've learned so far, PowerPoint has advanced features that can stretch the impact of your presentation even further. Combined with accessory applications such as WordArt, you have a full complement of tools to add sizzle and pop to your slides. This chapter introduces you to a few of these topics.

In this chapter, you learn to

- Use colors and patterns effectively
- Handle fonts
- Create and edit tables
- Use special backgrounds
- Create special text effects
- Add mathematical equations

Using Colors and Patterns Effectively

As you've seen in several earlier chapters in this book, color is an important tool for creating successful presentations. Color provides many elements in a presentation beyond making pretty pictures. Understanding good color relationships can be very useful in creating a successful presentation. Color can add emphasis to items in a slide and lend balance to a slide's appearance, or it can be a distraction that interferes with your presentation's message. Thus, you should choose colors carefully when building a color scheme.

VI

Advanced Techniques

Creating Emphasis and Balance with Color

A common impulse is to use numerous color mixes to break up the monotony of a long presentation. Learn to resist this impulse. Effective color use lends unity to an overall presentation concept. A good rule of thumb for text slides (which constitute the majority of the slides you make) is to use color rather than text style for emphasizing lines or values in text.

You can use colors and patterns to direct attention to important points, data, graphics, or chart elements in a slide. In color printouts or overheads, you can apply a bold and striking color to the most important series for emphasis. You can apply lighter shades of the same color to the other series in a chart. For on-screen presentations, use light or bright colors for emphasis. For black-and-white overheads and slides, show the most important items in the darkest pattern. Shades of gray and patterns aid in readability and are just as important as color choices.

Warm colors, such as red, orange, and yellow, draw the eye's attention, offering more visual punch and activity. Cooler colors, such as greens, blues, and violets, provide rest for the eye. Use cool colors for backgrounds to set off areas of warmer colors, such as a movie clip depicting a bright outdoors scene.

Understanding Color Relationships

Colors have complementary relationships. Complementary colors are certain hues and shades that get along well with each other, regardless of their essential character. On a color wheel, for example, the primary colors of red, green, and blue are drawn with secondary colors of yellow, cyan, and magenta. Colors located on opposite sides of the wheel from each other are complements, such as the frequently used blue and yellow.

Tip

Avoid red-green color combinations. It is a simultaneous contrast, and, almost 10% of the population is red-green color-blind.

Another tool in using color is a *split complement*, which expands on the range of complementary colors for a more subtle effect. For example, on our RGB color wheel, light green is located next to yellow. Light green is a split complement color that goes well with dark blue, which is normally the complement of yellow. The color templates offered in PowerPoint follow the concepts of using complementary colors and split complements for their color schemes.

By the same token, large areas of complementary colors bordering each other is visually disturbing and annoying. This nasty effect is called *simultaneous contrast*. This type of contrast is hard to look at.

> **Note**
>
> To avoid the problem of simultaneous contrast, a good technique is to place a black, gray, or white border around the surrounded color object. An even better technique is to avoid having two large areas of complementary colors present. You also can lower the saturation of each color to produce a milder effect.

Two Color Wheels

But wait, you say, aren't red, yellow, and blue the real complementary colors? Unfortunately, the answer is yes and no. There are two different methods of creating color: *subtractive* and *additive*. Subtractive colors begin with white, and color is removed to leave the desired color. This method is used in the old reliable red-yellow-blue scheme. You begin with a white piece of paper and begin painting. If you use all your paints, a big black blot results, which blocks white light from reflecting off the paper.

Additive is opposite of subtractive. Your television is an example, shining some colors and letting others pass. If you put your nose close to the screen, you would see tiny red, green and blue dots. The television translates the color signal into different intensities of these three dots. If all the dots were on at full power, the screen would be white. Your computer screen works in a similar fashion, so your color choices are based on the additive color wheel, also known as RGB.

With some basic tips for good color relationships behind you, it's time to take a closer look at PowerPoint's color mixing system.

Understanding PowerPoint's Color Mixing System

PowerPoint relies on two color mixing schemes for color creation: RGB and HSL (Hue, Saturation, Luminance). These schemes are adequate for any color work in a presentation.

◀ See "Studying PowerPoint's Color Schemes and Basic Color Palette," p. 481

The red-green-blue color model defines how much of each of the three colors is added to the mix in order to arrive at the final color. PowerPoint provides a scale for mixing RGB-based colors, with the range for each color being from 0 to 255 in brightness value. The higher the number for each color, the closer the mix is to white—the brightest possible color. If all three values (red, green, and blue) are zero, the color is black. This is the easier of the two color systems to use and understand.

In the HSL color definition, *hue* is the basic color mix—red, green, blue, yellow, or any other basic color in the spectrum. *Saturation* and *luminance* affect the actual purity and brightness of the color, respectively. The more saturation, the more purity a color displays. Luminance controls the effect of light on the color, and is also shown when you adjust the brightness values of the red, green, and blue mix.

Creating New Colors

The Colors properties box provides several important tools for creating new colors and for understanding exactly how color works in the program. There are two ways to get to a Colors properties box. From the Format menu, select Slide Color Scheme or Custom Background (see fig. 23.7 later in this chapter under "Using Special Background Effects").

Notice at the bottom edge of the histogram (see fig. 23.7 later in this chapter), gray and black predominate. The colors grow brighter at the top of the histogram, reaching their highest intensity at the top edge. Histogram colors diminish in intensity at the bottom. The color hues change from the left edge to the right in the histogram.

If you change the value in the Hue control box, the crosshair in the histogram moves to the left or right. Movement in either direction changes the color.

You adjust saturation from top to bottom. If you change the value in the Sat control box, the crosshair in the histogram adjusts straight up or down. If the crosshair moves down, the color is less vivid and less intense, with more gray mixed in.

Notice that when you adjust the saturation, the Red, Green, and Blue values in the control boxes to the right all change at the same time. Depending on the hue, RGB values may adjust up or down when the saturation is changed. For example, if you have a blue hue selected, and you adjust the saturation down, the Red and Green values increase and the Blue value decreases.

When you adjust the saturation, you can watch the color intensity slowly change on the adjacent bar (the arrowhead bar that you use to adjust luminance).

The Lum (Luminance) control box does not affect the position of the crosshair. Instead, the arrowhead alongside the adjuster bar to the right of the histogram moves up or down. Drag the arrowhead up or down to adjust the luminance (brightness). If the arrowhead moves down, the brightness of the color is decreasing.

> **Note**
>
> Keep in mind that when you make adjustments to any values, you may not see results of color adjusting on the monitor. The colors you see are determined by the color range that your video card can display. If you're running Windows in 256-color mode, the colors you can specify are much less substantial than in other video display modes.

Understanding PowerPoint's True Color Support

The Colors properties box is a good place to illustrate what True Color support means for the PowerPoint user. If you're using a video card that supports 16 million colors in 640 x 480 resolution, 800 x 600 resolution, or even 1024 x 768 resolution, you can use True Color on your screen. With True Color, the monitor is capable of displaying the exact color that your eye normally sees (unless, of course, you're color-blind to some degree). PowerPoint's histogram looks markedly different. Color contrasts are much smoother and the adjuster bar is one continuously darkening band of color. True Color support is invoked automatically by PowerPoint if your video equipment is capable of the higher resolution.

When using True Color display, the two color thumbnails—Color and Solid—at the bottom left of the dialog box consistently display the same color when color mixing values are adjusted. Conversely, if your monitor normally displays 256 colors, the Color and Solid thumbnails are almost always different, because the selected color cannot be adjusted as finely.

> **Note**
>
> The terms *True Color*, *16 million colors*, and *24-bit color* all describe the same thing. When you use 24-bit color, your video card uses 24 bits of data to determine the color value of each pixel on-screen. When you're using 256 colors on the screen display, it's often referred to as *8-bit mode* because the video uses only eight bits of data to define each pixel's color.

If your monitor is capable of True Color, you have access to many more colors and the opportunity to adjust them more precisely. In addition, the visual results of your presentation can be much richer (especially if you use an on-screen slide show). Color shading and patterns are more subtle and attractive. You eliminate color dithering (the practice of mixing a color with dots and patterns of other colors to create new ones to compensate for a more limited display color palette). You also can import photo-realistic pictures into a slide or template, and the pictures look more realistic (which substantially increases the size of your presentation file).

Using Postscript Fonts

Postscript is the professional standard for fonts and typefaces on computers. If your computer utilizes desktop publishing and drawing programs such as Aldus Pagemaker or Adobe Illustrator, it may have some of these typefaces installed already. Adobe Systems is the inventor of the Postscript language for laser printers, which is widely used today. Adobe and a host of other type foundries have created a massive library of computer fonts; among the type families are the TrueType fonts you've been using throughout this book.

◄ See "Setting Up Your Printer," p. 455

You can use Postscript fonts in the same ways you use Microsoft's conventional TrueType fonts. Postscript fonts are special because they are the standard for service bureaus. Thus, many professionals prefer Postscript fonts for computing tasks.

Almost invariably, when you send any kind of file to a service bureau for output, they ask you to use Postscript fonts in your files. That's partly because Adobe font names are accepted as the standard names for typefaces (TrueType fonts usually have imitative names but can't be named identically because of copyright restrictions), and also because most companies consider TrueType a technically inferior standard.

TrueType is a low-cost competitor to Postscript, but realistically it doesn't compete with Postscript's professional quality. TrueType is aimed at the average Windows user who doesn't want to bother with building an expensive font library but wants to produce good-looking output without resorting to a service bureau.

Postscript fonts are available in many laser printers; many people probably have a printer with Postscript capability attached to their computer. If you don't have a Postscript-type printer, you can use another alternative, called Adobe Type Manager. ATM is a high-quality font control program that enables your Windows machine to display and print industry-standard Postscript fonts whether or not you have a Postscript-type printer. Most Windows users have either ATM or TrueType, or both, on their systems. TrueType is included with every copy of Windows, and PowerPoint comes with a selection of TrueType fonts.

> **Note**
>
> If you use Postscript fonts in your presentation, you may need to bring them along with the presentation if you take it to a service bureau for output. All service bureaus don't carry all typefaces, so you need to check first to see if your chosen font is included in their system.

The advantage of using Postscript fonts is the comfort of knowing you're using industry standard, professional fonts. Keep in mind the disadvantage: you can embed TrueType fonts into a presentation, but you cannot embed Postscript fonts. If your presentation will be viewed or printed on a machine other than your own, typeface availability could be a problem, so pay attention to the preceding note.

Using Alternative Table Editing Techniques

Instead of building table creation features into PowerPoint, Microsoft elected to enable users to take advantage of Microsoft Word for Windows 6 to build complex row/column tables. However, if you don't own Word for Windows 6 or later, you cannot use PowerPoint's OLE 2.0 features to embed a table from Word into a slide.

The same is true if you don't own Microsoft Excel 5. PowerPoint offers a tool for editing and inserting row/column datasheets using Excel 5. The process, as with Word for Windows, uses OLE 2.0. PowerPoint does not offer a native method for editing and creating datasheets for display in a slide; even Graph's datasheets only create charts and cannot be displayed in the program. Essentially, you can take full advantage of PowerPoint's table creation and datasheet creation tools only if you own Word 6 and Excel 5.

Fortunately, you have many alternatives. Almost every Windows user has at least one major word processing program, such as Lotus' Ami Pro, WordPerfect for Windows, or half a dozen other alternatives available in the Windows market, including older versions of Word for Windows. The same is true of spreadsheet programs, and many users own programs such as Lotus' 1-2-3 for Windows, Improv, or Borland's Quattro Pro for Windows.

Inserting Tables From Other Programs

If you own Ami Pro, Lotus Improv, an older version of Excel or Word, or Word-Perfect for Windows, you easily can use any of the programs to create a table or datasheet. In doing so, you're using object linking and embedding. All the programs mentioned in the preceding paragraph support OLE 1.0, which is sufficient for your needs, thus the following steps are relatively generic:

1. Choose Insert, Object.

2. When the dialog box appears, choose the appropriate program object type from the Object Type list.

VI

Advanced Techniques

3. If you're creating a new table or datasheet, click the Create New option button; if you want to use an existing file, click the Create from File option button.

4. Choose OK or press Enter. If you're creating a new datasheet or table, the program that you use to create the new object appears, ready for editing. If you're creating the object from an existing word processing or spreadsheet file, the table or datasheet pops up on your current slide. Double-clicking the new object opens its originating program for editing.

Troubleshooting

When I double-click the table or datasheet created with a non-Microsoft application, it doesn't come up.

You probably linked the file instead of embedding it. Programs like WordPerfect for Windows, Ami Pro, Quattro Pro, and others (including the older but still very useful Microsoft Excel 4.0) use OLE 1.0. You still can embed and link objects from these programs in your slides, but if you link an object in a PowerPoint slide from one of these programs, double-clicking the object may not bring up the other program. You must open the other program separately, do your edits, and then update the link.

However, many OLE 1.0 programs appear if you double-click a linked object originally created in them. Microsoft's OLE 2.0 enables this feature with programs that support it. Check to make sure the other application program is installed properly.

Creating Tables Directly in PowerPoint

You can create simple tables directly on the PowerPoint slide. Although typing and editing a simple table on a slide is fairly inflexible and doesn't offer the formatting capabilities of a sophisticated word processor like Word, WordPerfect, or Ami Pro, you have a few advantages:

- You don't need to run another application program.

- All of PowerPoint's basic editing tools are available, including line spacing, text formatting, and ruler tab setting.

- Because you're typing in unformatted text for your table, the text is considered just another PowerPoint object. You can apply background coloring and shading, as well as shadowing and text colors.

When you want to create a table directly in PowerPoint, follow these steps:

1. In PowerPoint's Slide view, display the slide where you want to write your table.

2. Choose <u>V</u>iew, <u>R</u>uler.

   This step is optional, but PowerPoint's Ruler is a valuable tool for creating tables on a slide.

3. Click the Text button on the Drawing toolbar.

4. Type your tabular data. Press the Tab key between each field of data. At the end of each table row, press Enter.

   As you enter your data, the Ruler changes its appearance to reflect the growth of the table, as shown in figure 23.1.

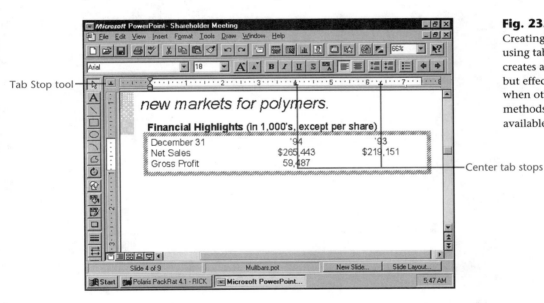

Fig. 23.1
Creating a table using tab stops creates a simple but effective table when other methods aren't available.

You can use four different types of tab stops in a table format: Left, Right, Center, and Center with Leader. The Tab Stop tool in the top left corner of the document window (adjacent to both rulers) enables you to cycle between the four tab types to select the one you want.

VI

Advanced Techniques

5. To add tab stop formatting on columns in a table, click the mouse in any text item in the column you want to format. Do not select any text, because then tabs cannot be set.

6. Click the Tab Stop tool to select the tab style you want.

7. Click the mouse inside the top ruler to place the tab markers. The entire column adjusts. Figure 23.1 shows the table with two center tab markers used to align the values.

You may set colors for borders of a table because it is just another text object. You can boldface and underline a top row of labels (see fig. 23.2).

Fig. 23.2
The completed text table, using bold, underline, and italics for emphasis on the column heads.

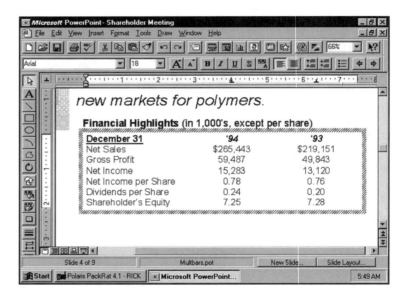

Unfortunately, PowerPoint has no provision for adding borders to individual table cells. Because the table you're creating is only a simple text object, you cannot easily structure the table with borders around each value.

Using Special Background Effects

PowerPoint offers some interesting background effects beyond those used for most of the examples in this book. First, let's review briefly what's involved in changing this type of effect.

You can change background effects for one or more slides by using the Format, Custom Background command. In addition to a selection from the color scheme palette, you have five additional choices from a drop-down menu (see fig. 23.3):

Shaded	Available in one or two colors and in a variety of alignments.
Patterned	A mix of lines, checkerboards, and other geometric patterns.
Textured	12 textures come with PowerPoint, including cloth, sand, marble, and oak. You also can add your own texture from paint and clip art files.
Picture	Choose from a variety of pictures, including PCX and TIFF files.
Other Color	Choose a color from the palette or create your own.

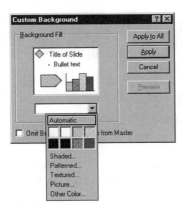

Fig. 23.3
The drop-down menu for Background Effects enables access to a wide variety of special effects.

You can preview all background styles for their effect, either in the small preview area in the dialog box or in the actual slide by choosing the Preview button. If you use the Preview button, you may need to move your dialog boxes if they block the view.

Shading

Styles are split into six categories in the Shaded Fill dialog box (see fig. 23.4):

Horizontal	Four styles, from top to bottom or from the middle in both directions.
Vertical	Four styles, from left to right or from the middle in both directions.
Diagonal Up	Four styles, from top left to bottom right or from the halfway diagonal line in both directions.

Diagonal <u>D</u>own	Four styles, from top right to bottom left or from the halfway diagonal line in both directions.
<u>F</u>rom Corner	Four styles, originating in one of the corners with shading parallel to sides of the page.
From T<u>i</u>tle	Two styles, with color radiating from the slide title.

Fig. 23.4
The From Title shading variant, chosen in the Shaded Fill dialog box, lends a distinctive emphasis to a slide title and to its overall appearance.

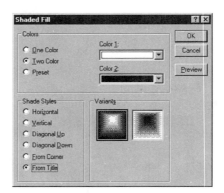

Each style is available in PowerPoint's default colors or a color you select. You also can combine two colors by selecting <u>T</u>wo Color.

An interesting shading style worth noting is the From T<u>i</u>tle variant set. When you change the size of a title on a slide that has this type of shading variant applied, the shading changes its shape to conform to the new title size.

Wherever you move the title, the shading adjusts to match. Use the From T<u>i</u>tle shading style sparingly, though, because it tends to draw attention to the title, which can be a detriment to the clarity of the message conveyed in the slide. Nonetheless, the effect is very striking, because the eye is also drawn downward to the object below the title, in a spotlight effect.

Patterns

PowerPoint offers 36 different patterns in your choice of colors from the color scheme palette or a custom color (see fig. 23.5). Previewing your choices here is important; choosing complementary colors can lead to a very strong contrast that can interfere with the content of your presentation.

Textures

PowerPoint includes 12 textures that offer an interesting effect when placed in the background (see fig. 23.6). The warning sounded earlier is also appropriate here—use textures sparingly and with caution, as they can easily overpower a slide or entire presentation.

Fig. 23.5
The Pattern Fill dialog box offers 36 different patterns in two-color combinations. Be careful in your choice of colors; the effect can make your presentation unreadable.

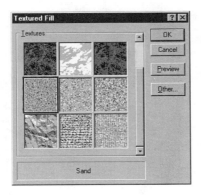

Fig. 23.6
Textured fills are art files with unique textures you can place in the background. Other textures are available from clip art vendors.

You also can include textures from other clip art libraries:

1. Choose Other from the Textured Fill dialog box.

2. In the Look In box, select the folder or drive where the images are stored.

3. Choose Find Now to begin the search.

4. Double-click the file you want from the list.

Pictures

In addition to using art as an element in your slide, you may use a PCX or other graphic file as your background. Because PowerPoint doesn't automatically assume you want to use Microsoft Office clip art, you'll need to direct the search. After locating the file, select from the list and click OK. Choose Apply to use it as a background for the current slide, or Apply to All to use it for the entire presentation.

Many vendors offer clip art packages for specific applications that also can be used with PowerPoint, including Lotus and WordPerfect. Others are available from art vendors, such as Image Club. Image Club has a wide variety of backgrounds on CD-ROM in TIFF format. These can be purchased by category or in one large package.

Other Color

◀ See "Studying PowerPoint's Color Schemes and Basic Color Palette," p. 481

Other color is probably the easiest choice of all. If you don't want to use one of the colors from the color scheme, you can choose another color from the Color properties box by selecting the Custom tab (see fig. 23.7). Select a color available from the Standard page, or choose a custom color from the palette using RGB or HSL parameters.

Fig 23.7
The Colors properties box with the Custom color tab selected. From here, you can select any color available on your computer.

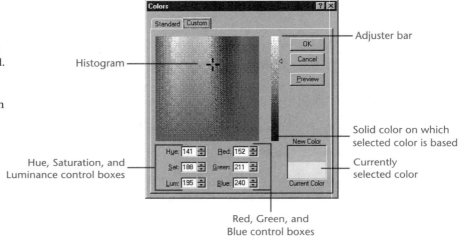

Histogram

Hue, Saturation, and Luminance control boxes

Adjuster bar

Solid color on which selected color is based

Currently selected color

Red, Green, and Blue control boxes

Troubleshooting

What can I do to ensure an effective black-and-white or gray-scale presentation?

Colors don't always translate well into gray-scale or black-and-white. A good practice is to use more pattern fills in your objects to help visually distinguish them. This is particularly useful for laptop users.

The vast majority of PowerPoint users rely on overhead transparencies or black-and-white handouts for their presentations. According to Microsoft, only 2-3 percent of PowerPoint users employ on-screen slide shows for their work, so you'll probably use gray scales on a frequent basis. Microsoft provides a large selection of black-and-white overhead templates in the program, along with templates for color slides and overhead transparencies.

Adding Special Text Effects with WordArt

WordArt is a mini application, or applet, that is a companion to PowerPoint. With WordArt, you can make text fit curves or shapes, rotate and stretch text, add shadows, and more—all in endless combination. However, the same warning applies here that applied to the use of any other special effect: too much of a good thing can be downright ugly. Use these abilities sparingly, and their effect will be amplified.

To insert a WordArt object, follow these steps:

1. Choose Insert, Object.

2. From the list of object types, choose Microsoft WordArt 2.0 and click OK.

3. WordArt begins with the art frame in the middle of the screen, and a smaller text frame just below it. As a starting point, the program adds, "Your Text Here" (see fig. 23.8).

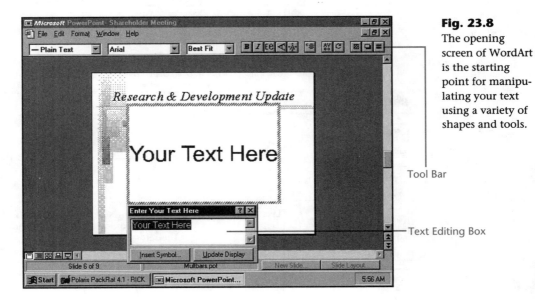

Fig. 23.8
The opening screen of WordArt is the starting point for manipulating your text using a variety of shapes and tools.

Tool Bar

Text Editing Box

Type your text in the text editing box below the display. When you want WordArt to show your text or any subsequent changes you make, choose Update Display. If you need to add special characters, like trademark or copyright symbols, choose Insert Symbol and select the symbol from the character map.

VI

Advanced Techniques

4. Special effects are available from the toolbar. On the top left are options for fitting text to a curve or shape, and changing the typeface and size. Simply choose the arrow next to the item to expand the list and apply the attribute you want (see fig. 23.9).

Fig. 23.9
Choosing the drop-down menu of special effects reveals a wide variety of curves, lines and boxes that can be applied to your text.

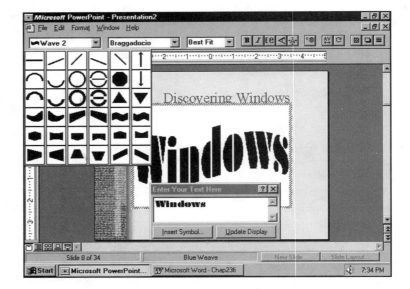

The following table describes the toolbar buttons and what they do:

Button	Name	Effect
B	Bold	Makes the text boldface.
I	Italic	Makes the text italic.
Ee	Even Height	Increases the sizes of all characters, uppercase or lowercase, so they are the same height as the tallest character.
◁	Flip	Each character is rotated 90 degrees.
⁺A⁺	Stretch	The text is pulled to all edges of the frame, usually creating distortion.

Button	Name	Effect
	Alignment	Justifies text to the center, left or right of the frame. Three other options also are available: Justify Letter justifies the text to both margins by adding space between letters; Justify Word adds space between words; and Justify Stretch pulls the text to both margins by distorting the letters.
	Character Spacing	Increases or decreases the amount of space, called tracking, between each letter.
	Special Effects	Two options are available: sliding and rotating. (Sliding tilts the text to the left or right by decreasing or increasing the value beyond 50 percent.)
	Shading, Shadow, and Line Thickness	These are all text coloring attributes, where you can specify patterns, different types of drop shadows, and thickness of the character outline.

The key to mastering these effects is to open WordArt and start playing with the attributes. Keep track of what you do, so when a good idea develops, you can recreate it. A simple method of learning the capabilities is to apply one effect at a time to text that describes your actions (see fig. 23.10).

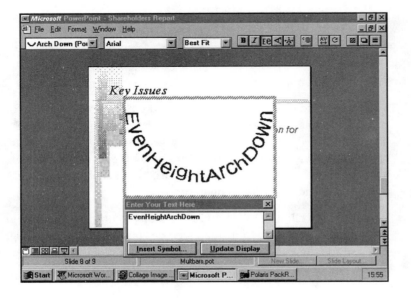

Fig. 23.10
Fitting text treated with the Even Height icon to a curve. Printing examples this way gives a graphic and written reference for repeating the effect later.

VI

Advanced Techniques

Using the Equation Editor

The Equation Editor is another separate application provided with PowerPoint for the creation of mathematical equations for your slides. If you use math in your work, you'll appreciate this program, which is an OLE 2.0 application. This section provides just a brief explanation of basic features, but Equation Editor has a great deal to offer to users interested in advanced math topics. Follow these steps to use the Equation Editor:

1. Choose Insert, Object.

2. When the dialog box appears, choose Microsoft Equation 2.0 from the Object Type list.

   The Equation Editor toolbar and menus appear, as shown in figure 23.11.

   A white editing area surrounded by a grayed border also appears, displaying a blinking insertion point.

Fig. 23.11
The Equation Editor toolbar buttons offer lists of math symbols.

Top row contains mathematical value symbols

Bottom row contains equation templates

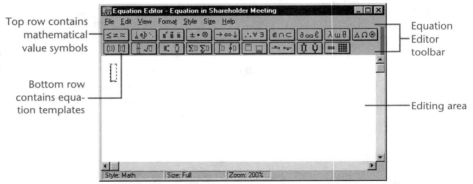

Equation Editor toolbar

Editing area

3. Type your equation in the editing area. For the current example, type **27**.

   Now it's time to choose a template. The Editor's toolbar is divided into two sets of tools. The top row of buttons on the toolbar is a set of Symbol Palettes used to enter mathematical value symbols, and the bottom row of buttons is a set of Template Palettes used to insert mathematical templates for fractions, matrices, integrals, brackets of various types, and other elements of math equations.

   Whenever you click an Equation Editor toolbar button, a drop-down list of symbols attached to the button type appears. For example, figure 23.12 shows the template list attached to the Fraction and Radical Templates symbol button.

4. Click the Fraction and Radical Templates button as shown in figure 23.12. This toolbar button offers formatting for fractions, radicals, and long division.

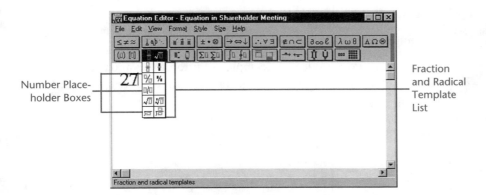

Number Place-
holder Boxes

Fraction
and Radical
Template
List

Fig. 23.12
Choices available from the Fraction Template button include three basic styles of division marks and two choices of radicals, including basic square root. User-added numbers are indicated by boxes.

5. To add a fraction symbol to your equation, you can click any of several template buttons on the drop-down list.

   For example, when you choose a fraction template, it's inserted into your equation. Fraction templates automatically contain two placeholders for numbers that you replace to finish the mathematical expression.

6. Type a number in the top half of the fraction template, press the down arrow key to move the insertion point to the bottom of the fraction template, and type another number. Press the right arrow key to move to the next position for a number or mathematical expression.

   The Equation Editor applies the fraction template and adds numbers to create the fraction.

   The results appear somewhat like figure 23.13.

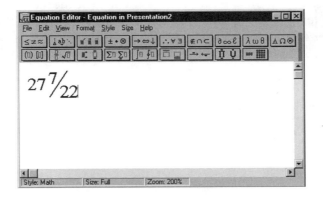

Fig. 23.13
A fraction template is completed by entering the numerator, pressing the down arrow key, typing the denominator, and then pressing the right arrow key.

VI

Advanced Techniques

Tip
You can include other equation templates as part of the current equation by selecting additional templates from the toolbar. For example, a radical could be added as the denominator in a fraction.

Fig. 23.14
This completed equation will be inserted into your presentation by clicking outside of the Equation Editor area.

7. To add a multiplication sign or other operator to your equation, click the Operator Symbols button on the Equation Editor toolbar. Choose the multiplication symbol from the drop-down list. The multiplication symbol is inserted into the equation. Press the right arrow for the next element.

8. For our example, type **32**.

9. Click the Fraction and Radical Templates button again and add another fraction template. Type in the numbers you want and press the right arrow key.

The results should resemble figure 23.14.

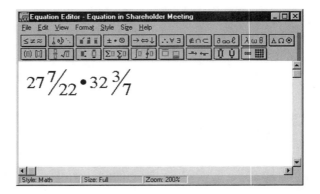

The last steps in this exercise show you how to resize the equation to a larger font:

1. Highlight the equation text.

2. From the Equation Editor, choose Si<u>z</u>e, <u>D</u>efine.

The Sizes dialog box appears, enabling you to define the default point sizes for the fonts in your equations. You can specify point sizes for the full-size font, subscript and superscript fonts, mathematical symbols, and math subsymbols.

3. For our example, type **40pt** in the Full text box.

4. Choose OK or press Enter.

The results appear similar to figure 23.15.

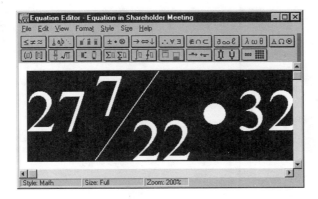

Fig. 23.15
To maintain the quality in the final presentation, size your equations the same as corresponding text in the section where it is located. When used as a figure or illustration, an equation should be at least the size of a headline (44 point).

5. Click anywhere outside the editing area in the Editor to embed the equation into the slide.

6. To edit the equation again, simply double-click the equation object. The Editor appears, displaying the equation for further work.

You now should know enough about the Equation Editor to get started with equations in your presentations. This book cannot begin to explain all the details of Equation Editor; it is a powerful and complex application program all by itself.

Troubleshooting

I can't get the Equation Editor or WordArt to start up. It's not listed in the Insert Object dialog box.

You probably didn't install these applets. Fortunately, you can easily install them by using the PowerPoint Setup program and choosing to install components that weren't previously installed in your computer. Double-click the PowerPoint or Microsoft Office item available through the Add/Remove Programs icon of Windows Control Panel.

All the chapters up to this point have covered many important issues—from simple to complex—about creating your own presentations. If you let your coworkers know about your new knowledge, chances are you'll have people asking you how to use PowerPoint, or even design their presentations together. Go ahead and show off—you've earned it.❖

Chapter 24

Customizing PowerPoint 95

by Rick Darnell

Some people like to start their day with a clean desk, while others leave it piled from the day before. PowerPoint gives you the flexibility to change your work environment to fit how you use it. You can change toolbars, adding, removing, rearranging, or even creating your own custom toolbar. Default settings associated with your presentations, such as color and text, can also be changed. When you finish customizing, you can save the changes and apply them to future presentations.

In this chapter, you learn how to

- Change PowerPoint's defaults
- Create custom toolbars
- Modify existing toolbars
- Change PowerPoint's default editing options
- Set PowerPoint to prompt for file information

> **Note**
>
> For the instructions in this chapter, it's assumed that PowerPoint has been installed in the C:\MSOFFICE\POWERPNT directory. If you installed PowerPoint in a different directory, please substitute your directory's name in the following examples.

Tip
Don't use the
Printer button on
the toolbar to
access the Print
dialog box. This
button is a fast
shortcut to print-
ing your whole
document.

Understanding PowerPoint's Defaults

Defaults are the guidelines used to determine how PowerPoint will operate when it is launched. These initial settings can be changed at any time. If you used other Windows applications (such as Word for Windows), you're prob-ably already aware of the advantage of defaults: they allow you to start using the program immediately to create results you need. For example, you can create a document without first choosing the page size, layout, or other im-portant settings. In PowerPoint, these settings cover all aspects associated with creating and publishing a presentation.

> **Note**
>
> Defaults allow you to begin work quickly after you're familiar with the program. Until you're comfortable with PowerPoint, create your presentations using the default settings.

You don't have to assign any default settings before you create your first presentation, which makes it easy to get acquainted with PowerPoint's com-mands at your own pace. When you're learning how to use the program, default settings are a good place to begin, and these settings are adequate for most presentations. PowerPoint's defaults are saved in a file called Blank Presentation. Later on in this chapter, you learn how to change this file.

Printing Defaults

◀ See "Setting Up
Your Printer,"
p. 455

Any printer installed in Windows can be used to produce your presentation. PowerPoint's printer settings are determined by the type of printer currently selected for use by all Windows applications, but you can change these set-tings within PowerPoint. To see which printer is currently selected, choose Print from the File menu, or press Ctrl+P. The Print dialog box appears, dis-playing the selected printer at the top (see fig. 24.1).

If you want to change the default printer, click the down arrow next to the printer name to view the list of available printers. Then click one of the listed choices. The Printer Name section of the dialog box immediately displays your change.

To view current printer settings, including page size, orientation, and graph-ics treatment, choose Properties. If you change any pages on this sheet (see fig. 24.2), choose Restore Defaults to revert to the original settings.

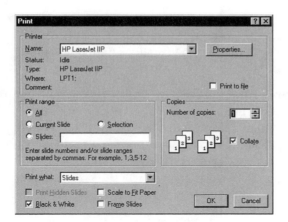

Fig. 24.1
The Print dialog box with the selected printer shown at the top.

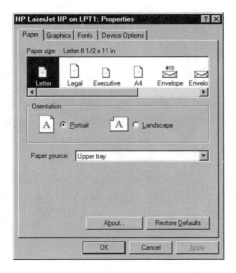

Fig. 24.2
Use the Print Properties sheet to display print settings.

VI

Advanced Techniques

There are four pages available on this sheet which may be selected using the tabs:

■ *Paper.* The size, orientation, and paper source for your printer are selected from this page. If your presentation is being sent to a service bureau, make sure their capabilities and equipment match your choices.

■ *Graphics.* This page controls the overall resolution of the printed sheet and how images are handled by your printer. Resolution is expressed in dots per inch—higher numbers result in smoother curves and cleaner text, but are slower and require more memory. Dithering relates to the treatment of colors, especially on black and white printers. Again, the finer the resolution, the longer the print time and more memory required. Intensity is how dark each dot is that makes up your picture. It is especially noticeable on gradations from one color to another, or across shades of gray.

- *Fonts.* PowerPoint can send TrueType characters to your printer in one of two ways. The first, Send as a Soft Font, is the fastest way. This is how most documents are printed, whether they're in PowerPoint, Word, or any other text-intensive application. Send as Graphics is slower but is necessary for special effects. If you have hidden part of a title with a graphic for visual effect, the text will still appear if it is printed as a soft font. As a graphic, it is treated like any other graphic on the page.

- *Device Options.* Printer memory tracking tells PowerPoint how hard it should try to print your presentation. If your presentation contains many fonts, complex graphics, and other hard-to-print items, your printer may run out of memory. PowerPoint keeps track of what memory is available on your printer and will not print if it doesn't think there is enough. The more conservative the tracking, the less likely a document is to print, even though there may be enough memory. If PowerPoint tracks aggressively, it may send your presentation to the printer even though it is likely to run out of memory.

Changing Text Defaults

◄ See "Editing Text," p. 173

Title objects in PowerPoint have a default text style of Times New Roman 44 Regular, while body object text uses Times New Roman 32 Regular. Initially, all text is centered. Text boxes receive the Adjust Object Size to Fit Text feature.

To change default text editing settings, change the text size and style as desired in one of the Master Views. If you press Shift while you select the Slide or Note Pages view, the Master view appears. With the Outline and Slide Sorter views, press Shift to display the Handout Master view. Then follow one of the two methods described in the next sections to save the default settings.

Changing Color Defaults

The following eight colors are available in the default color scheme:

Area	Color
Background	WHITE
Lines & Text	BLACK

Area	Color
Shadows	GRAY 5
Title Text	BLACK
Fill	BLUE 5
Accents	GREEN 4
Accents	RED 8
Accents	GRAY 6

To change default color scheme settings, use the Color Scheme option on the Format menu. Then follow one of the two methods described in the next sections to save the default settings.

◄ See "Changing a Slide's Color Scheme," p. 488

Changing Object Defaults

Drawn objects are transparent (not opaque), framed in black, filled with white, and unshadowed. The default line style is the thinnest line in the menu, without arrowheads.

To change a default object setting, select new object attributes and follow one of the two methods described in the next sections to save the default settings.

Saving New Default Settings

PowerPoint settings for new presentations are stored in the Blank Presentation file. You can save default settings for all future presentations or for the current project only.

◄ See "Creating and Using Templates," p. 139

To save new default settings for new presentations, follow these steps:

1. Open a new presentation and use the commands on the Format menu (Font, Slide Layout, Slide Background, and Slide Color Scheme) to select the setting you want to change.

   Or, you can open an existing presentation that contains the settings you want to use as defaults.

2. When all settings are correct, choose File, Save As. The Save As dialog box appears.

VI

Advanced Techniques

3. In the Save as File Type box, double-click Presentation Template. Enter Blank Presentation in the name box, and click OK to save the file. The next time you create a presentation from the File menu, your settings will be the defaults.

> **Note**
>
> The Blank Presentation is available when you start PowerPoint or when you choose File, New. Use the New icon on the toolbar to load a different Blank Presentation that never changes.

To save default settings for only the *current* presentation, follow these steps:

1. Select the Arrow button on the Drawing toolbar. Doing so ensures that no objects or text in the active presentation are selected.

2. Use the commands on the Format menu (Font, Slide Layout, Slide Background, and Slide Color Scheme) to select the settings you want to change.

   Because you changed the settings without selecting text or an object first, PowerPoint automatically saves the new settings as defaults for the active presentation.

Customizing Toolbars

PowerPoint allows you to display, modify, and create toolbars to suit your needs. Specifically, you can:

- Add or remove buttons from any of the supplied toolbars
- Rearrange the buttons on toolbars
- Create a custom toolbar

> **Note**
>
> If you don't have a mouse, you should set the Accessibility options in the Windows Control Panel to allow keyboard control of the cursor.

Adding and Removing Buttons on the Toolbar

To add a button to a toolbar, follow these steps:

1. Click the toolbar area using the right mouse button, and then choose Customize from the shortcut menu; or choose Tools, Customize. The Customize Toolbars dialog box appears (see fig. 24.3).

Fig. 24.3

You can create your own toolbars using the Customize Toolbars dialog box.

2. Select a button category from the Categories list. Notice that each selection determines the items shown in the Buttons area in the dialog box.

3. Select the button you want and then drag and drop it onto the toolbar.

4. Add more buttons by repeating steps 2 through 3.

To remove buttons from a toolbar, follow these steps:

1. Click the toolbar area using the right mouse button, and then choose Customize from the shortcut menu; or choose Tools, Customize. The Customize Toolbars dialog box appears.

2. Drag the button you want to remove from its toolbar. As you drag, the button's outline follows the mouse pointer.

3. Release the mouse button when the button is no longer on the toolbar.

4. Remove more buttons by repeating steps 2 and 3. You can close the Customize Toolbars dialog box after you finish removing buttons.

Troubleshooting

I can't see some of the buttons on a toolbar when the toolbar is placed on the sides of the screen.

Change the toolbar to a "floating" toolbar by dragging the toolbar near the center of the screen until its shape changes to a rectangle.

(continues)

VI

Advanced Techniques

(continued)

I wanted to remove a button from a toolbar by dragging it, but I just selected the button.

Display the Customize Tools dialog box by clicking the right mouse button while the pointer is on the toolbar. You can now drag the button to remove it.

I accidentally removed a button from a toolbar.

No problem. Choose Tools, Customize to display the Customize Tools dialog box. Select the name of the toolbar missing the button from the Categories list. Locate the missing button and drag it to the toolbar on the PowerPoint screen.

Rearranging the Contents of a Toolbar

You may want to organize buttons in groups by inserting spaces between buttons, or you may want to simply move a button to a new location on the toolbar. To move a button on a toolbar, follow these steps:

1. Move the mouse pointer to the toolbar you want to modify, click the right mouse button, and choose Customize. The Customize Toolbars dialog box appears.

2. While the Customize Toolbars dialog box is on-screen, move the mouse pointer to the toolbar and drag the button to its new location on the toolbar.

3. Release the mouse button to complete the operation.

To group tools together, do the following:

1. Move the mouse pointer to the toolbar you want to modify, click the right mouse button, and choose Customize. The Customize Toolbars dialog box appears.

2. While the Customize Toolbars dialog box is on-screen, move the mouse pointer to the toolbar and click the button at the end where you want to insert a space.

3. Drag the button to the right and release the mouse button to complete the operation. A space should exist between the dragged button and the button to its left.

Troubleshooting

I tried to swap the position of two buttons on a toolbar, but I just get additional space between the two buttons.

Make sure you drag the button past the center of the adjacent button. Be careful not to drag the button off the toolbar; you'll remove it completely.

Creating a Custom Toolbar

Create your own toolbar by following these steps:

1. Choose <u>V</u>iew, <u>T</u>oolbars. The Toolbars dialog box appears (see fig. 24.4).

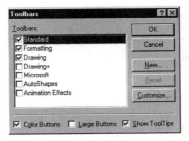

Fig. 24.4
The Toolbars dialog box.

2. Click <u>N</u>ew and type a name for the new toolbar in the small dialog box that appears. Choose OK and an empty custom menu appears on-screen, along with a Customize Toolbar dialog box.

Note

You can display the Customize Toolbars dialog box in several ways. You can display the dialog box by choosing <u>T</u>ools, <u>C</u>ustomize, or by choosing <u>V</u>iew, <u>T</u>oolbars and then clicking <u>C</u>ustomize in the dialog box that appears.

Tip

You can add the same button to more than one toolbar. If you're using a particular button frequently, add it to the Drawing toolbar as well as the Standard toolbar. When you need the button, click the closest one.

3. Select a button category from the Categories list. Notice that each selection determines the items shown in the Buttons area in the dialog box.

4. Select the button you want and drag and drop it onto the Custom toolbar.

5. Add more buttons by repeating steps 3 and 4.

> **Note**
>
> As you create and customize toolbars, you may find it helpful to "float" the toolbar on the PowerPoint screen. To "float" a toolbar, drag it away from the top or sides of the screen until its outline changes to a rectangular shape. Release the mouse button to place the toolbar.

> **Note**
>
> Toolbars may slow down PowerPoint, especially if you are using Windows with just 4M of RAM. To increase performance, remove all toolbars and create and display a custom toolbar.
>
> It's helpful to group like tools together. Use the default groupings of tools on toolbars as an example. For example, on the Drawing Toolbar, all the drawing related buttons are grouped together, the text button is by itself, and the Fill and Shadow buttons are grouped near the bottom of the toolbar.

Enabling and Disabling ToolTips

ToolTips are a feature to help understand what each button does. After you place your cursor on a button for a few seconds, a small box pops up with the name of the button. If you're not sure what a button does, this is a quick way to find out without actually trying anything.

PowerPoint's default is to enable ToolTips. To disable it, choose Tools, Customize, or choose View, Toolbars, and then click Customize in the dialog box. At the bottom right of the dialog box is the ToolTips selection. Click the box to enable or disable it. This will be the default for all future presentations, or until the option is changed again.

Changing PowerPoint Options

In addition to defaults associated with presentations, you can set preferences by using the Options dialog box shown in figure 24.5. There are option tabs for Edit, View, Advanced and General. Choose Tools, Options to display the Options dialog box with its four categories. To disable or enable an option, simply select it. The options are described briefly in table 24.1, and then in more detail in the sections that follow.

Fig. 24.5
The Options
dialog box
includes four tabs.

Table 24.1 Options in the Options Dialog Box	
Option	**Result**
General	
Show Startup Dialog	Displays the Startup dialog box when you start PowerPoint.
Show New Slide Dialog	Displays the New Slide dialog box when you start PowerPoint or select File, New.
Print in Background	Sends printing to the background to allow work to continue.
Recently Used File List	Displays a list of recently used files on the File menu. You can specify the maximum number of files to be displayed in the Entries box.
Prompt for File Properties	When saving a presentation for the first time, PowerPoint asks for more information about the slide show.
Full Text Search Information	Enables Windows Explorer to search the presentation when looking for files.
Edit	
Replace Straight Quotes with Smart Quotes	Replaces straight quotes with Smart, which curve in the appropriate direction to either open or close the quote.
Automatic Word Selection	Selects text a complete word at a time as you drag. Turn off this option to select words one character at a time.
Use Smart Cut and Paste	Text pasted from the clipboard is pasted with appropriate spaces between words.

(continues)

VI

Advanced Techniques

Table 24.1 Continued	
Option	**Result**
Edit	
D̲rag-and-Drop Editing	Selected text and objects can be moved by using the mouse.
A̲lways Suggest	Always suggests an alternative word when encountering a spelling error.
View	
Status B̲ar	Displays the status bar at the bottom of the screen.
Vertical Ruler	Displays a ruler along the side of the screen when rulers are selected.
Pop-up Menu on Right Mouse Click	Display the annotation and slide control menu in a slide show.
Show Pop-up Menu Button	Display the button for the slide show pop-up menu on the bottom of the screen.
End With Black Slide	Ends a slide show with a blank black slide.
Advanced	
Maximum Number of Undos	Sets the amount of actions that are stored for undoing.
Render 24-bit Bitmaps at High Quality	Displays graphics at best possible quality, sometimes at the expense of system speed.
Export Pictures	Determines whether pictures will be prepared for printing or screen.
Default File Location	Chooses the folder where you want presentations stored unless otherwise specified.

Replace Straight Quotes with Smart Quotes

Smart quotes are special characters used by typesetters. This option is enabled by default in the English version of PowerPoint.

When Smart Quotes are enabled, double (") and single (') straight quote marks you type are replaced with double (") and single (') Smart Quotes, respectively. Also, existing quotes are not affected; any existing quotes must be changed manually after you enable Smart Quotes.

Note

The Smart Quotes feature also controls apostrophes to make sure they curve in the proper direction.

Automatic Word Selection

Marking this option enables the Automatic Word Selection feature of PowerPoint. Automatic word selection causes entire words to be highlighted as you drag the I-beam pointer into the word. This feature is helpful if you tend to reword titles or bullet text frequently. If this option isn't marked, the letters of words are highlighted one at a time.

Use Smart Cut and Paste

When Smart Cut and Paste is enabled, PowerPoint pastes text from the clipboard with some intelligence. That is, PowerPoint adds or removes the necessary spaces between words as needed. To illustrate this feature, consider the following sentence:

"The quick fox jumped over the lazy dog's back."

Now suppose you have copied the word *brown* from another sentence onto the clipboard. With Smart Cut and Paste disabled, pasting the word directly after the word *quick* would yield the following:

"The quickbrown fox jumped over the lazy dog's back."

With Smart Cut and Paste enabled, pasting the word after *quick* yields:

"The quick brown fox jumped over the lazy dog's back."

The feature added a space after *quick* to make the sentence read properly. The feature also removes extra spaces between words, as necessary.

Tip

If you have difficulty selecting individual letters of a word, try turning off the Automatic Word Selection feature and editing the text again.

Troubleshooting

Each time I paste a word into a line of text, I have to delete or add spaces.

Turn on the Use Smart Cut and Paste option under <u>T</u>ools, <u>O</u>ptions.

VI

Advanced Techniques

Spelling

When Always Suggest is enabled, the Spelling dialog box always suggests an alternative when a misspelled word is encountered.

Status Bar

Select the Status Bar option to remove the status bar from the bottom of the screen. It slightly increases the available screen for displaying slides but won't noticeably improve PowerPoint's performance.

> **Caution**
>
> Disabling the Status Bar option makes you rely more on your memory. If you have difficulty remembering which slide you're on, or how to perform a procedure, turn the status bar back on.

Prompt for File Properties

The Prompt for Summary Info option, which is enabled by default, displays the Summary Info dialog box whenever you save a file for the first time. You can disable this option and access the Summary Info dialog box whenever you want by choosing File, Summary Info. Use this dialog box to enter descriptive information about your presentation (see fig. 24.6).

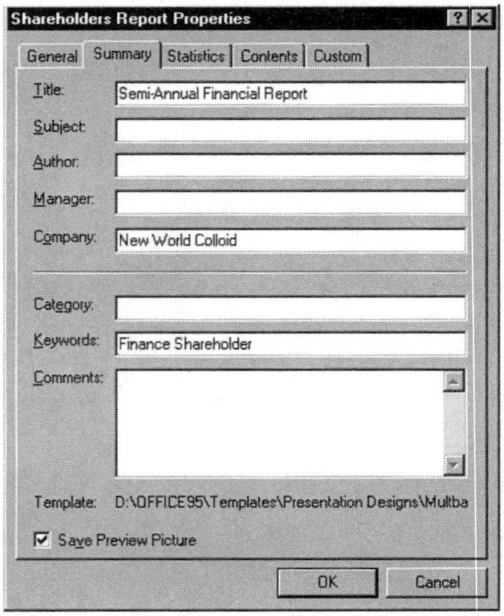

Fig. 24.6
The File Properties sheet with the Summary page selected. This is the best place to store information about your presentation for future reference or archiving.

Troubleshooting

I find it irritating that the Summary Info dialog box appears every time you save a file.

Disable the Prompt for Summary Info option under <u>T</u>ools, <u>O</u>ptions.

Whenever a file is saved for the first time, PowerPoint prompts you for descriptive notes or summary information that make finding the presentation easier later on.

Note

You can add summary information to a presentation any time. To do so, first make sure that the presentation is open. Choose File, Summary Info to display the Summary Info dialog box. Type descriptive text in the fields (up to 255 characters) and then choose OK.

General Options

To display PowerPoint's startup dialog box each time you start PowerPoint, enable the Show Startup Dialog option. The startup dialog box gives you options for creating new presentations and for opening existing presentations. If you become proficient at locating and using options such as the AutoContent Wizard and the Pick a Look Wizard, you'll speed your startup process by disabling the Show Startup Dialog feature.

Enabling the Show New Slide Dialog feature displays a New Slide dialog box each time you start PowerPoint—if you're not using the AutoContent or Pick A Look Wizards to begin your presentations. The New Slide dialog box allows you to choose the layout of the tiles and the text of your slides.

If you frequently use the same set of files, the Recently Used File List option saves you time. By default, PowerPoint displays the last four files that were opened and closed at the bottom of the File menu. Select the Recently Used File List option to hide the list, or adjust the number of files displayed on the list by specifying a different number in the Entries box.

In this chapter, you explored PowerPoint's defaults and customization options. Refer to chapters throughout this book for more details about the many PowerPoint features mentioned here. After you've used PowerPoint for awhile, you may want to come back to this chapter to customize the program to best meet your needs.❖

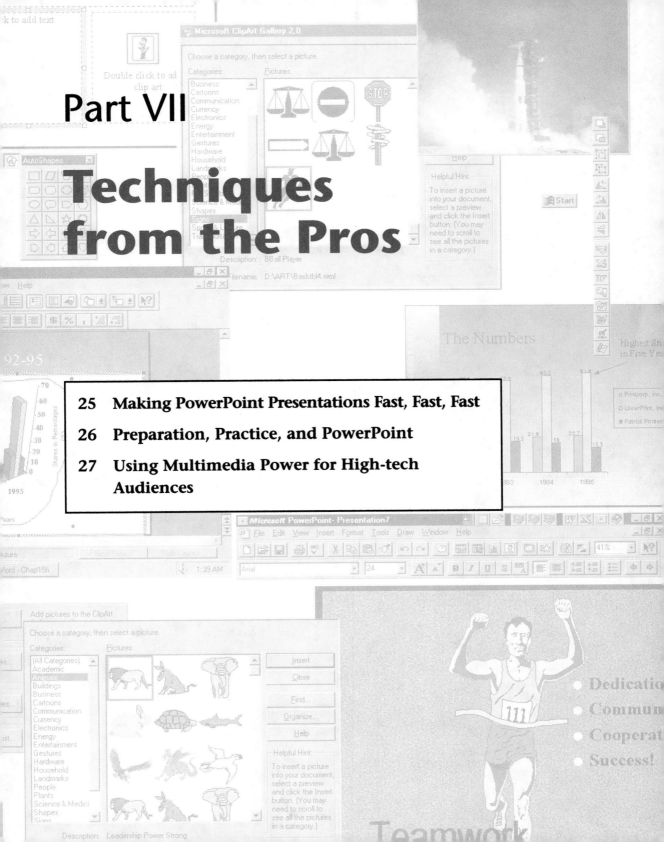

Part VII

Techniques from the Pros

Chapter 25

Making PowerPoint Presentations Fast, Fast, Fast

Harry Newton is a key figure in the telecommunications and computer press. He is the founder and publisher of *Teleconnect*, *Computer Telephony*, *Call Center*, and *Imaging* magazines. He also is the author of a best-selling 1,200 page telecommunications dictionary and of several other books. His research has been quoted in the Wall Street Journal, *Business Week*, *Forbes*, *Newsweek*, and the New York Times. He holds an economics degree from the University of Sydney, New South Wales, Australia, and a Harvard Business School MBA.

Harry Newton is considered the telecommunications industry's most popular and widely known speaker. He speaks at literally dozens of different telecommunications conventions, such as the Information Industry Association, the Telecommunications Association (TCA), and the Armed Forces Communications and Electronics Association. He travels routinely to the Far East, Europe, and throughout the U.S. to deliver PowerPoint presentations and speeches on various telecommunications topics. These presentations often show more than 200 slides.

The widely read industry periodical *ComputerWorld* writes of Newton: *"With Harry, telecommunications is a metaphor for life. Every occupational group should have a Harry Newton. Harry is the patron saint of communications, the exemplar of what can be. He addresses his audience members as though they were a family, chiding them and urging them to realize their potential. He really cares for them."* Nicknamed "Hurricane Harry" by some of his peers, Newton offers a torrent of advice and ideas on PowerPoint as a dynamic tool for the live presenter.

Techniques from the Pros

Interview with Harry Newton by Rich Grace

Q **This book includes various tips and techniques from the pros. What are some of your favorite techniques with PowerPoint?**

Techniques from the pros, eh? Well, I'll give you a few. Even though I do hundreds of slides, you'll have to remember that there's only so many slides that you can throw at an audience. Obviously, the limit is 30 per second—the frame rate of a television. Don't believe anyone who says that you should show only one slide per minute or one every 30 seconds. People are used to watching TV, and they're used to watching film, so the more slides you throw at them, the better.

The second thing to remember is that a series of slides that tells a story, one after another, is more interesting than having one slide with so much information that no one can read it. A lot of what I have in these 240-odd slide presentations is screen shots showing people as they move through demonstrations of software—because I do a lot of that—and those screen shots are done using a typical screen capture program.

Q **What kind of system do you use when you deliver these long presentations?**

If you're doing a program with that kind of graphics load—and my presentation files tend to run about 36M-40M on disk—there are a number of things you need.

The first thing you must use is a Pentium laptop. Mine has 40M of RAM in it. I also set up Windows' swap file to at least 150M. Windows combines the memory and disk space for the swap file, and shows that as the system resources I found; also you don't have to have quite as much memory as long as you have the disk space allocated, and then PowerPoint will run with all those slides. I once tried to deliver a long presentation on an old 486 laptop without enough space allocated, and it froze up halfway through.

You also should put a red Avery label on your Page Down button. When I'm delivering in front of an audience I use the Page Down key, because with a lot of newer laptops the mouse clicker button is located way down on the bottom of the laptop, and it's very hard to get to. But the Page Down key is usually very close to the end key, and I've made the mistake of hitting End when I wanted to hit Page Down, and scrolled all they way to slide 242 instead of number 40. Then I have to click backwards in front of a thousand people. Yes! This has happened to me!

I've also discovered a product called MindPath Remote Control. For $60, it's a little thing that plugs into your serial port, and it gives you an infrared pointer. You hold the little pointer towards the projection screen, and it allows you to page up and page down. It also allows you to move the cursor (the Annotate tool) around the screen, and has five programmable buttons.

Q So that means you can be a lot more relaxed when you do your presentation.

This device could be a godsend, because the worst thing you can do when you deliver a presentation is to stand behind a podium. The audience can see only your face and your shoulders, and you look like a talking head, and everybody goes to sleep. What I do now is I have a hand-held microphone but then I have to rush back to the machine to push the button (to advance the slide)! That, of course, is stupid. I'd much rather have a microphone in one hand and a pointer in the other. Now it looks like I'll be able to do that, to experiment.

Q How do you deal with external graphic sources?

When we're importing into PowerPoint, the best graphic format to use is PCX. It's the easiest format. We find that we can scan in graphics and take a lot of stuff out of the Macintoshes—we use a lot of Macs in our publishing operation—and we can drop the files directly into our PowerPoint presentation. A key point is to tell your artists that you must save at no more than 640x480 resolution.

Q Why use typical VGA resolution on a laptop?

There's no point in doing anything else, even if your laptop can do higher resolutions on an external screen, because the projectors that you meet at trade shows don't do anything else besides VGA anyway.

Q How do you account for different languages? Since you deliver in front of international audiences, is this a problem?

Well, of course I normally do English, but it's also all high-tech. Everything that I'm talking about—telecommunications, and various aspects of computing, and LANs (Local-Area Networks), imaging, and so forth—it's all high-tech, and all those audiences are in English. The most important part is that when you do the talk, you've got to put the words on the slide. This sounds like a really basic point, but at least the audience has some reference on the slide of what the heck you're talking about.

With my typical slides, I will not have any text on them that is smaller than about 48 point. My traditional size that I'll go with is 60 point to 90 point. The reason for that is with a big audience, you just can't see that small type from the back. Even though you might have a 20-foot screen and you might be backlit, and have a $100,000 Barco, it doesn't do any good if the audience is a hundred feet away because they can't read it. So they just go to sleep.

So in preference to having a busy slide with five hundred words on it, I'd rather have a series of slides with much less verbiage on them. I never have more than, say, a title and three points, then a title and three points for the next slide. I'll often have the same title on six to ten different slides. I also never do any fancy stuff, like dimming points, or using transitions or build effects where the points slide over one by one. I just give them the information.

Q You don't use transitions or Build effects?

I don't do any of that. Whenever I've experimented with them, a transition takes too long. If you're doing 242 slides in an hour and a half, or as I did today in an hour and 25 minutes, you don't have time for that stuff. People want fast, fast, fast. Most people in the United States now—or in the world for that matter—were brought up on Sesame Street. The longest time that Sesame Street will stay on one scene, without moving the camera or chopping it to another camera angle is about 25 seconds. Anything more than that is too long.

You've got a very, very short attention span to deal with in many cases. That's the reality. It's true of audiences worldwide. They just expect slides to move very fast. Now, in between these things, what I do is I often run little video clips, and I'll run multimedia presentations as well, but I don't include them in PowerPoint. I've tried a little ScreenCam (a way to record and play back a series of on-screen software procedures, such as making menu selections or clicking a tool button) during a show, but I just find it's too difficult. If I want a video, I just go into another application, and load it and run it. With 36M of extra RAM, I can run one or two more applications without a problem.

What type of laptop do you use?

I use a Toshiba 4900 laptop, which is the top of the line now, with a Pentium-75, an 800M hard disk and the 40M of RAM. Naturally, if you have to ask how much it costs, you won't be able to afford it. But can you afford not to have it, when you're doing a presentation and trying to sell something to 1,500 people? If you divide the cost of the laptop, which is five or six thousand dollars by that fifteen hundred people, it's nothing. You might as well throw it away at the end of the presentation—it's cheap! It's certainly cheaper than giving them a bag of handouts and stuff to carry away! You might as well throw the thing away at the end. Of course, I wouldn't.

 But is it cheaper in the long run than building packets of handouts for an audience of your size?

It's a more powerful thing. You've got a captive audience, and it behooves you to do these things in as professional a manner as possible. I still do a lot of multimedia in certain situations. People present me with little clips and I drop them in using a lot of different sources, like Intel ProShare, or ScreenCams, and other things. I also ask manufacturers for clips or sets of slides, and they give them to me because they know I'm presenting their stuff in front of audiences. I try to make a point with the program.

A problem with a lot of presenters is that they don't really make a point with their presentation. They tend to say things like, "The trends in the industry are this way, or that way," and they never bother to show any supporting evidence. They say something like "Ads are becoming very sexist," but they don't show you any ads. If I'm doing something, on say, voice processing, I will mention that "a trend in the industry is toward fax servers, or integrated messaging," and then I'll show them examples of what the darn things are. Let's face it, you can give people these technology words, you can talk to them about word spotting in voice processing and recognition as much as you like, but they won't get it unless you explain to them what it is. Don't take it for granted that the whole audience always knows what you're talking about.

 That seems like a really basic thing to keep in mind. Does everyone?

Well, most people make terrible PowerPoint presentations. The biggest mistake that everyone makes when they give a presentation is talking about their company, and forgetting to talk to their audience and make an interesting presentation. They just take some standard set of slides that they've given 400 times.

I just gave a keynote speech today with PowerPoint at a big IBM show, and came back with a book that the company was handing out. I was sitting and reading it on the way home. There are PowerPoint slides in there, and down at the bottom of the slides it reads "Copyright 1994." This is halfway through 1995 and IBM is giving out slides from last year. Why give people a reason to dismiss the information because it doesn't *appear* to be current, even though it still might be? At least fix the copyright before you give the show! That's just stupid stuff. In any case, I don't normally use dates after the first slide.

Q What kind of color depths do you typically use in your presentations?

I usually run it at the maximum that the laptop will support. There again, you're limited by what the projector will support. Another thing is that sometimes I'll get slides from other places and have to clean them up before I use them. For example, if I get a slide that has a fancy drawing or graphic on it, frequently it takes too long for the graphic to draw when the slide appears. You can often redraw them so that the slide will change much faster. Sometimes, you'll need to simplify a slide. Watch what happens when you run a slide transition. Watch the slide draw itself when it goes from one slide to the other, and watch what comes out last. You can often just remove that last bit and the slide will move very much faster.

You don't want to hit Page Down and wait 10 seconds for the stupid thing to do something. You may be giving a speech and talking very quickly, or have good momentum, and then you hit Page Down and you have this long wait. You might think you hit the wrong button, and go over and hit it again, and suddenly you're two slides ahead. Then you wind up going backwards and forwards and you look like a jerk! You're in Presentation Hell.

Before you start your PowerPoint presentation in front of your audience, completely reboot your machine and load Windows again from scratch. Windows has a nasty habit of remembering all the other stuff that was in there (Author's Note: Windows 95 still does this to some extent), and tying up resources for things that aren't even there any longer. Never run a PowerPoint presentation without doing this.

The discipline of doing this stuff is very critical.❖

Chapter 26

Preparation, Practice, and PowerPoint

Dr. Grace Beatty and **Dr. David Gardner** are business and marriage partners. Residents of northern San Diego County, they are accomplished public speakers and frequent Power-Point users. Their book publishing credits include the best-selling *Never Be Tired Again,* from Harper & Row, and a successful series of *Visual Learning Guides* for beginning computer users.

Q **What types of public speaking engagements do you and Dr. Gardner specialize in?**

Well, we just finished a speech in San Francisco entitled "Sex, Business, and the Internet." It was for a group of 500 Australians who were here as prize winners in a sales contest for an insurance company. We work through speaker's bureaus across the country. We really enjoy it, because it's a real adrenaline rush. It's fun to speak in front of hundreds of people.

Q **What formats do your presentations usually have? Do you use a lot of multimedia, for example?**

We normally just use basic slides, without a lot of multimedia or effects. Our presentations are very interactive, and we use a lot of audience participation, so we don't get into the multimedia things. In our San Francisco trip, we had a computer hookup so that we could project from the computer screen up onto the big screen for the hall.

Techniques from the Pros

Interview with Dr. Grace Joely Beatty and Dr. David C. Gardner by Rich Grace

We were showing them actions like "cruising the Internet," browsing, what it (the Internet) looks like, and other things. In this particular speech, we not only had slides, but a live demonstration. This is the exception and not the rule.

How long is your typical slide show?

Our speeches range from an hour or so to a full day. This particular one was an hour, and we had a lot of audience participation, so we might have had ten minutes of slides during the talk. We might have, in a longer speech of two or three hours, 20 to 30 slides. We have what I call "Canned" presentations that we draw upon. There's another one that we do called *Never Be Tired Again*, based on one of our books, and that ranges over wide periods of time. We pick a choice depending on the projected length of the talk. We have another one on interpersonal relationships that we build on for varying lengths.

How do you handle the actual delivery of the presentation?

We always use hand-held remote-control clickers, regardless of whether our audience has dozens or thousands (of people), which has happened a couple of times. The last speech that we did, the facility had a control booth at the back of the auditorium, which they used to control the slides. I didn't like that. We prefer to manage the slide shows ourselves.

We've learned the hard way that the colors that you see on your screen can be deceiving. They don't look the same way on the projector screen as they do on your monitor. They look really pretty on the screen but may not project well. They don't magnify well. You want to go for contrast—for a light background you want dark type, and for a dark background you want light type, for example. Not white, however. Ideally, you don't want text to just drop out of the background in a projection. You'd have to use light yellow as opposed to white. Then there's an actual shape and not just a cutout.

Somehow, that makes a difference in how it's perceived when it's blown up to huge proportions by a projector or a Barco (a Barco Vision large screen projection system). Obviously, basic rules apply, such as not putting too much on a slide. You're better off showing a few slides in sequence than you are trying to cram everything onto one slide.

If you know that you're going to talk for a while about a particular topic—that doesn't have direct bearing on the slide that you're seeing—take the next slide and make it a black one. It blanks out and then people's attention isn't torn between you and what's on the screen. A really common problem in presentations that have a lot of slides is that the speaker gets lost in the information. The audience then tends to focus on the slides and not on you. That gets boring, because then all you're doing is presenting a lot of information. You need to set up your speech so that there's a good mix, and so the audience can set up a good relationship with you as the speaker.

Q Are there any ideas that you can share about tailoring your presentation to your audience?

One of the things that we do that has been very successful is to ask for the names of two or three people who are good representatives of the audience group. I literally call them on the phone before the show, and tell them I'm giving a speech called "Blah, blah, blah…" at their convention. I ask them questions about the things they want to get out of that speech, what interests them about the topic, and what would make them happy that they learned during the speech. I get invaluable information by doing that. This also gives me names of people that I can mention at the beginning of the presentation, to establish a clear rapport with the group or the audience. Frankly, it's a pain in the neck to do, because most of the people we talk to are very busy people in their own right, and have their own lives going on.

Q Just like what we've been trying to do for the last week— getting this interview arranged. It's a lot of work, isn't it?

It's exactly like that. But it's well worth it, and I highly recommend doing that. Another thing that we do is to make sure we get there early. It's a big caveat—get to your presentation site early so that you can field-test the equipment. It's absolutely essential. I would allow a minimum of an hour in advance of speech time, and preferably two hours. And speak to whoever it is who's setting up this speech—if it isn't you—and tell them that you want to do this. They always understand, because it's essential to them, too, that things go well. We always go in early and do a run-through with the slides, one by one, because you never know what can happen. We've found slides upside down, or backwards. You catch equipment that doesn't work. You catch little clickers that don't work.

Try on your mikes and make sure that they work, that you're not getting feedback from the P.A. system. Do a sound check. All of these things are important, because they're the things that people remember—the little annoyances that grate on the audience's nerves. And that's what they remember about your speech. They don't hear you if they're thinking, "What is that hissing?," "What is that noise?" or whatever. They don't hear what you're saying anymore, and you've lost them.

Because we're there early, another thing we do is that when people start to wander into the hall or the room, we go around and introduce ourselves to people individually. We ask the same questions about why they're interested in this seminar as opposed to the 17 others that are going on. You can get some great feedback, or even good lines that you can use in the beginning of your speech. You get a good rapport with 10 or 20 people out of this group, and it can be very effective.

Q **I've been to a number of conventions, particularly Comdex and New Media Expo in Los Angeles, and some of the presentations and group discussions of the various topics at these shows are below par. These are usually pretty technically accomplished people, or they're veteran marketers in the computer and new media industries, but all they do is sit at a desk, using clickers to advance their presentations.**

Fortunately, as a member of the press, I can go in and out of these meetings at will, but the person who spends $250 for a two-hour seminar is usually trapped, because they want to get their money's worth. The point is: Can you offer any tips on how others can improve their deliveries?

That's a good point, because many people get lost in the technology. They think that because they're giving people really cool technology, they're doing their job as a speakers, and they're not. To me, this is just presenting information. That's not your job as a speaker. Your job is to engage the audience, to get them excited about what you're saying, and to get them beyond the technology. It's very old rules for public speaking, but nothing has really changed.

Eye contact is important. One of the horrible things about our last speech in San Francisco is while we were speaking, they projected your face up on this huge screen, so that everybody had a good audience perspective. Unfortunately, from the speaker's perspective, I had these huge beacons glaring in my face, and I couldn't see a darn thing! So I had no eye contact with anybody, and I had to try to maintain kind of a friendly looking face, and look like I was making contact with people when all I could see were these blinding lights. It was awful, and I hated it.

 Almost like being a rock star, right?

Typically, that's not the situation. Don't think of it as speaking to 500 or a 1,000 people. Try to personalize it. People are paying us thousands of dollars to do this stuff, so we have to put in the extra effort.

 A lot of speakers are prone to the "talking head" syndrome, where they anchor themselves firmly to a podium and never move. What do you do to avoid this?

We never speak from behind a podium. We walk back and forth across the stage, go down into the audience, and get some elements in our speech to get the audience involved, even if it's just raising their hands to answer a question. God forbid you should read from notes. There's nothing worse than sitting for an hour or an hour and a half, in a boring presentation. A cardinal sin is to read from notes throughout your speech. You're better off forgetting something and maintaining personal contact than you are reading from a list.

So you think the utility of Notes Pages is limited?

I think they're very limited. To me, Notes Pages would be used for really key points and there might be one or two things on a page. But never, never use a script. Number One, never use a script. Inevitably, you'll forget it and then you'll panic. It sounds canned, and it sounds like you're reading something. You might as well hand it out to people so they can read it at their leisure.

> **Q Since you don't rely on this tool, what do you do to ensure that your speeches come off well?**

Practice. Speakers who don't practice and time themselves are crazy. We absolutely rehearse. There are some speeches that we've been giving for years, such as "Never Be Tired Again," which we've been doing for five years. Every time we do it, we ask ourselves, "How long will this take? What slides do we use?" and so on. We do run-throughs. People are paying us thousands of dollars to speak, and it's our professional obligation to do that. Plus you look like a fool if you don't.❖

Chapter 27

Using Multimedia Power for High-tech Audiences

Christine Andresen is a graphic artist and technical illustrator in Intel's Corporate Speech Development group. She and two colleagues actually build the PowerPoint presentations that Intel's top executives (including CEO Andrew Grove, founder Gordon Moore, and vice-presidents David House and Craig Barrett) use when they deliver speeches across the globe.

Because Intel is the world's premier microprocessor manufacturer, Christine Andresen and her colleagues bear a heavy responsibility to ensure that things go well when the leaders of this multi-billion dollar technology company appear before packed audiences. Especially compared with the other interviews in this book, Christine's outlook on technical effects in presentations is markedly different. "Multimedia and animation can express an idea much more clearly than simple words or pictures ever can." Christine's views and experiences are of great value to any serious presentation user.

Q **Can you give me a sense of the typical PowerPoint presentation you produce for Intel's executives?**

Most of the time, our presentations have lots of embedded video. They're either shots taken from a video camera or animations that are converted to AVI files (a video playback file standard under Windows). We also use a lot of clip art. I've created an entire CD of clip art using PowerPoint's drawing tools, including company logos,

Techniques from the Pros

Interview with Christine Andresen by Rich Grace

which are used throughout many of our presentations. We use a lot of scanned art, and a lot of bitmaps and pictures as well as lots of text. We also use sound files in many places. Our usual file winds up being about ten megabytes, but we've had them at as many as a hundred.

Q So your presentations run the gamut of all different types of computer data. How long are your typical slide shows?

We can do anything with PowerPoint. Our slide counts depend on the length of the speech. Usually, it's about 25 slides for a half-hour speech, and we've done as many as 120 for a two-hour speech. David House gives a lot of those, because he likes to show things off, and he uses a lot of Builds and fancy stuff.

Q When you hand the PowerPoint files over, what do you do to make sure that the slide shows come off properly?

Most of the time, we provide presentation systems along with the PowerPoint files. We have a number of presentation systems set up for executive use only, and everybody is taken care of when Intel executives go as a group to give talks, for example, at sales conferences. We set up anywhere between 10 to 50 different systems, and we'll load up all of them with all the different files, pack them up, load them and bring them into the site. We always have primary and backup systems available. We do all the last-minute changes and rehearsals up there, on-site, with the executives. They do dry walk-throughs so they feel comfortable with the slide sequence before their speech. We use either an AirMouse, an infrared mouse, or an actual mouse placed on the podium. The AirMouse is like a garage-door remote control. You can point it in any direction and it will advance the slides in the system.

A lot of the executives like to have freedom to move about on the stage, while some prefer to stay at the podium. Sometimes we have demo systems placed on stage, so the executives can move around to work with those as well.

We use new Sharp projectors that are about the size of a suitcase, and they're really slick. They're much brighter than the old Barco machines that are used everywhere.

Q **What kind of presentation systems do you normally use? Pentium laptops?**

Yes, we have several Pentium laptops, running 24 megabytes of RAM and things like that. Typically, we use thousands of colors on the screen, and sometimes millions, unless we have a problem. Occasionally we'll run across a piece of funky clip art that will crash the system at higher color depths, so we convert them down to thousands of colors and it usually fixes it. Sometimes, other people will do presentation files and give them to us, and we clean them up, and apply the right template to it.

Q **Though this book is about PowerPoint 95, all the interviews done here are with strong PowerPoint 4 users. PowerPoint 4's multimedia support is a little scanty. How do you manage to work around this?**

We fudge to make things look right. For example, we might embed a video clip on a slide, and we want the presenter to be on the slide, click the mouse to start the video, and cleanly return to the slide when the video is finished running. We also might want the video to hide when it isn't playing. Sometimes we'll take a still of the last frame in the video and have it on the slide, and have the actual video running in a window over PowerPoint. So the executive can click again to run the video, have the video end on the last frame and on the still. He then clicks and moves on. What we do is make two slides. The first slide has just the still on it, and the second slide has the embedded video with a still of the last frame pictured on top. When you click through it, it looks like it's all on one slide when it's really not.

We have all kinds of little work-arounds to make things look right. Another artist that's in my group just did a mock-up version of a virtual-reality Internet session. He's got an animation embedded in PowerPoint that has an executive's face on a virtual body, and he walks into a room—it's all embedded videos in mocked-up PowerPoint slides—and the user clicks on a button, and the virtual body walks into a hallway, and explores the hallway to look up something on any subject, such as "Cars." He clicks on a button for that subject, and the virtual head talks. Then he's walking down this 3-D aisle with columns and marble floors, with a big banner on top that reads 'Nissan,' 'Ford,' and so on. He walks around, turns around, and talks! It's all in a PowerPoint presentation, and it looks great! It looks like something that would be in MacroMedia Director.

Q You're really going to like PowerPoint for Windows 95. It has greatly enhanced multimedia and animation features. How do you manage to make this stuff work in PowerPoint 4 without having Windows hang every ten minutes?

It's the RAM in the laptops, to start with. We also make sure that the machines are restarted before the show.

Q Have you had a chance to use PowerPoint for Windows 95?

No, I haven't. I was contacted by the PowerPoint people, and they asked my opinion on things that I would like to see in the next version, and the other artists and I sat down and wrote up a whole list of things that we would like to see in the new version. I wanted to be able to customize my own page layouts. I wanted to see a better charting tool. Its text wrapping feature is not very good, and it causes me a lot of problems.

Q Since you usually place your presentations on portable systems, you can get around the problem users have when they have to bundle up their files for transport to another site, with the collection of OLE linked files and so on. But when you have to deal with that problem, what do you do?

If we don't support the system, what we do is tell the people, "Look, here are all the files, and this is where they should all go when you install them, say, in the C:\POWERPNT directory, and everything should run fine." When we embed video and sound files, we download them onto our hard drive into the PowerPoint directory before we use them—we don't insert them off the server or off of some other machine. We do those things the same way every time.

PowerPoint is really cool for bringing in clip art from lots of other programs. You can bring anything in. You just have a lot more freedom in PowerPoint over other programs from an artist's point of view.

Q If PowerPoint doesn't have a direct file format filter for a type of drawing, like CorelDRAW! 5.0, then what do you do?

Then you just copy it into the clipboard and paste it in from there. That is usually good, and if the program drops things from the drawing (which happens once in awhile), you just export it as a bitmap. You can't use OLE in that case, but CorelDRAW! 5 supports OLE 2.0 and you can then use it right alongside PowerPoint, so most of the time, there's no need to import.

Q **Given that you're producing these presentations for some of the most powerful executives in the computer industry, there must be considerable pressure to make sure that this stuff is successful, and that it works properly before you give it to them. Is there any tension on the job as far as making sure that everything is the way they want it to be?**

Oh, yes, of course there is. I can tell you one story. One time we were backstage, running the backup systems and the primary, and David House was up on the stage with all the executives, and they were doing a wrap-up of a big conference. He was making changes while he was up on the stage. We would get the changes from his controlling the primary, and we were on the backup system rearranging the order of the slides, and then we would switch Dave to the backup so he could click through it with the correct order.

But the tension is part of the job. You know, the job is really fun. It's exciting, and I get a kick out of it. Sometimes we're really pushed for deadlines, especially when everyone's making last-minute changes and we have to get the presentation systems loaded and ready to go to the airport. Then we get to the site and we pull our hair out, getting things started and rolling on the first day. By the second day of a conference like Comdex things start to smooth out and we can begin to enjoy ourselves. We usually pull all-nighters when we first do it.❖

Glossary

Terms

16-bit   In Windows, this refers to the way memory is accessed. 16-bit applications access memory in 16-bit "chunks" (2-bytes). Most pre-Windows 95 applications are 16-bit (see *32-bit*).

16550A UART   The name of the most modern chip controlling the serial port. Older chips could not support the data throughput that today's high-speed communications protocols and modems support.

32-bit   In Windows, this refers to the way memory is accessed. 32-bit applications access memory in 32-bit "chunks" (4-bytes). Large portions of Window 95 and many of its new applications are 32-bit applications, and may run faster because it has become more efficient to access chunks of memory.

A

accelerator key   A keyboard shortcut for a command. For example, Shift-Delete is an accelerator command for the Edit, Cut command.

activate   To bring a window to the front and make it active.

active printer   The printer that will be used by programs.

active window   The window that is currently being used. Active windows show the "active window color" in their title bar (settable through the control panel). Other windows are inactive. To activate an inactive window, you must click somewhere in the inactive window or use the taskbar to select the window (see *taskbar*). On the taskbar, the active window looks like a pressed button; inactive windows are represented by unpressed buttons.

address book   A list of persons, phone numbers, and other information used by various Windows 95 programs, including Microsoft Fax and HyperTerminal.

Adobe Type Manager (ATM) An Adobe program that enables you to work with PostScript fonts in Windows 95.

Advanced Program-to-Program Communications A communications standard defined by IBM. The APPC standard is intended to allow multiple users to share the processing of programs.

airbrush In "paint" and graphics programs, a tool that "sprays" dots in a randomized pattern around the point indicated by the user. In most programs, the output of the airbrush can be configured to modify the color, pattern, and density of the dot pattern.

alert message A critical warning, confirmational, or informational message appearing in a dialog box.

annotate To add notes. For example, you can add your own notes to Windows Help.

ANSI A standard for ordering characters within a font.

anti-aliasing A graphics technique used to hide the diagonal edges and sharp color changes ("jaggies") in a graphic or font. Because a computer screen possesses limited resolution, such changes highlight the pixels on the screen and don't look smooth. Using anti-aliasing smoothes out the changes and makes them appear more attractive.

Anti Virus A program included with Windows 95 that helps eradicate viruses (see *virus*) from your hard drive or floppy disks.

API See *Application Programming Interface.*

APPC See *Advanced Program-to-Program Communications.*

applet A small application unable to run by itself. When you purchase Windows 95 or another application, it may come with additional applets. For example, Word comes with applets for manipulating fonts (WordArt), drawing graphs (MS Graph), and creating graphics (MS Draw).

application A computer program.

Application Programming Interface (API) A set of interface functions available for applications.

archive bit A single bit stored in a disk directory to indicate if a file has been changed since it was last backed up. Backup programs clear a file's archive bit when they back up the program. Modifying the program resets the bit and a backup program knows to make a backup the next time you do a backup.

ASCII characters   A subset of the ANSI character standard.

ASCII file   A file consisting of alphanumeric characters only. Although virtually every file can be converted to an ASCII file, all formatting (for example, bold, italics, underline, font size, and so on) will be lost in the ASCII file.

associate   Linking a document with the program that created it so that both can be opened with a single command. For example, double-clicking a DOC file opens Word for Windows and loads the selected document.

AT command set   A set of commands originally developed by Hayes for modems. Its name originates from the fact that each command starts with "AT" (attention). Today, most modems support the AT command set, enabling Microsoft to supply the Unimodem driver with Windows 95.

ATAPI   A specification for devices to attach to EIDE buses. This specification is almost identical to the EIDE specification.

ATM   Asynchronous Transfer Mode is a high-speed, but expensive, networking solution. ATM networks reach speeds of 155 Mb/s.

attribute   A property or characteristic.

attributes (FAT)   Settings for each file indicate if the file is used by an operating system, has read-only status, has its archive bit set, or is a hidden file.

auto arrange (Explorer)   In Explorer, auto arrange organizes the visible icons into a regular grid pattern.

B

background operation   A job performed by a program when another program is in the active window. For example, printing or creating a backup can be done by Windows 95 as a background operation.

Backup   A program that comes with Windows 95 and enables the user to back up the files from a hard disk to a floppy disk, tape drive, or another computer on a network.

backup set   The set of duplicate files and folders created by a backup program (see *Backup*). This set is stored on tapes, diskettes, or other storage media that can be removed and stored safely away from your computer. See *Full System Backup*.

Basic Input/Output System (BIOS)   A program—usually residing on a ROM-based storage device in your PC—that handles instructions to and from the system bus.

batch program   A text file that instructs Window 95 to perform one or more tasks sequentially. Used for automating the loading or execution of programs. Batch files have a .BAT or .CMD extension.

Bézier curve   A mathematically constructed curve, such as the one used in drawing programs.

bi-directional printer port   Bi-directional Printer Communications sends print files to your printer and listens for a response. Windows quickly identifies a printer that is unable to accept a print file.

binary   A numbering system with only two values: 0 (zero) and 1 (one).

binary file   Any file containing characters other than text.

binary file transfer   A data transfer in which files aren't converted. Typically used with a modem to send programs or complex documents from computer to computer.

binary transfer protocol   When using a communications program to transmit binary files, it is very important to ensure that errors are not introduced into the data stream. Various binary transfer protocols check for matches between the data transmitted and the data received. The most common protocols are Xmodem, Ymodem, and Zmodem.

BIOS   See *Basic Input/Output System*.

bit map   A screen page in memory. Most bit maps represent some sort of viewable graphics. You can use a "paint" program to edit graphic bit maps and make modifications to them. However, although objects such as rectangles and circles may appear in a graphic bit map, these objects cannot be edited as objects. You must modify these objects one bit at a time using the paint tools in the program.

bits per second (bps)   A measurement of data transmission speed, usually over a serial data link. Roughly equivalent to baud rate. A single character requires approximately 10 bits, so a transfer rate of 9600 baud results in about 960 characters per second (cps) being transferred. This speed, however, varies depending on the make of your modem.

boot partition   The hard-disk partition that contains the Windows 95 operating system.

bound media   In networks, this refers to traditional cabling connecting the nodes of a network together, and to a server, if any. See also *unbound media*.

bridge   In networks, a device that joins two separate LANs but restricts LAN frame traffic to either side of the bridge (unless forwarding is required). Bridges process LAN frames (not network packets) and are governed by IEEE standards. A bridge should not be confused with a router (see *router*), which uses an entirely different layer of protocol and information for forwarding packets (not frames).

browse   To search through or examine a directory tree of files, directories, disks, workstations, workgroups, or domains. Often done via a Browse button in a dialog box.

Bulletin Board System (BBS)   An electronic service that can be accessed via a modem. A BBS typically includes collections of files, notes from other computer users, and many other services. Examples of commercial BBSs include CompuServe, Prodigy, Delphi, GEnie, and America Online (AOL). Information about Windows 95 and Windows 95 applications can be found on all these BBSs.

burst mode   A mode used in MCA and EISA computers and devices to facilitate greater flow of data through the bus. When bus mastering is employed, a bus master and its slave can establish a connection and send large blocks of data without CPU intervention. Without burst mode, each byte requires CPU attention to gain control of the bus, and send a byte of data.

bus   The interface between devices in a computer. PCs incorporate bus designs including ISA, EISA, MCA, PCI, and VLB (VESA Local Bus).

bus mastering   A function used to off-load I/O processing to a processor on the interface card. Bus mastering is only truly effective when used with a bus design that can control bus master access to the computer bus, as is the case in EISA, MCA, and PCI computers. Bus mastering alone does not fully utilize the capabilities of this design unless implemented in conjunction with accessing the 32-bit burst mode and streaming data modes of EISA, MCA, and PCI computers.

bus network   One of various network topologies. A bus network is one in which all of the computers on the network are connected to the main wire of the network.

C

cache RAM A small collection of very high speed RAM. In general, modern microprocessors can process information much faster than standard dynamic RAM can even supply the information. Nevertheless, fast dynamic RAM is very expensive. Instead, a very small amount (typically 256K or 512K) of very fast "cache RAM" acts as a buffer between the CPU and the dynamic RAM. If the information needed by the CPU is in the cache, it can be processed without waiting to retrieve it from the dynamic RAM.

Calculator A program that comes with Windows 95 and enables you to perform standard or scientific calculations.

capture text In Hyperterminal, this refers to capturing and saving the text that appears in the terminal window to either a file or the printer. This is handy when reviewing the session at a later time.

Cardfile A program that comes with Window 95 and enables you to record information cards and sort through them by using their index lines.

cascade (Windows) To arrange all the windows so that they are neatly stacked; only their title bars show behind the active window.

cascading menu A submenu that appears (usually to the left or right of the main menu item) when a menu selection is made.

CD File System (CDFS) An optimized, 32-bit, protected mode file system that significantly improves the throughput of data from a CD-ROM drive.

CD-ROM drive A CD-ROM drive uses discs (not "disks") as the storage media. These discs look much like audio CDs, but can store about 600M of data on a single disc. They can only be read by a normal CD-ROM drive (hence the Read-Only Memory portion of the device's name), and take special equipment to create (write) them. CD-ROM drives are rated in multiples of the original (1x) drives that transfer data at the same rate as audio CD players (150kb/sec). Today, 1x drives no longer exist, and 2x drives (300-330kb/sec) are cheap. 3x (450 kbs), 4x (600 kb/sec) and even 6x (900kb/sec) drives are available. 4x drives fulfill basic requirements needed to achieve decent performance when playing animations from a CD-ROM.

CD Player A program packaged with Windows 95. CD Player lets you play audio CDs from your CD drive in the background while you are working in another application. It offers many of the controls found in stand-alone audio CD players. As a result, it looks and operates in a similar fashion. In addition, it allows you to edit your playlist. Thus, the tracks play in the order you want.

character-based   Usually used when referring to non-Windows applications. Character-based applications display information using the ASCII character set, or characters normally found on the keyboard. Also known as "text-based."

character formatting   In word processing, this refers to formatting that is applied to individual characters. This type of formatting includes font, effects, size, and color.

chat room   A place on Microsoft Network where you can have a live conversation with other MSN members. They see your comments immediately.

check box   A square dialog box item that takes an off or on value. Clicking in a check box adds or removes an X in the box, indicating whether the setting is on (checked) or off (unchecked).

checksum   A method for creating a calculated number, frequently used as a part of an error-detection protocol. Normally, a checksum is calculated against a copy of a file or other data, and compared to the checksum calculated for the original file/data. If the two numbers match, then it is very likely that the copy matches the original. Checksums are used in some forms of transmission protocols (for example, Xmodem) as well as in part of the Anti Virus program.

choose   A term used in many instructions in this book and in Windows books and manuals. Usually means opening a menu and clicking a command. Also can refer to dialog box items, such as "Choose LPT1 from the drop-down list."

clear   Typically refers to turning off the X in an option or check box.

clicking   Quickly pressing and releasing the mouse button.

client   As opposed to *server*, a client is a workstation that connects to another computer's resources. A client also can include the server, and doesn't necessarily have to be another workstation. Basically, a client is just another application or workstation that utilizes resources from another process.

client application   In OLE context, a program that uses an object (such as a graphic) supplied by another application (the *server* application).

client/server networking   As opposed to *peer-to-peer* networking, an arrangement in which central computers called *servers* supply data and peripherals for use by *client* computers (workstations). Typically, a server contains a large, hard disk that supplies not only data, but also programs. It even executes programs. A server might also supply printers and modems for clients to use on the network. In other words, client/server refers to an architecture for distributed processing wherein subtasks can be distributed between services, CPUs, or even networked computers for more efficient execution.

clip art   A collection of images you can use in your documents. Clip art is often distributed on CD-ROM in large collections (thousands of clip art pieces) organized into categories. Various clip art formats are sold, and the most popular are CGM, WMF, BMP, and GIF format files.

clipboard   A temporary storage area in all versions of Windows used for storing various types of data (for example, text, graphics, sound, and video). The clipboard can hold one piece of information at a time for use in a program or to pass information between programs.

Clipboard Viewer   A Windows 95 program enabling you to store and save more than the single item that the clipboard can hold.

clock   An area at the far right edge of the task bar that displays the time (and date if you leave the mouse pointer over the time). You can configure the task bar to show or hide the clock.

close button   A button in the upper-right corner of a window with an "x" in it. When clicked, it closes the program running in the current window.

cluster   Segment of space on a hard drive. Each file, no matter how small in actual size, takes up at least one cluster on the hard drive. As drive sizes increase, so does the cluster size. Thus, if you have a large drive and many small files, you may waste a significant amount of space on your drive. To avoid this, physically partition the drive into multiple "logical drives" of a smaller size. These smaller, logical drives also use smaller cluster sizes, wasting less space.

coaxial cable   A type of shielded cable used in wiring networks together. Although coaxial cable sufficiently shields network signals from outside electrical noise, "coax" is stiff and difficult to work with, and more difficult to run through walls and ceilings than twisted pair cable (see *twisted pair*).

codec   A technique for compressing and decompressing files, typically sound and animation files. Common codecs include Cinepak, Indeo, Video 1, MPEG (see *MPEG*), QuickTime (see *QuickTime*), and RLE.

collapse folders   To hide additional directory (folder) levels below the selected directory (folder) levels. In Explorer, you can collapse the view of a folder to hide the folders stored within by double-clicking the folder in the left pane (tree view) of Explorer. When a folder contains no additional folders, a minus sign (–) appears next to the folder.

color pattern   A color selection made up of two other colors.

color rendering intent   Provides the best ICM settings for three of the major uses of color printing, for example, presentations, photographs, and true color screen display printing.

color scheme   A selection of colors that Windows 95 uses for screen display of applications, dialog boxes, and so forth. The color scheme is set from the Control Panel.

COM   Refers to the serial port, usually to attach a mouse and/or a modem to the computer. Most computers have two serial ports, labeled COM1 and COM2. The serial port transmits data in a single-bit stream. This serial transmission of bits gives the port its name.

command   Usually an option from an application's menus. Also refers to commands typed in from a command-prompt session or from the Run dialog box from the Start Menu. In essence, it's a way of telling an application or Window 95 to perform a major chore, such as running an application or utility program.

command button   A dialog box item that causes an action when clicked.

compare files   Compares the files in a backup set to make sure they match the source files on the hard disk.

complex document   See *compound document*.

component   A portion of Windows 95. When installing Windows 95, you have the option of installing (or not) various components. For example, you might choose to not install Hyperterminal (you might have a better terminal program). Later, you can go back and add/remove components using the original install disks or CD-ROM.

compound document   A document (created using OLE) that includes multiple types of data. For example, a Word processing document that includes a Paint picture is a compound document.

compressed volume file (CVF)   A file, created by DriveSpace (see *DriveSpace*), that is treated like another "volume" (logical disk drive). It even has a drive letter (for example, "D:") assigned to it. When you save or retrieve files compressed by DriveSpace, they are written or read from the compressed volume file. The compressed volume file exists on a hard drive (called a "host drive"), and looks like a regular file to the FAT (see *File Allocation Table*).

connection (HyperTerminal)   In HyperTerminal, a connection sets and saves all the configuration parameters for one party you wish to contact.

connection (network)   A communication session established between a server and a workstation.

container object   An object that contains another object or several objects. For example, a Word document might be the container object that holds the Excel object. See also *compound document*.

control menu   A menu that exists in every window and enables you to modify its parameters or take global actions, such as closing or moving the window.

Control Panel   A program that comes with Windows 95 that enables you to make settings for many Windows 95 actions, such as changing network, keyboard, printer, and regional settings. Some programs (including many video card drivers) may add sections to the control panel for you to use to configure that program.

conventional memory   Memory located in the first 640K.

cover page   The page preceding a fax message. The cover page often includes such information as your name, company, telephone number, and return fax number. Windows 95 includes a program (Fax Cover Page Editor) that enables you to create your own fax cover pages.

CPU   Central processing unit. Also known as a microprocessor (see *microprocessor*) or processor (see *processor*). The 80386, 80486, and Pentium are examples of CPUs built by Intel.

cross-linked file   A disk error (which can be found using ScanDisk) in which at least two files are linked to data in the same cluster.

current directory   The directory that activates if you log onto the drive at the command prompt by typing the drive letter and pressing Enter. When you switch drives, the operating system remembers the directory that was current when you switched away. It will still be the active/current directory when you switch back; it becomes the default directory. Applications will store or look for files on that drive if they're not specifically told which directory to use. This concept also works in Explorer—when you switch back to a drive, the last active directory (or *folder*) is still the active one.

current window   The window that you are using. It appears in front of all other open windows (see *active window*).

cursor   The representation of the mouse on the screen. It may take many different shapes.

Cylinder/Head/Sector (CHS)   An addressing scheme that allows IDE drives to exceed the original 512 megabyte (1/2 gigabyte) size limit. With CHS, an IDE drive can be up to 8.4 gigabytes.

D

database   A file or group of related files that are designed to hold recurring data types as if the files were lists.

data bits   The number of bits used to transmit a piece of information. Usually 7 or 8.

DCI   The Drive Control Interface is a display driver interface that allows fast, direct access to the video frame buffer in Windows. Also, it allows games and video to take advantage of special hardware support in video devices, which improves the performance and quality of video.

DDE   See *Dynamic Data Exchange.*

DEC printer utility   The DEC printer utility adds features to the standard Windows 95 print window and updated printer drivers. The utility includes a very detailed help file for configuring both local and network printers. Additionally, it creates an enhanced set of property menus for configuring DEC printers.

default button   The command button in a dialog box that activates when you press the Enter key. This button is indicated by a dark border.

default printer   The printer, which is established using the Printer settings, to which documents will be sent if the user doesn't specify another printer.

deferred printing   This enables people with laptop computers to print even though their laptops are not in docking stations. Once connected in a docking station, it will automatically print. This also refers to computers whose only printer access is to a network printer, and the computer is temporarily disconnected from the network. When the network connection is reestablished, the print job starts.

density   Density is a brightness control that lightens or darkens a printout to more closely reflect its screen appearance and to compensate for deficiencies in toner or paper quality.

desktop   The screen area on which the windows are displayed.

desktop pattern   A bit map decorating your desktop. You can select one of Windows 95's patterns or create one of your own.

destination document   The document into which a linked or embedded document is placed.

device driver   A program that provides the operating system with the information it needs to work with a specific device, such as a printer.

Dial Up Networking   Dialing into a network from a remote site by using a modem.

dialog box   An on-screen message box that conveys or requests information from the user.

differential backup   A differential backup backs up only those files that have changed since the time a backup was made. Normally, a backup philosophy will involve making a full system backup (which includes all files on the hard drive), and then making periodic differential backups. Windows 95 can determine which files have changed (or been created) since the last backup by the condition of the archive bit (see *archive bit*). To restore a system that has been backed up using this philosophy, first restore using the full system backup, and then successively apply the differential backups *in the same order they were made.*

Direct Memory Access (DMA)   A PC has eight DMA channels that are used for rapidly transferring data between memory and peripherals such as hard disks, sound cards, tape backups, scanners, and SCSI controllers. DMA is very fast because it doesn't need the computer's microprocessor to access memory.

Disk Defragmenter   As you use your hard drive, blocks of information for a file spread across the hard drive, wherever there is room. This fragmentation of the information in a file can lead to a significant slow-down in file access times because the disk's read/write head must move all over the disk, looking for the various portions of a file. Disk Defragmenter arranges the blocks of information for a file into adjacent blocks on your hard drive, which may significantly improve file access times.

dither pattern   A pattern of dots used to simulate an unavailable color or gray scale in a printout or graphic. Most frequently used when specifying a printout of a color graphic on a monochrome printer or simulating more colors in a graphic than are available in the current graphics mode.

docking station   For a portable computer, an external device that provides additional resources such as speakers, CD-ROM, keyboard, empty card slots, and so on. A docking station is typically plugged into a portable computer using the port replicator connection.

document   A file created using an application. For example, you might create a text document using a word processing application (such as WordPad) or a picture document using a graphic application (such as Paint).

document formatting   In word processing, this refers to formatting that is applied to a whole document. Document formatting includes margins, headers and footers, and paper size.

document window   The window in which a document appears.

DOS   A term used to refer to any variation of the Disk Operating System (for example, MS-DOS and PC-DOS).

double buffering   The process of displaying the screen currently in the frame buffer while painting the next screen in another portion of RAM. Then the new screen is quickly copied to the frame buffer. This makes video playback and animation appear much smoother.

double-click   To press the mouse button twice in rapid succession while keeping the mouse pointer motionless between clicks.

download   Retrieving a file from a remote computer or BBS (see *upload*).

drag   To move an object on the screen from one place to another by clicking it with the mouse, holding the mouse button down, and pulling it to where you want it to be.

drag and drop   "Drag and drop" describes a particular action you can make with the mouse. Click an object such as a folder, then hold down the mouse button as you drag the object to a new location. You drop the object by releasing the mouse button.

DriveSpace   DriveSpace is a program included with Windows 95. It enables you to compress your disks and free up more space.

DriveSpace for Windows supports drives that were compressed using Double Space (which was included in MS-DOS versions 6.0 and 6.2) as well as DriveSpace for MS-DOS (which was included in MS-DOS version 6.22). You can use DriveSpace and DoubleSpace drives interchangeably. For example, you can use floppy disks that were compressed using either DoubleSpace or DriveSpace. However, such floppy disks can be used only in computers that have DriveSpace for Windows or DoubleSpace installed.

If you have drives that were compressed using either DoubleSpace or DriveSpace, you can configure them by using DriveSpace for Windows.

drop-down list   A dialog box item showing only one entry until its drop-down arrow is clicked.

dual boot   The ability to reboot and enter either Windows 95 or Windows 3.1 (or whatever version of Windows you had running before installing

Windows 95). This option is offered during installation, and involves not installing Windows 95 over your previous Windows installation. If you choose dual boot, you will have to reinstall your Windows programs under Windows 95.

Dynamic Data Exchange (DDE)   A feature of Windows 95 that allows programs to communicate and actively pass information and commands.

E

echoing keystrokes   In a communications program, you may type information at your terminal. If the receiving system doesn't "echo" your keystroke back to your terminal, then you can't see what you type. By setting your own system to echo keystrokes, you can see what you have typed. Systems that echo your keystrokes for you are termed "full duplex"; systems that do not echo your keystrokes are termed "half duplex".

editable fax   An editable fax is a file transfer between computers, with the additional option of a cover page. Once received, the editable fax can be edited in the application that created it—or another application capable of reading that file type. For example, if you send a document created in Microsoft Word for Windows, which is a .DOC file, the recipient can open it in Word, WordPad, AmiPro, or WordPerfect, using import filters if necessary.

ellipsis   Three dots (…). An ellipsis after a menu item or button text indicates that selecting the menu or clicking the button will display an additional dialog box or window from which you can choose options or enter data.

embedded object   Data stored in a document that originated from another application. Differing from a linked object, this type of object doesn't have its own file on the disk. However, it runs its source application for editing when you double-click it. For example, a Paint drawing embedded in a Word document.

Encapsulated PostScript (EPS) file   A file format for storing PostScript-style images that allow a PostScript printer or program capable of importing such files to print a file in the highest resolution equipped by the printer.

Enhanced Integrated Drive Electronics (EIDE)   A design that improves on the drive limitations of the IDE design. EIDE designs can use up to four devices (split into two pairs). For each pair of devices, one of the devices is the master; the drive electronics on the master control both the master drive and (if applicable) the secondary slave unit attached. Unlike IDE, EIDE supports devices in addition to hard drives, including CD-ROM drives and tape drives. EIDE devices can be up to 8 gigabytes in size, improving on the 524-megabyte limit of IDE devices. As with IDE, this type of drive is inter-faced to a computer bus with an EIDE host adapter, not a controller. How-ever, most newer computers include an EIDE host adapter right on the motherboard.

Enhanced Meta File (EMF)   The process of converting generic Spooling print instructions to the instruction set "understood" best by a particular printer. This conversion has the capability to create faster printouts of better quality.

Enhanced Small Device Interface (ESDI)   A drive controller type that utilizes a hard drive as a slave unit. ESDI controllers generally drive only two disk drives and have an on-board processor to translate drive geometry, man-age I/O requests, and provide caching.

escape codes   A set of codes that appear in a text string on a terminal (see *terminal emulation*). Although these escape codes (which provide formatting information) aren't visible in terminal emulation, they will show up as non-text characters if you capture the text to the screen or printer. In fact, some escape codes may cause the printed output to skip pages, switch into bold mode, and other undesirable effects because the codes may conflict with printer command codes.

Ethernet   One of the earliest and least expensive network types. Ethernet is capable of speeds of 10Mb/s, and employs Bus and Star network types. When attempting to transmit over an Ethernet network, the transmitting worksta-tion must "listen" to the network line to ensure that it is clear (another work-station is not currently transmitting). If the line is not clear, the workstation must wait until the line clears.

exit   When you are finished running Windows applications and Windows, you must not turn off the computer until you correctly exit Windows. Win-dows stores some data in memory and does not write it to your hard disk until you choose the exit command. If you turn off the computer without correctly exiting, this data may be lost.

expand folders   Views the structure of folders that are stored inside other folders. In Explorer, you can expand the view of a folder that has a plus sign (+) next to it to see the folders stored within by double-clicking the folder in the left pane (tree view) of Explorer. When a folder does not contain any additional folders, a minus sign (–) appears next to the folder.

expanded memory   Memory that conforms to the LIM 4.0 standard for memory access. Windows 95 has the capability of converting extended memory (see *extended memory*) to expanded memory (using EMM386.EXE) for programs that require it. However, most modern programs no longer use expanded memory.

Explorer   A program in Windows 95 that helps you view and manage your files.

Extended Industry Standard Architecture (EISA)   A computer bus and interface card design based on 32-bit bus mastering. EISA is an extension to ISA (Industry Standard Architecture) bus design and enables EISA and ISA interface cards to be used in a single type of bus interface slot in the computer.

extended memory   Memory that can be accessed by Windows 95 beyond the first megabyte of memory in your system.

external command   Unlike an internal command, a command that requires a separate file to run.

F

FDDI   Fiber Distributed Data Interchange is a network type that requires fiber optic cable (see *fiber optic*). Although expensive, it is immune to electrical interference and can achieve speeds of 100 Mb/s.

fiber optic   A type of cable that transmits information via light signals. Although both the cable and the decoders are expensive, such cabling is immune to electrical noise, and is capable of much higher transmission rates than electrical (coaxial or twisted pair) cables.

FIFO buffers   First in, first out buffers. In communications programs that use FIFO buffers, the first information added to the buffer is also the first information transmitted when the transmission restarts.

file allocation table (FAT)   The native DOS file system that uses a table, called the file allocation table, to store information about the sizes, locations, and properties of files stored on the disk.

file converter   File converters take the file format and transform it to a format that the application can read. During a file conversion, text enhancements, font selections, and other elements are usually preserved. Sometimes, however, these elements are converted to a similar format, and then converted to ASCII format.

file name   The name that a file system or operating system gives to a file when it's stored on disk. File names in Window 95's file system can be 256 characters long. Additionally, Windows 95 assigns a file name compatible with older DOS (eight characters with a three-character extension) naming conventions.

file name extension   The three-character extension that you can add to a file name—either the standard eight characters of DOS and Windows 3.1, or the long file names of Windows 95. The file name extension is only visible in Explorer if you enable the appropriate option. Otherwise, the extension is hidden. Nevertheless, the extension is still part of the file name, even when you can't see it — it is this extension that Windows 95 (as well as earlier Windows) uses to associate a document with the application that created it.

file set   In the Windows 95 Backup program, a collection of files to back up and the destination to back them up to. By saving a file set in Backup, you won't have to reselect the files to back up the next time.

file utility   A program that can directly manipulate the information available on the disk that defines where files are found, sized, and other attributes. It is important to NOT use file utilities that were designed for earlier versions of Windows, as Windows 95 stores some file information in different places — and earlier file utilities could scramble the file information, destroying the file.

fixed-space font   Fonts that have a fixed amount of space between the characters in the font.

folder   Folders represent directories on your drives. Folders can contain files, programs, and even other folders.

folder window   A window in Explorer that displays the contents of a folder.

font   A description of how to display a set of characters. The description includes the shape of the characters, spacing between characters, effects (for example, bold, italics, and underline) and the size of the characters.

foreground operation   The program in the active window.

forum   On The Microsoft Network, a folder with a collection of related documents and sub-folders.

frame   A unit of data that is exchanged on a LAN. Frame formatting implements an access protocol for the purpose of enabling communications between nodes on a LAN (Ethernet, Token Ring, and so on). A frame should not be confused with a packet, which is encapsulated within a frame for transport across the LAN.

full system backup   A backup set (see *backup set)* that contains all the files on your hard drive, including Windows 95 system files, the registry, and all other files necessary to completely restore your system configuration on a new hard drive.

G

grid   A background pattern that defines regular intervals — for example, a 1/4" grid displays dots in the background every quarter inch in a rectangular pattern. Many graphics programs make a grid available. Even when turned on, a grid won't print. When you "snap to grid," your graphic endpoints are constrained to fall on a grid point.

H

handshake   A protocol used between two devices to establish communications. For example, a portable computer and a PC card "handshake" to set up the communications between the devices.

header information   Data sent to a printer to define aspects of the printout and prepare the printer prior to printing. PostScript documents include header information.

heap   An area of memory (also known as the System Resources area) that Windows uses to store system information (such as menus) about running applications. If the heap fills up, you may get an "out of memory" error, despite the fact that you have plenty of regular memory (RAM) available. In Windows 95, you have much less chance of getting an "out of memory" error. Although Windows 95 still uses a 64K heap to store systems information for 16-bit applications, a lot of the information that was stored in this area by older versions of Windows is now stored elsewhere. As a result, there is much less chance of your application failing due to this error.

Hearts   A card game included with Windows 95 for up to four players. The winner is the player who has the fewest points.

At the end of each round (each player has played all 13 cards), the following points are given:

1 point for each Heart you collected.

13 points for the Queen of Spades.

If one player wins all the Hearts and the Queen of Spades (called Shooting the Moon), then that player gets zero while all other players are penalized 26 points.

Help   A program that gives you information about how to run Windows 95 and its programs, including how to use the Help program.

hexadecimal   A base-16 numbering scheme with values ranging from 0 to 9, and A to F. Used in many programming languages. Not particularly relevant to users, except that memory address areas are frequently stated in hexadecimal. Hex is used whenever the actual internals of the computer are being revealed, as in memory addresses and I/O ports.

hidden file   A characteristic of a file that indicates that the file is not visible in Explorer under normal circumstances. However, by selecting the View Option to view all files, hidden files will still be visible.

hierarchical   A way of displaying text or graphics in a structure. In a hierarchical structure, items closer to the top of the structure are considered "parents" of items connected to them, but which are lower down in the structure. The tree structure of Windows Explorer is an example of a hierarchical structure.

home page   A document on the World Wide Web dedicated to a particular subject. From a home page, you can use hyperlinks to jump to other home pages to gain more information.

host drive   The physical hard drive upon which a DriveSpace compressed volume file exists (see *compressed volume file*). You can choose to either show or hide the host drive when working with Explorer.

hot docking   For a portable computer, "hot docking" refers to the ability to insert the computer into a docking station (which may provide additional resources such as a CD-ROM, speakers, a hard drive, and so on) and have the computer recognize that the new resources of the docking station are now available.

hot swapping   For a portable computer, or any other computer that uses PC cards, "hot swapping" refers to the ability to remove a PC card and/or insert a new card, and have the computer recognize the change.

HP JetAdmin   The HP JetAdmin utility is a tool that can be used to install and configure networked Hewlett-Packard printers using the HP JetDirect network interface. The HP JetAdmin utility appears as a substitute for the Windows standard Printer window. This utility can also be used to interface printers connected to a NetWare LAN.

hub   A wiring concentrator or multiport repeater (see *repeater* and *wiring concentrator*). Hubs may be active or passive.

hue   The numerical representation of the colors of a color wheel. It is almost always seen with saturation and brightness.

hyperlink   A link in a document that, when activated (often by clicking it), links—or jumps to—another document or graphic.

HyperTerminal   HyperTerminal is a program included with Windows 95, that enables you to easily connect to a remote computer, a bulletin board, or an online service. It replaces Terminal from Windows 3.1.

Hypertext Markup Language (HTML)   A hypertext language used to create the hypertext documents that make up the World Wide Web.

I

I-beam   The shape the cursor takes in the area of a window where text can be entered.

icon   A small graphic symbol used to represent a folder, program, shortcut, resource, or document.

Image Color Matching (ICM)   Image Color Matching (ICM), a technology developed by Kodak, creates an image environment that treats color from the screen to the printed page. Microsoft licensed ICM from Kodak to be able to repeatedly and consistently reproduce color matched images from source to destination.

import   An OLE term. In Object Packager, you can import a file into a package and later embed it into a destination document.

inactive   An open window that is not currently in use. On the task bar, the active window looks like a pressed button; inactive windows are represented by unpressed buttons.

Inbox   Inbox holds incoming and outgoing messages and faxes that are sent or received over Microsoft Exchange.

incremental backup   See *differential backup*.

Industry Standard Architecture (ISA)   This term describes the design of the 8/16-bit AT bus (sometimes called the "classic bus") developed by IBM in the original IBM PC.

in-place editing   A feature of OLE 2. With in-place editing, you may edit an embedded or linked object without that object being placed into an additional window (the way it was in OLE 1.0). Instead of creating an additional window, the tools for the object you want to edit appear in the toolbar for the container object (see *container object*). Also, the menus for the object you want to edit replace the menus of the container object. In-place editing is less disruptive; it is much simpler to ensure that the changes you make to an embedded or linked object are updated to the original complex document.

insertion point   A flashing, vertical line showing where text will be inserted.

Integrated Drive Electronics (IDE)   A later drive design that incorporates an embedded controller on a smaller (3 1/2 inch) disk drive. IDE drives can be connected together, but the second drive must be a slave to the first, using the primary disk controller and not its own embedded controller. This type of drive is interfaced to a computer bus with an IDE host adapter, not a controller.

Integrated Services Digital Network (ISDN)   A special phone line that supports modem speeds up to 64Kbps. However, these phone lines can be quite expensive to acquire. Many ISDN adapters support two-channel access.

interface   The visible layer enabling a user to communicate with a computer. In DOS, the interface consists largely of typed commands and character-based feedback. Windows 95 is an entirely graphical interface, using a mouse, menus, windows, and icons to allow the user to communicate his instructions and requirements to the computer.

interframe compression   A technique that achieves compression of a video file by eliminating redundant data between successive compressed frames.

internal command   A command embedded in CMD.EXE, the command interpreter for Windows 95, or in COMMAND.EXE, the MS-DOS equivalent. Internal commands don't require additional support files.

Internet   The Internet is a "network of networks," a global linkage of millions of computers, containing vast amounts of information, much of it available for free to anyone with a modem and the right software. The Internet is an aggregation of high-speed networks, supported by the NSF (National Science Foundation) and almost 6,000 federal, state, and local systems, as well as university and commercial networks. There are links to networks in Canada, South America, Europe, Australia, and Asia, and more than 30,000,000 users.

Internet Explorer A web browser bundled with the Windows 95 Plus kit. It takes advantage of features in Windows 95, such as shortcuts and long file names.

Internet Protocol (IP) A network protocol that provides routing services across multiple LANs and WANs that is used in the TCP/IP protocol stack. IP packet format is used to address packets of data from ultimate source and destination nodes (host) located on any LAN or WAN networked with TCP/IP protocol. IP provides routing services in conjunction with IP routers, which are incorporated into many computer systems and most versions of UNIX. IP Packet format is supported in NetWare 3.11 and 4.0 operating systems, and is used throughout the Department of Defense Internet—a network of thousands of computers internetworked worldwide.

interoperability Compatibility, or the capability for equipment to work together. Industry standards are agreed upon or used by vendors to make their equipment work with other vendor's equipment.

interrupt request line (IRQ) A line (conductor) on the internal bus of the computer (typically on the motherboard) over which a device such as a port, disk controller, or modem can get the attention of the CPU to process some data.

intraframe compression A technique that compresses the video by removing redundancy from individual video images.

I/O address Input/Output address. Many I/O devices, such as COM ports, network cards, printer ports, and modem cards, are mapped to an I/O address. This address allows the computer and operating system to locate the device, and thus send and receive data. Such I/O addresses don't tie up system memory RAM space. However, there are a limited number of I/O addresses. You can access an I/O port in one of two ways: either map it into the 64K I/O address space, or map it as a memory-mapped device in the system's RAM space.

IPX Internetwork Packet Exchange (IPX) is a network protocol developed by Novell to address packets of data from ultimate source and destination nodes located on any LAN networked with NetWare. IPX also provides routing services in conjunction NetWare and third-party routers. An IPX packet has information fields that identify the network address, node address, and socket address of both the source and destination, and provides the same functionality of the OSI Network layer in the OSI model.

J

jumpers Jumpers are small devices that complete a circuit between two pins of a multi-pin header, specifying various aspects about a card—for example, which IRQ, base memory address, or I/O port address to use. Jumpers are not normally used on a card that is compliant with Plug and Play, but were common on "legacy" (pre Plug and Play) cards.

K

kernel The core of an operating system, usually responsible for basic I/O and process execution.

kernel driver A driver with direct access to hardware. A hardware driver.

keyboard buffer Memory set aside to store keystrokes as they're entered from the keyboard. Once it's stored, the keystroke data waits for the CPU to pick up the data and respond accordingly.

keyboard equivalent See *keyboard shortcut.*

keyboard shortcut A combination of keystrokes that initiates a menu command without dropping the menu down, or activates a button in a dialog box without clicking the button.

kiosk In the Microsoft Network, a download-and-run document that contains additional information about a forum. Kiosks are usually found in forums.

L

legacy Refers to pre-Windows 95 software or hardware. Legacy cards don't support Plug and Play, and legacy software is older software (although you may have just purchased it!) typically designed for Windows 3.1 or Windows for Workgroups 3.11.

license Refers to the agreement you are assumed to have acceded to when you purchased Windows 95. As with much other computer software, you don't own your copy of Windows 95, but instead, just license the use of it. As such, there is a long list of legalese-type things you supposedly agree to when you open the envelope containing your copy of Windows 95. These legal agreements are part of the license.

line by line   When using terminal emulation (see *terminal emulation*), some primitive terminals only allowed you to edit text on the single line on which you were working. Once you pressed [Enter] to move to the next line, you couldn't go back and change something on the previous line(s) because those lines had already been sent to the host computer. The PC emulated a terminal. In line-by-line editing, there is a line length limit as well, so you can't simply type an entire paragraph before pressing [Enter].

linked object   In OLE terminology, data stored in a document that originated from another application. Unlike an embedded object, this type of object has its own file on the disk. The source application is run for editing when you double-click it. For example, a Paint drawing linked to a Word document. Linking saves space over embedding when a particular object must be included in more than one other document, since the data does not have to be stored multiple times. Additionally, you can directly edit a linked file, and all the documents that link to the file update automatically.

list box   A dialog box item that shows all available options.

local area network (LAN)   A limited-distance, multipoint physical connectivity medium consisting of network interface cards, media, and repeating devices designed to transport frames of data between host computers at high speeds with low error rates. A LAN is a subsystem that is part of a network.

local printer   A printer connected directly to your computer.

local reboot   The ability of Windows 95 to close down a single misbehaving application. When you use the Alt+Ctrl+Delete key sequence, Windows 95 queries you for the application to shut down. In this way, you can close down only the application you want, without affecting other running applications.

logical block addressing (lba)   A type of addressing scheme for IDE disk drives that allows the drive to exceed the original 512 megabytes (1/2 gigabyte) IDE size limit. With logical block addressing, an IDE drive can hold up to 8.4 gigabytes.

logical drive   A drive that isn't a physical drive, as in the floppy drive A or B. Instead, a logical drive is a drive created on a subpartition of an extended partition and given an arbitrary letter such as C, D, or E.

long file name   A reference to Windows 95's ability to use file names up to 256 characters long.

lossy compression   Compression techniques that lose some of the data when compressing the file. Although lossy compression isn't acceptable for compressing application files and certain types of data files (for example, database, word processing), it is often acceptable to have a low degree of loss when compressing video or graphic files, since you likely won't notice the missing data. Also, lossy compression can gain considerably higher compression ratios than "lossless" compression. However, when using lossy compression, you don't want to decompress the file, then use the result to recompress, as the loss of data gets worse with each cycle.

LPT   The parallel port used for printing. Most computers have a single parallel port (labeled LPT1), but some may have two. The parallel port transmits data one byte (8 bits) at a time. This parallel transmission of all 8 bits gives the port its name.

luminosity   When working with colors, indicates the brightness of the color.

M

macro   A sequence of keyboard strokes and mouse actions that can be recorded so that their playback can be activated by a single keystroke, keystroke combination, or mouse click. Unlike Windows 3.1 and Windows for Workgroups, Windows 95 does not come with a Macro Recorder.

mailing list (Internet)   An e-mail discussion group focused on one or more topics. The mailing list is made up of members who subscribe to that mailing list.

map network drive   The act of associating a network drive makes the drive available in My Computer. Windows 95 uses the next available drive letter, and you can access the network drive just like any other hard drive.

maximize button   A button in the upper right corner of a window with a square in it. When clicked, it enlarges the window to its maximum size. When the window is already at its maximum size, the maximize button switches to the restore button, which returns the window to its previous size.

media control interface (MCI)   A standard interface for all multimedia devices, devised by the MPC counsel, that allows multimedia applications to control any number of MPC-compliant devices, from sound cards to MIDI-based lighting controllers.

menu   A list of available command options.

menu bar   Located under the title bar, the menu bar displays the names of all available menu lists.

menu command   A word or phrase in a menu that, when selected, enables you to view all the commands.

Micro-Channel Architecture (MCA)   A proprietary 32-bit computer and bus architecture designed by IBM to improve bus bandwidth and facilitate bus mastering. MCA is not backward-compatible with ISA and requires exclusive use of MCA devices.

microprocessor   A miniaturized processor. Previous processors were built in integrated circuit boards with many large components. Most processors today use high-tech, silicon-based technology that improves performance, reduces heat generation, and increases efficiency.

Microsoft Client for NetWare Networks   Windows 95 Microsoft Client for NetWare Networks allows users to connect to new or existing NetWare servers. It permits you to browse and queue print jobs using either the Windows 95 network user interface or existing Novell NetWare utilities. The Microsoft Client for NetWare interfaces equally well with both NetWare 3.x and 4.x servers.

Microsoft Exchange   Microsoft Exchange provides a universal Inbox that you can use to send and receive electronic mail (e-mail). In addition, you can use the Inbox to organize, access, and share all types of information, including faxes and items from online services.

Microsoft Fax   Microsoft Fax is a program included with Windows 95 that enables you to send and receive faxes directly within Windows 95.

Microsoft Network, The (MSN)   Access to The Microsoft Network, a new online service, is a feature of Windows 95.

With The Microsoft Network, you can exchange messages with people around the world; read the latest news, sports, weather, and financial information; find answers to your technical questions; download from thousands of useful programs; and connect to the Internet.

MIDI   Musical Instrument Digital Interface. Originally a means of connecting electronic instruments (synthesizers) and letting them communicate with one another. Computers then came into the MIDI landscape and were used to control the synthesizers. Windows 95 can play MIDI files.

Minesweeper   A game of chance and skill included with Windows 95. When playing Minesweeper, you are presented with a mine field, and your objective is to locate all the mines as quickly as possible. To do this, uncover the squares on the game board that do not contain mines, and mark the squares that contain mines. The trick is determining which squares are which.

If you uncover all the squares without mines, you win; if you uncover a mine instead of marking it, you lose the game. The faster you play, the lower your score. You can use the counters at the top of the playing area to keep track of your progress.

minimize button   The button in the upper right corner of the window that has a line in it. When clicked, it reduces the window to display the task bar only.

mission-critical application   An application program considered indispensable to the operation of a business, government, or other operation. Often, these applications are transaction-based, such as for point-of-sale, reservations, or real-time stock, security, or money trading.

modem   A device, usually attached to a computer through a serial port or present as an internal card. A modem makes it possible to use ordinary phone lines to transfer computer data. In addition to a modem, a communications program is required. "Modem" is short for "modulator/demodulator" — the processes whereby a digital stream of data is converted to sound for transmission through a phone system originally designed only for sound (modulator) and the conversion of received sound signals back into digital data (demodulator).

motion JPEG   Developed by the Joint Photographic Experts Group, motion JPEG is a compression /decompression scheme (codec) for video files. It is a variation on JPEG, this group's codec for compressing still pictures. It uses only intraframe lossy compression (see *intraframe compression*, *lossy compression*), but offers a tradeoff between compression ratio and quality.

mounting a compressed drive   When you are working with removable storage media— such a diskettes— that are compressed, you must mount the compressed drive if it wasn't present when the computer was started. Mounting a drive links a drive letter with a compressed volume file (CVF). This enables your computer to access the files on the compressed volume files. Mounting a compressed drive is done using DriveSpace.

mouse pointer   The symbol that displays where your next mouse click will occur. The mouse pointer symbol changes according to the context of the window or the dialog box in which it appears.

MPEG   Created by the Motion Picture Experts Group, MPEG is a specification for compressing and decompressing (see *codec*) animation or "movie" files, which are typically very large. Although extremely efficient at reducing the size of such a file, MPEG is also very processor-intensive.

MS-DOS-based application   An application that normally runs on a DOS machine and doesn't require Windows 95. Many MS-DOS-based applications will run in Windows 95's DOS box, but some will not.

multimedia   A combination of various types of media, including (but not necessarily limited to) sound, animation, and graphics. Due to the generally large size of "multimedia" files, a CD-ROM is usually necessary to store files. Of course, a sound card and speakers are also necessary.

multitasking   The capability of an operating system to handle multiple processing tasks, apparently, at the same time.

multithreading   A process allowing a multitasking operating system to, in essence, multitask subportions (threads) of an application smoothly. Applications must be written to take advantage of multithreading. Windows 95 supports multithreading.

My Briefcase   An icon present on the Windows 95 desktop. My Briefcase is the way that portable computer users can take data with them as they travel. When they return to the office, Windows examines the files in My Briefcase and updates the contents of their desktop computer.

My Computer   An icon present on the Windows 95 desktop that enables you to view drives, folders, and files.

N

NetBIOS   An IBM protocol (and packet structure) that provides several networking functions. NetBIOS was developed by IBM and Sytek to supplement and work with BIOS in PC-DOS-based, peer-to-peer networks. NetBIOS protocol provides transport, session, and presentation layer functions equivalent to layers 4, 5, and 6 of the OSI model. The NetBIOS software that is used to implement this protocol is the NetBIOS interface.

NetWare   A trademarked brand name for the networking operating systems and other networking products developed and sold by Novell.

NetWare Core Protocol (NCP)   A NetWare protocol that provides transport, session, and presentation layer functions equivalent to layers 4, 5, and 6 of the OSI model.

Net Watcher   A tool included with Windows 95. Net Watcher allows you to monitor and manage network connections, as well as create, add, and delete shared resources.

network   A group of computers connected by a communications link that enables any device to interact with any other on the network. The word network is derived from the term "network architecture," which describes an entire system of hosts, workstations, terminals, and other devices.

Network Interface card (NIC)   Also called a network adapter, an NIC is an interface card placed in the bus of a computer (or other LAN device) to interface to a LAN. Each NIC represents a node, which is a source and destination for LAN frames, which in turn carry data between the NICs on the LAN.

Network Neighborhood   An icon that Windows 95 displays only if you are connected to a network and Windows has been installed for a network. Double-clicking the Network Neighborhood icon displays all the resources available on any network to which you are connected.

non-volatile RAM   RAM memory on a card that is not erased when power is cut off. Cards that don't use jumpers often store their resource requirements (IRQ, I/O Base address, I/O port, DMA channel, etc.) in non-volatile RAM. Non-volatile RAM is not normally used on a card that is compliant with Plug and Play, but was common on "legacy" (pre-Plug and Play) cards.

non-Windows program   A program not designed to be used specifically in Windows. Most non-Windows applications or programs are character-based in nature (for example, DOS programs).

Notepad   A program that comes with Windows 95 and enables you to view and edit text files.

null modem cable   A serial cable link between computers. Standard modem software is often used to transmit information, but because there are no actual modems in the connection, very high transfer rates with good accuracy are possible. The cable must be different from a regular serial cable, however, because several of the wires in the cable must be cross-connected to simulate the modem's role in acknowledging a transmission.

O

object   Any item that is or can be linked into another Windows application, such as a sound, graphics, piece of text, or portion of a spreadsheet. Must be from an application that supports object linking and embedding (OLE).

object linking and embedding   See *OLE.*

OEM fonts   OEM fonts are provided to support older installed products. The term OEM refers to Original Equipment Manufacturers. This font family includes a character set designed to be compatible with older equipment and software applications.

offline   A device that is not ready to accept input. For example, if your printer is offline, it will not accept data from the computer, and attempting to print will generate an error.

OLE   Object linking and embedding is a data-sharing scheme that allows dissimilar applications to create single, complex documents by cooperating in the creation of the document. The documents consist of material that a single application couldn't have created on its own. In OLE, version 1, double-clicking an embedded or linked object (see *embedded object* and *linked object*) launches the application that created the object in a separate window. In OLE version 2, double-clicking an embedded or linked object makes the menus and tools of the creating application available in the middle of the parent document. The destination document (contains the linked or embedded object) must be created by an application that is an OLE client, and the linked or embedded object must be created in an application that is an OLE server.

OLE automation   Refers to the capability of a server application to make available (this is known as exposing) its own objects for use in another application's macro language.

online   Indicates that a system is working and connected. For example, if your printer is online, it is ready to accept information to turn into a printed output.

Open Data Link Interface (ODI)   A Novell specification that separates the implementation of a protocol and the implementation of the NIC hardware driver. Novell's MLID specification enables NIC drivers to interface through Link Support Layer with IPX ODI and multiple ODI-conforming packet drivers.

option button   A dialog box item that enables you to choose only one of a group of choices.

orientation   For printer paper, indicates whether the document is to be printed normally (for example, in "portrait" mode) or sideways (in "landscape" mode).

OSI model   Open System Interconnect 7-layer model is a model developed by International Standards Organization to establish a standardized set of protocols for interoperability between networked computer hosts. Each layer of the model consists of specifications and/or protocols that fulfill specific functions in a networking architecture. Novell's UNA was patterned against the OSI model. The OSI model consists of specific protocols that are nonproprietary and offered in the hope of unifying networking protocols used in competing vendors' systems.

P

packet   A limited-length unit of data formed by the network, transport, presentation, or application layer (layers 3-7 of the OSI model) in a networked computer system. Data is transported over the network, and larger amounts of data are broken into shorter units and placed into packets. Higher-layer packets are encapsulated into lower-layer packets for encapsulation into LAN frames for delivery to the ultimate host destination.

Paint   A program that comes with Windows 95 and enables you to view and edit various formats of bit maps.

palette   A collection of tools. For example, in Paint, there is a color palette that displays the 48 colors available for use in creating a graphic.

pane   Some windows, such as the window for Explorer, show two or more distinct "areas" (Explorer's window shows two such areas). These areas are referred to as "panes."

Panose   Panose refers to a Windows internal description that represents a font by assigning each font a PANOSE ID number. Windows uses several internal descriptions to categorize fonts. The PANOSE information registers a font class and determines similarity between fonts.

paragraph formatting   In a word processing program, this refers to formatting that can be applied to an entire paragraph, including alignment (left, center, right), indentation, and spacing before and after the paragraph.

parallel port   A port (usually used for printing) that transmits data 8 bits at a time. This parallel transmission of 8 bits at a time gives the port its name.

parity   An additional portion of data added to each byte of stored or transmitted data. Used to ensure that the data isn't lost or corrupted. In HyperTerminal, parity is used to ensure that the data is transmitted and received properly. Parity is also used in RAM chips to determine if RAM errors have occurred.

partial backup   See *incremental backup*.

partition   A portion of a physical hard drive that behaves as a separate disk (logical drive), even though it isn't.

path   The location of a file in the directory tree.

PC Cards   Formerly called PCMCIA cards, these are small (usually only slightly larger than a credit card) cards that plug into special slots provided in notebook computers. PC Cards can provide functionality for additional memory, modems, sound, networking, hard drives, and so on. PC Cards normally identify themselves to the computer, making configuring them quite simple.

PCMCIA   The old name for PC Cards (see *PC Cards*).

peer-to-peer   A type of networking in which no workstation has more control over the network than any other. Each station may share its resources, but no station is the sole resource sharer or file server. Typically less expensive than client/server networks, peer-to-peer networks are also more difficult to administer and less secure because there is no central repository of data.

personal information store   The personal information store is Exchange's term for the file that contains the structure of folders that make up your Inbox, Outbox, sent files, deleted files, and any other personal folders you may choose to create.

Phone Dialer   Phone Dialer is a program that is included with Windows 95 that enables you to place telephone calls from your computer by using a modem or another Windows telephony device. You can store a list of phone numbers you use frequently, and dial the number quickly from your computer.

picon   Picons are small, bitmapped images of the first frame of your video clip. They can be used to represent the in and out source of your video segments.

PIF   A file that provides Windows 95 with the information it needs to know in order to run a non-Windows program. Unlike earlier versions of Windows, there is no PIF editor in Windows 95. Instead, you set up a PIF file from the properties for the file. Access the file properties by right-clicking the file from My Computer.

Ping   A network utility that determines if TCP/IP is working properly. Simply executing the Ping command (from a DOS prompt) and specifying the IP address should produce a response (the response will depend on how the remote machine has been programmed to respond to a Ping), but virtually any response that references the remote machine's identity indicates that the Ping was successful and TCP/IP is working correctly.

play list   In CD Player, a list of tracks from an audio CD that you want to play.

Plug and Play   An industry-wide specification supported by Windows 95 that makes it easy to install new hardware. Plug and Play enables the computer to correctly identify hardware components (including plug-in cards) and ensures that different cards don't conflict in their requirements for IRQs, I/O addresses, DMA channels, and memory addresses. In order to fully implement Plug and Play, you need an operating system that supports it (as stated, Windows 95 does), a BIOS that supports it (most computers manufactured since early 1995 do) and cards that identify themselves to the system (information from these cards is stored in the Windows Registry). If you have hardware, such as modems that aren't Plug and Play (so-called "legacy hardware"), then Windows 95 will prompt you for the information necessary for setup, and store such information in the Registry.

pointer   The on-screen symbol controlled by the mouse. As you move the mouse on the desk, the pointer moves on-screen. The pointer changes shape to indicate the current status and the type of functions and selections available.

polygon   A multisided shape, in which each side is a straight line.

port   A connection or socket for connecting devices to a computer (see *I/O address*).

port replicator   On portable computers, a bus connection that makes all bus lines available externally. The port replicator can be used to plug in devices which, in a desktop computer, would be handled as cards. Port replicators are also the connection used to connect a portable computer to its docking station.

Postoffice   The machine in which all mail messages are stored for the workgroup.

postproduction editing   The steps of adding special effects, animated overlays,and more to a "production" video.

PostScript   A special description language, invented by Adobe. This language is used to accurately describe fonts and graphics. Printers that can directly read this language and print the results are termed "PostScript printers."

preemptive processing   In a multitasking operating system, multiple tasks (threads) are generally controlled by a scheduler that preempts or inter-rupts each process, granting processor time in the form of a time slice. This enables multiple tasks to run at the same time. However, each task runs for a time slice and is then preempted by the next process, which in turn is pre-empted — rotating processor time among active threads. In preemptive multitasking, the operating system is empowered to override (or preempt) an application that is using too much CPU time, as opposed to cooperative multitasking, where the application is responsible for relinquishing the CPU on a regular basis.

primary partition   A portion of the hard disk that can be used by the operating system and that can't be subpartitioned like an extended partition can. Only primary partitions are bootable.

printer driver   A Windows 95 program that tells programs how to format data for a particular type of printer.

printer fonts   Fonts stored in the printer's ROM.

printer settings   A window that displays all the printers for which there are drivers present. You can select the default printer from the installed print-ers, as well as configure each printer using the shortcut menu and the Op-tions dialog box.

printer window   For each installed printer, you can view the printer win-dow. The printer window displays the status of each print job in the queue, and enables you to pause, restart, and delete the print job.

processor   The controlling device in a computer that interprets and exe-cutes instructions and performs computations, and otherwise controls the major functions of the computer. This book discusses Intel 80x86-series pro-cessors, which are miniaturized single-chip "microprocessors" containing thousands to millions of transistors in a silicon-based, multilayered, inte-grated circuit design.

program file   A program that runs an application directly (not via an association) when you click it.

program window   A window that contains a program and its documents.

property sheet   A dialog box that displays (and sometimes enables you to change) the properties of an object in Windows 95. To access a property sheet, right click the object to view the shortcut menu, and select Properties from the shortcut menu. Property sheets vary considerably between different objects.

proportional-spaced fonts   Proportional-spaced fonts adjust the inter-character space based on the shape of the individual characters. An example of a proportional-spaced font is Arial. The width of a character is varied based on its shape. Adjusting inter-character spacing is really a function of kerning, which is similar but not exactly the same. For instance, the letter 'A' and the letter 'V' are typically stored in each font as a kerning pair, which means they will be spaced differently when appearing next to each other. In a mono-space font versus a proportional font you will see a difference in the width of the letter 'i'.

protected mode   A memory addressing mode of Intel processors that allows direct "flat memory" addressing (linear addressing) rather than using the awkward "segmented" scheme required by real mode, which was pioneered on the Intel 8088 and 8086 processors. Protected mode derives its name from the fact that sections of memory owned by a particular process can be protected from rogue programs trying to access those addresses.

protocol   Rules of communication. In networks, several layers of protocols exist. Each layer of protocol only needs to physically hand-off or receive data from the immediate layer above and beneath it, whereas virtual communications occur with the corresponding layer on another host computer.

Q

QIC   A formatting standard for tapes used by various tape backup devices. The amount of information that can be stored on a tape varies by the QIC number. Windows 95's Backup program supports QIC 40, 80, 3010, and 3020 formats. It also supports QIC 113 compression format.

queue   Documents lined up and waiting to be printed, or commands lined up and waiting to be serviced. Use the Printer window to view the print queue for a printer.

Quick Format   A quick way to format a floppy disk, Quick Format doesn't actually wipe the whole disk, nor does it test the media for bad sectors. It just erases the FAT.

Quick View   A program included with Windows 95 that enables you to view files stored in 30 different file formats without needing to open the application that created the file. Quick View is available from the File menu of Explorer if a viewer is available for the selected file type.

QuickTime   Developed by Apple, QuickTime is a compression and decompression (codec) scheme for animation files. It is unique in that versions are available for both Windows and Macintosh, enabling software designers to provide their data in a format compatible for both platforms.

R

RAM   Random Access Memory. Physical memory chips located in the computer. Typically, Windows 95 machines have 16 million bytes (16M) of RAM or more. However, Windows 95 will run on machines with 8M of RAM.

raster font   A font in which characters are stored as pixels.

read-only   Characteristic of a file indicating that the file can be read from, but not written to, by an application. Note however, that a "read-only" file can be deleted in Explorer, although you will get a warning (beyond the normal "are you sure" you normally get when you try to delete a file) if the file is read-only.

real mode   As opposed to *protected mode*, real mode is a mode in which Intel x86 processors can run. Memory addressing in real mode is nonlinear, requiring a program to stipulate a segment and memory offset address in order to access a location in memory. Originally appeared on the Intel 8086 CPU and has been the bane of PC programmers ever since. Although subsequent CPU chips supported protected-mode linear addressing, backward compatibility with the thousands of real-mode applications slows the evolution of operating systems. Note that all Intel CPUs boot in real mode and require specific software support to switch into protected mode.

Recycle Bin   An icon that appears on the Windows 95 desktop. To discard a file, you drag the file from Explorer, My Computer, or any other file handler to the Recycle Bin. This action hides the file—but doesn't actually erase it from the disk. You can "undelete" the file by dragging it from the Recycle Bin back to a folder. To actually delete the file, select the Recycle Bin menu selection to empty the Recycle Bin.

registering a program   The act of linking a document with the program that created it so that both can be opened with a single command. For example, double-clicking a DOC file opens Word for Windows and loads the selected document.

Registry   A database of configuration information central to Window 95 operations. This file contains program settings, associations between file types and the applications that created them, as well as information about the types of OLE objects a program can create and hardware detail information.

Registry Editor   The Registry Editor ships with Windows 95. Using this tool you can fine-tune Windows 95 performance by adjusting or adding settings to key system information. Since Windows 95 has placed WIN.INI and SYSTEM.INI file settings in the Registry, the ability to remotely edit these parameters is an extremely powerful tool. Warning: you can totally destroy a workstation using this tool!

repeater   A device that repeats or amplifies bits of data received at one port and sends each bit to another port. A repeater is a simple bus network device that connects two cabling segments and isolates electrical problems to either side. When used in a LAN, most repeaters take a role in reconstituting the digital signal that passes through them to extend distances a signal can travel, and reduce problems that occur over lengths of cable, such as attenuation.

resize button   A button located in the lower left corner of a non-maximized window. When the mouse pointer is over this button, it turns into a two-headed arrow. You can click and drag to resize the window horizontally and vertically.

resource (card)   When installing a card, certain "resources" are needed; these often include a DMA channel, I/O Base address, and IRQ. Although these are detected and set automatically with Plug and Play-compliant cards, you will have to set them using jumpers or the setup program to store the resource values in non-volatile RAM when installing a "legacy" (pre-Plug and Play) card.

restore button   A button in the upper right corner of a window that has two squares in it. When clicked, it returns the window to its previous size. When the window is at its previous size, the restore button switches to the maximize button, which returns the window to its maximum size.

restore files   Copies one or more files from your backup set to the hard disk or to another floppy.

rich text format (RTF)   RTF (rich text format) is compatible with several word processors and includes fonts, tabs, and character formatting.

ring network   One of a variety of network topologies. Ring networks connect computers by using an In and an Out port for data. Each computer sends information to the next computer down the wire. Data flows from one computer's Out port to the next computer's In port.

ROM (Read-Only Memory)   A type of chip capable of permanently storing data without the aid of an electric current source to maintain it, as in RAM. The data in ROM chips is sometimes called firmware. Without special equipment, it is not possible to alter the contents of read-only memory chips, thus the name. ROMs are found in many types of computer add-in boards, as well as on motherboards. CPUs often have an internal section of ROM as well.

routable protocol   A network protocol that can work with non-proprietary routers. Traditional routers use the network packet header fields to identify network addresses (network numbers)/node addresses for ultimate source and destination nodes (or hosts) for packets of data. This scheme for routing packets across internetworks is used by OSI, NetWare (IPX), TCP/IP, and AppleTalk network protocols.

router   In a network, a device that reads network layer packet headers and receives or forwards each packet accordingly. Routers connect LANs and WANs into internetworks, but must be able to process the network packets for specific types of network protocol. Many routers process various packet types and therefore are termed multiprotocol routers.

S

safe mode   A special mode for starting Windows 95 that uses simple default settings so that you can at least get into Windows and fix a problem that makes it impossible to work with Windows otherwise. The default settings use a generic VGA monitor driver, no network settings, the standard Microsoft mouse driver, and the minimum device drivers necessary to start Windows.

safe recovery   An installation option provided by Windows 95 to recover from a faulty or damaged installation of Windows 95.

saturation   When working with colors, saturation indicates the purity of a color; lower values of saturation have more gray in them.

ScanDisk   A program used to check for, diagnose, and repair damage on a hard disk or diskette. Part of your routine, hard disk maintenance (along with defragmenting your hard disk) should include a periodic run of ScanDisk to keep your hard disk in good repair. In its standard test, ScanDisk checks the files and folders on a disk or diskette for *logical* errors, and if you ask it to, automatically corrects any errors it finds. ScanDisk checks for *crosslinked* files, which occur when two or more files have data stored in the same *cluster* (a storage unit on a disk). The data in the cluster is likely to be correct for only one of the files, and may not be correct for any of them. ScanDisk also checks for *lost file fragments*, which are pieces of data that have become disassociated with their files.

screen fonts   Font files used to show type styles on the screen. These are different from the files used by Windows to print the fonts. The screen fonts must match the printer fonts in order for Windows to give an accurate screen portrayal of the final printed output.

screen resolution   The number of picture elements (or "pixels") that can be displayed on the screen. Screen resolution is a function of the monitor and graphics card. Higher resolutions display more information at a smaller size, and also may slow screen performance. Screen resolution is expressed in the number of pixels across the screen by the number of pixels down the screen. Standard VGA has a resolution of 640 by 480, although most modern monitors can display 1024 by 768, and even higher (larger monitors can usually display a higher resolution than smaller ones).

screen saver   A varying pattern or graphic that appears on the screen when the mouse and keyboard have been idle for a user-definable period of time. Originally used to prevent a static background from being "burned into" the screen phosphors, this is rarely a problem with modern monitors. Many screen savers (including those that come with Windows 95) can be used with a password—you must enter the correct password to turn off the screen saver and return to the screen. However, someone could simply reboot the machine, so a screen saver password is not very sophisticated protection.

scroll arrow   Located at either end of a scroll bar, it can be clicked to scroll up or down (vertical scroll bar) or left or right (horizontal scroll bar). Clicking the scroll arrow will move your window in that direction.

scroll bar   Scroll bars allow you to select a value within a range, such as what part of a document to see, or what value to set the Red, Green, and Blue components of a color to.

scroll box   A small box located in the scroll bar that shows where the visible window is located in relation to the entire document, menu, or list. You can click and drag the scroll box to make other portions of the document, menu, or list visible.

SCSI Configured Automagically (SCAM)   The specification for Plug and Play or SCSI buses. This specification makes it unnecessary to set a SCSI ID, as the configuration software negotiates and sets the ID for each connected SCSI device (that is Plug and Play-compliant!).

select   To specify a section of text or graphics for initiating an action. To select also can be to choose an option in a dialog box.

selection handles   Small, black boxes indicating that a graphic object has been selected. With some Windows applications, you can click and drag a selection handle to resize the selected object.

serial port   See *COM.*

serif fonts   Serif fonts have projections (serifs) that extend the upper and lower strokes of the set's characters beyond their normal boundaries, for example, Courier. San-serif fonts do not have these projections; an example is Arial.

server   A centrally administered network computer, which contains resources that are shared with "client" machines on the network.

server application   In OLE terminology, an application that supplies an object, (such as a drawing), to a client application, (such as a word processing program), for inclusion in a complex document.

shareware   A method of distributing software, often including downloading the software from a BBS or The Microsoft Network. With shareware, you get to use the software before deciding to pay for it. By paying for the software and registering it, you usually receive a manual, perhaps the most up-to-date version (which may include additional functionality). Shareware versions of software often include intrusive reminders to register—the registered versions do not include these reminders.

shortcut   A pointer to a file, document, or printer in Windows 95. A shortcut is represented by an icon in Explorer, on the desktop, or as an entry in the Start menu. Selecting the program shortcut icon or menu entry runs the program to which the shortcut "points." Selecting a document shortcut runs the application that created the document (provided the document type is associated with a program). Dragging and dropping a document onto a printer shortcut prints the document. Note that a shortcut does NOT create a copy of the program or document itself.

shortcut keys   A keystroke or key combination that enables you to activate a command without having to enter a menu or click a button.

shortcut menu   A popup menu that appears when you right-click an object for which a menu is appropriate. The shortcut menu displays only those options which make sense for the object you select and current conditions.

Small Computer System Interface (SCSI)   An ANSI standard bus design. SCSI host adapters are used to adapt an ISA, EISA, MCI, PCI, or VLB (VESA Local Bus) bus to a SCSI bus so that SCSI devices (such as disk drives, CD-ROMs, tape backups, and other devices) can be interfaced. A SCSI bus accommodates up to eight devices; however, the bus adapter is considered one device, thereby enabling seven usable devices to be interfaced to each SCSI adapter. SCSI devices are intelligent devices. SCSI disk drives have embedded controllers and interface to a SCSI bus adapter. A SCSI interface card is therefore a "bus adapter," not a "controller."

Small Computer System Interface-2 (SCSI-2)   An ANSI standard that improves on SCSI-1 standards for disk and other device interfaces. SCSI-2 bandwidth is 10 Mbytes/sec, whereas SCSI-1 is 5 Mbyte/sec. SCSI-2 also permits command-tag queuing, which enables up to 256 requests to be queued without waiting for the first request. Another SCSI-2 feature is the bus' capability to communicate with more than one type of device at the same time, where a single SCSI-1 host adapter only supports one type of device to communicate on the bus.

soft fonts   Depending on your printing hardware, soft fonts may be downloaded to your printer. Downloading fonts reduces the time taken by the printer to process printouts. Although downloading soft fonts is done only once (per session), benefits are realized through subsequent printing.

Solitaire   A card game included with Windows 95 for a single player. The object of Solitaire is to turn all the cards in the seven face-down stacks face-up on top of each of the four aces for each of the four suites.

Soundblaster   An extremely popular family of sound boards, developed and marketed by Creative Labs. Because of the popularity and large market share of this product family, most sound boards advertise themselves as "Soundblaster-compatible," meaning that drivers provided in Windows, Windows 95, and programs such as games will work with these boards. However, some boards' compatibility is not perfect.

source document   In OLE, the document that contains the information you want to link into (to appear in) another document (the destination document).

spool   A temporary holding area for the data you want to print. When printing a document, it can take some time (depending on the length of the document and the speed of your printer) for the document to come off your printer. By spooling the data, you may continue using your computer while the document is printing, because the computer "feeds" the spool contents to the printer as fast as the printer can handle it. When the print job is completed, the spool file is automatically deleted.

star network   One of a variety of network topologies. Star networks connect computers through a central hub. The central hub distributes the signals to all of the cables that are connected.

Start menu   A menu located at the left end of the task bar. Clicking the button marked "Start" opens a popup menu that makes Help, the Run command, settings, find, shutdown, a list of programs (actually, program shortcuts) and a list of recently accessed documents available for you to run with a single click. For some items (such as the Documents item), a submenu opens to the side of the main item to display the list of choices. You can configure the Start menu to specify which programs are available to run from it.

Startup folder   A folder that contains any programs that you want Windows 95 to run whenever you start up. You can drag and drop program shortcuts into the Startup folder to add them to the list of programs to run.

static object   In OLE, where some objects have a "hot link" to their original application, static objects are simply pasted into a destination document using the clipboard. These objects are not updated if the original object is updated. This is the simple "pasting" that most Windows users use on a daily basis.

stop bits   In a communications program, the number of bits used to indicate the "break" between pieces of information (see *data bits*). Usually 1 or 2.

stroke font   A font that can have its size greatly altered without distortion.

submenu   A related set of options that appear when you select a menu item (see *cascading menu*).

swap file   A file that gives Windows 95 the capability to use a portion of hard drive as memory. With the use of a swap file, you can load and run more programs in Windows 95 than you actually have RAM memory for.

A swap file allows Windows 95 to "swap" chunks of memory containing currently unused information to disk, making room in RAM memory for information you need to run the currently selected program. Using a swap file is slower than holding everything in RAM memory, however.

system disk   The disk containing the operating system, or at least enough of it to start the system and then look on another disk for the support files.

system fonts   System fonts are used by Windows to draw menus, controls, and utilize specialized control text in Windows. System fonts are proportional fonts that can be sized and manipulated quickly.

system monitor   A program that enables you to monitor the resources on your computer. You can see information displayed for the 32-bit file system, network clients and servers, and the virtual memory manager, among other things. Most of this information is highly technical in nature and most useful to advanced users. You can display the information in either bar or line charts, or as a numeric value.

system policies   Policies, established by a system administrator, which override Registry settings on individual machines. By setting up policies, a system administrator can restrict a user from changing hardware settings using Control Panel, customize parts of the Desktop like the Network Neighborhood or the Programs folder, and maintain centrally located network settings, such as network client customizations or the ability to install file and printer services. This program can also control access to a computer, enable user profiles, and maintain password control.

System Resources   See *heap*.

T

tab (dialog boxes)   In dialog boxes, there may be multiple panels of information. Each panel has an extension at the top that names the panel. This small extension is called a "tab."

TAPI   Telephony Applications Programming Interface, or TAPI, provides a method for programs to work with modems, independent of dealing directly with the modem hardware. All the information you give Windows during the modem configuration is used for TAPI to set up its interface. Communications programs that are written specifically for Windows 95 will talk to TAPI, which will then issue appropriate commands to the modem. This is called device independence.

taskbar   An area that runs across the bottom of the Windows 95 desktop. The Start button (see *Start menu*) is at the left end of the taskbar, and the clock can be displayed at the right end of the taskbar. Running applications are represented as buttons on the taskbar, the current window is shown as a depressed button, and all other applications are displayed as raised buttons. Clicking the button for an inactive application activates that application and displays its window as the current window.

task list   A list of currently running applications. You can switch tasks by clicking an item in the task list. The task list is accessed by pressing Alt+Tab on the keyboard.

TCP/IP   Transmission Control Protocol/Internet Protocol is a set of networking protocols developed in the 1970s. TCP/IP includes Transport Control Protocol, which is a connection-oriented transport protocol that includes transport, session, and presentation layer protocol functions, which is equivalent to layers 4, 5, and 6 of the OSI Model and Internet Protocol, and a widely used routable network protocol that corresponds to layer 3 of the OSI model. User Datagram Protocol (UDP) can be substituted in cases where connection-less datagram service is desired. TCP/IP is an entire protocol stack that includes protocols for file transfers (FTP), termination emulation services (telnet), electronic mail (SMTP), address resolution (ARP and RARP), and error control and notification (ICMP and SNMP). TCP/IP is used extensively in many computer systems because it is nonproprietary — free from royalties. Its use was mandated by Congress for use in computer systems for many government agencies and contract situations. TCP/IP is also used in the Internet, a huge government and research internetwork spanning North America and much of the world. TCP/IP is the most commonly used set of network protocols.

terminal emulation   In the "old days" of computing, a "terminal" was an input/output device that was a slave of a CPU, such as a terminal for a minicomputer or mainframe. Generally, terminals had no computing power of their own, but simply provided an interface to a remote host computer. "Terminal emulation" refers to a mode (character-based) in which a PC emulates one of these terminals to communicate with a remote host — typically a BBS computer or a corporate mainframe that only "knows" how to talk to a terminal.

text-based   See *character-based*.

text box   A space in the dialog box where text or numbers can be entered so that a command can be carried out.

text file   A file containing only text characters.

thread (BBS/Communications)   A set of messages pertaining to one general idea.

thread (program execution)   A "thread" is a chunk of a program. In a multi-threading environment such as Windows 95, multiple threads (multiple portions of a program) can execute at the same time—provided the program has been programmed to take advantage of this feature.

thumbnail   A miniature rendition of a graphic file. A thumbnail gives an idea of what the full-size graphic looks like, and is usually used as a gateway to view the full-size graphic.

tile   To reduce and move windows so that they can all be seen at once.

time slice   A brief time period in which a process is given access to the processor. Each second is divided into 18.3 time slices; multiple tasks can be scheduled for processing in these slices, yet outwardly appear to be occurring simultaneously.

time-out   A time period after which a device or driver might signal the operating system and cease trying to perform its duty. If a printer is turned off, for example, when you try to print, the driver waits for a predetermined period of time, then issues an error message. In computer terminology, the driver has *timed out*.

title bar   The bar at the top of a program or document window that shows you what its title is. The control menu, maximize, minimize, restore, and task bar buttons can be accessed in the title bar.

token ring   A network type developed by IBM. It is more expensive than Ethernet to implement, but can run at 16 Mb/s. Unlike Ethernet, where the workstations must listen for a clear line before transmitting, workstations on a token ring take turns sending data — passing the "token" from station to station to indicate whose turn it is.

toolbar   A collection of buttons that typically make the more common tools for an application easily accessible. Although often grouped in a line under the menus, a toolbar can be located on the left or right side of the working area — or even be relocated to any area of the screen the user wishes. In some applications (for example, MS Office applications such as Word), the toolbar is user-configurable — the user can display different toolbars, and add or remove tool buttons from the bar.

topology   The layout or design of cabling on a network.

TrueType fonts A font technology developed by Microsoft in response to Adobe's success in the scaleable font business with its own Type 1 and Type 3 PostScript fonts. Used as a simple means for all Windows applications to have access to a wide selection of fonts for screen and printer output. TrueType fonts greatly simplify using fonts on a Windows computer. The same fonts can be used on Windows 3.1, Windows NT, Windows 95, and other Windows products, such as Windows for Workgroups. Consisting of two files (one for screen and one for printer), hundreds of TrueType fonts are available from a variety of manufacturers. Depending on your printer, the TrueType font manager internal to Windows, in conjunction with the printer driver, generates either bitmapped or downloadable soft fonts.

twisted pair Cabling that consists of lightly insulated copper wire, twisted into pairs and bundled into sets of pairs. The twists enhance the wire's capability to resist "crosstalk" (bleeding of signal from one wire to the next). This cabling is used extensively in phone systems and LANs, although even moderate distances in a LAN require "repeaters" (see *repeaters*).

U

unbound media In a network, this refers to connections that are not implemented using traditional cabling. Instead, unbound media are wireless—implemented through use of various portions of the radio wave spectrum.

unimodem driver A universal modem driver supplied by Microsoft as part of Windows 95. The modem driver assumes that the modem supports the Hayes AT command set (most do).

uninstalling applications When you install an application in Windows 95, it places the necessary files in many different places on your hard drive. You can't remove all of a program by simply erasing the contents of its main subdirectory. To uninstall the application — and remove all the files it placed on your hard drive — you must run a special program that should have been included with the application. Many applications do not include the "uninstaller" program, although, to be certified under Windows 95, the uninstaller program must be included.

Universal Naming Convention (UNC) With UNC, you can view, copy, or run files on another machine without assigning it a drive letter on your own. It also means if you are running short of logical drive letters, you can get to servers that you use only intermittently with a simple command from the MS-DOS prompt.

unprintable area   The area, usually around the extreme edges of the paper, in which the printer is incapable of printing. For example, a laser printer cannot print in the 1/4" at the left and right edges of the paper. It is important to know the unprintable area, since graphics or text you place in this area will be cut off when printed.

upload   The act of sending a file to a remote computer (see *download*).

V

VCACHE   Windows 95 uses a new 32-bit VCACHE that replaces the older SmartDrive that ran under DOS and previous versions of Windows. VCACHE uses more intelligent caching algorithms to improve the apparent speed of your hard drive as well as your CD-ROM and 32-bit network redirectors. Unlike SmartDrive, VCACHE dynamically allocates itself. Based on the amount of free system memory, VCACHE allocates or de-allocates memory used by the cache.

vector fonts   A set of lines that connect points to form characters.

video for windows   A set of utilities and protocols for implementing full-motion video in Windows 95.

virtual machine   A "logical" computer that exists inside a PC. Multiple virtual machines can be running in a PC. Applications that run on one virtual machine are unlikely to affect the applications running on a different virtual machine. 16-bit applications (for example, Windows 3.1 applications) all run on the same virtual machine in Windows 95, thus, if one crashes, it is likely to make the rest of the 16-bit applications unusable as well. However, such an occurrence will likely not affect 32-bit applications that are running simultaneously.

virtual memory   The use of permanent media (for example, a hard drive) to simulate additional RAM (see *swap file*). This allows large applications to run in less physical RAM than they normally would require. When RAM runs low, the operating system uses a virtual memory manager program to temporarily store data on the hard disk like it was in RAM, which makes RAM free for data manipulation. When needed, the data is read back from the disk and reloaded into RAM.

virus   A virus is a computer program written to interrupt or destroy your work. A virus may do something as innocuous as display a message, or something as destructive as reformatting your hard drive—or almost anything in between. Your computer can "catch" a virus from a floppy disk, or even from a file downloaded from a remote source, such as a BBS. Once your computer has become "infected," the virus may spread via connections on a network or floppy disks you share with others. A variety of virus-detecting software exists, (including one packaged with Windows 95).

ViSCA   A protocol for daisy-chaining up to seven video devices together and connecting them to a single serial port.

volume   Disk partition(s) formatted and available for use by the operating system.

volume label   The identifier for a volume (see *volume*) or diskette. This is specified when formatting the volume or diskette.

W

wallpaper   A backdrop for the Windows desktop, made up of a graphics files. The graphics can be either *centered*, appearing only once in the center of the desktop, or *tiled*, repeating as many times as the graphic will fit.

WAV files   Named for the three-character extension .WAV (for sound wave) these files have, a WAV file is a file containing a digitized sound. Depending on the sampling rate and resolution, the sound recorded in the WAV file seems realistic (provided you have the sound card and speakers to hear it). These files can be quite large, running into the multi-megabyte range for high-quality recordings.

Web browser   A software program that enables you to view home pages and retrieve information from the Internet.

What's This?   A new feature of Windows 95 help. In a dialog box, click the small button with a question mark (?) on it. Then, click where you want help. A small description should pop up to explain what the item is and how to use it. Click in the description popup to remove it.

Winpopup   Winpopup is an applet that is included in the Accessories group when you install the network component of Windows 95. This tool normally sends short messages from one computer on the workgroup to another (or from a shared printer to a workstation). It is designed so that when a message is received, the program will pop up over anything else on the screen and show the message.

wiring concentrator   In a network, a multiple-port repeating device used in Ethernet LANs to connect multiple cable segments into one LAN. Sometimes called a "hub" (see *hub*) or "multiport repeater" (see *repeater*), this device isolates cabling problems by separating each workstation connection on an isolated cabling segment.

wizard   Microsoft's name for a step-by-step set of instructions that guide you through a particular task. For example, there are many wizards included with Windows 95 for installing new hardware, configuring the Start menu, and changing other aspects of the environment.

WordPad   A program included with Windows 95 that enables you to do basic word processing and save the results in plain text format, Word 6 format, or rich text format.

word wrap   In word processing, this refers to words that cannot be completed on one line automatically "wrapping" to the beginning of the next line. Most word processors use word wrap automatically — an exception is Notepad, where you must turn on word wrap.

workgroup   A collection of networked PCs grouped to facilitate work that users of the computers tend to do together. The machines are not necessarily in the same room or office.

World Wide Web (WWW)   The fastest growing part of the Internet, the 'Web,' or WWW, is a collection of hypertext documents. It provides access to images and sounds from thousands of different Web sites, via a special programming language called **H**yper**T**ext **M**arkup **L**anguage, or **HTML**. This language is used to create "hypertext" documents, which include embedded commands.

WYSIWYG   Short for "What you see is what you get," this term refers to the ability of an application to display an accurate representation of the printed output on the screen.

X

x coordinate   The position of an item relative to the left side of the screen. Values increase as you move to the right.

Xmodem   An error-correction protocol (see *binary transfer protocol*) used by the DOS application XMODEM and many other communications programs. Xmodem uses CRC (cyclical redundancy check), a means of detecting errors in transmissions between modems or across wired serial links.

Y

y coordinate   The position of an item relative to the bottom of the screen. Values increase as you move down the screen.

Ymodem   Another form of Xmodem that allows batch transfers of files and (in Ymodem G) hardware error control.

Z

Zmodem   Zmodem is a fully functional streaming protocol where Xmodem is a send and acknowledge protocol that causes delays in the transfer equal to twice the modem lag on a connection. Zmodem is the preferred way of exchanging data since it is reliable, quick, and relatively easy to implement.

Index of Common Problems

Indexes

Text, Notes, and Tables

If you have this problem...	You'll find help here...
Text doesn't appear when you print handouts	p. 216
When you click Insert Word Table, nothing happens	p. 241
Only one row resizes when I use the column selector on the ruler	p. 254

Drawing

If you have this problem...	You'll find help here...
While drawing freeform you made a mistake	p. 269
An object is too pale to see on screen	p. 265
A placeholder won't move when you drag it	p. 295
So many files in your ClipArt Gallery make it hard to find the one you need	p. 322
Images you added to your system don't show in the ClipArt Gallery	p. 322
A category name you used to store images is no longer accurate	p. 322
Can't find an image you deleted from the Gallery	p. 322

Charts

If you have this problem...	You'll find help here...
Columns in a chart are in the wrong order	p. 366
Can't add titles to a pie chart	p. 380
Value labels on a chart overlap the axis titles	p. 380
Can't add captions while in the Graph program	p. 392
Colors on your chart have been changed and you need to return them to default	p. 403
Shading effects don't work on objects drawn in Graph	p. 416

Charts

If you have this problem...	You'll find help here...
Double-clicking an organizational chart placeholder doesn't open the OrgChart program	p. 424
Selecting a group of people to set as co-managers gives you an error message	p. 426
Scatter chart data markers are almost invisible on-screen	p. 545
Some axis tick mark labels disappear when a chart is displayed	p. 553
Can't create combination charts using 2-D and 3-D chart types	p. 562

Output and Color

If you have this problem...	You'll find help here...
Can't find a Genigraphics printer on the printer list	p. 458
Output on a black and white printer is dark	p. 460
It takes too long to print black and white output	p. 460
Genigraphics only offers you the option of paying by credit card, even though you have an account	p. 462
Can't transmit a presentation using GraphicsLink	p. 464
Call waiting is disrupting transmission of a presentation	p. 464
Color schemes don't look good	p. 493
Can't find color tools	p. 506
While trying to apply a color to one slide, you applied it to all by mistake	p. 506
Colors used to create a black and white or gray scale presentation don't look good on overhead transparencies	p. 678

Using Advanced Features: OLE and Multimedia

If you have this problem...	You'll find help here...
Several linked files won't run when I use them on another computer	p. 524
Can't embed Excel datasheets or Word tables in a slide	p. 535
OLE doesn't work with Windows 95	p. 531
Media Player doesn't load sound files	p. 615
CD soundtrack won't play	p. 628
Double-clicking a table or datasheet doesn't bring up a non-Microsoft application	p. 671
Now you need applets you didn't install with PowerPoint	p. 682

Customizing PowerPoint

If you have this problem...	You'll find help here...
Some buttons on a floating toolbar disappear off the side of your screen	p. 693
Can't remove a button from a toolbar	p. 693
After removing a button from a toolbar, you want to get it back	p. 693
While trying to switch the place of two buttons, you just get more space between them	p. 694
When you paste text into a line, you get extra spaces you have to delete	p. 699
Don't want the Summary Info dialog box to appear every time you save a file	p. 700

Making Effective PowerPoint Presentations

If you have this problem...	You'll find help here...
The pace of your presentation is too slow or fast	p. 703
Text on your slides is too small to be read by the audience	p. 705

Making Effective PowerPoint Presentations

If you have this problem...	You'll find help here...
A complex graphic or transition causes a delay in a slide appearing during a presentation	p. 705
Can't decide which hardware to use for presentations	p. 717
You have problems with equipment at a presentation site	p. 717

PowerPoint Gallery of Presentation Examples

3-D Bar Chart

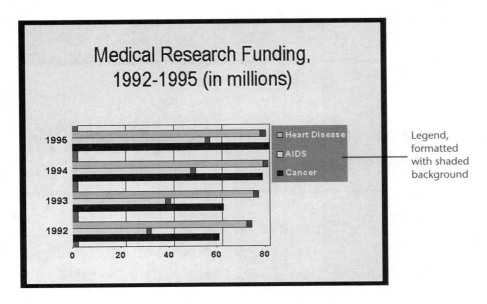

3-D Pie Chart

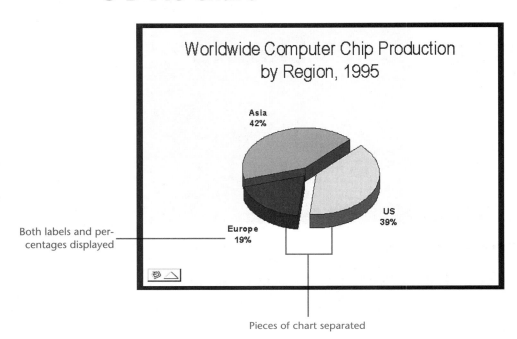

Both labels and percentages displayed

Pieces of chart separated

Title, Clip Art and Text Placeholder Layout

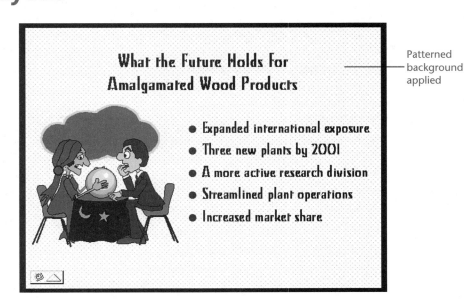

Patterned background applied

Title and Text Placeholder Layout

Textured background

Title placeholder moved to bottom of page

Text moved in front of inserted clip art

Blank Layout with Inserted Clip Art and Text Boxes

Title Placeholder with Word 7 Table

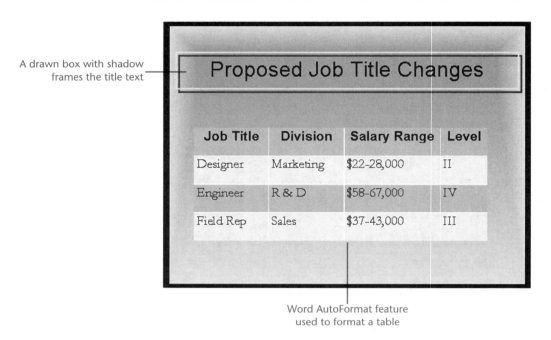

A drawn box with shadow frames the title text

Word AutoFormat feature used to format a table

3-D Line Chart

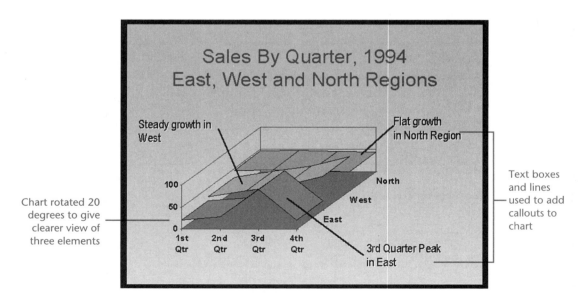

Steady growth in West

Flat growth in North Region

Chart rotated 20 degrees to give clearer view of three elements

Text boxes and lines used to add callouts to chart

3rd Quarter Peak in East

Clip Art Used to Frame Text

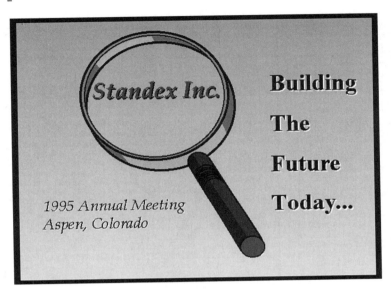

3-D Area Chart

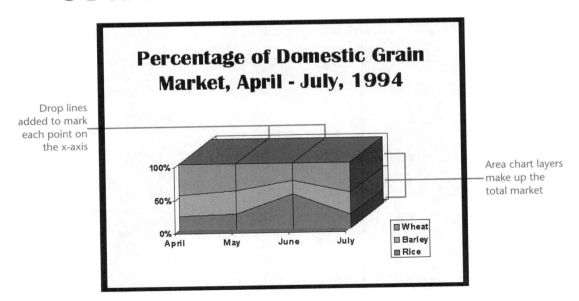

Drop lines added to mark each point on the x-axis

Area chart layers make up the total market

Custom 3-D Column Chart

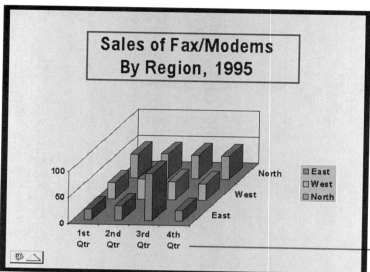

Rotation (20 degr
and elevation (20
degrees) used to s
bar elements clear

Title and Two Text Placeholders Layout

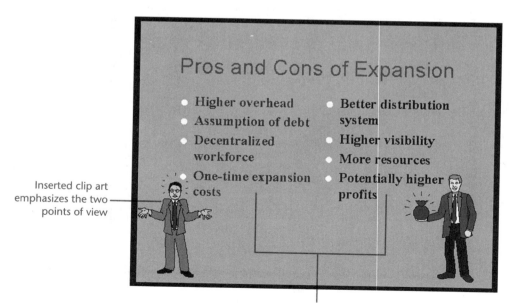

Inserted clip art
emphasizes the two
points of view

Two text placeholders work
well with comparisons

Title, Chart and Text Placeholder Layout

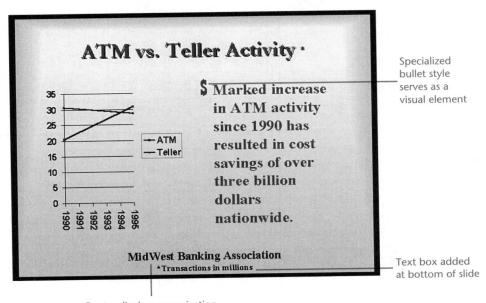

Index

Symbols

? button (dialog boxes), 80
? tool (toolbars), 50, 51
... (ellipsis), defined, 736
16-bit defined, 723
1655OA-UART defined, 723
2-D charts
  building, 361
  combination charts, 555-557
    creating, 557-559
    customizing, 584-586
    formatting, 559-562
    titles, 562-564
  converting to 3-D charts, 407
  doughnut charts, 567-569
  elements, 355-357
  gridlines
    displaying, 386-388
    scaling, 389-390
  line charts, 542
    creating, 543-544
  radar charts, 564-567
  scatter charts, 545-548
  stock charts, 548-550
    creating, 550-551
    formatting, 551-555
  trendlines, 586-589
3-D charts
  area charts, 573-574
    deleting legends, 574-575
    formatting, 576
  coloring walls, 405-406
  converting 2-D charts to, 407
  elements, 357-359
  rotating
    3-D perspective changes, 411

    mouse method, 409-410
    rotation values, 408-409
  surface charts, 569-571
    adjusting views, 571
    gridlines, 572
    legends, 572
  trendlines, 586-589
32-bit defined, 723
35mm slides, 83, 452
  Genigraphics, 462-463
  printing, 454-455

A

About Microsoft PowerPoint dialog box, 74
accelerator keys
  defined, 723
  see also keyboard commands
activating windows, 723
active presentation title bar, 47
active window, defined, 723
Add New Pictures dialog box, 308
address book, defined, 723
Adobe Type Manager (ATM), 724
Advanced Program-to-Program Communications (APPC) standard, 724
airbrush tools, 724
alert messages, 724
Align command (Draw menu), 296

aligning
  objects, 295-297
  placeholders, 202
  table cell data, 248
  text, 191-192
animation effects, 28, 120-121, 647-650
  builds for text, 650-651
    sounds, 652
    special effects, 651-652
  dimming objects, 653
Animation Effects toolbar, 647-649
Animation Settings dialog box, 121
  After Build Step options, 653-654
  Build Options drop-down list, 611-612, 650-651
  Effects section, 652
  Play Options drop-down list, 607-608, 621-623
  Reverse Order checkbox, 654
  Start When Previous Build Ends checkbox, 654
Animation toolbar, 49
annotating slides, 32, 661
  defined, 724
ANSI standard, defined, 724
Answer Wizard, 25, 75
Anti Virus programs, defined, 724
applets, defined, 724
Application Programming Interface (API), 724
application window, 41

F

X-Y-Z

Also by Thomas C. Renner

My Life in the Mafia (with Vincent Teresa)
Vincent Teresa's Mafia (with Vincent Teresa)
Wall Street Swindler (with Michael Hellerman)
Mafia Princess (with Antionette Giancana)

MAFIA
ENFORCER

MAFIA ENFORCER

Cecil Kirby and
Thomas C. Renner

VILLARD BOOKS

NEW YORK | 1987

Copyright © 1987 by Thomas C. Renner and Cecil Kirby
All rights reserved under International and Pan-American Copyright Conventions.
Published in the United States by Villard Books, a division of Random House, Inc.,
New York.

Library of Congress Cataloging in Publication Data
Kirby, Cecil.
Mafia enforcer.
1. Kirby, Cecil.
2. Mafia—Canada—Case studies.
3. Crime and criminals—Canada—Biography.
I. Renner, Thomas C.
II. Title.
HV6453.C2K577   1987   364.1'5'0924   [B]   86-40329
ISBN 0-394-54459-5

Designed by Mary Cregan
Manufactured in the United States of America

9 8 7 6 5 4 3 2

First Edition

To my wife, Nancy, who makes all things possible, and to my daughters, Dawn, Elaine, Jacqueline, and Sandy for their patience and love.

—T.C.R.

TYPICAL ORGANIZED CRIME FAMILY

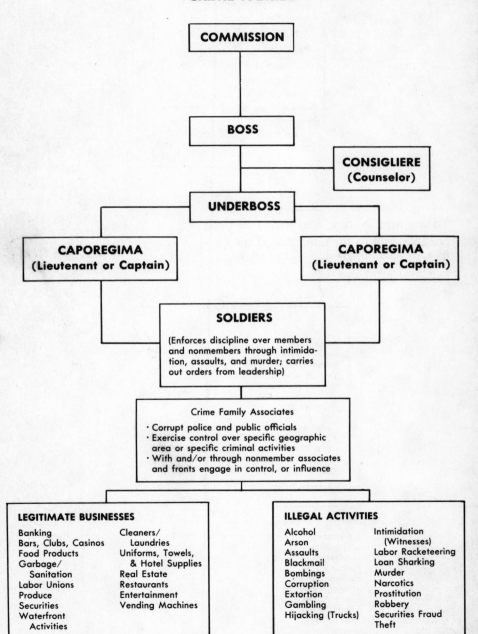

COMMISSION

BOSS

CONSIGLIERE
(Counselor)

UNDERBOSS

CAPOREGIMA
(Lieutenant or Captain)

CAPOREGIMA
(Lieutenant or Captain)

SOLDIERS

(Enforces discipline over members and nonmembers through intimidation, assaults, and murder; carries out orders from leadership)

Crime Family Associates
· Corrupt police and public officials
· Exercise control over specific geographic area or specific criminal activities
· With and/or through nonmember associates and fronts engage in control, or influence

LEGITIMATE BUSINESSES

Banking
Bars, Clubs, Casinos
Food Products
Garbage/
    Sanitation
Labor Unions
Produce
Securities
Waterfront
    Activities

Cleaners/
    Laundries
Uniforms, Towels,
    & Hotel Supplies
Real Estate
Restaurants
Entertainment
Vending Machines

ILLEGAL ACTIVITIES

Alcohol
Arson
Assaults
Blackmail
Bombings
Corruption
Extortion
Gambling
Hijacking (Trucks)

Intimidation
    (Witnesses)
Labor Racketeering
Loan Sharking
Murder
Narcotics
Prostitution
Robbery
Securities Fraud
Theft

TYPICAL MAJOR MOTORCYCLE GANG CHAPTER

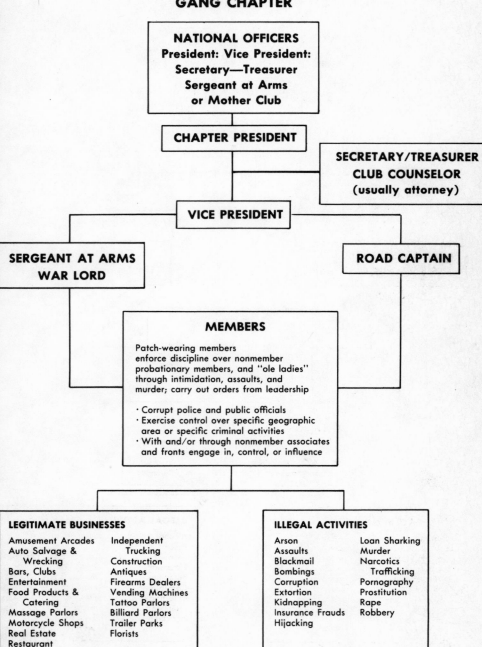

NATIONAL OFFICERS
President: Vice President:
Secretary—Treasurer
Sergeant at Arms
or Mother Club

CHAPTER PRESIDENT

**SECRETARY/TREASURER
CLUB COUNSELOR
(usually attorney)**

VICE PRESIDENT

**SERGEANT AT ARMS
WAR LORD**

ROAD CAPTAIN

MEMBERS

Patch-wearing members
enforce discipline over nonmember
probationary members, and "ole ladies"
through intimidation, assaults, and
murder; carry out orders from leadership

· Corrupt police and public officials
· Exercise control over specific geographic
  area or specific criminal activities
· With and/or through nonmember associates
  and fronts engage in, control, or influence

LEGITIMATE BUSINESSES

Amusement Arcades
Auto Salvage &
  Wrecking
Bars, Clubs
Entertainment
Food Products &
  Catering
Massage Parlors
Motorcycle Shops
Real Estate
Restaurant

Independent
  Trucking
Construction
Antiques
Firearms Dealers
Vending Machines
Tattoo Parlors
Billiard Parlors
Trailer Parks
Florists

ILLEGAL ACTIVITIES

Arson
Assaults
Blackmail
Bombings
Corruption
Extortion
Kidnapping
Insurance Frauds
Hijacking

Loan Sharking
Murder
Narcotics
  Trafficking
Pornography
Prostitution
Rape
Robbery

Foreword

Cecil Kirby may well be the most disarming professional criminal I have
ever met—and I have met hundreds during my thirty-three years as a
journalist-author, twenty-six of those years as an organized crime investiga-
tive reporter.

Kirby is many things to many people. Charming, soft-spoken, deceptively polite, he does not fit the public mold of the outlaw biker or the
perceived characterization of an underworld enforcer. Yet he is both—
the first and only outlaw motorcycle gang member and leader to become
the chief enforcer for a Mafia-type crime family.

To the former attorney general of Ontario, Roy McMurtry, he is
Canada's Joe Valachi, the "first real breakthrough in penetrating the
conspiracy of silence" that shrouds the Honoured Society or Calabrian
Mafia and other Canadian organized crime groups, including outlaw
bikers.

John Schiman, a veteran FBI agent who worked with Kirby in Connecticut to save a woman's life, describes Kirby as a "suave, self-assured
[criminal who] knows how to handle underworld figures . . . the best
double agent I have met in my ten years as an FBI agent."

And the leadership of the Honoured Society and outlaw motorcycle
gangs in the United States and Canada consider Kirby so dangerous that
a price of $100,000 or more has been promised to killers who can find and
assassinate him.

Foreword

Since becoming a Canadian informer and witness, Kirby has saved the life of the mistress of a Connecticut Calabrian Mafia leader; at least temporarily prevented the murder of a Toronto Mafia chieftain; solved more than seventy bombings, arsons, and attempted murders; and provided authorities with information, evidence, or testimony that resulted in the conviction of at least thirty-six criminals, including three high-ranking Calabrian Mafia leaders.

At age thirty-five, Cecil Kirby has lived a life of crime that spans the highs and lows of the organized underworld. More than sixty arrests fill his criminal file. There are multiple convictions for break and entry, assault, extortion, crimes for which he has spent a total of less than four years in jail. And there is a controversial immunity agreement, necessary to obtain his testimony and the recorded conversations of criminals, that exonerates his participation in more than seventy crimes ranging from extortion, bombings, and arson to assault, attempted murder, and homicide as a result of a bombing.

Kirby's curly, reddish-blond hair frames an impish, almost boyish face that often breaks into an infectious smile. Sky-blue eyes twinkle with a devilish delight as he engages interviewers in word duels, smiling broadly when he knows he has disarmed or shocked them. Yet the infectious smile and musical laugh can change suddenly to a deadly scowl while eyes harden to steely coolness in unexpected moments of anger. In those moments the taut, muscular chest and arms of an avid weight lifter flex, the mouth hardens, and language that only moments before reflected what appeared to be a mild-mannered young businessman suddenly mirrors the gutter vocabulary of a vicious enforcer and assassin and the criminal underworld Kirby lived in and often dominated for nearly fifteen years in Toronto.

I first met Kirby on September 13, 1983, in an office provided by Canadian journalist James DuBro, who was trying to convince Kirby to appear on a television show with him. Kirby wanted to have a book written about his exploits. My concern, at that time, centered on the threat of organized crime that was proliferating to an awesome extent and with growing sophistication in Canada and the United States.

Kirby and I decided to meet again before I left Toronto. As a sign of good faith, Kirby provided me with a stack of documents and news clips

that he had brought with him in a brown leather briefcase. He agreed to permit me to use them and whatever information we taped in subsequent meetings for news articles I hoped to write about the new criminal groups I had been investigating.

Of particular interest to me then and now were the growth of the Calabrian Mafia and the apparent lack of intelligence about it by American law enforcement. More important was the public's ignorance of its existence. As early as 1975, I had written about the operation of a Calabrian Mafia group that had come from Siderno, Italy, and were known as the Sidernese. They were then active in counterfeiting, extortion, murder, business infiltration, and the pizza industry, but little was known about them except what was being compiled by Canadian authorities, particularly the Ontario Provincial Police, the Royal Canadian Mounted Police, and Canadian Immigration.

It has been my primary objective in writing books—first on Vincent Teresa, later on Michael Hellerman, and more recently on Antoinette Giancana—to provide the public with hitherto unpublished views of organized crime from people who have either been a part of it or have lived with it. Cecil Kirby provides a unique point of view on this world.

When Kirby and I met for the second time, there was no advance notice, only a ring of a telephone, Kirby's voice on the other end, and, within what seemed like seconds, a pounding on the door of my room at the Royal York Hotel. As I peered out from behind the door, I could see two burly plainclothesmen, members of a three-man team from the Special Enforcement Unit (Canada's equivalent of the U.S. Marshals' witness protection section), standing in front of my door.

"You Tom Renner?" one of them asked.

I nodded affirmatively, noticing a walkie-talkie he held in one hand and the high-powered pistol he had under his coat. "That's right," I said. "Who are you?"

The plainclothesman flashed a police identity card for the Toronto Metropolitan Police and asked me for some identification, but said nothing more.

I ushered the detectives into my room. While I showed my New York driver's license and police press pass to the plainclothesman, his partner

checked every nook and cranny of my room, including the door to an adjoining room, closets, and under the bed.

Once the room, the hallway, and stairway exits of the floor on which I was staying had been thoroughly searched, the detective I had first talked to spoke into the walkie-talkie and told Kirby it was safe for him to come up. Within a minute, he and two other men appeared. Making sure the door was locked, they left Kirby in my room, with two men stationed at either end of the hallway. Kirby sat down, a walkie-talkie at his side, to begin the first of what was to be a series of interview sessions that were to span two years and take place in less desirable locations throughout Canada.

During that first, four-hour interview, I fully realized Kirby's importance in showing the links that had been forged between outlaw motorcycle gangs and so-called Mafia groups. Law enforcement had for some time suspected that there were criminal links and business ties between cycle gangs and Mafia groups. Until Kirby surfaced, however, no member of a cycle gang had stepped forward as an informer-witness to make his role with both criminal groups public. Formerly a club vice president, Kirby, in fact, is still the only high-ranking member of an outlaw motorcycle gang to become the chief enforcer for a Mafia-type crime family.

Disclosures of business ties between motorcycle gangs and Mafia groups were beginning to surface in 1983. In Philadelphia, members of the Pagan motorcycle gang were engaged in drug trafficking with members of the Angelo Bruno crime family. Rebellious members of the Bruno family recruited bikers for hits on others within the family. A special report prepared by the office of U.S. Attorney Dan K. Webb in Chicago found that there was a "sinister criminal association" and a "loose alliance" between gangster flunkies of Chicago mob boss Anthony (Big Tuna) Accardo and the Outlaws, a motorcycle club that resorted to extortion, kidnapping, and murder to supply for profit nude dancers and prostitutes for Chicago mob clubs and massage parlors. There were other investigations in Detroit, Arizona, California. None provided the graphic documentation that Kirby did.

By 1985 both the Federal Bureau of Investigation in the United States and the Criminal Intelligence Service of Canada agreed on one thing: Outlaw motorcycle gangs represented significant organized crime threats

to both countries. Their hypothesis was supported by a growing body of evidence from U.S. Senate committees and federal trials from Philadelphia to Chicago, which details extortions, kidnappings, murder, narcotics trafficking, counterfeiting, white slavery, and brutality at a level that is difficult for even the most hardened observer to comprehend.

A new sophistication has emerged among outlaw bikers. The image of the apelike, "dirt-bag" bikers who took over towns to rape and pillage has evolved into that of a computer-age mobile criminal who uses electronics, computers, and high finance to thwart law enforcement and the courts. Outlaw bikers now invest in real estate, bars, restaurants, motorcycle shops, and other business ventures. Their reputation for brawn and unbridled violence has enabled them to obtain contracts to act as strikebreakers for an international oil company; to provide drugs and bodyguards for an internationally famous country singer; to muscle in on rock concerts and rock groups; and to engage in multi-million-dollar narcotics-smuggling enterprises.

An internal FBI report entitled "Outlaw Motorcycle Gangs," dated June 1985, placed the total membership of the four major U.S. gangs—the Bandidos, Hell's Angels, Outlaws, and Pagans—at more than 3,800, and that figure did not include the 800 smaller gangs, whose membership may exceed 2,000. A CISC annual report released to the media in Canada in 1985 put total Canadian outlaw motorcycle gang membership at more than 725.

A frightening add-on increases those membership figures. Police and federal agencies on both sides of the border say that for every known member of an outlaw biker gang there are ten associates. That means there are 65,000 bikers and associates dealing in crime in Canada and the United States.

Those associates have been described by the Ontario Provincial Police as the "support group—businessmen, prostitutes, lawyers, fellow travelers, recruits, hustlers, and con men who cooperate with outlaw bikers in crimes ranging from robbery and theft to murder and mayhem."

Cecil Kirby was an upper-echelon member of Satan's Choice, once the most vicious and powerful motorcycle gang in Canada. As a chapter vice president, he knew and traveled with members of other outlaw cycle gangs, including the stateside Outlaws. He possessed accurate, docu-

mented information about outlaw biker crimes ranging from murder and extortion to white slavery and narcotics trafficking.

In Chicago, Philadelphia, Arizona, and California other witnesses have testified about outlaw biker gangs, but they could testify only about their gangs, and the scope of their knowledge was generally regional. Their gangs—the Hell's Angels, the Outlaws—were international, with branches in Australia, Austria, Brazil, Denmark, England, France, Holland, Switzerland, and West Germany as well as Canada and the United States.

The scope of Kirby's experience goes far beyond painting a portrait of the international outlaw biker. Kirby became the only non-Italian to be accepted by the inner circles of the Honoured Society, to become their trusted chief enforcer and hired assassin of a "locale's" (crime family branch's) boss.

The Honoured Society is an emerging crime organization in both the United States and Canada. Its existence in Canada has been documented since the late 1950s, when large numbers of Italian immigrants, mainly from Siderno Marina in the southern Italian province of Reggio di Calabria began arriving in Canada, and later in the northeastern United States, primarily New York, New Jersey, and Connecticut.

In August 1971, Toronto Metro Police uncovered a twenty-seven-page, handwritten document while searching the home of a Toronto man for unregistered guns and counterfeit money. Translated from Italian, the document disclosed the rituals, responsibilities, and penalties for members of the Honoured Society, a secret organization that had flourished for hundreds of years in southern Italy. Similar documents were uncovered that same year in Australia, where another branch of the organization operates. The society was strikingly similar to the Sicilian Mafia, with its code of *omertà,* (silence), blood rituals for membership, close blood-family ties, and a ruling council similar in structure and responsibilities to the Mafia's and Cosa Nostra's separate boards of directors known as the *commissions.*

Though the Sicilian Mafia was the dominant criminal secret society, the Honoured Society was *the power* in southern Italy, corrupting every level of government, controlling the construction industry, and forcing local police and the judiciary to dance to its tarantellas.

Police in Italy and Canada found that the Honoured Society often worked closely with the Sicilian Mafia where mutual concerns coincided in major crimes. In recent years, Italian police are known to have warned Canadian authorities that the Canadian branch of the Sidernese Honoured Society may be the most insidious and dangerous criminal organization to emigrate to North America in decades.

By 1973 New York and Canadian police documents indicated that the Honoured Society's members were operating in Indiana, Ohio, Massachusetts, and Pennsylvania as well. In all there were an estimated 1,000 members in the United States, 400 in Ontario, at least several hundred in Australia, and approximately 2,000 in Calabria. They were heavily engaged in counterfeiting, the construction industry, pizza parlors, the smuggling and sale of illegal weapons, and narcotics trafficking. Police discovered there was even a hit-man exchange.

While Canadian law enforcement, in particular, had credible evidence of the existence and operation of the Calabrian crime organization, and had made some arrests, they had been unable to penetrate the inner structure of the organization during nearly a decade of investigation. American authorities had had far less success, depending almost entirely on the tidbits of intelligence provided by their Canadian counterparts.

That set the stage for Kirby, the outlaw biker who had become the trusted Calabrian enforcer and wanted immunity for past crimes in return for his testimony and an eventual agreement to carry a body mike. With that body mike he would record Honoured Society bosses and others ordering him to commit crimes including extortion, arson, assault, and murder.

Kirby, with a flair for derring-do, recorded the conversations of Honoured Society crime bosses and helped police at least delay the planned murder of Toronto mob boss Paul Volpe. He is also responsible for saving the life of a Connecticut woman by convincing mob bosses he'd carried out a contract to kill her while FBI agents kept her in hiding.

On the witness stand Kirby was equally poised. At least seventeen criminals, many of the major Honoured Society mafiosi, are now serving long prison terms, at least one for life, for murder, arson, assaults, extortion, and a host of other crimes. Scores of other major crimes have been solved through Kirby, resulting in perhaps as many as one hundred arrests on charges of murder, arson, narcotics trafficking, and robbery. His infor-

mation tipped off a plot to take over the small Caribbean nation of Dominica and foiled plans to blow up nightclubs.

Kirby will always live in danger, with a bounty on his head that has been estimated at between $100,000 and $250,000—a bounty that will more than likely never be paid to the outlaw bikers and Honoured Society mafiosi sworn to hunt him down and kill him.

Because of this bounty and attempts on his life and those of some members of his family, Kirby has had a deep reluctance even to mention the fact that he was married and divorced and that he had a daughter by that union. Both the ex-wife and daughter are currently living somewhere in Canada under secret identities. Kirby is honestly and deeply concerned about their safety. He is also concerned about the safety of his immediate family—his father, mother, and brother—and about his ability ever to see any of those in his present and past families without endangering their lives. As a consequence, Kirby feels that the less known about them and his relationship with them, the less likelihood that a crazy biker or wild Calabrian hit man trying to make a name for himself will target them in an attempt to flush him out. It has been tried, unsuccessfully, largely because of protective measures taken by law enforcement agencies in Canada.

Today Kirby lives by his wits, the sixth sense of a streetwise criminal. He is a fox who has often gone to the protected henhouse to gather information about those hunting him. His mobility and the chances he takes to keep his intelligence alive worry many who have protected him. He, and those who may be with him, is at risk every moment of every day.

There is nothing heroic about Cecil Kirby. He has lived a violent, often brutal life and has hurt a great many people. He has killed, he has lived off the proceeds of prostitution, he has blown up restaurants, intimidated contractors, plotted murders, and stalked his victims like a hunter tracks animals in a jungle. When he faced the likelihood that his own life might be terminated by the very bosses with whom he had plotted the deaths of others, he took the route of the informer to survive.

The deal he cut with the Ontario attorney general is very controversial. In return for his testimony, Kirby was given immunity from prosecution for past crimes. He was also guaranteed subsistence and protection for five years or until he concluded his testimony.

Without Kirby, there would have been no penetration of the Honoured Society and no conviction of its bosses. Calabrian-ordered murders, extortions, arsons, and other crimes would have been carried out. At least one defense attorney has grudgingly admitted in private to media representatives that he advised at least one of his clients to plead guilty to charges rather than face Kirby as an avenging witness because "he is so devastating" on the witness stand.

Because of his life of violent crime, Kirby has been reviled for eluding jail, for receiving subsistence for himself and his family from Canadian authorities, and for being allowed to work on a book with me for his own profit. In 1984 and 1985, public pressure led to attempts to introduce legislation in Canada to prohibit Kirby or any other criminal from profiting from any book or media production based on their criminal lives. Crown prosecutors who had extolled Kirby's worth as a witness and arranged for his immunity and subsistence waffled under media heat, claiming that they didn't know he was writing a book, that he shouldn't profit from past crimes.

Kirby, through it all, has kept his word. He has been brutally frank about his criminal life and has made no apology for being what he is. He has fought openly and publicly with prosecutors over subsistence agreements, with the support of his attorney. He has broken free of the protection once provided by Canadian law enforcement to survive on his own, moving from area to area while assassins still hunt him. It has not been easy.

Since I have known him, Kirby has moved at least a half dozen times, at least twice in the belief that outlaw biker assassins knew his location and were on their way to kill him. He has had to work for minimum wages, seldom enough to pay his way, because subsistence checks were as much as two months late. He has tried to obtain work under his new identity only to be turned away because some of his so-called protectors provided prospective employers with his criminal record without specifically identifying him as Cecil Kirby. Many of the government's promises of job training, relocation, family protection, funds to move to safe harbors, and help with a new life have not been fulfilled.

I have worked with scores of witnesses over the last decade or more. All have had problems with witness protection programs, some valid, some

not. In my judgment, it would be nothing short of a miracle if any other witnesses made a deal with Canadian prosecutors unless they had public guarantees that they would not have to face the indignities and broken promises that Kirby has had to live with.

I have written from the personal accounts of scores of criminals. Each has added to the public knowledge of the world of crime. Kirby provides something extra—a rare inside view of two different organized crime groups and how they prey on the public.

Thomas C. Renner

Contents

Contents

PART ONE

Outlaw Bikers

CHAPTER 1

No Honor Among Thieves

The Honored Society [L' Onorata Societa] is a secret organization of criminal parasites, like an insect that attaches itself to a flower and bleeds it. It infiltrates all the economic fields in Calabria.

> Dr. Alberto Sabatino Chief Commissioner
> Criminal Intelligence Branch
> Central National Criminalpol of Rome, Italy

It was May 1979 when I first began to suspect that my safety as the personal enforcer–hit man for Honoured Society crime boss Cosimo Commisso might be in jeopardy. My suspicions were aroused as we sat together eating at the Casa Commisso, his banquet hall and the Calabrian Mafia's meeting center, which he and his brothers, Remo and Michele, owned and operated not far from Toronto's Little Italy. There were no threats, no special incidents, nothing unusual said, just a sort of eerie feeling that I got in my gut as I listened to Cosimo talk about murders and vendettas and the traditions of Calabria.

I knew he was talking about the Calabrian Mafia, or the Honoured Society as it's generally called, but the actual names were never mentioned. In all honesty, I can't remember hearing him or his brothers use either name. When they said anything it was usually in terms of "our people" or "our family," not the "Mafia." I've also heard police call his group the Sidernese Mob or Mafia.

3

* * *

Cosimo and his brothers were born in a small southern Italian town called Marina di Gioiosa. It was a town of about 25,000, on the water, and very close to Siderno Marina. Siderno is the birthplace of the Calabrian Mafia or Sidernese Mob of Canada and the United States.

Cosimo was just fifteen when he came to Canada with his mother, Emilia, in 1961. He didn't grow up on the streets as a fighter and hustler like me, but he did grow up with a tradition that had its roots in Calabria and in the family.

He told me his father, Girolamo, was killed in some sort of Mafia shoot-out in 1949 in Siderno. And his family knew Michele (Mike) Racco, the old Siderno mafioso who was sort of the godfather of all the Calabrian hoods in Ontario and even New York before he died of cancer in 1980.

From the time Cosimo and Remo were kids in this country all they, particularly Remo, could think about was avenging their dad's murder. Remo was always calling people in Italy mafiosi and relatives, and sometimes traveling to handle contracts or what Cosimo would call "affairs of honor." It was, I suppose, from this tradition and because of Racco that Cosimo and his brothers became big shots in Toronto and eventually headed their own crime family.

By the time I met Cosimo through a trucker friend in 1976, he was what they call the capo bastone, or crime boss of one of several Calabrian crime families. A lot of coppers think Remo is the brains behind Cosimo and may really be the boss, but they don't know.

I know, because I worked for them both. Cosimo is the boss, and Remo pays him the respect due a boss and an older brother. Remo is like a lightning rod. He draws a lot of the heat because he's out front on a lot of deals, like going to Italy all the time and meeting with other bosses. But it's Cosimo who's calling the shots, running an outfit that's become known and feared as Canada's Murder Inc.

Cosimo was only thirty-four at the time I was sitting with him in the Casa Commisso, but he was a Mafia boss in every sense of the word. He weighed about 180 pounds, which is 60 pounds more than he weighed when he was in jail a year or so ago. He had an Italian accent so thick that at times I could hardly understand what the hell he was saying. He was married and had two kids. His wife was Jewish, strange enough when

you think about his Calabrian traditions, but she was quiet, you never heard from her, and he treated her with respect whenever I saw them together at home. But when he stepped out of his home to meet me or some of his Mafia friends at the Casa Commisso or at pool halls or even in cars and restaurants, he was a different man.

Cosimo pushed himself back from the kitchen table at the Casa Commisso. He belched with satisfaction as he wiped tomato sauce from his mouth and brushlike mustache and picked at the last remnants of meat stuck in a lobster-tail shell on the plate in front of him.

He gulped down some red wine, belched again, rubbing his belly. A peculiar smile crossed his face as he watched me toy with the small plate of spaghetti and lobster in front of me, eating slowly, savoring the flavors that his cook, a soft-spoken Italian woman in her fifties, managed to brew into the dishes she created. She was a great cook, a real nice lady who was always whipping something delicious together for me whenever I showed up at the Casa Commisso. With all her cooking talents and her kindnesses to me I could never remember her name. I still can't.

"It's good, no?" Cosimo asked.

I nodded. "It's good, yes," I answered and continued eating. Cosimo kept talking, but the conversation wasn't about food.

"You know, it's not too long ago when one of my uncles, he's involved in a war between our family and another family back in Italy . . ." Cosimo said softly, glancing around the kitchen to make certain we were alone and no one was listening.

"We went after that other fuckin' family," he said. "They had this big fuckin' house in this village near Siderno. It took awhile, but we got into this house when the whole family was there and we shot and killed everybody in the place—even the little *bambino* in the crib."

For a split second I thought he was bullshitting me until I looked up from my food at that round, moonlike face and that unbrushed, scraggly hair of his. His sleepy, dark brown eyes danced with a hidden deadliness I'd come to know over the years. I knew this was no tall Mafia tale. It was a matter-of-fact, you-kill-everyone-opposed-to-you true story, told without emotion but with obvious satisfaction.

He was giving me a little historical lesson in the ways of the Calabrian

Mafia in Italy, particularly Siderno. But there was more to it than just a little tale of vengeance. "But why kill the kid in his crib?" I asked.

Cosimo sort of smirked as he answered. "If you don't kill the kid as a *bambino,* he will grow up and kill you, kill your family later. It's the way of Vendetta."

Cosimo was working his way up to something that he wanted me to handle, and there was something about the way he was doing it—about the story of the murdered family, about the tales of his father's murder —that was bothering me. I wasn't squeamish about the murders. What the hell, I'd been around murder and violence for a long time as a biker and as Cosimo's enforcer. But I got antennae that sense things that are wrong for me, and those antennae were vibrating and warning lights were going off mentally.

I had worked for Cosimo and his brothers for about three years. While I never really questioned what they wanted to do, I always had an uneasiness about some of their assignments.

Maybe it was because they had short arms when it came to paying for the work I did. They were always shortchanging me or pleading poverty or claiming they hadn't been paid for the jobs they'd hired me to do.

Maybe it was because I wasn't Italian. I knew that I could never be a real member of their organization and that Irish-Canadians are expendable to Calabrians. They talked in Italian a lot when I was around—like they didn't want me to know about something.

Anyway, I always had the feeling that they didn't really trust me any more than I trusted them. But they needed me, and I knew a helluva lot about their operations and the crimes they were involved in. Because of that I figured that I would either disappear or I'd be killed at some meeting, like my predecessor.

So I took precautions. I usually picked the places where we'd meet, places I knew, places where I could control things around me. I'd pick the time, usually on short notice, and I'd never tell them where they could find me. In fact, I carried a telephone pager around on my belt so that they could reach me without ever knowing exactly where I was.

I was also careful about the assignments I took from them. Whether I was handling a bombing, setting up an arson, or plotting a hit, I did things my way, without giving them any details of when or how I would strike.

Cosimo, like his brother Remo, still had close ties with mafiosi in the old country. Remo, for example, had gone back to Calabria to handle a hit in the early 1970s. That trip was a revenge hit—a hit that involved some of those behind the killing of his father. It also had something to do with "family honor" in the village where the brothers had strong family ties.

Remo never forgets. Neither does Cosimo. Because of that I'll always be looking over my shoulder for them or their relatives and family members. They want to kill me more than they want to eat, and maybe one day they will.

Cosimo told me that Remo was in a car in Italy with some other Siderno Mafia members looking for some of those responsible for the slaying of his father. His enemies must have known about it, because they ambushed the car and machine-gunned it. Two of the men he was with were killed. Remo escaped, but his trench coat was riddled with holes.

Remo brought the coat back to Canada to show his family how close he'd been to death. It was like a medal, a badge of honor. He even showed it to me one day and laughed about the bullet holes and the scar he got on his face in the shoot-out.

On June 7, 1976, the body of an eighteen-year-old kid named Salvatore Palermiti was found shot to death in a place in Toronto called the Bayview Ghost, an old, ruined apartment building that was left half finished by a builder who ran out of money.

I never knew exactly how the kid's murder and Remo's shot-up trench coat and trip to Italy fit together, but there were two stories told by the cops and friends of the Commissos. At first, the cops' story rested on this Palermiti kid's shooting out the windows of a Calabrian shop owned by the relative of a Mafia friend of Remo's. Remo's friends had another version. They claimed the Palmeriti kid was involved in the Siderno shoot-out.

The coppers, in later years, questioned me about this murder and about the kid's relationship to Remo, who they said was one of the last people to be seen with him. They said the kid was sent to Toronto by his father. Among the people the kid went to see while his father tried to cool things down with the mafiosi in Calabria were the Commisso brothers. It didn't work. They weren't about to forgive and forget. The cops also were told,

but could never confirm, that the Palermiti kid was one of those who shot up Remo's car in Calabria.

The bottom line to Cosimo's stories at the Casa Commisso was a rather wild murder plot he wanted me to carry out—not in Canada or the United States, but in Calabria. And his target wasn't just any Italian or Canadian hood, it was Girolamo (Momo) Piromalli, the most powerful Calabrian boss in southern Italy.

"Cec," he said, "we got this job for you and it's important, very important!"

Now when Cosimo said a job was important, it was *important*. Usually jobs were just jobs. I'd handled extortions, bombings, beatings, card game rip-offs, plotted murders—you name it. For me the bottom line was always money. For Cosimo, the bottom line was always results. Up to this point, he had never said that anything was as important as this was supposed to be.

"What's the job," I asked, "and how much are we talking about?"

"It's gonna pay good," he answered. "It's worth ten thousand dollars, and we pay all your expenses. We arrange everything for you."

"What's the job?" I pressed.

"We want you to do this person," he said. "We get you to Italy. We arrange for all your travel there and back. We set things up—*booma boom*—it's over. You got the money in your hand and we get rid of this pig."

Piromalli lived on "a big estate" in Gioia Tauro, a steel-making town in southern Italy. The area is also supposed to be one of the best for growing olives, oranges, and mandarins. Cosimo said the estate had guards all around it, but they had a way of taking them out. "If you do this job for us," he said, "it's gonna help all of us—it's a big thing for me and my friends."

"Why not use someone over there to kill this guy?" I asked.

"No, no, no," he said. "It must be kept a big secret. We can't use anybody from there to do this job. It'll leak out. We need you."

My father didn't raise a stupid son. Curly-haired, blondish, blue-eyed Canadians who don't speak Italian don't exactly blend into the scenery of the mountain country of Reggio di Calabria. It's a place where the mob runs everything from shops and hotels to politicians and cops.

"Hey, Cosimo, I'll stand out like an Arab sheik in a Dublin pub," I said. "They'll spot me in a second, and even if I could do the job, I'd have less chance of surviving than a snowball in hell."

Cosimo waved his hands excitedly in the air, shaking his head vigorously. "Don't you worry," he said. "We got this plan—we get you in and we get you out and you get your money, no problem."

Cosimo emphasized over and over the importance of maintaining secrecy—that absolutely no one must know about the plot, that I couldn't talk to anybody about it, not even his brothers.

Cosimo told me that Piromalli was the mafioso who bossed a big kidnapping ring in Calabria, one that in July 1973 had kidnapped J. Paul Getty III, the then sixteen-year-old grandson of the oil billionaire J. Paul Getty. For his safe return, Cosimo said, Piromalli's people had demanded a $2.9 million ransom. The kid was finally released after being held for five months, but not before Piromalli's men cut off one of his ears and sent it to the Getty family to force them to pay the ransom. Piromalli was arrested with six others and then acquitted because the cops couldn't come up with enough evidence.

Cosimo said that there were fifteen or twenty in the kidnapping group, who collected nearly $200 million in ransoms in less than five years. The racket was booming until 1978, when Italian police arrested fifteen more Calabrians, including Piromalli's brother Giuseppe.

Before those arrests, Piromalli and his Honoured Society had kidnapped more than a hundred people, including industrialists and heirs to big fortunes, and collected some really big ransoms. A year before Cosimo talked to me about Piromalli, I remember having seen stories about their collecting a $600,000 ransom for the release of an Italian businessman named Giovanni Fagioli.

I knew that this couldn't be a scheme that Cosimo'd hatched all by himself. Remo and others in Calabria had to be involved, and in my gut I just knew that I wasn't supposed to come out alive—that maybe this was their way of getting rid of a non-Italian hit man who knew too much about their affairs.

"I don't know, Cosimo," I said, rubbing my chin and looking as deep into his eyes as I could to see if there was something he was hiding from me, something else I should know. "I'll have to think about it and let you know."

"Okay, Cec," he said. "You think. Guaranteed—it's ten thousand dollars and it's safe."

Cecil Kirby in Calabria—it didn't make sense. I had a nagging feeling that it was a setup, that I was going to be taken there to hit this Piromalli fella and then they were going to do me on one of those back roads of theirs or leave me by the body of Piromalli or something like that. My sixth sense told me no, but the money made it interesting. I liked the intrigue and excitement. It was something to think about—carefully.

The Piromalli murder scheme, I learned later, was all part of a Mafia struggle for leadership in Calabria that had gone on since the 1949 murder of the Cosimo's brothers' father. But their father, police told me later, was never higher than what they call a *Sgarrista E. Cammista,* the same thing as a soldier in the Cosa Nostra. He was the kind of guy who approached businesses to extort money, and he could give orders to members of his group, associates that are called *Picciotti,* people like me, who place the bombs, beat up the victims, apply the muscle, and collect loan-shark debts or other fees.

Cosimo said that Mafia power in Calabria was so absolute that even international companies knuckled under to their demands. He said that in the early 1970s a hotel chain came to Siderno to build a big hotel. About halfway through construction it was bombed. The Mafia didn't want outsiders in their town. If there were going to be any hotels, they'd own them and build them.

The big Honoured Society boss before Piromalli was Antonio Macri. He controlled all the Calabrian families like a boss of bosses, but he didn't like change. Most Calabrians don't. They stick to the old ways of making money. New ways, like narcotics trafficking, were not allowed. But the money was too big, and Piromalli was too ambitious. In 1975, Macri was gunned down when his chauffeur-driven car stopped at a main intersection in Siderno. Cosimo said that five or six men jumped from nowhere and shot everyone in the car except Macri's right-hand man, a guy named Frank Commisso, who was a distant cousin of Cosimo's.

Piromalli tried, but couldn't get the power that Macri'd had. He remained a local boss, not a boss of bosses, and rivals hated him for killing Macri. The Commisso brothers had sided with factions that opposed

Piromalli. That's why Remo had gone to Calabria and gotten involved in some firefights. That's why, I supposed, they had turned to me to handle Piromalli's killing.

I had bought a pass on the plan to kill Piromalli only because Cosimo kept putting it off and he died from natural causes.

Finding a way out of a Calabrian organization that sometimes kills just because they're insulted isn't the easiest thing. I knew that there was only one way it would end—I'd be lured someplace by Cosimo or his brother to collect some money or plot some job and I'd be killed.

In October 1980 I was facing trial for break and entry as well as extortion and assault. They were the latest in a series of criminal charges, acquired since my youth, that now numbered more than sixty. I was certain I would be convicted on one, probably the B&E, and, if I was, I'd do big time.

My choice was doing a long stretch in jail and probably being killed there by one of the Commissos' people or be done by the Commissos outside prison walls. The trouble was, I didn't know who the hell to talk to. I had never found a cop I could trust.

I had tried trusting a cop named Terry Hall of the Ontario Provincial Police (OPP). Hall was a particularly tough cop who had become a thorn in the ass of the Vagabonds, one of Toronto's worst motorcycle gangs. He had become their shadow—turn around in a bar and he was there. Step out of the house, and there he was on the street. Always hounding them, breaking their balls, making their lives miserable. He had put the fear of God into them. He was a tough cop and an honest cop, and they were afraid of him. I couldn't understand why all these big, rough bikers were so afraid of just one cop.

One night in 1978 I heard from a biker friend of mine, Armand Sanguigni, that the Vagabonds had put out a contract to kill Hall. Hall, he said, had hounded them too much and charged too many of them with crimes. He said they were busy collecting money to pay for a hit man to do him in. "They're desperate to get rid of this copper," he said.

I figured I'd do myself and Hall a favor by tipping him to what was happening. I called him, met him, and told him about the murder plot. I figured I'd get some consideration down the road from him if I was

charged with something. Well, I was charged later on, but I got no consideration from him at all—not even a thank you for saving his fuckin' life. I should've let them do him. Anyhow, I knew I couldn't turn to him to get any help on this case. He'd already told me to go to hell.

On October 11, 1980, I took a chance and called the Toronto Royal Canadian Mounted Police (RCMP) National Crime Intelligence Section and asked to talk to someone. I got a break that day—I got to talk to Corporal Mark Murphy.

I didn't identify myself to him that first day. I simply told him that I was a former member of the Satan's Choice motorcycle gang and that I could provide him with a lot of good information if he could help me with some charges I had pending. He didn't promise me anything, but we talked some more and I gave him some information that he found was accurate.

At first he wasn't impressed. He still didn't know my name and referred to me only as "Joe." Still no promises. Then I began feeding him information on narcotics dealers, on prison beatings and murders, on robberies and other crimes, and I dangled promises that I could deliver much, much more, including information on everything from arsons and murder to the Commissos and their organization.

Up to that time I had no intentions of becoming a witness or doing anything but providing tips to Murphy. All I wanted in return was a light sentence. Murphy was willing to talk to Crown prosecutors for me, but he was opposed by biker cops from the Toronto Metropolitan Police and the OPP, including Hall.

That really jammed me. If I didn't keep cooperating, one of those cops could put the word out on the street that I was an informer, and I'd have bikers and rounders [independent street hoodlums] out to kill me along with the Commissos. If I did keep talking, I'd still go to jail for a long term because the cops wouldn't listen to Murphy.

It was the Commissos who gave me the bargaining chip I needed. They handed me a $20,000 contract to kill a good-looking broad in Stamford, Connecticut, Helen Nafpliotis, the girlfriend of Nick Melia, a convicted receiver of stolen goods and the brother of a ranking member of the Calabrian Mafia in Canada and Connecticut.

I was certain that this hit contract was really part of a plan to take me

out. They wanted this Nafpliotis woman killed, all right, because she was costing them money—money they were losing because Melia wasn't paying attention to business. But I knew that if I took the contract, the chances were they'd do me after I'd done her. If I didn't handle it, they'd have her killed anyhow, their suspicions about me would be raised another notch, and I'd probably be hit anyhow.

It was February now, the Commissos were pressing, and I hadn't told Murphy. As I tried to make up my mind about what to do, I found myself wondering where it had all begun. How the hell had I gotten myself into a mess where my future, my life, rested on the whims of some cops and some crazy Calabrians?

CHAPTER 2

Born to Violence

I was born in 1950 in Weston, a suburb of Toronto, and from the time I was in kindergarten I was fighting with kids around me, fighting to survive. My parents weren't rich—they had to work like hell to make enough money to support the family—but we weren't poor either. I mean I never wanted for food or clothes. I may have had to use an outhouse at the cottages we lived in or I might have had to walk a mile or more to get water for the house, but there was always good, wholesome food on the table and plenty of it, and there were always enough decent clothes for everyone.

Where we lived was a tough neighborhood. I guess you'd say there was an ethnic balance. There were Irish and English, Jews and Poles, Italians and Greeks, but there weren't any Latins or blacks, or any Orientals that I can remember. An Irish kid, like myself, had to stand his ground and fight his way through kids of other nationalities who were out to establish their reputations and uphold their origins. So I fought, and I was always getting into trouble for playing hooky or running away. I just didn't like school.

I didn't go look for fights, don't get me wrong, but there were kids who would try to push me around, and I wasn't one to be pushed. Someone would give me a shove and bang! That was it. I'd lose my cool and start fighting. Many a night, I'd come home bruised and bloodied and my dad would give me hell and then ask, "You whip him?" and I'd nod my head and say, "Yeah, I beat him." He'd say, "Good. Go get cleaned up."

Sometimes it was a draw and sometimes I got the hell kicked outta me, but as far as I was concerned I was a winner 'cause I didn't knuckle under to anyone. I never told Dad I lost. He wouldn't have wanted to hear that anyhow and I didn't need sympathy.

By the time I was ten, my parents moved to Wasaga Beach, a small resort community about one hundred miles north of Toronto on Georgian Bay off Lake Huron. My mother, Muriel was her name, wanted to change my environment, hoping the fights would stop and I'd do better in school. It didn't do any good. The fights went on, and I missed as many as one hundred days of school in a year.

During the summers I played baseball for a team in Stayner, about four miles from where we lived, and it was there that I began hanging around with other kids who broke into cottages. The break-ins were mainly for excitement. We never got much money or valuables. The idea was to fool the coppers, watch 'em scramble. The satisfaction was in never being caught.

Within three years my parents were divorced. They just stopped getting along. They were always fighting. My dad, Kitchener Kirby, moved back to Weston. He'd never liked Wasaga Beach, and he'd had trouble earning a living there. My mother stayed there, and after a few months I told her I wanted to go live with my dad. There was a helluva argument, but finally she agreed to let me go.

My dad and I were pretty close. I guess I've always admired him. He's got a lot of courage. During the war Dad was a motorcycle dispatch rider in Europe with the Canadian army. When he came back he became a trick bike rider in the circus. He used to ride the barrel and take the bike through hoops of fire and everything. There wasn't much he couldn't do with a bike, and a lot of the bike-riding skills that helped me be a top biker with the outlaw biker gangs, like Satan's Choice, were developed through him.

Dad was also a regular playboy. He'd been married three times, and when he wasn't married he always had all kinds of girlfriends. For twenty to twenty-five years he was a waiter in hotels. He was also a hotel bouncer. He could always handle himself and still can, even though he's in his seventies. Until a short time ago, he could still ride a motorcycle with the best of them.

Dad had remarried when I moved in with him, and at first I resented

my stepmother. But I found she really wasn't a bad person after I got to know her. Dad tried his damnedest to reform me, but there was no way. We'd argue a lot, but even with the arguments we got along. My stepmother, Mary, was good to me. She always stuck up for me, and both of them were always bailing me out of jail.

Mary died in 1979. She'd been an invalid for almost a year, but she didn't complain. Neither did my dad. No matter what happened they both always stood behind me.

It wasn't long after I moved in with my dad, maybe two months at most, before I got kicked out of Weston Senior Public School for fighting. It was a helluva fight, the biggest they'd had in the school's history. I took on this big, tough senior who'd been trying to push me around. Within minutes we were battling all over the grounds, with a crowd of more than two hundred students cheering and urging us on.

Both of us were covered with bruises and blood before some teachers came out and stopped it. The next day we were called before the principal and disciplined, but I was warned that if I got into a fight again, I would be bounced from school. Easy to say. There were too many wise guys who wanted to see how tough I was. Within two weeks I was in another fight and bounced.

I moved on to Roseland Public School in the Mount Dennis area of Toronto. In the first month, I must have gotten into ten fights, all of which I won. My reputation as a tough kid was following me, and every so-called tough in the school was trying to take me on. It was sort of like being the fastest gun in the West—there was always some wise guy who thought he was faster and tried to draw on the guy with the reputation. So I beat them up, one at a time, sometimes two. Things got so bad that by the end of the spring semester my desk was in front of the principal's office.

I got thrown out of Roseland by the summer, but not before I had met and either fought or become associated with a number of students who were, like me, to become members of motorcycle gangs. Some of them were to fight with me, others against me as members of rival gangs. Our lives would never be the same.

I can't say there was anything about the environment, or our economic stature, or our ethnic backgrounds that made us that way. It just happened. I think we just drifted into the gangs and got into trouble. The

only thing we all had in common was that we played hooky a lot. We all bumped around on the streets and hung out in garages because we wanted to become auto mechanics. It seemed everyone in school wanted to be an auto mechanic then.

The principal, I forget his name, was glad to see me go. A month before the end of the semester, he called me in and said he was tired of seeing me. "Go home, Cec," he said. "Let's figure you've passed everything without taking any tests." He and the teachers just wanted me out. They passed me to a higher grade so I wouldn't return to their school the following year.

I was supposed to go to George Harvey High School as a ninth grader after that, but the summer break came and I never went back. Instead, I went to work driving a truck for a Ford dealership in Toronto.

I had turned sixteen by then, and I'd started buying old cars—1956 Fords and Chevrolets—reconditioning them, and selling them. I enjoyed that. But I was still getting into fights even then, hanging around in parks with youth gangs. That was also the year I got my first conviction and taste of jail.

The trouble started when I visited some old friends at Wasaga Beach. We drove to Collingwood, which was about six miles away. We went into this restaurant and got into a fight with three other guys. Two of my friends took off and left me on my own. But I was a tough kid by then, and I beat the hell out of those guys. As soon as I walked outside the restaurant, I was arrested.

Later that week I appeared in court with the three stiffs I'd wound up beating up. They got a $50 fine each for causing a disturbance and fighting. The judge had other plans for me. After giving me hell for being a troublemaker and a street tough, he told me I'd learn more if I spent some time behind bars. I got ten days in jail even though it was my first time in court. It doesn't pay to win a fight sometimes, even when you're outnumbered, a lesson that came back to haunt me again and again.

The ten days were no picnic. The judge sent me to the Barrie County Jail, fifty miles north of Toronto. On my second day there some guard handed me a rag to wash the floors with and I refused. I wound up doing the next nine days in solitary confinement.

Spending nine days in the hole—in solitary—was probably, in the long

run, better than spending it with the others in the jail, who were hard core. At least it was quiet, and I didn't have to fight my way out of some lousy creep's attempt at a jail-house rape. They gave me a Bible to read, and I fooled them—I read the whole thing. Those nine days in 1968 prepared me for what I had to face later.

The next time I was in jail I was just seventeen, and it didn't have any impact on me. That time I went to Toronto's Don Jail for a weekend, until I could raise bail. A year later, after I was convicted of a minor assault, the judge sentenced me to thirty days in the same jail.

The Don Jail was like an old castle, but it was the wrong place to put teenagers. All the rabble are in a place like that—the drunks, the homosexuals, the perverts, the sadists, the killers—you name them, they're there. You might as well go to a sewer. The smell there is the same. It might be cleaner, but the smell is the same.

I remember this sixteen-year-old kid was having a terrible time. I don't know what he was in for, but he cried all night that first night. I expected to see him hanging in his cell the next day. You see things like that, young kids being abused by other prisoners. They shouldn't be put in a place like that. They should be in minimum-security jails, away from the hard-core criminals and perverts.

The routine in a place like Don Jail was boredom. All you could do was sit around, read books, or play cards. They'd let you out in the yard for fifteen to twenty minutes every day. You'd walk around about ten times and then you were back in your cell and that's where you sat the rest of the day. There was no weight room, or recreation room, no nothing. They had me in dorms half the time and cells the rest. I must have known a dozen guys in there, a lot of them bikers, who seemed to always be in the can.

When I got out of jail, I was still fighting and changing jobs. Then in late 1968 I started working for a concrete company. It was there that I met "Jimmy G," who was a member of the Toronto chapter of Satan's Choice motorcycle club.

At the time I owned a Triumph motorcycle, and I had a real love for cycling. But you don't do much cycling alone—not if you want to avoid trouble. You've got to belong to a club or an association, something. Other than the hell-raisers I sometimes hung out with, I had no one to ride with.

So, after almost a year of associating with Jimmy and his friends, I asked him if he would help me become a member of Satan's Choice.

In August 1969, with Jimmy G's sponsorship, I started "striking." Striking is a probationary period that bikers go through before they are accepted into the club. For the Choice, striking lasted eight weeks. During that time I had to do whatever I was told to do, from cleaning the bikes of other members to proving that I could handle myself in fights. Sometimes those fights were on bikes, sometimes in hotels, other times in the clubhouses.

During the striking period I was asked to do a lot of what would be seen as sensible things. I was asked, not told, to help in fights or to steal motorcycles. And there were some stupid things, like running to the store for hamburgers for the whole club or cleaning the bikes of all the members.

Striking was showing that you were man enough to be a member of the club. Just to get to the striking position you had to prove you were good enough to someone in the organization so that the membership would vote you in as a member.

It was, in a way, something like being initiated into the Mafia. Your sponsor had to be a member, he had to be willing to be responsible for you, and you had to go through a probationary period of proving yourself before you were accepted. If you cheated a member, violated his rights, or became an informer against club members, you could be voted out, beaten to a bloody pulp, or killed, and very often members were. Outlaw bikers like myself have codes of silence that we had to live by.

There were a couple of big differences from the Mafia, of course. You didn't have to be Italian or from one ethnic group to be a member, although blacks were usually banned. Instead of going through a rite of initiation—in which blood was drawn and mixed while the recruit was required to swear eternal fidelity on pain of death—biker recruits or strikers sometimes had to literally eat shit while swearing loyalty to the club.

There was one biker, Howard (Pig Pen) Berry, who loved to make new recruits squirm by dumping buckets of pigshit and urine over their heads and not letting them clean themselves off all day and night. Berry was a

tough biker. He had a reputation as a killer in North Carolina, where he rode with the Outlaws for a while. He loved fights, and he was a master biker, but he could be a mean bastard when he was riled. He wore thick glasses, which made a lot of people think he was a patsy—until he hit them. When Berry hit, it was like being hit by Man Mountain Dean. In Florida one time, while hiding out with the Outlaw motorcycle gang to avoid an attempted murder rap in Canada, Berry got into a street brawl and had his nose and jaw broken. He went out and got a gun and shot the guy who had pushed in his face. He did time for that job, and for shooting another guy in the belly with a rifle in Canada.

The public has an image of the biker as a hairy-ape type, with long smelly hair, World War II helmet, iron crosses, full beard and mustache, dirty pants and boots, with a total disregard for people, their feelings or property, or any sense of morality. All those are probably true and then some.

In truth, most members of biker gangs in the States and Canada like scaring the individual so he spreads fear through stories, often exaggerated, of how terrifying bikers are. Fear was and is our principal weapon —it's the bikers' badge of honor, their way of intimidating the common folk and the businessman and making it pay off for them. A biker can spread fear because he has the safety of numbers. If he was one on one with the ordinary guy, he wouldn't be so brave. The thing that stops the ordinary guy from taking him on is the fearsome look and the patches that signify membership in a gang.

When I joined Satan's Choice in 1969, I joined a gang that was very much in that public image. The violence, the smells, the dirty clothes— all those intimidating things the public's come to expect—were part of the Choice. The public feared us. We were the biggest outlaw gang in Canada, and we had close relationships with the Outlaw motorcycle gang, which had chapters in Florida, Illinois, and North Carolina. It was more than friendship.

Satan's Choice supplied the Outlaws with Canadian Blue valium and speed from our labs and with women for their topless joints or for prostitution. Some of the women were sold for $1,500 or more, others were given away. Sometimes the Outlaws supplied us with the same things. But more

often than not we provided each other with cooling-off places—places where members could hide while the cops searched for them on either side of the border. If a Choice biker was wanted for murder or assault or robbery in Canada, Big Jim Nolan, the head of the Outlaws, would make sure he had a good hideaway in Chicago or Fort Lauderdale. And while he was in hiding he was given women and drugs or whatever else he wanted.

Big Jim's doing double life for some murders in the States, but he'd beaten Florida charges of shotgunning three Hell's Angels and dumping them in a rock pit in 1974. There were also stories circulating among biker gangs about his skinning some Hell's Angels bikers alive before he killed them, but he was never convicted of anything like that. The Hell's Angels and Outlaws have been warring for years, killing each other, killing and beating members of other gangs that associate with either one. If they'd ever stop fighting and work together, the cops would have a helluva time trying to tame them.

I knew from the beginning that trouble and violence were part of life in Satan's Choice. I knew there might be a shooting and I'd be there; I knew that I might be in the same room or the same house when someone raped some broad and we'd all be charged with it; I knew there would be other crimes that I'd probably participate in with them. I didn't care. It wasn't that I joined the gang to do something like that. It just came, and I wanted the excitement.

Satan's Choice was, by then, Canada's largest and strongest motorcycle gang. It had fifteen chapters in places like Montreal, Ottawa, Kingston, Toronto, Peterborough, Richmond Hill, Hamilton, Kitchener, Saint Catharine's, and Windsor. Each chapter had ten to fifteen members, but people in the community thought a chapter had as many as three or four hundred because they were so loud and violent and because members of other chapters would often join one chapter on a run on a town. But the most that were in the Choice while I was in were about 220 active, full-time members.

Today all that's changed. Now there are only a few chapters left, because the club split up in 1977. There are maybe fifty to sixty Satan's Choice members now in Toronto, Kitchener, and Peterborough. The rest are all part of the stateside Outlaws and Hell's Angels gangs, which set

up chapters in Canada and are now fighting and killing each other, mostly in Quebec.

The image of the scraggly bunch of bikers who went around raping girls has also changed. Some bikers have gotten smarter and richer. A lot of them wear three-piece suits. They invest in business and real estate, they run narcotics rings, they testify at public hearings, and they often present an acceptable public appearance. They are still as violent as they ever were, just smarter. They have no intention of blending into the main-stream, of society. They are outrageous outcasts and they love it. It's one of the reasons we called ourselves the one-percenters, the worst 1 percent of the population. We wore a patch to show we were outcasts.

In all the years I was a motorcycle gang member, and those were seven long years, I found maybe only 10 percent of all the members—whether they were from Canada or the United States or wherever—could handle themselves and fight one on one. The rest, for the most part, would never get into a fight unless there were ten guys to back them up, because they couldn't bloody well fight. A lot of the members had joined because they needed and wanted the protection of the rest of the members.

Strikers are at the lowest level of the club. It's like being a plebe at West Point—all the upperclassmen can give him orders. It's the same with a striker. It's a chance for the club to see if you have what it takes to be a member or if you're just an idiot who wants to get in on the pack's action.

Sometimes it took a lot of guts to finish the striking period, to pass all the tests members wanted. I remember one striker who was told to hold up pop bottles in his hands while members shot at them with a .22 caliber rifle. He survived with a few cuts and some bleeding, but he could have refused. If he had, though, he probably wouldn't have made the club.

You are told when you start striking that you do not have to break the law if someone asks you to. But you have to be nuts if you think you're going to join a motorcycle club like ours or some of the others around North America and not break the law. I mean, it's part of our life-style.

Jimmy G told me when I joined I would find that I'd always have very close and reliable friends in the chapter, that members helped each other

out when they had trouble, and that they always stuck together wherever they were. That was true up to a point.

The Toronto chapter was a diverse group. Jimmy G was a laborer. I was a truck driver. We had a plumber, a stock market office executive, an electrician, three narcotics dealers, an insulation installer, a couple of professional motorcycle thieves, some safecrackers, and an explosives expert. It was with this group that I got my baptism of fire, my skill as a bike thief, a burglar, and an enforcer. And it was here that I saw my first murder.

CHAPTER 3

Clubhouse of Assassins I

Some members of Satan's Choice wear a patch on the backs of their jackets that says simply, "In Memory of John Foote." I never wore that patch, but it was Foote and maybe two or three other members of the Choice who trained me in the fine art of crime. Foote is dead now. He was killed in November 1975 by a friend of mine in a fight over a dope deal. Before he died Foote taught me much of what I needed to know to handle explosives and use them for cracking safes, extorting contractors, and blowing up buildings.

Before he became a member of the Choice, Foote was what they call here in Canada a rounder. It's a term that's been used for more than twenty years to describe street criminals who can operate around bars and clubs and hotels and sell drugs, set up gambling operations, negotiate street deals for stolen goods, or run high-stakes, back-room card games. Rounders are tough people who live by their wits and are always around the right places to make the deals. That's why they're called rounders. They're all-around street hoods, who can handle just about any kind of deal.

Foote was one of the toughest of the rounders. He was a vicious street fighter when challenged. He'd killed more than one man in his travels. He was also a brutal enforcer when he had to be for those who paid him enough. He was originally from Scarborough. He weighed only 175 pounds, but he could bench-press 450 pounds.

For years Foote had worked for a well-known Toronto bail bondsman when bail was still used in the Canadian court system. He got to know a lot of the criminals in Toronto because of that association, including outlaw bikers. He often dealt with bikers when they were setting up safecracking jobs or wanted to use explosives to scare the hell out of some businessman who wasn't paying tribute to Choice members, or when they were doing break and entries of businesses and homes. He also collected loan-shark debts from street hoods and businessmen who sought out an ex-bondsman for shylock loans. Those that were delinquent in payments frequently got visits from Foote.

When I first met Foote, he wasn't a member of Satan's Choice, but he was often at the clubhouse and he frequently turned up at field days, when biker clubs and bikers showed off their skills by competing against each other. It was just before one of these events, in the summer of 1973, at a popular resort known as Rice Lake, that Foote introduced me to the first murder victim I'd ever seen.

I'd arrived at the clubhouse early one morning to get ready to leave for the event. Foote came to the house and confessed to another biker and me that he had the body of a Choice club member in the trunk of his car. The victim was a popular biker named James Lyons.

"We were doing this B&E [break and entry] at a farmhouse in Pickering," he said, "when Jim opened the door to the house and was shot in the shoulder by this farmer. I was hiding in the brush when I saw the farmer walk over to where Jim had staggered and fallen and I saw him shoot him in the head. When the farmer went back to the house, I ran over, picked Jim up, and carried his body to the car. When I left I could hear sirens in the distance," he added.

At first we didn't believe him, but we went to his house in Scarborough. He took us to the rear of the driveway, where his car was parked. Three other Choice members were also there. Foote opened the trunk and lifted a blanket, and I saw Lyons lying crumpled with a bad wound in his shoulder and his head distorted and bloodied.

I never really understood why Foote told us or showed us the body. He just did, and then he and one of the Choice members, a burly, bearded character named Jim, took Lyons's body and buried it on a farm in Brighton. The body has never been found. In fact, Lyons's murder has

never been reported as a murder. None of us believed Foote's tale. We all thought he'd killed Lyons himself.

Foote had a terrible temper, and he was homicidal when he got mad. Lyons was really killed because he cheated Foote on a drug deal, ripped him off, so Foote blew him away, blew away half his head with a shotgun at close range. Outlaw biker drug deals usually ended up with some sort of violence. Everyone's paranoid—everyone thinks he's being cheated or there's an informer in the group. That's why I never dealt in drugs except as a courier.

As for Jim, he's the only one who knows exactly where Lyons's body is. He's involved in narcotics and he's a police informer. In October 1982 I found out that he was stopped by police at Blind River, Ontario, near Sault Saint Marie. He was carrying a high-powered rifle, a .357 Magnum revolver, and two pictures of me, as well as a quantity of cocaine. He told police he was on his way to see a man both of us knew in Sault Saint Marie, a town where I was supposed to appear two days later, on October 21, to testify in a mob extortion case. The police couldn't prove anything, but I've always been certain that he was there to kill me as part of a contract. There was also another motive. By killing me he would eliminate one of the few remaining people who could identify him as a participant in the Lyons disappearance.

I told the RCMP about Jim and the Lyons murder and where I believe Lyons was buried, but they never did anything about it, probably because Jim was working for them on other cases.

To stop questions about Lyons, Foote and members of the club spread the word that Lyons had taken off for Vancouver. Nobody ever questioned that. His only relatives that I knew about were his mom and dad, and they didn't know he was dead until I talked. He was never close to them, so they didn't ask questions either.

The only real danger to Foote or gang members was Lyons's girlfriend. They sold his big Harley-Davidson motorcycle and some other belongings, gave her the money, and told her to take off and keep her mouth shut. They bought her off cheap. She knew he was dead, but she never talked. She never knew that club member Mike Everet, who is now doing four years for dealing in drugs and having illegal guns, took the diamond and

gold rings from Lyons's fingers to wear himself. Any doubts I might have had about honor among thieves were laid to rest right then.

Foote used to keep large quantities of explosives in a warehouse he had in Scarborough. If they'd all gone off at one time, he'd probably have blown half the town up. He didn't just keep dynamite there. He had C-4 plastic explosives and all kinds of timing devices. It was impressive. Most of it was stolen.

By the time I met Foote I knew something about explosives, but not a helluva lot. I'd learned a little from a gang member we called Rupert, who showed me how to handle dynamite and put blasting caps in with fuses. The fuses I'd used with Rupert were crude, made with gunpowder. I learned to figure, by the length of the fuse, how long it would be before the spark reached the percussion blasting cap to explode the dynamite. The trouble was, some fuses burned faster than others, and that could be a real hazard.

I remember my first experience with a bombing device came with the Twelfth Division of the Metropolitan Toronto Police Force. I was with a biker named Jesse, who had a real buzz on for the coppers and wanted to throw some dynamite through the window of the division's headquarters. I talked him out of it. I had visions of a bunch of coppers being blown up and our becoming the object of a continentwide manhunt. It would have been a disaster. The alternative I got him to agree to was to let me throw the bomb he'd made at the rear wall of the division. He waited in his car for me to do the job.

He had a full stick of dynamite, but I cut it in half and used a fuse of less than a foot. I put it in a bag, lit the fuse, and threw it at the cement wall. It never quite made it to the wall, because as I threw it a cop drove up. I just turned and started running. It went off faster than expected— while I was still running across a nearby field about a minute later. The whole incident was hushed up by the cops, who never reported it to the newspapers. They never caught either of us. The bomb only blew a hole in the ground. But before now only a handful of cops and bikers knew that Satan's Choice members had tried to blow up Metro's 12th Division.

Foote's instructions eliminated a lot of the risk. I wouldn't have to run

like a deer to escape the effects of a bomb because he taught me about different timing devices—how to hook explosives up to alarm clocks, how to use pressure switches to set off bombs, how to set mercury switches. He gave me a lot of on-the-job training with all the different types of switches and bombs. He constantly reminded me, "Remember, Cec. In this business, your first mistake is always your last mistake—you never get a second chance." I found that wasn't necessarily true. I made a number of mistakes in rigging bombs and I survived, but I admit I was damned lucky.

Foote had a lot of sophisticated bombing techniques that he'd used successfully, but I learned some on my own through studying various books. Without Foote's instructions—and he spent three years on and off teaching me the ropes with various devices at the warehouse, in isolated areas outside Toronto, and while doing safecracking jobs—I would never have been equipped to do the kind of extortion bombings I had to do later on. A lot of the techniques he taught me I used later when Cosimo Commisso and his buddies hired me to intimidate rivals and contractors who stood in their way.

The use of explosives was really a sideline of Foote's. Crime in every form was where he was at. It didn't matter if the victim was a friend or a former business associate. One of those associates was a tough bodyguard for a businessman Foote dealt with and sometimes worked for. The bodyguard had been busted for selling hot diamonds without telling the businessman he was supposed to be protecting. So the businessman decided to teach his bodyguard a lesson, and he used Foote as the teacher.

Foote told me that the businessman had told him his bodyguard had a lot of money stashed in his house and that if we broke in at a certain time we could keep all we found. So we cased the house for a few nights and finally broke in. We even waited for the bodyguard to come home. Foote wanted to grab him and beat the hell out of him until he told us where the stash was. So we sat and sat and sat—for six hours we sat and the bodyguard didn't show.

Finally Foote said to hell with it. But he wasn't about to leave empty-handed. He took statues, collectibles, rifles, anything he thought he could peddle for a few bucks. Then, at his direction, we wrecked the house—a really beautiful, expensive place. The final touch was left for the dining

room, where the bodyguard had this costly mahogany table that was so polished you could see your face in it. Foote was always calling this bodyguard a "rat," so while I stood with him, he took a knife and carved the word *rat* in the middle of the table. Then he looked up at some antique paintings on the wall and he slashed them to shreds.

There was a weird smirk on his face as he finished slashing. "That'll teach the son-of-a-bitch for not bein' around to show us his stash," he said with a chuckle. "This'll drive him wild." When Foote saw his business-man friend the next day, he told him what had happened, and the businessman gave us each $100 because we didn't get as much as he'd promised us.

Foote was finally killed in 1975 by another close friend of mine and his, biker John Harvey. Harvey's about thirty-two now. He has a long record of convictions for obstructing justice, theft, assault, possession of stolen property, and manslaughter. The manslaughter conviction came in April 1977, and was the result of Foote's shooting.

Both Harvey and Foote, as members of Satan's Choice, were dealing speed [methamphetamines] that had been manufactured in one of the club's secret drug labs. The speed, sometimes called Canadian Blue, was popular with bikers and other street people both in Canada and the States. The Choice labs, for a long while, were the among the chief drug suppliers for the stateside Outlaw gang.

An argument over a split on the take in one of their drug deals led to Foote's death. Harvey told me that Foote suddenly went wild as they argued, shouting, "I'm gonna kill you just like I killed Lyons." Harvey said he walked up to his apartment and got his gun, a .38 caliber revolver that I'd sold him about a year before. It was one of several guns I sold bikers and rounders that were later used in homicides. Harvey said he then walked downstairs to an apartment that Satan's Choice was leasing. Foote was there. Harvey shot him once in the chest but it didn't stop Foote. He just kept coming at him. Harvey had to shoot him two more times before he stopped him and killed him.

There were three other members of the Choice in the room at the time. Harvey ran back upstairs and dropped the gun in a hole in the wall near the stairs. The cops investigated the shooting, and three weeks later Harvey was charged with murder. He got two consecutive two-year jail

terms for manslaughter instead of a life murder rap because he had a smart lawyer. Besides, in Canada you don't get much for doing a bad guy. Harvey's attorney, Clayton Ruby, had painted a pretty black picture of John Foote the criminal.

Murder was almost a way of life for members of motorcycle gangs. The same summer I saw Lyons's body in the trunk of Foote's car, I saw two members of Satan's Choice stuff the body of a young white male into the trunk of a car at the Choice clubhouse in Toronto. The kid—he was in his early twenties—was a victim of club discipline, a discipline that says if you testify about club members being involved in crimes, expect to get killed.

People who want to testify against outlaw bikers—whether they are Outlaws in Florida, Hell's Angels in New York or California, or Pagans in Philadelphia or Long Island—can expect to be the targets of intimidation, beatings, or even murder. This kid had been warned to keep his mouth shut, but instead he told the cops about the two club members who were involved in an armed robbery and a drug rip-off attempt in Collingwood, a small town outside Toronto.

When I arrived at the clubhouse I saw two bikers and club members, Mike Everet and Armand Sanguigni, putting the kid's body into the trunk of a car. Sanguigni told me that they had picked the kid up at a well-known motorcycle shop run by a Choice member. They shoved him into the car and drove away. When I saw him he was gagged, his hands and legs were tied up with rope, and he wasn't moving. He'd had the hell beaten out of him by those involved in the drug rip-off. He'd apparently lived through the beating, so they decided to silence him permanently. One of those involved injected battery acid into his arm. By the time I saw him he was dead.

I found out from Sanguigni, who was killed himself several years later, that he and Everet took the kid to Peterborough. From there Howard Berry and another biker took the body to Rice Lake and dumped it in. They didn't do the job right. They anchored him when they dropped him in the lake, but he still had air in his lungs. A few days later, the body broke loose from the weights and bobbed to the surface. The cops raided

the clubhouse in Toronto and the Peterborough clubhouse in hopes of finding evidence. They didn't get what they were looking for, and no one was charged with killing the witness. It's still listed as an unsolved homicide.

Intimidation of witnesses has been a technique that outlaw bikers have used for a long time both in the United States and Canada. Most of the bikers I knew, whether they were in Toronto or Fort Lauderdale, had long criminal records but very few convictions. The reason was simple. They all used threats and bribery and beatings to make witnesses disappear. Sometimes witnesses ended up like that guy in Rice Lake, but more often than not it was the fear of what bikers might do that made witnesses lose their memories or take long vacations.

Back in 1974, I stabbed a guy during a fight in a bar in Toronto's West End. I had been in there drinking with a girl when about ten Indians started mouthing off. They were high on firewater. A couple of them shouted something at the girl, so I calmly got up, walked over to them, and motioned to them, saying, "You, outside. Not just one of you—all of you fuckin' assholes—all of you outside!"

The first guy I said something to followed me, and as I got out the door, I wheeled and stabbed him right in the gut the first time, and in the chest the second time. He stood there, dumbfounded for a minute, then he stumbled back and fell into the arms of some of his buddies, who by then had all started to come storming out the door to take me on. I started fighting like a wild man.

I had a baseball bat in my van in the parking lot. I made a dash for the van, got the bat out, and began dealing with it. Two other guys in the tavern who knew me came out to help me fight the mob of Indians —three of us against ten.

I remember one of the Indians shouted, "Oh, you think you're tough with a bat, eh?"

I said, "Yeah, I'm tough—you take the bat," and I gave it to him. I beat the hell out of him without the bat, and within two minutes I had the bat back and I was working some other Indians over. And the guy I'd stabbed had returned to fight some more.

31

Two weeks later the cops charged me with assault and wounding. They had four witnesses against me. One of the Indian's girlfriends had gotten the license number of my van before I took off.

It took a little doing, but I found out where the witnesses lived and paid them a visit. "Look," I said, "here's two hundred dollars. Take a vacation around court time." So the guy I stabbed, his girlfriend, and the rest of his family took off just before I had to be in court.

When I did appear to face the charges, the cop that had filed the complaint took the stand and testified that the witnesses had disappeared. The Crown prosecutor explained to the judge, "Your Honor, we're going to have to drop the charges. We can't find the witnesses to subpoena them." Then he added, looking over at me, "And I don't think I will ever find them." He made it sound as if I'd killed them and dumped them somewhere. He thought he was making me look bad by that. But the judge dismissed the charges because there was no evidence, and by intimating I'd killed the witnesses, the prosecutor had added to bikers' mystique among the general public. After hearing or reading that, who in his right mind would testify against Cecil Kirby, outlaw biker—or any outlaw biker?

The more intimidation is used, the more it adds to outlaw bikers' prestige, despite what cops try to do to stop it. A lot of members of outlaw gangs joined to become part of that intimidation, to scare people on the street in a group because they couldn't do it by themselves. They didn't have the guts. They also figured it was a way of getting girls. For some reason broads flocked to outlaw bikers, to become part of that atmosphere of fear and violence.

There were others who used the gangs as a cover for narcotics operations. A lot of independent narcotics operators get ripped off—are robbed of their money and their narcotics stashes—because they aren't members of Mafia gangs or outlaw biker gangs or Colombian mobs, or some other group. So some of these independent drug dealers joined the bikers or teamed up with a biker gang. It was sort of an insurance policy. The premium was splitting some of the profits with the gang. But more often than not, many of these independents wound up getting killed or ripped off by the bikers who were supposed to be giving them protection. The money is big and the greed is bigger.

CHAPTER 4

Clubhouse of Assassins II

One of the earliest criminal ventures I got into when I joined Satan's Choice was safecracking. I learned the business after I transferred from the Toronto chapter to the Richmond Hill chapter, where I met two brothers, Duke and Chuck Bernard. Chuck was an expert safecracker who had spent half his life in jails in Dorchester and Kingston.

I didn't know the first thing about cracking a safe when I met them, but it wasn't long before I realized that not only was Chuck an expert but he had someone who was tipping him off about the places to hit. Sometimes it was an employee of the company he hit, who wanted a quick buck. Sometimes it was a girlfriend who worked in the place or knew someone who worked there. Sometimes it was a deliveryman or a salesman who told him what to look for or that the company kept more cash than usual in the safe on certain nights or on weekends. Whatever information he could get he used to his advantage. I learned that technique, as well as others, from him. I also learned safecracking isn't the most risk-free criminal activity to get involved in.

My first job with Chuck was a bearing company in Malton, Ontario. We cased the place for a couple of days first. By that I mean we found a way to gain access either by applying for work, posing as deliverymen or salesmen, or shopping in the area. The idea was to see where the safe was located, to find out what type it was, and to check out the burglar alarm systems. We'd also carefully find out if there were guards or dogs

and when they might be around. If a place looked too well protected, we'd pass.

The bearing company wasn't, and we got $1,500. On that job I was "keeping six." That's a safecracker's code name for someone who is assigned to watch at a window for cops or to check out and deactivate any alarm system that might screw up the job. While one man is keeping six, two others are either peeling or blowing the safe.

In the more than dozen jobs I went on with Chuck, we almost always went through the roof to bypass the alarm system. We'd use a fireman's ax and a railway bar to cut through the roof. Most roofs were made of sheet metal that was easy to cut open. The exceptions were wooden roofs, which took a lot longer to break through.

We already knew the whereabouts of any alarms. Once inside, we'd either deactivate or bypass the alarm, then we'd turn the safe over on its front and cut the back open with an ax. That's called peeling the safe. The safes that we picked to work on were generally made of the same material—sheet metal on the outside, three inches of asbestos rock with wire mesh after that, and then one more sheet of metal and you're inside. At least most of the time. A notable exception was a safe we hit at a market named Food City in the town of Oakville.

When we cased the Food City job we noticed that there was a wire going into the safe, but we figured it was just a door wire. Although I didn't have Chuck's experience, I had a funny feeling about the wire. As Chuck started cutting the wood away around the safe, I told him not to hit it.

"Let's use a torch this time," I said. "I got a feeling there might be a sensor inside there, or a bugged line."

Chuck and another member of our B&E Team didn't listen. They hit the safe and suddenly all hell broke loose. Alarms went off at the safe. We grabbed our equipment and ran like hell out the fire door. More alarms went off. They were going off everywhere. We ran to the yard behind the store, jumped into our car, and saw the cops coming. There was no way we could outrun them on the road, so we pulled the car into a nearby driveway and lay down on the seats while the cops came past us from every direction. Then, while the cops searched the area, we drove off quietly—unseen and empty-handed—but at least not heading for the jail house.

None of the safes we hit, including the Food City safe, was solid steel. They were all the cheap sheet metal safes that could be peeled with the ax through either the back or the top. We never went through the front door of the safe. That would have taken too long unless we were using explosives, as I did once at a restaurant with Foote. Peeling a safe took at the most twelve or fifteen minutes.

Weather very often played an important role in planning a job. We did most of the jobs when it was raining or there was a snowstorm. We hit restaurants, supermarkets, catering establishments, and bakeries. In the dozen jobs we did, we got maybe a total of $32,000. It wasn't very profitable, but it gave us pocket money. With all the new technology and alarm systems, safecrackers are a dying breed. It just isn't worth taking the risks.

The job I remember best was the Community Credit Union in Collingwood in early September 1971. I remember it for two reasons. First, it was the first safe job that I was convicted for. Second, Collingwood was a community where I had left a lasting impression as a biker.

I had cased the place pretty well. I'd walked in and, using a phony name, asked an employee about opening an account. He took me to the safe to show me how secure my money would be. The safe he showed me was a Dominion Safe, about five feet high and four feet long. There were obviously no alarm wires going to it, but there was a silent system for tellers to alert police to a holdup. Later in the day I went around back and cut the telephone wires going into the place. My mistake and that of my partners was not noticing that there was someone in the area when I did that.

Chuck and I sat in a grocery store parking lot and watched to see if the police came after I cut the wires. Nothing happened, so we figured it was safe. We came back that night and broke in through a basement window in the rear of the building. Then we went upstairs. There were no wires on the window then, but you can bet there are now—it's really bugged today. Anyhow, we rolled the safe over into the corner and peeled it apart with fire axes and a big crowbar. It was just like opening a can with a big can opener.

We were expecting to find a lot more money than we did. We opened all the cash boxes in the safe, and all that was inside was $5,000. There

was a lower part to the safe where I was sure there was a lot more money, but we'd already been in the place fifteen minutes, and we couldn't spend more time breaking that drawer open.

A few days later, I was arrested. My lawyer told me that it was a tough case to beat and that I'd be better off pleading guilty.

"The most you'll get is six months," he said. He was right. I had been charged with break and entry and theft, but my lawyer cut a deal and I pleaded guilty to willful damage of a public improvement—cutting the telephone wires. I got a year's probation. The copper that charged me with the job was furious.

"You get the hell out of this town, Kirby," he shouted, "and don't you ever fuckin' come back. I'm sick of you and all your biker cronies."

He had good reason to be sick of me. A year before I'd partied with some Satan's Choice gang members and gotten a little high. I told them I was going to make Collingwood remember the Choice. So I got a bucket of special paint, went to the top of the town's tallest water tower, and, standing on the railing, painted "Satan's Choice" all over the tower. Next to it I added, "Fuck the World."

I don't know why, but it took about three years before they painted it over. For all that time, every daylight hour the people who lived and worked in that town had to look at "Satan's Choice—Fuck the World." It drove the police chief crazy. He knew I'd done it, but he couldn't prove it. He couldn't even remove it. All he could do was look at it and fume and listen to angry residents.

Between safe jobs and other crimes, I was moving up in the organizational structure of Satan's Choice, first in the Toronto chapter and then in the Richmond Hill branch. In my first year as a member, I was made road captain, a very important post in any outlaw biker gang. It's the road captain who, with the chapter president and other officers, is responsible for mapping out the route that the members are to follow when they go to a function. He also has to ride up and down the line of bikes to keep them in formation, divert traffic, and stop it at intersections if necessary. The road captain always rides up front, at the left side of the chapter president. To do all that, you've really got to know how to handle a bike, and you have to move at speeds of up to eighty to ninety MPH. Later

on I also acted as sergeant at arms—a sort of enforcer who walks around with a baseball bat or some other instrument to whack guys in the head when they get out of order at club meetings. And I was vice president of the Richmond Hill chapter. But it was as road captain that I got my spurs in field events.

Field events are competitions where outlaw biker club members who aren't warring get together in the States, Canada, Australia, or Europe to test their skills as cyclists. They are also times when bikers have a helluva party. They get drunk or stoned, they play cards and gamble, and sometimes they tear up the nearest town if they're not properly welcomed. For the most part, though, field events are chances to test your skills as a biker and have a good time.

Field events would be advertised a month or two ahead of time. Flyers would be sent to all the outlaw clubs: the Vagabonds, the Outlaws, Hell's Angels, the Crossbreeds, Satan's Choice, the Paradice Riders, or a half dozen other clubs in the United States and Canada. Tickets would be sold at five bucks each to get in, and the sponsoring club would sell beer and hotdogs through the day. Sometimes there would be a party the night before on the location, sometimes the night after.

On the day of the competition, there'd be ten or twelve events, and trophies for first and second places. The events were in two classes, an A class for Harley-Davidson motorcycles with 1,200-cubic-centimeter motors, and a B class for the smaller bikes, 500 to 750 ccs. There were competitions for individuals and for teams. There were drag races for a quarter mile or less; there was the body pickup race, where we had to race to one end of the field, pick up a passenger, and race to the other end.

One of the most popular events was called the balloon race, where each biker had a passenger with a balloon tied around his neck or his back and a paper baseball bat. Bikers would ride around in circles while their passengers tried to destroy the balloons of others with the bats. The last biker and passenger with a balloon were the winners. Very often people got hurt in these events because there'd be twenty, thirty, or more bikes whirling around in a cloud of dust running into each other. If you had a grudge against someone from another club, this event would give you a chance to smack him right in the teeth and just about knock him out. Many a fight between outlaw clubs began this way.

The most controversial event of all, however, was the chicken race. It got the Animal Humane Society all over us—they stopped the race for a while when they found out what we were doing. The event called for a live chicken or turkey at one end of the field and the bikers at the other. Everyone would race up, and the passenger on each bike would jump off and try to grab the chicken or turkey, which was staked out and, of course, alive. Whoever came back with the biggest piece of the bird or the whole bird was declared the winner. Very few chickens or turkeys survived. They were usually torn apart by the bikers' passengers, who'd return to the finish line covered with blood.

Then for laughs there was a shit race. We'd put a golf ball in a bag of manure, usually pig or cow shit. Bikers were to race into the field, and the first one to find the ball and come back with it was the winner. I remember seeing one guy come back with the ball in his mouth. There were some real weirdos in those competitions.

Of course, there were the power turn races, where you lean your bike over and go around in circles, tearing up the ground with your wheels in high-speed turns. I won a couple of those.

As good as some bikers were, they often watched in awe when my father would ride a motorcycle. Dad didn't like the outlaw club, but he accepted the fact that I was a member and that I loved motorcycle riding. He gave me the love of biking. I can't remember when he didn't have at least three or four bikes around the yard.

When I was very young, about ten years old, he used to sit me in front of him on the gas tank of the bike. Then one day, as we were riding like the wind, he shouted in my ear, "Cecil, you want to hold the handlebars?" I nodded excitedly and he added, "We'll go down the street—now hold the handlebars and keep the bike up." I was excited, steering the bike for the first time, sure that the whole of Weston was watching me. They weren't. I looked behind me and there was Dad, standing on his head on the rear of the seat.

He used to tell me that when he was younger he rode his bike down Dundas Street, a main thoroughfare of Toronto, where they had streetcar tracks. He said he'd lock the throttle, get on the side of the bike, put his feet on the steel rail, and slide along with the bike pulling him. He was also a great one for riding his bike along the river in the wintertime. He'd

put his ice skates on and ride with his bike beside him. He was young and crazy and he loved daredevil riding.

In Canada or the United States, the theft of motorcycles is a major problem for insurance companies and law enforcement. Almost every biker I knew or met from Fort Lauderdale to Toronto had a stolen Harley-Davidson or was using parts from one to keep his bike running. It's big business for outlaw bikers, who not only steal parts but sell the parts from stolen bikes through motorcycle shops they own in nearly every community where bikers operate. In fact, the theft of motorcycles got so bad in Manitoba that insurance plans there will not include theft coverage for bikes.

The best of the outlaw biker thieves was Bob Gray of the Paradice Riders. He was about six feet four, 250 pounds, and extremely strong. He also had a very loud mouth. At a party he was always the center of attention. As loud as he was, he had the stealth of a fox approaching a henhouse when he was supplying speed to Outlaws and Choice members or stealing motorcycles. I don't think there was anyone in the States or in Canada who had ever successfully heisted as many motorcycles as Gray had.

For a time I helped him steal motorcycles. I was a piker next to him. In my lifetime as a biker, I stole maybe thirty or forty motorcycles. That might be a month's work for him when he was moving around. As good a thief as he was, if you were his partner in a deal, you had to watch him. Greed would go to his head. He'd take the gold out of your tooth if you kept your mouth open too long. I learned to keep my eye on him in any deal after he slid one by me at a pop festival in 1971.

The festival was being held at Rock Hill. By the time I got there, Gray had already stolen one bike. That was no small trick when you consider that police covered every entrance and exit. It seemed like hundreds of coppers from the Ontario Provincial Police were there. When I saw Gray he was looking for a way to get the bike off the festival grounds without having the coppers inspect it and discover it was stolen. He said he wasn't the only one who'd stolen a bike, that a biker called Al from Satan's Choice had also taken one.

"Look, Bob," I said, "wait here awhile while I think of a way to get you and the bike outta here."

"Okay," he said, "you figure a way and we split what I get."

So I checked out the grounds and found a barn near the entrance. When no one was looking, I set the barn on fire and returned to where Gray was. By that time the flames were roaring into the sky, smoke was curling overhead, and people were yelling and screaming while the coppers and firemen raced to put the fire out.

I hopped on my bike and shouted to Gray, "Bob, you follow me with that bike, right now."

He was laughing like hell. "Cec, you're a pisser," he shouted, started the bike, and roared off behind me.

When we got to the gate, the coppers were just waving everybody through. They didn't stop anyone. There was too much confusion. Right behind us was the Choice biker, Al, with his stolen bike, but he decided not to follow us. "I'll take it out later," he said. The next morning he tried to get the bike out and was stopped and charged with bike theft.

Now Gray and I couldn't get far because there wasn't enough gas in the stolen cycle, so Gray had to abandon it at the National Park on Airport Road that night.

"I'll go back and get it later," he said, hopping on the back of my bike.

Two or three days later, when I saw him again, I asked about the bike. He said he'd gone back and found it gone. I shrugged and didn't think much of it until another Paradice Rider, Warren Smith, who had been in a prison reformatory with me, told me about some bikes he'd stolen.

"You know I went with Bob Gray out to this park on Airport Road one day and damned if he didn't come up with a Harley he'd hidden in the bush there that he said he'd stolen at the festival."

So Gray had ripped me off. He'd gotten the bike, sold it, and kept everything for himself.

I remember one day we were in a suburb of Toronto together when he saw a Harley sitting in a guy's driveway. The poor guy was cleaning the bike, and Gray went over and watched him working for a minute and then he began talking to him. Suddenly the bike owner left to get something. As soon as he entered the house, Gray was on his bike and gone like the wind.

Gray had other techniques, too. He used to read the newspapers like

a hawk to see what bikes were on sale. When he found one that interested him, he'd visit the seller and convince him that he should take it for a test drive. That would be the last that seller ever saw of the bike.

Gray would even steal stolen bikes from the guys who sold him bike parts that he'd stolen in the first place. Like Charles (Chuck) Yanover, who in 1970 was just a small-time hood like the rest of us. He owned the City Custom Cycle Co. in Toronto and from there sold stolen bike parts that bikers brought to him. Later he was convicted of theft and possession of fifty stolen motorcycles, charges that resulted in two and a half years in jail. At the time, Gray was selling him hot bikes, I was, dozens of guys were. I remember I stole a brand-new Triumph with only ten miles on it. I took it apart and sold the damn engine to him for only forty dollars. He was making a fortune on the deals, and bikers were getting ripped off when they sold to him.

One day, Gray decided to steal Yanover's personal bike. Yanover went bonkers. He ran screaming to the police, who were laughing so hard they were crying when they took his theft report. I ended up with the bike. A member of the Richmond Hill Satan's Choice sold it to me. Then Gray came to me and said he could make even more money and get back at Yanover for chiseling us on other bike deals. Together we stripped the bike and sold it, piece by piece, back to Yanover. We sold him all but the front end. When we were through Gray told him he'd been buying back pieces of his own bike. Yanover didn't say a word. His face was red as a beet, but he didn't say a word. About five years later, I showed him a bike I was riding and pointed to the front end. "There's your front end, Chuck," I said with a chuckle. He didn't think it was funny but he didn't say anything—just walked away.

Stealing motorcycles, I learned, was one of the easiest rackets around. It was also very profitable. On the average we'd get $800 to $1,000 a bike if we didn't have to take it apart. If we stripped it and sold it for parts we'd get more than double—$2,000 to $3,000, depending on who we were dealing with. Harleys were selling at from $6,000 to $7,000 apiece new then.

To steal a bike, the most important thing to do is case the area—map

out the easiest and safest routes of escape, check out neighborhoods to prevent being spotted, and watch the bike owner to see how careless he is.

A lot of bikes were spotted through newspaper classifieds, or at motorcycle shops, or in neighborhoods where we knew bikers hung out. Once we spotted a bike, we'd take a couple of days to case the area and then drive up in our van. We had a big set of bolt cutters in the van that could cut any chain or lock that could be used on a bike. We'd break the lock, usually at night, wheel the bike down the street quietly, and put it in the waiting van.

Sometimes there were close calls. The owner of a bike I'd selected to steal in Richmond Hill came home earlier than expected and I got jammed between his car and the bike. I slid underneath his car to hide. When he walked by I could have grabbed his foot, that's how close he was to me. He went into the house. Within seconds I was out from under that car, on his bike, starting it, and taking off.

When we stripped a bike, we'd usually sell the parts to other outlaw club members. Fenders, gas tanks, windshields—there was always someone in the biker gangs who needed parts for his bike, and we could get those parts faster than a shop could, even one that had the franchises for Harley-Davidsons and Triumphs.

Among the popular items were cylinder heads. Everybody looked for cylinder heads. We sold ours to a motorcycle shop owner named Sissy, who gave us top dollar and would buy all we could lay our hands on. And we kept our own spare parts shop in a garage in Richmond Hill.

I preferred selling the bikes as is, without stripping them. It was a pain in the ass to strip a Harley. It could take eight hours, and my back would be killing me afterward. Some bikes, smaller ones, might take only four hours, but it was still back-breaking work. A lot of the time was consumed pounding the identification numbers away with a ball-peen hammer or drilling the numbers out, then placing an aluminum weld over the hole and stamping the casing with new numbers.

When we did a strip job—and most biker clubs wherever they are do this—we took the bikes apart right down to their nuts and bolts. We'd drill the numbers out of the transmission casings, out of the frame, and sometimes out of the engine casings. Most of time we'd throw away

the engine casings because it was too difficult to get the numbers off them. When it was too much trouble to drill off the numbers of the engine or transmission, we'd take them to a lake or a construction site and dump them. For those we kept we'd weld over the numbers, grind the weld down, and leave it like that, selling it to someone who was making a customized bike, who was willing to put the motor over the frame numbers, and who knew he was getting a hot product but didn't ask questions and paid the price. Or, when possible, we'd restamp the engine casing, which was made of aluminum, and repaint the part.

Sometimes we felt the theft hadn't been reported, so we'd send someone down to the local police department saying they were interested in buying the bike and asking them to check the numbers of the bike on their hot list to make sure it wasn't stolen. If it wasn't listed, we'd get a document from the police to show that the numbers had been checked and therefore the bike couldn't be stolen.

There were also insurance scams. Brothers in one club would report a theft while the other would cannibalize the bike, rebuild it, and sell it as a home-built bike. They'd get the $8,000 insurance claim for theft and the sale price of the home-built, maybe $4,000 to $5,000. Some of the Harleys were valued at as much as $12,000, and the insurance companies paid off. I made thousands that way. I also landed in Guelph Reformatory in 1972 with some other bikers because we'd stolen motorcycles from a cycle shop.

Guelph Reformatory is a medium-security prison about sixty miles west of Toronto. It's not the worst prison in the Canadian system and it's not the best. The food was terrible and they made you work hard on the bush gang. The bush gang is a bastardized version of the southern U.S. prison chain gang, only without the chains. It got the name *bush* because heavily guarded prisoners worked in cedar brush and forests in parks owned by the Ontario provincial government.

The prisoners had to cut down the cedar trees, parts of which were sectioned off into fence post sizes and sent back to the reformatory, where other prisoners stripped them. Other parts of the trees were stripped, finished and formed, and made into picnic tables, which, in turn, were sent back to Ontario's parks.

When I started on the bush gang, I wasn't the strongest guy around,

but working with axes and saws, and lifting the trees started to build me up. It also gave me some incentive to work out with weights with another Satan's Choice member, John Murdoch. When I started I couldn't press much more than 120 pounds. By the time I left Guelph less than a year later, I was pressing nearly 330 pounds. I was also ready—through associations I'd made at the prison with other outlaw bikers—to graduate to the higher and more violent levels of crime.

CHAPTER 5

Girls for Sale

Girls are as much a part of outlaw biker life as are drugs and violence, and they are probably our weakest link. They often carry our guns, hide our drugs, front for our businesses, gather information for us about cops and other bikers or places we want to rob, and act as our couriers in drug deals and other crimes. That gives them access to a lot of evidence that could put members of biker clubs in jail. So cops do their damnedest to get the girls to talk. Bikers often kill some of the women to protect themselves, because they think they have become or might become informers.

That's one of the reasons many girls—some of them from Canada—disappeared or were tortured and murdered in Florida by members of the Outlaws. The cops would find them in pieces, or crucified, or they'd just never find anything because the bodies were dumped in the Everglades, where the animals finished them off.

Girls disappeared for other reasons, too. Sometimes they had worked as prostitutes and dancers in topless bars too long—become too old and used physically at sixteen and seventeen and eighteen. Others tried to run away from the club members who owned them. Some cheated on the money they were supposed to turn over, and some just weren't making enough money.

I can't say if any of them were actually killed by Satan's Choice bikers, or the Paradice Riders or Vagabonds or other Toronto gangs. I didn't see any killed, but I know a lot disappeared across the border and haven't been

seen or heard from since. A copper I know once said to me that there was no way of knowing how many women disappeared from Canada in white slavery and were killed. "It's like trying to document missing children," he said. "They're just swallowed up in the traffic and there's no one around to trace them."

He was right. Bikers from the Canadian clubs were selling girls for from $500 to $2,000 apiece across the border. A biker just had to make the right arrangements in the States and deliver the girl to the border, and members from the Outlaws, Satan's Escorts, or some other gang would take over. Some of the girls were as ugly as sin or so spaced out they never knew where they were, but they brought bucks to the bikers, who made them work for still more bucks. "If they got four limbs and a hole they're worth money," a biker friend of mine once said.

The Outlaws are one of two biggest cycle gangs in the United States, and they're now very big in Canada. In the 1970s they were our allies and they used to come to Canada to buy drugs from members of Satan's Choice. They also bought and sold weapons, bought and sold counterfeit money, and bought some of our women. Sometimes the women were given to the Outlaws to hustle in their body rub shops [massage parlors] and topless bars in Florida and Chicago.

The public thinks we get most of our broads through fear or rape or kidnapping. That's what the media likes to play up—the kidnapping of some girl who's held captive and raped by all the gang members. Well, there is some of that, but for the most part bikers don't need to grab women off the street and rape them—the women flock to them like bees to honey. That's the truth.

Biker women are worse than rock star groupies. Most of them come asking for sex and companionship and to be someone's "old lady." They have no families or they're on drugs, and they need money. So what happens to them happens to them. Their families don't even care enough to tell the cops they're missing.

In 1970 a lot of bikers hung around the Yorkville Village, one of a number of hippie hangouts. The girls hanging around clubs like that always needed money to buy dope. So a lot of the bikers, myself included, would show these girls where to go and hook, peddle their bodies.

We'd send them to special hotels and bars on Front Street or on

Charles Street, where there were a lot of men looking for action. They were told that they had to give us a percentage of what they made to guarantee protection from pimps. Some guys took 50 percent, some guys took it all and gave the girls drugs to keep them working. When the girls weren't making enough money for them, or when they said they wanted to go on a trip with their biker pimp-boyfriend, they'd be taken to the border and sold to some other biker gang member. The Outlaws or other gangs would use them for a while and either sell them again or kill them because they'd seen or heard too much.

Satan's Escorts members would come to Canada to socialize a lot with members of Satan's Choice. Some of the Choice members would set them up with girls to take back to the States. They'd just deal them to the Escorts as a favor or sell them for as little as $100 or $200. Some of the broads were sold a bill of goods—promises of a vacation, a trip to sunny Florida, a good time. "Work for them [the Escorts]," the Choice bikers would say, "and come back in six months if you want." They were conned. I never saw one of them come back and dozens of them left.

It worked in reverse, too. There were times when the Escorts and Outlaws sent American girls to Canada to work for Canadian biker clubs. A lot of them disappeared, too.

I wasn't any better than the rest of the bikers who had their own stables of girls working for them. I didn't sell any of the girls that worked for me and I only took 20 percent from them, but I was pretty much doing the same thing as everyone else. I had four girls working for me at one time, but I only did it for six months.

On good weeks the girls were pulling down from $200 to $500 a day each, and I was collecting from $200 to $800 a day. That wasn't every day of the week—maybe three or four, but it was a nice income. Plus there were some fringe benefits, like making love to them.

I was making it with all of them—sure I was. I'd have been a fool if I didn't. I'm human and I don't need to rape some broad to get what I want. But they were a pain in the ass with their jealousy, and after a few months I got tired of it and just had one working for me. The others took off.

I didn't chase them down, beat the hell out of them, and make them

go back to work for me like most of the bikers would have. What was the sense? If they don't want to work for you they don't want to work for you and they weren't really working for me. I was their insurance policy.

Now some of the other bikers were hustling the girls, really pimping for them, and I didn't like that. I wasn't about to hustle tricks for some broad. That's why I took a small percentage. I was just giving them protection, not drumming up business for them. I wasn't a pimp. If anybody tried to beat them up or rip them off, I'd catch up with the guy and beat the hell out of him.

I remember one of my girls was a really gorgeous blonde called Cindy. She was about twenty-three. She wasn't a hippie, just a good-looking woman who wanted to hustle for a buck. I met her in Cedar Beach, where she was working at the hotel. Cindy was drinking at this bar when I picked her up. We started talking, and before long she told me she wanted to leave waitressing and get back into being a hooker. I told her I knew some good spots she could work, spots some of my other ladies worked.

Cindy went right to work. I'd drive her downtown and drop her off at the places where she'd pick up the johns and work them. She had trouble only once. One of her johns beat her up. She called me and I found out who he was. I called him at his home. His wife answered the phone.

"I got some business with your husband," I said, "lemme talk to him."

She didn't argue or give any excuse that he wasn't there, just called him to the phone. When he got on, I said, "Friend, you got a choice. I can talk to you or I can talk to your wife about the girl you went out with last night." He didn't answer. So I continued talking. "I'm her boyfriend. You can come out and talk to me privately or I can come to your house and talk—and your wife can hear it all. Either way."

"No, no, no!" he said excitedly. "I'll come."

"Okay," I answered. "Meet me at the North Hill parking lot and bring some money. Come alone if you're smart."

He hung up and met me where I'd told him I'd be. I got into his car, grabbed him by the collar, and put a gun up to the side of his head.

"You beat my girl up when you got through," I said, "and you didn't even pay her, louse. Give me the two hundred dollars."

He was shaking as he handed me the money. Right then I punched him hard in the jaw. You could hear it crack. I left him lying there and drove

away. I never heard a word from him. Neither did Cindy. I gave her all but fifty bucks.

The hippies turned hooker were always high, always having problems with some john or pimp who wanted to muscle them, and I'd have to come in at all hours of the day and night to settle the problem. All the bikers did.

There were a number of guys in the biker clubs who would pick up one or two girls hanging around the streets near the Yorkville Village, bring them back to the clubhouse nearby, put some clothes on them, and send them back out on the street. When the girls would come back, the bikers would take some of the money from them, give them some dope, and send them back out on the street again. It was real easy. The bikers just had to give them some dope. To pay for the dope these hippies, some them were fifteen, sixteen, some older, had to work the streets.

Some professional pimps, mostly black, tried to take the girls over by beating them up and hassling them. We didn't have that kind of trouble too often though. The pimps knew the girls were protected by the bikers, and they would stay away. They didn't want the trouble.

Some of the bikers weren't satisfied with shaking down the hippies and regular prostys for their street money and free lays. They had a thing about taking women off the street or grabbing them in the clubhouse and raping them, getting clubhouse gang bangs going.

When we were hanging around the Villager and the women were all doped up on the street, some gang members would grab them, drag them back to the clubhouse, and start screwing them. Before long everybody in the clubhouse was joining in. Sometimes members cut loose their own women and let them get raped. Very few girls who were raped ever went to the cops.

One was attacked by two brothers and a biker they called Larry. The brothers said that some girls had told them to stop and see them. So we stopped at an apartment and one of the brothers went in and came out about a half hour later. We left without anyone saying a word.

Two days later I was driving around and I got stopped by the police for indecent assault. I said, hey, what the hell is this all about? The cops asked me was I with Larry and these two brothers when they assaulted

a woman in a Keele Street apartment. I didn't know what the hell they were talking about, but I found out. The brother that had come out of the apartment like nothing had happened didn't tell any of us he'd raped the woman. We were kept in jail for two weeks without bail. When we went back to court, the case had been withdrawn. I don't know who did it, but somebody got to her—threatened her life, I guess—and she withdrew the charges.

I knew one biker in prison like that. We called him Nutty. His real name was Gary. If he found a broad in the biker clubhouse alone, he'd rape her—you could count on it. Almost 99 percent of the rapes that took place in the clubhouse in Richmond Hill involved him.

I know there's been a lot of talk about bikers that have forced cars off the road and attacked women and entire families. In all the time I was a biker I can only remember once when it happened and Nutty was involved. He forced a whole carload of girls off the road and grabbed one of them and threw her on his bike. She just thought she was going for a ride, but she ended up being thrown in a biker's car and getting screwed by about twenty guys.

The sale of women and drugs between the Outlaws of the United States and Canada's Satan's Choice really heated up in the 1970s. When I first met and visited with a lot of the top Outlaw members in Florida in 1974 and 1975, they weren't as big as they are today, but they were every bit as tough. They hated the Hell's Angels as much then as they do now. The war between those two gangs—the two biggest in the world—has been going on for more than twenty years, and wherever they rumble across the same turf, bodies drop. I guess more than one hundred on both sides have been killed either in Canada or the United States in various "battles."

I went to Florida to meet some of the Outlaws with "Mother," then the national president of Satan's Choice. Mother's real name was Garnet McKuen, and he was about thirty years old. He was from Saint Catharines and had six convictions, including an assault on a cop and being caught with narcotics. With us was Drago Salajko of the Choice's Kitchener chapter.

In Miami we were treated like royalty by the president of the Outlaws, Big Jim Nolan. He and a guy named Pete of the Outlaws' Hollywood,

Florida, chapter picked us up and drove us to Nolan's house in Hollywood in a specially equipped van. The house was small, nothing impressive, but it was like a fortress. It was a two-bedroom bungalow that was very efficiently protected by the latest in alarm systems. Big Jim had two huge Great Danes who would just as soon chew you into pieces as look at you. He always had a handgun in the living room, and there were two or more high-powered rifles in other rooms of the house.

Two girls were living there, one who worked in a body rub place and was Big Jim's special girlfriend, the other a broad who just worked and hustled for him. It seemed to me at the time that almost every broad associated with the Outlaws worked in body rub parlors, or topless joints, screwing anyone and everyone willing to pay the price. All the money they made went back to Outlaw members like Big Jim, who provided them with places to live, clothes, food, booze, and whatever drugs they wanted within reason.

The Outlaws were making a fortune off women. They had the body rub parlors and topless bars from Orlando to Fort Lauderdale, in Chicago, and all across the country, and they had an endless supply of women who danced and worked as prostitutes. Those broads, hundreds of them, were bringing in as much as $2,000 to $3,000 a week each.

Big Jim was an impressive man with an impressive reputation. Only a few months before I met him he had been accused of ordering the execution of three Hell's Angels enforcers. He'd had them shotgunned to death in April 1974. Their bodies were found in Fort Lauderdale, face down at the water's edge, with their hands tied behind their backs and cement blocks tied to their feet.

There were stories that Big Jim had personally skinned other Hell's Angels alive. He certainly was big enough and tough enough to do a job like that if he wanted to. He stood about six feet eight in his stocking feet and weighed about 250 pounds. Whether his reputation was true or not —and he wasn't convicted on either story but for something else—I found him to be a nice guy. It was obvious he had lots of money—profits from the hustle of his broads and from the sale of drugs by the club. On every finger he had rings of all shapes and sizes—all gold and diamonds, some big, some medium, but all expensive as hell.

Mother, Drago, and I stayed at his place for two days before moving

on. Whatever we wanted we got, whether it was booze, women, or drugs. All the while we were there so was Big Jim's trusted bodyguard Pete, who roamed around the house carrying a fourteen-shot Browning semiautomatic handgun.

We were given the "honor" of attending the Outlaws' club meeting that week, but there wasn't much to it. It was short and sweet and to the point. Nolan introduced us to the membership and told them to treat us like we were one of their own. They did. We also got to see a clubhouse they had just rented and were rearranging. All the windows had been bricked in. Two bricks were left out of each at the middle as gun ports. They also had rattlesnakes around the place to keep out any unwelcome strangers.

In the time we were there, I met and talked to about ten Outlaws other than Nolan and Pete. They looked and acted like stone killers. They were really crude- and cruel-looking guys, let me tell you. They put a chill in your spine just lookin' at them.

After a few days we went to Key West with some of the Outlaws. We stopped at a house that was owned by their former national president, a guy they called Surfer, who I had met once before at a field day in Kitchener. While we fished, Surfer told me he had a job teaching school there.

Surfer was forty and he'd retired as a biker, but he entertained any of the Outlaws and their friends when they came through. I suspected the retirement was only partial. I figured they were moving things like guns and drugs through his area. They had plenty of bucks, those Outlaws. Some of them had to be millionaires with the kind of places they lived in and the businesses they owned.

Just before I left Florida I had a talk with Big Jim about bringing some girls from Canada with me the next time I traveled south.

"Can you get them jobs in your body rub shops?" I asked.

He burst out laughing. "You mean the massage parlors?" he answered. "Sure. You're welcome to come back anytime with any of your girls. I'll get them jobs, and you'll make plenty of money."

I tried to get a couple of the girls across the border in my van with one of my bikes, but I was turned back by immigration agents. I should have worked something out with one of Big Jim's people, but I wasn't trying

to sell these girls. I just wanted them to work for me in Florida while I took it easy. It wasn't worth it to keep trying. I didn't want to get busted on some stateside white slavery rap.

Mother had a few broads that he'd shipped there from Canada to work in the joints the Outlaws controlled. One of them was named Cindy. A few months after I left, I found out she had died in a fire in a body rub place. When Mother came back he was a little shook up over it, but he never explained what had happened. We all figured she probably had seen something she wasn't supposed to see.

The last thing I heard about Big Jim was that he had come to Canada to have members of Satan's Choice hide him while he ducked a warrant. They eventually caught him and returned him to the States, where he was convicted and sentenced to a double-life jail term.

Some of the evidence and testimony that helped send Big Jim to jail came from a Canadian member of the Outlaws, a kid named Willy Edson, who had been one of Big Jim's enforcers. Before Edson became a protected federal witness in the States, he was supposed to have been one of the Outlaws who worked out a deal to supply the Chicago Mafia with women for its topless joints and body rub parlors.

When the law came after Edson, he hid in a number of Outlaw chapters in the States. Then they smuggled him across the border and hid him in Canada at Satan's Choice chapters in Windsor, Kitchener, and Montreal. Choice members gave him phony new identification, weapons, and a radio to monitor police calls, but he got caught going to a liquor store in Kitchener and was deported.

In November 1982 there was a trial of some Outlaws and their business associates in Chicago. Five were convicted, including Robert Burroughs, a Canadian biker and drug supplier for the Chicago Outlaws. Burroughs worked for the president of the Outlaws' Chicago chapter, Thomas Stimac, who was also jailed in the case. Stimac, who was a friend of Big Jim and knew a lot of Choice bikers, was identified at the trial as one of those who met with members of the Chicago mobs way back in 1977.

One of the women the Outlaws had supplied to the mob was named Betty Darlene Callahan. She'd been kidnapped in North Carolina when her boyfriend didn't come up with money he owed the Outlaws for drugs. After killing her boyfriend, they raped her and forced her to become a

prostitute for them in Chicago. Her story was like that of a lot of girls. The big difference was the Callahan woman became a protected federal witness like Edson. She was able to testify about the Outlaws handling millions of dollars in cocaine, marijuana, and Canadian Blues because she'd been around long enough to see a lot and she remembered. When she got her chance to make a break and talk to the feds, she did. It saved her life. If Stimac or the others had had even a hint of what she was going to do, they'd have killed her. Like I said before, women are the weak link of bikers.

CHAPTER 6

Nothing Is Secret

If the police want to know what outlaw biker gangs are doing or what biker is dealing dope or stolen goods or women, they usually turn to their special biker squads. The squads have informers on the street and in biker gangs. The biker squad cops talk to street people—like pimps, prostitutes, burglars, bartenders, gamblers, and nightclub owners—people who see and deal with bikers regularly.

The information they gather from these people usually can't be used in a court of law. It's not evidence. It's what they call raw intelligence. That's hearsay stuff that can provide valuable leads to dope pushers, bookie joints, holdups, burglary rings, and extortions. It can even prevent murders or stop gang fights, or it can help cops find guys that are hiding out. Intelligence is what makes biker squads and other special police units tick. Without it, police wouldn't know a damned thing about bikers, or any other crime group for that matter. It's their eyes and ears on crime.

While cops use intelligence to catch crooks, bikers have their own intelligence system to help them survive on the street. The bikers' system is probably better than the one the cops have because bikers can do things illegally to get information about what the cops are up to.

We needed intelligence to keep tabs on each other as well as the cops. The truth is that there is very little trust among outlaw biker gangs and even among bikers in the same clubhouse. Yesterday's friend may be tomorrow's enemy, and it's best you have a record on him. When you

know more about your enemy that he does about you, you win battles and you win wars between gangs. While the cops were using us, we were using the cops to get information and to eliminate our enemies either through firefights or the cops themselves. All biker gangs did the same thing. The Choice, the Outlaws, and Hell's Angels were the best at the intelligence game in Canada and in the States.

One of the best intelligence sources we had in Satan's Choice was one who had access to the Canadian police computer. Gary Cuomo of the Choice had acquired that source. Club members carried her number around in their wallets. All a member would do, if he was worried about the cops, was call her number. She'd access the police computer to see if there were any warrants on him. We could also see if there were outstanding fugitive warrants on rival gang members when we'd spot them. If there were, we'd have someone in the club call the cops and tip them off to where the rival gang member was and who was with him. We could also check out anyone's criminal record through that computer. That helped us spot people from rival gangs or from the cops trying to infiltrate us.

Biker clubs used the sergeant at arms to rap with cops and pump them. Sometimes we used club members cops had hassled a lot. The cops figured they had them hooked, afraid that they were going to go to jail. Whoever they were, they'd been told by club officers to cozy up to cops to get information, even if it meant giving some up themselves.

While the cops were pushing those bikers for information, the bikers were using them to find out who the cops were looking for, what bikers were in trouble, where cops were concentrating their power—all kinds of tidbits that would help bikers avoid arrests or other trouble with the cops.

For quite a while, members of Satan's Choice had a gal working in the police dispatch office of the Ontario Provincial Police. She tipped us for years about things like when they were going to raid a biker clubhouse or homes. A lot of guys were able to skip out before raids. Large amounts of guns and drugs were moved and hidden because of tips we got from her.

There were other ways we would gather intelligence. One of the most important was through pictures. Bikers were forever taking pictures of each other. They took them at parties screwing broads; they took them

when they were high on drugs; they took them at field events and at funerals—pictures, pictures, pictures. They filled album after album of bikers. They filled desk drawers and closets in clubhouses. Cops grabbed them on raids and more pictures were taken. Why?

Pictures are a record of what a guy looks like. Descriptions are never adequate—they can't fill the bill like a picture can. If the day comes that you want to have a guy hit, and you need an outsider to get next to him, what's better—a picture or a description?

I had been looking for a former member of the Toronto Outlaws. The Last Chance club members hid him out. They wouldn't turn him over, and I was unable to break into their clubhouse because they had it secured so well. So I did the next best thing. I took a bat and smashed the windows of four of their cars, bending some of the fenders as well.

The Last Chance bikers never forgot. They had pictures of me that they'd gotten at a field event or some other affair. They had one picture enlarged and, I'm told, it now hangs in their clubhouse with big block letters saying, "Wanted, Dead or Alive—Reward $200,000."

Many outlaw bikers in Canada and the States have pictures of me in their clubhouses or in their wallets. That way they can recognize me if they spot me and inform club members so a death squad can come after me. There are a lot of pictures of every biker in every club floating around. Someday they may be used the way the Last Chance bikers and other clubs are using my pictures.

Every biker club has its friends, its associates and hangers-on, people the cops like to call their support group. The cops say that for every biker there are ten support group members that help them. I think they are low on the estimate. It's a lot more than ten.

When I was a biker some of that so-called support group were citizens we used to get us inside information. Some held key government jobs where they had access to special and sensitive information. Like in the Driver Suspension Branch of the Department of Transportation. For years, I have had a source there who could go to the computer and check out auto license numbers. It was helpful. We were able to identify RCMP unmarked cars and other people who were doing surveillances on us that way.

I never overused that source, and it never cost me that much. Cops would like to think big bribes are paid for such information. It's just not so. I used to have plate numbers checked out maybe twice a month, and all it cost me was a bottle of good booze. My source was just a good friend. You don't really have to pay off good friends.

My government source has been a lifesaver for me, even today. If I didn't have a source like that, I'd be in a lot of trouble, particularly if there was someone tailing me or watching my house to set me up for a hit. I could call cops I know who are supposed to be available to help me in an emergency. By the time I got to them, if I could find them, and had them check out numbers like that, I could be dead. It takes them a helluva lot longer to do a license check than it does me.

I wasn't the only biker with a source in the Department of Transportation. There were bikers from the Vagabonds, Satan's Choice, the Paradice Riders, and other gangs who had girlfriends or associates that either worked in the department or had contacts there. In one instance, the wife of one of the Choice bikers was working in a government office. The cops found out about it and had her fired. But since there were other wives of members working in that office, the cops didn't stop the flow of information.

What information we couldn't get from corrupt government employees we sometimes got from people we dealt with in banks, and Bell Canada, the telephone company. My banking source, for example, could check the records of any bank to find out how much some guy or gal had in his or her accounts. Information like that was very useful when I wanted to set up an extortion or put pressure on someone to take on a "new partner." It also gave me a way of finding out if a guy was really what he said he was in business. It stopped a lot of ringers from slipping through the cracks.

The tipster I had in Bell Canada was equally important. She could provide me with any unlisted telephone number in Canada within two hours after it was activated. She could get me the numbers and the addresses of people I wanted to check out. That made her very valuable, particularly when I wanted to harass or threaten someone in an extortion or when I wanted to be sure that I had the right address for a bombing target. A number of bikers that I know of had sources in Bell Canada.

Some provided the information because they liked the biker, others because they were paid, and still others because they were afraid the biker would hurt them or their families.

Very often bikers need new identification—like driver's licenses and credit cards—to hide from the cops or just to run up tabs on somebody else's credit. While I was a biker, one of my best sources was a Canadian postal worker. He could come up with driver's licenses and major credit cards—like American Express, Visa, and Mastercard—whenever I needed them. He'd snatch them from the mails for me, and all he wanted for his troubles was a bottle of whiskey. Sometimes there were bonuses of twenty dollars for a credit card and fifty dollars for a license, but that was it.

At one time I had five different driver's licenses. I can't count the credit cards I got from him and used to buy thousands of dollars' worth of goods. Scores of other bikers had similar sources, who could get them the documents they needed for identity changes. Hell, we supplied other bikers, many from the States, with licenses and credit cards and other identity documents that they needed to hide from the cops.

There were other biker sources who gave up information for some drugs, like cocaine or speed or Quaaludes. Still others wanted to be entertained by women, and that's something all biker clubs had plenty of —women who did what they were told. Whatever the price, the bikers in every club had information networks that kept them aware of what the cops were doing and who they were looking for and what rival biker gangs were up to.

To hide from cops or rival gang members you needed more than new identities. Just as important were places to hide—safe houses. Every gang had safe houses, safe harbors, or cool-off areas that wanted gang members could hide out in.

Because of our relationship with the Outlaws in the States, members of the Choice had places they could hide out in North Carolina, Georgia, Florida, Tennessee, Indiana, Illinois, and in the Southwest. The Outlaws, in turn, could smuggle their "hot" gang members into Canada to hide in our safe houses in Richmond Hill, in Concord, or up in the remote areas of the North, where we owned farmhouses and other places under the names of people who fronted for us.

I recall one Choice member who was easily identifiable because of his

tatoos. We called him Charlie Brown, but that wasn't his real name. Mother, who was a tatoo expert, changed all his tatoos. The club even got him a job for a transfer company in Saint Catharines and told him to keep a low profile and stay away from the clubhouse.

Charlie Brown did what he was told and stayed hidden for a long time. It was as though he had disappeared from the face of the earth. Charlie finally broke the rules and was eventually caught and sent back to the States, where he was wanted for a number of crimes. If he had paid attention to the rules, the cops would still be looking for him. We knew every move the cops made in trying to find him through people we had who kept tabs on car dispatches, fugitive warrants, and police computer information.

Howard Berry of the Choice's Peterborough chapter was wanted in Ontario for shooting a guy in Peterborough at point-blank range with a .303 caliber rifle. Needless to say, the guy he shot died, so Berry took off. He was smuggled across the border and went to Georgia and a safe house of the Outlaws. I heard later Berry was tested by the Georgia Outlaws to see how tough he was. They beat him up once, but not before he'd beaten the hell out of some of them. They accepted him after that.

Berry had always been tough—one of the toughest of the Choice. But in Georgia he went bananas. He got involved in some homicides with the Outlaws, and he was charged with stealing military equipment—automatic weapons and a tank—from an army base. When the cops grabbed him, they found he was wanted in Canada for the shooting and he was deported. He got eight years. Like Charlie Brown, he didn't stay cool, so the cops caught him. I guess nobody can stay cooped up in safe houses for long. Bikers got to be out doing things—usually bad—and that leads to their downfall.

PART TWO

Hustling with the Rounders

CHAPTER 7

World of the Rounders

Between the violent, undisciplined life of the outlaw biker gang and the secrecy and tradition of the Calabrian Mafia is a strange, independent criminal world the public knows little or nothing about—the world of the rounder. It's a world I grew close to early in my life as a biker and later as a enforcer–hit man for Calabrians like the Commissos.

In a sense, Canada's rounders are like the criminals that police in the States call crime associates, of the Cosa Nostra or the Mafia. They operate independently in gambling and loan-sharking, they set up dope deals and hijackings, and they sell their services to organized groups like the Mafia. In Canada the rounders, unlike stateside crime associates, don't owe allegiance to anybody but themselves, and they deal with all types of organized groups, whether Chinese tongs and triads, outlaw bikers, or Calabrian and Sicilian Mafia crime families.

The term *rounder* has been used in Canada for the last twenty years or more. A rounder is really a street person who knows hundreds of other people that operate around bars and clubs, that sell dope, gamble, and deal in stolen or hijacked goods. Rounders always dress well. No matter where you go, whether it's a high-class or average hotel, whether you barhop, whether you go to the best clubs, you'll find a rounder or maybe several, and you'll always find them in classy, expensive clothes.

They are the people with connections. They're rough, they're tough, and they know where to get the things you need and want. At one of the

better bars, Joe the Rounder can get you a pound of grass on a moment's notice, if you got the money and if someone's vouched for you. And there's Ken the Rounder at one of the class hotel discos. If you come with the right word and enough money, he can hustle up an ounce or more of coke faster than you can reach for your wallet.

Rounders answer to no one—not to the Commisso brothers, not to Paul Volpe when he was alive, not to Vincent Cotroni before he died, not to Danny Mo of Toronto's Kung Lok Triad before he went to jail for robbery, not to members of Satan's Choice or Hell's Angels or any other gang. They answer to themselves. They're on the street to make money and to survive. They deal with other street people, but it's their connections—for guns, for drugs, for women, for gambling, and for stolen goods—that make them important to the criminal world.

Go to a racetrack where everybody seems to know each other and you'll see little cliques there, groups of ten guys or less hanging around, working out deals. These are the people that the Italian mobs would come to see if they wanted to find out something. They are the people that the cycle gangs would go to learn about jobs, or places to deal speed, or people to unload guns and counterfeit currency with. They are the guys who can cut deals for anyone and everyone. They all think they know people in the mob. A lot do and a lot more don't, but they shoot the shit about it, and when push comes to shove they use the right connects to get the job done.

Rounders would rather stay away from bikers, but they can't because a lot of them were bikers before they became rounders.

One of the toughest rounders I ever knew was Andy the Rounder. He and two of his fellow rounders, a guy they called Bobby and a black man named Billy, were tough enough to take on eight of the toughest members of the Toronto chapter of Satan's Choice in a bar called The Trick. The Choice bikers dragged them into the parking lot, beat them and then ran over one or two of them. Andy kept on fighting, even though he was outnumbered four or five to one. He really mauled one of the bikers— broke his jaw with just one punch. When he got through wrecking him, Andy went after a biker who had tried to run him down. The biker finally escaped, but not before Andy had smashed the car's windows and windshield with his fists.

Andy the Rounder was about five foot nine and about 170 pounds with curly, blond hair. Sometimes he wore a beard and sometimes he was clean shaven, but he was always dressed in a suit or slacks with a sharp shirt and he was always neat. I personally found out how tough he was at a hotel up at Wasaga Beach. I was there with another rounder, who was a sort of friend and business associate, when I heard some loud yelling in a hotel across the street. I went over to see what was going on. I saw that the guy who was screaming all kinds of curse words at Andy was a member of the Toronto Choice.

Right then and there I should have turned around, walked back into the hotel, and minded my own business. I didn't, and suddenly the Choice biker jumped Andy, knocked him down, and began pounding his head on the floor. My rounder friend decided to help Andy. The next thing I knew I was in the middle. A friend of Andy's decided I was the enemy and took a swing at me. I knocked him out. Then Andy turned and came after me. He said something I didn't like, and I hit him as hard as I could—knocked him down. He got right up and I knocked him down again. This time I kicked him in the head to keep him down. It was like kicking a block of wood.

Whew! What a guy! No matter how many times I knocked him down, he got up. Now we were in the street, and cars were roaring by, and we were still swinging. I grabbed him and tried to push his head into the wheel of a car. It didn't work. By then the cops were on the scene, and Andy was fighting them.

I saw no point in hanging around. I took off to get away from the cops. What set Andy off that night? He just didn't like bikers, and he was in the hotel drinking when some members of the Toronto Choice came in. He decided he was going to fight them.

Funny thing. About a year after that brawl, Andy started hanging around with some members of the Choice that I knew, and they began bringing him to the clubhouse, where he started to make some friends. By then he had calmed down and was busy making dope deals with the bikers. He was handling a pound of speed and more at a clip that he bought from a biker who'd been a rounder and had organized a drug ring that manufactured hundreds of pounds of speed, selling it at $8,000 a pound.

Andy and the more important rounders during the late 1970s hung out at one of the bars at the Hyatt Hotel. The Hyatt bar was popular with the rounders because one of them, a guy I'll call Roger, had two waitresses working for him. Their job was to spot trouble, usually in the form of cops trying to slip in undercover. When they spotted the cops or any other people who might be there to cause trouble, they were to tip him off. He, in turn, would tell us and the rounders he dealt with so we could cool any deals we had working before the coppers got onto us. Only Roger knew who the waitresses were.

Roger controlled the distribution of cocaine to rounders at that club. It wasn't unusual to see a dozen or more rounders meet with Roger to make multiounce buys. Sometimes they'd buy even more. Sometimes Roger the Rounder was a buyer instead of a seller, particularly when it came to speed. He could handle two, three, or more pounds at a time. He wanted pure speed, not speed that had been stepped on, or cut.

Roger's demand for pure speed and the willingness of Satan's Choice lab suppliers to deliver it to him were what eventually brought a lot of heat down on everyone, costing a lot of people some really big money. Roger drew the attention of some crooked narcotics investigators. Eventually they caught him with a big load of the pure speed. Instead of busting him, they took his supply as a patch or payoff and said good-bye. It was the beginning of a lot of patches for dope dealers after that. A patch means they took your proceeds from crime—like drugs, or illegal guns, or gamblers' money—and kept it and you said nothing about what they did if you wanted to stay out of jail.

Roger kept his mouth shut and took the loss as part of the cost of business. Later on, he went to jail on another big speed bust. Other dealers —most of them rounders—had the same business expenses, since the narcs started hustling everyone.

These payoffs went on for years in the 1970s. The favored technique was to hit a gambler or a drug dealer with a minor summary charge that could land him six months or more in jail. If the Rounder gave the narcs the patch without any trouble, they would either drop the charge in court or they'd make sure he got probation or a fine with no jail sentence. That way they covered their asses on the bust and no one was the wiser. It wasn't only narcs pulling that scam—there were other coppers involved, and none of them ever got caught to my knowledge.

One of those who had to shut his mouth about a patch was Jim Lyons before he was murdered. His patch was a little different than some of the others. He had been charged with assault and was facing a long jail sentence. One day some coppers told him they could help him out if he came up with six handguns for them. Lyons didn't have them, but he went to a lot of his friends to get them. I supplied him with a .357 Magnum, a brand-new one I had just gotten. Other bikers gave him some other handguns. I helped him put the handguns in a sandbox on the side of Woodbine Avenue, as he was told to by the cops. Then we sat back where nobody could spot us and watched the cops drive up and put the guns in their unmarked car. The charges against Lyons were dropped a short time later.

I recall one time when I was charged with a break and entry. The guy I had with me had picked the wrong place to hit—the home of a cop's sister. Someone spotted us leaving the house and got the license number of the car we were driving. Two weeks later I was arrested. That was the day I found out that the house I'd hit was that of the arresting cop's sister. Now this cop was no graft taker. He wasn't looking for a patch, but he played the same kind of game that some of the patch takers did.

"You know the house you broke into was my sister's," the cop said.

"No, I didn't know, honest," I replied.

"No, eh?" he grunted. "Well listen to me, Cec. You just make sure that everything you took gets back. If you do, I'll see to it the charges get dropped."

I got the message loud and clear. As soon as I got out of the courthouse, I gathered all the stuff that we'd taken and put it in a plastic bag. Then I placed it on the side of the road in front of an old Satan's Choice clubhouse and called the detective involved. He picked it up. A few days later I appeared in court in Richmond Hill and the charges were dropped. The detective told the judge that the police had no way of identifying me with the case and that, as a result, they wanted to withdraw the charge. And that's what the judge did.

A little over two years ago that detective was killed while he was on patrol. He was gunned down in front of a warehouse where somebody was involved in a break and entry. I was sorry to hear about that. He was a decent cop—one I could trust. He had given his word to me and when

I delivered he kept his end of the bargain. He wasn't a crook. He just stretched the rules a bit to help his sister.

There were a lot of rules we played by with the cops that were unusual. There were times, for example, when we—whether we were bikers, rounders, or Mafia hoods—got caught cold turkey on a crime and we'd try to cut a deal through our attorneys before the preliminary hearing. We might want to plead guilty and take a six-month sentence rather than face a long jail term or an extended trial that cost a lot of money and took us out of circulation for a long time.

One time, six members of Satan's Choice and myself were charged with break and entry and the theft of motorcycles and other stolen property, including a handgun. I wasn't there when the cops raided the Choice garage and found the stolen motorcycle parts, but I got charged with a couple of deals. To make sure they'd nail me, the cops took my handgun, which they'd found in the raid, and wrote my name on the back of the holster. Our attorney told all of us after the preliminary hearing that we were cooked—that we'd better make a deal before the case went to a higher court for trial. If we fought it, he said, we'd get a minimum two years in the pen. If we didn't fight it, we'd get between four and six months each.

It was clear to all of us we couldn't beat the charges. What evidence the cops didn't get they'd rigged. So we made the deal and I got six months.

One of the most active areas for rounders was and still is Toronto's Airport strip, an area filled with bars, motels, and hotels. There were several popular hangouts there in those days—Attilla's Cave at the Hilton Hotel and the Skyline Hotel—where most of the gambler rounders used to hang their hats.

One of the most active was Walter (Wally) Chomski, a professional gambler–loan shark who worked with a Greek gambler who always made sure Wally won in the high-stakes card games at the Skyline. Chomski and the gambler rounders worked a strictly nighttime operation, ending their games at five or six in the morning, after $50,000 or more had changed hands.

For a long time Chomski was close to Johnny (Pops) Papalia, one of

Ontario's most important crime bosses. While he was operating around the Skyline and other rounder hangouts, Chomski got in some heavy trouble with Johnny Pops. The word among the rounders was that he owed Johnny Pops a lot of money. The next thing I knew, in December 1974, Chomski had his right leg torn off when a bomb that had been planted in his Lincoln Continental exploded. The cops said the force of the explosion ripped the transmission loose and sent it up through the car, tearing up Chomski's leg.

They never solved the bombing. There were too many suspects, they said, and no one was talking, least of all Chomski. I heard he took care of his problem, whatever it was. He must have. He was allowed to keep operating, and he had no more trouble with the mob. In 1984 he and his son were arrested on charges of running a $750,000-a-year loan-shark operation.

There were a number of rounder gambler operations going every night. Chomski and his partner might work the Skyline on a given night, while other groups of two to four rounders would be working games at the Cambridge Hotel across the street.

There were also other groups working games at banquet halls like the Casa Commisso, where one of the Commissos' uncles controlled the action. The uncle knew all the cardsharps, and sometimes he'd let them in, and sometimes he wouldn't. When he did, he'd tell them that they had to pay a kickback on all their winnings to the Commissos. Then he'd let the suckers sit down and get taken—all but his close friends and relatives.

The gambling rounders had games all over town—at the Royal York, the Care Inn, the Holiday Inn, the Bristol Palace Hotel, and the Constellation. Their general routine was to hang out in the hotel bars or the coffee shops to make their connections. They weren't big drinkers because they had to keep their minds on business. They didn't cut deals with the hotel employees or management because they didn't want to share their money with anyone. They trusted no one. I've seen them, after they'd played cards, search each other to see if they were cheating. It was crazy.

To set up their games, they'd get rooms to play in, sometimes through hotel security people, who they did pay off to make sure they weren't raided or ripped off. They would target particular hotels when they knew

there were to be big banquets or conventions or stag dinners. Some of the rounders were members of Kiwanis, the Lions Club, the Rotary, and through those memberships they would get lists of upcoming events to hit. They would know a week or two ahead of time where to go for the action, whether it was Ottawa, Montreal, Saint Catharines, Niagara Falls, Saint Thomas, or London.

No matter where the gambling rounders played, they rigged the games, set the gaff. They always had a gaff for something. They used dice that were mercury loaded. The heat from their hands would make the mercury set on the numbers they wanted to turn up. Sometimes they switched dice so fast no one spotted what they were doing.

I remember one rounder playing a high-stakes dice game at the Beverly Hills Hotel in Toronto. He was throwing the dice out and everyone was losing. It was about 2:00 A.M. when he rolled the dice again, and this time three of the suckers came clicking out. His hands moved like greased lightning. He grabbed the fuckin' things so fast no one else noticed, but I saw it and I thought to myself—oh shit, nobody saw it because they were too busy drinking. He was palming two dice as he threw out dice to make the number he wanted, and that once, one of those palmed dice slipped.

There was a game where they spun a top. The way the rounder spun it he always won. The sucker always spun it the wrong way and lost. The cards were rarely marked. They didn't have to be. The rounders dealing could make any card they wanted come up, and I defy anyone to spot what they were doing.

One event stands out in my memory above all others. It happened on the Mariposa Boat, a place owned by Don Pressey, one of the Commissos' associates. The event was a stag party for a rounder named George.

George was one of several guys who had robbed a bank in Winchester more than fifteen years before, getting more than a million bucks in cash, money that was for the payroll of the Windsor racetrack. George and his friends were caught after they tied up all the bank employees. So he went to jail. When he was paroled, he was broke, so the rounders of Toronto decided to hold a stag and raise money to give him a new start.

At the time, I was working for the Commissos. They knew I was going to work with the rounders to help raise money for George. At the club were a lot of outlaw bikers from Toronto and Kitchener. Among other

things, most bikers are degenerate gamblers. They piss their money away in games, and half the time they know those games are rigged. But in this case they didn't believe the games were rigged because I was playing, and I wasn't known to be a gambler—in fact, I had never played poker before.

I sat down at a table with one of the rounders I knew, who had given me some general instructions on how to play. I was sitting in the game for a rounder who couldn't make the party. A number of bikers were playing, among them Ernie, the president of the Toronto chapter of Satan's Choice. He was blowing $500 every hand. So were some others in the game. I just sat there drinking—almost drunk—as the rounders dealt me winner after winner—flushes, full houses, three aces, straights, you name it, I got it. Finally, Ernie stood up and started to leave, but before he did he looked me up and down and shook his head.

"Kirby," he said, "I never seen you play before, but I gotta tell you—you are the luckiest mother I ever saw pick up a card." Then he turned around without another word and left the club. He had dropped more than $4,000 in the game.

That night I won over $10,000. The other rounders in the game dealt me the hands that couldn't lose. They knew no one would suspect it was a crooked game with me as the big winner.

Several times they tried to deal me some losers so it wouldn't look too bad. I almost screwed up their strategy by drawing cards when I wasn't supposed to. A couple of times one of the rounders had to kick me under the table, hard, to make me stop playing bad hands that didn't have a prayer of winning and that I was supposed to fold with or only lose a small amount on.

When the game was all over, I met the rounders and gave them all but $100 of the money I'd won.

"Look," I told them, "just give me a hundred bucks and you keep the rest for George."

They all laughed, shook my hand, and bought me a few drinks. I was supposed to have kept half, but I'd had a helluva lot of fun and they'd really done all the work. It was worth it for me to see some of those bikers get ripped off, especially Ernie. He'd figured he was gonna clean me out in that game. It was worth it all to see the expression on his face when he left with his pockets empty.

Ernie should have known better in the first place. When you gamble with the rounder cardsharps, you'd better check to see if you still got your pants after a game. They can't play without cheating. It's in their blood. They've just gotta have that extra edge—they've gotta get something for nothing.

Ron the Rounder was like that. He was one of the best Italian rounders in the business, and he was an expert at gambling. I met Ron while I was a biker, and we quickly became friends. He had style, Ron did. He did everything with a flair. He made and lost literally millions of dollars in card games from Buffalo and Niagara Falls to Toronto and Montreal. He survived because he was close to the Italian mob, the Cosa Nostra in Buffalo, and the Calabrians in Niagara Falls. He played high-stakes card games with them, but Ron never cheated while playing with his Mafia friends. That's when he lost big sometimes, playing with them. They hustled him but he didn't hustle them. It wasn't healthy.

Because of his close association with the different Italian mob groups, Ron had a lot of action steered his way—suckers the mob dealt with but told him it was okay to work over. Of course, they expected and got a piece of his action.

Sometimes Ron worked the suckers with the best gambler in all of Toronto, Eddie Neuff. I could introduce you to a dozen gambler rounders and they'd all tell you the same thing—before he was killed, Eddie Neuff was *the best*. He was an independent, a rounder, but he lacked the protection some of the rounders like Ron had, who worked with different mobs. Eddie was well known in the States. He'd been barred from a number of casinos in Las Vegas and Atlantic City because he was too quick—a professional counter who could tell you how many aces or how many fives or whatever had been dealt and used that ability to make big bets on hands when the percentages favored him.

One of the suckers that Ron and Neuff really worked over was the owner of a prominent Italian food company in Toronto. The food dealer —I'll call him Giuseppe—was the kind of guy who'd bet on when the next raindrop would fall. He wouldn't listen to anyone—not his brother, not his family, not his friends—he just had to play in the high-stakes card games that Ron and Neuff were operating in a room at the Seaway Hotel.

Ron told me later that he had never played with a sucker for punish-

ment like Giuseppe. Night after night he would show up and play, and each night Ron and Neuff would take him off for $20,000, $50,000, $80,000. It was a dream come true for them.

Then one night Ron told me that Giuseppe had paid off in tens and twenties the night before. "He had a bag full of cash," he said, "and when he left he still was carrying a lot with him, maybe twenty thousand dollars or more."

"Does he keep all that money at home?" I asked.

Ron looked up at the ceiling like he saw a pot of gold on top of the rainbow instead of at the end. He reached into his pocket, took out Giuseppe's address, and handed it to me.

"Why don't you break into his house some night?" he said. "There's a helluva lot of money in there. This guy always pays in cash, and he comes to the game straight from his home." He paused for a minute, letting what he'd said sink in. "You get into his place and sack it and whatever you get just give me half—the rest is yours."

I knew I couldn't handle it alone, so I called a biker friend named Brooks to help me and we headed for Giuseppe's home. No one was there and we broke in. We couldn't have been inside ten minutes when Giuseppe pulled in his driveway. We both ran out the back door, and as we ran Brooks shouted, "Cec, I got some money out of a fuckin' bag—I don't know how much. There was a lot more—but I didn't have time to grab it, goddamnit."

We got back to the car we'd parked near a school and started counting the money. There was over $8,000 in fifty- and one-hundred-dollar bills. We'd missed the big bundle, the big stash because we hadn't made sure he was gonna be gone for a lot longer before we broke in. I gave Ron $4,000, and Brooks and I split the rest.

Ron laughed when I told him what had happened, but not so hard that he didn't take his cut. Later he told me that every gambling rounder in town tried to get in on the action, get a piece of this food dealer. Ron and Eddie had milked him for hundreds of thousands, but like all good things it came to an end. Giuseppe's family found out he was squandering their profits, and they forced him to stop. Not long after that, Giuseppe died.

Ron was so good that he started to run his own school for card cheats,

particularly for some of his Italian mob friends—charging them $100 for each lesson. He got a lot of people hot at him for doing that. It was really stupid. He was teaching newcomers a technique that's supposed to be kept inside the gambler-rounders' organization. There were maybe thirty professional card cheats in the city who worked the big card games. For a lousy $100 a lesson, Ron was giving away the road map to a gold mine.

Neuff, on the other hand, wasn't so lucky. He became the target of a gunslinger rounder friend of mine who had also been a member of Satan's Choice for a while. Neuff ran into this rounder and his sidekick, a biker who was later killed because he knew too much about this particular rounder.

I'll have to call the rounder Billy and his sidekick Al. Billy the Rounder has a number of convictions, but none of them is for murder. He doesn't leave witnesses around. He's been involved in one way or another in at least six killings, but he always slips through the cracks. They never nailed him for the Neuff case. There was one guy who could have nailed him for Neuff and for some other cases, and that was Al. He was an eyewitness, but he's not around anymore. The irony is Al wasn't the kind of guy who would have become an informer against Billy. He thought the world revolved around that rounder buddy of his.

For years, the coppers thought that Neuff had crossed some Mafia bigwig or some other big organized crime guy and been knocked off. His body was found January 5, 1979, stuffed in the trunk of a car at the Toronto International Airport. He'd been shot repeatedly. It took four days to thaw out his body at the Metro morgue and figure out how he'd been killed.

The last he was seen alive was in a Toronto restaurant on December 12, 1978. He was supposed to be married three days later. Five years later they found the body of Toronto Mafia boss Paul Volpe shot and stuffed in the trunk of his car at the same airport. For a while some cops speculated that Volpe may have been killed by the same assassin. Maybe he was.

Al told me before he was killed himself that Billy the Rounder did Neuff, and I know he was telling the truth, although I wasn't there to witness it. Seems Al and Billy had a guy in New York who was giving them some terrific tips on football games—on what teams were going to win and by how many points. This guy was right about 90 percent of the time,

according to Al. Al said that he and Billy were paying this tipster for his information. He got a kickback on the money they won by taking off all the bookies in Canada with their bets.

For weeks they were having a field day busting out a lot of bookies. One of those they busted took off before paying off thousands of dollars. Billy the Rounder and Al went looking for him. They searched for him at his home, at his clothing store, at all his regular haunts, but he was nowhere to be found.

Billy was furious. "I'm gonna get that bastard, Cec," he shouted one night. "So help me I'm gonna get that little fuck and bury him." I don't know if he did, but he also made one other promise that night. "The next fuckin' bookie that rips me off, I'm gonna fuckin' do him," he said.

Al told me that that next bookie was Neuff. They started betting heavily with him and winning. He smelled a rat and on the last bet wouldn't pay off. So they shot Neuff and dumped him to make an example of him. Bookies throughout Canada understood the message.

While rounders would turn themselves inside out to help a fellow rounder like George, a lot of the rounders I knew had a cheap streak, too. Most of them never paid a bill in a restaurant. They were good at this —really good. They had a technique that few people could follow. All but one of the rounders in a group would leave, and the last guy, the guy with the bill, would walk up to the register. The waitress would be watching him. But he'd stick the bill in his pocket and ask the gal or guy at the register for change for the phone. That was it. He'd be handed the change, the waitress would think he'd paid his bill, and he'd walk to the phone so the person at the register would think he was making a call. They'd stop watching him, and before they realized it he'd be gone. No one would figure it out later, either, because the bill would never turn up to show a cash register shortage.

Rounders, like a lot of outlaw bikers, were also boosters, store thieves who either acted like shoplifters or did the smash-and-grab bit at jewelry stores—smash the front window, grab what they can, and be far from the scene in less than three minutes. Ron was a great booster of Royal Doulton china and figures, and he was good at it.

One of the best smash-and-grab thieves around was a Satan's Choice

biker, Armand Sanguigni, who was found dead with his girlfriend on October 15, 1984, from a heroin overdose—a hotshot that someone he trusted had given him. Whoever dosed him figured Armand was a junkie, and junkies sooner or later talk if they can't get their supply of dope. So a friend did Armand. It's always a friend who does you in this business. That's why you try not to trust anyone. Sooner or later, though, we all make that one mistake. I'm trying not to get suckered that way, but you never know.

Sanguigni was Italian. He'd grown up in Toronto's Little Italy. When he wasn't racing around on his bike with members of the Choice, or peddling dope, or hustling counterfeit bills, he was busy boosting from jewelry stores. It was a sideline that he made $3,000 to $4,000 a month at.

Sanguigni wasn't a particularly good fighter, but he sure as hell was no coward. He was only five foot seven in his stocking feet, and I can't remember him ever weighing over 145 pounds, even when he wore a heavy black beard and mustache and his hair long.

Sanguigni was a fast talker, and his main topic was always sports or gambling. He was always at the track when it was open, gabbing with friends and rounders and betting his shirt. One day in 1978 he and a friend of his, a rounder turned biker turned rounder named Kenneth Goobie, came to the house of a friend of the Commissos to pick up some funny money. I was at the house when they made the pick up—$300,000 in counterfeit U.S. twenties. The next day they had sold it all off— peddled it all over Toronto after paying the Commissos fifteen cents on the dollar.

It couldn't have been two days later before there was a story in the paper about the town being flooded with the counterfeits, which became so hot nobody wanted to touch them.

The funny thing was that the counterfeit money had been hot for a couple of years. The Commissos and the Calabrian Mafia had peddled the stuff around New York—particularly in Long Island and Brooklyn. And they'd pushed it in Connecticut through pizza parlors the Calabrian Mafia controlled or could influence.

They moved hundreds of thousands of dollars of the funny money in the States, and they moved a lot of it in Vancouver with the help of the

Vancouver mob and an Italian friend of theirs named Carmelo Gallo. In 1976 the roof caved in on that operation because they sold the money to an undercover agent. They were all convicted.

Later Gallo was part of a plot they wanted me to get in on to take down an armored truck in Vancouver that was supposed to be carrying a couple of million bucks. That scam fell through, but Gallo was busted a short time later in an international heroin scheme. He got a life sentence, but he escaped before he could do his time.

For a while things cooled down over the money that Goobie and Sanguigni flooded the market with. But a lot of people—a lot of bikers and rounders—had to sit with thousands of dollars' worth of the phony bills. Andy the Rounder got stuck with a big bundle. Goobie even got burned. He gave $20,000 in bills to a biker they called Jerry, who was a member of the Last Chance. Jerry was supposed to sell it, but he ended up losing it. Rather than face Goobie, he took off.

Goobie tried to hunt him down. I even went with Goobie one night to try and find him. No luck. Goobie did the next best thing. He took Jerry's bike and sold it about a year later. I got about $200 out of the deal.

But that didn't end the tale of the counterfeit twenties. About a year later, in 1979, I did a favor for Cosimo Commisso, and he told me he had some counterfeit money I could have if I wanted it. I thought, what the hell, it's cool now, maybe I can move it and make a quick buck, so I said sure.

"You know, Cec," he said, "that money's been nothing but a pain in the ass. I got pinched with it. Remo, he got pinched with it. Everybody that's touched that fuckin' stuff's been caught."

Cosimo let it sink in. He was letting me know I could land in trouble if I handled the money he was offering me.

"When we first got this stuff," he said, "we had this whole room just piled high with the money. We had about twenty million bucks."

Cosimo didn't say where they had held the money, but he said he had a guy that was still holding $20,000. "You get in your van," he said, "and you drive down to this place on Bloor Street. You park your van in the parking lot, leave your doors unlocked, and take a walk for about an hour. When you come back, the money, she'll be waiting for you. But you be careful when you try to unload. It's jinxed."

I did what he told me, and when I came back the money was there waiting. It was the same kind of funny money that Goobie had gotten. I took it north to a cottage I had and buried it. About a year later I came back to move it. When I dug it up it was soaked, even though I'd wrapped in carefully and put it in a container.

I didn't let a little water discourage me. I took it back to the city, dried it out, and then examined it to see if it could be used. The bills must have been cut by a butcher. Some were short, some were long—it was terrible. I picked up, stacked, and wrapped it and brought it to Ron, who gave me $300 for the whole load. The last time I saw that funny money was in November 1980, when biker Gary Barnes came out of prison. He stopped by my house to say hello and pulled out a roll of the bills.

"For chrissake, Gary," I shouted, "where the hell did you get that shit? Get that crap outta my house. I'm tired of seeing it. It's the same stuff we had years ago."

Gary had gotten the money from Goobie and Sanguigni, who were supposed to be his friends. The trouble was, they didn't tell him how hot the money was.

It couldn't have been a week later when Barnes started passing the money. Somebody took a license number off the car he was using and the cops traced it back to him and busted him. I felt bad about that when I heard it. I liked Barnes. He was a pretty easygoing guy, not the world's smartest, but tough and a stand-up guy, who stood up with you in a tight spot. I remember when I came back from vacation in Acapulco in February 1978—he was sharing a place with me at the time—I had pneumonia. I was with my girlfriend and I drank a bottle of tequila. The next thing I remember was Barnes carrying me into the Humber Memorial Hospital in the West End of Toronto. I probably would have died if he hadn't taken care of me.

CHAPTER 8

Call Them Treacherous

Burglary, safecracking, counterfeiting, murder, arson, extortion, prostitution, motorcycle thefts, insurance frauds, gang wars—all of that and more was a part of my everyday life as an outlaw biker. You either live with it, become part of the action, or you don't survive—you become an outcast and sooner or later you become very dead.

At least some of these activities provide a source of income to the biker. But for the biker who was ambitious and wanted to make a bigger buck, moving narcotics was where the real action and the big money were. It was also where the violence could always be found, where gang wars started and where killings were part of the territory.

I first got involved in the narcotics traffic through Ken Goobie. A lot of bikers that I knew dealt in narcotics, but, until I hooked up with Goobie, I'd pretty much steered clear of it except for smoking a reefer now and then. I never thought much of the dope dealers. I still don't. They can't be trusted and Goobie was no exception, although it took me a little longer than usual to realize it.

I first met Goobie in 1970. He was only twenty-two then, but he was big and tough, with a quick and violent temper that had already cost him more than a year in jail for assault. We took an almost immediate liking to each other because, I think, he was such a good fighter, and in those days he backed off to no man. He was six foot, 170 pounds, a little bald on top with long hair down the sides, and he wore a mustache—he was

never without that mustache. He had done some amateur boxing, winning two or three while fighting at the Lansdown Boxing Club.

He had already earned a reputation as a tough rounder in the downtown area of Toronto, where he battled in bars, dabbled in selling small quantities of dope, ran around with lots of women, and burglarized homes whenever he was broke. He was forever joking around and shadowboxing with everybody in bars and restaurants that he frequented. Behind all that fun loving and kidding around was a cool character who had a brain that was always click-clacking—figuring ways to make a quick buck.

In the beginning, I went on some burglary jobs with him after a friend of mine, a gambler we called Johnny the Hat, told me Goobie was like a cat when it came to pulling a job. He was right. Whenever we were broke, Goobie would come up with some place we could break into that had coin collections or money stashes or some other gimmick. He had good connections who tipped him, and we used them to get some loot to fall back on. It wasn't always wine and women though. There were some tough times. I remember days and weeks when things were so bad moneywise that we slept in the car of another biker because we didn't have enough for a room. But that didn't last long.

In 1972 Goobie, after I'd introduced him to a number of members, decided he wanted to join Satan's Choice. He did his striking period, and within a year he'd stepped up the ladder to become one of the biggest outlaw biker dealers in narcotics. Two of his suppliers were my friends Harry the Hat and Patsy Perry, both gambler-rounders who had connections for large quantities of speed from biker methamphetamine labs on both sides of the border.

Harry the Hat and Perry, who's dead now, could come up with five to ten pounds a week for Goobie, who was paying them $4,500 a pound for the speed and selling it to bikers and rounders, to pimps and prostitutes in the hotels and bars around Toronto's West End for more than $8,000 a pound after he'd diluted it once or twice.

In the early stages of his operation, Armand Sanguigni was Goobie's number-one guy—his trusted courier and distributor. I became his banker and a sometime courier. Many times I would have to take the money that Goobie and Sanguigni were pulling in from the operation to a restaurant

to meet Harry the Hat, pay him for dope that had already been sold, and insure future deliveries.

It was an operation with high profits and equally high risks. Typical of those risks was a period when a lot of American money was coming in to pay for drug buys. Goobie told me he and Sanguigni were selling quantities of speed to a rounder and safecracker known as Irish Danny. Danny had some kid working for him named Larry, who was caught by the Horsemen (the RCMP).

The Horsemen turned this kid into an informer, and before long they were buying the narcotics from Goobie and others using American money. Eventually, Harry the Hat, Perry, and Goobie were all busted for trafficking in speed, but Goobie beat the rap. They never got to me, although I was the one with the American money, and I was the one using about ten different banks to convert it to Canadian currency.

The Horsemen never knew, or never had enough evidence to prove I was involved, and they never charged me with anything. By then I was making better than $1,000 a week, which isn't a helluva lot to some big-time cocaine dealer, but in 1973 and 1974 it was more than most of the big industrial executives and politicians were making as salaries, and it was a helluva lot more than any of the Horsemen were making.

It wasn't long after that that the Horsemen got Sanguigni. The day he got nailed he'd been at my apartment. I watched him as he crossed the street to his car. He was throwing a gym bag he carried up in the air like a basketball—higher and higher—playing catch with himself. The bag was filled with speed, better than two pounds.

As I watched him I remember thinking to myself—what a dummy! He's walking across that goddamned parking lot throwing $13,000 up in the air like it's nothing. He got into his car and he made it almost to the heart of Toronto when the Horsemen stopped him—smashed into him and drove him off the round. That ended his effectiveness as a courier. He got two years in jail for it.

With Sanguigni in jail, I had to do a lot of the courier work for Goobie, and he had to watch over the money. By 1976 he had developed another major source of supply and he was selling big amounts to the Peterborough

Satan's Choice, to the Kitchener Choice, and to some of the more trusted rounders, including one I called Roger the Dodger.

I made most of the big deliveries to Roger. I was storing the stuff in a gym that I bought later on and turned into a health club. I used to stash the speed in the boiler room on top of the vents—usually ten pounds or more at a time.

Goobie would make the connection with the buyers and come to the gym to tell me where to meet them. I'd take out the amounts he had sold and deliver them to a drop-off location. I'd make sure the buyers picked it up, but I never took any of the money. Goobie saw to it that they paid him. For every pound I transported I got a lousy one hundred bucks. Goobie was getting ten times that. I was being hustled by Goobie and I knew it, but I wanted the money and I liked the excitement.

Goobie had an almost foolproof system. With one exception, he never touched the dope he was selling. As his courier, I never met the guy who was delivering the loads. That was my insurance policy. Goobie would send me to a place like York University, to a particular garbage can where a bag containing ten or fifteen pounds of the stuff had been dropped. If the cops showed up, all they would see was another bum rifling through a garbage can looking for some chicken parts or something.

Of course I took precautions to be sure I wasn't being followed. Sometimes I'd use different cars for pickups, other times a van. When I made deliveries, they were to people who Goobie or I knew. We never made deliveries to strangers. I had to be confident enough to meet with a buyer. I had to have known him for at least two or three years. When you sell to people you know, it's less likely you're going to get caught. There's always that chance, but it's less likely. The best system in the world is to sell to those you've known a long time. If you're stupid enough to sell to strangers, you might as well go into the cop shop and give yourself up.

The speed we were getting was like a rock. It was being brought from a biker lab to drop-off points where Goobie would be notified it was stashed. Usually it was in a locker at Oakdale, or at the Hillcrest Mall in Richmond Hill, or I'd find it underneath the rear of a trailer in a private parking lot late at night or inside a garbage container or garbage can at York University. It was never at the same location—always someplace

new, and each load would be ten to fifteen pounds, about the size of a briefcase. The most I picked up in one day was fifteen pounds in a suitcase left at the Hillcrest Mall. It was four inches thick and twenty inches long, and it was so hard I had to use a hammer to break it up for distribution.

I would put the stuff in a special briefcase, take it back home or some other place, and chop it up into five- and ten-pound pieces. Then I'd hide it at the gym or in a toolshed at my dad's or high in the rafters of a garage we had down the street.

Goobie never went near the dope himself except once that I can remember. He had decided to bypass me as a courier and save himself a couple of thousand. He sent the buyer to a parking lot off Yonge Street, telling him the load was stashed under a trailer. When the buyer got there he couldn't find it and came back to me and Goobie at the Beverly Hills Hotel screaming: "The stash isn't there, you bastard!"

"It's gotta be there," Goobie shouted back. "I'll get the shit myself."

Goobie calmed the buyer down and took off for the parking lot with me. When we got there, Goobie got out of the car and spent nearly an hour crawling around under trailers and cars until he finally found the stuff. What had happened was that the guy who owned the trailer had moved it and parked another car in the spot where the load had been stashed. Goobie found it underneath the car. It was the only time I saw Goobie handle a load of narcotics himself.

By 1977 I was pissed off about getting only one hundred dollars a pound, and I told Goobie how I felt.

"Look, Kenny," I said, "I want at least two hundred dollars a pound to handle this stuff. I'm doing a lot of work here—taking a lot of risks. I want a raise to two hundred dollars."

He agreed to up the ante to $150, and I accepted it. It wasn't long after that—maybe a few weeks—that I was stopped by the cops as I was driving a black van I owned. In the van was better than two pounds. The cops searched and searched but didn't find a thing. The load was stashed behind the panel of a back door.

It wasn't the first or the last time I had a close call. I was once following Sanguigni's car with my van when he suddenly speeded up and got about ten cars ahead of me. As I tried to keep sight of him, he went through an intersection. I had to stop for the light. Within seconds two Mounties'

cars went barreling through the red light after him. About an hour later I phoned him and asked what happened.

"Whaddya mean what happened?" he said. "Nothing. What should've happened?"

"Didn't you see the Mounties chasing you?" I asked.

"Hell no, there were no Mounties chasing me," he said.

"Armand—you're an asshole," I said angrily. I was transporting more than three pounds of speed. If the Mounties had stopped me after missing him I'd have been cold meat. I was lucky that time.

Later on Goobie and a guy from the Vagabonds developed a way to package speed that made it easy to slip by the Mounties and other narcotics agents. They molded the speed into a pie-plate shape—they called it pie-plate speed. It came in different sizes and weights, but the shape was the same. For a long time, the narcotics agents didn't realize that the "pies" that bikers were delivering and receiving were actually quantities of speed.

Goobie was making millions. I know because I was his banker. Every week I'd take $20,000 to $30,000 or more and move it through the banks, changing the money from Canadian to American currency. I can't remember ever being questioned by anyone at any of the banks. I'd usually change about $2,000 at each bank, never more than that, so they wouldn't ask questions. Once the money was changed, I'd arrange to wire it to relatives of Goobie's in the States, particularly California. I was just one of his couriers, and I handled over three hundred pounds of speed in a two-year period. That alone represented more than $2.4 million in sales, and Sanguigni must have handled double that or more before he was jailed.

What Goobie and Sanguigni didn't send across the border, they gambled away—especially Sanguigni. They were being taken like any suckers at a black crap table in the Yorkville area. Those blacks just loved Goobie and Sanguigni.

The games were rigged, of course, with loaded dice. Goobie dropped an average of $2,000 a night for months, sometimes more. He had the fever, and they kept his temperature high. You see, he wasn't smart enough to figure out why he was losing so much. He just had to throw those dice. He gambled in a lot of clubs in the area, and he bet his socks

on football games. I saw him bet $10,000 in just one day. Sanguigni was just as bad. He was blowing thousands a week on bookies and the tables. It was god-awful to see.

You would have thought that making money like that would have satisfied Goobie. After all, he had the Satan's Choice colors—that meant he was protected. He wouldn't get ripped off. If an outsider tried, the gang would come after him. That protection was implicit while you were a member of the Choice. It was an insurance policy for the narcotics business. Of course there were exceptions. You could become the target of members of another motorcycle gang, who would rip off your stash, or worse, kill you doing it.

Dope rip-offs became a way of life in the narcotics trade, and outlaw bikers very often used techniques that they saw police use in busting dope rings. In Satan's Choice we had a number of techniques, but the most popular and successful one was to use a girl or someone known on the street to buy dope from the dealers we wanted to set up. That's the way the cops did it. They'd have an informer or undercover agent make a buy and when they got the signal that the buy had been made and the dealer was carrying dope, they'd bust in to make the arrest.

Well, we did a variation on that technique. Our "agent" would be sent in to make a buy from the dealer, usually an ounce of speed or cocaine, and leave, making an arrangement to buy a couple of ounces on the next visit. The agent would reappear in a day or two to make the two-ounce buy. By then the dealer had confidence in our agent and was ready to be set up.

The agent would then make arrangements to buy a pound or more on a special date and at a prearranged place. Once he or she went in to make the buy, we came charging in behind, our guns drawn, shouting "this is the police" as we flashed phony identification. The dealer would freeze without a fight. Convinced we were the cops, the dealer would surrender his gun and say nothing as we confiscated his narcotics and weapons. It was only when we tied him up and left that he'd realize he'd been had.

We all knew who the dope dealers were and what quantities they handled before we hit an operation. When I went on a job, I always made sure we had it thoroughly cased. Because of that we never had a problem

on a dope rip-off. Others who handled rip-offs weren't always that careful.

There were always reports of a lot of shootings and beatings, like in the Rice Lake case I mentioned earlier. That started off as a drug rip-off, and two of the Choice bikers ended up shooting a guy, who they believed was a dealer. He was hit in the spine and ended up a cripple. There were four witnesses in the case, and one of them just happened to turn up at a motorcycle shop that was used by bikers. Armand Sanguigni and another biker recognized the witness. They grabbed him and brought him up to the Satan's Choice clubhouse at 7 Woodbine Avenue, where I saw him tied up and gagged in the trunk of the car.

About a week later I read in the paper that they'd found the guy in Rice Lake. The cops came and searched the clubhouse for the rope they used and other things, but nobody was ever charged with anything.

To me it didn't make sense to get rid of just one witness, but Sanguigni and the others thought it would scare off the others. It didn't. They testified, and Bill Dollack and Bob Cousins were convicted of assault and jailed. The cops never did solve the murder of the witness they found at Rice Lake.

Goobie's biggest rip-off was one that didn't require a phony holdup, just a phony story. The guy he took was our supplier, the chemist who manufactured the stuff for biker gangs at a hidden lab up near Sault Sainte Marie.

Goobie's principal supplier was a former Vagabond who ran a pinball machine company. The guy was also a pilot, and he had access to a plane that was used to fly to speed labs throughout Ontario, pick up loads, and peddle the speed wholesale for the biker clubs to guys like Goobie. Goobie, in turn, sold it to dealers of various biker clubs on both sides of the border.

One of the biggest operations was on a small island in the bush at Sault Sainte Marie, where some members of Satan's Choice had a big lab that manufactured speed and PCP, a hallucinogen that was very popular among college and high-school students. The lab operators eventually got busted, and more than one hundred pounds of PCP and speed was seized.

In 1977, Goobie spotted a newspaper report that said that one of his biggest buyers, an associate of the Vagabonds, had been arrested at the Detroit Airport with a "large quantity" of speed. What the article didn't

say was that the quantity was only two pounds. Goobie had just gotten fifteen pounds from our supplier. He told him that the buyer he'd sold the fifteen-pound load to had been busted and the entire load had been seized. He showed him the article and he bought the story. What really happened was that Goobie had sold off the fifteen pounds, including the two pounds, to his Detroit biker buyer, collected the money, and lost it all—more than $100,000—at the gaming tables. He lost so much at the black crap tables and with the bookies, in fact, that he fell behind in mortgage payments on one of his houses. The next thing I knew the house had burned down and Goobie had collected on the insurance. Funny thing about that fire. The only things that didn't burn to a cinder were about ten or twelve photo albums of his.

About a year later, the source Goobie had been using offered me the same deal he'd given Goobie. He'd provide me with the speed in whatever quantities I wanted and when I'd sold it off, I'd pay him. He wanted the same $4,500 a pound he was getting from Goobie wholesale. I turned the deal down. The risks were too great. After three years with Goobie and his crew, I knew you couldn't trust anyone you were dealing with. It wasn't worth it to me.

Until that happened, Goobie, Sanguigni, Mike Everet, and myself were a tight little clique in Satan's Choice. If one of us got in trouble, the rest would be there to help him. If one of us got involved in a fight, everyone jumped in to help, even when the odds were heavily against us. Sometimes we got into trouble helping a friend. Like Gary Barnes.

When Barnes got out of prison in 1978, he stayed with me for a short time. He borrowed a .22 caliber pistol I had with a silencer. Barnes got himself in trouble shooting up a tent full of people in Peterborough. He didn't hit anybody, but he shot it up, and he was jailed for parole violation and then charged with possession of a weapon dangerous to public peace.

When I went to his place the day after to get the silencer, I found out he'd used my .22 to shoot up the tent. I talked to Goobie, Evert, and Sanguigni about what had happened and about the witnesses that were stacked up against Barnes. We decided to see if we could help him by trying to persuade some of the people he was charged with shooting at not to testify in court.

When we got to the place where one witness was staying, we ran into

trouble that we didn't expect. We hadn't threatened him yet—we were just talking to him through a partially opened door, but I could see that he had a friend with a gun trained on us.

"Look," I tried to reason with him, "tell your friend we just came here to talk. We don't want trouble—we just want to talk."

The guy wasn't listening. His friend kept the rifle in his hands pointed at my belly. Then he started shouting at the four of us. I knew that if we stayed around it could only end up in a shoot-out, so I told the guy that we were going to leave and that we wanted no problems with him.

Two months later, in early 1979, we were charged by Terry Hall and some other biker cops with attempted obstruction of justice and attempted murder. We were all acquitted in a trial before a jury.

Under ordinary circumstances, we might have pleaded to a lesser charge, but a source I had knew a cop in Toronto Metro Police who was involved in the investigation. The cop, a detective from the thirty-first Division, had talked to some people about the case before we were arrested and said we were going to be charged with a crime. He didn't say exactly what the crime was. The cop also predicted after we were bailed out that we'd beat the case if we fought it—that there wasn't much evidence against us. My source heard about it and told us all we had to do was get a good lawyer. It was another instance of our sources being better than the cops'—good enough to help us beat charges that might have cost us a jail term.

There was a lot of drug smuggling going on in the late 1970s between motorcycle gangs in the States and Canada. One of the more profitable businesses that I knew about involved hashish smuggling from Jamaica to Toronto. It was run by members of the Last Chance and the Toronto Outlaws, who later became the Rebels. At that time moving cocaine wasn't as big as it is now, and bikers zeroed in on things like grass, hash, and speed.

Three of the bikers, including a former president of the Toronto Outlaws, had each invested $10,000 in the business. They'd send one of their girlfriends to Jamaica, where she'd pick up the load of hashish and hash oil, strap the stuff to her legs, and fly back via New York, where she'd change flights.

Once they sent three girls down, after giving them $15,000 each to pay

for the loads they were to bring back. The girls left Jamaica without any problem, but en route to the States they started partying and a sharp stewardess noticed that one of the girls had something taped to her legs. The stewardess, with the help of the pilot, tipped off customs before they landed in New York, and the customs agents pulled the girls off the plane, had them searched, and confiscated the hashish loads.

The bikers who had the big investment wanted to have the girls killed because they'd been so stupid, but they didn't. Two of them got tried in the States and got three years. The third girl was never extradited or tried, but the bikers lost one profitable smuggling business. Hash oil, in 1979, was selling for $500 a vial, an ounce, in Canada. The bikers were buying the stuff for $500 a pound in Jamaica, and each trip they were moving twenty pounds—loads worth $160,000 in Canada. That's a helluva return on a $30,000 to $45,000 investment.

A couple of years before I got out of the narcotics business with Goobie, I gave up my membership in Satan's Choice. It all happened in March 1976. At the time I was vice president of the Richmond Hill chapter.

The Choice was involved in insurance frauds that used phony thefts of motorcycles. What we would do was have some guy register motorcycles in his name. He'd then report them stolen, and the insurance company would send him a check, of $7,000 or more each, to cover the loss.

One of the front men we were using was a young guy who was rooming with a black kid. I'd had some trouble with both of them and had been a little nasty to his roommate. I didn't like blacks then—still don't. Outlaw bikers don't trust blacks, and it's rare to see a black biker riding with white bikers. You can say we're prejudiced. We do business with some of them, but we don't ride with them.

Anyhow, I'd chewed out this white guy for being late on some payoffs to us. He'd noticed, I guess, that I didn't take to blacks, and he decided to use that to get me. A week or so after I'd had problems with this kid, my wife started getting threatening letters and phone calls. The letters were written in a way to make her and me think that they were from a black.

I was wild. No black was going to threaten my wife or me. So I went to this black's house, but before I left I tucked a gun in my belt and went

to the Choice clubhouse to get some backup. There was just one guy there, Billy the Bum.

"I'm going down to face this nigger," I said to Billy, "and I wouldn't mind having you back me up in case something happens. All you gotta do is sit out in the car and keep an eye open in case some other people show up."

This bearded giant of courage looked up sort of lazily from where he was sitting and said, "Gee, Cec, I can't leave yet. I just ordered a pizza."

That blew my mind. I had helped this guy out of a few jams and never hesitated. I was steaming. It was a club rule that you always helped a fellow biker when he was facing trouble—you stood with him and fought with him. I'd always lived by that rule.

"You son-of-a-bitch," I shouted. "You just stay where you are and eat your fuckin' pizza. I'll do what I gotta do without you."

So I went alone that night to this black kid's boardinghouse. He'd moved to a different room after he and his roommate had a fight. I went there and talked to him calmly, all the time fingering my gun in case I ran into trouble.

First I pulled out the letters my wife had received. He looked them over and shook his head vigorously.

"I didn't write no letters to your wife," he said nervously. "I got no reason to."

"Maybe you did and maybe you didn't," I said. "You willing to give me a sample of your signature and handwriting and come to the clubhouse later? I'll make sure your ex-roommate is there and make him sign a piece of paper. I think he might have written them and tried to get you in trouble for it."

"Sure," he said. "I got nothin' to hide."

We set a time to meet, and as I left six big black bucks were out on the street waiting for me. Each of them had a gun. If anything had happened with the kid, they were going to gun me down. They let me pass without any trouble.

The next night the black kid and his ex-roommate showed up at the clubhouse. The white guy's girlfriend waited for him in a car outside. I shoved a piece of paper in front of the white kid and made him sign it. He was shaking like a leaf, but he signed his name. It was a match to the handwriting in the letters.

I grabbed a .410 shotgun, pulled the hammer back, and pointed it right in his face. As I did that he pissed all over himself.

"You're the bastard who's been writing letters to my wife—not this kid," I said, pointing to the black. "I should blow your fuckin' brains out right here. Now there's the door. You better get outta here while you're still alive. I ever see you in the West End again doing anything, I'll put you in the hospital for a year."

The kid ran out of the clubhouse, wet pants and all, straight to the car with his girlfriend and drove off like his life depended on it.

I met the next night with the chapter president, a guy we called Monk.

"Here's my colors," I said, throwing them on a chair in front of him.

"What's the matter, Cec?" he asked.

I pointed to Billy. "One, you see this guy here?" I said. He nodded. "I was in trouble and I asked him to help. I'd helped the bastard before when he was in tight spots. He was a fuckin' coward. All he said was he was gonna eat some pizza. He's not a man. I won't be associated with someone like that." I paused a minute, letting what I'd said sink in. "You want me to stay?" I asked.

"Hell, yes, we want you to stay," Monk answered.

"Well, then, throw the bastard out," I said.

Monk took a vote of the chapter's membership, but there weren't enough—you need 90 percent—to vote him out. Only seventy-five percent wanted him out. He had some friends who depended on him to get them dope that he was buying from some dealers including Goobie.

So I quit. I was the vice president and the road captain of the chapter at the time, but I quit. I just walked out after the vote and threw my colors on the chair as I left. The irony was that a year later he quit anyhow.

It wasn't long after that that I teamed up with Cosimo Commisso and the Calabrian Mafia to begin a new and even more violent career in crime.

PART THREE

Mafia Enforcer

CHAPTER 9

The Enforcer

Ron The Rounder paved the way for me to start working for the Commissos. It wasn't something that was planned. It was just a question of timing, and need. I was the right person to fill a need, and Ron was around to recommend me. It was as simple as that.

In the spring of 1976, Ron found out that I had left Satan's Choice. I hadn't seen him for a while. At the time, I was busy hustling a buck in a part-time job as a tractor-trailer driver for a construction company. Ron had been out of town working high-stakes card games for the Niagara Falls Italian mob. We bumped into each other at one of the rounders' hangouts in Toronto's West End.

"Where have you been hiding, Cec?" he asked. "I've been looking all over town for you for some friends of mine."

"What friends are you talking about?" I asked.

"The Commissos," he answered. "They'd like to have you working for them."

Now I had heard about the Commisso brothers. Anyone who worked the streets as I had had heard about them. They were the bosses of a rough and tumble outfit that was shaking down contractors and businessmen in a large segment of Toronto. The guy who was their godfather, so to speak, the head man of respect for the Calabrians, was an old-timer named Mike Racco.

Racco, his real name was Michele Racco, ran a popular bakery shop in

Toronto. It was particularly popular with a lot of the old so-called members of the Calabrian Honoured Society or Calabrian Mafia. They all used to meet there.

Racco was the Carlo Gambino of Toronto. I remember reading about Gambino playing the role of the godfather at a popular bakery and confectionery in New York's Little Italy. The old and even some of the young Italians would come from all over New York to get Don Carlo's blessing and help. Well, Racco was like that in Toronto. Everyone who needed the help of a godfather in the Calabrian community, including the Commissos, would come to the bakery to see Don Michele.

The Commissos bossed their own family, but they took their orders from Don Michele when push came to shove. So did the bosses of two other Canadian Calabrian families, police and underworld friends of mine have told me. Racco, before he died in January 1980, was the Capo Crimini, the boss of bosses for the Calabrian Mafia in Canada and the United States. Later I was told there was no one higher than him among the Calabrians, not even the Calabrian Mafia bosses in Siderno.

Nobody in Satan's Choice had ever dealt with someone like Racco or the Commissos because, up to that point, they lived in different worlds. Calabrians stuck with Calabrians and kept to their own traditions and secret society. There was a frame of mind among mafiosi like the Commissos and Racco and his son, Domenic—bikers and the Mafia don't mix.

With that in mind I wondered out loud why the Commissos would want to hire an ex-biker, and an Irishman to boot. I certainly didn't fit their mold. I also wondered what happened to the guy that was their former enforcer. Where had he gone? Had he been killed?

"Come on, Ron. What the hell would the Commissos want with me?" I said. "I'm not Italian. And worse—I was a biker."

Ron shook his head. "Look, Cec," he explained, "they've heard of you—they've heard a lot about you. I've been talking to them about you." He paused for a minute, looked around to see if anybody was listening to us, and then kept talking. "You got a good reputation as a solid person—a solid rounder. They want me to bring you to the Casa Commisso. If things work out you could make a lot of money." He reminded me that for years members of the Niagara Falls Italian mob, as well as people like himself, had worked with members of the Saint

Catharines Outlaws in drug deals and occasional beatings that had to be given to street people.

So I agreed to go with Ron to meet the Commissos the next day. I was a real fish out of water there. I'm certain, now that I think back on it, that I was the only non-Italian in the damned place. It didn't bother me at the time. I expected it to be that way.

The three of us sat down at a table near the kitchen, where Cosimo felt nobody could listen in, and Ron introduced me. Then Ron got up and walked over to some other men so Cosimo and I could talk privately.

"How you like to work for me?" Cosimo asked in heavily accented English.

"Depends on what you have in mind and how much it pays," I answered matter-of-factly.

A trace of a smile crossed his face before he answered. "Ronnie, he says you can be trusted. He says you're tough—you do good work. I give you some jobs—we see how good you are." He was giving me the once-over as he talked. I think he was wondering what happened to the long hair, the stubbly beard, and the dirty jeans and black leather jacket he expected a biker to be wearing. I had changed that look even before leaving the Choice. I'd shortened my hair. I'd shaved the beard. All I had was a mustache, and I was always cleaned up and dressed up when I went out. So I suppose I was a surprise to him and to his brothers, Remo and Michele, who had joined us at the table.

"Fine, but what about the money?" I asked.

"You'll be paid well," he said. "We put you on the payroll when we see how you do the first job."

I suspected they would test me on a few minor jobs before giving me any major assignments, if they ever did. Ron had told me I'd probably make about $500 a week to start, but that the money would escalate if I did well for them. I had other concerns besides money. I wondered where I would stand if there was trouble with other mobs as well as with the cops.

"Look," I said, "before I jump into this I'd like to know something for my own protection. Just who is running Toronto? The Raccos, you, Johnny [Pops] Papalia, Paul Volpe? I don't want to get done myself 'cause I don't know the players."

Cosimo looked around and motioned to his brothers. "We run this area," he said. "We run it all. We control Toronto."

He and his brothers weren't saying they shared things with anybody or that they answered to anybody. He was saying they were running things and that Toronto was their pie. They were saying if I worked for them I wouldn't have trouble with other mobs.

I was impressed and I nodded in agreement. "Okay, that's fine," I said. "I just wanted to know what position I'm in. What if I get caught doing anything for you in the future?"

Cosimo looked at his brothers and, still smiling, answered, "We have a lawyer for you and we pay all your expenses. We'll look after you."

With that we shook hands, and I gave them a number where they could reach me. "Just call," I said, "and I'll meet you someplace to talk about whatever job you want done."

Cosimo nodded. "We'll be in touch."

In early August 1976, I met with Cosimo and received my first assignment. A contractor owed him money, and Cosimo wanted me to give him a message to pay or else. He gave me the contractor's name, the location of his office, and a description of what he looked like. His instructions were to deliver a message, not to hurt anyone, yet.

So I located this guy's office—I don't recall his name now—and I went up to see him. I just walked into his office, up to his desk, and laid it on the table to him. No open threat, just a subtle intimidation.

"I don't want to say this more than once, my friend," I said. "You owe a friend of mine a considerable amount of money. Now I suggest you pay him, because I don't want to have to come back." I looked at him real hard, the muscles in my jaw twitching. "I hope you're smart enough to understand."

The contractor understood, but as I left I decided to leave a reminder —just in case. I flattened all the tires on his car. Cosimo never said how much the contractor owed, but when I saw Cosimo a couple of days later, he was obviously pleased.

"You're on the payroll, Cec," he said.

The next job was on a bookie. It was sort of a spur-of-the-moment thing. I was in a pool hall one evening when Cosimo walked in.

"There's this fella over here," he said. "We want him to pay the money to us, but he needs the persuasion." He pointed to a middle-aged bookie who I'd seen operating at the pool hall quite often and who was pocketing better than $10,000 a week in profits without paying anyone for the privilege. "That's him," Cosimo said. "Persuade him."

I walked over to the bookie and pressed him pretty hard. He was up against the wall, shaking like a leaf as I sort of whispered in his ear while I jabbed him hard in his lower gut. He got the drift and that night started paying the Commissos a percentage of his daily take.

He wasn't the only one to get a message from the Commissos that night. They had me come with them to visit a boxing promoter they called Bernie, who had been holding out on them—not paying them a percentage of the money he was taking in promoting fights and shylocking some of his own fighters.

The Commissos laid it on Bernie pretty heavy. While I held his arms they stuck guns in his face and cocked the hammers. Suddenly Bernie smelled like a miniature cesspool. He'd crapped all over himself in fright.

All of these assignments were tests. There were four before I got a major assignment, but not all went off without a hitch. The last of the tests had a few twists and gave Cosimo a big laugh.

My job was to beat the hell out of a guy who apparently owed them a bundle of money. Cosimo had given me the guy's address and his phone number, and I called to see if he was in. I couldn't tell him who I was or why I really wanted to see him—not if I wanted to get him out of his apartment. So I came up with a tale I thought would make him come down.

"This Mr. Smith?" I asked.

"Yeah, you got him," he said.

"Look, I'm sorry, Mr. Smith, but I just backed into your car down in the parking lot," I said. "You want to come down and look at the damage and figure out how much I owe you?"

"I'll be right down," he said, anxiously.

I already knew where his car was parked because I'd cased his operation pretty well beforehand. When he arrived at the car I was standing there, my head bent over to hide my face. I whipped around suddenly with a

blackjack in my hand and clobbered him across the head, knocking him cold. Then I worked him over good.

Several days later I went to see the Commissos, and Cosimo greeted me. He handed me $500 and was laughing like hell.

"You didn't do the right guy," he said, still laughing.

"I don't get it," I said. "If I did the wrong guy, why are you so happy?"

"It's all right," he said. "You did his partner. This smart ass. He sent his partner to meet you. The partner that you did, he's gonna spend two months in the hospital. So the guy we wanted done, he's paying up. He doesn't want to go to hospital the same way."

My target had gotten suspicious, knowing the Commissos were after him, and had sent his partner to double-check the car damage, believing nothing would happen to him. I had a description of the guy I was supposed to beat up, but it was dark, and so the wrong guy got worked over. The blackjack I used on him was made in Brazil—eight or nine inches long, flat, thick at the end. It didn't leave a muscle that wasn't blackened, not to mention a few broken bones.

While the wrong guy had been put in the hospital, the results were the same. The Commissos had gotten their money. I was now ready, they were convinced, for bigger, tougher assignments. I didn't know it at that moment, but I was about to become their new top enforcer.

People like me aren't concerned with history. We probably should be. If I had known as much about the Calabrians as I do now, I probably would never have gotten involved with them, and I wouldn't be in the kind of situation I am.

When I agreed to work for the Commissos, I knew very little about the Calabrians. In fact, all I knew were some stories I'd read about the arrest of an Italian named Francesco Caccamo. Toronto Metro had raided his home back in 1972 and found some guns and explosives. But more important, they'd found some papers that were supposed to describe the initiation ritual that Calabrian Mafia members—the Honoured Society—have to go through.

Those documents—they came to be known as the Caccamo Papers—were the first real evidence, I'm told, that the public was given of the Calabrian crime organization. Caccamo was no informer like Joe Valachi

in the States, but those papers were as important as anything Valachi had to say about the Cosa Nostra. Valachi could describe how he was "made" as a member, a soldier of the Cosa Nostra, when he testified before the U.S. Senate in 1963, but he had no document that spelled out what he was talking about. Caccamo didn't say anything, but the documents the cops grabbed said it all—more than he could have—and made it more believable. There it was in black and white.

That was history and I didn't know much more about it. If I had, I would have understood more about the first major assignment that the Commissos gave me. It was in October that Cosimo called me to the Casa Commisso. It had been quite a while between jobs, and I figured they were still testing me. I was living a fairly straight life then, still driving the tractor-trailer. Working for them was a sideline.

The target for this job was a salesman by the name of Antonio Burgas Pinheiro. He was about thirty-eight years old, and he lived in Brampton, Ontario, with his wife and four kids when he wasn't working for the Appia Beverage Company of Queen Street, West Toronto.

"We don't want this man hurt," Cosimo explained. "Just blow up his car or his pop truck. We'll take care of things from there." Remo just sort of stood there, nodding in agreement, letting Cosimo do the talking. Cosimo always did most of the talking.

I found out later that Italian soft-drink beverage companies, according to the police, had been at the center of some serious extortions by the Calabrians from Siderno in the late 1960s. A couple of murders and the bombing of the Appia plant in 1972 were involved. Two officials of the Cynar Dry Ltd., an Italian soft-drink company that employed a relative of the Commissos, had been murdered.

The first one was Salvatore Triumbari, president of Cynar. He was gunned down as he left his home in a Toronto suburb in January 1967. The next guy killed was Filippo Vendemini, who was from Calabria. He had been involved in delivering illegal alcohol for some big Calabrian Mafia hoods, like Paolo Violi from Montreal and Vincenzo (Vincent) Melia. I had to deal with Melia later in a murder plot in Connecticut. Vendemini was shot three times in front of his shoe store in Toronto.

The reasons behind the murders were never made clear, by police or anyone else. It was part of a Calabrian problem and a fight for control of

the Italian soft-drink market by people like the Raccos and Commissos.

I found it interesting that Violi was picked up and questioned about Vendemini's murder. Just as interesting was the fact that somebody had spotted a Montreal license plate leaving the area at the time. Cosimo told me later that the cops traced the license number and the car to a place where the car owner was supposed to be staying. The car owner was there with Cosimo and Remo playing cards. He was grabbed, but they had to release him because there was nothing to prove that he was driving the car. The Commissos weren't charged with anything either. Still, it was quite a coincidence that they were all together and that they all had connections to Vendemini and Cynar employees.

Knowing that history in advance would not have made a difference in how I approached the job, except maybe I would have wanted more than the $1,000 they offered me for it.

On October 23, 1976, I drove out to Brampton. Pinheiro's truck wasn't there that night, but his car, a 1974 Chevrolet, was in the driveway. After parking my truck where no one would notice it, I went back to his car with two sticks of dynamite under my coat and a five-foot fuse.

In a matter of minutes, I placed the dynamite between the frame and gas tank of his car, stretched out the fuse, lit it, and drove off in my truck. I was far enough away when the bomb went off that I didn't even hear it—but half of Brampton did. It exploded at 11:00 P.M. and caused more than $1,000 damage to the car. Later that evening I called Pinheiro's home and threatened him. The cops taped the call but could never identify my voice. They stayed that night, and watched him for a couple of weeks after that because he was so badly shaken.

Pinheiro told them that he didn't have any idea who was behind the bombing. Maybe he didn't, but his boss, Liberato Simone, told the press that the people behind the bombing were trying to drive him out of business. He never identified the Commissos or anyone else. His problem was that his soft-drink company was competing—the Commissos wanted to control the business.

The Commissos were more than happy with the way I operated. They were busy shaking down people all over the city, using the bombings and beatings I had handled for them to intimidate others. Sometimes they worked, and sometimes people needed personal object lessons. A drywall

contractor, who the Commissos said needed such a lesson, lived in an expensive neighborhood in King City.

I got the call to meet Cosimo and Remo at the Casa Commisso. As usual, I parked my car in the nearby parking lot of a Kentucky Fried Chicken store and came in through the banquet hall's rear entrance so I wouldn't be spotted if the cops were watching.

The guy they wanted shaken up was Andy Pozzebon. He owned the Pozzebona Construction Company. They told me that Pozzebon owed a large plastering bill to a friend of theirs.

"If you do a good job and he pays his bill," Cosimo said, "you gonna make ten thousand dollars."

I smiled at that figure and nodded. "Sounds good," I said, looking at Remo to see if he was in agreement.

Cosimo said he would go with me to show me the location and what he wanted me to do. We drove to Pozzebon's home and to the business so I would have a good feel for the area. He told me he wanted me to put a stick of dynamite in Pozzebon's mailbox in front of his home and then to call his office.

That's exactly what I did on November 11. I told Pozzebon's secretary that my name was Thompson and that she should call her boss at home and tell him to look in his mailbox for a special message that I'd left in it. She called Pozzebon, and when he went to the mailbox he found the dynamite. He called the York Regional Police.

A couple of days later I called the Pozzebona Construction Company again and talked to the same secretary.

"Did Mr. Possebon receive my message?" I asked.

The woman was nervous—obviously upset—and she struggled to answer, stuttering a little. "Ye-e-s, he, he got your message," she said.

"Good," I said. "Now tell him he better pay his plastering bill, or the next time I'll blow up his car."

She delivered the message, and Pozzebon must have paid the Commissos. They paid me $1,000 with the promise of more to come. I never got the extra, but they were famous for that.

Extortion, bombs, beatings, threats—they were becoming routine. But in December 1976, the Commissos changed the routine. This time murder was their game.

CHAPTER 10

The Contract Is Murder

The push and shove, phony names, and telephone threats came to an end at a meeting between Cosimo and me at the Casa Commisso.

"Cec, I want you to do a guy for me," Cosimo said. "It's worth ten thousand dollars."

I was still ticked off about the payoff the month before, and I let him know it.

"You mean ten thousand dollars, like in ten thousand dollars you were going to give me last month for Pozzebon?" I said. "Come on, Cosimo. No more bullshit."

"Cec, that was not my fault, not Remo's fault," Cosimo explained. "We don't get everything we're supposed to get. When we get it, you get it. You have my word."

"Okay, okay, Cosimo," I said shaking my head. "Who do you want done?"

"This fink, this Dennis Mason," he said. "He's a witness against a friend of mine. I want him shut up—permanently and fast."

Mason was a relatively young guy who worked in a place called Pizza-Pizza in a shopping plaza. He was a witness against a Commisso associate who had been charged with possession of counterfeit money. It was the same junk that had put so many of the Calabrians, their friends, and bikers behind bars. It would even cause the attempted murder of another witness, Long Island pizza parlor owner Giuseppe Magnolia, who was shot

six times in 1978 by a couple of Canadian Calabrian hit men who screwed up their job.

He was involved in a lot of deals, but in this one he was facing long jail time because of Mason's testimony. He had supposedly sold $2,000 worth of counterfeit to Mason.

Cosimo gave me Mason's address, and we drove first to his home and then to his pizza parlor. After we split up, I began stalking this guy—planning his murder.

It was cold, and it snowed during the next couple of weeks as I watched this kid. I watched him drive home, drive to work. I followed his routine until I had it down pat. There was a pattern to his work. Most of the time he delivered pizzas to private homes. That became the frontpiece of my murder plan. The pizza delivery.

My initial plan was to gun him down from a wooded area across the street from a home where I planned to have him deliver a pizza. The location I had selected was perfect. It was under the large branch of a big Christmas tree.

It was snowing the night I called the pizza parlor from a phone near the Prince Hotel. I parked the van and sat underneath the Christmas tree, waiting for Mason to show. It was very dark, about midnight. I was almost certain he would be the one to deliver the pizza because it was so late. I sat under this tree for thirty, forty minutes. Nobody saw me. The delivery vehicle showed up at the house.

A young guy stepped from the truck and rang the doorbell. Just as he delivered the pie and turned back toward the truck, I got ready to step out and blow him away. As I looked down my gunsight at the door, I could see it wasn't Mason—it was someone he'd sent.

I tried a couple of other ambushes, but they didn't work either. Finally I decided on a bomb. I was going to blow this kid to kingdom come the day after Christmas in his mother's driveway.

The dynamite I was using had been given me by Cosimo. I should have known better. I took the sticks he'd given me and a stick I had, wired them to the dash of Mason's car, and rigged it so that when he turned the ignition key it would go off. The hookup was relatively simple. One wire went to the windshield wiper fuse under the dash, and the other was wound to a bolt connected to the master cylinder. The wiper fuse remains

inactive until you turn that ignition switch. Once it's on, an electrical circuit is made, and *boom!*—off goes the bomb.

After wiring the car and making sure everything was set, I left for home. A day later, the front page of a newspaper had a story about a guy who got minor injuries in a car in a bomb explosion.

Minor injuries! Jesus Christ, I shouted, how the hell can you get minor injuries with six sticks of dynamite? This kid had to have had a guardian angel sitting on his shoulder that day. All he got out of it was some minor cuts. One stick of dynamite should have killed him. The five bad sticks that Cosimo gave me and the stick I had just gave him some cuts.

To add insult to injury, the kid I had been stalking and almost killed, was the *wrong* Dennis Mason. Cosimo had not only given me bad dynamite but bad information. He'd screwed up from start to finish. For all my troubles I got a lousy $2,000, but then I hadn't done Dennis Mason, the witness. As for Commisso's associate, he went to court two weeks later and the real Mason showed up to testify. When the associate saw him, he pleaded guilty in a plea bargaining and got two years out of the deal.

In addition to murder contracts, I was responsible for a homicide. It happened May 3, 1977, when I blew up the Wah Kew Chop Suey House in Toronto's Chinatown. The murder was accidental, but it was a murder nevertheless. It could have been avoided if the Commissos had done their homework before handing out the contract.

The Commissos, I learned later, had taken a contract to blow up this place through members of the Kung Lok Triad, the Chinese crime syndicate that controls gambling, extortions, and drug peddling in Chinatown. The Kung Lok is kind of a Chinese mafia, a secret society, complete with bloody initiation rituals and secret oaths, that came to Canada from Hong Kong and, like the Calabrians, shakes down the people of its own community.

Restaurant owners, gambling dens, tailors, all kinds of small shops pay some sort of extortion to members of the Kung Lok. Those that don't get visits from their enforcers. The next thing you know, merchants and customers have been beaten up and sometimes killed. That triad has Chinatown locked up tight.

Even the old Chinese tongs that used to run Chinatown and its mer-

chants knuckle under to the Kung Lok and hire their enforcers for protection. All the Oriental gambling dens in Toronto are supposed to be protected by the Kung Lok.

One of the gamblers who wasn't paying for protéction was a big shot at the Wah Kew Chop Suey House. Cosimo told me that this guy had been using the place for some gambling, running phony dice games and Chinese games after hours without the Kung Lok's permission. In fact, he was cutting into the business receipts of one of the gambling dens the Kung Lok were providing protection for.

Because the Kung Lok was under pressure from the Toronto police, they decided to get somebody outside Chinatown to handle the job for them. When Cosimo got the contract in late April, he called me in to tell me about it.

"You gonna get paid fifteen thousand dollars for this job," he said. "When you do the job, make sure there's nothin' left. Level it. Do it at six in the morning. Nobody be there then." Remo stood there nodding. He was certain no one would be there when the bomb was to go off.

Famous last words!

I had to case the layout of the place. The next day I went to the Wah Kew and gave them a take-out order. While they were busy cooking it up, I walked around, looking for rooms where I might set the charge. Finally, I checked out the washroom. I noticed there were some loose ceiling tiles. After jamming the door to be sure no one would surprise me, I stood on the toilet seat and pushed the ceiling tiles up. It was perfect. Plenty of space to put a bomb and timer where nobody would spot it. I also checked to see when the restaurant emptied out. By 3:00 A.M., it was closed and everybody was gone.

The next order of business was to get the dynamite and the blasting caps I needed. I figured it would take about one hundred sticks with a couple of blasting caps made up into two separate but identical bombs. Each bomb was to have fifty sticks of dynamite, a blasting cap, a standard twelve-volt flashlight battery, a small clock, and a positive and negative wire that ran from the blasting cap to the clock. I drove to Windsor and got the dynamite from the Satan's Choice chapter there. They always had dynamite available because of extortions they handled and the gang wars. It was usually stolen stuff, but it was dependable.

At about 7:00 P.M. the night of May 2, I put on some glasses, changed my hairstyle, and went back to the restaurant carrying a gym bag and a briefcase with the two bombs. The idea of the two bombs with two clocks was if one didn't work, the other would—sort of a safety valve.

I ordered a couple of egg rolls and coffee to go and went back to the washroom with a doorstop in my pocket to jam the door while I worked. I stood up on the toilet seat again, lifted the ceiling tiles, and gently eased the bombs, one by one, into place. With each bomb, I left a wire loose —I always left a wire loose—the final wire that made the connection for the bomb to go off. I kept it loose until the last minute, just in case something banged or screwed up. It was lucky I followed that procedure. If I hadn't I probably wouldn't be around today.

One bomb was resting on a ceiling tile ledge that had a slight downward slant. I had something in my pocket—I can't remember what the hell it was—that I took out and dropped. I started to bend down to retrieve it. I had the bomb above me with the connecting device taped on but not hooked up. I took my hand off for a split second and then I saw it falling as if in slow motion—falling, falling—I said to myself, "Oh, my God." I heard it hit the floor. I blinked, involuntarily threw up my arms to protect myself—a foolish act in itself—and looked at the floor. There was a momentary silence, but I could hear my heart pounding like a sledge-hammer. I thought to myself as I looked at the bomb, "Christ, I'm still here."

I was breathing again. When my hands stopped shaking, I wiped the sweat from my brow and my hands. Then I gently lifted the bomb and put it back on the tiles. When everything was in place, I set the clocks to go off at about 6:00 A.M. and hooked up the final wires, closing the ceiling tiles carefully behind me. Then I left, picking up my take-out order as I went.

I guess it was about 2:00 A.M. that I telephoned the restaurant just to be sure nobody was there. The phone rang and rang but there was no answer. If someone had answered I would have told them—"Hey, get the hell outta there—there's a bomb about to go off." But there was no answer, and after I hung up the phone I thought no more about it.

The bombs went off about a half hour early. Official reports said the explosion occurred at 5:33 A.M. The bombs tore the hell out of the place.

Working in the kitchen, which shared a wall with the washroom, was a cook who was later identified as Chong Yim Quan. He was killed by the blast. Three other employees were injured. They had come to the restaurant in the early morning hours to begin preparing meals for the day's customers. I'll never know why any of them didn't answer that damned phone.

I heard about the homicide on the morning news, but I didn't see Cosimo and Remo until about a week after the bombing. We were in the Casa Commisso.

"Great information you and Remo gave me, Cosimo," I said. "I thought you said no one was gonna be in the restaurant."

"Ah, Cec, so what?" Cosimo said nonchalantly. "It's no big deal. It was just a Chink."

That was typical of Cosimo and his brothers. They didn't give a damn who got killed or who got hurt as long as the contract was fulfilled and they got their money. They didn't care as long as it wasn't their family.

I shrugged at his answer, and figured I could be just as calculating as Cosimo or his brothers. "You got my money?" I asked.

He nodded and shoved an envelope across the table. "Here's your money," he said.

I opened the envelope and counted it out. There was $18,000 in cash. For the first time he'd paid me more than he'd promised. I didn't ask why. I knew. I pocketed the money and left without another word.

I never found out how much Cosimo and his brothers got for the job, but the restaurant damage was estimated at more than $168,000. He probably pocketed twice what he paid me. But then that's what crime bosses do. They take the lion's share. That's why they're bosses.

If the murder of the Chinese cook was accidental, there was nothing accidental about the Commissos' plot to murder millionaire Montreal stock promoter Irving Kott in April 1978.

From the time I had first met the Commissos until May 1979 there had really been only two contracts for murder and a bombing that turned into murder.

The Mason hit was a case of mistaken identity and only faulty dynamite and a switch of deliverymen had saved his life. The planned Piromalli

murder fell through because Piromalli died of natural causes before they could send me to Italy to do the job. If I had gone, I doubt I would have lived to tell this story or become a witness against the Commissos.

The murder of Kott was probably the most important hit assignment the Commissos had come up with, except for Piromalli. There were more significant hits they wanted me to handle a little later on, but by that time I had decided to bare all and become a secret RCMP informer.

For more than twenty years Kott had wheeled and dealed in the securities business in the United States and Canada. In 1962 he'd been fined $10,000 by the Quebec Securities Commission for trading in unregistered stocks. Police then thought he was being financed by Montreal Mafia boss Vincent Cotroni. The Cotroni brothers, Vincent and Frank, were Calabrians and close to the Commissos.

. In 1967 the Quebec Securities Commission ordered a halt to the sale of stock for a company known as Allegheny Mining & Exploration Co. of Quebec because its owners were dealing with Kott, who was involved in stock deals under investigation in Florida, New York, Denver, Toronto, Vancouver, and Montreal.

In 1973, while he was living in New York, Kott was sued in U.S. District Court for more than $8 million. A British tycoon, Iain Jones, claimed Kott had defrauded him out of a multi-million-dollar calculator business. A year later Kott and eight others were arrested for fraud in the sale of Somed Mines Ltd. stock to investors in Ontario, Quebec, and Europe.

One of those arrested with Kott was Stanley Bader, a swindler who became an informer against Johnny (Pops) Papalia, a Toronto mob boss, and Cotroni. Bader was shot to death in front of his guarded northeast Miami home in March 1982.

In 1975 Kott pleaded guilty to conspiracy in the Somed Mines case and paid a $500,000 fine, but not before he and eighteen others were charged in the $5.5 million swindle of Continental Financial Corp. of Montreal, an American-owned subsidiary of Industrial National Corp, the owner of the Industrial National Bank of Rhode Island.

Through all this Kott was supposed to be operating with the blessing of the Cotronis until 1978, when they were blitzed in one of his stock

operations. I bring up this history because it explains why the Commissos, in particular Cosimo, went to such lengths to make sure I handled this job.

The price to hit Kott, Cosimo said, was $25,000. He said he was acting as a "broker" in the deal for Kott's partner, who would benefit from Kott's death. I never believed that was the real reason or source for the contract. I was convinced then, as I am now, that the Cotroni mob had given the Commissos the contract to kill Kott because they believed Kott had swindled them. Later on Kott's bodyguard, Michael Pozza, was gunned down in Montreal after he'd been subpoenaed in a Quebec crime inquiry into Mafia control of the garment industry in Montreal.

Cosimo gave the Kott hit plot a personal touch.

"This is a very important job, Cec," he said. "I'm gonna meet you in Montreal and I'm gonna show you where this guy works, where he lives. I'm gonna show you everything about this Kott." He paused for a minute and looked straight into my eyes. "I'm not rushing you," he continued. "You can kill this guy whenever you feel it's right, but we want him killed soon. *Capice?*"

I understood, and for $25,000 I'd put icing on the job if he wanted it. He was saying don't rush, but hurry. It's not good when you have to hurry jobs like this.

Cosimo's plan was for me to fly to Montreal. He was going to drive. The following day we were to meet in front of the Bonaventure Hotel.

We met, and for the next day or so, Cosimo drove me to every haunt of Kott's. He knew the guy inside out. We went to where he lived and where he had breakfast every morning at a small place not far from his home, which was in a Jewish neighborhood. While we were casing the house, Kott suddenly came out, climbed into his gleaming new Mercedes-Benz, and drove right past us. Cosimo was furious.

"If I had the gun," he shouted, "I'd've killed the no good son-of-a-bitch right then."

That told me there was something very personal in this contract. For Cosimo to say that he'd have handled the hit personally on the spur of the minute was extremely unusual. He wanted this done and done right to impress someone.

We didn't stick around too long after that. Cosimo took me to an Italian district in Montreal, where we stopped at a coffee shop and had a sandwich.

"We'll just eat here and take off fast," he said. "We don't wanna hang around too long because people know me in the area and I don't wanna be seen in Montreal."

After we finished casing Kott's business location, his home, and his hangouts, Cosimo gave me the address of a girlfriend of Kott who was also his employee. "He stays at the girlfriend's sometimes," he said quietly. "Sometimes he stays the night, sometimes a couple nights."

Then we split. I flew back to Toronto to construct the bomb I'd need and get a .22 silencer to go with a special .22 handgun I'd acquired for the hit. I also went to a Mercedes-Benz dealership in Toronto to check out their cars and see the best place to put the bomb.

Before I was ready to handle the job, I traveled back and forth to Montreal a couple of times, staying a different place each time as I stalked Kott's every move. I wanted this guy down pat before I blew him away. The Commissos had given me $1,000 for expenses.

The first time I went I had taken the .22 and silencer and the dynamite with me—all ready to hook up to his car. I planned to go through a side window of his house and hit him inside. Just as I was going through the window, somebody walking his dog on the street spotted me. That caused a little unexpected heat, and I had to leave the area. Everyone thought it was a burglar.

I had to lay low for about two weeks. Then in late August I returned. This time I planned to attach the bomb to his car and rig it so it would explode when he turned on the ignition. Later I had to change that plan.

When I got to Montreal I found out Kott was in court. I parked near the courthouse and walked around most of the afternoon, trying to find Kott's car in the parking lot. It might have been in the underground garage, but I wasn't about to look. There were too many cops in the area, so I walked on by, got to my car, and left.

I was concerned about being seen. I remember driving by a cop at one point. It was early morning. I was figuring I might have to shoot the cop if he stopped me. He kept on going, never looked at me, so I just took off.

I had no photograph of Kott, just a good description. I'd seen a photo, but I never carried pictures of the victims I was after. Cosimo had handed me a piece of paper with addresses and directions. I memorized most of it. I had trouble memorizing the phone numbers. If I knew a number was in the telephone directory, I'd destroy it. If not—if it was an unlisted number—I'd keep it inside my sock.

Every time I went to Montreal to case Kott's movements, I stole a new set of plates off a Quebec car and put them on mine. I figured I had at least twelve to twenty-four hours before the theft was discovered and reported to the cops. It would take them another couple of hours to alert their cars to the stolen plates. In that time I could keep tabs on Kott's movements.

I took other precautions. I changed the type of clothes I'd wear and my appearance each day. Sometimes I'd comb my hair down, wear a baseball cap or a winter hat with a tassel. Sometimes I'd wear sunglasses or tinted eyeglasses and dark clothes. It always was different, and I'd always look for the quickest way to exit an area before parking or walking around.

One day I sat outside Kott's office for six hours, waiting for him to go to lunch. I didn't realize it, but he had a kitchen in his office and he'd usually have his secretary make his lunch.

The next day I called his office to make sure he was there, then I went to his place of business, the Highland Knitting Mill Inc., and spotted his car parked in an underground parking lot. I retrieved the bomb from my car, set the wiring, and returned to his Mercedes. There was a parking attendant maybe two hundred feet away from where I was. He never spotted me.

The bomb—five sticks of 75 percent nitroglycerin taped together—was placed on top of his exhaust pipe, almost exactly beneath where he sat. I ran electrical wires back to a battery that I hid behind one of the car wheels on the inside, below the axle.

I had a pressure-sensitive ignition starter button on top and placed it under his tire so that at the slightest movement of the tire, it would go off. Once it was in place, I slipped out quietly and drove back to Toronto.

I figured at most Kott would get into his car within a couple of hours, and *poof!* up he'd go. If he sat in his car on top of that dynamite, his

asshole would be on the third floor of the warehouse of his firm. Wrong.

Kott never used the Mercedes. Instead, he climbed into his wife's Jaguar and drove to the airport. While he was away the parking attendant was sweeping under the cars and saw the button under the Mercedes. It was very dark. I still don't understand how he saw it. I should have put it on top of the tire, not under—it was my mistake. I hurried the job too much.

It was about 5:10 A.M. on August 28, nearly nine hours after I had set the bomb in place. The attendant looked at the button, pushed it, and *ba-boom!* it went off, sending him flying halfway across the lot. Another person who was walking nearby was knocked to the ground.

The attendant lost part of his hearing in the explosion, but he wasn't badly hurt otherwise. Neither was the bystander. Kott's car was demolished, and two other cars parked nearby were badly damaged.

I didn't know that Kott had escaped injury when I reported to Cosimo back in Toronto. He was pleased. Then he found out that Kott wasn't hurt.

I saw Cosimo about three weeks later. Surprisingly, he wasn't all that upset. I guess those who had ordered Kott hit weren't that upset either. Maybe the explosion had sent a message to Kott that he understood and, as a result, had taken care of their problems. Whatever happened, Cosimo handed me $3,000 more for my trouble. It wasn't the $25,000 I'd been promised, but then I hadn't nailed Kott either. I hadn't expected to get anything.

"Well, I guess Kott knows who's after him now," I said.

"Well," Cosimo said, "he knows who he owes money to—but there's others who are after him."

"You want me to go back and do the job right?" I asked.

"No. Never mind, Cec," he said. "Remo, he's going there to kill him."

I know Remo never went, and Kott is still alive. I never did figure out why Cosimo said that. Whatever the reason, I was $3,000 richer for botching a job. If they hadn't been in such a hurry to take him out—just as they'd wanted Mason done in a hurry—Kott and Mason might not be around today.

CHAPTER 11

Everything Has a Price

Whether it was concrete or cement, plumbing or plastering, electrical wiring or trucking—if it had anything to do with the construction industry, the Commissos and their Calabrian Mafia friends had a hand in it somewhere, and usually that hand was reaching in and taking, either with threats or as part of a mob agreement.

Michele Racco and his family had a piece, Paul Volpe and his people were in it, and so was the Luppino crime family of Hamilton. The infiltration of the construction industry by mobsters, some of them from the Mafia, some of them associated with the Mafia, was so widespread that it even resulted in an investigation by a Royal Commission under Judge Harry Waisberg. There had been many bombings and shootings in the industry, which the commission documented in an investigation that lasted more than a year and produced a 770-page report. That was back in 1974.

What the report and the investigation didn't produce was public evidence of the Raccos' and Commissos' operations in construction. That was probably because the coppers knew little about the Calabrian Mafia at that time and even less about the Commissos. The Commissos were young then. They hadn't reached the status of bosses of a crime family that could rattle the cages of other mobs from Long Island to British Columbia.

The people who drew most of the heat for the bombings and shootings,

the shakedowns of contractors, and the infiltration of unions from 1970 to 1973 were bosses like Paul Volpe, or Natale Luppino, or people representing the Stefano Magaddino crime family of Buffalo.

When I started working for the Commissos, I learned quickly that their big thing for making money was the construction industry. They probably made more from extortions in that industry than from their trafficking in heroin, and it was a helluva lot safer.

They had a lot of ways to make money in construction. One of their most successful was making the law that contractors depended on to collect debts work for them. It could take years for a guy to collect through the courts. In fact, contractors could and did go broke waiting for the law and civil suits to settle their claims. Even when the courts made awards favoring a contractor, he often found out that the guy he was suing had a dozen different corporations and the corporation he'd been dealing with was legally bankrupt. The debtor had simply moved his money from one corporate account to another.

What that did was make room for guys like the Commissos to become "collection agencies" for contractors. For a slice of the money owed, the Commissos would collect, and they didn't let legal technicalities or stalling tactics get in the way.

Take a major contractor—let's call him Builder X. To complete his project he subcontracts electrical, plumbing, and plastering work out to smaller, specialized contractors. Mr. X promises to pay these contractors $300,000 more or less to complete their work.

Now the electrical contractor finishes his job and comes to Mr. X and says, "Pay me." Mr. X doesn't have the cash right then, so he says, "I'll have to pay you later." The electrical contractor has employees to pay, supplies to pay for, bills to meet. He sues in court to recover his money. Maybe two or three years down the road he collects—maybe he doesn't. Meanwhile, Mr. X has used the electrical contractor's $300,000 and similar amounts from the plumbing and plastering contractors to invest in some other project that makes him an even bigger profit.

That was the system for a long time. It took the Commissos to find a way to make big money out of it. Now the subcontractor goes to his friend down the street who knows "the Mafia, who knows the Commissos." The Commissos then go to see Mr. X or send someone like me to hassle and

threaten him. They collect, they get a piece, and the subcontractor gets most of his money back. That's the way it's done here.

By 1978 I was getting a number of contracts from the Commissos to squeeze contractors who they wanted to extort money from, who they told me were not paying bills they owed to subcontractors. The first of these involved Ben Freedman.

Freedman was the main contractor on a construction project in Toronto. He had hired a couple of subcontractors to do some electrical work that cost more than $175,000. When it came time to pay, Commisso said Freedman suddenly came up with short arms and long pockets. There was no money, he told them, either wait or take him to court.

The subcontractors, both of them Italian, turned to Remo and Cosimo for help. They wanted their money and they wanted it now and they didn't care what had to be done to get it. That's when Cosimo called me in.

We meet at the Casa Commisso on February 13, and then drove to Freedman's home in North York.

"Bomb his house," Cosimo said, "but don't hurt anyone. I just wanna shake this guy so he pays up what he owes."

The fee to do the job was $2,000. Originally Cosimo wanted me to put the bomb on the side door of the house. I didn't see any problem until I got there that night on my own.

I was in a jogging suit, which I wore so that anyone who saw me would think I was just another one of those health nuts jogging up and down streets in the area. People don't take much notice of joggers. The jogging suits I wore were usually black or dark blue, which made it even harder for anyone to see enough to remember. I also wore a cap.

I had two sticks of dynamite with me and a five-foot fuse that I connected to a percussion cap that I'd hooked to the dynamite. When I got to Freedman's house, I spotted some kids' bicycles and a baby carriage around the front. I decided against a bomb at the door. I didn't want some kids to get maimed or killed because they were playing at the wrong place at the wrong time. So I chose to bomb Freedman's car, which was parked in the driveway.

I put the bomb between the wiper blades and the windshield, set the fuse, and jogged away. I was long gone when the bomb went off. The next

117

day I read in the paper that the car had been totaled, but that no one was injured.

A couple of days later Cosimo went to a public telephone booth and called Freedman to explain why the car had been blown up.

"Be smart, Mr. Freedman," he said, carefully speaking the words so his accent wouldn't be obvious. "Pay your bills. That way no one—no kids —get hurt."

Cosimo paid me the $2,000 and said I'd done a good job. Cosimo, however, had not kept his word. He had told me that when I handled these extortions for him, I would get a percentage, as much as one-third of what was collected as a result of my intimidation of the victims. I never got anything beyond the $2,000. It was another pipe dream.

Once the Commissos delivered for a subcontractor, they were in a position to muscle him or make deals to collect for him on other projects. In effect, they became his private collection agency and silent partner. That was the case with the electrical contractor who had collected from Freedman because of my bomb. There were other contractors who owed him money, big money, and the Commissos were going to cash in collecting those debts.

The biggest of the targeted contractors were a pair of apartment and condominium building owners named Jerry and Roman Humeniuk. They were brothers and partners. In March 1978 I got the first of several assignments from Cosimo and Remo to force the brothers to pay more than $196,000 they owed. The contractor had done a lot of work at this exclusive and very expensive condominium complex and hadn't been paid for it.

Before taking on the job, I checked out the area to see what the best escape routes were and how many people were around at different times of the day and night. I finally settled on doing the job in the underground parking lot of the condo, where I figured it would be least likely to kill anyone.

I took two sticks of dynamite with a three-foot fuse which I'd gotten from the Commissos and lit the fuse a few minutes before 9:00 P.M. When it went off it blew out plate-glass windows that partitioned the parking area from an underground lobby.

Not long after, I telephoned some people who were living in the complex—people whose names I'd gotten out of a telephone book.

"Look, you don't want to get hurt, right?" I asked.

A woman in the room was crying and the man who was on the phone was asking, "Why us? Why are you calling us? We haven't done anything."

"Just tell that landlord of yours to pay the money he owes to his contractor," I snarled. "He'll know who I'm talking about. Tell him to give up the money he owes or I'm coming back and blow the fucking apartment house apart—and I'll blow up your fucking place with it."

The woman was hysterical now, screaming into a telephone extension: "He isn't here. Please! Leave us alone!"

"Lady," I answered, "just give him the message." I hung up.

The Commissos gave me $2,000 for the job. Two months later, they wanted me to go back.

"This building owner," Cosimo said, "he hasn't paid up. We want you to go back again—blow up his car."

This time he wanted me to zero in on the home of Roman Humeniuk in Oakville.

I drove by the place first to look around. There were kids in the yard and in neighboring yards. I didn't think it would be safe. Blowing up the car might cause a fire because the car was very close to Dr. Humeniuk's garage. Then the fire would spread to the house. I didn't want some kid trapped in that house by fire. So I figured out an alternative plan.

Early on the morning of May 15, I threw one stick of dynamite on the lawn and put a big hole in it with the explosion. I almost screwed up with that one. I used a short fuse, about a foot. That gives you about forty seconds after you light it to get the hell out of the area. I hit a red light just as that one went off at about 12:15 A.M. I could hear the explosion, feel the van rock a little, as I waited to get on the Queens Expressway. Humeniuk's house was just a short distance from the expressway exit.

Still nothing. The Commissos were mad as hell. Humeniuk hadn't paid, and the contractor was pressing them for results. So in July I went back to the condominium again, this time to the other side of the garage, where there were two concrete supporting pillars. I rigged a bomb with four sticks of dynamite, a six-foot fuse, and a blasting cap. When it went off

at 12:05 A.M. the morning of July 21, it shook the entire complex and sent debris flying more than sixty feet onto the nearby golf course. The bomb was designed to cause more fear than damage, and that's exactly what it did.

I called the same tenants again and went through the same routine. The woman was almost a basket case by then. The idea was to get the people to tell the Humeniuks to pay what they owed or they'd move out. When they moved out, the owners would lose money. Rather than lose money and have an empty condo, they'd pay what they owed.

I don't know if it worked. The Committee claimed the Humeniuks never paid up, but they never called me back to squeeze them anymore either, which made me believe that their contractor was a satisfied customer. I figured they were just trying to get out of paying me any part of that $196,000 that the Humeniuks owed the contractor. All I got out of all my work was about $3,000.

It was apparent to me that by the time I got the Humeniuks' extortion contract the Commissos had a lot of the construction industry subcontractors lined up, ready to pay them to do what the courts weren't doing. Even while I was handling the Humeniuks' bombings, I got the nod to start extorting money from developer Max Zentner and his millionaire partner, John Ryan, the owner of the engineering firm of John Ryan and Associates.

In May, Cosimo told me to try to go after Ryan and Zentner, who he said owed an electrical contractor "friend" of his more than $200,000 for work he'd done on a project. The contractor was supposed to be suing Ryan in court to recover the money, but Ryan's lawyers were stalling.

Cosimo showed me Ryan's home in Hamilton, his Cadillac, which was usually parked in the driveway at his home, and his office in Toronto. He said I should also muscle Zentner, who lived in Montreal.

"Break his legs," Cosimo said of Ryan. "You break his legs and rough him up good."

So in May I went to Ryan's home at about 5:00 A.M. and flattened the left rear tire of his car. I waited in my car for him to show up. I figured I'd waylay him when he tried to fix his tire. The trouble was, by 9:00 A.M. he still hadn't come out of his house. So I left. About five days later I returned. I changed my facial appearance with a mustache, a wig, and

glasses, walked up to the front door, and knocked. When he opened the door, I knocked him flat with a blackjack to his face.

I then traveled to Montreal and telephoned Zentner, telling him to get his partner to pay up or he'd get the same treatment Ryan had just gotten. Nothing happened, but Cosimo paid me $1,000 in cash that Remo pulled out of his pocket. The money was to cover my expenses.

About two weeks later, I returned to Hamilton. It was about 1:30 A.M. when I got there with two sticks of dynamite and a five-foot fuse. I spotted a 1977 Firebird in the driveway that I knew belonged to Ryan's daughter. I set the bomb on top of the rear tire, set the fuse, and took off. I heard it go off just before I hit Main Street in Hamilton. It sounded like two trains colliding.

Later I saw a picture in the *Hamilton Spectator*. The car was wrecked. Pieces of it were found two or three houses away, and the bedroom window of a neighboring home was cracked, but no one was injured. The Ryans and their daughter were staying at some cottage near Parry Sound. A witness said she'd seen a sports car leave the scene when the bomb went off. Hell, I was driving a sports car, but she couldn't have seen me. I was about a mile away when that bomb went off. Witnesses sometimes have vivid imaginations.

After the bomb went off, Cosimo wanted me to call Ryan and tell him that the next time a bomb went off, his son or his daughter would be in the car that was blown up. I tried getting Ryan, but his secretary never let me talk to him. I was never certain that he'd paid the $200,000 to the contractor, but the Commissos didn't ask me to go back. They just paid me the $2,000 they said they'd pay and that was that.

One thing that drove me wild with the Commissos, was that they were full of promises of big money, but rarely delivered. Sometimes I'd get so pissed off that I'd pull out of jobs I'd promised to do unless they paid me the money up front. Take the case of Alphonso Gallucci, the owner of Gallucci Construction in Toronto.

The Commissos' said Gallucci owed a friend of the IRS more than $54,000 and had stalled paying. Cosimo's face was flushed with anger when he told me what he wanted.

"You break this guy's arms and legs," he said angrily. "You break them slow so he feels the pain longer."

"How much am I going to get for this?" I asked.

"We give you a percentage," Cosimo said.

"No good, Cosimo," I said. "I'm tired of promises. I want my fee up front. Like the Chinamen say, 'No tickee, no shirtee.' No money, no legs broken."

Finally, after a lot of arm-twisting, I said I'd do the job, and Cosimo drove me to Gallucci's home and to his business. In October 1980, after a couple of months of haggling with Cosimo and Remo about up-front payment, I pulled out of the deal. As far as I know, Cosimo never got anyone else who was willing to do the job.

Shaking down contractors to make them cough up money owed builders and subcontractors they were collecting for produced only a small part of the Commissos' take from the construction industry. They were also very active in bid rigging on municipal contracts, like hydroelectric projects, buildings, or highways. When they wanted to rig bids, the Commissos would threaten the competition facing the contractors they were dealing with. Once their man got the bid, they became his partners, and their people—plasterers, electricians, plumbers, cement suppliers—would be used on the job. They'd inflate the cost of the job, pocket the profits, and run like thieves while the public or business paid the price.

I recall one dam project that the Commissos wanted to control in British Columbia. They wanted to use a friend of mine to do it. The friend was "Charlie Tuna." That wasn't his real name, but he didn't do anything wrong, so I'm not going to name him. He was the son of the owner of one of Canada's largest construction companies, which had bid on the project.

They wanted me to shake down Charlie Tuna, rough him up if need be, to put pressure on his old man. I refused. Charlie Tuna was a friend of mine who eventually joined the Rebels motorcycle club. He used to work out and hang around at an athletic club that I owned and operated. I remember trying to talk Charlie out of getting involved with the cycle gangs.

"You're a nice guy, Charlie," I told him at the gym. "You don't want to join a motorcycle club. You'll just wind up in trouble."

Charlie Tuna's father ran a big outfit. They had millions, and Charlie

used to drive around in a souped-up Porsche and a special truck that was worth $40,000 or $50,000. He was a big, strong kid, about five foot ten. Long before he teamed up with the Rebels bikers, he rode around on a Harley-Davidson.

Charlie Tuna and some of his Rebel friends were grabbed one day at the border by customs or immigration. They were hassled but they never got into any real trouble. Charlie finally got out of the biker clan and went back to working for his family. It was the smartest thing he ever did.

When Cosimo wanted me to make a move on Charlie Tuna I said, "Look, I don't do friends. I'm not extorting him or his family."

"Cec, don't say no," he said. "Think about it."

"There's nothing to think about, Cosimo," I said. "I'm not shaking down Charlie or his family. That's it."

"Okay, okay, Cec," he said. "We gotta see if we can get through to this company some other way, work something out with them."

He smiled as he looked at me. "If they don't cooperate, I'll get my friends in the unions in British Columbia and we'll close this company down with a strike. You'll see. They'll fall in line."

I don't know if they did fall in line or if the Commissos got a piece of the pie at the dam project, but there was no doubt in my mind about Cosimo's influence with the unions, particularly the plasterers' union. One day Cosimo gave me the address of their union hall and told me to go there and sign up. "Once you sign up, you'll be a member," he said. "You'll get a check for five hundred dollars every week."

I said no to the offer. I knew that if I went to that union and signed up, the guys in the union would sooner or later know who I was working for and start talking. One night the guy who ran the union would come to me and say, "You're Cosimo's friend. I want you to burn this house or break this guy's head." It would have been stupid. I could have taken down an easy $500 a week, but why take the chance? It wasn't worth it.

The plasterers' union was only one that the Commissos had their hooks into. Just before I began working as an informer, I'd heard them talk about forming some sort of protection union for the construction industry.

Their plan was simple. They were going to use this union to shake down contractors who were being shortchanged by companies they did work for. For a fee or a percentage of what was owed, they would send union goons

to the company that owed the money. The company either paid up or faced beatings of employees by union muscle, wildcat strikes, and other forms of intimidation. I never found out what union they took over or whether they actually put the plan into operation. By that time, I'd become a witness against them and was no longer able to get that kind of inside information.

The Commissos were also busy controlling the mobile lunch trucks that provide workers with sandwiches, coffee, soda, and other goodies at construction sites. It's a damn good way to make a buck if you're sitting at a catering hall, like the Casa Commisso, pressing all the buttons while everyone else does the work.

The mobile lunch truck business is so lucrative that the boss of the Joseph Bonanno family in New York, Philip (Rusty) Rastelli, got into it and wound up in jail after a federal jury in Brooklyn, found him guilty of extortion. Rastelli was more than once a guest of mob members in Toronto and Montreal, where the Bonanno family had a lot of friends and connections for their narcotics business and for other rackets they were involved in in Canada.

The Commisso version of Rastelli's racket was geared toward the construction sites themselves. The Commissos and the Raccos controlled most of the catering trucks in Toronto. When there were rivals, they usually didn't blow up their trucks or threaten them, they went after the construction site superintendent and squeezed him—made him keep the competition off the site.

Cosimo brought me to the owner of one of the mobile catering companies, who was close to Michele Racco. He was having a problem with a construction site superintendent who was letting a rival company service the workers.

"What my friend wants," Cosimo said, "you do for him. You'll get paid well."

I didn't trust this friend of Cosimo's and Racco's. He wanted me to rough up the site superintendent—break his legs if I had to—to make him open the site to his lunch trucks. When I was through with that, he said, he wanted me to burn some trucks of another catering company in another part of the city. There was something about the way this guy talked—the way he wanted to grind his competitors under his heels—that

made me uneasy. I figured he'd double-cross his mother, let alone me, so I refused to handle his work. Cosimo wasn't happy about it, but he didn't press me. He knew I'd made up my mind. The lunch company caterer was greedy. He already had trucks operating all over the city—at construction sites, industrial complexes, garages, you name it—and he wasn't afraid to handle hot goods to increase his profit margin.

Some time after I turned down that assignment, Cosimo told me that the lunch company caterer's trucks were going to handle a $100,000 load of cigarettes, stolen from the Imperial Tobacco Company, that I was arranging to sell to Cosimo for some friends. The cigarettes were from a trailerload that Ken Goobie and Armand Sanguigni were trying to peddle for $40,000 through a middleman named Richard Corbett. Cosimo finally agreed to take the load for $30,000.

With all those lunch trucks, he said, they could move a trailerload of stolen cigarettes in a day and no one would ever be the wiser, least of all the cops.

Funny thing about the hijacked cigarette deal. At the last minute Cosimo had second thoughts about his friend. When he got the cigarettes, he arranged to sell them to another mobile lunch company owner —a rival. This guy promised Cosimo a bigger profit than the guy Cosimo'd wanted me to work for. That was always Cosimo's downfall—his greed.

In the end, the whole deal blew up in Cosimo's face. After paying about $12,000 of what he owed on the cigarettes, Cosimo lost everything when a sharp-eyed citizen spotted his Calabrian flunkies unloading 127 of the original 317 cases of cigarettes in a rundown garage in Toronto. The citizen called the police, who seized the cigarettes and arrested four men who later pleaded guilty to possessing stolen cigarettes. The Commissos had to provide lawyers, bail money, and expenses for the four. It was a fiasco for the Commissos; for Goobie, Sanguigni, and Corbett; and for me. I'd expected to make a good piece of change out of the deal, but all I got for my troubles was a headache and a lousy $100.

CHAPTER 12

Hustling a Buck

Working as an enforcer and hired assassin for the Commissos had some good paydays, but it wasn't exactly lining my pockets with enough gold to live on easy street. The money I received for blowing up the Chinese restaurant and for contractor extortions and the attempted murders of Mason and Kott went fast. Too fast.

There was a new Corvette, there were a lot of fast women, and there were even more slow horses. I went to the track too often and bet more often than not on the wrong nag.

I had recognized early in my relationship with the Commissos that I'd have to supplement my income with side deals of my own. For a while, I continued operating as a courier for Goobie's narcotics. I also handled a number of drug rip-offs with some bikers that added thousands to the stash in my safety deposit box. I was averaging $75,000 to $80,000 a year, but it wasn't nearly enough. I had become a rounder of sorts myself, and I was always looking for new ways to make money.

Through a chance meeting with two international gambler friends— I remember them only as Bob and Roman—opportunity came knocking. Roman was a good friend of Eddie Neuff, the murdered gambler, and he was pretty close to Ron the Rounder, who had introduced us. We'd all done some drug rip-offs together. On this particular night, we were at a hotel in downtown Toronto tossing down a few when Roman asked me if I'd be interested in taking a trip to Bogotá.

Roman's objective was to locate a source for cocaine that he and Bob planned to smuggle into Canada. They had a front they were convinced would get them through customs. They were leaving for Colombia to have some parts made for a plumbing operation they were running. Their plan was to have the parts produced on a massive scale and smuggle coke inside some of the parts being shipped to them. It wasn't a foolproof plan, but it was successful for them.

I decided to go along for the hell of it. I'd just finished blowing up the Chinese restaurant, and I wanted some high living without worrying about coppers or the Commissos or anyone else looking over my shoulder. I wasn't the least bit interested in smuggling narcotics. I considered that too risky.

We spent about a week living it up in the city and sightseeing. During that stay, we met a high-ranking official of the Bogotá Chamber of Commerce at a Colombian bank where we were changing Canadian currency into pesos. One thing led to another—before I knew it the discussion went from pesos to plumbing supply parts, cocaine, and finally to guns.

"Can any of you get guns?" he asked. "We need guns, all kinds of guns —rifles, machine guns, bazookas, ammunition."

Roman and Bob were dumbfounded. They were trying to set up a supply source for a cocaine smuggling operation and here this guy was talking about reverse smuggling—moving guns from Canada to Colombia. They both shook their heads, figuring that their lack of contacts for weapons was going to cost them in trying to set up the drug-smuggling operation. At that point I surprised them with an offer of help.

"There's a guy I know," I said. "He's sort of a friend. His name is Chuck Yanover." Roman's face brightened as I spoke, and the Colombian business official leaned close to listen to what I had to say.

Of course I knew Yanover, but we weren't close friends, just sometimes business associates. Like a lot of members of Satan's Choice and other biker gangs, I had sold stolen motorcycle parts to Yanover for years. I'd lost track of him for a while, but after he was in prison he apparently graduated to the big time. He got hooked up with Nathan (Nate) Klegerman, a convicted diamond swindler and international con man who was Paul Volpe's right arm. In 1974 the Royal Commission that investigated

the construction industry identified Yanover as part of the Volpe mob that was shaking down and bombing contractors. Two years later he was busted with Volpe, Klegerman, and three others for trying to smuggle $1.5 million in diamonds into Canada.

With all that, Yanover still managed to get an arms dealer's license. He used to brag about that to me whenever I saw him. He was the Ontario agent for Fabrique Nationale, a Belgium arms manufacturer. The joke was that as the agent for the Belgium supplier he was helping arm the Ontario Provincial Police. He said he was negotiating a contract to sell the police a special rifle they were after. When Yanover told me that, I didn't know whether to believe him or not. Chuckie was always bragging, talking about million-dollar deals and international plots to take over countries.

From the tip of his balding head to his pudgy feet, from his thick glasses to his weasellike face, there was nothing about Yanover to remind you of a cold-blooded mercenary capable and ready to kill whoever stood in his way. Yet that was exactly what he was. And he had a lot of mercenary friends—gunmen for hire—he'd met while peddling arms for the Belgians.

Yanover was full of schemes in those days. He was living on the fifth floor of a building owned by Volpe. We used to meet there occasionally, usually in the boiler room of the building, when I wanted to buy some diamonds or some guns from him. It was at one of these meetings that Yanover offered me a murder contract.

"I got a couple of things for you to do if you want some work, Cec," Yanover said.

With Yanover you never knew what to expect, so I was cautious in expressing interest.

"Yeah, well, what have you got in mind?" I asked.

"First of all," he said, "I can guarantee you a million bucks if you'll handle a contract to kill Fidel Castro."

I looked at Yanover as if he'd lost all his marbles. "Come on, Chuck, you're not serious," I said.

"I sure as hell am," he snapped. "The only thing is it's going to take a helluva good shot. You're going to have to take the shot at him from a quarter of a mile away. That's as close as you'll be able to get."

I started to chuckle, but I saw Yanover getting almost beet red with

anger, so I coughed and frowned and speculated that the job was a suicide mission.

"Chuck, be reasonable," I said. "I don't speak Spanish. I wouldn't last ten seconds there after taking a shot at Castro. The people would tear me apart. Even for a million bucks I don't think I'd be interested. I don't have a secret desire to kill myself—not yet."

He never said much more about it, but I got the impression that the plan to hit Castro was something hatched up by some mob guys who wanted to get back into the casino business in Cuba. Castro had cost the Italian and Jewish mobs millions when he took over their hotels and threw them out of the country. Since then the papers and U.S. congressional committees have reported a number of plots to kill Castro, some sponsored by the Central Intelligence Agency, who wanted to use the mob, others planned by stateside mobsters who had dreams of getting back their casinos.

When I turned Yanover down, he didn't bat an eye.

"Okay, maybe I got something else for you," he said. "I got something personal you can handle. I'll give you ten thousand dollars and all your expenses will be paid."

The target of his vendetta was some poor slob who was working a Caribbean cruise ship. The guy had made the mistake of taking off with a girlfriend of Yanover's. Yanover didn't like people chasing his women, even if he was chasing three or four at a time himself.

"You go down to Miami and you get on this cruise ship," he said. "You grab him and just dump him off the boat and forget about it."

"Let me think on it, Chuckie," I said. "Maybe I can do something."

Later on he had a guy he wanted me to get rid of in Switzerland. I don't remember his name, but he wanted this guy hit in the worst way. Friends of mine and the cops told me later that some guy who was a witness against Yanover was shot in Switzerland and nearly killed. I never was certain whether that was the guy that Yanover wanted me to hit.

It was about a month after we'd talked to the Colombian businessman that I arranged a meeting with Yanover at the Prince Hotel. Roman, Yanover, and myself sat down. I was acting as sort of the middleman, figuring I'd collect from both sides on the deal.

"I have this Colombian," Roman explained to Yanover. "He wants to

buy automatic weapons, bazookas, tanks, and whatever else he can get his hands on, and he's willing to pay whatever it takes to get them."

Yanover sat there nodding, wiping his glasses. "You just have him send the money up and I'll ship them whatever they want—planeloads of tanks, guns, munitions—you name it, I'll get it, and the prices will be right."

Both Roman and Yanover sort of glided over the costs. Nobody got specific about the price of a tank or a machine gun or anything. They just talked in generalities.

"How are you going to get weapons like that to them in the quantities they want without attracting too much attention?" Roman asked.

"Look," answered Yanover with a just a hint of anger in his voice. "I've handled shipments like this lots of times before. We just report the plane lost at sea after we deliver the weapons. Just go back to Bogotá and have them draft some money to a bank here and we'll start delivering the guns and tanks they want."

Roman never went back and he never saw Yanover again to my knowledge. The last I heard he was living in England.

As for Yanover, we kept on dealing together. From guns and cocaine to arsons, from a plot to overthrow a Caribbean island called Dominica to a plan to assassinate the president of South Korea. The government overthrow plots happened later, when I became an informer and witness. In the late 1970s Yanover's biggest value was as gun supplier.

He had a supply of handguns and machine guns available on almost a moment's notice. He could get anything I wanted—grenades, machine guns, plastic explosives, antitank guns, even tanks themselves. His suppliers weren't just the Belgian manufacturer. He also had sources in New York and Chicago, sources he didn't talk about. I used to buy a lot of guns from him—guns that I sold to bikers, to the Commissos, to rounders I knew.

Cosimo was always in the market for guns. If he wasn't buying them from me, he was getting them from two Italian gunsmiths who had a shop in downtown Toronto. The gunshop owners themselves were in the market for special guns, even those that were hot. I recall selling one of the owners a collector's Winchester carbine. It was hot—stolen in a burglary —but they didn't care. They had a customer who wanted it, no questions asked. Cosimo sometimes bought hot guns from the youngest gunshop

owner. On one occasion, the owner promised Cosimo he'd have ten guns coming in from a source he had in the States within a couple of days.

Collector's guns—any guns—were always wanted by bikers, who were constantly checking out gun collectors and gun stores that they could heist later. There were times when everyone in Toronto seemed to be in the market for a gun of some kind and no one asked questions. Bikers and rounders in particular were always either buying or selling guns. I didn't have to go look for them. They would come to me to sell their wares. If someone really wants a gun, he can always buy one on the street—whether it's in Toronto, Montreal, New York, or Miami. They are out there for people who know people, and it doesn't take too much to find and get to know the right people.

When I was dealing heaviest in guns between 1978 and 1980, I always had two or three of my own just sitting around for possible sales or jobs. Keeping guns around sometimes got me in trouble. I already described how Gary Barnes took a gun of mine and shot up a tent full of people.

The worst incident I can recall resulting from my trafficking in guns came out of my giving a .32 caliber handgun to James Munro, a rounder friend of mine, in May 1980. Munro was short on money and he was an old associate. So when he asked me for a gun and said he'd take care of me later, I didn't ask what he planned to use the gun for. It wasn't any of my business. Munro was a hustler. I knew he handled burglaries and heists, but that was his business.

On May 14, Jimmy and his brother, Craig, tried robbing George's Bourbon Street Tavern, a Toronto nightclub. A Metro cop, Constable Michael Sweet, interrupted the robbery and was shot. That brought out an army of cops, and for a couple of hours Craig, who was older and crazier than Jimmy held the cops at bay with the gun I'd given Jimmy. All that time, Constable Sweet was bleeding. He bled to death from the shots that Craig later admitted firing at him. Both Craig and James Munro got life for murder. I was never charged in the case, because the Munros never implicated me. When I became a witness and got immunity for past crimes, I admitted giving Jimmy Munro the gun just one day before the shoot-out. I felt bad about Sweet. He was a good cop with a wife and three kids. He was just in the wrong place at the wrong time.

* * *

While I was moving deals on the side with people like Yanover and the Colombians, I was still very active with the Commissos. In 1978 alone I handled seven arsons and bombings, some of which I've already described. Probably the most violent and the one that was supposed to bring me the most money was that of the Laramie Sports Store in Guelph, Ontario.

It was strictly an insurance blowout, set up by the store owners, Bruno Spizzichino and his partner, Armando DiCapua, with the help of another Italian friend, Rocco Mastrangelo. Mastrangelo was the connection to the Commissos. He knew Remo very well. I'm not sure whether the connection was through friends in Italy or from contacts in the Calabrian community of Toronto.

Their plan was to bomb and set fire to the store, collect the insurance, and pay the Commissos $20,000 for the job. DiCapua and Spizzichino went to Italy to borrow the $20,000. Then they flew to Las Vegas and then, after a short stay at one of the casinos, to Guelph. The idea was to make it look like they had won the $20,000 they were bringing into Canada while they were in Las Vegas. Once in Guelph, they deposited the money in the Bank of Commerce and, after a short wait, took the money to Mastrangelo. He, in turn, paid Remo and Cosimo for the job.

I found all that out later when I wore a body mike and recorded their recollections of what happened after the Commissos had been arrested and jailed. In 1978 all I knew was what Cosimo told me, and that wasn't a helluva lot.

I was working out at a gym in early June when Cosimo called me and told me it was important that I come to see him at the Casa Commisso. When I arrived he said he had a job for me.

"I got friends in Guelph," he said. "They got a business that's not good. They wanna burn it—blow it up and collect the insurance."

"How much is my end, Cosimo?" I asked.

"Eight, maybe ten thousand dollars when the job's done," he said.

The next day we met at a pool hall and Cosimo told me he wanted to drive to Guelph and introduce me to the owners. I didn't like the idea too much, but Cosimo said that the owners were friends of his family and that, for my protection, he would identify me only as "George."

I finally agreed to go, but I said I'd drive. The following afternoon, Cosimo and I drove to Guelph in my Corvette. When we got to town,

I parked the car about a block away and then walked to the store, where Cosimo introduced me to DiCapua.

DiCapua gave me a tour of the store and the building. He showed me a disco and an after-hours club on an upper floor and a karate club in the basement. Then he took me to a storage area in the back of the store and showed me a door that he said led to an alleyway. While I was there I studied some gas pipes that led downstairs, and I told him that I would probably place the bomb downstairs near the pipes to set fire to the place.

"I'll be back in about a week with the materials I need," I said to DiCapua.

"Okay. I'll be waiting for you to return," he said.

On the way back to Toronto, Cosimo made a promise. A few days after I had finished the job, I was to come to the Casa Commisso to collect my $10,000.

Before I returned to the store I ran into a problem. I'd gone to a cottage I owned to get the dynamite and blasting caps I needed. All told, I had twenty sticks of dynamite. But I had no fuse, and I knew it would be difficult to get fuse, do the job, and not be identified later by inquisitive cops as someone who had bought fuse at some store. My biker friends didn't have any fuse and neither did the Commissos. My alternative was to try using a sparkler, the kind you see used at fireworks displays.

I went to a nearby novelty store and bought a large package of long sparklers—about two feet long. I had no way of being certain my idea would work without testing it, so I returned to the cottage, took a blasting cap, and went out in the backyard. I put a sparkler in the blasting cap. It fit perfectly. Then I lit my makeshift fuse and watched, timing how long it took for the sparkler to reach the cap and blow. It took about two minutes.

That afternoon, June 20, about 6:00 P.M., I arrived in Guelph. It was sunny and hot, and I was sweating as I looked at the package I had filled with the dynamite lying beneath the glove compartment of my Corvette. I was a little nervous, partially because of the heat and its possible effect on the dynamite. I drove around the block where DiCapua's store was. As I drove by, a police paddy wagon passed me. I pulled over to the side of the road a considerable distance from the store, parked in a lot next to a fire station, and waited to be sure the paddy wagon wouldn't return.

At a little after six, I walked back to the store with the dynamite in a gym bag. I was wearing my gym clothes and driving gloves. The door of the store was locked, but as I turned the doorknob, DiCapua appeared and let me in.

He was fidgety—something I didn't need at a time like that.

"I was expecting you last night," he said. "You never showed up so I phoned this man—Rocco—to see what was keeping you."

"I had a problem getting some materials," I said, "that was all. This Rocco—I never talked to him."

As I spoke to him, I unzipped the gym bag and showed him the contents. His eyes sort of bulged out a bit, and he seemed to be shaking, but it didn't stop him from chattering like a magpie.

"Wait 'till late, 'till about one in the morning before you start the fire," he said. "I need plenty of time after I close the store to get home."

Then he walked me to the back door again, opening it to show me the main street behind the building.

"This isn't an alleyway like you told me before," I snapped. I was angry —more at myself than anything for not casing the place better on my own the first time.

DiCapua was clearly afraid, but he kept his head. He gave me the telephone number of the karate club that was adjacent to his store basement.

"Please," he said, "phone them about ten or eleven tonight. Make sure no one's there."

"Don't worry about it," I said. "Of course, I'll check. I don't want anyone in the building any more than you do. Nobody's gonna get hurt. Don't worry."

With that he left, and I went to the basement and sat in the storage area for nearly three hours, listening to the people at the karate club work out. I could hear them through the wall as they kicked the heavy pad, threw each other down, and shouted their so-called battle cries.

When I didn't hear any noise for a while, I dialed the club's number on the phone. I let the phone ring for a long time, hung it up, and then phoned back to be doubly sure no one was there.

While I was listening to the people in the karate club work out, I had carefully pulled the dynamite from the bag and taped it together. I'd also

put in the blasting caps with the sparklers inserted. Before I set the bomb, I walked quickly up the back stairway leading to the door and pulled one of the bars open to make certain that the door would open when I came running back up the stairs. I checked my watch—it was about 12:30 A.M. DiCapua had had plenty of time to establish his alibis. I went back downstairs and started two fires in the storage room area.

As the fires burned, I went to the boiler room and placed the bomb inside. I wanted it to blow the cast-iron boiler and hit the gas main next to it. That would trigger still another explosion and blow the place sky high. Later I learned I had blown open a one-and-a-half-inch gas line that just sent out puffs of flame.

When I set the bomb in the boiler, I placed newspapers around one of the sparklers. As I left, I lit a match and touched the sparkler to the newspapers. They were burning as I dashed from that room, passed the storage room where the other fire was burning strongly, and ran up the stairs and out the back door.

Just as I came out the door I spotted the police paddy wagon I'd seen earlier. It was pulling into a parking lot across the street, and two people were walking up the street toward me. I slammed the door with my right foot, uncertain whether it closed tight or not, put the hood on my gym suit up, and started jogging up the street as if I were working out.

I had used three sparklers to set the bomb off. That gave me six minutes to get out of the area. I jogged down the street, hurdled some guardrails, ran across the railroad tracks and down the street to where my car was parked. By the time I reached the fire hall parking area and my car, the alarm bells hadn't gone off, so the fire hadn't been spotted. It had taken me about a minute to reach the car.

My palms were sweaty, and there was a chill along my spine as I started the car and drove off unhurriedly down some city streets to Highway 7 and then to Route 401.

I went to see Cosimo two days later at the Casa Commisso and collect my money.

"You got the money you owe me, Cosimo?" I asked.

He shook his head. "I'm sorry, Cec," he said. "I gotta go to Guelph and get the money from these people. Come back in few days."

So I did, and he handed me $2,500.

"Where's the rest you promised me?" I said angrily.

"That's all they gave me," he said. "They say the fire department, she come, put out the fire—the building, it no burn."

I didn't believe him. A few days later I drove to Guelph to check. I noticed as I drove by that the windows were all black, and those that weren't were all boarded up.

I then drove around the side of the building to the other block, where a hotel was located. I checked the outside wall and part of the sidewalk —they were intact. The bomb hadn't worked as planned. It had blown the boiler apart and destroyed the room it was in, but it had missed the gas line it was intended to set off. I didn't learn until later that I had just missed by a few feet the city's main gas line, which for some strange reason ran through that building. If I had hit that, blown it up, I'd have taken a whole city block and probably killed a lot of people—something I hadn't even thought about.

The building had burned all right, but not to the ground. The store was destroyed and there was $100,000 damage to other shops in the building, but the building wasn't leveled the way they had planned. Fire investigators never realized the place had been bombed until years later, when I became a witness. They had thought all along that the fire was caused by a gas explosion. No one had even suspected arson or a bomb.

It took me nearly four years to find out that the Commisso brothers had stiffed me on that job. They had collected the $20,000 from the store owners up front. Among crooks on the street, there is a code of honor of sorts. When it came to the Commissos, there was no honor. There was more of a code of honor among biker gang members than with the Commissos. Two sixteen-year-olds breaking into a house had more of a code of honor than these Mafia men did. The only code they had was to look after their "family." I was an outsider. I wasn't Italian or Calabrian, so they stuck it to me.

CHAPTER 13

Shaking the Disco Beat

The Commissos once pitted me against bikers. From the time I became a biker and before, nightclubs, bars, and discotheques were the targets of shakedowns, of extortions, of biker-run prostitution. It didn't matter whether we were in Orlando or Fort Lauderdale, Montreal, Toronto, or some small suburb, the bikers singled out night spots and hotels for all sorts of money-making schemes.

Talent agencies run by bikers or biker associates supplied the topless clubs and the strip joints with strippers and topless dancers. More often than not, the places where the bikers sent their women became centers of prostitution and muggings, and frequently attracted violence between rival biker gangs. Since I had "officially" left the street and biker clubs, nothing had changed except the names. Bikers still had talent agencies, still supplied women, and still muscled clubs that didn't want to do business with them.

The women who work for these agencies don't realize what they're getting into when they go to them for jobs. They think they're dealing with legitimate agencies. Most of them are young, just out of high school. Some of them are girlfriends of bikers who are told to go to the agency and work or else. Still others are starry-eyed kids who think that the agency is really a talent agency, a stepping-stone to stage or television or movies.

Once they start dealing with those running the agency, they're hooked. They're told they have to pay an agent's fee and give a percentage of their

salary to the agency so that the agency can provide them with protection while they strip or dance. Most of the girls don't object. Those who do either get roughed up or find they can't get jobs.

Some of the clubs that the girls dance and strip in are owned by bikers. The Outlaws and the Pagans owned a lot of topless bars, discos, and stripper joints in Long Island, Philadelphia, and Orlando. They were hidden behind corporate fronts, biker relatives, or biker associates, but the club members were the real owners. The vast majority of clubs where bikers' women worked, however, weren't owned by bikers. They were extorted and shaken down by bikers and forced to use biker women as their performers.

Biker club members would go to a nightclub, a small bar, or a disco. They would promise the owners a kickback of the money they collected from the broads the bikers supplied. They'd also promise to look after the broads.

Now the bar owners would go for those tales, those promises because they didn't want bikers to come in and break up their places, and that threat was implied by the bikers.

"Look, if you don't want my women in here, fine, but tomorrow night there may be twenty-five Vagabonds here having a r-e-a-l good party," the biker would say.

So hundreds of bar owners all across the United States and Canada signed contracts to hire dancers, strippers, and entertainers that were supplied by the biker agency. If it was a small club or bar, the owner was also usually invited to use the shuffleboards, pinball machines, and video games that the bikers or their friends owned or controlled. The bar owners still made their profits, and they avoided violence and damage in their clubs and attacks on their employees and patrols.

The biker agency meanwhile put ads in the papers for more dancers. The bikers also muscled in on the talent that other agencies provided for the hotels, bars, and discos on both sides of the border.

A good example of what I'm talking about involved the owner of a disco in Toronto. He was a Greek who went by the name of Cosmo. I was introduced to him by Cosimo.

"Cosmo, he's having trouble with the bikers," Cosimo said. "They

...atan's Choice, outlaw bikers, led by captain Cecil Kirby (*right*) down Airport Road ...Toronto.

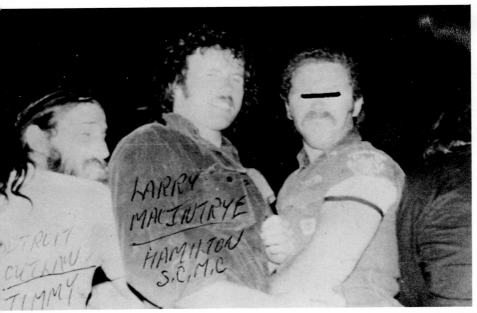

...ecil Kirby partying at the Green Parrot in Key West with Satan's Choice biker ...arry McIntyre (*center*) and Timmy, Detroit biker.

Killer blast. Wah Ken Chinese Restaurant, Elizabeth Street, Toronto, after Kirby set off 100 sticks of dynamite in a Mafia contract bombing. One man was killed and another injured in the blast on May 4, 1977. TORONTO STAR SYNDICATE

eft: Mafia leader Paul Volpe's fortresslike home where Kirby arranged a faked *b*micide and later secretly met with the crime boss. TORONTO STAR SYNDICATE *ight*: Paul Volpe, member of the Stefano Magaddino crime family, murdered in a *l*ngland struggle for power. CANADA WIDE FEATURE SERVICES, LTD.

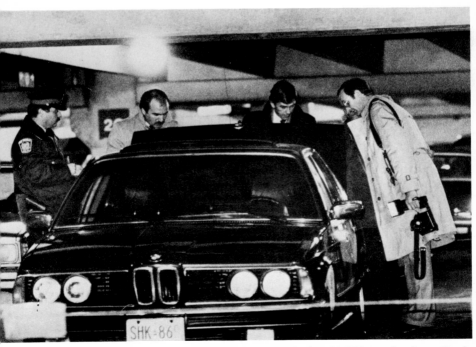

*P*earson International Airport, Toronto. Police search the BMW trunk where Paul *V*olpe's body was found November 13, 1983, two years after Kirby saved his life. *T*HE GLOBE AND MAIL, TORONTO

Rocco Remo Commisso, Calabrian Mafia leader now serving a fourteen-year sentence for extortion and conspiracy to murder as a result of Cecil Kirby's testimony.
CANADA WIDE FEATURE SERVICES, LTD.

Mick Rocco, the godfather of the Canadian Calabrian Mafia, is laid to rest.
THE GLOBE AND MAIL, TORONTO

Left: Philadelphia associates meet with Peter Scarcella in Toronto under the watchful eyes of the police, March 1981.
Right: Police photo shows meeting between Peter Scarcella and Paul Volpe just before Kirby is given the contract to kill Volpe.

Left: Antonio Rocco Romeo, convicted in the plot to kill Helen Nafpliotis, former Connecticut girlfriend of a Calabrian Mafia leader's brother.
Right: Helen Nafpliotis, saved in a daring rescue by Kirby in cooperation with the FBI. THE STAMFORD ADVOCATE

Police surveillance photo of Michele Commisso entering a car with an unidentified male after meeting with Kirby to pay him for a contract outside a Howard Johnson hotel in Toronto.

Cecil Kirby leaves the Howard Johnson hotel with Cosimo Commisso in Kirby's bugged car during one of a number of clandestine meetings in which plans for murder and extortion were recorded. (These photos, along with police recording helped convict Commisso.)

Police surveillance photo of Cosimo Commisso and Kirby meeting at the Toronto disco Faces to plan crimes.

Cecil Kirby (*back to camera*) holds an animated conversation with Cosimo Commisso as police record discussion with a body mike worn by Kirby.

The meeting breaks up with Commisso (*left*) walking off and Kirby (*right*) crossing the parking lot to his car to meet with police. Within weeks, Commisso was arrested.

been causin' fights, damage in his club. They even raped his waitress and one of his customers."

"Which bikers?" I asked.

"The Paradice Riders," he answered. "They cause him lotsa trouble." Then he added, "You talk to them—get them to stay outta the place for a while. If they do, this guy, he'll pay—we'll all make some money."

"Okay," I said, "I'll see what I can do, but tell your friend it's probably going to cost him. Bikers don't do things for nothing, and you know I don't."

So I went to see a friend of mine at the Paradice Riders—one of the top officers—and I talked to him about the problem and about the rapes. I told him one of his biker members, a guy named Terry, and some of his friends had raped this waitress twice and one of the customers.

"Look," I told my friend, "stay out of the disco for a while. The guy, this Cosmo, is willing to pay me money if you do. We'll all make money."

At first my friend was against the idea. "Hell no, Cec," he said. "We don't want any fucker tellin' us to stay outta his place. Nobody tells us where to go."

"Okay, okay, I understand what you're saying, but just stay out of there for a while—as a favor to me," I said. "I can make a few bucks. You know, one hand washes the other."

So he agreed. I offered him a kickback—a couple of hundred bucks for him and some of the boys to have a night on the town—but he refused. He was doing it as a favor, and you don't get paid for favors. I told him to tell Terry I'd get the girl off his back—stop her from testifying against him.

With the deal cut, I went back to Cosmo, and we sat down with the disco owner.

"My friend here," Cosmo said, "he's talked to the bikers. They know him and they're gonna stay outta your place. But it's gonna cost you. Nothing's for free."

Cosmo understood. He came up with several thousand dollars to pay for the protection that Cosmo was providing through me. He also had a long talk with the waitress. She agreed to forget what Terry and his friends looked like. Terry never came back. He went into hiding in the

States with another biker gang because the coppers had warrants out for his arrest on that rape and some other similar assaults. And the club— it burned down a couple of months later. I was never sure whether the bikers did it or it was an accident. I didn't care. I'd collected the money and Cosimo had kept maybe $500.

In May 1979 I set up the Superior Fitness Centre. I bought the club from a friend of mine who wanted to get out of the health/fitness business. I wanted in because I needed a business as a front and because I thought I could make some money out of it. It was a dumb move.

It wasn't long before I was commingling gun smuggling, bombings and arsons, and plots to shake down discos in the health club. I didn't pay attention to the business, and as a result I lost money on it.

I soon found out that I wasn't a particularly good health club businessman. By August 1980 I'd sold out and just about broken even on the deal. For over a year, it did provide a good front for my operations and for meetings with the Commissos and others I had criminal deals with.

Early in the summer of 1979, not long after we had straightened things out for the Greek disco owner, the Commissos told me they were convinced there was gold to be mined in Toronto's discos. Because I was an ex-biker with a lot of contacts among biker gangs and the rounders, I was the key to the plan.

The idea was simple—use biker gangs to break up clubs and muscle club owners and then, for a fee, promise them protection from biker intimidation. Of course, the bikers would get some of the profits, and they would only be asked to stay away from a club that was paying for protection *temporarily*. After a few weeks or months they could go back and terrorize it some more, and the Commissos would collect all over again. It was the first real semialliance between some of the biker gangs and the Calabrian Mafia. It was at best shaky, because no one trusted anyone, and for good reason.

The first test of the extortion alliance, as I'll call it, came when Cosimo came to see me at the health club. He knew a disco owner named Mike who ran an after-hours club. The place had become a target of the Vagabonds, who the owner had mistakenly tried to keep out. They kept coming back to break up his club and harass his customers.

"I don't know, Cosimo," I said. "You don't tell bikers to stay out of places. They don't care about the money. It's a matter of pride."

"Try, Cec," he said. "See Mike. See what you can work out."

I set up the meeting with the disco owner at Harvey's Restaurant and talked to him about his problem.

"Maybe I can get the bikers to stop breaking up your joint, Mike, but it's going to cost you," I said.

"How much?" he asked.

"Two grand now—maybe some more later, but at least you'll be in business," I said. "The way things are now, you're just about shut down."

"Okay, see what you can arrange," he answered. Then he reached in his pocket and handed me $1,000. "Here's half on account."

I went to see a friend of mine at the Vagabonds and explained that I was rousting this disco owner for a quick buck.

"Look, get the guys to stay away from this joint for a few weeks, maybe a month," I said. "That'll give me a chance to make some money off the guy and I'll look after you. Besides, we've helped each other before."

My friend agreed. "Seeing it's you, Cec, okay," he said. "This guy's an asshole. When you've gotten what you want outta him let me know. Then we'll go back and break his lousy club up again."

I laughed, slapped him on the back, and left. For the next two weeks I collected $1,000 a week from Mike. I was supposed to split with Cosimo, but all he asked for was $500 and that's all I gave him. He figured I was splitting with the bikers. I gave my friend some, but I kept most of it.

There were other clubs we shook down the same way. Some worked, but one didn't—a place called the Peaches on Pears Disco. It was owned by a guy named David Freedman, who I knew through the gambler friends that I'd gone to Colombia with. Cosimo knew about Peaches on Pears and he knew about Freedman, who he said had plenty of money and would be an easy extortion.

Freedman had helped me out a few times, and I wasn't about to shake him down for Cosimo. While I gave a nodding agreement to Cosimo to handle the deal, I secretly called Freedman at his apartment in Hyde Park to warn him.

"Look, Dave, some people want me to lean on you, you know," I said.

"Remember that other place, that disco that burned down not far from your place? Be careful—you don't need their kind of trouble."

Freedman was quick to show he had no fear of the implied threat that I was trying, in my own way, to warn him about.

"I don't know what you're saying to me, Cec," Freedman said, "but if anyone is trying to put the arm on me, they're gonna get nothing. If they burn my place down, they'll be doing me a favor."

"Dave, forget it," I said. "I'm just trying to give you a friendly warning —nothing more. Just make sure your insurance premiums are paid up."

I went back to Cosimo and said to him, "Forget about Freedman and his club. No way are you going to extort the guy. He's not going to pay up."

Not all of the disco owners were targets for shakedowns by the bikers and the Commissos. At least one, Harold Arviv, had his own ideas about how to make money and get rid of business partners.

Arviv pleaded guilty in 1986 for his role in a conspiracy to blow up his disco on January 9, 1980. That's when Gi Shik Moon, the Korean ex-sergeant and partner of Yanover, took thirty sticks of dynamite and blew the disco sky-high, causing over $700,000 in damage. Yanover and Michael Gerol, who supplied the dynamite, were convicted when Moon testified against them. Moon said that Arviv offered him $10,000 "front money" and 25 percent of the insurance to blow up the place. Moon agreed to do the job after talking it over with Yanover, who was in prison at the time and was to split the proceeds. I'd introduced Yanover to Arviv —but I'm getting ahead of myself.

I first met Arviv in November 1977 through a Satan's Choice biker friend of mine, Frank Lenti, who frequently worked out at the health club that I kept in shape in by lifting weights.

Lenti at first told me that he had a million-dollar burglary setup that he wanted me to go in on. The burglary was to be that of a house owned by a Jack Mamann. Arviv and Mamann had been business partners in a place called the Hippopotamus Restaurant, which I later robbed, on January 15, 1978, for Arviv.

Lenti said that the information on the setup came from Arviv, who

wanted us to rob Mamann's house and split the money we found with him. I agreed. The terms were I would take 50 percent of whatever we got, and Lenti and Arviv would split the other 50 percent. I was taking the lion's share because I had the experience and I'd be doing most of the work planning and executing the job.

I did a surveillance on the house and kept track of the people who were in and out at different times. On the day I decided to break into the place, I telephoned to be sure there was no one in and then donned a postman's uniform I had in the trunk of my car.

I drove past the house again, making sure no one was around, parked a few blocks away, hoisted a mailbag with a crowbar inside over my shoulder, and walked to the house. I rang the doorbell, waited a minute or so for an answer, and, when there was none, went to the rear of the house and broke in through a glass sliding door.

I searched the den, the bedrooms, the whole damned house for about seven or eight minutes before the phone started ringing and ringing. I had a feeling I might have been spotted by a neighbor who was calling to see if someone was home or if I was in there alone. So I left—empty-handed.

I was steamed over finding nothing, and a few days later I told Lenti. He went back to talk to Arviv, who claimed that there was money in the place and that he wanted me to go back and try to find it.

I told Lenti the only way to do the job now was to stage an armed robbery. In December 1977 I recruited a couple of friends who had just come out of jail to handle the job, Gary Barnes and a friend of his.

I took them to the house, showed them the layout, and told them what I wanted done. Then I supplied them with two balaclavas—handcuffs— and one revolver, a P-38 that I gave to Barnes. His friend had his own gun. I drove them to the house that evening. I parked about two blocks away while they went to do the robbery.

They got inside when someone opened the door and handcuffed one of Mamann's older sons. Mamann was not at home. They said the family was upset—the kids were crying, so was the wife, and she denied that there was a big stash of money in the house. All they got was some jewelry and a few hundred bucks in cash. When they met me at the car, I drove off, checked the jewelry, and found Mamann's name engraved on a gold

bracelet. There were also some rings. I told my friends to keep the money, but the jewelry I threw out over the roof of the car into a vacant lot near a car-wrecking lot.

When I saw Lenti again he told me that Arviv had told him that Mamann had taken the money out of his house two days before the robbery and had had it deposited in an account in a Swiss bank.

I wasn't too happy about all the trouble I'd gone to for nothing, and I told Lenti that I wanted to see Arviv personally. A meeting was arranged at Arviv's disco, which was under construction at the time. It was early January 1978.

When I went to meet with Arviv, I was carrying a .22 caliber High Standard automatic with a silencer in the front of my pants, hidden by my coat. I was prepared for anything. Arviv, Lenti told me, was a former Israeli army commando. I suspected that he could be violent and might have armed himself for the meeting.

Arviv didn't know me as Cecil Kirby. Lenti had never told him or his contacts who I was. He knew me only as "George," a name I used frequently when Cosimo introduced me to some of his "clients."

"You owe me some money, Mr. Arviv," I said. "You owe me for a B&E and a robbery—and I figure those two jobs were worth twenty thousand dollars."

He agreed that he owed me money for what I'd done for him and said he'd pay me $10,000. There was a problem, however. He said that because his expenses were running high at the disco he was building he'd have to cover what he owed with several payments.

All the time he talked, I felt the gun cool and hard against my gut. Because of the way it was positioned in my pants, it was damned near impossible for me to sit down, so I paced up and down slowly, keeping my jacket on to conceal what I had. If he made a move—tried anything —I was ready to blow him away right where he sat. But he didn't. He didn't give me a hard time at all.

The next day we met at the Hungarian Gourmet Restaurant, where he paid me $2,000 in cash and later, at another meeting, paid me another $1,000. It was then that he told me he had a friend that was the manager of an after-hours club and that he would talk to this guy to arrange a fake robbery of the night deposits. He figured I'd get at least $10,000

from the job, and I could keep that plus the money he'd already given me.

On January 15 I held up Yvo Sajet, the manager of the Hippopotamus —the club Arviv told me to hit—using his description of Sajet and his European sports car.

I parked about a block away from the parking lot of the Hippopotamus and waited for a couple of hours. First, some women who appeared to be waitresses got into a car and left. I walked back down the street cautiously and stood at the edge of the parking lot, about seventy-five feet from the manager's sports car.

I saw a man come out of the club and walk to the car carrying some boxes, which he put on the car roof. I appeared out of the dark behind the guy. He was about six foot three, 210 pounds—a big man.

As he opened the car door, I said, as Arviv had told me to, "You have something for me?"

Sajet hesitated for a minute, then answered: "Yes, I do." One box was still on the roof of the car. He pointed to it. "This is what you want."

"Turn around and bend down a little bit," I said, disguising my voice as best I could. As he did I hit him with a blackjack I was carrying. The blackjack flew from my hand in front of the car. Sajet was semiconcious, lying on the ground. I grabbed the boxes, and as I walked around he said there was still something in the car. I looked inside, saw another box, grabbed it, and then walked to the front of the car, picking up my blackjack.

"Give me about ten minutes," I said to him, "then call the police." Then I jumped the fence, ran behind some apartment houses, down the street to my car, and opened the trunk, throwing the boxes inside. When I checked the boxes out I found only $4,800 in cash and some charge receipts.

When I saw Arviv again, I told him he still owed me $2,000—that his friend wasn't carrying as much as he'd promised. Arviv said he realized that, but he couldn't pay me the $2,000 right away because he was short on cash. In the months that followed, Arviv kept his word and paid me what he owed. He seemed to be a gentleman among the criminals I had known.

There was an attempt at extortion after that. One of my original

contacts and some other guys, one biker from Satan's Choice, went to him and tried to shake Mamann down. They hadn't talked to me about it—it was something they did on their own, and they were caught by the cops.

Arviv really hated Mamann. He never really explained why. He said he had started the Hippopotamus and that Mamann and his brother were his partners. After a bitter separation, Arviv went into a clothing business that went under. He said he tore the store down and then started building the disco on money he borrowed from lawyers and other people. I couldn't figure out why he was having so much trouble getting money. His father-in-law was Louis (Lou) Chesler, a multi-million-dollar Canadian financier who was chairman of both the General Development Corp., which sold Florida homes and lots through the mails, and Universal Controls Inc., a big electronics firm. Chesler had also worked in the Bahamas as part of a group that developed a gambling resort at Freeport.

In October 1978, when I was on a diamond-buying visit to Yanover, Chuckie asked me if I knew Arviv. I told him I did and he said his friend Gi Shik Moon had lost a ring of his in a fight at Arviv's Disco.

"You want me to see if I can get the ring back?" I asked.

Yanover nodded.

The next night, Lenti and I picked up Yanover and went to the Oriental Palace, where we met Moon, who told me what happened at the fight. Leaving Moon behind, the three of us went to Arviv's Disco and sat down with Arviv. I introduced Arviv to Yanover and told him about Moon losing the ring. Arviv said he had found the ring after the fight and had turned it over to police because no one had claimed it. While we sat there drinking his booze on the house, he sent one of his flunkies out to the police and within an hour had the $3,000 ring back in Yanover's hand. That meeting was to lead to the Moon contract to blow up the disco for Arviv.

Maybe ten months later I brought Cosimo to the disco. Arviv had told me he was tired of running the place and wanted very badly to sell it. Since Cosimo wanted to get into the disco business while he was using me to shake down most of the owners in town, I told him that the disco was for sale and that it might be an opportunity for him. He could use a front man to operate it.

Cosimo had other ideas. He tried to strong-arm Arviv and shake him

down for the business. Arviv was too smart for that. He suggested that if Cosimo wanted the place he come up with a million bucks and, lacking that, be a nice guy and sip the free champagne. Cosimo backed off on his extortion try after that—I was never certain why, but it could have been because of Arviv's father-in-law. Chesler had some heavy friends—people like Meyer Lansky, the American syndicate's financial wizard, and Trigger Mike Coppola. Those friendships and the respect Chesler had with mob people probably made Cosimo think twice.

A couple weeks after that, in the middle of August 1979, I returned to the disco and Arviv told me that he couldn't sell the business so he'd decided to blow it up.

"Can you do the job?" he asked.

"For fifteen thousand dollars I can do it," I said.

"Make it ten thousand dollars, after it's done," he said. "I'll get the money to pay you then."

"I'll need money for the dynamite," I said. "It'll take a big bomb here in this room." The room we were in was at the rear of the bottom floor.

At first he wanted to supply the explosives, but I told him no—I wanted to buy the dynamite and be sure of the stuff I got. He gave me $300 to make the buy. The bombing was to be done within a few months. I did buy some dynamite, but I never went back to see Arviv or deal with him. In 1981 I turned the dynamite over to the Ontario Provincial Police after I had become an informer.

On January 8, 1980, Arviv's Disco blew sky-high. Nobody was hurt. For a while I couldn't figure out who had done the job. I thought I was the only bomber in the city. In 1983 the truth came out. Moon pleaded guilty and got a five-year sentence. He testified against Yanover, who got nine years, and Gerol, who got seven.

Arviv at first fled the country and holed up in Miami. He finally was extradited to Canada, where he was freed on bail put up by his mother-in-law, Molly Chesler. She put up $250,000 cash, a $250,000 surety bond guaranteed by a condo. There were two more $100,000 bonds guaranteed by property owned by a popcorn company executive and a real estate executive.

As an added guarantee, Arviv had to surrender both his Canadian and Israeli passports. He's still awaiting a trial that I'm supposed to testify at,

but it's been stalled for more than two years by his lawyers. Moon and Yanover were convicted and jailed—even Sajet was jailed for thirty days for misleading police with the false robbery report. Arviv pleaded guilty in April 1986, just before I was scheduled to testify at his trial. He was to be sentenced in September. There's still more than $100,000 on my head and a lot of people standing in line, waiting for an opportunity to get me out in the open once more.

Cosimo too often acted on impulse. It was a part of his personality that often seemed to cause him problems, and where his family was involved the impulse could be violent. An insult to his family could have an injurious if not fatal impact on the lives of innocent people. One incident in particular involved a restaurant in downtown Toronto.

There was fire in Cosimo's eyes when he began pounding on a table and cursing in Italian as I entered the office at the Casa Comisso.

"Hey, Cec," he said. "I got a job for you."

"Whatcha want me to do, Cosimo?" I asked.

"I'll give you two grand to blow up this *ristorente* downtown," he said. "I want you to throw a bomb right through their fuckin' window, you understand?"

"Sure," I said, "through the window. But what place are we talking about?"

"It's this fuckin' Napoleon Ristorante," he shouted.

While he was talking—his face flushed—he was counting out $2,000 on the table in front of me. That was unusual and gave me a hint at the depth of his anger. He almost never paid for a job up front.

I asked him why he wanted the place hit and he explained that the night before his wife and his mother-in-law had stopped at the restaurant. While they were there his wife had an argument with the woman who owned the restaurant.

"This woman," he shouted. "she threw my wife and the mother out and my wife, she's very upset and insulted." He pounded again on the table. "Throw the bomb right through the fuckin' window."

"Suppose there's people in there," I asked.

"I don't care," he snapped. "You do it Sunday night, when the owner is there. I don't care if there's anybody else inside at all. Fuck them. Just blow the inside of the place right out, you understand?"

148

"Okay, okay," I said. He was very agitated, and it was no time to question him. "I'll do something similar to what you want," I said.

So I went to my cottage and made up a bomb that consisted of two sticks of dynamite, a battery, and a timer and brought it back that same night. I cased the restaurant and then parked my car on a nearby corner.

I slipped down the side of an alley on the east side of the restaurant and put the bomb on a window ledge. For a split second I took my eye off the bomb as I reached into my pocket to get something. I felt like I was suspended in time watching my own killing as I saw the bomb fall from the ledge to the ground. It took only seconds, but I thought it was in slow motion and that my hands were frozen to my pants. As it hit the ground, my heart literally stopped.

If I had had it wired to the blasting cap and I had had the cap in the dynamite, I wouldn't be here to tell this story. They'd still be scrapping pieces of me off the buildings.

After I caught my breath, I picked the bomb up slowly, put it back on the window ledge, made sure it was firmly in place, set the timer, and left. I was in the North End of Toronto, about twenty miles away, when it went off.

The next day I read in the paper that the bomb had injured three women. Now that wasn't what I had intended. Despite Cosimo's orders, I had phoned the restaurant before I arrived to make sure that nobody was inside. I had let the phone ring about thirty times, and when nobody answered I figured it was safe.

When I placed the bomb, I couldn't see inside because the window was so thick and there were no lights on. But I guess the owner and two of her friends had returned to the restaurant after I'd left and were sitting inside when the bomb went off, sending glass flying through the air like razor-sharp missiles.

Police told me later that one of the iron bars outside the window next to the bomb was blasted loose and thrown across the room where the women were. The police said it narrowly missed the owner's head and struck the wall. If it had hit her it might have decapitated her. They were all hurt, cut up pretty bad. Later, they received awards for damages and injuries from the criminal compensation board, but they at least survived.

And Cosimo? He was pleased as hell over the results. He didn't give a damn about the women. The insult had to be avenged and it was. For

a time, however, the papers blamed it on French terrorists. The bomb had gone off at 8:45 P.M. on May 4, 1980, the anniversary of Prime Minister Margaret Thatcher's taking office in England. She'd opposed French separatists' plans to have the Province of Quebec declared a separate country.

There was one other club owner, a restaurateur really, that Cosimo put the arm on. He wasn't trying to collect for himself on this one—he was trying to collect a debt that Willie O'Bront, the French rackets friend and money launderer of crime boss Vincent Cotroni, said was due him. O'Bront lived in Hallandale, Florida, where he was accused by U.S. drug agents in 1983 of operating a $50-million-a-year narcotics trafficking ring.

In early July 1980 I went to see Cosimo about the job. The target was Maury Kalen, then the owner of Mr. Greenjeans Restaurants in Toronto.

"This Kalen, he owes money—a hundred thousand—to a friend of mine, to Willie O'Bront," Cosimo said. "I want you to send the message to him with a bomb."

Now I knew who and what O'Bront was, but I knew nothing about Kalen, so I took Cosimo at his word. I also took his word that he knew where Kalen lived when he gave me the address of his house in Toronto. I had a description of his car and the locations of his office in Village Grange and of the restaurants, one on Lombard Street and the other in the crowded Eaton Center. The Greenjeans Restaurants weren't anything elaborate, but they were popular for their salad bars and food.

Cosimo wanted me to set off a bomb in Kalen's house or his car, but on looking over the area, I figured the best thing to do was drop a couple of sticks of dynamite taped together without a fuse in the mailbox at his home.

I ruled out bombing the car as being too dangerous. The restaurants were out as far as I was concerned because there were too many people around them. I figured the bomb in the mailbox was as good a message as any explosion, and that way no one would get hurt. If something more violent was needed later—well, that was another story.

The job was worth $2,000, and Cosimo paid me the fee. Late on the night of July 7, I dropped the two sticks in the mailbox. I learned later that two guys in a room where Kalen was supposed to be saw the two sticks

land inside their mail cage by the door. They called the cops, and early on the morning of July 8 the Metropolitan Toronto Police Explosive Disposal Unit came out to remove the dynamite.

A week later I got a call from Cosimo and met him again at the banquet hall.

"Cec, this Kalen, he moved from Heath Street just before you put the dynamite there," he said. "I want you to go to his new home and bomb it. I'll give you two thousand more."

The new location was the Palace Pier.

"Cosimo, that place is crawling with security guards," I said. "It's too tough to hit."

Cosimo smiled broadly. "Don't worry, Cec," he said. "I'll take care of the guards. I know people there."

"You mean that the security guard will let me in to place a bomb at the fuckin' door!" I said.

"Well, maybe not," he said.

I told him I wouldn't handle the job, and later I learned from police that it wasn't Kalen that owed O'Bront money, but supposedly his father. Not only was Cosimo stupid about what he thought could be done, but he did lousy homework on addresses and his victims.

CHAPTER 14

False Hopes, False Starts

Today, Montreal's Mafia is supposed to be run by a Sicilian "man of respect" who they call Nicholas Rizzuto. He divides his time between Canada and Venezuela, where he has a business. I don't know Rizzuto personally. I do know that he and the Commissos were close. I also know that for many years before Rizzuto took over, Montreal's Mafia was ruled by Vincent Cotroni and the three Violi brothers—Paolo, Rocco, and Francesco. All of them had two things in common. They were Calabrians and they had gotten to where they were in Montreal because of Carmine (Lillo) Galante.

Galante was Joseph Bonanno's underboss before he was killed in July 1979. While he was with Bonanno, he was sent to Montreal to organize a branch of their New York crime family. That, along with other things, caused Buffalo mob boss Stefano Magaddino to complain about Bonanno ignoring other mafiosi to plant "his flags" all over the world. I'm told that the Cotroni brothers and the Violi brothers were, like Galante, among the most vicious killers and Mafia men ever to walk the streets of Montreal.

Galante's top men at first were Giuseppe and Vincent Cotroni. The youngest brother, Francesco or Frank, moved up later. At the same time, the Cotronis' closest supporter and enforcer was Paolo Violi. The only guy who wasn't a Calabrian was Galante—he was born in the States. His father was supposed to be an immigrant fisherman from Castellammare del Golfo, the same Sicilian village that Bonanno came from.

They formed a Bonanno family branch that ruled Montreal and provided a smuggling route into the United States for heroin that was imported from Sicily and Marseilles. Public hearings in the States and narcotics agents later confirmed that.

The Montreal Bonanno branch then became a full-fledged Canadian crime family run by Vincent Cotroni. Galante eventually became Bonanno's successor and got greedy. He tried to take over the narcotics supply routes of some other bosses of the American Cosa Nostra, and they had him knocked off by his own people, replacing him with Philip Rastelli, who had a lot of friends in Toronto. Before Galante was killed, Cotroni went to jail for a couple of years and Paolo Violi became the acting boss of the Montreal family, according to a Quebec crime commission inquiry.

I first became aware there were problems between the Commisso brothers and the Violis on February 11, 1977. That was a couple of days after Francesco Violi, the youngest brother, was killed at the headquarters of a Violi importing and distributing company. He was supposed to have been backed against a wall and shot in the face by a shotgun. Another killer made sure he was dead by pumping some bullets into him from a handgun.

Cosimo called me and told me it was very important I come as quickly as possible to the Casa Commisso. When I arrived, Cosimo was pacing up and down and Remo was nowhere to be seen.

"So I'm here," I said. "What's the big hurry?"

"I need some guns—some pistols and shotguns, and I need them fast," Cosimo said.

"How many?" I asked.

"I need five, six, maybe more if you can get them," he said. He was very agitated.

"What the hell you need them so fast for?" I asked.

"You ask a lotta questions, Cec—maybe too many," he snapped.

He looked at me, his eyes flashing a bit. I was starting to get pissed off myself now, and I made sure he knew how I felt.

"Oh for chrissake, Cosimo. You want guns I'll get you guns," I said sharply. "I don't really give a damn why you want them."

His voice softened, and for the first time he sat down. "I'm sorry, Cec," he said. "You see the stories about Frank Violi?"

"Yeah, sure," I said.

"Well, the people in Montreal, they think me and Remo killed him," he said. He paused and lowered his voice. "We may have to go to Montreal to kill the rest of the family—like we get this guy."

Had he and Remo killed Francesco Violi? I had only what he said that morning and the way he was acting to go on. Just because he said they got Francesco didn't mean they did, but he was desperate for guns at that moment. I didn't press him any more on what had happened. Within a day or two I had acquired all the guns he wanted. When I was ready to deliver them, I called the Casa Commisso and asked for Cosimo. He wasn't there, but Remo was.

"I got that package ready that you need," I told him.

"Forget it, Cec," he said, "we're not going to need them."

Almost a year went by before the Violis made headlines again. This time it was Paolo who hit the front page.

"Blood spilling is feared after Mafia boss killed," was the headline of the January 24, 1978, *Toronto Sun*. The story was about how Paolo Violi was killed in his Jean Talon bar and restaurant on January 22 when two masked men burst in from the street to gun him down while he played cards. Both of the killers were using shotguns, a favorite Italian Mafia weapon. Four men, Sicilians, were arrested and later convicted of conspiracy to murder Violi.

Were the Commissos involved? I remember going to their banquet hall the day after the murder. We were constantly meeting at that time, handling hijacked cigarettes, arsons, extortions, assaults.

"Where's Remo?" I asked Cosimo.

"He's in Montreal," Cosimo answered.

"Wasn't that where Violi was killed in his restaurant?" I asked.

"Yeah, isn't that funny?" he said with a smirk on his face.

It was funny, all right, but I found something else that was strange. Both the Violi brothers had been gunned down with shotguns. Remo's favorite weapon was the shotgun. He loved skeet shooting, but he also said the shotgun was his favorite weapon in Italy. They were also close friends of Rizzuto, the guy who took over the Montreal mob from the Violis.

On October 19, 1980, the last of the Violi brothers, Rocco, was killed by a single shot in the heart while he sat at his kitchen table with his wife

and two children in his home in the east end of Montreal. The cops said the shooting was by a professional killer. I remember wondering at the time if the Commissos were involved. It was their style. They wouldn't hesitate about killing a guy in front of his wife and kids. Any family that would kill whole families in Italy, including a baby in a crib, would kill a rival in front of his family. They had no ethics—no honor about murder —when it came to wielding power.

For some reason, 1978 and 1979 were years when a lot of the Commissos' extortions and arsons went wrong. It had to do with their lack of planning, their rush to do things without checking them through thoroughly. Some Calabrian friend would want them to burn down his place right away to collect insurance and they'd hand me the job and say go do it without even looking it over. If someone got hurt or even killed because they were careless, they didn't care.

The Avala Tavern was typical. It was located in Toronto and was owned by a friend of the Commissos who was never fully identified to me. Remo, who could speak the King's English when he wanted to or pretend he needed an interpreter when he was in court, just handed me a key to the back door and told me to use garbage bags filled with gasoline to start the fire.

I'd never been in the place before, never had a chance to see where things were, so when I got there on the night of July 6 it was like groping in a dark unfamiliar closet.

I was carrying a jerrican filled with a mixture of kerosene and oil. Wherever I went in the damned place I kept banging into things. I finally found my way to the basement, where Remo wanted me to start the fire, but when I got there I couldn't find a light switch. There were none. I couldn't find the damned door to the upstairs either. I left the can lying behind me and I was lighting matches, trying to see where I was going, because like a dope I hadn't brought a flashlight. From the beginning, this assignment had been a disaster because it hadn't been planned.

I finally found a couch downstairs, and I took the jerrican and poured the stuff I had in it all over the couch. Now Remo wanted me to shut the back door to the basement behind me and lock it. What that did was cut off all the air. Since I couldn't find the upstairs door to open so the

fire could spread to the upper section of the tavern, this fire had nowhere to go but out.

At 4:38 A.M., the Metropolitan Toronto Fire Department was called to the scene by a police constable who spotted the fire. The damage was limited to the couch, and the blaze had virtually gone out by itself by the time the firemen arrived.

The Commissos only paid me about a hundred dollars because the place hadn't burned down. Even if I'd burned the place to the ground, I would have gotten only a few hundred bucks. Later on some young Italian was hired by someone to go back to the tavern and torch it. The kid got caught in the fire he set. He was convicted, but he needed a lot of medical treatment first.

A month later the Commissos had another arson scheme that was almost as bad. This time the place was a restaurant and banquet hall in Niagara Falls called Vaccaro's Italian Gardens. It was owned by another of their Calabrian friends.

This time I went to the restaurant with Cosimo. He drove while his driver, Vince, sat in the backseat. It gave me an uneasy feeling, like it was a setup, but I shrugged it off as my imagination. It was.

I went with Cosimo because I wanted to plan appropriately. I wasn't going to get caught groping in a dark basement without a light again. When we got to the restaurant, we all took a tour, outside and inside. I went up to the roof and looked around, noticing a giant Ferris wheel nearby, and I checked other buildings in the area. When I was through, we all sat down to a dinner with wine that had been prepared by Cosimo's friend. We talked first in general terms, then more specifically. Even then I felt uncomfortable, because stragglers and wise guys were coming in and wandering around while we talked.

What bothered me most was the way Cosimo's friend wanted it done. He wanted me to bomb the building next door so that his place would catch fire by mistake.

"That's too dangerous, Cosimo," I complained. "It'll take too damned much dynamite to do what he wants. If I put dynamite between the buildings, I can't guarantee that it'll work properly, and somebody could get hurt."

"Don't worry," Cosimo said. "It's worth ten, fifteen thousand dollars if you do the job right."

"I'm telling you, Cosimo, it's too risky to do it the way he wants it," I said. "I can take this place down good if I put the bomb in the kitchen. And there's less chance of somebody getting hurt."

Cosimo's associate wasn't sure he could pay the price. He wanted time to check his insurance policy and told me to come back again later.

A couple of weeks went by, and I didn't hear from Cosimo. Finally I asked him about it.

"Forget it, Cec," he said, "it's all been taken care of."

I learned later that the restaurant had burned to the ground. I never did find out how it was done, and I didn't care.

Sometimes I think carelessness was the Commissos' middle name. They were forever making mistakes, mistakes that injured innocent people or damaged the wrong location. They were reckless. They were like the gang that couldn't shoot straight. The only difference was they could shoot straight, they just didn't shoot or beat up the right people.

As careless and stupid as they seemed to be even to me, they were still making millions, whether they did nickel-and-dime extortions or rattled the cages of a whole industry, like construction. For them there was nothing too big or too small to make money from.

Typical of the nickel-and-dime jobs they managed to screw up was one involving a business called Cook-O-Matic, a pots and pans distributor that operated three miles from the Casa Commisso. The owner of the business was a man named Frank Mauro. Cosimo and Remo had tried a number of times to extort money from him without much success. So they turned to me and I, in turn, went to a friend of mine, a kid I'll call Jimmy Tires.

Jimmy was a young hustler and tough who wanted to make some money on the side, so I told him I'd pay him a few bucks if he hassled Mauro for me while I handled some other work. Jimmy did what he was told. He went to Mauro's business location, flattened all the tires on the guy's car, and then poured paint over it. Then he made some threatening calls to Mauro. It wasn't enough.

Cosimo complained that Mauro still wasn't paying. Finally, one night in December, Cosimo and I drove by Mauro's business. Two men were standing in front of the office loading boxes into a parked car.

"That's him," Cosimo shouted, "that's the fuck that refuses to pay."

"Which one?" I asked.

He pointed to one guy holding a box. "That's him," he said. "I want

you to break his arms like this." He angrily snapped a toothpick between his fingers.

"Screw it," I said. "I'll do it right now." With that I parked the car around the corner, got out, and walked toward the man that Cosimo had identified as Mauro. My head was down so neither man could make out my face.

I caught him cold turkey on the chin. He was bleeding as he fell back and hit his head against the wall. I took off in a dead run around the corner, jumped in the car, and drove off.

It wasn't until years later I found out it was the wrong guy. The guy I'd banged around was the warehouse manager of Cook-O-Matic, a man named Peter Antonucci. I'd hit the guy Cosimo pointed out, but he'd pointed out the wrong man.

Maclean's magazine on June 21, 1982, identified Carmelo Gallo as a key figure in what they called "the Italian Connection" of a multi-million-dollar international opium, heroin, and cocaine smuggling scheme that stretched from Italy and the Middle East to Vancouver and Southeast Asia. They described him as a thirty-five-year-old "cheerful grocer" who had singlehandedly extended the 1981 narcotics trial by four months when he escaped from a Vancouver hospital bathroom during the trial. He was sentenced to life for conspiracy to traffic in heroin, and they gave him another twenty years for conspiring to deal in cocaine. The cops didn't see him again until January 1983, when he gave up to appeal his conviction.

I knew Gallo by a different standard and a different name. When I met him in March 1979 with Cosimo, he was introduced as Carmen Gallo, their "family" man in Vancouver. He was not only their main West Coast connection for heroin, but since 1976 he had been their primary source for counterfeit money. It was the same counterfeit American money that caused so many Calabrians and my biker friends to get either busted or shot.

I met Gallo at the Casa Commisso. He was nicer than most of the Calabrians that I'd met at the banquet hall or with Cosimo. He was a little guy, sort of quiet, always smiling, with a sense of humor and and the kind of laugh that made others laugh. He was only about thirty-two years old

at the time, with wavy brown hair and brown eyes. That was one thing about the Commissos' Mafia family. They were almost all young. There weren't any old-timers, any of what they call the Mustache Pete types.

When Cosimo introduced me to Gallo, he told me that after Gallo returned to Vancouver, he would be calling to arrange for me to join him on the West Coast.

"Carmen's gonna give us information for a big robbery that you're gonna handle," he said.

Cosimo went on to describe what they had in mind. It involved a courier who left an underground location in downtown Vancouver carrying a bag full of money—$200,000 to $500,000.

"They've been doing this for years," he explained. "They got no security—no guards, no cops, no gun, nothin'. This courier, he just takes the bag of money—he brings it out to the docks and pays the fishermen. They do it for one week steady, every day and that's it. We get only one shot at the jackpot."

"Okay," I said, "I'm ready to leave any time. Just get ahold of me the usual way."

A week or so later I got a call and flew out to Vancouver, where I met Gallo again, this time at an Italian restaurant. He took me to a twelve dollar-a-night hotel in the Jewish section of town and got me a room.

"I'll be back in the morning to take you down to the place we want to hit," he said. "I'll have a driver to get you there. You'll have a gun, handcuffs, everything you need for the job."

I should have known right then to case the courier and the location on my own. The trouble was they had never given me details on the location, what route the courier followed, the times he left and arrived—nothing.

The next morning Gallo showed up at the hotel. There was no driver with him, no gun or handcuffs, and he wasn't smiling as he usually did.

"We missed it. We missed the last payroll yesterday," he said dejectedly. "I tried to call Remo but it was ridiculous. He wouldn't listen. You can't talk to him."

With the right information and the right time it could have been a simple job. I would have just had to flatten the tire on the courier's car and when he changed the tire, knocked him out, thrown him in the trunk,

159

and left with the bag of money. I'd have been back in Toronto by the time he got out to report the heist.

I was supposed to get one-third of whatever was in that bag. Gallo was to get a third, and the Commissos would have gotten a third. The truth is, I'd planned to take half to make up for all the money they still owed me. It was just another false hope, a false start on another plot that failed.

Probably the worst arson plan of all was the one carried out at the Dominion Hotel in Acton, Ontario. I was supposed to blow it up, but like with Vaccaro's Italian Gardens I insisted on certain preconditions, so I didn't handle the job.

I was upset by the plan from the beginning because Cosimo had brought the client, the owner of the hotel, to the Casa Commisso to meet me. That was unusual, and it made me nervous. I didn't like meeting the people who were hiring me through him even though I was always introduced to them as "George." Meetings gave Cosimo a two-on-one edge if any arrests should result from the crimes. The worst part of it was I always had the feeling that I was being set up or used. I never knew if a so-called client was what Cosimo said he was or some Calabrian getting ready to do me in.

As George I met with the hotel owner, Cosimo Mercuri, in early August, just before going to Niagara Falls. Cosimo identified him as Cosimo Val-Currie, not Mercuri. They talked some in Italian first, which I didn't understand, then the hotel owner, who I later testified against as Mercuri, said he wanted me to me to burn the hotel down.

"I'll come up and look at it and tell you the best way to do the job," I said. "Maybe it can be bombed, maybe burning is best." Then I added a word of caution. "There are two things I want to be sure of. I want to be certain there are no people inside, and I want ten thousand dollars up front before I do any planning on this job."

Mercuri admitted there were people living in the hotel, but he didn't seem concerned about it.

"Then they have to be taken out somehow," I said. "You got to make some arrangement so there's no one inside when it goes up—maybe a phone call saying there's a bomb in the building."

"I don't know," Mercuri said. "I don't have the money right now. Give me a week to get the money."

I never heard from him again, but on August 19, 1979, the Dominion Hotel burned to the ground. A fifty-nine-year-old guest named Howard Gibbons was trapped in the fire and died.

Mercuri and two others—Michael McCrystal, one of his hotel employees, and Leonard Cripps—were arrested. Cripps was acquitted, but Mercuri and McCrystal were convicted after I testified about Mercuri coming to me with Cosimo. Mercuri went to jail for twenty-five years while McCrystal got two years.

Vaccaro Gardens, Mercuri, and a dozen other plots that I never got paid to do—they were all part of an increasing mistrust that was developing between us. I had been screwed out of more than $30,000 in promised fees in 1979 alone.

Up to then I had pretty much trusted the Commissos. I knew they had been cheating me, but that wasn't all that unusual in the underworld. Everybody chisels. Everybody's hustling. That's the way of the street. Even so, there was always a nagging feeling at the back of my mind about why they had chosen me as their chief enforcer. I wasn't Calabrian. I wasn't a sworn member of their Honoured Society. I played by my rules, not theirs.

I had always figured that the Commissos had gone outside their group because they didn't have anyone within the group who was straight enough, with the capabilities I had—the experience—to handle their jobs. Yet I knew that there was a possibility, a likelihood, that they might eventually kill me because I knew too much about their operations, had handled too many jobs for them.

While that uncertainty bothered me, it didn't concern me enough to fear for my life. In truth, I didn't really worry that much about living or dying. The day I started working for the Commissos, I had been divorced by my wife. It was my own fault for fooling around with other women. I had lost her and my daughter, and I really didn't have a handle on where my life was going.

I remember asking Cosimo when I started working for him in 1976 about my predecessor.

"I know you had to have somebody working for you—doing what I'm going to be doing," I said. "What happened to him?"

"Oh, he went back to Italy," Cosimo said. "He didn't want to stay in Canada."

I didn't really believe him then, and I still don't. I figured that the guy had been killed and that sooner or later that was what was in store for me.

I think what made it jell more for me mentally was seeing one deal after another go down the tubes and fewer jobs being offered. The uneasiness was the worst when I saw how Cosimo dealt with other people who worked for him, like Anthony Carnevale.

Carnevale was a drug dealer, a street punk, a guy who robbed card games and pool halls for the Commissos with other street hoods. The Commissos would set up the games and promise to provide protection for them. Then they would turn Carnevale and his thugs loose to hold them up. The robbers would take from $3,000 to $20,000 or more from people who were so-called friends of the Commissos. Carnevale and his men would take the piece allotted to them and give the rest to the Commissos, who planned the jobs. The Commissos made hundreds of thousands of dollars from holdups like that, many of them never reported to police, all of them handled by their stickup men.

On January 12, 1980, Carnevale was killed by a shotgun blast through the window of his parents' home. His girlfriend, who was with him, was badly wounded but she survived. I heard that Cosimo had been tipped that Carnevale was a police informer, yet he'd done nothing to hurt the Commissos or anyone involved in the dozens of robberies they had arranged.

PART FOUR

Government Witness

CHAPTER 15

Let's Make a Deal

He was tall and gangling and there was something that reminded me of Jimmy Stewart in the way he walked and talked. Beneath his cap was a shock of dark brown hair and a mischievous, Irish face. His eyes sort of sparkled with excitement when he talked. When he had something to say, I knew I was listening to the voice of an honest man.

I liked Corporal Mark Murphy from the first moment I met him under a phony name in the parking lot of the Casa Loma. There was nothing devious about the man. He was what he said he was—a tough, dedicated Royal Canadian Mounted Policeman who wanted to fight organized crime in Canada more than he wanted to eat, almost more than he wanted to be with his wife and children, who he really was devoted to.

He had been a important investigator in Operation Oblong, a big RCMP intelligence-gathering mission aimed at the crime organization of Paul Volpe. He was familiar with and had worked on Nate Klegerman, Volpe's top lieutenant in the loan-shark rackets, and he knew Chuck Yanover and what he was up to almost as well as I did.

Murphy and the investigators he worked with had spent thousands of hours looking at Volpe's rackets—loan-sharking, diamond smuggling, casino investments, arson, you name it. Their investigation had led them to Las Vegas, to New Jersey and Atlantic City, and finally to the convictions of some of Volpe's flunkies—Yanover, Murray Feldberg, and Jimmy Bass—for extortion.

His knowing all that and more about organized crime made my meeting with Murphy all the more important. It was a freak—a stroke of luck that changed my life and is probably the reason I am still alive today.

By November 1980 I knew it was only a matter of time before I would become one of the Commissos' victims. Assignments were coming fewer and farther apart, and each seemed to be more reckless than the last. It was almost as if they were handing me jobs that they hoped would result in my getting killed or caught by police.

My initial suspicions, as I said earlier, were raised when they wanted me to go to Italy to murder Momo Piromalli, the Calabrian Mafia boss. The Commissos swore they had a plan for my escape, but in the back of my mind I knew they didn't, I knew I was going to be wasted by some grubby little roadside in Italy and buried in some field where I'd never be found.

In May 1980 Cosimo insisted on bombing Napoleon's Restaurant, a stupid act of pure vengeance that nearly resulted in the death of three women because Cosimo's wife had been insulted. And then in October, there was what I considered his reckless order to bomb Maury Kalen's apartment despite heavy security. If I'd carried out that plan the way he wanted me to, I'd have been killed by one of those security guards the moment the bomb had gone off.

There were also a lot of little things, things I couldn't put a handle on, but that nevertheless made me uncertain. I could enter a room at the Casa Commisso and talk would stop. Cosimo, Remo, and I could be talking about something in English and when a friend of theirs entered the room, someone I knew spoke and understood English, the language suddenly turned to Italian. Remo was using cousins and relatives to contact me at the health club for meetings or to deliver messages and money to me. I had the feeling they didn't trust me and yet I'd never, up to then, talked to a cop or done anything suspicious.

Being cheated out of money I had coming to me was causing friction, arguments. I knew it wasn't healthy for me to protest so loudly about the money they owed me or to refuse to handle their assignments. There was no room for a rebel in the Commissos' organization. It might give

younger, impressionable members ideas about discipline and whether Cosimo should be a boss.

With all these insecurities, I was also facing the likelihood of a long jail sentence for an old break and entry that involved an assault and extortion. The Commissos had always seemed suspicious about the delays my lawyers got in the case. There was something in their questions about those delays that made me think they thought I was whispering in some cop's ear. There was also no better place for the Commissos to have me wasted than in jail. A prisoner with a shiv, a prison fight—suddenly I'm history and they've got no one to worry about.

I had to find a way out, to protect myself, to cut a deal, and to work something out with someone in law enforcement. If I could trade important information for help in getting my sentence reduced or even dropped to probation, I'd have breathing space and maybe a chance to survive.

My first attempt had been with Terry Hall of the Ontario Provincial Police. I told him that his life was in danger, that the Vagabonds had a contract to kill him. He didn't even say thanks, let alone talk about seeing what he could do for me on the charges I was facing—charges he and Ron Tavenor of Toronto's Metro Police biker squad were responsible for.

There was little chance of my getting anywhere with them. They'd take whatever I gave them, but they wouldn't help me make a deal. If I couldn't talk to them, who could I talk to? I had to be careful, very careful.

On November 10 I dialed the number for the RCMP National Crime Intelligence Section.

"RCMP, can I help you?" the voice at the other end said smartly.

"Who am I talking to?" I asked.

"Corporal Murphy, Corporal Mark Murphy," was the reply.

"Look, Corporal Murphy, we don't know each other, but I can help you," I said. "I can solve a lot of cases for you, maybe even some murders."

"I'm listening," Murphy said, "but you haven't told me anything yet."

I told Murphy I was a former member of the Satan's Choice and that I could give him information on robberies that had happened and were about to take place. I also told him that if he played it straight with me I could give him information about organized crime, particularly the Commissos.

"All I want is someone to put in a good word for me when I'm sentenced on a B&E. For that you get a lot of heavy stuff." Then I added: "If you're interested, meet me in a half hour in the parking lot of the Casa Loma. Come alone, and no wires or we don't talk."

"What's your name?" he asked.

"No names for now," I said. "Just be there."

The Casa Loma Castle is a tourist attraction in downtown Toronto. It was built in 1911 and took three years to complete. It's advertised in magazines as North America's "most famous castle," and they are probably right. I can't remember ever seeing a castle anywhere else that had gold-plated bathroom fixtures and porcelain troughs for horses. But that and its ninety-eight rooms weren't what made me select it as a meeting place.

The castle is set up in such a way that it's easy to spot people in the parking lot or coming from various vantage points. It's also not the kind of place that mafiosi or bikers come to too often. By getting there before Murphy, I could see if he was followed or if there was anyone else there that looked like a cop or a hood.

I watched Murphy come up from Austin Terrace and pull into the Casa Loma driveway. He parked where I told him to, climbed out of his unmarked police car, and stood up, towering over the roof of the vehicle. I jotted down his license number so I could check it out through a friend later. When I was certain there was no one following him, I walked up behind him.

"You Corporal Murphy?" I asked.

"That's right," he said. "What do I call you?"

"Call me Jack, Jack Ryan for now," I said. "When we know each other better, I'll give you my real name."

As we talked, my eyes tracked the entire parking lot and the overhead terraces of the castle for anything, anyone out of the ordinary. I saw no one. I patted him down to see if he was wearing anything. He wasn't.

"It's not that I don't trust you," I said, "but cops aren't my favorite people, and so far the ones I've dealt with haven't been too trustworthy."

"Let's get on with it," Murphy said, a little annoyed by all my precautions.

"One more thing before we talk," I said. "I've already supplied good information to Terry Hall of the OPP. He double-crossed me on a case in court. I don't want to deal with him anymore. That understood?"

Murphy nodded.

"I'm not asking to have charges against me dropped," I said. "I just want you to assist me at my sentencing—put in a good word for me. I can't beat the B&E. I'm looking at two to four years. I just want to minimize the sentence."

Murphy understood, but he guaranteed nothing. "I can't promise you anything," he said. "If what you tell me is helpful, useful, I'll talk to my superiors—see what can be done for you. But you've got to produce."

"Good enough," I answered. With that I began to supply him with information on some drug deals, some armed robberies, and some burglaries. We talked about bikers, about the Mafia, and about guns.

"I'm in the business of guns," I said. "I sell them. I sell them to bikers, to rounders, I sell them to the Commissos. Some are handguns, some are rifles, some are machine guns, and I know where they are. Sometimes when I sell these guns, people are shot." Then I added: "Maybe if things check out the way you want, I can give you some unsolved murders."

With that I left, telling Murphy to take some time checking things I told him out. "I'll get back to you in a few days, and then we'll see where we go from there," I said. "Just don't double-cross me. I won't forget it. I may even have to come after you."

When we separated that day there were problems, some of which I was unaware of. I had given Murphy my true name, but when I called him I used the name Jack Ryan so that no one else knew that it was Cecil Kirby who was talking to him.

The veiled threat had made an impression on Murphy. So did the relationship that developed between us in the year that was to follow. He considered me dangerous, and he said so in a confidential RCMP report dated November 2, 1982: "[Kirby's] dual personality ranges from a very kind person to a vicious, hot-tempered violent individual who is quite capable of killing. He might also be described as an opportunist. I quickly perceived Kirby to be an experienced criminal who had tremendous potential as an informer."

Murphy was cautiously optimistic that I could be helpful to him, but Hall and Tavenor and some of their superiors didn't see it that way. On November 26, at another meeting with Murphy, I was secretly watched by Hall and Tavenor, who had put me under surveillance and tailed me to the meeting. They recognized Murphy.

Tavenor and his superiors at Metro called Murphy. They demanded to know what I had been talking to him about. Murphy told them, but warned Tavenor not to say anything because I had made a veiled threat to Murphy if he told Tavenor and Hall I was talking.

At the meeting I'd had with Murphy, I had given him information I'd just received from a rounder friend on a stash of one hundred pounds of hash hidden in a store.

"If you want," my friend said, "we can hit this place—rip them off. All we have to do is pull our guns, tell them we're cops, tie them up, and leave with the load of hash."

I told him it was a great idea, then I went to the meeting with Murphy to tell him. He said I would have to talk to a narcotics sergeant of the RCMP about it.

I talked to the sergeant, told him I'd stall my friend as long as possible. "If you hit it in the morning," I said, "be sure you have a cop outside and that he's visible."

"How the hell do you know it's there?" the sergeant said, a little testily.

"Look, it's there. I guarantee it," I said. "If you don't go, I'm going to fuckin' go with someone else and take it for myself!"

On November 28 my friend and I drove down to hold up the drug dealers. As we approached the store, I pointed to a uniform cop in front of the store.

"We better get the hell out of here," I said. "There's a cop there." We drove off as my friend cursed our bad luck.

The RCMP wasn't so unlucky. They had seized 42 pounds of hash, 900 hits of LSD, pornographic film, and a stolen stereo. The haul was worth over $150,000, and they had arrested three people to boot. Murphy suggested I be paid $2,000 for supplying the information. It wasn't unusual to be paid for giving such good information. It was done all the time. His request was turned down. I got nothing, and the narco squad took all the credit.

Less than a week later I was pulled out of court during my trial by Hall.

"You're talking to the Horsemen," Hall said. "Get this straight, Kirby. You'll get no help on these charges unless you talk to us."

"I don't trust you, Hall," I said. "I'm not dealing with you."

It wasn't that I thought Hall or his superiors weren't honest. As far as I knew they were. I just felt Hall wouldn't keep a promise. Telling him how I felt didn't help. For the next month or more, Hall, Tavenor, and the brass they worked with did everything they could to stop Murphy from helping me.

I was caught in a tug-of-war between rival agencies.

The RCMP has Canada-wide authority, like the FBI in the United States, and they operate with local agencies the same way. They like to operate on a one-way street. They like to take information, but they don't give it unless they have to, because either they don't want to share the credit for a big arrest or they don't trust the local agency they're supposed to be working with.

The result of all these rivalries and mistrust is that organized crime profits. Members of different mobs learn to work together because it means saving their own skins and making big money. That's something police at national levels haven't learned to do yet. Until they do, the mobs will always slip through the cracks.

In this case, though, the big hang-up was with the locals. They didn't want the RCMP in the form of Murphy coming in and taking over a case or a possible informant. They threw up every roadblock possible. It seemed to me it was more jealousy than anything else.

As far as Murphy was concerned, I had proved I could be a valuable informer. But it still wasn't enough for his bosses and for Sergeant Robert Silverton of Metro, who supervised the operations of Hall and Tavenor. Then I dropped information on another important case in Murphy's lap.

There had been a robbery of a jewelry store, the Dolly Jewellers in Toronto, on January 15. On the day of the robbery, I was maybe a half a block away from the store when I bumped into the two guys who'd held it up, Nicolino Pallotta and Richard Cucman. I knew them both from the street, and they told me they'd just held up Dolly's and had a bag full of jewelry.

"Sounds like you got a lot," I said, after listening to them brag. "Look, if you have any trouble getting rid of the stuff, let me know. Maybe I can help out."

As I talked, my mind was spinning with possibilities. I could use what I knew about the robbery as a bargaining chip with Murphy and those he worked for, and maybe I could make myself some money by recovering the jewelry and selling it.

Less than a week after I'd seen them, on January 20, I called Murphy.

"You know that Dolly Jewelers' robbery?" I asked.

"Yeah, what about it?" said Murphy.

"If I can get some help at the court, if someone will speak to the Crown for me, I'll solve their robbery for them," I said. "I'll give them the names of the holdup men on a silver platter."

"I'll see what I can do," Murphy said.

Murphy tried. He talked to Silverton. He said Silverton wouldn't even consider speaking to the Crown for me. He said he then asked two inspectors he reports to intercede with Silverton's boss, Inspector Don Banks of Metro. According to Murphy, they refused.

When Murphy told me that none of the coppers involved with him or with my case were willing to go to bat for me, I was furious—not at Murphy, but at the people who he worked for, who were so goddamned narrow-minded.

"Maybe if you give me the names, some proof, I can get them to agree," Murphy said.

"I'll have to think about it," I said.

A few days later Pallotta and Cucman came to me with the bag of jewelry and asked me to sell it. I took it, but I couldn't sell it because they were asking too much for it. So I returned it to them. It was mostly junk jewelry, anyway, about one hundred diamond rings, gold chains, knick-knacks. They also had about one hundred used watches they'd grabbed, and I told them to throw them down the incinerator of the apartment we met at or police would track the stuff back to them. I found out later on that they had tried to sell the jewelry to the Commissos.

Finally, I decided to give Murphy the names of the holdup men. The cops arrested them both, and they were later convicted, but it didn't impress Murphy's two superiors, particularly Inspector James McIlvenna,

who was the boss of the Joint Forces Special Enforcement Unit that was later to provide protection for me.

Murphy said that McIlvenna told him he wouldn't touch my case "with a hundred-foot pole."

"McIlvenna and Inspector [J] Wylie said I should let you go to jail, Cecil," Murphy said. "I just want you to know I'm not giving up. So don't you give up."

I didn't and he didn't, but a year later Pallotta and Cucman pleaded guilty to the robbery. Their attorney, Earl Levy, charged, in a grandstand play to the press outside the courtroom, that I had "ripped off" $140,000 worth of stolen jewelry from them. Cucman, who got two years, made the charge because the Commissos told him to. They were trying to show I had lied as a witness.

It didn't take McIlvenna long to jump on the bandwagon after Levy's charge appeared in the press.

"Did you keep the jewelry from those two?" he roared.

"If I had one hundred thousand dollars in stolen jewelry, I damn sure wouldn't be here talking to you," I snapped back. "I'd be in Florida, where I wouldn't have to listen to your shit."

Pallotta, who got three years because he was carrying the gun during the robbery, wouldn't confirm Cucman's story. He told the cops that I did give all the jewelry back, and he took a lie detector test to back up his claim.

McIlvenna never once said he was sorry for suspecting me, but then he had never wanted Murphy or the Crown or anyone to deal with me. He wanted me in jail and, I'm certain, if he had had his way, I would never have become a witness. But because of Murphy, he and some other shortsighted brass hats didn't get their way. The trouble is that in the end Murphy paid a terrible price for being as supportive as he was.

When I took the step of calling Murphy, I never considered the possibility of becoming a witness. It also never dawned on me that the Commissos would call me in to have me handle a murder in the United States.

Just after I told Murphy that I knew who held up the jewelry store, I was summoned to the Casa Commisso.

"I got a job for you, Cec," Cosimo said. "It's very important."

Cosimo seemed edgy as he spoke. He paced from one side of the empty banquet hall kitchen to the other. It seemed as if he was avoiding looking directly at me as he usually did. Suddenly he stopped in front of the table where I was sitting and looked squarely into my face, his eyes searching mine as if what he saw would tell him something he didn't know.

"There's this woman in Connecticut," he said. "She's a big problem to some friends of ours. She's gotta be done and I want you to handle the job."

"Why me, Cosimo?" I asked. "Why don't your friends have an American handle the job? Why don't they do the job?"

"Because it's a family matter. It's gotta be handled by an outsider who knows what he's doing and who can do the job right," he said. "That's you, and it's worth fifteen, maybe twenty thousand to you."

"I don't know," I started to answer.

"We'll take care of everything," he said. "Your expenses, that gun, everything you need to know about the girl, we give you."

"Let me think about it, Cosimo," I said. "I need the money for the lawyers on the case that's before the court, but I don't know if there's time. Let me think about it."

We didn't talk much more about it for a while after that. For nearly two weeks I didn't say anything to Murphy. I was worried. I'd never killed a woman before, and I didn't like the idea. Suppose the whole deal was a plot to get rid of me? What better way? I go to the States, I blast this broad, and then I get wasted. There's no witness to the conspiracy, they get rid of the broad, and they unload me, an outsider who knows too much about their Honoured Society and its members.

Over and over something kept clicking in my head. "They're gonna waste you any day now. They're gonna bury you with this job. Do yourself and the broad some good. Call Murphy." Still I waited.

I guess I knew from the start that if I didn't handle the job they'd get someone else to kill the woman, which, in fact, they tried.

While I stalled Cosimo, he went to Ken Goobie, who he'd met through me, and offered Goobie $25,000 to kill the woman. Goobie went to Gary Barnes to handle the job, and Barnes told me about it later.

Finally, on February 17, I called Murphy to tell him about the contract. I didn't want to see the woman killed, but I didn't know how to prevent it without Murphy's help, so I called him.

"I've got a contract, Murf," I said, "and I don't know how to handle it. We've got to talk."

We met again at the Casa Loma parking lot. This time Sergeant Norman Ross was with him.

"Take the contract, Cec," Murphy said. "Find out who the woman is. I'll get office approval. We'll go to the States, see the woman, and remove her from danger. You can then return to Canada and tell them there was just too much heat and police around, so you couldn't handle the murder."

I didn't want to follow Murphy's suggestions, but I figured I had no choice.

"Okay, but don't hang me out to dry on this, Murf," I said. "I've got to meet Cosimo and someone else at two o'clock."

Murphy told me to go ahead with the meeting and he would go to his office to get money to pay for the trip to the States to save the woman.

"How about wearing a tape machine to that meeting?" Murphy asked.

I was taken aback at first and then I refused. "Look, Murf, it's too dangerous right now," I explained. "They got a habit of touching you, putting their arms around you. And here I'll be meeting with some strange guy. He may want to check me out, pat me down. It's too risky."

"Where are you meeting?" he asked.

"On Dixon Road, near Faces [a discotheque] and Howard Johnson's," I answered. "One other thing, Murphy. I'm broke. I haven't enough to buy a drink right now."

Murphy had repeatedly asked his superiors for expense money for me. Each time they refused, although I had, by this time, given them inside information that helped them solve dozens of burglaries and robberies and a number of murders.

"Here, Cec," he said, reaching into his pocket, "here's ten bucks. It's all I can swing right now."

So I left with Murphy's personal ten dollars to finance what was probably one of the most significant meetings I ever had. I felt like a complete

jerk. Here I was, about to deal with a mafioso on a $20,000 murder contract, and all I had in my pocket was a lousy ten bucks, enough to buy maybe one round of drinks.

It was crazy. Murphy was crazy and so was I. Only crazy people try to beat the Mafia this way. What kind of copper was I dealing with anyway?

At 2:00 P.M. I met Cosimo at Howard Johnson's. Antonio Rocco Romeo was with him. We sat down at an isolated table, and Cosimo began talking in low monotones.

"Cec, this here's Antonio Romeo," he said. "He's the man who's gonna put you together with a friend named Vince in the States. It's Vince who wants this woman done. Vince'll take care of everything. He'll show you the woman, get what you need to do the job."

While I was having no problems in negotiating with Cosimo, who I was supposed to meet again on February 19 to get final instructions and $300 to pay for the airline tickets to New York, Murphy was running into one roadblock after another.

He asked for backup to accompany him and me to the States. He told the brass that he had no way of knowing how I would react in the States. He said he didn't know how reliable I would be and pointed out that I was an ex-biker with a reputation for violence. His request for support people was turned down.

Murphy's troubles were only just beginning. Nobody told him it was illegal or against RCMP rules, so he decided to take his service revolver along for self-protection. He declared the gun at U.S. Customs. He didn't know it then, but in doing that he sealed his fate. Those who opposed him used that as one of the charges against him for what they called conduct unbecoming an officer of the RCMP. When he explained that he took the gun because he felt the need for protection since he had no backup, his excuse was brushed aside. He didn't realize it at the time, but powerful forces in the RCMP were at work to get him for defying past suggestions that he let me rot in jail. If I had known that then, I would have told them all to go to hell.

On February 19 Cosimo and I met again. He advanced me $300 and said that when I got to New York, I was to get transportation to Stamford,

Connecticut. There I was to meet Romeo and Vince at the Marriott Hotel the next day at 9:00 P.M.

"When you meet Vince there," he said, "you'll get the gun, expense money, and five thousand dollars advance. You'll get the other ten thousand when you finish the job."

I just nodded and went to meet Murphy and buy my airline tickets. The next day we left. The tickets cost me $260, and Murphy had to give me $50 more out of his pocket so I'd have some money for expenses. Unless something happened, I would be going to jail on February 26. I was beginning to wonder whether I had been stupid in trying to make a deal with the RCMP and save this woman's life.

CHAPTER 16

The Connecticut Caper

I felt the American Airlines jet engines roar to life as we hurtled down the runway of Toronto International. I looked across the aisle and to the rear. From the corner of my eye I could see Murphy looking past me as if I didn't exist. Not the slightest sign of recognition passed between us as the jet rose and headed toward La Guardia Airport.

My hands felt clammy and cold as I leaned back and watched the flight attendant pass out drinks. I ordered juice, and I remember looking out the window at the clouds wondering how in the hell I had been talked into this trip.

Nothing had been resolved about my sentence before we left. I was still looking at from two to four years, and no one but Murphy was in favor of suggesting to the Crown or a judge that I be given a break for helping police. Yet here I was, flying to New York with an RCMP officer, preparing to meet with Calabrian Mafia hoods who wanted me to kill a woman I'd never seen before in my life.

I had boarded the plane using my true name, but once I hit New York, I would be operating under a fictitious name with phony identification in a strange country among people I didn't know. I thought to myself, "Cecil Kirby, you've got to be crazy doing this." Even as I wondered if I'd lost my marbles, the warning words of Murphy kept echoing in my head.

"You know too much, Cecil," he said. "Sooner or later, the Commissos have got to dispose of you. They can't let you live."

"You're just working on my head," I remember snapping as we talked about what he expected me to do after I had taken the contract from Cosimo to kill the woman.

"Be realistic," Murphy said. "First they owe you forty thousand dollars by your own estimate. Why should they pay that much if they don't have to? Second, you've become a liability to them. You're a non-Italian working for the Honoured Society. You're not one of them. You don't live by their codes. You could put them in jail for a long, long time. So you're a liability." Then Murphy struck a chord that made even more sense to me.

"Remember Ian Rosenburg?" he asked. "He became a liability to the Volpe crime group. So what did they do? They bailed him out of jail and killed him and his girlfriend. If you don't work with us, that's what could happen to you."

"You mean they might be setting me up for a hit on this Connecticut caper, don't you?" I said.

"It's a possibility. It's something to think about," he said. "What better way to get rid of you? They have you enter the United States under an assumed name. They get you to a small place like Stamford, and after you do in the woman, or even if you don't do her, they kill you. Who would really be concerned about an ex–Satan's Choice biker if, in fact, they ever found your body?"

Those words were still ringing in my ears as the plane dipped toward New York.

When we touched down I quickly passed through customs and caught a cab for the Holiday Inn near the airport. Once there I called a detective at the New York City Police Criminal Intelligence Bureau, leaving him my phone number and room number as Murphy had instructed. The name I used was Jack Ryan—the same name that I used to registered in the hotel.

It couldn't have been more than an hour before Murphy was knocking on my door. With him were two FBI agents. Within minutes we were in a bureau car and on our way to Connecticut.

Just before we stopped at a hamburger place for a quick bite and a phone call to some agents in Darien, Murphy spotted a car with a couple of black guys in it counting bundles of cash.

"Did you see all the money they were counting?" he asked.

"Yeah," I said. "They probably held up a bank or just sold a load of dope."

Murphy jotted down the license number, but the two FBI agents, one of them was a guy named Nick Mott, registered no reaction at all. Mott had all of two years as a bureau agent, and he was from a Midwest farm. New York was obviously unfamiliar territory to him. Even so, what Murphy and I saw didn't excite him, and he made no attempt to call Connecticut State Police to give them the car's license number as Murphy suggested. It was like it was an everyday occurrence, and what the hell could they do about it anyhow?

When we arrived in Darien I was introduced to several other agents, including John Schiman, Donnie Brutnell, and David Cotton, all from Connecticut. I was brought to a room at the Holiday Inn, where I briefed the agents. I told them I was supposed to meet Romeo, who was coming in from Toronto, at the Marriott Hotel in Stamford at 9:00 P.M. He was supposed to be with someone named Vince, who would provide me with the money, keys to the apartment of the victim, photographs, and a gun to kill the woman with.

I half expected either Murphy or the agents to ask me to wear a body mike to the meeting. I wouldn't take that chance. My main concern was to find out who the victim was, not blow the whole deal before it happened.

Just before 8:30, I took a cab to Stamford. I got out at the corner near the hotel and was met by Schimen and Murphy. With barely a word passing between us, I walked into the hotel lobby and waited for Romeo to appear.

I sat there for several hours. Nothing happened. Finally I got up, hailed a cab, and went back to the Holiday Inn.

I had to find out what happened. There was a problem. How was I going to find out what it was? I had no idea of where to reach Romeo or his boss, Vince, and I hadn't brought my phone book, so I didn't have Cosimo's home phone number.

I was stymied, but I told the agents to give Romeo until the next day. "Something must've held him up, eh?" I said.

At that point a light went on in my head. There was a way to reach Cosimo. I called my ex-girlfriend, Linda Cadwell, and asked her to go to Cosimo's home.

"Have him call me at this number," I said. "Have him call me as soon as possible."

Cosimo didn't call, but he gave Linda a message to relay to me when I called her back early the next morning.

"He said to tell you that the guy you were supposed to meet with last night was delayed by weather," she said. "He said he'll be there today, and he'll meet you at the same place and the same time."

As soon as she got off the phone, I called Murphy, who was in the same hotel. What I didn't realize was that he was in a room next to mine.

"He got held up in Toronto by fog," I said to Murphy. "He's coming into La Guardia today. I'm supposed to meet him tonight—same time, same place."

While I stewed in my room, Murphy was busy with Agent Mott and New York City detectives at La Guardia Airport, looking for Romeo. When they spotted him, he was moving from phone booth to phone booth, making calls.

When I saw Murphy later, he was upset. He said Mott had almost blown the surveillance by pulling the bureau's car to within fifty feet of Romeo as he stood by the curbside waiting for a cab to Stamford. Murphy said he had to insist that Mott get out of the car and open the trunk as if he were unloading luggage to avoid having Romeo spot them.

Things sometimes have a way of getting worse before they get better, and Murphy said that was what happened as they tried to tail Romeo. He said that Mott made a bad identification on the cab Romeo drove away in. The assisting surveillance cars lost him as he left the airport. They finally spotted him on Route 95, ten miles out of New York, heading toward Stamford. This time they kept the tail tight with other surveillance cars from the bureau and New York City police playing leapfrog so Romeo and his cabbie wouldn't notice.

It was early afternoon when my phone rang.

"This George?" the voice on the phone asked.

"Yeah, who's this?" I asked.

"This is Vince," he said. "We meet the same time, same place to-night."

"Okay," I said. "I'll be there."

After hanging up, I called Murphy again and told him that I'd gotten a call from a man who called himself Vince.

"I think it's the guy who gave Commisso the contract," I said. "He must have gotten my phone number from Cosimo."

"I've got to get you out of that room—now," Murphy said. "I don't want them to be able to watch you—set up a counter-surveillance—understand?"

Within minutes, Murphy was at my door and we left the area.

At 9:00 P.M. I entered the lobby of the Marriott Hotel in Stamford for the second time. There were agents everywhere, but they blended into the scenery. They were impossible to spot.

Vincenzo (Vincent) Melia didn't look all that impressive to me as he stood there with Romeo in the hotel lobby.

Romeo clearly treated Melia as though he was very important, like a boss. Romeo was about twenty-four and Melia was more than twice his age, fifty-two, I was told later, but Romeo treated him like the mob treated Don Corleone in *The Godfather*, with a great deal of respect.

"Please, Mr. Kirby," he said, "I'd like you to meet Vince Melia. He's the man you're s'pos to meet."

I stood up and shook hands with Melia. He was medium in height, with dark brown wavy hair, a thin, clean-shaven face, and piercing brown eyes.

Melia was as important in Connecticut as Cosimo was in Toronto. He was the boss of a family, and he didn't take a backseat to many people. He was very close to Mike Racco, the old man who had been the boss of bosses for the Calabrian Honoured Society families in the United States and Canada until he'd died in 1980.

Melia was an Italian citizen who had moved to Toronto from Siderno and then to Stamford, where he operated a construction business. No one, not the community, not his neighbors, not the FBI, knew what he really was.

In the lobby of the Marriott, he was quiet, but careful. The lobby

wasn't a good place to talk, so we went to a bar in the hotel, ordered some drinks, and sat down at a table.

"Look, before I do anything," I said, "I want five thousand dollars up front."

"Tomorrow, I'll have it for you tomorrow," he said.

"What about the gun?" I asked.

"You get that tomorrow too," he said.

"I'm going to need a picture so I know what she looks like," I said. "Who is this broad anyhow?"

"Her name is Helen," he said. "A relative, he lives with this woman. He's not to be harmed. Remember that. I don't want him killed. He's family. The woman, she's blond—a good-looking hairdresser."

He was somewhat nervous as he spoke. His eyes shifted from table to table in the darkened bar, searching for someone he might recognize.

We couldn't have been there more than ten minutes when Melia leaned over to me and whispered, "That guy at the table over there—he looks like he's a cop."

"Nah," I said, glancing at the guy he had motioned to. "There's no cops in here."

Melia was nervous now. He was suspicious about everyone in the bar, and he wanted to leave.

"Let's go outside," he said. "I got someone I want you to meet."

We left the table and began to walk outside. I knew the FBI was watching. So was Murphy. But I didn't see any of them. Before I got outside, Romeo took me aside as Melia continued on ahead.

"Look," he said, "I don't want these guys to tell you what to do. You do what you gotta do. You do your own thing and we'll look after you." He spoke in clear English, with a trace of Italian. In court, he and his attorney said he couldn't speak English.

Outside, Romeo and I caught up with Melia, who walked me to the hotel parking lot and a Cadillac driven by another of their *paisans*.

"This is Jerry Russo," Melia said. "He's going to drive you to the house of the woman you are to take care of. He'll show you the house and her car. Then he'll take you to a hotel and a room we got for you. We also got a car for you."

"Don't want any of that," I said. "You keep the room and the car. I

got my own equipment and no one knows where I stay. I do things my way. Incidentally, I'm not too happy about taking a ride with your chauffeur."

"Don't worry, don't worry," he said. "He's all right. But you can tell him to forget he ever saw you. He'll know what you mean."

He looked around, reached into his pocket, and handed me some keys. "Here," he said, "here's the keys to her house and her car." He fumbled in his pocket for something else. "Here's three hundred dollars for expenses and my phone number," he said. "Before you kill her, call me so we can be sure the relative's not there. Okay?"

I nodded. "Okay. And the five thousand dollars?"

"We meet here tomorrow. Two o'clock," he said. "You get everything then."

So I climbed into Russo's Caddy. I had noticed it as I walked into the hotel. I remember feeling a sense of satisfaction knowing that I had spotted it and made the connection. They—Melia, Romeo, and Russo— had all come in that Caddy early and checked me out as I arrived. Obviously, they'd spotted nothing, or the meeting and our conversation wouldn't have taken place.

While I drove off with Russo, Melia and Romeo climbed into Melia's yellow Ford and headed in another direction. I noticed a bureau tail car following them at a discreet distance.

Russo, about twenty-four, was a gofer. Melia was his boss, and he did what he was told. I guess women would think Russo was good looking. He had carefully cut, wavy dark hair, a manicured mustache, and sharp, expensive-looking clothes. All that on a thin, five foot seven frame. Soaking wet he couldn't have weighed more than 150 pounds.

We drove to the woman's home in Stamford. As we went by slowly, Russo pointed out which side of the house she lived in and which room she slept in. He pointed to her car, a Toyota as I recall. We continued past the house, a small bungalow, for about half a block and I asked him to stop. He pulled over to the sidewalk and I got out.

"Stay here," I said sharply. "I'm gonna take a quick look around. I'll be right back."

While Russo watched me, as did some unseen eyes of the FBI, I walked back toward the house and jotted down the license number of the car. As

I turned to return, one of those supposedly unseen eyes came roaring up the street past me. I kept waving—keep going, don't stay around. Russo didn't spot anything luckily. The overprotective surveillance was understandable. The FBI was worried. Overall, they were super—concerned, professional, and tough.

The FBI had cautioned me before I met with Melia about staying out of the house and the yard. Murphy had told them the Commissos might be setting me up as well as the woman.

"Stay away from that house," one of the agents said. "Don't go in wherever it is. You could get blown away. This could be a setup, even with the cops. There could be a cop in there waiting to blow you away because they've been tipped you'll be breaking into the house." The message was clear enough. The Melias could have friends with the local coppers, and the agents didn't want any chances taken. Every step I took, every place I went, I was watched, and those I was with were photographed.

As Russo and I returned to the hotel, I carefully began pulling on some black driving gloves I had in my pocket.

"Word to the wise," I said menacingly to Russo. "You better forget who I am. And you better forget what I look like." I watched his face twitch slightly around the jawbone in the subdued light from the dashboard. Then for emphasis I added, "I don't want to have to make another trip down here."

When Russo dropped me off at the Marriott, I stood at the entrance for several minutes. I then hailed a cab and, after a few side trips downtown to be sure Russo hadn't the balls to track me, I headed back to Darien to meet with Murphy and the agents at the Holiday Inn and turn over Melia's phone number, the license number of the woman's car, her keys, and her address. The money I kept. Nobody said I shouldn't, so I kept it. I was tired of living off the nickels and dimes that Murphy had to scrape out of his pocket because the RCMP refused to provide support money.

I briefed the FBI and Murphy on what had happened and what I had to do the next day. Then I went to bed.

It was 2:00 P.M. Sunday when I got to the Marriott lobby. Melia was waiting.

"The girl will be back tonight," he said. "You'll have to kill her tomorrow—not today. Kill her tomorrow after ten in the morning. Somebody is with her up to ten. Wait 'till he leaves and kill her after that."

"What?" I said, registering surprise. "You don't want me to kill the guy she's with?"

"No, no, no, no. He's family," Melia said excitedly. "Don't kill him."

"Why do you want her hit?" I asked.

"She's caused trouble, a lot of trouble, and the guy she's going with is messing up," he answered.

He said nothing more but motioned for me to follow him out to the parking lot. We stood by Melia's car waiting for Russo to show up with the $5,000 and the gun.

"You know if you want to come back down here," Melia said, "I got other work for you to do—places to burn. I got lots of work here."

"Well, I'll have to think about that," I answered. "You'll have to talk to Cosimo about that."

"I know Remo many years—longer than Cosimo," he said. "I talk to them both."

"When do I get the other ten thousand dollars?" I said, as we waited.

"What other ten thousand dollars?" he said with a look of surprise. "You're supposed to get another five thousand dollars after you get this five thousand dollars."

"Hell, no," I snapped. "Cosimo said the job was worth fifteen to twenty thousand dollars. Now you're telling me ten thousand dollars!"

"It's ten thousand dollars," he said, his face darkening a bit with anger. "If you make sure she disappears and isn't found, I give you a bonus— an extra one thousand dollars. That's it!"

"Okay," I said. "I'll see what I can do. But the deal was for more."

Just as things started to get a little heated, Russo drove up in a silver Capri. He got into Melia's car. Out of the corner of my eye I could see Agent Schimen in a telephone booth maybe twenty-five to thirty feet away. There were agents hidden all over the place, snapping pictures of everything that was happening.

Russo handed me $4,000, and Melia reached in his pocket and pulled out an additional $1,000. Russo then pulled a bag from beneath his shirt

that had been tucked under his belt. The gun was in the bag. I took the gun out and examined it.

"This isn't a fuckin' .38, it's a lousy .22," I said angrily.

"Well, that's all we got," Melia answered.

I took the clip out to make sure it was loaded, and I checked to see if there was a bullet in the chamber as well as in the clip. There was. It was a Sturm Ruger, nine-shot automatic. I noticed a long, thin silencer at the end of the barrel. I tried to remove it, but I couldn't. It was handmade, and probably would work, but it wasn't the kind of silencer I felt comfortable with. Silencers usually screw into the barrel. They're usually custommade for the weapon. A bad silencer can cause all kinds of problems. I made Melia know I wasn't happy with the weapon. I thought to myself, "some Mafia bunch this is."

With the gun they handed me a picture of two women. One was a blond. Melia pointed to her. "That's the one I want killed," he said. "Remember, if she disappears, there's a bonus."

"Consider it done," I said.

With that we shook hands and I walked off, watching them as they drove away in Melia's Ford. When they were out of sight, I grabbed a cab for the Ramada Inn up the street, where I thought I was supposed to meet some agents and be picked up. I wasn't.

I stood there with the gun and the money for almost a half hour. I felt exposed, naked, in a dangerous spot. A local cop might check me out and find the gun. Finally, I hailed another cab and returned to the Holiday Inn in Darien. I sat in the lobby. Sooner or later, I figured, the agents and Murphy would find me there. The best thing to do was wait.

It was a little after 3:00 P.M. when a couple of agents spotted me in the lobby and escorted me to a room on the second floor. Murphy was there, so was Agent Schiman.

I drew the gun from my belt line and threw it on the bed. Schiman jumped up and grabbed it. I removed my jacket, dropped the $5,000, and threw it on the other side of the bed. Nobody touched it as I sat on the bed next to it. As far as I was concerned the money was mine and nobody was contesting that. I didn't say a word. I just scooped up the

money and put it in my pants pocket and waited for them to debrief me.

Murphy was later reprimanded for not seizing the money. He couldn't. I'd warned him that if the RCMP wasn't going to pay my bills, then the Commissos were. Besides, I was helping save a woman's life, and Murphy's people weren't doing a damn thing to help me with my court problems.

After more than a hour of debriefing, the agents asked me to come with them to the woman's house. By now I knew she was a Greek hairdresser and the mother of a six-year-old girl. They wanted to set up a surveillance of the house in the morning and familiarize themselves with the neighborhood. Beyond that no one was really sure of what was going to be done the next day.

When Murphy and I returned to my room, he asked me to take out the money. "Let me record the serial numbers and take some sample bills," he said.

I agreed, and we spent more than an hour recording the numbers and carefully placing bill samples from four different stacks of the money in a special evidence envelope that Murphy had with him. He had $150 in sample bills, some of which I suppose had Melia's and Russo's fingerprints on them.

It wasn't until the next day that I knew what the FBI was going to do with the woman. They were going to keep her under surveillance, and when she and her boyfriend separated, they were going to snatch her.

"Can I come along on the surveillance?" I asked.

"Sure, why not?" Schiman said.

They put me in a van they had equipped with cameras, and I sat there with a couple of agents waiting and watching the house while other agents were parked in the area in other cars.

I guess it was a little after 10:00 A.M. when Helen Nafpliotis opened the door and walked to the car. I was looking at her through the Telephoto lense of the camera, and I snapped the first picture of her. She started the car, went back into the house, and came back out. This time the agent was doing the picture taking. I watched from a van window.

A minute or two later, a man about six foot, in his mid-forties, came out and climbed into her car. He was Nick Melia, the brother of Vince.

I sat in the van as agents in other cars followed the couple at a discreet distance.

I was sitting outside the Holiday Inn in a car with two agents when the agents returned with Nafpliotis. They had waited until she dropped Nick Melia off in downtown Stamford. Melia at the time was appealing a state sentence in connection with a shooting in Stamford.

When the agents were convinced Melia had left the area, they flagged down the woman's car on the highway, flashed their identification, and told her it was urgent that she come with them to Darien. A bureau agent, meanwhile, took her car and hid it.

For the next three hours, the agents and Murphy questioned her while I sat in the car outside. I later read a statement that Murphy compiled of what she had to say.

She was born in Greece on July 26, 1947, and she had lived in the United States for about ten years. For all but six months of that time she had been living, on and off, with Melia, and out of that relationship came a six-year-old daughter, Christina. She also had three other children by a husband she'd split up with in 1977. He'd gone back to Greece and taken her kids with him without her knowing it.

She said that Melia had been arrested by the police for the shooting of Antonio Ianniello, a Stamford hairdresser that she had worked for for several years. The charges were dropped nolle prosequi, four years later.

For a while, she told Murphy and bureau agents, she had worked in Melia's shop, Continental Coiffures. That lasted until she was threatened, beaten and hospitalized for five days, she said. Charges against her attacker were dismissed in October 1981, when she failed to appear in court.

There were other incidents after that. The tires of her car were slashed. After they were replaced, new tires blew out as she was driving, causing her to lose control and almost roll her car just before Christmas of 1980. A year earlier, on November 3, 1979, her car had almost rolled over because of slashed tires that blew.

She said she finally couldn't take any more threats and flew off to Greece, where she stayed for five months. She said Melia's brother, Vincent, had told her it would be smart for her to leave.

She said she had tried, unsuccessfully, to break off her relationship with Melia several times, but each time he found her and made her return. She supported herself by working at a $300-a-week job and renting out two apartments in her house for $450 a month each. She had no other place to go.

"Where can I hide?" she asked the FBI. "Even if I go to God, Nick will find me."

She was really afraid of this Melia. He'd moved to Canada from Italy when he was nineteen. He'd come to Connecticut when he was in his twenties. She said she never saw him work. She knew he'd been accused of having stolen jewelry and of shooting Ianniello, but she didn't know anything about his "family" connections.

They had been to Atlantic City the weekend before I arrived and the weekend I had been provided with the money to kill her, they had been in Queens.

When the interview ended, Murphy, Schiman, and I had another meeting. They were going to provide protection for Nafpliotis, but they couldn't hide her forever. If the Commisso mob and the Melias found out she was still alive, I'd be a dead man.

"You're going to have to become a witness," Murphy said. "It's the only way we save her, and you."

I sat there for a while, thinking about it, looking for a way out. There wasn't any, and we had to return to Toronto. It was Monday, and as things stood I was supposed to go to jail Thursday. Without some sort of agreement, some deal with Murphy, with the Crown prosecutors, I was a dead man.

"Look, Murf," I said, "I'll be your witness. I'll help you get the evidence you want on other cases, but I can't do it without protection. If I talk to you about everything I know, if I help you, I want immunity from prosecution for past crimes. The Crown's got to support my family and me, relocate us, and give us something to live on when it's all over, when I'm through testifying."

"I can't promise that, Cec," he said. "I can't promise anything. I'll do all I can to help, but that's all I can promise."

"You get me what I want and I'll give you what you want," I said. "One thing more. I work with you, not somebody else."

Before we boarded our plane for Toronto at La Guardia, Murphy took a big gamble. He called Crown attorney Al Cooper and told him the whole story, and he held out the chance that they could wipe out the leadership of the Commisso crime family.

"We could do a lot of damage to organized crime in Toronto, Al," I heard him say. "Without him, we have nothing. With him we can do a lot. But not if they make him go to jail on Thursday."

Cooper, unlike Murphy's superiors, saw the dangers and the possibilities. He made no promises, but he agreed to meet with Murphy the next morning to see what could be arranged.

Even as they spoke, the FBI was busy in Stamford. They'd taken Helen Nafpliotis back to her house, let her gather her jewelry and a few belongings, and then staged a kidnapping that witnesses reported to police. They secretly sent her back to Greece, but it wasn't the last I was to hear of her. Even though I never saw her again, she and the FBI almost got me killed.

CHAPTER 17

The Informer I

Corporal Mark Murphy's superiors at the RCMP were clearly not happy. By going to Crown prosecutor Al Cooper, Murphy had leapfrogged the chain of command that wanted me in jail, not running around gathering evidence against organized crime. Instead of being praised for saving a woman's life and doing a helluva job with me, Murphy was in deep trouble.

His bosses were furious that I had been permitted to keep the $5,300 Melia had given me. They were angry that I hadn't been forced to wear a body recorder. And they were critical of Murphy for going to Cooper. Trouble or no, Murphy met with Cooper as promised. They then went to see two prosecutors familiar with my B&E case—Steve Leggit, head Crown prosecutor in Toronto, and Frank Armstrong. Leggit and Armstrong were as inflexible as Murphy's bosses and biker squad officers Hall and Tavenor. It looked hopeless.

Some time after 6:00 P.M. on February 24, Cooper and Murphy were called to meet with the deputy attorney general of Ontario, Rod McLeod. At that meeting, Murphy told McLeod that in addition to putting the Commissos behind bars for conspiracy to murder the Connecticut woman, the Crown could also clear up most of the bombings that had taken place in the city of Toronto over the last seven years as well as extortions, arsons, and bombings in Guelph, Hamilton, and Montreal. All

told there were more than twenty-three major criminal acts that could be solved and more than a dozen arrests effected.

McLeod wasn't as shortsighted as the others. He saw the potential and assured both Murphy and Cooper that I wouldn't go to jail on Thursday and that I would be made available to meet the Commissos and gather further evidence. The next day McLeod ordered Leggit to hold my case over. A deal was in the works.

"You're going to have to wear a body mike," Murphy said, as we talked about the promise McLeod had made. "You're going to have to wear a mike and get evidence to nail these guys."

I wasn't happy at all about the prospect. Becoming an informer for Murphy had been difficult, a gut-wrenching experience. It was against everything I had grown up to believe in. Up to that point I had justified it mentally by not fingering the crimes of friends—and I wasn't testifying against anyone. I could even excuse the Connecticut deal. I had helped save a woman's life and I had stiffed the Commissos and their mob for a change. Besides, I wasn't a witness.

"There's no way around it, Cec, you're going to have to testify—be a witness," Murphy said again.

I wanted to puke. It sucked—it really sucked. I was faced with doing what I was willing to kill others for doing. I tried to find a way out.

"Christ, I don't know, Mark," I said. "It'll never work. The Commissos, their friends—they're always putting arms around me, touching me, poking at me. They're sure to find any tape I'm wearing."

"They won't. I guarantee it," Murphy said. "Besides, I'll be close by."

"I don't know." I stalled.

"There's no other way," he said harshly. "Either you play the game or you go to jail. And you know what happens when they find out that the girl isn't dead, that the FBI grabbed her and you took their five thousand dollars."

"Sure. I'll be another unsolved homicide," I said. "I should never have come to you people. You got me between a rock and a hard place." I paced up and down, shaking my head. I was certain I was a dead man—I just wasn't in the box yet.

"What guarantees have I got?" I said.

"Only my word," Murphy said, "and these consent forms I want you to sign."

The consent forms were my ace in the hole, the protection for my backside that Murphy and I had talked about in Connecticut. They later became a center of controversy with the Crown prosecutors and with Murphy's brass, who disciplined him for living up to his word and using them to protect my interests.

Under the agreements, I had promised to wear a body mike and record conversations I had with the Commissos. Murphy had added a clause at the bottom and he attached these to the transcript of every recording I made. The clause, in effect, held that the Crown and police could not use the tapes or any conversations on the tapes without my consent, and if I consented, I would be protected against self-incrimination for any crimes discussed on the tapes or in testimony I later gave. Murphy had agreed to insert it to protect me if police or prosecutors welshed on their promises.

"Okay, Mark," I said. "But get that agreement drawn up and approved as fast as you can."

We both agreed that meetings with the Commissos should be arranged, as much as possible, away from the Casa Commisso. It was too difficult a place to surveil and record conversations at. The industrial nature of the area could cause interference in transmissions, and it would be difficult for Murphy and whoever was with him to get to me once I was inside.

I called Cosimo to arrange a meeting. He wanted it to take place at the Casa Commisso, but I convinced him to meet me at the Howard Johnson's.

I was nervous as they taped the body pack on me, and I was cautious. I wore extra clothing—a heavy sweater—to conceal the taping device and anything I thought might be bulging.

"Calm down," Murphy said. "He isn't going to spot anything. You'll do just fine."

I nodded, but I wasn't convinced. I worried about whether the body pack would break down. In future meetings, I would be equipped with a backup transmitter.

I felt clammy as I parked my car and walked toward the hotel. Droplets of cold sweat trickled down from my armpits, and I checked behind my jacket, under my belt, to see if I could reach the gun that I had slipped in there without Murphy seeing. Although I had not yet signed an agreement, I felt more secure with it. I wasn't supposed to carry a gun. What the hell.

At 1:15 P.M., Cosimo and I met. Parked nearby were Murphy and his immediate superior officer, Sergeant Norm Ross. They snapped pictures as Cosimo and I greeted each other.

Almost immediately Cosimo noticed the extra clothing. "Why you got so many clothes on?" he asked.

"I'm cold as hell," I said. "I been living up north and I'm just cold." I clapped my gloved hands together and stamped my feet. A sort of involuntary shiver went through my body.

He didn't poke me or put his hand on me or his arm around me as I expected, and I remember feeling relief. I wasn't sure how I'd react if he did.

"How're you?" Cosimo asked.

"You told me fifteen thousand," I snapped, catching him off guard, letting him know I was unhappy with what had happened in Connecticut. My purpose was to put him on the defensive—make him talk about the murder conspiracy—so Murphy and the Crown would have evidence to prosecute with. The body tape confirms the success of that strategy.

"Vince, he give you the money?" Cosimo asked.

"He paid me five—he didn't give me ten," I said.

"Five thousand?" Cosimo said.

"Yeah," I said.

"You do the job?" he asked. "When did you do it? Tuesday?"

"Hell no, Monday," I said.

"Monday night?" he asked.

"I don't want to get into details, okay?" I said. "Vince said to me—he said he'd pay me extra if she was a missing person. He's something else, that fellow. That's why I want the fifteen thousand."

Cosimo was surprised and somewhat puzzled. He didn't understand what had happened. My mind was working like a computer now. Set up an alibi, I thought. Protect yourself in case someone saw an FBI agent

195

or Murphy with you. I was in high gear now, and my nerves were steady. I was in a game of cat and mouse, and I was enjoying it.

"I'll tell you why, okay?" I said. "I took another guy down there, okay? They didn't see him, okay? He didn't see them. I figured maybe I'd want an extra guy with me in case, you know, I get any static. We got the broad out okay? She's gone. They'll never find her again. There's a lotta lakes around there. They got a big fuckin', you know, strait there, or sound— Long Island Sound."

"There's a lot of things to be done over there," Cosimo said, indicating that he had other jobs in mind, that Melia wanted me to handle other jobs for him. "Never mind this. You gonna get it. I'll make sure he gives it to you—the five—right away."

"I want it," I said. "I'm going to Vegas. Leaving at noon tomorrow."

"I'll try. Whatever I can get now for tomorrow, Cec," Cosimo said.

"Look, I told him [Vince Melia]. I said you want her missing, I said, I want an extra thousand. Six thousand, okay?"

Cosimo nodded his head. "Okay. Six thousand."

The discussion then turned to my court case, and I explained that everything had been postponed until April 10. Cosimo seemed to understand. He was appealing a conviction of his own. We agreed to meet again on March 10, at which time he said he'd pay me $5,000 more.

"We meet Marcha 10," he said.

"All right, March 10, here, at twelve o'clock," I said. "I don't want to go near the bakery, okay?"

"I come—I come and see you at your house," he suggested.

"No, no, I'm never home," I said. "I tell you, I got this other broad, okay, up in Barrie. I don't want to be seen around too much, you know. When the court case is over with, okay, fine, but for now I'm keeping low. I don't want to go near the bakery anymore."

"All right," Cosimo answered.

"I worry about cops every time I go around there," I said, showing my concern. "I don't want the heat."

Cosimo didn't like the idea of returning to where we were now standing. He didn't have the control here. His friends and family weren't here. My friends were.

"Stop at my house," he said. "Nobody else comes to my house—you understand what I mean."

"Sure, I know that," I said, "but you never know—you might have the cops watching. I don't need the heat."

"All right," he said with resignation.

"March tenth—here at twelve o'clock," I said. "I want the fifteen, I want the six thousand."

"All right," he said again.

"And the rest later, a month later, okay?" I asked.

"Okay," he said with a shrug. "Have a nice time."

The recording session had gone well, but there was still no agreement. Murphy had outlined what I wanted at a special meeting of police brass representing RCMP, OPP, and Metropolitan Toronto Police. He also said that I would not work with anyone but Murphy while I was on the street, acting as their agent. I agreed to talk to others after an agreement was signed, but not before.

I was, by now, desperate for money. I owed more than $4,000 in legal fees, some $2,000 in credit-card charges, another $2,000 to my father, and I had a bank loan payment, alimony, and other bills to take care of. All that and no money coming in.

March 10 was on the horizon, and Cosimo was scheduled to pay me $5,000. Murphy said I had to turn that money in for evidence.

"Look, Mark," I said, "all I've gotten from your outfit up to now are two $100 expense payments. That don't pay the bills. You tell them they'd better pony up the money so I can pay the bills."

We met again on March 10.

"You got the money?" I asked.

Murphy shook his head. "Inspector McIlvenna said he'd have the five thousand in my hands before the meeting, but I haven't gotten anything. Look, Cec, you can't keep the money Commisso gives you. I'll have to seize it as evidence."

"The hell you say," I shouted. I was fuming and I let Murphy have both barrels. "You can tell the RCMP, McIlvenna, Sergeant John Simpson, and all the rest of them that they can go fuck themselves. The deal is off. I'll meet Commisso later tonight and get the money when you're not around."

Murphy pleaded with me to be reasonable, but for me there was nothing reasonable about the jam I was in, the bills I was facing, and the

way his bosses were dancing me around. I knew they didn't have enough to make a case without another recording and without me.

Murphy got out of my car and walked back over to the car of Sergeant Ross. He told Ross what I had told him. Then he came back to my car and again tried to change my mind.

"Mark, I'm tired of getting fucked. I'm tired of their fuckin' promises that they never keep," I said angrily. "The only way I go through with that meeting for you is for you to promise, right now, that you don't take that money."

Murphy threw up his hands. He really didn't have much choice, and it was almost time for me to meet with Cosimo. "All right, Cec," he said with a sigh, "you have my word. I won't seize the money."

The meeting went down as planned.

"You look sick, Cosimo," I said.

"Feel sick," he said.

I smiled, made light of his problem. "And me—all sunburned. I went to Florida instead."

Cosimo was mildly surprised.

"Yeah, I couldn't get to Vegas," I said.

"By yourself you went?" he asked.

"Nah, with a friend of mine," I said. "We went down to the Keys, the only place it was warm. It was just freezing everywhere else."

"It was freezin' there?" he said with surprise.

"Oh, it was cold near the top of Florida," I said, "so I went down the Keys, went fishing for a couple of days. I got sunburned out on the boat. I still don't feel well."

"I'm tired," Cosimo answered.

"You got the money?" I asked.

"Don't worry about it," Cosimo said. "I went and borrowed it for you."

"So how much is here?" I said.

"Five," he said.

I shook my head. "All right, you know, I told you [Melia] said he'd give me an extra thousand."

"Yeah, because you kill her, eh?" Cosimo asked. "The car—she disappear too? Her car?"

"Yeah, in a roundabout way," I said. "They'll never find it. She'll be

a missing person sooner or later. That's it—it's better for everyone."

Cosimo was happy, and he promised to get the additional six thousand from Melia. I told him I had to pay my accomplice for helping me dump the woman and the car in Long Island Sound. Then he dropped the bombshell. He had a new contract for me. He wanted me to kill Peter (Pietro) *Scarcella*, one of crime boss Paul Volpe's associates. He wanted it done before he had to go to jail on the counterfeiting charges.

"When am I gonna see you?" he asked. "How can I get in touch with you?"

"It's hard," I said. "I'm with this broad. And she didn't even get a phone where we're at—out in the country."

"Still things to be done," Cosimo said.

What he wanted done was to hit Scarcella. He didn't identify him then, and he didn't say how much it would be worth to me. All that he would tell me a week later at his home.

Murphy, meanwhile, had to hold off the wolves. He went to Cooper, the prosecutor, and told him what had happened—that the RCMP hadn't come up with the money as promised and that he'd had to let me keep the money that Cosimo paid me because I would have shut down the investigation and taken the money without any photos or any tape.

Cooper took the problem to Howard Morton, the Crown attorney who had been assigned to handle the Commisso case. Morton wasn't that upset. "It doesn't really matter a row of beans if the money was seized or not," Murphy said he said. "The fact it was paid by the Commissos to Kirby is what really mattered."

By now my car, a Chevrolet, had been carefully bugged by Murphy's people. I had the body pack, and they had also rigged a transmitter inside a belt buckle. With all that equipment, it was sometimes difficult to get Cosimo into the car. Cosimo was suspicious of cars, of clothing, of telephone pagers, and strange buildings. He was afraid of being bugged by police. I always had to be creative, fast on my feet with my thinking cap screwed on right.

I remember on one occasion, Murphy wanted a clearer recording of our conversations, which often took place outside the Faces Discotheque and

Howard Johnson's, where there would sometimes be the roar of overhead planes and nearby trucks.

One conversation Murphy had difficulty recording took place when Cosimo asked me to get him a gun.

"You mean one like this?" I said as I pulled out a .32 automatic from the small of my back.

"Yeah, something like that," he said, surprise registering on his face. "Why you carry the gun?"

"I got some problems," I explained, "so I carry a gun." Then I put it back.

From that point on Cosimo and his brothers knew I carried a gun. They knew I carried it either behind my back or in a pocket or behind my belt buckle in the front of my pants.

Knowing that, I think, had something to do with Cosimo not patting me down—checking to see if I was carrying anything unusual on me. I think he was always a little afraid of me because I had the balls to carry the gun and show him I was carrying it when we met.

The gun gave me a sense of security, but I wouldn't have been so secure if I'd known what the RCMP learned when I turned it in after all the meetings with the Commissos had ended. I had borrowed that gun from two rounders who were friends of the Commissos, but I had never had the chance to test it because I was always in the city working with Murphy and other investigators. When I finally turned it in, Murphy sent it to the RCMP laboratory to see if the weapon had been used before in a crime. He found that the gun had a faulty firing pin. If I had ever tried to use it to protect myself I'd have been hung out to dry. A cap pistol would have been more effective.

Losing most of my conversation with Cosimo about the gun and lacking clarity on some of the other tapes concerned Murphy. He was also worried about my safety and about the evidence they collected on the recordings.

To allay those fears, I showed up one day for a meeting with Murphy at the Skyline parking lot equipped in an unusual way. As Murphy stood by the car, I took off my shoe and my sock and pulled an elastic bandage from my jogging suit pocket. I wrapped the bandage around my ankle and looked up smiling.

"Guaranteed I get Cosimo in the car today," I said with a chuckle. Murphy was smiling from ear to ear as I drove off to meet Cosimo.

Cosimo spotted me as I pulled into the Faces parking lot and walked over.

"Get in," I said to him.

"Cec, you know I don't like to talk in the car," he said. "The cops, they could have bugged your car."

"No chance, Cosimo," I said. "The people I sent over to your place to do the debugging check the car out all the time. I never take chances. Besides, I can't walk. I can't get out of the car."

"What's the matter?" he asked.

I opened the door and pointed to the bandaged ankle and foot.

"Your foot—what's the matter with it?" he asked.

"I went jogging this morning," I said, "and I sprained—maybe broke —my ankle when I fell running down the street."

"Ah, that's a shame," Cosimo said, climbing into the car. The conversation that followed was clearly recorded without any feedback.

There were instances, though, when the bug—the transmitter that they'd hidden behind the dash—caused some problems. On the last day before the cops wrapped up the Commisso conspiracy investigation, I had to meet with Michele Commisso in the car. Michele wasn't as reluctant to get in the car as his brother was. He'd generally just jump in, no problem, and start talking. On this occasion, just minutes before he was due to meet with me, I turned on the radio. The transmitter started buzzing—giving off static right through the radio. I just told him that the radio wasn't working right, and he never suspected a thing.

There was one time, April 23, 1981, that Cosimo didn't even hesitate about getting into my car. I still remember the circumstances.

I was at Howard Johnson's waiting for him, when he arrived in a taxi instead of his car. He paid the driver, walked over to my car with a slight limp, and climbed in.

"Where's your car?" I asked him. "Why are you riding in a taxi?"

"I was just in a car accident," he said as his hands seemed to flail at the air in frustration. "I hurt the leg—banged my leg against the dash."

After he paid me a thousand dollars our meeting ended and I drove him to the Cambridge Hotel parking lot and let him out.

As he started to get out of the car, I shouted to him, "Hey, start limping down the street. The cops are down there. You'll have witnesses, and you can put in for an insurance claim."

He turned and looked at me with sort of a smirk on his face. "Yeah, yeah, you're right, Cec," he said. "Good idea. The leg. It's swollen and I got the whiplash."

"Got another idea, Cosimo," I said. "Better than that. Put your fuckin' leg in front of the car and I'll run over it. Then you'll really collect."

Cosimo looked back, shaking a fist at me. "Fuck off, Cec," he said laughing. He slammed the door behind him, started to walk over to a car in the lot, then remembered and started limping again while the surveillance cameras snapped.

Murphy and those who helped him monitored and recorded the conversations in a specially equipped van. It was a three-quarter-ton, blue-step vehicle with a big square box in the back and dual wheels on either side. It had glass windows on the back with a one-way mirror window. The coppers could look out, but nobody could look in while they were taking pictures.

The van was my security blanket, literally. It was a rolling recording and movie studio. It was loaded with sensitive electronic recording equipment —cameras of all types with special Telephoto lenses—and there were pictures all around of Cosimo and me together.

There were other vehicles that could pick up the conversations and record them, but the van was usually the one Murphy used, particularly when he was alone. There were at least five occasions that he had to cover me without any backup because of problems in his office.

I look back now at some of things that happened—the bickering and shortages of equipment and personnel while I was out meeting these Calabrian mafiosi—and I marvel at the fact that I lived through it.

It was a little after noon of St. Patrick's Day when I drove up to Cosimo's house in North York. It was a nice home, a little on the conservative side, but comfortable. Cosimo was smart enough to know that if he lived too high off the hog—in too plush surroundings—he'd attract attention, and that's something he tried not to do. He tried, not too successfully, to keep a low profile with police.

I knocked on the door. There was no answer. I knocked again. Still no answer. I began to wonder if Cosimo had forgotten the meeting. I started to walk up the street toward Remo's house, talking as I went so that

Murphy could record and understand what I was doing without becoming too concerned.

"Just going up the street here, to Remo's house for a second," I said as I walked. The recorder picked it up.

Within a minute or two I ran into Remo.

"How you doing?" I asked.

"Going," he said without elaborating.

"Where's Cosimo?" I asked. "He's supposed to be here at eleven thirty."

"He's home," Remo answered.

"I knocked on the door," I said. "There's no answer."

"He's home, for sure," said Remo. "I just called."

"Jesus, he must be deaf then," I said. "Must be sleeping, you know."

I returned to Cosimo's house and banged on the door. Just then his wife drove up with the kids.

"Is Cosimo sleeping?" I asked. She shook her head. "He must be deaf."

"Deaf?" she said.

"Deaf," I said. "I rang the doorbell, banged on the door about ten times."

She opened the door wide to let me in. I shouted inside. "You getting up, Cosimo?"

"Yeah, I'm ready," he answered.

As I started to walk inside, his wife cautioned me to take off my boots. Before I pulled them off, I turned to her and said, "I got my car running. If he's not going to be too long I'll just leave it running."

Cosimo entered the room then, and I showed him I was a little agitated about the delay. "I was out there a half hour waiting for you," I said. He appeared surprised. Before he could say anything else, I put the boots back on and started out the door. "I'll wait for you outside. I got the car parked out there and I don't want to get a ticket or anything, you know. Where we gonna go? Where do we have to go? north? south? Got enough gas?"

"South a little bit," he said.

"South of what? I only got a half tank of gas. Is that enough?" I asked.

"Yeah," he said.

I got into the car. While I waited, I talked into the transmitter, telling Murphy that we were going south on a particular road. I had to wait

another twenty minutes before Cosimo finally climbed into the car.

We talked about Remo and three friends he had in a car. I got Cosimo to identify the car as a Pontiac and confirm that one of the men in the car was a big guy but he didn't say what they were doing. He did confirm my observation that I'd never seen them around before. He also promised to have the rest of the money from Melia by the end of the month. We hit a traffic jam and he gave me new directions.

As we drove there was a lot of small talk about my upcoming sentencing, which I said would be postponed again. When Cosimo asked if I'd seen Ken Goobie recently, the purpose of all the driving came into focus. It was to show me where Peter Scarcella hung out.

Scarcella was only thirty, but he had become one of Paul Volpe's important associates. I don't recall ever meeting him or even seeing him until Cosimo brought him to my attention that day. Scarcella chauffeured Volpe to meetings; he frequently was seen at Volpe's home. He seemed to be one of the brightest young stars in the Volpe crime organization, even when he was charged with bribery of Metro Works employees at three incinerator sites in Toronto.

Now Cosimo wanted him hit and he was laying out the floor plan of his life-style, the places he lived and hung out, without explaining why he wanted it done.

I let Cosimo give the directions while I played the role of a tourist. He reeled off this street and that in an area where I grew up. He was directing me to an apartment that Scarcella used. I played dumb, repeating each street he named so the surveillance teams tailing us would keep up.

"Turn right, here," Cosimo said. "It's hard to get that guy."

"Hard to get him?" I asked.

"Over here, yes," he said.

"Why is it hard to get him there?" I asked.

"He lives with his family there," he answered.

"What is it, a house or an apartment?" I said.

"No. It's an apartment," he said.

"You got his name and everything?" I asked. Up to this point, he hadn't given me a name that I could record on the tape that day.

"Yeah, but, first I wanna show you another two, three places where he usually goes." Cosimo said.

He showed me Scarcella's father's place and a location where he went to play cards two nights a week.

"He goes to poker games," he said.

"Poker games? What, around here?" I said.

"No, they move it every night," he said. "There is a restaurant he goes to almost every night."

"Around here?" I asked.

"No, no. On Dufferin and Castlefield,—where Canadian Tire is," he said. "There's a restaurant on the corner. It's open twenty-four hours. He goes there every day."

He asked me how I was going to handle it—when I'd do it.

"I'll come back. I'll just keep watching this guy," I said. "There's no hurry for this, eh?"

"No, no," he answered quietly. "One other thing I want to give you, when it's time. I'll give you more, you know, particular details."

"Oh, I'll just watch," I told him. "I'll look around here, then I'll go to this restaurant. Does he drive his car by himself?"

"Most times, yes," Cosimo said. Then, as we drove from one location to another, he added that Scarcella parked his car outside his parents' apartment at Winston House.

"You got a license number?" I asked.

"Yes," he said. "Last three numbers are 747."

"Open this darn page," I said, "and write it in. Write his name down here so I can check it out myself, eh? Then the number where he lives with his mother and father."

I figured that if I got him to write down the information, it would be another nail of evidence to hammer in his coffin—an important nail.

"You got his first name?" I asked.

"It's Peter," Cosimo said.

"Peter?"

"S-A-R-C-E-L-L-A," he said, spelling it wrong at first and then correcting himself.

I tried to pry out of Cosimo why he wanted Scarcella eliminated. It came slowly, with great difficulty.

"He did something, the bastard," he said.

"What is he? A stool pigeon?" I asked.

"Look's that way," he said.

We got to the Branch Restaurant. It was the place Scarcella came every day to meet gamblers and a girlfriend who was a waitress. Then Cosimo dropped another nugget of information. Scarcella was going to be at the Commisso bakery the next day at 1:00 P.M.

"All right," I said, "I'll get a look at him. I won't come in, but I'll be around there, okay? I'll park across the street or something."

Cosimo nodded. "Just between twelve thirty and one o'clock."

"Between twelve thirty and one o'clock he's gonna meet you, eh?" I said. "And he'll be driving that car, eh?"

While Cosimo thought I'd be there watching, I wasn't. The members of the surveillance team were, and what they discovered was important. They spotted Scarcella at the Casa Commisso the day Cosimo and I met, and they tailed him that afternoon to the Four Seasons Sheraton Hotel in downtown Toronto, where he met with Paul Volpe and two other people. We didn't know it then but the Commissos were worried— worried about facing a gang war with Volpe and his people. They were busy plotting to strike first.

CHAPTER 18

The Informer II

I was still working for Murphy, the Combined Forces Special Enforcement Unit (SEU), the RCMP, and the Crown prosecutor without any immunity, or any agreement, and I was getting nervous about it. All that was supposed to change with a meeting between me and members of a special steering committee representing the agencies involved in the Cosimo investigation. It was supposed to, but it didn't.

We met at the Holiday Inn in Toronto just two days after Cosimo had given me a contract to kill Scarcella. As we started to sit down, Inspector Wylie of the SEU told Murphy to leave while they talked to me.

As Murphy walked toward the door, I stood up. "If Murphy goes, I go," I snapped.

"Wait," Wylie said. He motioned to both of us to return to our seats. "Corporal Murphy can stay."

"Mr. Kirby, we'd like you to work with Sergeant Al Cooke of Metro and Sergeant John Simpson of SEU," Wylie said. "They're better equipped to handle this case."

I shook my head. I knew Cooke. He was all right. I had nothing against him. But he wasn't Murphy. I also knew Simpson. I didn't like him. Besides, I knew and trusted Murphy.

"It's Murphy or no one," I said. "I've said that from the start, and that's the way it is. I trust him, period. If I don't work with him, I don't work."

I could see a lot of unhappy inspectors in the room. They were going to be even more unhappy before the meeting ended.

First, I rejected the agreement they had signed and asked me to sign. It met my conditions except the most important one—immunity from prosecution for all past crimes.

"Can't sign that," I said, "not till I get immunity. Without immunity I don't testify, and you can't use the tapes."

That really upset them. They had admissions on those tapes that represented solid evidence of two conspiracies to murder—and there was the promise of more to come. But they weren't worth a dime unless I testified and agreed to the use of the tapes. Stalemate.

"One other thing, gentlemen," I said. "I've got another payment of seven thousand dollars or so coming from the Commissos. I intend to keep it unless you people come up with money to pay my expenses and living costs."

They all agreed to pay my expenses, but the agreement was still unsigned when I left. I said I'd continue to work with Murphy as long as they took care of my expenses, but unless I had immunity, I was still a "confidential informant" of the RCMP, and I wouldn't have to testify. Murphy had given his word, and his bosses didn't like it.

For the next few days there were additional meetings, including one with Simpson, all designed to get me work with other investigators. None of them succeeded. Then another meeting was arranged with Cosimo at his house. Events started to move rapidly, a lot faster and in a lot more directions than we'd expected.

Cosimo was awake and waiting for me when I arrived the morning of March 27. The last thing I expected him to talk about was what he considered a developing Mafia war, but that's what he ended up doing. As he talked, the transmitter in my belt buckle and the body pack near my hip recorded it all.

"Listen, I got a few things to talk to you about—about this Scarc [Scarcella]," I said. "Want to go outside? Let's go outside. Few problems I've had."

Cosimo wasn't in any hurry to go outside to the car. He was comfortable where he was as I talked, so I didn't press it. I didn't want him getting

suspicious. I did, however, want to pick up the conversation where we'd left off the last time we met. The Mounties needed more on his plan to kill Scarcella. As a prod, I used information the Mounties had pulled together watching Scarcella from the moment he left his apartment to the time he went the Casa Commisso.

"You know the day you told me he was going to be at the hall there?" I asked.

Cosimo nodded. "We were there."

"All right," I said. "I went over to the apartment there about nine o'clock and I sat there. I saw him come out. I got the license number of his car and everything, eh?"

"Yeah," Cosimo acknowledged.

"Now I followed him from there. I had a different car, a broad's car," I said. "I followed him right down to the Four Seasons Sheraton Hotel downtown."

"Yeah," Cosimo said, "and . . ."

"In the morning, okay?" I said. "I parked the car, I went in there, and you know who he's standing there talking to?"

"Who?" asked Cosimo, his interest raised.

"Paul Volpe," I said. "How come? What's he doing talking to Volpe?"

"He's close to him," Cosimo answered. "That's okay. Forget it for now."

"He's close?" I asked.

"You don't have to worry about anything," Cosimo said.

"But who wants him killed?" I asked, really puzzled by the events and his answers. "Is it Volpe who wants him killed, or you, or what?"

"No, no, no, I'm . . ."

I interrupted. "You know like I saw Volpe and I said, what the fuck's going on here?"

"I'm wondering. Maybe he wants to do it to me," answered Cosimo, obviously concerned. "Him and this fellow."

"It's you that wants this done, or Volpe?" I asked.

"It's me, not Volpe," he said.

"Volpe doesn't know nothing about this?" I said.

"No, no. Why?" he said.

"You know, I didn't want to stick around the lobby too long," I explained, "I've seen Volpe before. I don't know if he's seen me."

"You ever meet him before?" he asked.

"Oh, I've seen him before, with Chuck," I said.

"Where?" he asked.

"You know where Chuck's place is," I said. We were talking about Chuck Yanover, who was a member of the Volpe organization and was supposed to be out of town, in hiding.

"Recently?" he said nervously.

"No, about a year ago," I said.

"Nobody saw you?" he asked with concern.

"No," I said.

"You tell anybody about this thing?" he asked.

"No, nobody knows about it," I reassured him.

"Things—they're bad over here," he said, deep worry showing on his face. "I don't know why these guys . . . I don't know. They want to do me and my brother."

"They what?" I said with real surprise.

"They want to do me and my brother," he said. "Maybe I can't trust any one of them."

Cosimo was telling me that he and Remo were targets of possible mob hits and that Volpe and his organization were behind the plot. Scarcella was some kind of double agent, playing both sides for his own interests.

"Who, Volpe does?" I asked. "You think Volpe wants to kill you and your brother?"

"This guy," he said, meaning Scarcella.

"What, with this guy?" I asked to be sure I was getting his story straight.

"Yeah. It's the two of them," he said.

"What? This Scarcella's playing both sides?" I asked. "He's telling Volpe everything about you and him?"

Cosimo shook his head. "No, nothing about me and him. It's just that I don't know what's going to happen next year, you know. We just don't know."

"So what do you want to do?" I asked. "You want to kill Volpe in the future?"

"No. Not for now," he said, his voice trailing off.

"Not for now?" I asked.

"Like wait for this guy [Scarcella] for another week or so, okay?" he asked.

"Pass on him for a week?" I said.

"Yes," Cosimo answered.

"All right, a week," I said.

"'Cause I'm waiting for an answer," he said. "I wanna be sure it's him." Then he switched back to questions about Yanover, who he was obviously concerned about. "You talk to Chuck about these things?"

"About this?" I said.

"Yeah," he answered.

"No, he's on the run, Chuck," I said. "People are looking for him."

"For what?" asked Cosimo.

"He ripped somebody off," I said. "He sold somebody a kilo of coke or something. Ripped him. Bought himself a new Cadillac and he's gone. Yeah, he's too much. All right, so wait a week or so on this guy, eh?"

He nodded.

"Now what do you want?" I asked, to try and get more details out of him. "Do you want his body left laying around? Do you want him disposed of, or what?"

"Which way can you do it?" he asked.

"I can do it whatever way you want," I said.

"Gonna do it. You with me," Cosimo said, looking at me with a smile.

"That's right," I said. "I just did this last one [the girl in Connecticut] with no problem."

"You were with me," Cosimo said, staring at me, trying to read what I was thinking. "You be with me because there's lotsa things will go on with this fuckin' town. You see what I mean?"

The message was loud and clear to me. As far as Cosimo was concerned, a gang war was coming, and he wanted to be certain I was going to be there to help him.

"I don't know. I stay away from this shit now, you know," I answered.

"Yeah, you stay away, but be sure you are with me," he said sharply, "not with those other people."

"That's right, that's right," I said, "you know that."

The conversation changed suddenly. Cosimo wanted me to see a man he called "Lillo" at a furniture store.

"There's two guys workin' there," he explained. "One older and the young guy. The young one's the one. Just give him, you know, a couple of smacks."

But I still wanted more on tape about the Scarcella hit.

"You want him left laying in the street where everybody sees his head, sees him and says look, here's a stool pigeon that got a bullet in his head?" I asked.

Cosimo wasn't certain, but he was concerned that Scarcella would be suspicious, a difficult man to to kill. "Some days, he's very suspicious," he said.

"I got a way of getting to him," I answered. "I got a dirty trick of my own I could get him with."

"You do?" he said with surprise.

"He's not going to be suspicious if I walk up to him and show him a badge and say, 'Here, you're under arrest. Come with me.' How can he be suspicious then?"

"That's right," Cosimo said with a broad smile on his face.

I reminded Cosimo that he still owed me $7,000 for the Connecticut job and that I was broke. He promised he would pay by the first week of April.

"You won't lose no money with me, you know that, Cec," he said.

"The point is you know I need it," I said. "I'm broke."

Still he was worried, worried about betrayal in his own camp, worried about being stabbed in the back by people he trusted, including me, particularly since I needed the money he owed me. I suspect that he wondered if I would sell him out for money. He didn't know it, but he'd already been sold out, for my life.

"You won't betray me, eh?" he asked. "You wouldn't go against me?"

"Never," I said.

"Thank you, Cec," he said.

"Never, Cosimo," I said again.

A feeling of exhilaration gripped me as I left. If the recording equipment had worked—and it had—the surveillance teams had some strong evidence from that meeting. I was certain Cosimo was convinced he could

trust me, at least for the moment. I was equally certain that if I actually handled any of the hits he had planned—whether Scarcella or Volpe— I would be wasted eventually myself.

Cosimo was a very suspicious man. He had been very close to Scarcella. He was someone he trusted. Now he was ready to sink that knife into him once he was certain that whoever was whispering in his ear about Scarcella was whispering truth. Even if not, the seed had been planted, and it was festering like an open sore.

For the next few weeks, Cosimo stalled. He stalled on paying the money he and Melia owed me. He stalled on setting a date to hit Scarcella. On April 8, he came close to making a commitment on Scarcella.

Cosimo was nervous as we sat in my car talking. He noticed that my ankle was wrapped in bandages, and he seemed to accept my explanation that I'd injured it when I fell while jogging. Then he noticed a small telephone pager I was wearing on my belt. Immediately his suspicion reached an almost fever pitch. He appeared convinced it was a tape recorder until I told him I had gotten the pager so that he could reach me when he needed me. I gave him a number.

"Here it is," I said, "R, eight, nine, four, seven."

"Just call and give the message?" Cosimo asked.

"Right, and just leave a number," I answered. "Don't say a name there."

"By tomorrow night, they gonna page you, okay?" Cosimo asked. "If you can, grab more information on the guy—Peter."

Cosimo's voice dropped to a whisper as he mentioned Scarcella's name. He was still nervous about the car and the pager I was wearing. I repeated the last name, Scarcella, then I tried to ease his suspicions again.

"It's all right, this car," I said. "I check this car all the time, every week."

"Then next week, Michele gonna call you," he said. "And, without mentioning the name, he gonna say yes or no, okay? If it's yes, go ahead, okay?"

"If he says yes, go ahead," I said.

"Yes," Cosimo said without hesitation.

They needed another week to decide whether they had to kill Scarcella.

Cosimo was planning a trip, to Vancouver. He was establishing an alibi. It would be up to his brother Michele to pass on the hit order.

"All right," I said, "what about Volpe?"

"No, no, for now, forget about him," Cosimo answered excitedly.

"You're gonna have to get rid of him sooner or later, aren't you?" I asked.

Cosimo looked at me for a long minute before answering, shaking his head slowly. "You talk about anybody? About him?"

"No, I don't," I said sharply. "I don't talk to fuckin' nobody. I don't even talk to anybody, okay?"

"About anything?" he pressed.

"Nobody," I said.

"I'll tell you what they say," he said. "They spoke to me in jail. They say there's gonna be a war involved—a war over here in Toronto."

"Is that right?" I said with a look of surprise. Then I hit him with some information I'd gotten from a biker about his relationship with Ken Goobie.

"I could tell you things that people around this fuckin' city are shooting their mouth off about, okay?" I continued. "I just don't pay any attention to them—and Goobie's one of them. He's got a big mouth. You don't tell him nothing. Okay?"

"No, no, no," Cosimo said.

"All right," I said. "'Cause everything you tell him he repeats, you know?"

"That's right," Cosimo said in agreement.

"He [Goobie] told Gary [Barnes] about this thing down in New York."

I watched as Cosimo's eyes widened in surprise. He was obviously upset that anyone on the street would have any knowledge about the plot to kill Helen Nafpliotis.

"Yeah?" he said in shock.

"Yeah," I said, "I didn't tell him, so you had to tell him."

"Well, he didn't know you went," Cosimo said. "He didn't know that it was done."

"He said to Gary, he said, you wanna make twenty-five thousand?" I said watching Cosimo's reaction. "He says, there's a broad down in New York that they wanna get rid of."

Cosimo was flustered, upset. He had gone to Goobie and told Goobie he would pay him twenty-five thousand to kill the woman as added insurance if I failed to do the job. He was going to pay this bastard more than he offered me. Goobie had gone to Barnes to get him to help. The last thing Cosimo expected was that I would find out about it. Finally he admitted talking to Goobie. His suspicions that I might be talking were sidetracked now by a much deeper suspicion about Goobie, and I played on that.

"Well, he's told Gary," I said angrily. "So how many other people has he told?"

Cosimo was really on the defensive now. "I don't know. Because I talk to him, not to nobody else."

"You got a big mouth," I said. "I told you. Stay away from the fuckin' guy. He's no good."

"I don't see him anymore," he said.

"And don't trust him. I'm telling you," I warned.

"I don't trust nobody," Cosimo said. "Ah, Cec, I trust you. Things they gonna be for the betterment. Things are gonna be smooth in this town."

Suddenly his mood darkened and his eyes narrowed.

"We wanna know if we can trust you a hundred percent," he asked. "You with us?"

"Yeah, well, I have been all the time," I said.

His face brightened a little and there was a trace of a smile. "All the time, you for us, yes?" he said.

It wasn't until April 21 that I met with Michele at Howard Johnson's. He didn't have the money that was promised, but he had information that jolted me.

Michele had been to the States two weeks earlier to see Vince Melia and collect the money that was due me for killing Helen Nafpliotis. Melia had stalled, and the Commissos were having trouble raising the cash. Cosimo's legal fees were over $15,000, and they had other commitments. With all the problems, Michele said he'd have $2,000 for me in a few days, but I'd have to wait until Melia came to Toronto for a wedding later in the month to collect the rest.

"Vince, he gave me the runaround," Michele said. "He says there was some money missing in the apartment, some jewelry."

I was stunned, but it didn't show. I didn't know it, but the FBI had, in addition to staging a fake kidnapping at her home in Stamford, let Nafpliotis take all her money and jewelry with her. Melia and his crew had apparently searched the apartment for the jewelry and money, most of it things Nick Melia had given her and wanted back since she was dead anyway. When they didn't find it, they asked questions and tried to convince the Commissos I'd gotten enough with the jewelry and cash and the initial payment.

"Yeah, well, I made it look good," I said to Michele.

"You know what happened to him?" Michele said. "I've checked it and it's true. His brother [Nick Melia] is into some trouble down in Kentucky. And he's out on a hundred and fifty thousand dollars bail. He's waiting for his brother to beat the case and come up with the money."

"That could be another two years," I said angrily.

"No, in May," he said. "He's either in or out. But this week, he's (Vince) bringing some money, that's for sure."

When I threatened to turn up at a family wedding, which was to be held at the Casa Commisso banquet hall, and grab Melia and shake it out of him, Michele excitedly told me to stay away and guaranteed I'd be paid. Two days later, on April 23, Cosimo and I met. He handed me $1,000 and promised to pay me $500 a week from a business he was taking over so that I wouldn't be broke anymore.

"You know, we gonna put you in payroll," he said. "So much a week. Then when things are done, you gonna have a bonus for it. You see what I mean?"

I shook my head in agreement. "It's about time I got some extra, some sort of . . ." He cut me off before I finished saying some sort of salary.

"Before, I couldn't do it," he said. "But now, I have something, ah, steady, inside." Then, without explanation he added, "Ah, Scarcella, forget about it for now."

"What?" I asked in surprise.

"Just don't worry about it for now," he said.

"For how long?" I asked.

"I don't know," he said. "A month, two months. We don't know yet. There's another guy I want to take care of."

"What?" I said.

"Another guy instead of him. [Remo] wants to do another guy," Cosimo said.

"So you don't want to do him [Scarcella]," I said, making sure that his orders to kill another man were being recorded clearly. "You want to do another guy? Who, who the fuck's this other guy?"

"I'll show you," he said. "Next week you'll see."

"Make up your minds," I said with annoyance. "What is he? A close friend of Scarcella's?"

"Yes," he answered.

"Not Volpe?" I said, so it was clear to everyone listening in.

"I'll show him," he said. "Maybe you know the guy a little bit."

"What's his name?" I asked, trying to squeeze out more information without arousing his suspicions. "Maybe I do know him."

"I'll tell you, but you don't worry about the name," he said. "You see him, okay?"

"What is he, a gambler?" I asked. "Another gambler?"

"Ah, you know," he said with a shrug. "Next week. Next week you gonna have two thousand."

"Vince is coming in Saturday, eh?" I said. "I'd like to be there. I'd like to kick his fuckin' ass when he comes in Saturday."

"You don't have to worry about that," he said. "I'll do it myself."

On the night of April 27, ten mercenaries, including Toronto Ku Klux Klan leader Wolfgang W. Droege, arrived at a marina near Fort Pike State Park in New Orleans in a truck loaded with weapons. With them were three undercover agents of the U.S. Bureau of Alcohol, Tobacco, and Firearms (ATF). When they got out to unload the weapons, ammunition, and dynamite they were transporting, agents of the FBI, the U.S. Customs Service, and ATF were waiting to arrest them.

Just four days before that happened, I reported to Mark Murphy that the mercenaries were going to invade a 300-square-mile island called Dominica. I didn't know much about the island except what I had been

told. It had been British, and it had been given its independence in November 1978. It was located between the French islands of Martinique and Guadeloupe and was about 400 miles southeast of San Juan, Puerto Rico.

All that and more had been told to me by Chuck Yanover, who I had seen at a discotheque while I was busy working for the RCMP on the Commissos.

Meeting with Yanover gave me an edge in my meetings with the Commissos, who were always afraid I would defect to Yanover's boss, Paul Volpe. Yanover was always a braggard and loved to talk about other people. As a rounder, he was in a position to hear about different rounders and hoods, including the Commissos. So I made a point of listening when he talked, because he could be a fountain of useful information when he wanted to. The last thing I expected him to talk about at one meeting was a plot to seize an island.

"Want a job, Cec?" he asked.

"Maybe," I said. "What have you got in mind?"

"How'd you like to go the Caribbean with me, to an island called Dominica?" he asked. "We're going to take it over."

Yanover said that he had been hired by Wolfgang Droege and James Alexander McQuirter, national director of the KKK in Canada. Droege was about thirty-four, and McQuirter was twenty-three. The two planned to take over the island and set up their own government. Yanover planned to be made one of their top officials, set up a casino with the help of Volpe, and become very, very rich.

The island had all kinds of potential as far as Yanover was concerned. It could be used for gambling, as a jump-off point and storage warehouse for narcotics, a place to hide felons, and a sanctuary for mob money through offshore banks they would set up. There was just no limit to Chuckie's dreams of riches.

Yanover and one of his buddies, Michael Gerol, had gone to the island on what was supposed to be a vacation. They had photographed all the island's important locations, including its police station, its small military post, and the best approaches to the island from the sea. Yanover had turned over the information and photos to the two Klansmen so they could prepare for the invasion.

"Join us," Yanover said, "you'll make a fortune."

I shook my head. "Thanks, Chuck, but that's not for me. I got too many problems here to take care of."

I told everything I knew to Murphy, and he reported it to the SEU, the RCMP, and the OPP, all of whom launched an investigation. At the same time, I was told, they notified the FBI, who, with other agencies, had already infiltrated the "invasion force." If they hadn't stopped the plot when they did, a lot of people might have been killed.

Their plan, I learned later, was to team up on the island with some Rastafarians, called "Dreads" on Dominica, who grew pot, kidnapped and killed island residents, and threatened officials who stood in their way. That would have been some crazy team—Klansmen who hate blacks, and Rastas, who hate whites and extort and terrorize their own people to push drugs and what they call a religion.

Funny thing. On May 15, shortly after the Dominica story broke in the papers, Cosimo mentioned that the island had been offered to his crime group some time before.

"Looks like they're [the police] after Yanover," I remarked. "Those people in that Dominica plot, they got pinched. They're looking at about fifty years."

"You know that the first people they talked to was us," said Cosimo. "They came to us two years ago."

"What? About that?" I said dumbfounded. The last thing I expected him to say was that he and his brothers were somehow involved in Dominica. I was really stunned. "They approached you on it?"

"Sure. Before anybody else," he said with a smile.

"What, the people down there?" I asked, still startled by what he'd told me.

"The people down there—from Dominica," he said. "I was down there."

"You went down there?" I asked.

"Hey, it's nice—beautiful island, beautiful island," he repeated. "Well, first it was too much money. Then—at the time they approached me— the people in power were the right people."

I was fascinated by what he had to say, and for the most part all I did was listen, with little more comment that an occasional "Yeah."

"Then there was an election and they lost it," he continued.

"Then it changed," I suggested.

"You understand," he said with a smile.

"And now it's the same people from before?" I asked.

"Ah no, but now they changed, okay?" he said. "So that's why we dropped the idea. "You know, we had people interested. Everybody was ready to go in. But then the people—they lost the election. These other people, they want nothing to do with it. The deal was twenty-five years we run a casino. Twenty-five years tax free."

"Is that right, eh?" I said. "Jesus. That would have been nice."

"What they wanted," he said, "was for us to build them a runway and an airport."

"An airport?" I asked.

He nodded his head vigorously. "Yeah, because they got no airport. There's no airport there at all."

"So you can't land a plane there," I said.

"Not a jet," he explained. "Just a small plane. So there was two million dollars' worth of work on the airport. They would give us the best side of land—five hundred acres farmland. For nothing. Just free. That way we'd be able to build on it."

"Yeah," I acknowledged.

"Okay—so much percent was to go to the prime minister there," he said. "That's all it was. Then this thing changed."

"Yeah, that's too bad," I said.

Cosimo was upset by the change, that was pretty obvious. The people he'd depended on were out, and there were new people trying to take over Dominica who had approached other people in Toronto. The new people wanted to overthrow the government and seize the island. Cosimo called that approach a waste of time.

"Dominica, it's beautiful, one of the best islands in the area and it's the most beautiful," he said. "There's just twenty-five thousand people on the whole island. It's one of the biggest islands. Bigger than Aruba. It's bigger than most of those islands up there."

He was really rambling on about the place, about the lost opportunity. Cosimo saw it as a gold mine for his group and a great place to spend his time.

"Like I said, that was no more than two, four, five years ago when we were approached," he recalled. "Then that thing in Vancouver happened [the counterfeiting bust] and then we layed around a little bit. A lotta things happened."

Cosimo was disappointed that his group hadn't been able to take over the island. But he was disgusted that Yanover had gotten involved and had blown the deal forever with the ridiculous invasion plot. The island paradise would never be a casino plum he could pluck.

Although the "invasion force" was arrested April 27, it wasn't until February 10, 1982, that McQuirter and Yanover were charged with trying to overthrow Dominica. Between those two arrests, Yanover had managed to get himself arrested for the Arviv Disco bombing and for a plot to assassinate the president of South Korea. He conned North Korean intelligence out of more than $600,000 with the help of Gerol, who played the role of a trained killer. Then he tried to con the RCMP and the American Central Intelligence Agency. He wanted to exchange pictures and tapes he had of the North Korean agents he was dealing with.

What Yanover had in mind was to have charges against him for the Arviv bombing and the Dominican plot dropped. He also wanted diamond-smuggling charges against his two bosses, Nate Klegerman and Volpe, dropped while he and Gerol were supposed to get immunity. Nobody was buying. Yanover eventually got two years running concurrent with his nine years for the Arviv bombing. Gerol got a year.

Nobody, so far as I was ever able to find out, got the pictures, the tapes, and all the other evidence Yanover said he gathered against the North Koreans. And all those North Korean co-plotters of his never turned up to try to collect their $600,000 back, but I'll bet Chuckie wishes he'd never taken them for that. Deep down, he probably also wishes he'd cut a deal with the RCMP and the OPP. The truth is when Yanover gets out of jail he's going to find that Communist agencies like North Korean intelligence don't like being ripped off and embarrassed. They have long memories, and they intend to make him pay—with his life. Yanover may find that to survive he'll have to make a deal with the coppers. They are the only ones who will ever be able to help him.

CHAPTER 19

The Last Contract

I felt more secure when I went to meet Cosimo on April 29 than I had in all the months I had worked for Murphy. For the first time I had a written agreement, signed the day they grabbed the Dominica "invaders," that guaranteed me immunity as a witness and protection and support for my family. I should have known then that all that glitters is not gold and things written on paper can always be altered. Promises made and sworn to are not always promises kept by men or their governments.

When I saw Cosimo at Howard Johnson's that day, I was concerned only with getting the evidence needed to wrap this thing up. I was tired and tense. Murphy was stretched to the limits of endurance—providing surveillance and protection for me and working long added hours checking out information I brought in. In his spare waking moments he was fighting with his brass, trying to get added physical and financial support for me. I have to say that I will always admire Murphy for his honesty, his integrity, and his guts. I'm alive today because of him.

Cosimo complained that he was still in pain from the injury he had received in the car accident. The leg still bothered him, and he was limping slightly. He looked terrible. His eyes were bloodshot, his round face looked drawn, and he was unusually nervous.

"I've got something I wanna talk to you about," he said. "Let's get outta the car for a second. I don't trust cars."

"All right," I answered. "Looks like you got a lot on your mind. Looks

like you haven't been sleeping too good. You can tell when your eyes are all red."

His tone was sharp, and there was an edge of suspicion to his questions.

"Why do you want my brother [Remo] here?" he asked.

"Well look, you told me last week that you're going to put me on a payroll," I said, trying to explain why I had asked him to bring Remo to the meeting. Remo had not come, and Cosimo was annoyed about that request.

"Now I wanted to just confirm it with him in case something happens to you," I added.

"Nothing happens to us," he said. "What could happen to me?"

"Well, suppose you get picked up?" I asked. "Get another charge. Then I won't see you anymore."

"Don't you worry about that," he said. "You don't see me anymore, you think I'm gonna die?" He stopped and pointed to my hip. "What's that?"

I looked down and smiled. "The pager. It's off now. If I turn it on, it starts beeping." To put him at ease, I turned it on.

Cosimo switched to problems with his people in Connecticut. It was out in the open. Melia and his friends didn't believe that the Nafpliotis woman was dead.

"They still don't believe that it's okay because even her suitcase is missing," he said, with just a trace of suspicion reflecting from his narrowing eyes.

"Yeah, well, I took care of all that, okay?" I said.

"He [Melia] said that all the jewelry is missing," he said.

"Well, my partner took some jewelry and some stuff," I snapped, grateful that early on I had established with him that I had had to take some help with me.

I'd originally created the fictional helper in the event someone from the Commisso crime group spotted me with Murphy or an agent in New York or Connecticut. Now that helper provided an alibi for taking the jewelry and cash that the FBI and the woman had cleared from her home without ever bothering to tell me or Murphy. Little mistakes like that can cost your life when you're dealing with people like the Calabrian Mafia.

The FBI hadn't given me or Murphy or the SEU a clue to what they

had done with Nafpliotis. They never told us they'd taken her back to the house to get her jewelry and her clothes. They didn't tell us she was back in Greece, trying to sell her home and other property from there. I knew they'd staged a kidnapping, because that was reported in the papers. But the kidnapping required two men. If I hadn't created a fictional helper, the Commissos would have been certain certain things were phony, and I'd have been dead. As it was, the FBI endangered me and the undercover operation, not intentionally, but it still made me scramble and it raised unnecessary suspicions.

"This was his," Cosimo complained. The jewelry had all been bought by Nick Melia, and he figured he'd been screwed out of the money he spent on her.

Think fast, Kirby. Come up with a story he'll understand. My mind was in high gear, and my mouth was about to catch up.

"We took the stuff out to make it look like she more or less went on a vacation," I said.

Then Cosimo dropped another hot rock in my lap.

"Just a minute," he said. "You know the radio, the American radio, she says that she's living in Italy, in Greece, or in Toronto."

A little bell went off in my head. This could be trouble—real trouble —unless I played hard and fast with Cosimo, kept him off balance with my questions and answers. They say the best offense is a tough defense. I believe in that and I used it.

"Who said that?" I snapped heatedly.

"The radio, but me, I'm not saying," Cosimo said defensively, afraid I was about to come after him.

"Radio? What radio?" I said. "Jesus Christ," I thought to myself. "Why the hell didn't the FBI tell us what was going on? The radio, yet. Jesus Christ what else?"

"Back there," he explained. "They didn't find the car yet. Where's the car? In the lake too?"

"Yeah," I said.

"That's where she died?"

"Yeah," I said again.

"Far away or nearby?" he asked.

"About thirty miles from there," I answered. "How fuckin' far do you want me to drive the car? Back to Canada?"

"No, no, no, no, that's good," he said nervously. "It's good, you know. Probably they just made those stories up. Give me twenty dollars."

"How much?" I asked.

"Give me twenty dollars because I'm broke," he said meekly now. "I'll give it back to you. Look, Cec, there's one thing, all of this—I think it's excuses because the guy is broke. So he's trying to, you know . . ."

"Look it, she's dead," I said.

"I know it," Cosimo said as sweat glistened on his brow.

"You got my guarantee on it, okay?" I said. "Do you want me to go show you where she's dead?"

He waved his hands in the air and then wiped his brow. "No, no, no."

"Well, why doesn't he fuckin' pay us?" I said. "My partner wanted to go back down there and see him, you know? What does he think? I got the broad shacked up here in Toronto or something?"

"Yes, that's what he says," Cosimo answered.

"Is that right, eh?" I said.

"Yeah," Cosimo said softly.

"Is he fuckin' nuts?" I growled. "Next time tell him to come with me. I told Michele the other day, I was gonna go out in that parking lot there and wait for him and give him a kick in the ass. You know, I still might."

Cosimo shook his head vigorously. "I know, but don't you worry about this money."

"If you can't trust me after this long . . ." I said.

"I trust you now," Cosimo said.

"I can see them being a little suspicious, okay?" I said. "But you know I'll go back down there. I'll show him where the fuckin' car is. He can go down there and swim. If she can hold her breath for fifteen minutes, she's the best swimmer I've ever seen in my life."

"Tell me one thing," Cosimo asked. "Was she dead when you . . ."

"Knocked her out," I answered, finishing his sentence. "I didn't use the gun. I threw the gun away somewhere else. I didn't know where this gun had been, all right? They hand me a fuckin' gun, and first of all it's supposed to be a .38 only it wasn't." I paused, looking at him, knowing he was on the defensive, convinced I had done the job despite what his friends from Connecticut had said. "They were making this up. You figure they were making this up so they won't have to pay you."

"That's what I think, but don't you worry about it for now, okay?"

I didn't. I knew he was convinced by what I'd said, and he was sore. He'd go back and collect now from Melia. It was time to turn the conversation to other important things, to Scarcella and to Volpe.

Cosimo was filled with surprises that afternoon. The plot to kill another man was off. There was no longer a need, as he had told me there was at a previous meeting, for him to take me to various locations and show me the victim's routine. Pure and simple, the hit was off and he had no name to give me. Then he dropped the other shoe. The plan to kill Scarcella was off too.

"You're in no rush to get rid of Scarcella?" I asked, surprised by his change of plans.

"No, no. We're gonna get him with us," he said, shrugging his shoulders and gesturing with his hands in the air.

"You're going to what?" I asked. I was floored by the turn of events, but I tried not to show it.

"I think we're gonna get him on this side now," Cosimo said with a smile.

"You're going to have him on this side now?" I asked, to be sure those listening in understood. Scarcella the cheese company owner, the former union organizer for Volpe, his trusted companion, was now on the side of the Commissos. If only Volpe knew.

There was no such change of heart when Cosimo turned his attention toward Volpe.

"Kill him," he said heatedly. "You understand what I mean?"

"I do," I said. "I know where he's at. Yanover told me where he lives, okay? You know where he lives?"

Cosimo shook his head vigorously. "Nothing," he said. "I have nothing."

"I do," I said confidently. "You want me to get him, kill him tonight?"

"All right," he said.

I knew I needed more time to get things arranged, to talk to Murphy and other SEU investigators. So I changed tactics and stalled a bit.

"I'll go," I said. "I'll see what I can do, okay? I'll work on it in the next week or two. I'll guarantee you he'll be dead in the next two weeks."

"All right. Fine," he said with a smile.

"He's got dogs around his place," I explained. "You got to be careful. He's a very suspicious man, you know."

For more than twenty years, Volpe had been the mob power in Toronto. He had connections with the old Joe Bonanno mob in New York City and then he teamed up in the distribution of narcotics for the Stefano Magaddino family, according to testimony in the U.S. Senate in 1963. He'd gotten heavily involved in property in Atlantic City, according to the newspaper. He and Vincent Cotroni were close. He had built his own crime organization in Toronto, but, for some reason I knew nothing about at the time, he hated the Calabrian Honoured Society and they hated him. Now they were going to do something about their hatred.

Cosimo was worried about my seeing and talking to Yanover. He was particularly concerned that I might have tipped my hand on the Volpe hit by talking to Yanover about him. I denied it. In fact, I noted, Yanover had invited me out to see Volpe's heavily guarded, fenced-in estate in Nobleton.

"You asked Yanover about this guy?" he asked.

"Did I ask anybody about him?" I repeated. "No, no, no, I don't ask anybody. I can find out on my own."

"This Yanover. Couldn't he tell you?" Cosimo asked.

"He said, you want to go up to his [Volpe's] place?" I said. "I said, yeah, I wouldn't mind going up. He told me where he lives."

"Where's Yanover gone?" he asked.

"He's downtown," I said.

"But he was to have been on the run, they told me. He was on the run for something," he said.

Since I was the one who had originally told Cosimo about Yanover being on the run for a drug rip-off, I had to come up with a plausible story now for his not being in hiding.

"Oh, yeah," I recalled. "He's always fuckin' somebody. That's why I think he wanted me to go up and see Volpe or something. He told me almost exactly where he lives. His name's on a mailbox out there. He said, Here's the address. Can you come up and meet me and meet him? But I never showed up."

"You still walk around with the gun on you?" Cosimo asked with concern.

"Yeah," I said with a half smile, knowing it worried him. We agreed to meet again on May 15 if I didn't go to jail May 5, when I told him I was scheduled to appear for sentencing on the B&E case after pleading guilty.

"I'll see you in here May fifteenth, two o'clock, all right? Read the papers," I said.

"Ah, don't you worry about it," Cosimo said. "You shouldn't be going in."

"I'm worried about you," I answered, "those accidents you're getting into."

Cosimo was smiling as we split, but I was worried. How was I going to show him that I had taken Volpe out without doing it? Did we have enough for a case, and if we didn't, what would I have to do? All those questions and more were to be answered by Murphy, but not without some problems from the people who gave him his orders.

Murphy was upset when we met later that day.

"What the hell are you doing carrying a gun?" Murphy shouted. "Are you crazy?"

"I feel safe with it," I snapped. "Besides, Cosimo knows. It keeps him honest."

"It's against the fuckin' law, Cec," he roared. "You could be in a whole lot of trouble and so could I because of a stupid thing like that. Jesus. Where the hell are your brains?"

I shrugged, reached under my belt, and pulled out the gun, handing it to him. "Okay, okay," I said apologetically, "but with the kind of support you're getting, what the hell do you expect me to do? You got one guy with you now, other times you're doing the fuckin' surveillance by yourself. Who's going to help me in time if things go wrong? Me—that's who. But here's the gun."

There had been references to the gun in prior conversations, but Murphy and the others listening in hadn't picked them up. It wasn't until months later that they transcribed all the tapes. They all assumed that we were referring to the telephone pager I carried when Cosimo asked me if I was carrying a gun or when I told him I was. That didn't cut ice with any of Murphy's superiors. They were convinced Murphy knew that I had

a gun all along. Later it was one of the charges when they reprimanded him. I think the real truth was that none of them had the guts to do what he did on the street, and when all the glory for the busts came they wanted to grab it and leave Murphy out.

I felt naked without the gun, and I was going to feel even worse about it when I had to step into the pressure cooker again on May 15 and explain to Cosimo why I hadn't called to say I was ready to kill Volpe. I said what I needed was time to get a good rundown on Volpe and his way of life. I didn't know it until later, but there was no one better for getting that information than my friend Murphy.

For years, Volpe had been the Buffalo Cosa Nostra's man in Toronto. In 1981, because of the Commisso investigation, he became Murphy's confidential informant. His code number in the RCMP was 0-1943, and the people who were Murphy's bosses in the operation involving me didn't have the slightest inkling of that relationship.

Volpe took his orders from the Stefano Magaddino mob in Buffalo, and that mob also gave orders to the crime family in Hamilton that was run by Giacomo Luppino. Murphy told me that Jimmy Luppino, the son of Giacomo, used to visit Volpe every day in Toronto until the Commissos gave me the contract to kill him. Publicly, no one has ever said who gave the Commissos that contract. I had information from some mob friends that it was Vincent Cotroni. He was a former member of the Bonanno crime family, but more important he was from Reggio di Calabria, and his Calabrian ties and associations were strong. Many contracts for the Commissos, who were called Canada's Murder Inc., came from Cotroni.

It was a long time before I knew what kind of information Volpe gave Murphy, but Volpe trusted Murphy, and that was to become very, very important in the weeks ahead. Murphy later told me that he'd met Volpe when he started a project that turned into Operation Oblong, an RCMP investigation that in 1975 had severely damaged Volpe's gambling empire.

Volpe didn't become the valuable informant he could have because Murphy's RCMP bosses refused to let Murphy talk to him or accept information that Volpe was willing to give him. All that came to pass later in the year.

* * *

Everything was about to come to a head when I met with Cosimo at Howard Johnson's on May 15. All those months of undercover work were going to end, at least temporarily, although I had no evidence of that when I met with him in my car.

"This thing with Volpe," I said. "How much you gonna give me for that? I want to know. I don't want no payroll or five hundred bucks. I want it all in one lump. I want to know how much you're gonna give me and then how much you can give me after that."

Cosimo hesitated. He didn't want to set a figure, and in the back of my head I knew he didn't really plan on paying me. My payoff if I killed Volpe was going to be two in the head, burial in a shallow grave, or my body dumped in the Bayview Ghost.

"Ah, Cec, I don't like . . ." he started to say. I cut him off.

"I want out. I want to fuck off out of the country," I said. "I've been out in the rain for the last two nights watching the guy's place for chrissakes. I'm gonna end up with pneumonia."

Cosimo was edgy. He was always afraid of being bugged, yet he still talked.

"Cec, how is this car? Is it still okay?" he asked.

"This car is safe," I said. "I had it checked out two weeks ago by what's his name—you know, my friend there. We took it to a garage, and they went through the whole fuckin' car. You know, I got a dog up there. Nobody gets near this fuckin' car. Nobody! I don't leave it for too long, I tell you. All right now?"

Cosimo appeared satisfied. He stopped looking at everything in the car and began talking again.

"Listen, let's move this way," he said. "You see, I don't want to promise you any more to put up until I'm one hundred percent sure."

"All right," I said. "Your word's good with me. Your credit's good with me, okay? You owe me five thousand dollars still, okay, from before."

"Yes," he acknowledged.

"All right, I just want enough money to get around in, and I want it after Volpe's killed. He'll be killed soon. I've been up there ten times. Do you know where this place is?"

"No, Cec," he said.

"It's out in the country, okay?" I said, "You can't park like here, like

you do in the city. It's hard. I gotta park at least a mile away where I got a good spoke. I got a mile to go through the bush. I tell you, I've been fuckin' soaked the last three days."

"In the morning, Cec," he asked, "how's it look in the morning?"

"Ah, I must have got there too late," I said. "I usually get there at nighttime, eh? I want to see the place at night. He's got Foxhill on the mailbox, with TV towers and a tennis court back there. He drives a maroon Cadillac, and he's got a station wagon too."

"He drives one of those Audis, you know, the car," Cosimo added.

I shook my head. RCMP and SEU intelligence wasn't all it was cracked up to be. They didn't tell me about an Audi, probably because they didn't know about it. Think fast.

"Haven't seen it up there," I answered. "Unless he's got it somewhere else. He's not bringing it home. Maybe he's switching cars in between, you know? I've done that before."

"You know him?" he asked.

"I know him to see him. Christ yeah!" I said sharply. "Couldn't miss him. I saw him come home one night in the Cadillac and I didn't have anything with me at that time. I wasn't even expecting to. But I got a good idea, you know, of his hours, when he comes home. I have a very good idea and it's beautiful. Nobody'd fuckin' hear it out there."

"There's no people?" Cosimo asked.

"There's no neighbors beside him," I said. "There's a house beside him, but it's up for sale and there's nobody in it. He won't be much of a problem. Just catching him at the right time is all I have to do."

"But you know him?" Cosimo said, making sure that there would be no mistakes.

"I know him," I said, showing my annoyance at his continued questioning on the point. "Tall, but sorta bald. Hair on the sides. He's had three-piece suits on sometimes. I saw him down at the Four Seasons with Scarcella. I've seen him around before. I saw him talking to Yanover one day, but I was off in the car, you know? He doesn't know me to see me."

"I wanna make sure, Cec," Cosimo said. "It's very important. You know what I mean, Cec. I wanna make no. . . ."

"There won't be no mistakes in this, okay?" I said, finishing his sentence.

"All right," he answered.

"Definitely okay," I emphasized. "All right now, how much? You're not talking about some idiot on the fuckin' street or some dope hustler, you know?"

"Cec, I know," he said.

"This guy gets knocked off. How about twenty thousand?" I asked.

"I couldn't give you that. I couldn't give it all at once, not that much money," he answered.

"All right, twenty thousand over periods of time," I said.

"All right," he agreed.

"All right," I said. "Soon after, the next day after it's done, I'm going to come and see you."

Cosimo shook his head. "Four days after."

"Four days?" I said. "Okay. Make sure you have at least five thousand on you or somebody."

He nodded his approval. "Okay, Cec."

"Either you or your brothers or somebody—make sure you have five thousand," I emphasized.

"All right, all right," he said impatiently. "And then I'll pay you after two months."

"All right, no problem," I said. "I'm waiting now, you know. Like I've been patient about this other five thousand bucks for the thing in the States."

"I know, Cec," he said. "It's just the wrong time. We mortgaged ourself over our heads—four, five properties. Buy here, buy there—see what I mean? If we don't pay the mortgage, we lose the property."

"What? You got your house mortgaged too now?" I asked.

"No, no, no," he said. "I have property in Richmond Hill. It's four thousand dollars a month—property in Mississauga, it's a few thousand dollars a month, property in Burlington, it's four thousand a month, property in King City—it's all property."

"You own that much land?" I said, surprised by the amounts he said he was paying out.

"Yeah," he said. "I'm broke. I have no cash, okay, but we have lotsa property—we have maybe ten million dollars' worth of property."

I let out a low whistle. "Ten million?"

"Maybe. You see what I mean?" he asked.

I smiled. I had a solution to his cash flow. "Well, give me a lot," I said. "Give me some—give me a piece of property."

Cosimo shook his head. Most of the land was in large lots and couldn't be split up. One section alone was worth two million dollars. There was also a ten-acre section of land in King City, and I registered my interest in that.

"You know how much I paid for that, Cec?" he said with a smile.

"How much?" I said.

"Half a million dollars I paid for it," he said.

I was really surprised. Cosimo and his mob were heavy into real estate investments. They owned a large land section north of the luxury estates where a lot of rich people lived, King Cross. He said he planned to subdivide it in a year and then maybe, he added, he'd have some land for me. But I'd have to be patient.

He said that the land he wanted to subdivide cost more than $100,000 just to service. "That's what happened," he said. "We mortgaged ourselves right up to here [pointing to his throat]. We're talkin' maybe twenty-two thousand a month in mortgages. It's a lotta fuckin' money."

Before we split up, I had one additional question for him. Normally there are rules about how you hit a Mafia man. Wives and children are almost always left out—not harmed. That sometimes complicates the planning of a murder. It's got to be timed so that only the target is hit. I knew that Cosimo and his brothers wouldn't care. They didn't live by the rules and they didn't kill by the rules, but I wanted others to know it. I wanted their ruthlessness on the tape so that others would understand how they operated.

"What if his wife's with him?" I asked. "I'm getting impatient, you know?"

"I leave it to you," Cosimo said.

"I'll do the wife," I said coldly.

"It's not likely that they go out together," he replied.

The next twenty-four hours turned out to be critical. One of the big holes in the investigation was Remo Commisso. The SEU and Crown attorney Howard Morton were convinced that the evidence against

Cosimo and Michele was sufficient for murder conspiracy charges, but the evidence against Remo was thin. He had said very little to me on tape. They had to get him out into the open. But how?

It was Lyle McCharles who came up with the idea. Why not stage a phony Volpe hit? Why not get Volpe to lend me his wallet and have me bring it to Remo while Cosimo was doing weekend jail time for the smuggling of aliens?

McCharles and Murphy floated the idea at a meeting of the SEU staff and Morton on April 30. Everybody laughed except Inspector Wilf Steferak, who had temporarily been assigned as officer in charge of the SEU. Murphy said he knew Volpe well enough to ask. Steferak said it was worth a try. The whole ball game was to go down on May 16. That morning Murphy called Volpe, who remembered him from past investigations. He told Volpe it was urgent that they meet.

Murphy and Sergeant Al Cooke of Metro Intelligence went to see Volpe at his home. They told him that there was a contract on his life and that there was one person involved who they lacked sufficient evidence to arrest. Would he help? Volpe said he would, provided he had Murphy's word that there would be no double cross. He got that, and Murphy got Volpe's wallet, complete with his driver's license, credit cards, and other identification.

Murphy and Cooke also got Volpe to agree to return to Toronto with his wife and to stay inside the RCMP headquarters on Jarvis Street for the entire day without talking to anyone. Murphy later told me he was surprised when Volpe agreed. Volpe had a condition, however. No one was to tell his wife, Lisa, why they were at headquarters. He would invent a story to explain it. Murphy and Cooke agreed, and they drove Volpe and his wife back to the RCMP.

Just after 11:00 A.M., I met Murphy at Bathurst and Steeles Plaza and he told me what had happened with Volpe. He handed me Volpe's wallet. By 11:15, I was at Remo's home. A woman answered the door. In the background I could hear a radio and a child's voice. I asked the woman if I could see Remo, identifying myself only as "George." Remo came out, and Michele was with him.

"I gotta talk to you," I told Remo. "Can I talk to you outside? I got something in the car I want to show you."

"You have something in the car?" he asked. "You want to take me to your car?"

"Yeah. Not in the house," I said. "There's something I got to show you."

Remo was suspicious. There was no way he was going to go to my car and talk. "Bring it to the house," he said. "We go downstairs some place to talk. I don't trust a car."

"I'll get it all right," I answered. "I know you don't trust cars. I don't trust houses."

"No, we go in the washroom," he said.

As I left his house to get the wallet I talked into the recorder to let those conducting the surveillance know what was going on. I knew my body pack and the belt buckle transmitter would get whatever he had to say on tape.

When I reentered the house I saw Michele with the kids and asked him if he was baby-sitting. He shook his head. Weekends, he said, he stayed at the house to play with the kids. "Atsa nice mafioso," I thought to myself.

Remo was standing nearby and motioned for me to follow. We went downstairs, through his recreation room to a washroom. He put his finger to his mouth. Then he turned the cold water tap on just in case there were bugs in the house. He signaled that we could talk.

"Volpe, he's dead," I said.

Remo looked surprised, almost at a loss for words. "How come?"

"I just killed him, an hour ago," I said matter of factly.

"What happened?" Remo asked.

"Well, Cosimo told me you and him wanted it," I said. "Want to go outside? Wanna talk in here?"

"George, you should never come here," he said. Remo was very upset, apparently fearful that police might be watching and that I'd lead them to his house.

"Well, look it," I said. "He's dead, so's his wife, too, okay?"

His face was clouded, and he was getting more and more upset. "You should never come here."

"Well, listen," I continued, "I need some money. I'm broke. I told Cosimo yesterday when I saw him. I said, I'm broke. I need some money

and I wanna get the fuck out of the country now. Okay? I want some money today."

"Tell me when I'm gonna get it to you, George," Remo said.

"Well, a thousand or something just to get me out of here," I said. I pulled out Volpe's wallet. "I took this right out of his back pocket."

"You should have thrown it away," he said excitedly as he looked it over and checked the identification.

"Well, listen, you people have doubted me in the past," I reminded him.

"All right," he said, "don't worry. We'll take care of you. You know we respect you like a brother. Don't worry about it."

"Yeah, but look at before," I said. "You've told me. Cosimo still owes me five thousand."

"You know you'll get the money from him," he answered.

"All right, but now there's two people dead," I said.

"I don't even want to talk about these things," he said shaking his head.

"All right. I got this thing on him partly just to prove to you," I said.

"That's all right," he answered, returning it to me. "Throw it away. Don't leave it."

"No, I'll get rid of it," I promised him. "I'll drop it down the sewer, far away from here."

"Where you wanna meet?" he asked. "Maybe tomorrow up here, or Monday?"

"'I need some money now, I wanna leave today," I said urgently. "I'll meet you down at the hall."

"Where'm I gonna get the fuckin' money today?" he asked.

"A thousand bucks," I said.

"All right, but it's not good to come by the hall," he said.

"Then where?" I asked. "Get Michele to meet me down at Howard Johnson's again, okay? At five o'clock. A thousand dollars."

"Okay," he said.

"I'll be taking off for a week or two," I said. "I want the rest of the money. I told Cosimo yesterday twenty thousand bucks, eh? I want at least five thousand."

"I know nothing about this," he said. "I didn't know that he told you to do it."

"But he told me a long time ago, you and him wanted this done," I said.

"Me?" he exclaimed. "I never said that. Oh come on, George."

"That's what he told me," I replied.

"Did you ever talk to me about this thing?" he asked.

"No, but he, hey," I said, "you didn't know this?"

"No," he said, shaking his head. "What's the difference? So what? All right. Michele will meet you at five."

"All right," I said, "I got to be back in two weeks. What about this other guy, this Scarcella?"

"Forget about him," Remo said. "We don't want to do nothing no more. No problem."

So I went, taking the wallet with me, back to the car and then to the location where all the cops were recording the conversations. A security detail that had been assigned two weeks earlier to protect me was waiting to escort me out of the area.

I handed the wallet to Corporal Danielle Bouchard, who was supervising the case. One of the supervising sergeants piped up, "That cinches it. You're finished."

"Are you sure?" I asked. "Don't you want me to meet Michele at Howard Johnson's and get the money off of him?"

"No, no," he said smiling, "we don't need it. We're finished. We've got them all."

I shrugged and walked off with my security guards. I remember saying to them, "You know what? I think they're going to want me to meet him."

We went to a bar, had a couple of drinks and about three or four beers, and then went back up to the room. Murphy was on the phone, and he was upset.

"Cec, you don't have to do this," he said.

"I know what you're going to fuckin' ask," I said. "You want me to go back there with Michele."

He laughed nervously. "You're right, Cec. You gotta go back and pick up that payment."

They had followed Michele after I left Remo's house and seen him go to the home of Domenic Racco, the son of the old Calabrian Mafia boss

and the man everyone was saying was going to succeed his father. At the house Michele got the money to pay me with.

The RCMP intelligence had information that Michele, and two other men who Volpe was in partnership with in some real estate, had gone to Buffalo to get a green light for the Volpe murder a couple of weeks earlier. The information came from Volpe. He said his two partners had been stopped at the border, but that Michele had slipped through and seen some people in the Buffalo Magaddino mob.

Volpe might have been right, but two weeks earlier a good friend of mine in the mob had told me that Racco had gone to Montreal to meet with Vincent Cotroni. My friend said it was Cotroni who gave the order to kill Volpe, and Racco had given the contract to the Commissos. Racco wanted the Commissos to have someone else do the job, but Cosimo had hired me, so they went to him for the money to pay me until they could figure out how to get rid of me later.

When Murphy arrived at the Holiday Inn where I was staying with my security detail, I got into the bugged car with him. We drove like we were at the Indianapolis 500 to get to the meeting on time. We must have been doing 90 MPH or more.

When we got there I had to piss, in the worst way, but I didn't have time. They had body-packed me. I had to pull in my stomach for the body pack, and I damn near pissed in my pants.

With all the problems, I got to Howard Johnson's and parked in front of the Faces Discotheque about five minutes before Michele arrived in his Oldsmobile. Murphy and his surveillance van were perfectly situated to get pictures and record. There was another special team of sharpshooters nearby ready to gun down anyone who tried to hit me.

I waited maybe ten minutes and Michele pulled up. There were four in the car, including three cousins of his. Michele got out of his car and walked to mine and handed me what he thought was $1,000. He didn't count right. It was $1,100.

"Who's with you?" I asked.

"My kid cousins—Claudio, Remo, and Johnny," he said. "We got to go to a wedding in Niagara Falls."

"Yeah, well, I'm going to Miami in about another hour," I said.

"Take care of yourself," Michele said.

I nodded. "How much is there?" I asked.

"One," he said.

"A thousand? Good," I answered.

"Take care of yourself," Michele said.

"I will for sure," I answered as I watched him leave.

When Murphy and the special marksman team spotted Michele's car with four inside, everyone got their rifles ready. If someone had gotten out of the car with Michele, the marksmen were all prepared to waste them on the spot.

I remember saying to Murphy, "But they were just kids on the way to a wedding."

"You're right, Cec, but at that moment we didn't know that, and we damned sure weren't going to take chances with your life," he said.

In the hours ahead Michele would be stopped for speeding and arrested on the murder conspiracy. Remo was arrested at the home of his girlfriend. Cosimo was charged in jail. It was a clean sweep.

CHAPTER 20

Bye, Bye, Paulie

Two weeks before the arrest of the Commissos, I was placed under the protection of the RCMP. I had bodyguards with me day and night. I was getting a $250-a-week allowance for my hotel room and my meals. It was like living in a prison only worse. In prison, what you can't see, you don't miss and you forget about. The way I had to live, I could see all the goodies of life but I couldn't touch. There was very little wine, women, and song —the high road that the news media and lawyers said I was strolling down —to enjoy. There were four walls, the faces of my protectors, some card games, and an occasional drive in a Chrysler leased for me by the government. Those drives were never alone. There were always a couple of bodyguards along.

The leased car arrangement, which strangely drew a lot of criticism from the media later on, was a necessity. I needed wheels, I needed to feel a breath of fresh air on my face, to get out of my room if I was to retain my sanity. Unless you've lived in an undercover situation, you can't know what it's like.

A car, like a motorcycle, was like an extension of myself. I had never been without one or the other. It was part of my way of life, the way I moved from place to place, saw people, did things, and, yes, committed crimes.

When the investigation of the Commissos began, the Mounties and the SEU had to use my car. If I'd suddenly changed to a new car, Cosimo

and Remo would have immediately become suspicious. So they bugged my car, they photographed it, wherever I went to meetings that car was with me. Only it wasn't really my car. It was my dad's.

Once the Commissos were arrested, the car had to be stripped of its equipment and returned to my dad. I couldn't use it again. It would be the first thing the Commissos and their associates would look for—Cecil Kirby and his Chevrolet. The alternative was the leased car, and that was only for a short time. Eventually, it became impractical for protective purposes. I was too hot a property to be allowed out in the open, even with bodyguards at my side. Not only was I in danger, but they were also in danger should some crazy Calabrian decide to take me out.

Picture the circumstances. What I'd done was about to wreck the crime careers of some of Canada's most powerful criminal leaders for at least a decade. They were naturally furious—mad enough to kill, mad enough to make it worth anywhere from $100,000 to $250,000 for someone to kill me. Of course, if anyone had succeeded, the chances of their living to collect that contract money were about one in a billion. Dead men can't tell tales, they can't be arrested and later forced to testify in courts.

With all that money on my head, the mission of the SEU and the Crown was to keep me alive, at any cost, and round-the-clock protection was a must. It wasn't always successful, but it was a must. When it wasn't successful, it was my fault, not that of those assigned to protect me.

For a street criminal, life in confinement is impossible. I was a socializer. I loved to hit bars and clubs where my rounder friends were. Now I couldn't, or I wasn't supposed to.

It would be safe to say that I wasn't exactly a model protected witness. It would also be safe to say that the art of handling protected witnesses in Canada hadn't been perfected. It still hasn't. The model they were using was the witness protection program of the U.S. Marshals, and that is one of the most criticized programs in the States. That criticism comes not so much from the press but from witnesses and other law enforcement agencies.

To protect me, the SEU assigned three-man details—one officer each from the RCMP, the Ontario Provincial Police, and Metro Toronto Police—to each shift. I didn't go to the bathroom without their checking out the room first. If we weren't in a hotel room—and many of our meals

were eaten there—I was on the road with SEU investigators, showing them where I'd planted bombs, where I had dynamite and blasting caps buried, the location of biker hangouts and other crime centers.

In early June stories were breaking in the United States and Canada about the plot to murder Helen Nafpliotis and the Volpe murder plot. The stories centered around attempts by the Canadian government to extradite Vincent Melia and Gerardo Russo to stand trial for conspiracy to commit murder.

One of the FBI agents, John Schiman, testified in federal court in Bridgeport, Connecticut, that the FBI had staged Nafpliotis's abduction to make it appear that she'd been kidnapped and murdered. He said he'd worked with me as I gathered evidence on the case and collected money for the planned murder.

"He was suave," Schiman testified. "He knew what he was doing. He was the best source I have ever seen. He knew how to handle underworld figures." As I read the story I remember thinking, "Yeah, but how do you handle living like this?"

It was so confining that a month after I was placed under protection I slipped out of my hotel room one night and went to the Beverly Hills Hotel for a couple of beers with an old friend. I was gone most of that night. I stayed at the home of a friend who worked for a catering company. Murphy, everyone, came down on me like a ton of bricks for my stupidity.

June 12 was another day of jangling nerves, a day I wanted to kick and yell about being surrounded constantly by dozens of noticeably nervous plainclothesmen. It was the day I had to appear in county court with Linda Cadwell, my ex-girlfriend, and Alan Stewart to plead guilty to charges of breaking into a home in metropolitan Toronto in 1979.

The court looked like an armed camp. Everyone was checked. The security people had me so tightly guarded it would have taken a team of commandos to reach me.

The charges against me stemmed from a planned theft from a gun collector Stewart had told me about. Stewart said he had a key to the place, that the collector was going to be gone and it would be a simple matter for us to get into the house and steal the guns. He estimated there were forty to sixty handguns there, guns I could sell to the Commissos

and others. The collection was gone when we broke in. It turned out Stewart didn't have the key, and all we found were five antique guns that couldn't fire bullets.

Sergeant Lyle McCharles of the OPP testified that my life was in danger. "I've received reliable information," he testified, "that a one hundred thousand dollar contract has been placed on Kirby's life." Crown Attorney Howard Morton told Justice Lloyd Graburn that my work as a police operative had resulted "in laying fourteen very serious criminal charges. My submission of sentence is he ought not to receive a jail term. It's not a submission the Crown takes lightly." As I listened, I found myself wondering what Morton would be saying if Murphy hadn't made them come up with the agreement that we all had signed.

Graburn passed sentence on June 14. Noting my previous convictions for assault, drugs, and theft, he placed me on probation for two years with the "special condition" that I testify in court when subpoenaed by the Crown. Linda and Stewart got suspended sentences of twelve and eighteen months. At the same time the Commissos were being held in Ontario Supreme Court without bail on conspiracy to murder charges involving Volpe, Scarcella, and Nafpliotis.

My having walked away from my security detail earlier and arguments I'd had with some of the investigators upset and embarrassed some people in the detail, who decided to put me in a squeeze play without telling the Crown prosecutors or Murphy. One of them, who is now a friend of mine, told other investigators that "we have to get a hammer to Kirby's head to make him testify."

The hammer they tried to use was Linda, who had been my girlfriend since 1978 and who was being provided protection and secret living quarters. Her whereabouts was a secret to those who wanted to use Linda to get at me.

I asked Murphy, as I often did, to call Linda so that I could talk to her to make sure she was all right. He placed the call and then put me on the phone. When she told me about the visit by the two investigators, I went wild.

I turned on Murphy like a cornered tiger and began shouting. "So that's the way you fuckers keep your word," I shouted. "You're trying to put me in jail, you bastards!"

"What the hell are you talking about?" he roared.

"I'm talking about two of this fuckin' outfit's flunkies going to Linda and trying to get her to testify against me, that's what," I shouted. "After all I've done, after all the risks I've taken, some people are still looking to shaft me. Hey, go to hell. Take this whole fuckin' thing and shove it. I'm getting out. I'll take my chances on the street alone."

I thought Murphy was going to go into orbit then and there. For two hours or more he tried to cool me down. I wanted to go out and get the two guys who Linda said had talked to her. Luckily, Murphy talked me out of that, but I told the detail that I was going to see Linda whether they came with me or not. They came and stayed in another room while Linda and I had a helluva argument. I finally belted her in the mouth.

Later the newspapers made it appear that I was in a jealous rage. One reporter tried to have the security guards and the attorney general publicly roasted for not arresting me for violation of probation for hitting Linda.

Linda never pressed charges. I admit I hit her. I lost my temper, knocked out one of her teeth, and cracked another. My troubles with Linda were to continue later.

My nerves were razor thin, and I was walking on the edge. There were nights when I went to bed hoping I wouldn't wake up. There were other nights when I seriously thought about killing myself or getting myself killed by going after some of those I knew wanted to do me.

Depression is a constant companion when you're an informer and a witness. You don't think too highly of yourself. You've cut yourself off from the people you know to enter a different world with people who don't respect you, don't like you, even hate your guts. I had nothing in common with any of those on my security detail or in the prosecutor's office. I was a means to an end for them, and they were my ticket to survival.

After the Cadwell incident, the strings that were binding me were loosened somewhat, and I managed to get along better with many of the men on the security details, who were really decent guys doing a tough job.

Murphy, meanwhile, never let up on providing me with the best security possible—not just through physical protection, but through street intelligence. One of his sources was Paul Volpe.

On July 29, Murphy met with Volpe secretly, and the old man provided him with information on those behind the contract to kill him. It was his belief, and he had ways of getting information, that some former partners of his in real estate both here and in Atlantic City were behind the hit order. The motive was greed, pure and simple—more than two million dollars collected in a sale and millions more that Volpe was laundering through land transactions. The former partners wanted it all, or so Volpe thought.

Volpe was also convinced that with a little pressure from the coppers, one of the former partners would roll over and begin talking. If he talked, he could bring down a lot of high-level people in organized crime. To this day, no one that I know of ever went to talk to that guy, and nothing was ever done to develop Volpe as an informer. In fact, Volpe was never given official RCMP informer status, although he was given the "O" number designation.

Volpe also predicted there would be no trial on the murder conspiracies. "The Commissos and their friends are going to plead guilty," he told Murphy. "They don't want this to go to trial."

Murphy said that Volpe was grateful to me for helping save his life. He wanted to show his good faith. He told Murphy he had heard that there were a lot of bikers in Canada, particularly Toronto, who were hot to kill me. He promised Murphy to do what he could to cool off the bikers through his underworld contacts. Murphy said he kept his promise, and many of the bikers that were actively hunting me turned their attention to other things.

Like clockwork, the three Commisso brothers and Romeo plea-bargained with Crown attorneys. Rather than face trials for conspiracy to murder, the four pleaded guilty in return for a guarantee of less than maximum jail terms. The Crown went for the deal because it would eliminate costly trials that they could not be certain would be decided in their favor.

Remo and Cosimo got eight years each, but they were going to face considerably more time in jail on charges relating to other crimes they'd hired me for. The charges in those cases would be based both on their admissions in the covert tapes I recorded and on recordings I made with others who admitted they had paid the Commissos to hire me to bomb and torch buildings for them.

Romeo and Michele Commisso got just two and a half years because they were more message carriers than actual plotters.

A couple of months passed before Volpe touched my life again. This time I was technically no longer under Murphy's protective wing but under that of the SEU and Corporal Ted Bean of the OPP. Nevertheless, the message from Volpe went to Murphy, and it probably saved my life and those of my security detail, including Corporal Bean.

On October 6 Volpe, believing Murphy was still protecting me, called to tell him that the detail protecting me had been spotted by some members of Satan's Choice.

"They spotted your friend Kirby and his three security guards in Aurora," Volpe told Murphy. "They're going to kill him and the guards."

Murphy was between a rock and a hard place when he got that call. He couldn't tell anyone that his tipster was Volpe, but the people on the security detail would want to know where the information came from to judge how valid it was. Murphy told me in confidence that the bikers had found out where I was staying and that they were going to kill all of us.

"We've got to figure a way to move you and the detail," he said. "And we have to do it without telling anybody that we know who tipped us."

I had no patience for the politics of the moment, and I didn't have to worry about the chain of command the way Murphy did. I called one of the detail supervising sergeants and told him. "The wrong people know I'm here," I said.

He didn't believe me, and he refused to order the detail to move me. "It's just another street rumor," he said. "More bullshit. You stay put."

That ticked me off. I didn't waste any time. I did the only thing I could at that moment to save our necks. I walked to the security detail's room, picked up the telephone, and called my dad.

"Dad," I said loud enough for everyone to hear me, "I just want you to know where I'm at before something happens. I'm here in Aurora, at the hotel."

The security agents stood there dumbfounded. "Jesus Christ," one of them yelled, "you've just blown our security."

"Good," I said. "I'll just take a taxi and get the hell outta here." And that was exactly what I did. It was the only way for me to get out of the area and to get the detail moved before something happened. I had to

figure a way out without blowing Volpe as the source. So I took off. I returned to the security detail about a week later. They were having fits, and Inspector McIlvenna wanted to have me thrown in jail as a material witness until he was told that he didn't have that right unless I failed to answer a subpoena or to appear in court.

Murphy told his bosses about the Volpe warning and that Volpe had also offered to turn over, no strings attached, information and evidence on a Korean international terrorist organization in Toronto. They didn't want to hear about it. They told Murphy he could not accept any information from Volpe and ordered him to cut off all further communication with him.

Talk about shortsighted people. They had a golden opportunity right then to develop Volpe as the most important informer in Canadian organized crime investigations. Volpe knew his days were numbered, and he was reaching out, like I had, to make a deal. He could have buried a lot of people.

Instead, nothing was done and Volpe was later killed before he could tell what he knew. I guess Murphy's bosses were afraid Volpe would use the RCMP and they'd get criticized for dealing with someone like that, but the law in the States has dealt with bigger guys than that to get testimony in major Mafia cases.

"They blew a helluva opportunity," Murphy later said. "With a little work Volpe could have been the most important informer in mob history." The government's attitude, particularly that of the RCMP, was that Volpe was trying to use the RCMP to escape some charges he was facing. The truth is Volpe probably was looking for a way out. He knew his days were numbered, just like I did. By turning him down, the knuckleheads who make these decisions blew the biggest source of information on organized crime in Canada. He could have provided them with a warehouse full of information on the States, on international mob plots and on casinos from Haiti and Cuba to Atlantic City and Las Vegas. It's amazing to me how shortsighted and jealous people get in law enforcement. That's why the mobs are always ahead.

Maybe a week after Volpe saved my life with his tip, I decided to see him. I told Murphy what I wanted to do.

"Have you lost your mind?" he asked.

"I don't think so," I said. "I want to see him. I want to thank him for what he did."

"You could be killed," he said. "You could get your head blown off."

"I'll take that chance," I said.

Without another word, I left the place where I was in hiding from the bikers, the mob, and my own security detail, and drove off in my car to Foxhill, the Nobleton home of Paul Volpe.

It was impressive. Behind the giant iron gates at the entrance was an almost palatial home, like that of some English lord. A castlelike turret with a circular, domed room was the centerpiece of the giant two-story home. The house had once belong to a retired judge from Toronto. I forget what Volpe paid for it, but it was worth hundreds of thousands of dollars then and maybe a million or more now. In the back was a big pool and two tennis courts. A little further back were overhead floodlights and some guard dogs led by a particularly annoying pet of Volpe's, a mongrel —part shepherd, part who-knows-what, named Caesar, who bit my leg three times while Volpe chuckled, barely scolding the dog.

When I arrived, Volpe's wife answered the door. I showed her my identification and asked to see Volpe. He wasn't home, she said, but he would be back by 5:00 P.M. I promised to come again.

I returned as promised. Volpe was there waiting. We met, for the first time, at the door. I showed him my driver's license and assured him that I was by myself and unarmed.

"Come on in," he said with a friendly smile. He was a tall man, maybe a little over six foot, bald, with sad eyes. He wasn't muscular or as strong as I was, but he wasn't in bad shape either. He could probably have handled himself pretty well if he'd had to, even at his age, which was about fifty-four then. He pointed ahead of me and said, "Come on downstairs where we can talk."

As I followed his directions, we walked through his living room into a kitchen with a long counter and a table off to the side. Off the kitchen was a staircase leading to the recreation room.

As I walked down the stairs, Volpe's damned mongrel bit me on the back of the leg, almost sending me sprawling into the rec room. I wanted to kick that bloody mutt in the teeth, but I held my mouth and my foot as Volpe called the dog off and mildly scolded him.

I was taken aback by the view of the rear yard through the huge glass windows and doors. Over to the side of the rec room was a small bar with a cappuccino machine on it.

"Can I get you a cappuccino?" Volpe asked. I shook my head. "How about some food? A steak maybe?" he said with a smile, pointing to his nephew, Anthony, who I'd seen up in the kitchen cooking.

"No thank you," I said, "I'm not hungry."

Without another word I opened my briefcase so he could see it was clean, with no tapes or bugs.

"Look, Paul, I got no tape," I said. "I just came here to thank you for helping me the other day." I opened my jacket so he could see there was nothing hidden there either.

He nodded with a broad smile on his face. "Okay, Cecil," he said, "I believe you."

He was warm and friendly. He smoked heavily, drawing long pulls into his lungs and watching the thin blue smoke curl out into the air in front of him as he exhaled. I felt like choking every time he took a puff like that.

He was attentive to what I had to say. I had a feeling of real sincerity when he talked, and his eyes were soft, sometimes a little animated, but never cold as we sat there. He had a rather gravelly voice. There wasn't the slightest hint of an Italian accent when he spoke, and I guess there shouldn't have been since he was born in Canada.

"Do the cops know you're here?" he asked.

I shook my head. "Nope, just Murphy," I answered. "He's the only one who knew I was coming to see you."

"Okay," he said. "I want your word that you're not going to give me up. I don't need that kind of trouble."

"You've got my word," I said. "Nobody's gonna know we met or talked." And nobody did until after he was killed. Everybody had something bad to say about the poor bastard after he was killed. I can only say good things about the man I met that day. He was a man and he talked straight—no bullshit.

"I want to thank you for saving my life," I said. "You saved the lives of some cops as well, but they don't know it. Probably never will."

We started talking about the case a bit and about the characters involved.

"I can't understand why they [the Commissos] would want to kill me," he said. "You know what jail they are in?"

"Kingston," I said.

He grinned, those sad eyes sort of twinkly as he spoke. "Got a lot of friends in there." He continued smiling, and said nothing else about the Commissos—nothing like I'm gonna get them or they're going to have an accident.

"You know, when I found out you were here I had you checked out with Chuck [Yanover]," he said. "He really has high regard for you. He says you're a very capable person."

"The truth is I don't like Yanover," I said looking him squarely in the eyes. "I don't trust him, and if I were you I wouldn't trust him. He set up one of his friends with my ex-girlfriend."

Volpe waved his hands, brushing aside the discussion. "It's foolish to have hard feelings over women," he said. "They aren't that important."

Volpe turned the subject toward my future. "Why don't you walk away from it [testifying and being a police operative]?" he said. "If you want I can get you a job down in my casino in the islands. You can stay there for a couple of years—work there for me and come back and I guarantee nobody I deal with is gonna fuckin' bother you. Of course, I can't guarantee the bikers. I have no influence with them."

Volpe didn't say what casino he was talking about or exactly where it was and I didn't ask. It was supposed to be in the Bahamas, but he didn't identify it. I knew he and his brother had operated a casino in Haiti at one time and some in other parts of the Caribbean and the Mediterranean as well. I just thanked him and said I'd think about it.

I did ask him if there was some way he could lend me a couple of thousand dollars. "I'll pay it back as soon as I can," I said. "You can go to the bank with that."

"I'll have to talk to my lawyer about it, Cec," he said. "Come back in about a week or so, about eight in the morning."

I gave him a number where he could leave a message for me without worrying about the cops. Then I thanked him and promised to see him the following week.

When I returned, we once again went to his rec room and for a second time that lousy dog of his nipped my ankle. I felt like kicking the fucker

through the glass window, but I restrained myself as Volpe whacked him lightly on the fanny and sent him off to another side of the room, where he lay staring at me. I could see in that dog's eyes I was dead meat if I ever made a move toward Volpe, not that I had any intentions of doing anything like that. For some reason that damned dog hated me from the start and I hated the dog.

"I haven't been able to talk to my lawyer about that loan yet," he said, "but I will. I'll have an answer for you next week for sure. Incidentally, I told Peter Scarcella about your being at the house. I'm expecting him here later today."

Now I didn't feel too great hearing that. Scarcella, I was convinced, had sold out to the Commissos to save his own skin. They had said as much in taped conversations with me. I thought to myself, that's not the kind of guy you should trust, Volpe, not at all. I sure as hell didn't trust him, and I didn't want to be around Volpe's house if Scarcella knew I was there.

Just then the telephone rang. It was Scarcella. When Volpe was through talking to him, he turned to me and said, "I told Peter that I had an old friend of his here visiting with me. I told him I wanted him to meet you. It's a shame. Peter said he couldn't come. He has a touch of the flu." There was a strange smirk on his face when he said that.

I wanted to say something but I bit my tongue. Instead I said good-bye and promised to see him again the following week.

Our third meeting took place outside his garage. That fuckin' Caesar was by his side again as I got out of the car, and again he went for my leg. Volpe called him off. "Caesar, I'm afraid, doesn't like you," Volpe said with a chuckle.

I didn't think it was too funny but I didn't say anything about it. "Talk to your lawyer yet?" I asked.

Volpe nodded. "I'm afraid he's advised me not to give you any money while you're working for the police," he said. "It could cause a lot of problems. I'm sorry, Cec, but I don't want the cops on my back and they would be if they knew I was lending you money."

"I understand," I said. "Don't worry about it. Nobody's gonna know we talked. I appreciate what you've done and what you tried to do."

It was months later, March 1982, that I heard that there was a contract

to kill Volpe. Murphy had been tipped, and he had asked his bosses for permission to warn Volpe and see if he could convince him to roll over and become an informer. The RCMP turned thumbs down on his request. He was told that he was not to speak to Volpe or have any further contact with him.

On November 14, 1983, I flew into Toronto International to meet with some security people about a case that was pending. The airport was swarming with cops. At 2:40 P.M. that day they had found Volpe's body stuffed in the trunk of his wife's BMW at the Terminal 2 parking garage. He'd been shot in the back of the head.

Who did Volpe in? I can't be positive, but I had good information that Vincent Cotroni had ordered the hit after he'd sent his brother Frank to Toronto to meet with a lot of Volpe's friends and enemies.

Frank Cotroni was facing heroin-smuggling charges in Connecticut, interestingly enough, in September, just two short months before Volpe bought it. I was told he met with Johnny (Pops) Papalia and an old Sicilian Mafia boss who was wanted by the Italian government on narcotics charges. A good source told me that a Montreal assassin and friend of Cotroni's was at that meeting. He was supposed to be in Toronto around the time Volpe's body was found. He was arrested on homicide charges in another case and, I was told, was questioned about the Volpe hit. He refused to talk to the cops about it because the Cotronis had been so close to him, like family.

They decided Volpe had to go. It was embarrassing to the Mafia. Here he'd been set up for a hit in 1981, and two years later he was still walking around, telling people what to do, running gambling in Toronto, making millions in real estate in New Jersey and Ontario, collecting from casinos around the world, and running big loan-shark rackets. It's probably true that he was living in fear behind the floodlights at his home, certain that someone would carry out the contract that had started when the Commissos tried to have me do the job. But he was still in business, still a boss.

On December 10, less than a month after Volpe was knocked off, four guys gunned down Domenic Racco, the son of the old Calabrian don. Now that couldn't have been done without approval from some Mafia bosses, but none of the four who were arrested and convicted in the case ever said who was behind it, and the Commissos were behind bars. Being

in jail, of course, never stopped a boss from running his business, and the Commissos were no exception.

One of the last people to see Volpe was his good friend Scarcella, who told the coppers that he'd had coffee with Volpe the morning of November 13, the last day Volpe was seen alive. Volpe had told his wife that he was going to meet someone at the airport. That's where they found him. For anyone to get a crime leader like Volpe required some planning and the help of someone he trusted. I've always thought I knew who that trusted Volpe friend was. What I am certain of is that with the killing of Volpe and Racco, the Commisso crime group became the most powerful of all the Calabrian groups in the United States and Canada.

CHAPTER 21

Run, Stoolie, Run

When I broke away from my security detail in October I was frustrated, bored, and upset. I'd be a liar if I said I wasn't worried when I learned that the bikers knew where I was staying with the security men. I was concerned about my life and the lives of the men protecting me. I knew bikers. I knew them better than any security supervisor at the SEU. I knew them better than the RCMP. When Volpe told Murphy that the bikers were coming to the hotel in Aurora to kill all of us, I knew that that was just what Satan's Choice would do. They'd have no hesitation about blowing me away and anyone who was with me.

Since I couldn't tell the detail who tipped me, blowing the location was the only choice I felt I had left. I wanted no one killed, least of all myself.

I want to make it clear that the men who provided me with protection during the years that I was a witness were really super guys. They were all different—guys that came and went—and I barely got to know them the way I would have liked to. Not all of them were lovable or even likable, and a few of them didn't like the idea of protecting a criminal like myself, but 99 percent of them were super guys with a lot of guts. You have to have guts to be on a detail like that.

I think most of them tried their damnedest to make life a little easier for me. They lived in a room next to me and tension was always present, as was the danger. Every move had to be thought out. Wherever we went, whether it was to a court proceeding or to an interview, the men of the

security detail preceded me and stood in front of me. If assassins had been waiting and started shooting, many of my protectors, most of them family men, would have fallen first attempting to save my life.

There were some light moments. When I wanted to go jogging, one or more of them would jog with me while others followed in special unmarked vehicles. The joggers had a hard time keeping up with me, and I'd often kid them about what lousy shape they were in when they ended the jog, huffing and puffing like old men.

We played cards together and pool, anything to provide a relief from the boredom of waiting, always waiting. One of the team members, a young guy named Byron, was a pool shark. He beat the hell out of anyone he played—me, the detail, anyone who challenged him. He literally made the pool cue talk.

At times we left the city to go to a place for a quiet drink. One location I remember vividly and enjoyed the most was a small island about 300 miles north of Toronto. We spent two weeks there just to relieve the tension and relax. It was a fantastic place to fish, to exercise, and to just plain talk.

As a team, the details were always heavily armed, alert, and damned well trained in the use of all types of firearms. They checked out each place we went thoroughly before they would let me go near it. They would also spend hours talking with me, picking my brain about people who might be looking for me, who might want to kill me. What did they look like? What kind of weapons would they use? Who were their friends? Where were their hangouts? The questions seemed endless, yet they were all designed to protect me and the detail from a surprise assault by assassins.

They had photographs of Ken Goobie, Armand Sanguigni, a dozen or more bikers, Calabrian mafiosi, rounders, every type of criminal who was a serious threat to my life.

I was convinced during that period, between 1981 and 1983, that my most serious threat was from bikers, not the Calabrians. There were so many damned bikers all over Canada and in the United States that you never knew when you'd run into them. In August 1981 I was taken to Florida for three weeks for security reasons and to ease the tension. While we were there, I remember worrying the most about running into bikers —Outlaws, Hell's Angels, Pagans—who had connections with biker gangs

in Canada. I was certain that pictures of me had been distributed to other gangs by Satan's Choice and the Vagabonds.

I often told detail members that outlaw bikers were more likely to make a stupid open hit than Mafia members, who were more conservative, more careful. The bikers were reckless. They didn't and still don't care who else might be killed in trying to get at me.

Some might think that going to bars or hotels or jogging was dangerous. It could be, except the element of surprise was to our advantage, and every location was checked out before we used it.

A lot of agents protected me—people like Murphy, Byron, Ted Bean, and Lyle McCharles—and their lives were in danger from bikers too. I know that Murphy was threatened. He had to take precautions not only for himself but for his family. He had to live on the edge for a long, long time. So did some others.

Bikers are persistent, if nothing else. I remember one ex-member of the Saint Catharines Outlaws, a guy named Jimmy, that I had real trouble with before I became a witness. He and another guy they called Gypsy had threatened to blow my head off. I caught up with Jimmy in a gym one day and beat the hell out of him. He couldn't open his eyes for a week. In fact, he had to use a seeing-eye dog to get around.

The trouble was over Linda. She and I had split up for a while. We had an on-again, off-again love affair that was often violent. Anyhow, they tried to make a move on her. I told them to keep away from her. One night they figured the best way to get rid of me was to lay in ambush outside her house with shotguns waiting for me to come to the door. I didn't show up, but not because I was tipped. It was only luck that they didn't nail me. When I did hear about it, I was very concerned.

First I went to the Saint Catharines Outlaws and told them that I wanted these two guys. I made it clear I was going to get them. They didn't care. Both Jimmy and Gypsy had broken with the gang and were on their own.

Gypsy was about six foot two, weighed about 220 pounds, and towered over me. I had a little trouble with him at first in the gym when he tried to wrestle with me. He didn't want to fight. But I broke loose and I gave him a helluva beating. He was bloodied, and I got my pleasure beating

his face in. I told him if I ever heard him mouthing off about me or making a move on Linda again, I was going to come back and kick his head in.

Linda was a problem for the security detail, mainly because of me. Being shut up with three men or in a room by myself drove me up a wall. There were times I felt I had to see her, despite our fights. She was living at a secret location arranged and paid for by the RCMP. When I wanted to see her or she wanted to see me, they'd work it out for us to be together. After she'd leave, we would always pick up and move to a new location. They didn't trust her, and for good reason, although I didn't agree with them for a long time. I had to be hit with a hammer quite a few times before I realized I couldn't trust her.

That relationship came to a head October 28, when Linda tried to set me up. I was still on my own, away from the security detail, when I learned that a warrant had been sworn out for my arrest for possession of a .308 rifle. I had gone to stay with my brother in Nottawasaga Township. My plan was to go up north and do some moose hunting with a rifle I had. I decided to test the gun at my brother's and fired three shells at a tree. Next thing I knew, some coppers came to find out what the shooting was about and my brother, Mark, said I had spent the night on the roof of my mother's house with a loaded rifle firing rounds into a tree to test the weapon.

Technically, I was on probation. When the coppers came and my brother came up with that tale, I had to get rid of the gun fast, and I did. Then I turned myself in when I heard there was a warrant for my arrest. I was charged with having a weapon dangerous to the public peace—a charge that was dismissed on January 28, 1983, in court.

Some members of the press played the hell out of the case. They used that and my troubles with Linda to try to have me jailed by having my probation revoked.

Then one night Linda called and said she was at a local Toronto bar, and asked me to go to her apartment to make sure her daughter was all right. She said that the baby-sitter was there watching her.

I told her I'd take a taxi and be there before she was. I went up to her apartment, knocked on the door, and got no answer. I tried the handle

and the door was open. There was a note on the floor, so I walked in. I don't know who the note was from, but it read: "Your daughter is next door." So I sat there and waited.

It wasn't long before I saw a Chrysler pull up instead of a cab, and out stepped Ronald Ambrose, a friend of Linda and her former husband. They came upstairs and rang the buzzer. I wasn't about to answer it. They left. About a half hour later, Linda came up the stairs. She entered the room and for a moment didn't notice me standing there. Finally she saw me. "Where's Lisa?" she said.

"Next door," I snapped.

She left the room to get the kid and put her to bed. When she returned the phone rang. It was Ambrose. She answered and all I could hear her say was, "Yeah, come on over." Then she turned to me with a sneer on her face and said, "You know who's coming here? You better take off, he might have a gun."

Ambrose lived in an apartment across the street, and I could see him come running across and through the front door of her apartment house with a rifle. He started ringing the buzzer. I yelled at him. "Look, I saw you coming across with the gun."

He yelled back, "Open the fuckin' door."

I didn't answer. I went to the phone, called the police, identified myself, and told them there was a man with a rifle standing in the hallway waiting to shoot me.

The cops got there fast, let me tell you. I was going to go out, but I decided I'd wait until I saw the cops. I looked out the peephole and there they were wrestling this guy out in the hall. I opened the door, and suddenly the cops were throwing cuffs on me, telling me I was under arrest. They didn't say what for, but I went along, figuring it was to get everybody under control.

The cops swarmed over the apartment, searching it. Linda was going nuts. She saw Ambrose in the hall being held by three cops. She wound up and hit one of the cops. Then she shouted, "Yeah, an' he [pointing at me] raped me."

I looked at her and started to laugh. "You better come up with something better than that," I said. "You should have said that when they came in the door instead of dreaming it up now." She wanted me so bad

she could taste it. She was willing to do anything, say anything to get me.

One cop had the rifle. He stood there beside me, pulled the bolt open, and the bullet popped out. I looked at him and said, "That fuckin' bastard was gonna shoot me." The cop, who had been looking down the barrel of that gun when Ambrose pointed at him, was upset. So were the other cops. They took the cuffs off me.

Ambrose was only twenty-four and a punk. But I'd have been out of my mind to go out to meet him without a gun. He was crazy enough to gun me down in the hallway for sure. His brother had been convicted in Nova Scotia for killing two RCMP officers—he made them dig their graves first, then shot them.

They charged Ambrose with pointing a loaded rifle at a policeman, and in April 1982 I was forced to testify in the case by his attorney, Michael Caroline. Ambrose's defense was that he acted because he thought Linda was in danger and he believed I was a man above the law because of what the media said about me. Caroline, who later became my lawyer, asked me in court what would I do "if a man like yourself, Cecil Kirby, came at you with a gun." I answered, "I would have gone out and bought a bigger gun." Ambrose still got convicted and sentenced to six months in jail.

In November the Ontario attorney general, Roy McMurtry, asked the press to keep a lid on stories about me. The reason was that I had been asked by the Crown and the SEU to carry a body mike to gather additional evidence against businessmen who had hired me through the Commissos to commit arsons, bomb buildings, or extort money. The plan was to nail down more charges against the Commissos and against those who had gone to the Commissos to hire me.

The idea of hitting the streets again, gathering evidence, jolted me out of my depression. My adrenaline was flowing, and the excitement of the hunt gripped me. I once again was working with a team of top investigators, including Corporal Danielle Bouchard of the OPP and SEU, who was going to pose as my girlfriend, but Murphy wasn't allowed to participate. He'd been transferred and admonished. He was eventually disciplined for standing by his promises to me in the face of orders to sink me by some of his superiors.

Most of those we approached and taped knew me only as "George."

259

They did not put "George" together with Cecil Kirby, and since the Commissos were in jail, they were unable to call them to see if I was still acting on their behalf.

Make no mistake, what we were doing—the investigators, myself, the security people—was dangerous. A slip of the tongue, a chance meeting with the wrong person could have cost me and them our lives. There was always the chance that one of them might have found out that George was Cecil or have made a successful effort to talk to Cosimo or Remo in jail about "George." If they had I would have been dead.

For a while it worked fine. I recorded admissions by a number of businessmen, including Armando DiCapua, Bruno Spizzichino, and Rocco Mastrangelo, who had paid Cosimo to have me blow up their sporting goods store in Guelph. I recorded admissions by Istvan Szocs, a real estate salesman who went to Cosimo in 1978 to get help in collecting $15,000 that he said Cornwall developer Hugh Fitzpatrick owed him from a 1973 land deal. Szocs paid me $200 to break Fitzpatrick's arms and legs and threaten his family. I never got to Fitzpatrick, but I spent two weeks trying. Szocs claimed he never collected the $15,000.

There were other cases, and there could have been more except that a reporter for reasons I've never been able to figure, broke stories about the immunity and support agreement I had with the Crown and charges from Linda and her attorney that I had beaten her while my security guards stood quietly by in another room.

The stories had an even more serious effect. They terminated the undercover investigation I was working on, endangering not only my life but those of Bouchard and other investigators on the case. On February 8, 1982, we tried to tape admissions from another Commisso associate. All we got were denials and claims of total innocence. I got the strong feeling that this guy knew who I was. My role as an undercover agent was over.

A reporter had created an atmosphere that made it impossible for me to continue my work for the Crown. Metro Police Staff Inspector Don Banks said that the stories carried "distortions of facts" that made my underworld connections "wary and on their guard. He was still making connections until the publicity made it impossible to continue." Banks

headed the intelligence squad and had worked closely with the investigators from the time I started working on the Commissos.

McMurtry was furious, and he went public to attack the press stories.
He said that "irresponsible reporting" had undermined my effectiveness.
He pointed out that until I had confessed under immunity, law enforcement in Canada had had no evidence against me for the crimes I talked
to them about. He defended the new agreement the Crown had with me
that provided me and those in my family with $1,950 in support plus my
living quarters and travel expenses. But he refused to disclose the terms
of the agreement, and I was and have been prohibited from disclosing
them. If I disclose more than I've been required to in court, all bets are
off—the Crown can walk away from me.

RCMP Chief Superintendent Donald Heaton, who was also upset by
the newspaper disclosures, said that police had known about the criminals
I'd worked on for twenty years. He said that despite millions of dollars
spent on investigations, no one had ever put them in jail. "For the first
time ever we had someone [Kirby] on the inside . . . and they [organized
crime figures] were going to jail."

It was over—the street work, the recordings, the moments of exhilaration and anxiety. All that remained now were the trials ahead and the
boredom.

If I had it to do over, I probably would never have become a witness.
I certainly wouldn't recommend that other criminals follow my path. The
reason is simple. Aside from the danger, the boredom, and the frustration
that a witness faces, there are the threats to his family, the spiraling costs,
a life constantly on the run without any stability, and the broken promises
of the government.

When I first signed an agreement on April 7, 1981, the government
promised me immunity from prosecution for past crimes. It also was to
provide physical protection for me and for my family during the criminal
proceedings, including all the trials. The agreement was revised on November 12, 1981. While it increased my expense allowances from about
$700 a month to $1,960 plus $550 for rentals, it was still inadequate.

Reporters and the public read figures like that and say, hey, I could live

on $32,000 a year plus very nicely, thank you. Sure you could, if you didn't have to live in hotel rooms, if you weren't required to move almost every week, if you didn't have to eat in restaurants most of the time, or to fly or drive hundreds and thousands of miles in the course of a month. When you live the life of a nomad—not by choice but by necessity—it's costly. I can't remember a week when I haven't been broke or the end of a month when all I had was more than five dollars.

It's a hell of an existence. There have been a couple of updated agreements, each one narrowing the promises made by earlier agreements, each one making it tougher and tougher to live.

There have been a lot of broken promises along the way. I've publicly challenged McMurtry for breaking his word. His answer was to deny me the help I wanted and then, in 1984, to get bodyguards for his personal protection because he thought I was going to hurt him. That had to be the dumbest thing I ever heard of. I might have been mad, but I'm not stupid enough to go after the Ontario attorney general.

The most important thing I wanted—more than the money I had requested—was a sense of security. I'm supposed to have a documented new identity. What good is an identity if there is nothing in the history of that identity to show you existed before 1981? Without a history, without something to show you went to school, someone to verify that you were employed someplace, it's almost impossible to establish credit or to get a job. Who's going to hire a man with no history? Dozens of times I've applied for jobs and the employer was ready to hire me until I was unable to come up with that history that says you exist, you are, you've worked and lived somewhere and gone to school.

So it's do an odd job here, an odd job there—nothing with security, nothing with a future, nothing where you can earn a solid salary.

You can't establish roots that way. You can't move into a community and try to buy a home if you have no background, no money to put down on a house, no steady job to pay the mortgage and the taxes and all the other bills that a man has to pay.

There should be some job training, something that would prepare me to work in something I hadn't done before. I can't drive trucks cross-country with bikers and the Mafia hunting me. The job training promises

turned out to be empty. The government hasn't made the slightest attempt to train me to earn a living.

I don't want to live from government check to government check. Too often they let you hang waiting—that check comes a week, two weeks, a month late. You call, you protest, your attorney does the same, and everyone ignores you. They don't need you anymore. They've got their big convictions, now they don't want to know you or live up to their word.

When I began taping the Commissos, not only did the RCMP never supply a car, there were times I was afraid that when Murphy and I had to go to locations for meetings I wouldn't have enough money for gas. They didn't give Murphy money, and I didn't get it. They just insisted that I continue using the car the Commissos were familiar with, my father's Chevrolet. It was only three years old then, with very little mileage on it. Once the Commisso investigations ended, the car was stripped of its electronic listening devices and returned to my father. There was no attempt to replace it, to pay for the maintenance, or to paint the car a different color.

That caused him problems. One evening two guys with full beards smashed into the rear of his Chevy and tried to force him off the road. They were bikers who had recognized the car and were trying to get at me through him. The car had to be sold later at a loss. In December 1982 my father's truck was shot up at my brother's cottage in Wasaga Beach. The bullet went through the tailgate and a steel box into the cabin of the truck, where it hit a steel jack behind the seat. It then cut through the seat and slammed through the glove compartment before finally stopping at the engine fire wall. Police found it was an armor-piercing, .303 rifle slug. An hour before that another bullet went through my uncle's house, two or three miles away. It went through the front door and whistled over his head while he was sleeping in bed. The papers reported it, the police investigated, but nothing happened—nobody was ever arrested.

You would have thought that after the shooting, police would have driven up and down the street a couple of times at night or sat out in front of the homes of my brother and my uncle for maybe a half hour. No such luck. Nobody provided protection or even offered to.

In March 1982 my brother, Mark, was arrested for selling a small

quantity of marijuana to an undercover detective. Mark shouldn't have been fooling with drugs, but he was all screwed up at the time. He had to fight his way in and out of bars as every biker tried to take him on. I appealed to the judge in the case, County Court Judge Donald Thompson, not to send my kid brother to jail. I told him it could cost the kid his life, that prisoners associated with the bikers or the Mafia could kill him in prison. Judge Thompson didn't listen. He said it was up to jail authorities to make sure my brother was safe. Then he sent Mark to jail for ninety days. That Mark survived without harm was a matter of luck. It wasn't because the Crown or the courts took any special precautions for him.

While I was testifying against the Commissos and others, the government did not provide protection for my mother or father, and both were subjected to threatening calls constantly. Almost every weekend, my mother would get calls from some biker's broad or some biker threatening her. They were messages to me, really. They were telling me, here's trouble for you, informer. And there's more to come. Here's how easy it is to get at your family if we want you. It was hell on both of them. It still is.

Since May 1981, it's been hell on my family, particularly my father. From the beginning, when my name hit print, he received threatening phone calls. The RCMP put a tap on his line to find out who was making the threats, but they got nowhere. Their answer to the problem was to tell him to sell his house, to move. When he did move, he lost $20,000 on the sale and the RCMP provided him with only $500 for moving costs. All told, he's had to move nearly a dozen times, and the government's provided just that one payment of $500. It costs that much to move all your belongings to a new location just once.

In addition to the threats, there have been endless attempts by bikers and the Commissos to frame me, to discredit me as a witness by attempting to show I was a liar or had committed crimes after signing my agreement. Anthony Speciale is a typical example.

I first met Speciale through Ken Goobie and Andy the Rounder. At the time he was on the run for shooting someone. Until I told police about the incident, they weren't aware that Speciale was involved in the shooting.

Speciale was pretty wild. He'd rather shoot you than fight you, and he always had a .38 snub-nosed revolver on him for protection or murder. I remember one night we all got stopped in a radar trap in Toronto. The cop was walking over to our car when Speciale, who was sitting in the back, reached for his gun.

"Jesus Christ, Tony," I said, "leave that fuckin' gun right there and don't say a word. Just let the cop give us the ticket and we'll leave."

He had a real cruel smile on his face, half sneer, half smile, and there was a kind of faraway glint in his eyes. He was ready to blow that cop away until I said something.

Speciale had a long record. He had gone to jail for assault, for car theft, for B&E, for robbery and wounding, but in 1978 he hit the heights—he got life imprisonment for killing three people, including a rounder named Stan Norman. Norman begged for his life, but Speciale just shot him through the head. Then he shot Norman's girl, Diane. She was shot twice and lay there, hearing him reload the gun to shoot her again. Somehow she survived to tell her story.

Now, I had been with Speciale that day just before the killings started. He was with me waiting for a guy, a courier, who we were supposed to rob. We waited a few hours, the target never came out, and we left the area. I dropped Speciale off at some girl's place in Mississauga. The next day I saw the Sunday paper, and splashed across the front page was the story of Speciale and the shootings.

While he was in jail for the murders he came in contact with Cosimo Commisso. In March 1984, while he was serving time in the same jail with Cosimo, Speciale tried to implicate me in the Norman murder. He charged I was with him when he killed Norman. Luckily, I was able to prove I wasn't but it was clearly an attempt by Cosimo to destroy me as a witness.

Cosimo had tried that before, in September 1982, when he got Nicolino Pallotta and Richard Cucman to claim that I had ripped them off, taken $140,000 in jewelry they'd robbed from the Dolly Jewelers in 1981, fenced it, and kept the money for myself. It was a lie, of course. I'd tipped Murphy off about the jewelry and the fact that they'd handled the robbery.

Then there was Satan's Choice biker Joe Ertel of Kitchener. Ertel had

a long record of convictions for robbery, assault, trafficking in drugs, and possession of stolen property. With a record like that and a hatred for cops, he still hated me more and charged that I had murdered another biker named Duke Coons. I was questioned by Crown prosecutors in the case and told them I knew nothing about the homicide. I took a lie detector test and passed it.

Today, I'm still on the run, still looking for a hole I can crawl into and survive in. Canada's a big country, but it may not be big enough. Wherever I've gone, I haven't been able to stay long because I was unable to get a job, unable to obtain credit and show a history of employment.

For several years the government was concerned. I was important to them in 1981 and through the trials that led to the conviction of more than fourteen criminals—people who burned down hotels, people who wanted to extort money, so-called respectable people who wanted other people's legs and arms broken.

I was important because they needed me to crack the Calabrian Mafia and put away their leaders, people like the Commisso brothers, and Vincent Melia, who's now free after serving only three years of a nine-year jail term for paying to have Helen Nafpliotis killed. I was important because they wanted my intelligence information, my tips—tips that led to major drug busts, to the arrests of gamblers and jewel thieves, to biker crimes and Mafia plans for murder.

But now all that's over. Prosecutors can't make headlines and further their political careers on sensational disclosures from Cecil Kirby. They can't win press notice by dueling with prominent defense lawyers who try unsuccessfully to discredit me as a witness. They are content with their press notices and, for some, new and lucrative jobs outside government that resulted from their "handling" of Cecil Kirby. So what happens to Cecil Kirby is no longer of concern to them. If members of the Outlaws find where Kirby's living, as they did in 1985, don't bother telling him. He's finished testifying, and it's not our responsibility to keep him alive forever.

In truth, the only ones that care are a few dedicated cops—members and former members of the SEU—who, after doing their jobs, were returned to their units with the RCMP, the Ontario Provincial Police or Metro Toronto. They've tried to help in many ways, but what they've

done, they've done on their own out of a sense of responsibility and decency.

I don't mind one bit saying that I'm bitter. I'm no angel, never pretended to be. I was a hardened criminal. But I've tried to follow a new path, keep within the law, and the bureaucrats that run this nation don't make it easy. If I survive, it won't be because they helped or kept their word. It'll be because I kept my wits and my instincts keen.

In the end, they and the public will be the losers. For while I've kept my word and done all I was asked to do, there won't be any other Cecil Kirbys willing to come forward. And without witnesses who trust the government as I once did, organized crime—whether it be outlaw bikers, the Mafia, or Chinese triads—will flourish, picking the pockets of American and Canadian citizens alike.

Epilogue

From Orlando, Florida, to Toronto, Ontario, Americans and Canadians alike are under siege. They are hostage to a new and increasingly dangerous organized crime intent on intimidation, extortion, drug trafficking, murder, and the infiltration of the consumer marketplace. Their aim—to accumulate wealth.

Motorcycle gangs larger in membership than the Cosa Nostra; Asian gangs with hundreds of thousands of members internationally, from Hong Kong to the Netherlands; the Calabrian Honoured Society that insidiously blends into the melting pot of North American society and Australia as well; Colombians who export death in the form of tons of cocaine; Russian émigrés who murder, steal, cheat, and sell doctored oil while evading hundreds of millions in fuel taxes; Israeli Mafia hoodlums who traffic in narcotics and dupe insurance companies out of millions; dozens of new and dangerous ethnic gangs that prey on their own people before branching out to victimize society in general; and the Cosa Nostra, the criminal enterprise that spans two nations and infiltrates every fabric of society—all are corrupting, murdering, and plundering society's resources.

It is a frightening array of criminal organizations that the law enforcement community and governments must face down and fight with an increasingly limited supply of weaponry and an even more limited number of experienced, qualified investigators.

Wiretaps, bugs, informers—all are vital to the battle. So are laws such

as the Racketeer Influenced Corrupt Organization statute, so successfully employed in recent years against the Cosa Nostra and other organized crime groups by federal authorities in the United States. Canada lacks such a law, but its law officers seek one.

The most vital and effective tool of all is the witness against organized crime. He has to be cultivated and nurtured. He has to be carefully used and, more important, his role as a criminal must be weighed against the value of the evidence he can provide.

Witnesses can be forced to testify, sometimes with the threat of jail or other dire consequences, but generally, in organized crime cases, they testify only when the government agrees to a deal. That deal frequently embodies immunity for past crimes, a promise of job opportunity and training after testifying, subsistence for the witness and his family while he's testifying, and a new identity.

Since the U.S. Congress authorized the creation of the Witness Protection Program, more than 6,000 witnesses have passed through that program after testifying for federal and state authorities. Under the control of the U.S. Marshals, the program has been often maligned, sometimes with justification, for failing to live up to the promises given to witnesses and to provide proper protection, identity documentation, and job opportunities.

Canada had a golden opportunity to learn from the mistakes of the U.S. program and provide a more stable future for its witnesses. It has failed miserably with Cecil Kirby.

Like him or not, Kirby made a deal with his government to gather evidence against the kingpins of organized crime in Ontario. He was successful beyond the wildest dreams of those who cultivated him. He was, unlike so many witnesses, a man of his word. He lived up to the promises he gave to testify. In fact, he went a giant step further, carrying a body mike after charges had been filed against a number of Calabrian crime leaders to gather more evidence against more criminals.

Without question, the Canadian government saved millions of dollars by using Kirby. He provided them with a wealth of intelligence on outlaw bikers and the Calabrian Mafia and led agents into the world of the rounders—all criminal societies with codes of silence that law enforcement had been previously unable to penetrate.

Kirby is owed a debt—a debt payable by promises made to him when he embarked on his dangerous adventure. While his subsistence has continued, the promises of job training and a solid, documented new identity have not been kept. Worse, Kirby has been left to his own devices, to survive on his instincts without the necessary protection, counseling, and guidance in relocation, reidentification, and job placement.

Incredibly, Kirby worked for government agencies for some months without immunity, without an agreement in writing, without subsistence or expenses. He lived by his wits. He was forced to use the funds collected from criminal conspiracies to pay his bills and feed his family. He was required to use his father's car, and quite often his father paid for the gas used to help the government gather its evidence.

By any standard of law enforcement undercover operations, the penny-pinching practices of the agencies involved were amateurish and patently dangerous. Kirby should have been properly funded and, as a result, never permitted to keep the proceeds of a criminal investigation, as in the case of the conspiracy to murder Helen Nafpliotis.

Unless a vigorous and carefully constructed witness program is developed in Canada, law enforcement officers and prosecutors will soon find that witnesses such as Kirby will not become willing weapons against organized crime. Sources of information and intelligence will dry up, and the word will spread in the underworld that the law and those who administer it do not keep their promises. Without trust, there can be no effective fight against organized crime in Canada or the United States. In a world where new organized crime groups are breeding like rats on the waterfront, that could have a profound and immensely costly effect on all of us.

Appendix I:
Convictions as a
Result of
Kirby Testimony

COSIMO COMMISSO

1981 Conspiracy to murder, three counts (Helen Nafpliotis, Pietro Scarcella, Paul Volpe): eight years each count, concurrent. Beating (assault): two years, concurrent.

1984 (March) Conspiracy to bomb (Guelph sporting goods store) and possession of stolen cigarettes: sixteen months, consecutive to time already being served.

1984 (April) Inciting to murder, bomb, arson, assault, and extortion (sixteen counts): eight years, consecutive to the thirteen years already being served.

ROCCO REMO COMMISSO

1981 Conspiracy to murder, two counts (Scarcella, Volpe): eight years each count, consecutive.

1984 (March) Possession of stolen cigarettes: six months, consecutive to the eight years already being served.

1984 (April) Assault, extortion, bombings, arson, and inciting to commit murder, seven counts: six years, consecutive to the eight years and six months already being served.

MICHELE COMMISSO

1981 Conspiracy to murder, three counts (Nafpliotis, Scarcella, Volpe): two and a half years each count, consecutive.

1984 (April) Planned arson: sentence suspended, two years' probation.

ANTONIO ROMEO

1981 Conspiracy to murder (Nafpliotis): two and a half years.

GERARDO (JERRY) RUSSO

1981 Conspiracy to murder (Nafpliotis): two years, ten months.

VINCENZO MELIA

1982 Conspiracy to murder (Nafpliotis): nine years.

COSIMO MERCURI

1982 Second-degree murder and arson (Dominion Hotel, Acton): life imprisonment, no consideration for parole for ten years.

MICHAEL McCRYSTAL

1982 Manslaughter (Dominion Hotel, Acton): two years less a day.

ARMANDO DI CAPUA

1983 Arson conspiracy (Guelph sporting goods store): two years.

ROCCO MASTRANGELO

1984 Arson conspiracy (Guelph sporting goods store): one year.

BRUNO SPIZZICHINO

1984 Arson conspiracy (Guelph sporting goods store): two years.

NICHOLAS PALLOTTA

1982 Robbery (Dolly Jewellers): three years.

RICHARD CUCMAN

1982 Robbery (Dolly Jewellers): two years.

ISTVAN (STEVE) SZOCS

1983 Attempted extortion: six months.

RICHARD CORBETT

1983 Possession of stolen cigarettes: three months.

ARMAND SANGUIGNI

1983 Possession of stolen cigarettes: three months.

In addition to the above, Kirby supplied information that led to the arrest and conviction of twenty more people, including disco owner Harold Arviv for the bombing of Arviv's disco; disco manager Yvo Sajet for filing a false report with the police in the robbery of the cash boxes from the Hippopotamus disco; and Charles (Chuck) Yanover for his part in the plot to overthrow the government of Dominica, possession of forty-two pounds of hashish (three people arrested), conspiracy to smuggle gold out of British Guinea (one person arrested), five robberies, two shootings, and information on six unsolved homicides.

Appendix II: Honoured Society

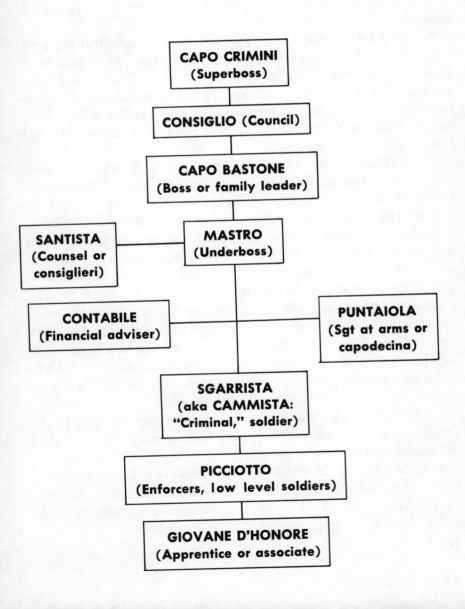

CAPO CRIMINI
(Superboss)

CONSIGLIO (Council)

CAPO BASTONE
(Boss or family leader)

SANTISTA
(Counsel or consiglieri)

MASTRO
(Underboss)

CONTABILE
(Financial adviser)

PUNTAIOLA
(Sgt at arms or capodecina)

SGARRISTA
(aka CAMMISTA: "Criminal," soldier)

PICCIOTTO
(Enforcers, low level soldiers)

GIOVANE D'HONORE
(Apprentice or associate)

1. CAPO CRIMINI: The highest-ranking boss in the Honoured Society or Calabrian Mafia. The equivalent of a "boss of bosses," but the title rarely exists. Last known boss of bosses was the late Don Antonio Macri of Siderno.

2. CONSIGLIO: The sitting council or ruling body, which includes the most influential bosses of the organization. The *consiglio* is roughly the equivalent of the Cosa Nostra Commission, with between nine and eleven members.

3. CAPO BASTONE: A boss. This is an archaic term that has been surplanted by the shortened title of *Capo* or *Head*. This includes all bosses in each area. There are fifty-four bosses in Calabria and three suspected bosses in Canada, including the late Mike Racco, and Cosimo Commisso. A *capo bastone* is the equivalent of a Cosa Nostra crime boss, such as Anthony Salerno of the Genovese family or Antonio (Ducks) Corallo of the Lucchese family.

4. MASTRO: Second in command of a Calabrian family. The *mastro* is similar in stature and responsibilities to the underboss of a Cosa Nostra family. He is the *capo bastone's* right-hand man.

5. SANTISTA: The family adviser, the equivalent of the Cosa Nostra's *consiglieri*. The santista gives counsel if asked to by the *capo bastone* or the *mastro*. He is usually an older man with experience who enjoys the respect of family members at both high and low levels. The name is derived from the Greek word that means "to act as an honorable person."

6. CONTABILE: The family's financial adviser, generally an attorney or accountant. He usually picks up money, gets bail for incarcerated members, and invests money for the *capo bastone*. He can be a businessman with legitimate business fronts. He is often in direct contact with the boss and directs communication on important financial matters. There is no equivalent of this position in the Cosa Nostra.

7. PUNTAIOLA: Roughly the equivalent in stature of a Cosa Nostra *capodecina* or crime captain. The name literally means "a stick with a nail at the end used to move animals," a prod.

8. SGARRISTA E. CAMMISTA (CAMORRISTA): The equivalent of a higher-than-average soldier in the Cosa Nostra. He approaches businesses for extortion and gives orders to associates and *picciottos* who work under him. He is a visible operator of the family.

9. PICCIOTTO: The worker, the out-front hustler and enforcer who plants bombs or beats loan-shark victims. He is the muscle of the Honoured Society and would be most associated with criminal activities. His equivalent in the Cosa Nostra is the soldier, the "made guy," the "wise guy."

10. GIOVANE D'HONORE: A person who wants to become a member of the Honoured Society. In the Cosa Nostra he would be known as the trusted associate vying for initiation as a member. He is required to do favors for the organization to prove his loyalty, have the right background and the right friends, and be sponsored by someone in the Honoured Society. Once accepted he is initiated, as are new members of the Cosa Nostra, in a ritualistic ceremony in which he swears loyalty to the organization and *omertà* (silence) on pain of death.

Index

Index

Index

Index

Index

Index

Index

About the Authors

CECIL KIRBY is living under an assumed name in Canada.

THOMAS C. RENNER has authored two best-sellers, the internationally acclaimed *My Life in the Mafia* with Vincent Teresa, and *Mafia Princess*, with Antoinette Giancana.

Renner is a veteran of thirty-two years on the Pulitzer Prize-winning *Newsday*. He has won recognition as an organized crime expert and was recently one of five reporters cited by the president of the United States for significant contributions in exposing organized crime. He was the first reporter in America to be assigned to investigate and write solely about organized crime and was a key member of the "Arizona Project," a prize-winning, investigation of corruption and crime in the southwest. Renner was awarded the coveted Louis M. Lyons Award for Conscience and Integrity in Journalism in 1983 by the Neiman Fellows of Harvard University. He is the recipient of numerous awards for excellence, integrity and community service.

7. Which of the following best describes your job title?

Administrative Assistant .... ☐
Coordinator .... ☐
Manager/Supervisor .... ☐
Director .... ☐
Vice President .... ☐
President/CEO/COO .... ☐
Lawyer/Doctor/Medical Professional .... ☐
Teacher/Educator/Trainer .... ☐
Engineer/Technician .... ☐
Consultant .... ☐
Not employed/Student/Retired .... ☐
Other (Please specify): _____ ☐

8. Which of the following best describes the area of the company your job title falls under?

Accounting .... ☐
Engineering .... ☐
Manufacturing .... ☐
Operations .... ☐
Marketing .... ☐
Sales .... ☐
Other (Please specify): _____ ☐

Comments: _____

9. What is your age?

Under 20 ....
21-29 ....
30-39 ....
40-49 ....
50-59 ....
60-over ....

10. Are you:

Male ....
Female ....

11. Which computer publications do you read regularly? (Please list)

_____
_____
_____
_____
_____
_____
_____
_____
_____
_____

Fold here and scotch-tape to

II""I"I"I"I"I""II"I"I"I"I"I"III"I.II"I"""II"I"I

INDIANAPOLIS IN 46209-9042
201 W 103RD ST
MACMILLAN PUBLISHING USA
MACMILLAN COMPUTER PUBLISHING
ATTN MARKETING

POSTAGE WILL BE PAID BY THE ADDRESSEE

FIRST-CLASS MAIL PERMIT NO. 9918 INDIANAPOLIS IN
BUSINESS REPLY MAIL

NO POSTAGE
NECESSARY
IF MAILED
IN THE
UNITED STATES

Complete and Return this Card
for a *FREE* Computer Book Catalog

Thank you for purchasing this book! You have purchased a superior computer book written expressly for your needs. To continue to provide the kind of up-to-date, pertinent coverage you've come to expect from us, we need to hear from you. Please take a minute to complete and return this self-addressed, postage-paid form. In return, we'll send you a free catalog of all our computer books on topics ranging from word processing to programming and the internet.

☐ .   Mrs. ☐   Ms. ☐   Dr. ☐

Name (first) ☐☐☐☐☐☐☐☐☐☐☐ (M.I.) ☐   (last) ☐☐☐☐☐☐☐☐☐☐☐☐☐☐

Address ☐☐☐☐☐☐☐☐☐☐☐☐☐☐☐☐☐☐☐☐☐☐☐☐☐☐☐

☐☐☐☐☐☐☐☐☐☐☐☐☐☐☐☐☐☐☐☐☐☐☐☐☐☐☐

City ☐☐☐☐☐☐☐☐☐☐☐☐ State ☐☐ Zip ☐☐☐☐☐ ☐☐☐☐

Phone ☐☐☐ ☐☐☐ ☐☐☐☐ Fax ☐☐☐ ☐☐☐ ☐☐☐☐

Company Name ☐☐☐☐☐☐☐☐☐☐☐☐☐☐☐☐☐☐☐☐☐☐☐☐☐

E-mail address ☐☐☐☐☐☐☐☐☐☐☐☐☐☐☐☐☐☐☐☐☐☐☐☐☐

Please check at least (3) influencing factors for purchasing this book.

Front or back cover information on book .... ☐
Special approach to the content .... ☐
Completeness of content .... ☐
Author's reputation .... ☐
Publisher's reputation .... ☐
Book cover design or layout .... ☐
Index or table of contents of book .... ☐
Price of book .... ☐
Special effects, graphics, illustrations .... ☐
Other (Please specify): _____ ☐

How did you first learn about this book?

Saw in Macmillan Computer Publishing catalog .... ☐
Recommended by store personnel .... ☐
Saw the book on bookshelf at store .... ☐
Recommended by a friend .... ☐
Received advertisement in the mail .... ☐
Saw an advertisement in: _____ ☐
Read book review in: _____ ☐
Other (Please specify): _____ ☐

How many computer books have you purchased in the last six months?

This book only .... ☐   3 to 5 books .... ☐
2 books .... ☐   More than 5 .... ☐

4. Where did you purchase this book?

Bookstore .... ☐
Computer Store .... ☐
Consumer Electronics Store .... ☐
Department Store .... ☐
Office Club .... ☐
Warehouse Club .... ☐
Mail Order .... ☐
Direct from Publisher .... ☐
Internet site .... ☐
Other (Please specify): _____ ☐

5. How long have you been using a computer?

☐ Less than 6 months   ☐ 6 months to a year
☐ 1 to 3 years   ☐ More than 3 years

6. What is your level of experience with personal computers and with the subject of this book?

	With PCs	With subject of book
New	☐	☐
Casual	☐	☐
Accomplished	☐	☐
Expert	☐	☐

Source Code ISBN:0-7897-0464-1